*Good Wives: Image and Reality in the Lives
of Women in Northern New England,
1650–1750*

*A Midwife's Tale: The Life of Martha Ballard,
Based on Her Diary, 1785–1812*

*All God's Critters Got a Place in the Choir*
(with Emma Lou Thayne)

# The Age of Homespun

# The Age
# of Homespun

## Objects and Stories
## in the Creation of an
## American Myth

## Laurel Thatcher Ulrich

*Alfred A. Knopf*
*New York*
*2001*

*For all the textilians*

THIS IS A BORZOI BOOK
PUBLISHED BY ALFRED A. KNOPF

Copyright © 2001 by Laurel Thatcher Ulrich
All rights reserved under International and Pan-American Copyright
Conventions. Published in the United States by Alfred A. Knopf,
a division of Random House, Inc., New York, and simultaneously
in Canada by Random House of Canada Limited, Toronto.
Distributed by Random House, Inc., New York.
www.aaknopf.com

Knopf, Borzoi Books, and the colophon are
registered trademarks of Random House, Inc.

Excerpt from "Children of Light" in *Lord Weary's Castle*,
copyright 1946 and renewed 1974 by Robert Lowell, reprinted
by permission of Harcourt, Inc.

Library of Congress Cataloging-in-Publication Data
Ulrich, Laurel.
The age of homespun : objects and stories in the creation
of an American myth / Laurel Thatcher Ulrich.—1st ed.
p.    cm.
Includes index.
ISBN 0-679-44594-3—ISBN 0-679-76644-8 (pbk.)
1. New England—History—1775–1865.   2. New
England—Social conditions—19th century.   3. New England—
Economic conditions—19th century.   4. Textile
fabrics—Social aspects—New England—History—
19th century.   5. Textile crafts—New England—History—19th
century.   6. Weaving—Social aspects—New England—
History—19th century.   7. Clothing and dress—Social
aspects—New England—History—19th century.   8. Material
culture—New England—History—19th century.   9. National
characteristics, American.   I. Title.

F8.U47 2001
974'.03—DC21        2001029862

Maps by George Colbert

Manufactured in the United States of America
First Edition

You must not go into the burial places, and look about only for the tall monuments and the titled names. It is not the starred epitaphs of the Doctors of Divinity, the Generals, the Judges, the Honourables, the Governors, or even of the village notables called Esquires, that mark the springs of our successes and the sources of our distinctions. These are rather effects than causes; the spinning-wheels have done a great deal more than these.

*Horace Bushnell, "The Age of Homespun," 1851*

Our fathers wrung their bread from stocks and stones
And fenced their gardens with the Redman's bones.

*Robert Lowell, "Children of Light," 1944*

What did they do, our grandmothers, as they sat spinning all the day? Are we not ourselves the web they wove?

*Anonymous toast, Mary Floyd Talmage Chapter*
*Daughters of the American Revolution*
*Litchfield, Connecticut, 1910*

# Contents

Prologue

3

*Introduction: The Age of Homespun*

LITCHFIELD, CONNECTICUT, 1851

11

*1. An Indian Basket*

PROVIDENCE, RHODE ISLAND, 1676

41

*2. Two Spinning Wheels in an Old Log House*

DOVER, NEW HAMPSHIRE, DATE UNKNOWN

75

*3. Hannah Barnard's Cupboard*

HADLEY, MASSACHUSETTS, 1715

108

*4. A Chimneypiece*

BOSTON, MASSACHUSETTS, 1753

142

*5. Willie-Nillie, Niddy-Noddy*

NEWBURYPORT, MASSACHUSETTS, AND NEW ENGLAND, 1769

174

*6. A Bed Rug and a Silk Embroidery*

COLCHESTER AND PRESTON, CONNECTICUT, 1775

208

*7. Molly Ocket's Pocketbook*

BETHEL, MAINE, 1785

248

*8. A Linen Tablecloth*
NEW ENGLAND IN THE EARLY REPUBLIC
277

*9. A Counterpane and a Rose Blanket*
KENNEBUNKPORT, MAINE, AND NEW ENGLAND, 1810
306

*10. A Woodsplint Basket*
RUTLAND, VERMONT, AFTER 1821
340

*11. An Unfinished Stocking*
NEW ENGLAND, 1837
374

*Afterword*
413

Notes
419

Acknowledgments
479

Index
483

# The Age of Homespun

# PROLOGUE

→>—<←

If this book were an exhibit, I could arrange it as a room, one of those three-sided rooms you sometimes find in museums, open on one side like a dollhouse, with a little fence or rope across. My room wouldn't represent a time or place but an idea—New England's age of homespun.

On the left wall, above the paneled fireplace, I would hang a fanciful embroidery—eighteenth-century Americans called it a chimneypiece—showing courting couples, winsome lambs, and an apron-clad maiden spinning with a drop spindle. On the opposite side of the room, on the curtained bed, I would arrange a real object of homespun, a blue and white bed rug made in Connecticut during the Revolution. Hannah Barnard's cupboard would stand against the middle wall, one drawer open to reveal a folded counterpane and a rough wool blanket embellished with a bright pink rose. Between the fireplace and the cupboard, I would stand two spinning wheels, one for flax and one for wool, scattering other emblems of household industry around them, a niddy-noddy partly wound with yarn, a weaver's shuttle, and a woodsplint basket filled with unspun wool. On the tea table in the center of the room, I would spread a homespun cloth with a netted fringe, arranging an embroidered pocketbook beside a little Indian basket twined from basswood and cornhusk. For poignancy, I would add to the wall near the bed Prudence Punderson's somber silk embroidery, *The First, Second, and Last Scenes of Mortality.* On the chair beneath it, I would drop an unfinished stocking still on its ancient needles.

To a scrupulous eye, my room would seem an improbable assembly of objects from different times, places, and sensibilities, as eclectic as a colonial revival house museum or a New England bed-and-breakfast. There is no arguing with that. But this room isn't meant to represent a moment in time. It is a memorial to the nineteenth-century Americans who saved all these things. Without them, this book would not exist.

I could try it another way. Honoring more modern curatorial practice, I could display each object with its kind, hanging the embroideries in the cool splendor of a textile gallery and exhibiting Hannah's cupboard in a furniture show on a low platform surrounded by other carved and painted chests from the Connecticut River Valley. In such a scheme, the unfinished stocking might have to go into storage, but the baskets could move to an ethnographic museum, joining wampum and a war club from the time of King Philip. The spinning wheels, massed with a hundred others, could introduce visitors to a linear display of textile technology from household to factory, with earplugs required in the mechanized weaving room at the end. In any of these spaces, pull-out drawers, safely encased in Plexiglas, could display flat textiles, like the linen tablecloth, their weave structures easy to see at close range.

That approach would provide a precise context for each object, but it would make it difficult to explore the mythology that connects them. As a place to begin, the three-sided room is better. It is compact, it is provocative, and it exposes the historiographic tension in my project. This is a book about cloth-making and about the production of history.

In *Good Wives*, I questioned the centrality of homespun in popular conceptions of early America. "For centuries the industrious Bathsheba has been pictured sitting at a spinning wheel," I wrote. "Perhaps it is time to suggest a new icon for women's history." Ten years later, I unraveled that argument when I chose homespun check as a metaphor for neighborly relations in eighteenth-century Maine. It was not just that Martha Ballard's diary allowed me to see things that weren't visible in earlier records. Things changed between the period of *Good Wives*, 1650–1750, and the age of *A Midwife's Tale*, 1785–1812. In seventeenth-century New England, as in Europe, weaving was a male occupation and only a minority of households owned spinning wheels. By the late eighteenth century, cloth-making was not only ubiquitous, it was the foundation of local patterns of barter and exchange that I called a "female economy."

How had this happened? Had the Revolution not only changed the meaning of women's work, but the work itself? My effort to answer these questions led to *The Age of Homespun*. As I burrowed deeper into the sources, I discovered that New England's female-centered production system developed well before the American Revolution and long before the introduction of waterpowered spinning turned women into weavers in other parts of the world. The feminization of weaving was part of a larger transformation in the northern rural economy as families adjusted to new market opportunities. In both Europe and America, this same period witnessed the beginnings of what other scholars have called a "consumer revolution." Far from being in opposition to one another, "store-bought" and "homemade" fabrics developed together.[1]

That discovery took me into the storage collections of museums looking for surviving fabrics. I was astonished by what I found. Packed into drawers and boxes, rolled onto storage tubes, or hanging from moveable frames were hundreds of ordinary household textiles rescued from New England attics. There were sheets, pillowcases, tablecloths, napkins, towels, quilts, blankets, grain bags, handkerchiefs, aprons, coverlets, and more. Rural families saved kitchen rags as well as embroidered bed hangings, Indian baskets as well as old spinning wheels, and Oxfordshire blankets as well as New Hampshire flax. The region's earliest museums had collected exotica—South Island seashells, cypress from Smyrna, spoons made from the horns of Alaskan mountain goats, and pestles and spear points from the graves of supposedly extinct Indians.[2] But in the last

*When this photograph was taken, circa 1900–1910, the garret of the Stephen Robbins Homestead in East Lexington, Massachusetts, was crammed with objects gathered over two centuries. Notice the woodsplint basket in the lower left-hand corner with the rim of a large wool wheel looming over it.*

COURTESY OF THE SOCIETY FOR THE PRESERVATION OF NEW ENGLAND ANTIQUITIES.

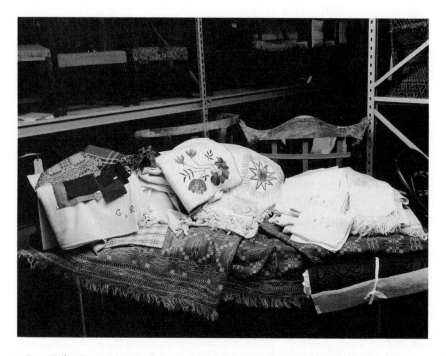

*Eliza Philbrick wrote dozens of handwritten labels identifying objects spun and woven on her grandfather's farm before 1816. Many can be seen here in a storage area of the Society for the Preservation of New England Antiquities. Notice the woven coverlets, the checkered blankets, marked towels, and tablecloths, some with netted fringes, and a pair of rose blankets.*

COURTESY OF THE SOCIETY FOR THE PRESERVATION OF NEW ENGLAND ANTIQUITIES. GIFT OF GEORGE O. SWASEY AND CLARA S. WOODBERRY, 1949. PHOTOGRAPH BY DANA SALVO

decades of the nineteenth century they discovered the detritus of rural households. For a people caught in the march of mechanization, antique tools and scraps of old fabric evoked a world that seemed simpler and more authentic than the one they knew.

Nineteenth-century Americans understood that objects tell stories. They wrote their stories in speeches, memoirs, and poems, and on scraps of paper that they pinned, pasted, or sewed to the things they saved. These were stories about patriotism, family pride, and household industry, about resolute farmers, disappearing Indians, and grandmothers who spun and wove by the kitchen fire. Other stories slipped through their hands, surviving unnoticed in tax lists, vital records, newspapers, censuses, letters, diaries, probate records, merchants' accounts, and in the objects themselves, waiting to be unpacked by genealogical research, historical reconstruction, and curatorial investigation. This is a book about the objects nineteenth-century Americans saved, the stories they told, and the stories that got away. It begins in Litchfield, Connecticut, in 1851, with a speech in which a Hartford reformer named Horace Bushnell gave "the age of homespun" its name. It then moves backward in time to trace the evolution of a mythology of homespun over two centuries of racial conflict, expanding gentility, and war.

My purpose is not to debunk the sentimental vision of the late nineteenth century, but to trace its origins, exploit its contributions, and perhaps in the process explain its persistence. Ironically, the nostalgic and seemingly indiscriminate collecting habits of the late nineteenth century can contribute a new unity to New England's early history. When examined closely, the objects in my imaginary room not only undercut colonial revival ideas about the simplicity and harmony of early American life, they challenge the compartmentalization of contemporary scholarship, forcing us to consider Algonkian baskets and English blankets on the same page, connect the study of household production with the study of expanding commerce, and rewrite the linear narrative of New England's transition from household to factory.

In a poem written around 1690, the Westfield, Massachusetts, pastor Edward Taylor found spiritual meaning in the fact that in a horizontal loom, fabric was wound onto the cloth beam as it was woven, leaving only a few inches exposed, until the entire web was complete. To him weaving was a metaphor for the guiding hand of Providence on the human soul. Although one might not be able to see the design while it was in process, at the end of life it would become visible.

> *Judge not this Web while in the Loom, but stay*
> *From judging it until the judgment day.*
> *For while it's foiled up, the best Can see*
> *But little of it, and that little too*
> *Shews weather beaten: but when it shall bee*
> *Hung open all at once, Oh, beautious shew!*
> *Though thrids run in and out, cross snarled and twin'de,*
> *The Web will even be enwrought you'l finde.*[3]

Taylor's metaphor could also describe the way hindsight allows us to see patterns in history. Looking back, we can see how an unobserved shift in the gender division of labor in the early 1700s created the female-centered textile economy later generations remembered as "the age of homespun."

Yet history gives us more than big patterns. Sometimes the most useful insights come from pondering the harnesses and treadles that move the interlocking threads of daily life. Here the big questions have less to do with overarching change than with the way ordinary people created meaning out of a world cross-snarled and twined. That is why this book focuses on the stories of individual people—makers, collectors, and users of ordinary household goods.

A book is not an exhibit. Words cannot display the texture of a bed rug, the sheen of old linen, or the curious geometry of a niddy-noddy. Nor can words replace the subtle measurements our bodies make as we look up at or down upon things. But with good fortune and sympathetic readers, a book about objects might move through the cluttered rooms of nineteenth-century memory and the ordered galleries of twentieth-century scholarship into that dimly seen and never fully realized space we call history, giving us blood and greed as well as beauty, exhibiting things that did not get saved.

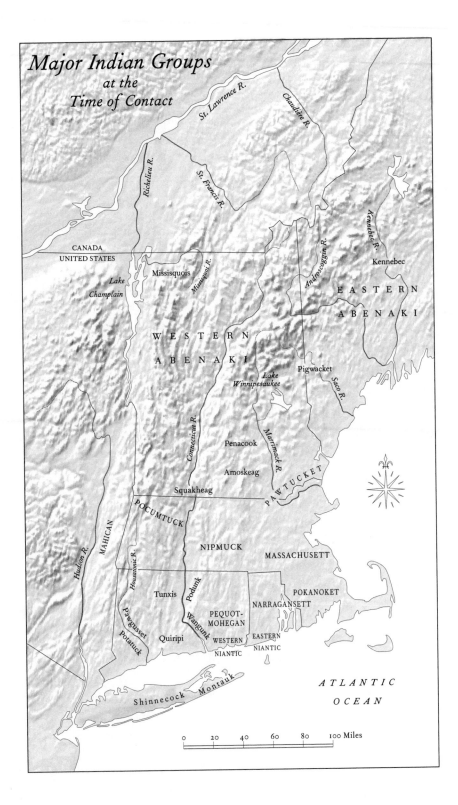

Major Indian Groups
at the
Time of Contact

*St. Lawrence R.*

*Chaudière R.*

*Richelieu R.*

*St. Francis R.*

*Kennebec R.*

*Androscoggin R.*

CANADA
UNITED STATES

Missisquois

*Mississquoi R.*

Kennebec

*Lake
Champlain*

E A S T E R N

A B E N A K I

W E S T E R N

A B E N A K I

Pigwacket

*Lake
Winnipesaukee*

*Saco R.*

*Connecticut R.*

Penacook

*Merrimack R.*

Amoskeag

P A W T U C K E T

Squakheag

POCUMTUCK

*Hudson R.*

MAHICAN

*Housatonic R.*

NIPMUCK

MASSACHUSETT

Tunxis

Podunk

POKANOKET

NARRAGANSETT

*Pawgusset*

Wangunk

PEQUOT-
MOHEGAN

*Potatuck*

Quiripi

WESTERN
NIANTIC

EASTERN
NIANTIC

*Shinnecock*   Montauk

*A T L A N T I C*

*O C E A N*

0    20    40    60    80    100 Miles

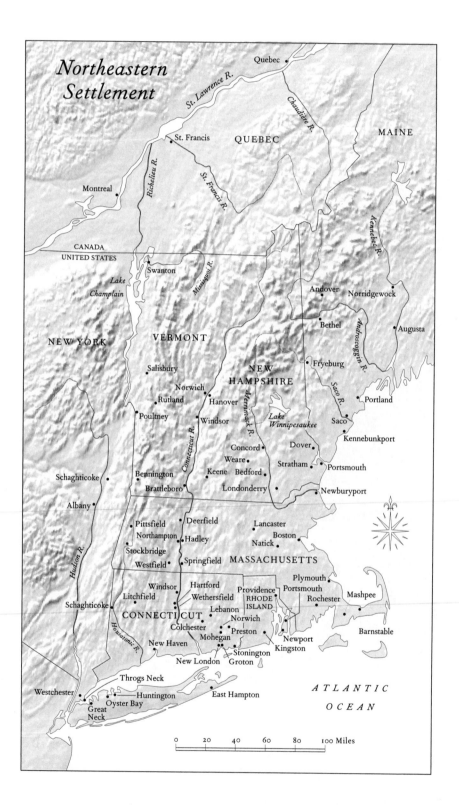

*Northeastern Settlement*

Quebec

St. Lawrence R.

Chaudière R.

MAINE

St. Francis

QUEBEC

Montreal

Richelieu R.

St. Francis R.

Kennebec R.

CANADA
UNITED STATES

Swanton

Lake
Champlain

Missisquoi R.

Andover

Norridgewock

Bethel

Augusta

Androscoggin R.

NEW YORK

VERMONT

Salisbury

Fryeburg

NEW
HAMPSHIRE

Norwich

Rutland

Hanover

Saco R.

Portland

Poultney

Windsor

Merrimack R.

Lake
Winnipesaukee

Saco

Connecticut R.

Concord

Dover

Kennebunkport

Weare

Schaghticoke

Bennington

Keene

Bedford

Stratham

Portsmouth

Brattleboro

Londonderry

Newburyport

Albany

Hudson R.

Pittsfield

Deerfield

Lancaster

Northampton

Hadley

Boston

Stockbridge

Natick

Westfield

Springfield

MASSACHUSETTS

Windsor

Hartford

Plymouth

Litchfield

Wethersfield

Providence

Portsmouth

Rochester

Mashpee

Schaghticoke

Lebanon

RHODE
ISLAND

CONNECTICUT

Colchester

Norwich

Housatonic R.

Mohegan

Preston

Barnstable

New Haven

Newport

New London

Stonington

Kingston

Groton

Throgs Neck

Westchester

Huntington

East Hampton

*ATLANTIC*

Oyster Bay

*OCEAN*

Great
Neck

0    20    40    60    80    100 Miles

# The Age of Homespun

### LITCHFIELD, CONNECTICUT, 1851

*What we call History, considered as giving
a record of notable events, or transactions,
under names and dates . . . I conceive to be
commonly very much of a fiction.*

*Horace Bushnell, "The Age of Homespun"*

The age of homespun wasn't born in Litchfield, Connecticut, but it was christened there on August 14, 1851, on the second day of the county centennial. Litchfield in that year was not the "colonial" town tourists know today, with its spired church and shuttered houses. The center village was poised somewhere between Greek Revival white and Gothic gray. Progress, not nostalgia, was in the air. The county had been in decline for almost a generation, its population siphoned off to the east by new industrial cities and to the west by more fertile states and territories, but under the watchful eye of the Village Improvement Society, the town of Litchfield was reviving. Residents had been tearing down dilapidated eighteenth-century fences and outbuildings, planting trees, and laying out granite fence posts to create the progressive landscape visible in the centennial engraving. Visitors stood under young elms in a *park,* not a *common.*[1]

"The Hill of Litchfield never showed so proud a spectacle," wrote the correspondent for the *New Englander. Ceremony* might have been a better word than *spectacle,* unless seeing a town double its population overnight was a spectacle. There were no fireworks, floats, or contests of skill, just a solemn procession and two days of speeches under the big tent rented from Yale College. Yet the crowd came. A reporter for the *New York Observer* thought there were as many as five thousand people in the pavilion on the opening day.[2] They came from all the towns and notches in the county, from Goshen, Canaan, Bantam Falls, Washington, Mudge Pond, and Kent. They came too from the statehouse in Hartford, from pulpits in Philadelphia, Boston, and Brooklyn, from the Supreme Court of Vermont and the Court of Queen's Bench in Canada. They arrived from industrial Waterbury and Stamford, from the college at New Haven, and from midwestern towns that only looked like Connecticut. Old Ebenezer Landon, age ninety-one, traveled three hundred miles from Lyons, New York, retracing the route he had taken when leaving Litchfield forty-six years before. "We have been wanderers

*Preceding page:*
*Julius Busch.* View of the Litchfield Centennial, *1851.*
COURTESY LITCHFIELD HISTORICAL SOCIETY

from our early homes," exclaimed Judge Amasa Parker of Albany. George Holley of Niagara Falls broke into dialect remembering the scenes of his youth.[3]

At 10:00 a.m. on the first day, the procession moved out from the Mansion House in the center of town led by a military band from the Watervliet Arsenal in New York. Behind the band marched Connecticut's governor and the general of the state's militia, the honorary president and vice presidents of the day, the orator and poet, the Central Committee of Arrangements, the town committees, the emigrant sons, the Odd Fellows, the Cadets of Temperance and other voluntary societies, and the male citizens at large.[4] There were a few clouds in the sky that day, but no rain. Perhaps a breeze touched the necks of the dignitaries as they marched in top hats and tailcoats along East Street, up North Street, circling back to the big tent, where the ceremonies began at eleven with a hymn to the tune of "Old Hundred." The correspondent for the *Observer* thought that "full half" of those in the tent "were the fair daughters of Litchfield County."[5]

The Reverend Mr. Horace Bushnell of Hartford was among the native sons marching in the procession, and he may have been among the dignitaries on the platform, but this was not his day. The speakers on the first day emphasized Litchfield's progress from a backcountry town to a center of education, enterprise, and trade, acknowledging the women in the audience with a few lyrical asides. Judge Samuel Church praised the hardworking colonial wives "to whom the music of the spinning-wheel and the loom was more necessary than that of the piano and the harpischord," and he told the story of how, during the Revolution, Litchfield women melted down an equestrian statue of the king brought from New York to provide bullets for the Continental Army, but like centennial speakers all over New England in this period, he focused on the biographies of leading men. In March he had written to the centennial committee asking the representatives from each of the county's towns to provide the names of the first minister and his immediate successors, the generals and field officers, chaplains and captains in the Revolution, lawyers, divines, physicians, authors, judicial officers, members of Congress, and other distinguished men who were natives of the county. His speech was a kind of parade. Allusions to domestic life were small trills above the drumbeat of his narrative.[6]

Church's discourse consumed two and a half hours, with time out for a recess at noon. The poet and wit John Pierpont followed. According to

one newspaper, he did not so much read his commemorative poem as *act*
it, playing upon the filial pieties of his audience by punning on the surnames of leading families. He too gave brief attention to the ladies, assuring them that their housekeeping talents were valued and that they, too,
had been beneficiaries of progress. In a particularly enthusiastic passage,
he described an exhausted colonial housewife sitting slumped beside her
wheel, "a heap of cotton lying by her side," when suddenly the steam
from her boiling teakettle rose, took the form of an angel, and spoke:

> *Woman, fear not, for thou shalt see the day,*
> *When I, yes I, the vapor that I seem,*
> *Of fire and water born, and baptized Steam,*
> *Will save you all this labor . . .*

There was no hint in Pierpont's poem that, even as he spoke, forty thousand women labored in New England's textile mills. In his view, steam,
not workers, produced calico.[7]

At half past ten on the second day, the centennial procession formed
once again, with Horace Bushnell at its head. The crowd in the big tent
had grown. Was it Bushnell's reputation as a speaker that drew them or the
notoriety of his recent conflict with the orthodox clergy of Connecticut?
His attempt to mesh a new theory of language with Christian theology
had outraged the less imaginative among his brethren, who had forced a
trial for heresy before the Hartford North Consocation. Though he was
acquitted, the controversy was still festering when he arrived at Litchfield
in 1851. The reporter for the *New Englander* thought some in the crowd
were merely curious "to see the man that has dared to bear Calvinism in its
very den." He was a handsome man, with a large head and a shock of dark
hair, slightly silvered, and he was about to surprise his audience.[8]

Bushnell deftly sidestepped theology, charming his listeners and dis-
arming his critics by offering neither a religious discourse nor a conventional history. He began with affected humility. Since Judge Church had
given such a complete account of "the principal events and names of honour by which our county has been distinguished, I am the more willing to
come after, as a gleaner, in the stubble-ground that is left."[9] He took as his
text Proverbs 31, the chapter describing the virtuous woman who "layeth
her hands to the spindle." Cloth-making—a subject that had been mere
miscellany in the judge's discourse and an object of humor and pathos in
Pierpont's poem—would be the organizing theme of his speech.[10]

*Jared B. Flagg. The Reverend
Horace Bushnell, before 1850.*
WADSWORTH ATHENEUM,
HARTFORD, CONNECTICUT.
ENDOWED BY C. N. FLAGG

The topic was not new. Since the 1820s, New England writers, particularly female writers, had been celebrating the productive colonial household, but unlike Church and Pierpont, Bushnell used this familiar material to challenge conventional notions of history.[11] "What we call History, as a record of notable events, or transactions, under names and dates, and so a really just and true exhibition of the causes that construct a social state, I conceive to be commonly very much of a fiction," he began. The causes of a nation's greatness had never been recorded, perhaps never could be, certainly not in the deeds of famous men. He told his audience not to go into burying grounds looking for tall monuments to important people. "It is not the starred epitaphs of the Doctors of Divinity, the Generals, the Judges, the Honourables, the Governors, or even of the village notables called Esquires, that mark the springs of our successes and the sources of our distinctions. These are rather effects than causes; the spinning-wheels have done a great deal more than these."[12]

Bushnell celebrated both the anonymity and the dignity of those he considered the true founders of Litchfield County. "Who they are by name we cannot tell—no matter who they are—we should be none the wiser if we could name them, they themselves none the more honourable. Enough that they are the King Lemuels and Queens of Homespun, out of whom we draw our royal lineage."[13] The image of Litchfield's pioneers as queens and kings of homespun was both a humorous recasting of the antiroyalism of the early republic and a pastoral corrective to the pomposities of the age of progress. If any old farmer and his wife could be a monarch, what did that do to the judges, the esquires, and the honorables marching in dignity through the streets?

Bushnell did not invite women into the parade. He eliminated the parade, substituting a verbal contra dance in which each sex played an essential part, sometimes joining hands, sometimes twirling separately in patterned unity. In the age of homespun, he wrote, fathers "climbed among these hills, with their axes, to cut away room for their cabins and for family prayers," and mothers "made coats, every year, like Hannah, for their children's bodies, and lined their memory with catechism." For both sexes, the virtues of neighborliness counterbalanced the failings of parsimony. The woman who haggled with a merchant for half an hour over some small trade was the first to invite the straitened schoolmaster to dinner. The compulsive farmer threshing by lantern light on a winter evening would not hesitate to drive through deep snow the next day to bring a load of wood to his minister. Formal entertainment in such communities "was commonly stiff and quite unsuccessful," but daily work created more spontaneous pleasure. When young "queens of the spindle . . . agreed to 'join works,' as it was called, for a week or two, in spinning, enlivening their talk by the rival buzz of their wheels, and, when the two skeins were done, spending the rest of the day in such kind of recreation as pleased them, this to them was real society" and far better in Bushnell's view than people going back and forth "with a card-case in their hand."[14]

Although Bushnell's vision of the past was as idealized as Pierpont's and Church's, his descriptions were more physical and immediate. His audience could hear the "thwack" of the weaver "beating up the woof" and the feel of rough wool on the body. Only a man who had himself been clothed in homespun could write of the "heavy Sunday coats that grew on sheep individually remembered—more comfortably carried, in warm weather, on the arm." He even managed a kind word for Calvinism. Rocky ground and cold winters nourished strong people. No matter if "the minister speaks in his greatcoat and thick gloves or mittens, if the howling blasts of winter drive in across the assembly fresh streams of ventilation that move the hair upon their heads . . . great thoughts are brewing, and these keep them warm."[15]

Family life, education, and religion all took their shape from an economy of homespun. "Thus, if clothing is to be manufactured in the house, then flax will be grown in the ploughed land, and sheep will be raised in the pasture, and the measure of the flax ground, and the number of the flock, will correspond with the measure of the house market—the number of the sons and daughters to be clothed—so that the agriculture out of doors will map the family in-doors." In such a society, there will be few distinctions among neighbors. The only "sign of aristocracy" will be that some are "clean and some a degree less so, some in fine white and striped linen, some in brown tow crash." The men of early Litchfield, having no excess money to spend in the tavern, found their entertainments at home. Their wives and daughters "spent their nervous impulse on their muscles, and had so much less need of keeping down the excess, or calming the unspent lightning, by doses of anodyne. In the play of the wheel, they spun fibre too within, and in the weaving, wove it close and firm."[16]

Most newspapers printed the speech in detail, though their reporters didn't know quite what to call it. "His sermon,—for that was the name given to the performance by the presiding officer,—was a masterly piece of pious humor," wrote the *Reporter*. The writer for the *Republican* concluded that it "might be called a Moral Lecture on Economy, rather than a Religious Sermon." The *New Englander* admitted that "though it would be pronounced by severer critics 'not much of a sermon,' " it was based on an ingenious idea, grouping sketches of early life in Litchfield around the theme of homespun. No one called it history. E. D. Mansfield of Cincinnati pronounced it "as strong a eulogy on the 'age of homespun' as can be expected from orator or poet." In his collected essays, Bushnell called it "a secular sermon."[17] Whatever its genre, it is a small masterpiece, a lyrical and cohesive rendering of one of the central myths in American history.


In the last half of the nineteenth century, the mystique of homespun spead. It attracted social reformers as well as conservatives, the arts and crafts movement as well as the colonial revival, and academic artists like Thomas Eakins as well as popular illustrators. By the 1890s, antique spinning wheels were everywhere, even in the mansion of a Montana mining magnate. In San Francisco, the Sequoia Chapter of the Daughters of the American Revolution displayed a New Hampshire flax wheel and a set of Vermont weaving reeds beside a "Paul Revere" lantern and a musket from Bunker Hill. At Hull House in Chicago, Italian, Greek, Dutch, Irish, Syrian, and Russian women offered spinning and weaving demonstrations alongside portrayals of colonial American, Navajo, Hindu, and Japanese textile crafts. In Kentucky, the suffragist Eliza Calvert Hall traveled the hills collecting weaving patterns and stories.[18] No construct with that sort of appeal can be interpreted easily.

In the case of Horace Bushnell, interpretation is further complicated by scholarly disagreement over his larger corpus. In 1978, Ann Douglas dismissed Bushnell as a prime specimen of the loss of intellectual rigor in American Protestantism. From this vantage point, "The Age of Homespun" is just another specimen of "the feminization of American Culture." Douglas's formulation has been challenged by Daniel Walker Howe, who argues that in his best work Bushnell compares "with some of the most original minds of modern times"; he anticipated the ideas of the presumed founders of modern social science, Emile Durkheim, Max Weber, and Sigmund Freud, and foreshadowed the themes of twentieth-century anthropology.[19] Although "The Age of Homespun" gives only a hint of this complexity, its argument for the importance of process over event mirrors many of the themes of modern social history. By shifting attention from political narrative to the unseen workings of ordinary life, Bushnell paved the way for later studies of the relationship between economy and culture.

There is a connection, of course, between his emphasis on social process and his presumed "feminization." As Nina Baym has shown, most histories in the early republic, even those written by women, concentrated on conventional themes of patriotism and military valor, portraying female actors, if at all, as victims of tyranny or as supporters of male heroism. Even Elizabeth Ellet, often considered the inventor of modern women's history, gave the impression that women were somehow outside history, that they were "far more effective on the sidelines as witness and testimony than in the fray."[20] By arguing for the primacy of culture over event, Bushnell was able to place women in the center of the story. Ellet and Bushnell were in total agreement over the character-building virtues of rural life and the importance of women's work in the domestic setting, but where Bushnell made that setting the center of the story, women's work remained for Ellet, as for most of her contemporaries, an acknowledged but undefined backdrop to the more heroic acts of revolution.

His contribution becomes obvious when the sermon at Litchfield is compared with other centennial addresses of the 1850s. At Northampton, Massachusetts, the keynote speaker admitted he really didn't know if it was true, as tradition claimed, that the wife of a colonial retailer used her father-in-law's sermons to line her patty pans. Though he was happy to report that "no old women in this town have ever been accused or imprisoned for witchcrafts," he was sure the more benign "witcheries" of the town's young women had often been felt in courtship. That was as far as he was prepared to go in acknowledging a female past.[21] The bicentennial at Natick, Massachusetts, was just as unapologetically male and probably a good deal less entertaining since the orator of the day, Calvin Stowe (Harriet Beecher's husband), chose to concentrate on theology.[22] At Middletown, Connecticut, in 1853, the Reverend Dr. Field, ailing with rheumatism, paraded the names of the town's clergy, physicians, and founding fathers through 120 pages, digressing only to quote from a 1737 "elegy on the death of a young sister" and to observe that when the "elder President Adams" attended worship in the town in 1771, he observed "a row of women all standing up and playing their parts with perfect skill and judgment."[23]

At Lancaster, Massachusetts, Joseph Willard managed to produce a detailed history, 140 pages in its printed version, that virtually ignored the town's most famous resident, Mary Rowlandson, author of an Indian captivity narrative.[24] At Bedford, New Hampshire, the newspaperman Horace Greeley extolled the brave men who first "let day-light into the woods" of New Hampshire and expressed satisfaction that such men could still be found in "the whaler in the Pacific, the packet-ship at Canton, the mining 'gulch' in California, or the lead 'diggings' of the Upper Mississippi."[25] A song "Written for the occasion by a young Lady" extended his theme:

> Pass on! sons of Bedford, press on in your glory;
> Pass on! deck your brows with the bright wreaths of fame,
> Generations, unborn, will rejoice at your story,
> For History just waits now to take down each name.

That the poet shielded her own name reinforced the message: daughters might offer "wreaths of fame," but only sons could wear them. Little matter. James O. Adams assured the women of Bedford that though their names "may not be recorded on the page of the world's great achievements," their reward would be "above the praise of human lips, greater than the honor which time can give, nobler than the recompense of heroes."[26]

Bushnell himself slipped into that kind of rhetoric in one highly suggestive passage near the end of his speech. "Let no woman imagine that she is without consequence, or motive to excellence, because she is not conspicuous. Oh, it is the greatness of woman that she is so much like the great powers of nature, behind the noise and clatter of the world's affairs, tempering all things with her benign influence only the more certainly because of her silence."[27] In the context of the speech as a whole, this is a minor concession to Victorian sensibility, but it shows one of the pitfalls of social history, which in abandoning the individualistic and institutional biases of conventional narrative sometimes substitutes one form of exclusion for another, freezing people into a collective anonymity that denies either agency or the capacity to change.

Bushnell's appropriation of lines from a poem by Lydia Sigourney exposes the problem. Although Sigourney had long since begun publishing under her own name, Bushnell acknowledged her only as "a favourite poetess of our own," quoting without attribution four short segments from a longer poem called a "Shred of Linen," in which the narrator uses a scrap swept up from the floor to imagine the history of civilization from antiquity to the present. It may well have been Sigourney's poem that inspired Bushnell to organize his sermon around the "article of homespun," though the approach he took was quite different from hers. Sigourney was less interested in women's work in the past than in the possibility of female authorship in the present.

The opening section of the poem lightly raised an old charge: literary women neglect domestic duties. The narrator is apparently sweeping the floor when she discovers the subject of her poem:

> *Here's a littering shred*
> *Of linen left behind—a vile reproach*
> *To all good housewifery. Right glad am I*
> *That no neat lady, train'd in ancient times*
> *Of pudding-making, and of sampler-work,*
> *And speckless sanctity of household care,*
> *Hath happen'd here to spy thee. She, no doubt,*
> *Keen looking through her spectacles, would say,*
> *"This comes of reading books."*

The speaker challenges the shred of linen to tell her of times gone by. When, after a hundred lines of earnest entreaty, it fails to inspire anything worthy of her effort, she resolves to throw it into the rag bag, hoping that it might emerge "stainless and smooth" from the jaws of a paper mill as a "fair page" for a better poet to write upon. Turning her scrap of linen into paper, Sigourney metaphorically chose cultural production over household production. Silence was not the crown she sought.[28]

Bushnell too understood that the labor of rural life left little opportunity for literary pursuits—for men or for women. He both welcomed and feared the opportunities for literary and artistic expression made possible by the industrial age. Too much work reduced life to drudgery, but too little led to shallowness, a fluttering obsession with surfaces. Significantly he described mechanization primarily in terms of women's work: "This transition from mother and daughter power to water and steam-power is a great one, greater by far than many have as yet begun to conceive. . . . If it carries away the old simplicity, it must also open higher possibilities of culture and social ornament. The principal danger is, that, in removing the rough necessities of the homespun age, it may take away also the severe virtues and the homely but deep and true piety by which, in their blessed fruits, as we are all here testifying, that age is so honourably distinguished."[29] That he used the word *ornament* to describe the advantages of the new economy suggests his ambivalence. In comparison, the piety of the age of homespun seemed "deep and true."

Had Bushnell been willing to push his analysis further, he might have arrived at a materialist critique of nineteenth-century gender roles. If women in early Litchfield acquired dignity through an encounter with the "rough necessities" of life, how could one argue against contemporary women's engagement with the work of the world? Was enlarged "social ornament" enough—for women or for men? Something very like Bushnell's vision of the age of homespun lay behind Charlotte Perkins Gilman's complaint that industrialization had created "an enormous class of nonproductive consumers,—a class which is half the world, and mother of the other half," and it was the observation that in ages past women had done "practically all the spinning, dyeing, weaving, and sewing" that led Jane Addams to ask whether modern women, even with the expansion of factory labor, were yet doing "their full share of the world's work in the lines of production which have always been theirs." Bushnell, however, resisted the implications of his own argument, seemingly incapable of imagining a reciprocity in modern industrial society such as that he so fully imagined in the age of homespun. If production had moved out of the home, the responsibility for "Christian Nurture" had not, and since personality was formed in childhood, and largely by unconscious means, the inculcation of piety required a domestic woman.[30]

Bushnell's idealizations of women were based in part on his own female progenitors. He remembered his maternal grandmother, Molly Ensign Bushnell, primarily for her piety and independence of spirit. She converted to Methodism shortly before she migrated to Vermont, where she organized meetings in her home, picking likely men to read the sermons. Although Bushnell saw her very few times in his life, he later attributed his own call to the ministry to her influence. "Whether it is that she made impressions on my childhood by means I do not recall, or whether, by sending me messages and verses of her own composing in the letters to my father, she knit into my feeling the conviction that she had religious expectations for me, felt but not expressed, I do not know."[31]

More important to his construction of early American women as "Queens of Homespun" were his memories of his own mother. Dotha Bishop Bushnell had no more than a common school education, but according to her son she was never self-conscious about her disadvantages. She clothed her six children in linen and woolen of her own making, administered a home dairy, boarded farm laborers, and during part of the year fed the workers in "a homespun cloth-dressing shop" attached to her husband's mill. She sent her children to the district schools—and Horace to Yale—clothed "in better, cleaner homespun than any others." All this work she accomplished year after year, working thirteen or fourteen hours a day, without a word of complaint. "What mortal endurance could bear such a stress of burden! And yet she scarcely showed a look of damage under the wear of it, but kept the appearance rather of a woman of some condition."[32]

There was a darker side to the family history that Bushnell was unable to acknowledge. When he wrote of the "young gentleman of homespun" who looked to his wife as "an angel of help," he was appealing to an ideal that was often betrayed in his own family's past. In 1789, his mother's father had abandoned his wife and three children, sailed to Virginia, and, as one historian described it, "cajoled an Anglican cleric into joining him in another marriage with a local woman of uncertain reputation." In his published descriptions of conjugal partnership, Bushnell bypassed such stories. He also ignored his own dismay over his mother's broken health when for the third time his father decided to try his fortunes in a new setting, uprooting his family for a last attempt in upstate New York. The manuscript version of Bushnell's "Age of Homespun" suggests that he struggled over the marriage section of his speech, writing and then crossing out phrases that located the "poetry of marriage" in its "truth to nature," its "sober constancy," or in "peace and love." He finally chose to end this section with humor, telling the story of a New England minister whose mother-in-law provided a wedding suit in the midst of winter by having "some of her sheep sheared and sewed up in blankets to keep them from perishing with cold."[33] His whimsical story silenced questions about the legal disabilities of early American women or the infelicities of colonial marriage.

Bushnell probably first encountered the "woman question" in the late 1830s when the antislavery activists Angelina and Sarah Grimké toured New England, creating an uproar because they dared to speak in public. In an 1840 sermon, Bushnell asked whether "rough publicity" would eventually turn ladies into "mere women," observing that "of the two women most conspicuous in the history of our Lord's trial-scene, Pilate's wife, who stayed at home, gave him some good advice, which it had been well for him to follow; while the busy maid, who went, actually faced down an apostle, and made him lie and swear as vilely as the worst man could."[34] Although he eventually accepted more public roles for women, he never fully resolved the tension in his own thinking between a Christian egalitarianism that refused to measure men and women by different standards and social conventions that elevated gender difference.

His 1869 book, *Woman Suffrage: A Reform against Nature*, epitomized his ambivalence. He acknowledged female oppression, argued for equal access to education, and applauded female advancement in literature and the professions, but simply couldn't imagine a society in which women took on the "rough-hewing" work of government. They had a "divinely superior ministry," one that placed them "above equality with men." He stuck to his position even though his daughter disliked it, his wife probably disdained it, and his friends in the women's suffrage movement were outraged. But he also admitted to his publisher that some passages in the book probably reflected his own "pains and discomposures more than my thoughts."[35]

The tensions apparent in Bushnell's thinking about women help explain the attractions of the age of homespun. In a world where economy and household were one, there was no need to choose between equality and domesticity. Locating the sources of American character in the preindustrial household allowed writers to elevate women's work without challenging the nineteenth-century trope of separate spheres. As a changing economy and a new political order drew men into the contentious worlds of commerce and politics, women could continue to model the domestic virtues of piety, thrift, hard work, and concern for the welfare of neighbors. Bushnell's celebration of household self-sufficiency challenged the materialism of his own age while leaving its structure intact.

By removing events from his story, he also avoided the dark underside of New England history. Bushnell was outspoken in his support for the rights of African Americans, including the right of freedmen to vote, but he showed little interest in American Indians. The only allusion to indigenous peoples in "The Age of Homespun" came early in the speech when he suggested that spinning and weaving marked a stage in the evolution of humankind from savagery to civilization. Since rude and primitive societies were characterized by clothing of skins, the creation of fabrics by spinning and weaving marked "a great social transition, or advance," one "not even yet absolutely perfected." He displayed neither the overt racism nor the ethnographic interest of his contemporary John W. DeForest, whose *History of the Indians of Connecticut from the Earliest Known Period to 1850*, completed in the year of the Litchfield centennial, described Connecticut Indians as "a people purely barbarous, whose nature was unsoftened by a single trait of civilization."[36] Like many writers before and since, Bushnell created an American pastoral by leaving Indians out, ignoring both the devastating wars of the colonial period and the persistence of native peoples.

There were Indians in Connecticut in 1851. They were farmers, housewives, blacksmiths, mariners, laborers, chair caners, basketmakers, cooks, preachers, and household servants, some visible to their neighbors as Indians, some categorized as "Negro" or "mulatto." A few weeks before the centennial, a young Hartford printer visited the jail overlooking the central green at Litchfield. Perhaps he was looking for news. Just as likely he was engaged in charitable work, bringing a message of salvation to the four men destined to die for a robbery and murder committed a year before. One of those men gave the printer a woodsplint hat that he donated to the Connecticut Historical Society a few weeks later with a note saying it had been made "by Henry Manasseh, an Indian, while in Litchfield Jail, under sentence of death." The rest of Manasseh's story is

*Henry Manasseh. Woodsplint hat made in Litchfield County Jail, c. 1850.*
COURTESY CONNECTICUT
HISTORICAL SOCIETY

lost, but his hat survives, witnessing his creativity and a lineage of native basketry central to New England history.[37]

Bushnell excised the troubling elements in Litchfield's past, but his ideas about the nature of history remain powerful. He said that the silent work of ordinary people in the past is like electricity, which, though unseen, "goes through and masters the world, holding all atoms to their places, and quickening even the life of our bodies." Electricity becomes historic only in a storm, "though it does nothing more in its thunder, than simply to notify us, by so great a noise, of the breach of its connexions, and the disturbance of its silent work." Historical events, then, are merely "points where the silence is broken by something apparently not in the regular flow of common life."[38] The obvious task for the historian, then, is to connect electricity and thunder. The objects nineteenth-century Americans collected can help us do that by calling attention to the unseen technologies, interconnections, and contradictions that lie beneath audible events.

No one knows when New Englanders first began displaying spinning wheels at public celebrations. Perhaps the idea developed out of Whig politicking of the 1840s. A New Hampshire town history notes that "an enthusiastic meeting of the Whigs of Hillsborough County" in 1840 included a "log cabin from Nashua, with the usual appendages."[39] There were probably many impulses behind the new emphasis on domestic life, including a desire to tame traditional holidays. In 1850, Boston reformers organized a parade of schoolchildren in fanciful costumes as a corrective to the rowdiness of typical Independence Day celebrations. Horace Mann, among others, ridiculed the "strange notion that there is any natural connection between wit, eloquence or ethics, on the one hand, and the burning of gunpowder on the other."[40]

Whatever the motive, towns in widely different parts of New England introduced vignettes of cloth-making into their historical celebrations. Three years after the Litchfield centennial, the citizens of Rockport, Massachusetts, included ten young ladies spinning and carding among the "emblematical" tableaux in their Fourth of July parade.[41] A YMCA fund-raising fair mounted in Boston in 1858 included costumed spinners in a replica of Benjamin Franklin's birthplace. The next year the citizens of Amherst, New Hampshire, erected a colonial hearth in their town hall, serving bean porridge and demonstrating flax- and wool-spinning as a part of their centennial celebration. The Hadley, Massachusetts, bicentennial of 1857 featured an ox-drawn wagon filled with spinning wheels and other antique implements. Its banner proclaimed the advance of civilization and the success of the Connecticut River Valley broom-corn industry: "Then the red man scoured the roofless room / Which now we sweep with the Hadley broom."[42]

In 1864, transplanted Yankees living in Brooklyn, New York, organized a fund-raising fair for the U.S. Sanitary Commission that included a "New England kitchen" with demonstrations of carding and spinning. Before the year's end there were similar exhibits in Philadelphia, New York City, Indianapolis, Poughkeepsie, and St. Louis. The Philadelphia exhibit honored colonial Germans, the one in New York City the Dutch, but those in Brooklyn, Indianapolis, and St. Louis were all billed as "New England" kitchens.[43] These were mere rehearsals for the displays of antique furniture and demonstrations of household crafts at Philadelphia in 1876 and Chicago in 1893.

Until the end of the nineteenth century some New England towns continued to march their leading citizens to the meetinghouse on public holidays for a long-winded and womanless narration of local history. This was especially so if the town had a notable military past. Yet even at Lexington, Massachusetts, in 1875, a fragment of linen appeared among the muskets in an exhibit of Revolutionary relics.[44] The triumph of homespun is exemplified in the evolution of public rituals at Dedham, Massachusetts, one of the commonwealth's oldest towns. In the two hundredth anniversary in 1837, the "ladies" were consigned to a private reception at the courthouse where they presided over tables of exotic fruits and performed at the pianoforte. Fifty years later, local women managed an "old-fashioned New England kitchen" in the church vestry, while in the parade, a mythical log cabin of 1636 draped with "fox, raccoon, skunk, and other skins" featured Miss Dolly Wale at her wheel.[45]

Henry Wadsworth Longfellow's 1858 poem "The Courtship of Miles Standish" helped to popularize the mystique of household production. Readers loved his story about the ascendancy of youth over age, love over power, and the New World over the Old. The real hero of the poem is not Standish, "the stalwart Captain of Plymouth," but young John Alden, whom Standish enlisted to court Priscilla Mullins on his behalf. When the reluctant go-between opens the door of the Mullinses' cottage, he sees a beautiful young woman seated at a spinning wheel with "carded wool like a snow-drift / Piled at her knee." As he explains his errand, Priscilla, "with eyes overrunning with laughter," asks why he doesn't speak for himself.[46]

An illustrated guide to the 1876 Philadelphia exposition featured the supposed desk on which John wrote love letters to Priscilla and claimed that a spinning wheel in the "New England Log Cabin" might have been "the very one which Priscilla, the Puritan maiden, whirled so deftly that poor John Alden could find no way out of the web she wove about him." During the Columbian Tercentenary, Priscilla and her lover appeared in a New York City parade alongside Columbus and Isabella. The organizers of a pageant sponsored by the Massachusetts Woman Suffrage Association featured John and Priscilla alongside Anne Hutchinson and other heroines of early feminism. "Was there a spice of feminine coquetry in her famous speech to John Alden?" one writer asked. "Or was it that she understood the dignity and worth of womanhood, and was the first in this new land to take her stand upon it?" Meanwhile, a Boston furniture manufacturer borrowed lines from the Longfellow poem to advertise parlor chairs made out of the discarded parts of old spinning wheels. By 1884, middle-class families could purchase plaster figurines of the famous couple, designed by John Rogers, a sculptor who was once an employee of New Hampshire's famous Amoskeag textile mills.[47]

Antiquarians, novelists, interior designers, settlement-house workers, museum curators, social theorists, architects, genealogists, entrepreneurs, journalists, political conservatives, and radicals joined in the frantic pursuit of the lost relics of colonial households. In Marion County, Pennsylvania, an inventor and illustrator named Linton Park added "The Flax Scutching Bee" to a panoramic series on rural life. In Deerfield, Massachusetts, two women trained at the New York Academy selected an abstract spinning wheel as the logo for their Society of Blue and White

*Scenes from the "New England Kitchen,"* Harper's Illustrated Weekly, *July 15, 1876.*

Needlework. In Boston, Dr. Mary Hobart encased the diaries of her great-great-grandmother, the midwife Martha Moore Ballard, in a home-made cover of linen. In Londonderry, New Hampshire, Justice of the Peace Robert Mack witnessed and then had photographed an affidavit signed by his wife attesting to the eighteenth-century origins of a scrap of handwoven towel. (Twenty years before, he had compiled a conventional, male-centered history of his town's 150th anniversary.) Academic historians too were touched by the craze. When Charles Andrews published the final volume of his magisterial history of colonial America in 1919, he selected as his frontispiece a photograph of "A New England Kitchen of about 1750" from the Essex Institute.[48]

The mythology of household production gave something to everyone. For sentimentalists, spinning and weaving represented the centrality of home and family, for evolutionists the triumph of civilization over savagery, for craft revivalists the harmony of labor and art, for feminists women's untapped productive power, and for antimodernists the virtues of a bygone age. Americans expressed these ideas in local and national celebrations, in family festivals, and in craft demonstrations. When they couldn't find appropriate objects in their grandparents' trunks, they invented or embellished them.

Alongside these celebrations of homespun, others were displaying so-called primitive crafts. Both the Women's Building and the Anthropological Building at the Chicago World's Fair featured exhibits of American Indian basketry, pottery, and weaving. Interpreters were divided over their implications. One writer, taking a feminist stance, argued that primitive women "were the originators of most of the industrial arts, and that it was not until these became lucrative that they were appropriated by men." Other writers emphasized the domestic quality of women's work over time. One even found evidence of mother love in a display of Peruvian mummies. These were "poor shreds and patches of humanity, yet so eloquent of mother-love, for who but a mother would have swathed those small bodies in softest feather cloth, and placed in the little hands food for that last long spirit journey."[49]

Was primitive woman a rung on the evolutionary ladder or a model for modern housewives? Had women in fact always been more civilized than men? The debate continued into the twentieth century. The author of a 1915 manual on basket-making explained that American Indian women stood "where Egyptian, Roman, Teuton, Frank and Briton women once were before their respective races attained civilization and culture." She found much to admire in their work. "While primitive man, of all races, waged war and hunted, of necessity, primitive woman was ever the constructive element in society, the homemaker, the conserver of industry and thrift, the manufacturer, through simple, homely processes, of the raw products of nature into useful and sometimes beautiful forms, the inventor of many crafts, the mother of the arts, the nurse of religion." Since progressive psychologists in this period argued that children recapitulated the history of the race as they grew, basket-making became an appropriate activity for summer camps and schools. By modeling themselves on primitive woman, youthful members of organizations like the Camp Fire Girls discovered the nonmonetary rewards of work and their own domestic destiny.[50]

Meanwhile, enterprising basket makers from throughout the northeast were capitalizing on the new interest in indigenous crafts. In 1884, Abenaki families from St. Francis, Quebec, established a summer camp at Intervale in the White Mountains of New Hampshire, where they made and sold baskets to tourists. Adopting some of the strategies of the "wild west" shows that were popular at the time, they dressed in Plains war bonnets and enacted stereotypical ceremonies that assured customers that the wastebaskets, pencil holders, and sewing and knitting baskets they sold were authentic. Similar encampments flourished at Niagara Falls, on Cape Cod, at Lake George, and on Mount Desert Isle. This was much more than an effort to exploit Anglo-American stereotypes for economic gain. By "playing Indian," northeastern Indians began their own colonial revival, recovering lost languages and restoring ethnic pride.[51]

On both sides of the cultural divide, exhibitors, collectors, and craft revivalists wrapped themselves in the past. For Anglo-Americans, class was a more insistent concern than ethnicity. Eliza Philbrick of Salem, Massachusetts, revised her family's history in the "colonial gown" she created in 1898 for a Daughters of the American Revolution party in Boston. She made the dress of rough brown wool spun and woven on her grandparents' New Hampshire farm almost a century before and saved uncut in her mother's trunk, but to the skirt she added a brightly colored panel purchased from an antiques dealer. She believed, no doubt correctly, that this panel had been "hand-wrought" before the Revolution, but it probably began life as a bed valance. She was photographed twice in this marvelous creation. By 1911, when the last picture was taken, she had replaced the antique embroidery with her own reproduction, adding new details to the neck and sleeves (see page 417).

*Eliza Philbrick, 1898.*
COURTESY PHILLIPS LIBRARY,
PEABODY-ESSEX MUSEUM,
SALEM, MASSACHUSETTS

*Eliza Philbrick's
"colonial gown."*
COURTESY PEABODY-ESSEX
MUSEUM, SALEM,
MASSACHUSETTS

No colonial dame ever wore a dress like Eliza's, but that was no matter. Her creation resolved any tension she may have felt between her rural ancestry and her desire for refinement. Eliza was a member of state and local chapters of the DAR, the Rebecca Nourse Association, the Association of the House of Seven Gables, and the Haverhill Whittier Club, as well as the Essex Institute. But she did not belong to the elite circle of ladies on Chestnut Street who presided over balls, pageants, and teas in their ancestors' silk gowns. In creating a colonial dress that combined homespun with fancy embroidery, she asserted both her independence from the ladies of patrician Salem and her desire to stand among them.[52] In an essay published in the *Essex Antiquarian* in 1897, she quoted a passage from a well-known memoir likening the motions of a woman spinning wool to the "graceful movement of the arms of a harpist and the action of the lawn-tennis player."[53]

A wall pocket made by the Maliseet basket maker Agathe Athanase for the World's Columbian Exposition in Chicago in 1893 is as exuberant as Eliza Philbrick's dress and as resoundingly eclectic. Hanging from the shelves, compartments, and lacy edges of this Victorian extravaganza are forty-five miniature baskets, twenty ash splint flowers, and tiny representations of snowshoes, a moccasin, a bow and arrow, and a birch-bark bowl. Athanase simultaneously honored the past and addressed the future. Porcupine quills trace the words FORGET ME NOT into the bar inside the circlet of flowers at the top. Along the bottom more porcupine quills spell WITH FOND LOVE TO THEE, REMEMBER RIV DU LOUP, CANADA, INDIAN WORK. Was this a plea that she as the maker might be remembered, or an acknowledgment of the values of an unknown purchaser? In any case, no one could doubt that this was "Indian Work." Like Philbrick, Athanase honored her ancestors by making something new. She did not, however, control the disposition of her own creation. After the fair, the head of the Ethnographic Division forwarded it "temporarily" to Harvard University's Peabody Museum. When the Quebec middleman responsible for the Maliseet, Naskapi, and Montagnais artifacts failed to return letters, the museum quietly accessioned the whole collection. Athanase was apparently never paid for her work though her wall pocket ensures she will not be forgotten.[54]

The contradictory impulses of the colonial revival animate the writing of Elizabeth Barney Buel, whose charming little book *The Tale of the Spinning-Wheel*, published in Litchfield in 1903, offered a vision of the past that was simultaneously more conservative than Bushnell's and more

*Agathe Athanase. Wall pocket made for the Chicago*
*World's Fair, 1892.*

explicitly "women's history." Born in New York City in 1868, Buel was
the sole woman in Columbia University's class of 1891. Like many educated women of her generation, she turned to club work after marriage,
founding a chapter of the DAR in Litchfield in 1899, and eventually serving as a national officer. Buel did not claim to be feminist, yet her prose
radiated a conviction that women mattered in the past and that they had
not been given their due. "The plough and the axe are not more symbolic
of the winning of this country from the wilderness, nor the musket of the
winning of its freedom, than is the spinning-wheel in woman's hands the
symbol of both," she began. Then she laid out the evidence: The women
of early New England not only made soap, candles, medicines, pies, pick-
les, jams, jellies, preserves, mead, metheglin, butter, and cheese, "they ran
bullets, as we very well know in Litchfield." Furthermore, they raised
flax, spun and carded wool, "knitted every pair of stockings and mittens,
wove every inch of linen and woolen cloth, and cut and made every stitch
of clothing" worn by their families. "No wonder a man could go to the

*Emily Vanderpoel.*
*Frontispiece for* The Tale
of the Spinning-Wheel.
*Litchfield, Connecticut,*
*1903.*

war for his country's independence, when he left Independence herself at
home in the person of his wife."[55]

The New York artist and Litchfield summer resident Emily Noyes
Vanderpoel created a frontispiece for Buel's book that perfectly captures
its spirit. A refined young lady dressed in the gauzy garb of the early
republic stands poised in a doorway with a great wool wheel, her stance

*Daughters of the American Revolution, Litchfield, Connecticut, c. 1900. Elizabeth Barney Buel, wearing medals, is in the front row.*

COURTESY LITCHFIELD HISTORICAL SOCIETY

securely domestic yet turned outward toward the world. The hub of the wheel, centered on her body, coyly alludes to her sexuality. She is both productive and reproductive, fitted to her sphere yet visible beyond it.

Buel dedicated her book to the "Mary Floyd Tallmadge Chapter, Daughters of the American Revolution," opening with a radically condensed quotation from Horace Bushnell: "Queens of Homespun, out of whom we draw our royal lineage." Since Bushnell had said that the citizens of Litchfield County would be "none the wiser" if they could name their ancestors, and "they themselves none the more honourable," the dedication is unintentionally ironic. By the end of her life, Buel had traced her own lineage to three colonial governors and nine *Mayflower* passengers and was simultaneously a member of the Colonial Dames, the Society of Mayflower Descendants, the United States Daughters of 1812, the Daughters of the Barons of Runnemede, the Martha Washington Memorial Association, the Daughters of Colonial Wars, and the Daughters of Patriots and Founders of America. She was also affiliated with the American Defense Society and the National Security League, organizations allied with the most conservative elements of the DAR.[56]

Buel was not indifferent to the changing industrial cities around her. In 1921 she revised and edited the DAR *Manual for Immigrants,* a handbook distributed by the thousands to incoming Americans. The hand of welcome and friendship, however, presupposed a willingness on the part of new immigrants to embrace a new culture. "Do not live in the crowded parts of a city, among those who speak a foreign language," Buel advised. "Associate with those who speak English and make friends with them. Live among them if possible. Learn their customs and the American way of living."[57] Similar ideas are reflected in the papers of the Litchfield Needle and Bobbin Club. When they contemplated offering lace-making instruction to the children of immigrants, a New York friend advised, "*Insist* that English *alone* be spoken—no foreign tongue. You can use these little lace centres as patriotic propaganda centres. You can interest the children in other things than lace." The same theme turned up, incongruously, in their work with the Sybil Carter Indian Lace Association, a group founded in the 1890s to teach needlework on reservations. "Lace, taught under these auspices, to the original natives of our continent, becomes an American industry," the secretary reported.[58]

In the half century since Bushnell gave his speech on Litchfield Hill, the age of homespun had passed from an alternative vision of history to a new kind of orthodoxy. The town had changed, too. In the late nineteenth century, wealthy urbanites began refurbishing their ancestors' homes and building new ones in the same style, combining romantic bay windows with Palladian doorways to create the "colonial" town visitors enjoy today. Litchfield's summer folk disdained the ostentation of nouveau riche Newport, glorying in a simplicity sustained by family pedigree. There were mild concessions to change. When the town celebrated its bicentennial in 1920, a historical pageant performed at the Litchfield Golf Links included, in addition to the requisite "Age of Homespun," a scene entitled "The New Leaven—Columbia Welcomes the Foreign Born." Antonio Da Rosa and the Italian Mutual Benefit Society portrayed the immigrants; Emily Vanderpoel played Columbia.[59]

Nineteenth-century Americans passed on a vision of New England's history saturated in sentiment and encrusted with contradiction. But they preserved artifacts and documents, rescued old buildings from demolition, aroused public interest in and support for historical institutions, revived dying arts, and stimulated new forms of scholarship. Their contributions are too important to be forgotten and their questions and assumptions still too much with us to be left unchallenged.

Horace Bushnell got some things right. In the late eighteenth century, cloth-making really was a cooperative enterprise, a neighborly as well as a household activity, and women were at the center of production. But the system he remembered had not been transplanted from the Old World to the New. The colonists who came from East Anglia to New England in the 1630s left a sophisticated manufacturing economy where men, not women, did the weaving. In Europe women had dominated cloth production from antiquity through the early Middle Ages. In fact, the word *wife* seems to be related etymologically to the word *weave*. But with commercial expansion in the late fourteenth and early fifteenth centuries, weaving became a male occupation. Guild regulations and municipal statues actually forbade weavers from employing their female relatives at the loom.[60]

The women and men who joined the great Puritan migration to New England in the 1630s brought this gender division of labor with them, but in the new setting, weaving became first a marginal enterprise and then a female occupation. The shift from male to female weavers was not just a change in the identity of workers, but a transformation in the nature of production. English weavers were apprentice-trained artisans; their colonial successors were domestic manufacturers who borrowed and traded implements with their neighbors, producing primarily for household use. Their work complemented rather than replaced foreign imports.

In the 1760s this largely invisible, seemingly retrograde cloth-making system acquired potent political meaning as Parliament's effort to tax the colonies provoked boycotts of British goods. Spinning meetings organized by New England's "daughters of liberty" became front-page news, taking a place of honor in spaces typically reserved for matters of state. "I presume there never was a Time when, or a Place where, the Spinning wheel could more influence the Affairs of Men, than at present, in this and the neighbouring colonies," exclaimed one writer.[61] A concern with women's work continued in the political discourse of the early republic, as Jeffersonians and Federalists debated the kind of economy the new nation would have.

The height of household production came in the early industrial era, not because economic circumstances forced families to work harder, but because machines made that work easier. Waterpowered carding mills took over the arduous task of preparing wool for hand spinning. Spinning-wheel makers perfected double-handed wheels and "accelerating heads" for handling finer grades of wool. Tiny spinning factories produced cotton warp and soft "candle-wicking" that supplemented home-grown fibers, and agricultural fairs celebrated household industry. Bushnell's claim that the "transition from mother and daughter power to water and steam-power" carried with it "a complete revolution of domestic life and social manners" was exaggerated.[62] Although mechanization had a powerful impact on middle-class women living in cities, hand spinning persisted in some parts of rural New England and in new states and territories into the 1850s. Rural women carried the values of the economy of homespun into early textile mills. In a series of strikes between 1828 and 1834, they revived the rhetoric of the Revolution, insisting on being valued as producers and as the daughters of free men.

The history of rural cloth-making is a story about the wealth that ordinary people created. But it is also a story about cultural conflict, violence, and death. In 1881, a farmer in Gill, Massachusetts, cut into a high point of land on a corner of his farm and discovered twelve bodies "buried with their feet resting on a circle about five feet in diameter, the heads radiating out like the spokes of a wheel." These bones ended up in Case D in the "Indian Room" in the Pocumtuck Valley Memorial Association's museum in Deerfield, Massachusetts, near a "Domestic Room" filled with antique spinning wheels, flax breaks, reels, hetchels, swifts, scarns, warping bars, swingling knives, and a loom.[63] Nineteenth-century Americans knew that their sheep grazed on Indian graves. Later historians have not been so quick to see the link between textiles and the conquest of North America. In the earliest years of colonial settlement, cloth literally transformed the landscape as Algonkian beaver passed into the hands of English felt-makers and English sheep began to graze on American meadows. The English conquered North America with spinning wheels as well as with guns.

From the beginning, cloth-making was also implicated in the expansion of New World slavery. As early as the 1640s, New Englanders began spinning West Indian cotton. In the 1760s, 70 percent of the cotton shipped into mainland North America came to New England states. Almost all of it was destined for household looms. After 1790, short-staple cotton exported from New Orleans or Charleston fed waterpowered mills.[64] New Englanders made cloth because they were farmers, lumberers, and mariners; because the flax they grew kept their daughters employed; because the ships that carried their fish and lumber to the West Indies brought back cotton as well as sugar; and because the rough land they cleared was suitable for sheep. There was no period when they were disconnected from the larger Atlantic economy.

When examined closely, the fourteen objects that organize this book show the intersection of Algonkian and English textiles and the interweaving of household production and commerce. The Indian basket, twined from basswood and cornhusk using techniques a thousand years old, is interlaced with unravelings of English wool. Molly Ocket's pocketbook also describes a series of exchanges across national and cultural divides. Designed to hold cash, it was twined from moose hair, then offered as a gift from an Abenaki woman to a colonial gunsmith. The woodsplint basket carries this theme into the early republic. Lined with Vermont newspapers from the 1820s, it tells us that its unknown maker was simultaneously an heir to a woodlands tradition and a participant in the market economy of the early republic.

The wool wheel is a direct descendant of those carried by commercial cotton manufacturers from the Near East to Italy in the twelfth century. The flax wheel, made in New England in the late eighteenth century, could have come out of a Dutch genre painting of the 1600s. Yet they sit in a seventeenth-century log garrison, a relic of New England's colonial wars. The embroidered blanket, woven on a household loom in northern New England in the early nineteenth century, puns on commercial "rose blankets" made in Oxfordshire and shipped everywhere in the Atlantic world. The cotton counterpane, an almost perfect replica of coverlets made in Lancashire in the same period, was woven at home from factory-spun yarn by the wife and daughters of a Maine shipbuilder. In examples like these, household manufacturing, industrial enterprise, and Atlantic commerce intersect.

Artifacts tell us most when they are imbedded in the rich texture of local history. As a work of pastoral embroidery, the chimneypiece is a reminder that idealizations of rural life long predated the colonial revival. It takes on deeper meaning, however, when related to the work of impoverished children gathered into Boston's spinning schools in the same period and to the contemporary clash between the embroiderer's father and the Mashpee Indians for whom he was guardian. Prudence Punderson's picture is equally complex. Interpreted for decades as an artifact of Puritan consciousness, it was in fact made by the Anglican daughter of a

Connecticut Loyalist on the eve of the American Revolution. Inspired by an eighteenth-century novel, it testifies to the limits of American liberty, not only in its portrayal of a diminutive slave standing beside a child's cradle but in its representation of an embroiderer who symbolically embraced death over seduction. Although stitched with imported threads, both pictures were paid for in part by a traffic in homespun.

Such works teach us that needlework was simultaneously a site of cultural production and a field for personal expression. Hannah Barnard's cupboard alerts us to something else—that textiles, homemade or store-bought, were a form of wealth and the core of female inheritance in a world where fabrics were so precious that rugs covered beds rather than floors, tablecloths were more valuable than tables, and an argument over yarn could lead to arson. The little niddy-noddy, the blue-and-white bed rug, and the tasseled tablecloth show how rural women created property, sharing tools and "changing works" in an economy of homespun celebrated but imperfectly represented in the rhetoric of the American Revolution and the political discourse of the early republic. Finally, an unfinished stocking, still on its ancient needles, witnesses the continuity in women's work over three centuries. The homespun yarn trails off the needles into two tight balls filled with the energy of its spinner.

The stories hidden in New England collections shatter Bushnell's vision of an innocent rural economy sustained by homespun, but they demonstrate the power of his central argument. To study the flow of common life is to discover the electricity of history.

# I

→>–<←

# An Indian Basket

*The rudest and most primitive stage of
society has its most remarkable distinction
in the dress of skins.*

Horace Bushnell, *"The Age of Homespun"*

The basket is four and a half inches high and four inches in diameter, about the size of a large tomato can, though smaller at the top than the bottom. When new it could have held a generous pound of meal or beans or twenty-four fathoms of wampum. Now light leaks through a weft ravaged by time and insects. The basket holds it shape through hundreds of invisible mends, the unseen art of a conservation lab. Tiny twists of rice paper bonded with unpronounceable adhesives like polyvinal acetate and polymethyl methacrylate fill gaps in a fragile fabric strengthened by multiple infusions of soluble nylon in ethyl alcohol. Would the basket be as precious without its story?

It came to the Rhode Island Historical Society in 1842 with a label carefully written by the donor:

> This little basket, was given by a squaw, a native of the forest, to Dinah Fenner, wife of Major Thomas Fenner, who fought in Churche's Wars; then living in a garrison in Providence, now Cranston, R.I. The squaw went into the garrison; Mrs. Fenner gave her some milk to drink, she went out by the side of a river, peeled the inner bark from the Wikup tree, sat down under the tree, drew the shreds out of her blanket, mingled them with the bark, wrought this little basket, took it to the garrison and presented it to Mrs. Fenner. Mrs. Fenner gave it to her daughter, Freelove, wife of Samuel Westcoat, Mrs. Westcoat gave it to her granddaughter, Wait Field, wife of William Field at Field's Point, Mrs. Field gave it to her daughter, Sarah. Sarah left it to her sister, Elenor, who now presents it to the Historical Society of Rhode Island.
>
> Field's Point, September, 1842.[1]

The reference to "Churche's Wars" led nineteenth-century antiquaries to date the basket to 1676, the year Captain Benjamin Church of Little Compton, Rhode Island, led New England troops in victory over the

Wampanoag leader Metacomet, or King Philip. No one since has doubted the attribution.[2] Displayed in the late nineteenth century alongside other relics of Rhode Island's first century, the basket quieted a troubling history of frontier conflict. Exhibited today as an icon of native art, it fulfills much the same purpose, shifting attention from the violence of the late seventeenth century to our own generation's hopes for multiculturalism.[3]

The details in Field's description line up like clues in a mystery: a garrison, milk, a Wikup tree, shreds from a blanket, and those evocative names—Dinah, Freelove, Wait. There was a Dinah Fenner who lived in Rhode Island in 1676, though in that year her name was Dinah Borden, and she was only eleven years old. She did eventually marry Thomas Fenner, a man who helped to defend Providence in King Philip's War, and they did have a daughter named Freelove who had a granddaughter named Wait. Yet there is much in the story that remains puzzling. If the basket was made by "a native of the forest," why would she have come to an enemy garrison in time of war seeking milk, a food repulsive to a people known today to be lactose intolerant? Was she a refugee? So desperately hungry she was willing to accept any food offered? If so, how does one explain the basket? The exposed warp is indeed rough, but the twined pattern is intricate and artful. Could its maker have stripped and soaked fibers from the inner bark of a tree, gathered husks from an abandoned field, then patiently sat on the bank of a river weaving in a time and place where even friendly Indians were in danger? That hardly seems likely, yet laboratory analysis tells us there are fragments of red and blue wool still clinging to the interior of the basket.[4] Could they have come from an English blanket?

The twentieth-century Narraganset historian and basket-maker Ella Sekatau once told a visiting scholar about a curious window in an old schoolhouse near her Rhode Island home. One pane was of "old, old glass," ridged and warped. Looking into it, people saw things that weren't there, like "a sea with Indian people, and it didn't match with the window next to it" or ancient figures standing by a big stone outcropping. Everybody saw different things, not the actual objects that sat on the other side of the window, but shadowy scenes from somewhere else. "My cousin's husband said you shouldn't have things like that, and he broke it."[5]

Dinah Fenner's basket is that kind of window. Some will use it to imagine a history more intimate and peaceful than the one in books. Others will find nothing in it they can trust. Interpreting such an object requires both imagination and skepticism, imagination to see new possibilities in

an old story, but skepticism about its placid surface. Here the important
question is not how a Rhode Island woman got her basket, but why milk,
a basket, and a blanket should appear in the same narrative. Rereading the
early history of New England with these objects in mind transforms an
apocryphal story into a powerful lens for understanding exchange relations in the first century of English settlement. To write about blankets is
to write about the expansion of English commerce. To write about baskets is to discover the little-known work of Native American women. To
search for the meaning of milk is to find the biblical vision that animated
the English quest for land. The history of Dinah Fenner's family brings
these themes together in unexpected and disturbing ways, providing a
solution to the origins of the basket that is less literal than Field's telling
yet true to its larger themes.

The English who came to the coast of what is now New England in the
early 1600s were not all alike. Some came to fish, some to pray, and
among those who prayed there were enough differences to keep them
squabbling and sometimes hounding one another from colony to colony
for generations. The people they found here also differed. Although
scholars sometimes refer to them collectively as Algonkians, they spoke
different dialects, inhabited different river basins, and assigned a bewil-
dering array of names to one another. In terms of textile history, however, Englishmen and Algonkians differed more from each other than
they did among themselves. The English came from a wool-producing
country proud of its blankets. Algonkians were renowned for their
basketry.[6]

Archaeological sites on coastal New England are littered with lead
seals once attached to bolts of fabric. As the Englishman Richard Hakluyt
espressed it in a 1584 treatise, the second purpose of colonization, after
advancing the "kingedome of Christe," was the vending "of the masse
of our cloths and other commodities." The English did that with a
vengeance.[7] Yet they were also fascinated with the unfamiliar fabrics they
found in Indian villages. Among the Algonkians, textile production was
women's work. Men worked in stone, metal, and wood, producing
impressive tobacco pipes, knot dishes, pendants, and other ornaments.
Women made netted, twined, sewn, and plaited textiles to cover their
houses, dry corn, trap fish, store provisions, carry produce, and line
graves. In the words of one English observer, they made baskets of

"rushes, some of bents; others of maize husks; others, of a kind of silk grass; others of a kind of wild hemp; and some of barks of trees, many of them, very neat and artificial, with the portraitures of birds, beasts, fishes, and flowers, upon them in colours." Men hunted and cared for tobacco fields. Women planted, hoed, and harvested food crops, storing them in containers of their own manufacture. Rhode Island's Roger Williams described heaps of maize "of twelve, fifteene, or twentie bushells a heap" drying on woven mats by day, covered with tarps of basketry at night.[8]

One writer claimed to have seen an immense basket buried in the earth that held sixty gallons of maize. Another said Indian containers ranged in volume from "a quart to a quarter" (in archaic usage a quarter was eight bushels).[9] Tightly woven bags of soft hemp held the parched maize called *nokake* in some dialects and *yohicake, yoheag, yokeg,* or *nokehick* in others, a food "so sweet, toothsome, and hearty, that an Indian will travel many days with no other food but this meal, which he eateth as he needs, and after it drinketh water." Williams claimed to have traveled with an Indian band "neere 100 miles through the woods, every man carrying a little Basket of this at his back, and sometimes in a hollow Leather Girdle about his middle."[10]

Although Europeans had their own basketry traditions, basketry was far more varied among the Algonkians. Thomas Morton wrote of mats made by stitching together long strips of what the English called "sedge" with "needles made of the splinter bones of a Cranes legge, with threeds, made of their Indian hempe." In preparation for netting or weaving, women spun fine fibers between their fingers or across their thighs. William Wood said that Indian cordage was "so even, soft, and smooth that it looks more like silk than hemp." Other writers admired the "curious Coats" or mantles of turkey feathers that women wove together "with twine of their owne makinge, very prittily." John Josselyn, who spent much of his time in northern New England, described "Delicate sweet dishes . . . of Birch-Bark sowed with threads drawn from Spruce and white Cedar-Roots, and garnished on the outside with flourisht works, and on the brims with glistering quills taken from the Porcupine, and dyed, some black, others red."[11]

Wigwams were also a form of basketry. Wood said that women framed them like an English garden arbor, "very strong and handsome," then covered them "with close-wrought mats of their own weaving which deny entrance to any drop of rain, though it come both fierce and long, neither can the piercing north wind find a cranny." Observing Indians along the Maine coast a little later in the century, Josselyn described similar structures "covered with the bark of Trees" and lined inside "with mats made of Rushes painted with several colours." Two different marsh plants—cattail (*Typha*) and bulrush (*Scirpus*)—yielded different fabrics. Sewn in overlapping layers, the leaves of the cat-o'-nine-tails swelled and exuded a gummy substance when wet, giving exterior mats their waterproof quality. Rushes, on the other hand, dried quickly and when combined with other fibers, such as the soft inner bast of cedar, could be woven into soft and absorbent mats as decorative as they were practical. These mats gave Indian dwellings their portability. "I have seen half a hundred of their Wigwams together in a piece of ground and they shew prettily, within a day or two, or a week they have been all dispersed," Josselyn wrote.[12] Wigwams moved because work moved. Coastal groups cultivated fields of maize, beans, squash, and tobacco in summer, moving to warm interior valleys in winter where game and fuel were more plentiful.

The most exotic textiles required both male and female labor. Men drilled and ground the beads called wampum from periwinkle, conch, and whelk shells or from the blue-black centers of the quahog. For ordinary exchange, these were strung into lengths the English measured in fathoms, but for ritual regalia, women wove the beads into "pleasant wild works" with warps of sinew and wefts of hemp. A wampum band worn by the Wampanoag leader Metacomet was nine inches wide and long enough to reach from a man's shoulders to his ankles. It was edged with red hair said to have been acquired in the Mohawk country. Metacomet's accoutrements, according to Josselyn, were worth twenty pounds in English money, or five times as much as all the clothing and bedding he recommended an English immigrant bring to New England.[13]

Although English writers admired Algonkian textiles, they had difficulty explaining their decorative qualities. The best analogy they could find was to the needlework of upper-class women, but since Indian women also did field work, this only confused the issue.[14] The most elaborate exploration of the problem is in a Latin poem with English translation published by William Morrell, who spent a year at Plymouth in 1623. Morrell compared decorative mats to the pictorial tapestries or "arras" found in English country houses and the "curious finger-worke" he found in Indian villages to *passementerie* or parchment lace.[15] Yet he puzzled over the fact that Algonkian women combined this delicate work with physical labor. "These hands doe digge the earth, and in it lay / Their fair choyce corne, and take the weeds away." Native women confounded English notions of class by combining outdoor labor with fine finger work and English notions of gender by performing agricultural labor the English assigned to men. While women worked, men, Morrell believed, spent their days "in play, / In hunting, armes, and pleasures."[16]

The division of labor among Native Americans was probably more complex than the simple male-female divide described in English accounts. Surely there was some heirarchy of age, skill, or status in textile production, and the sexual division of labor was not as fixed as it might seem. Williams said that men cut and set the long poles for houses, and that even in agricultural work, "sometimes the man himselfe, (either out of love to his Wife, or care for his Children, or being an old man) will help the Woman which (by the custome of the Countrey) they are not bound to." Williams no doubt idealized the noncompetitive virtues he wished to inculcate among his own people when he wrote of "friendly joyning" to break up fields, build forts, hunt, or fish, but his description of work parties of forty, fifty, or a hundred men and women corrects others' accounts of female drudgery and male leisure. His observations reinforce the larger point, however, that female as well as male labor was visible to and admired by outsiders.[17]

Nothing survives that can fully convey the complexity of seventeenth-century Algonkian textiles, but Dinah Fenner's basket read alongside archaeological fragments helps us to understand some of the techniques and materials used. The warp is of bark, the wefts of wool and of a flatter material that may have been cornhusk. The construction is complex. The weaver began with a plaited base, using three strands of bark for each warp, then moved to simple twining and finally to a technique called "wrapped twining" in which two wefts, one active and one passive, intersect the warp. By changing the color as she wrapped, she produced the pattern.[18] The technical details are important because they locate the basket in an ancient textile tradition. Shreds of twining very similar to that in Dinah's basket have been found in northern Vermont in archaeological sites dating from the Early Woodland period (1000–100 B.C.). One fragment even revealed a faint chevron created by weaving animal hair in two colors. Except for the wool in its weft, Dinah's basket could have been made a thousand years before the first European excursion to North America. It only hints at the variety of early textiles. Through electron microscopy, archaeologists have identified early baskets woven from the

*Top left: Pattern of ornamental weaving on Dinah Fenner's basket. Above: Pattern of quill embroidery on the Mohegan bag.*
DRAWINGS BY MINDY CHIOU

"bast" or stem fibers of wild hemp, dogbane, milkweed, and nettles, as well as the fibrous inner bark of slippery elm, black willow, cedar, and basswood. Excavations from later sites include plaited and sewn matting, coiled netting, and twined textiles of many kinds.[19]

Other bags and baskets thought to have been made in the early colonial period suggest the range of techniques and designs. On July 4, 1842, the same year that Eleanor Field presented her great-great-grandmother's basket to the Rhode Island Historical Society, a Norwich, Connecticut, man donated a twined bag to the Connecticut Historical Society in Hartford. It, too, came with a story. He said he had received it "from Cynthia, now 60 or 70, and daughter of Lucy Tocamwap, the first member of the Mohegan church. By tradition of her own family Cynthia believes the basket to be near 300 years old." He called it a Yohicake bag. If so, it was an extraordinarily large one. Measuring 13¼ by 9¼ inches, it could have held as much as three quarts of meal. The upper edge originally had twenty-four eyelets through which a drawstring could have been threaded.[20] Unlike Dinah Fenner's basket, the Mohegan bag is a soft textile, flat when empty. In each row, the weaver twisted two weft threads around each warp in a kind of spiral, then inserted porcupine quills in two shades to create the design. The banded design, though similar to painted motifs on later Mohegan baskets, is quite different from the stepped diagonals on Dinah's basket.

*Mohegan bag. Hemp and
porcupine quills.*
COURTESY CONNECTICUT HISTORICAL
SOCIETY. GIFT OF WILLIAM C. GILMAN,
1842

A third bag or basket with a New England provenance is closer in size to the Yohicake bag but closer stylistically to Dinah's. Called a wampum bag by its present owners, it ostensibly belonged to a Haverhill, Massachusetts, woman who was taken captive in the late seventeenth century. A later owner edged it with chintz and turned it into a sewing basket. This basket, like Dinah's, has strong diagonal elements with serrated edges and

*Wampum bag changed into
a sewing bag.*
PRIVATELY OWNED. PHOTOGRAPH
COURTESY NEW YORK STATE
MUSEUM, ALBANY

negative stripes.[21] A fourth example came to a Massachusetts museum in 1989. Although it has no history, textile experts believe it, too, is colonial. Like Dinah's basket, it mixes wool with bark. The handling of the materials is different, however. The warps are "plied" or doubled and the wool worked in later, as with the porcupine quills on the Yohicake bag.[22] The variations in the four baskets may reflect individual preferences, change over time, or stylistic differences among neighboring Algonkian peoples. The twining techniques, however, link all four to ancient American textiles.

Archaeological evidence documents the similarities and differences between European and indigenous fabrics. At a Wampanoag site on the west side of Narragansett Bay, archaeologists found sixty-six fragments of native basketry alongside seventy-three relics of European cloth. The European fabrics ranged from bits of a white wool blanket with end stripes of red, blue-green, and brown to a long coil of a trimming called "galloon" woven in yellow silk with twists of silver thread. The Algonkian textiles included ordinary matting as well as fabrics too complex and individual for an English loom—a belt of glass beads woven with sinew, a wampum collar skillfully shaped to fit the curve of a neck, and fragments of matting that incorporated as many as three techniques in a single swatch.[23]

Though made from different fibers and for different uses by people in radically different circumstances, many employed identical weave structures. A mat of undyed vegetable fibers, for instance, and a fabric of brown wool both exemplify "plain weave," the simple over-under technique that most of us learned in childhood. Another fragment woven in what textile specialists would call a "2/2 twill" is identical structurally to the pieces of English blanket found on the same site. Other samples demonstrate that Algonkian as well as English weavers knew how to vary plain-woven fabrics by combining warps and wefts of different materials or weights.[24]

What was different about the two sets of textiles was not their structural sophistication or the abilities of their makers, but their mode of production. In the Middle Ages, Europeans had perfected a method of producing large quantities of fairly simple fabrics through the use of spinning wheels and looms. Equally important were changes made in the early modern era in the division of labor. English fabrics traded in North America were made in an economy that divided work into many parts. A hierarchy of workers performed a small set of tasks over and over again, middlemen in one part of the kingdom selling wool, spun yarn, or undyed cloth to intermediaries in other towns who passed them along a production chain that stretched from one end of the British Isles to another and across the Atlantic to America.

For Europeans, flax was the most important vegetable fiber. Depending on soil and weather, it produced a long silky "line" used in linen or a shorter, rougher fiber called "tow." Sheep provided both "wool" and "worsted," a difference created not only by alternative ways of feeding the animals, but from different methods of preparing fleeces for spinning. Carding oriented the fibers of short, crimpy wool horizontally, so that when spun they formed a fuzzy surface or nap on the finished cloth. Fulling or pounding accentuated the effect, creating a dense surface that could be sheared. Long hairy worsteds, on the other hand, were combed longitudinally to create smooth fabrics that could be glazed or pressed.[25] Woolens were the basis of the heavy cloths historians call the "Old Draperies." By the early seventeenth century, lighter fabrics made of worsted, alone or in combination with linen, wool, or silk, became important. These were sometimes called "Tammies," from the French word *estame.*[26]

*Seventeenth-century broadside, reproduced in E. Lipson,* The History of the Woollen and Worsted Industries *(London: A. & C. Black, 1921).*

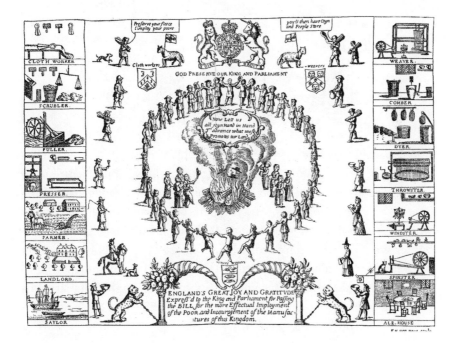

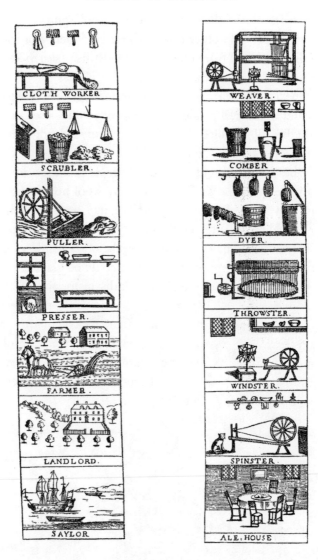

A broadside celebrating a parliamentary bill protecting worsted shows one artist's perception of the organization of English manufacturing. In the center, an unbroken circle of male weavers joins hands around the bonfire as giddy women, portrayed here as consumers rather than as workers, throw foreign imports into the fire. Smaller images around the border symbolize the many groups, from spinsters to landlords and from wool combers to alehouse keepers, sustained by worsted manufacturing.[27] What is remarkable about this image is its emphasis on the compartmentalization of production. Combing, spinning, dyeing, and dressing are as separate from one another as plowing and sailing.

What was true of worsteds was true of wool as well. In a famous description of the blanket makers of Witney in Oxfordshire, Robert Plot explained how wagons went weekly from Witney to London, returning with "fells" wool taken from animals slaughtered in "the furthermost parts of the Kingdom" and gathered into London for marketing. Witney manufacturers sorted the wool from these fleeces into half a dozen grades, shipping long stapled worsted to stocking manufacturers, reserving the best "Bay-wool" and "Head-wool" to make their most expensive blankets, and designating "Middle" and "Ordinary" wool for medium-priced products, some of which they mixed with local fleeces for the cloth they called "duffels." They used "tail-wool" for seamen's blankets and worked what was left into a rough fabric called "Wednel" used to stiffen collars, wrap bales, or cover barges. Plot estimated that Witney's blanketers kept 150 looms in active service, employing "3000 poor People, from Children of eight Years old, to decrepit old Age." Sorting, warping, weaving, fulling, dyeing, and finishing were men's work. The children and old folks did the carding and spinning.[28]

This was the division of labor Adam Smith theorized nearly a century later in *The Wealth of Nations* when he described a plain woolen coat worn by a day laborer. "The shepherd, the sorter of the wool, the wool-comber or carder, the dyer, the scribbler, the spinner, the weaver, the fuller, the dresser, with many others, must all join their different arts in order to complete even this homely production." Subdividing work increased productivity by reducing "every man's business to some one simple operation," by saving "the time commonly lost in passing from one sort of work to another," and by allowing the "application of proper machinery." By the time he wrote, both the subdivision of labor and the application of machinery had advanced considerably, but the general direction of change had been established much earlier. Seventeenth-century writers would have understood Smith's contrast between civilized and uncivilized economies. In "savage nations" everyone worked but everyone was at the same time "miserably poor." In "advanced and thriving nations," some people worked hardly at all and consumed ten times more than others, yet everyone was enriched. "It is the great multiplication of the productions of all the different arts, in consequence of the division of labour, which occasions, in a well-governed society, that universal opulence which extends itself to the lowest ranks of the people." Hence, an industrious peasant in an advanced society was more wealthy than an "African king" who was the absolute master of "ten thousand naked savages."[29]

*Massachusetts seal, Cambridge Press, 1672.*
COURTESY AMERICAN ANTIQUARIAN SOCIETY

*Massachusetts seal, Foster Press, 1675.*
COURTESY AMERICAN ANTIQUARIAN SOCIETY

American Indians were among the earliest models for the European notion of the "naked savage." An icon of a man dressed only in leaves was impressed in wax on the earliest official documents of the Massachusetts Bay Colony. Although the details of clothing and even the sex of the Indian on the colony's seal changed over time, most versions included the plaintive cry "Come over and help us," an adaptation of a passage in the Book of Acts describing the apostle Paul's vision of a man praying, "Come over into Macedonia, and help us." In the English view, New World "savages" needed both spiritual and material clothing. Christianity and good English cloth came together.[30]

Yet writers who emphasized Indian nakedness sometimes described Indian clothing in some detail. Williams's *Key into the Language of North America* included Algonkian words for coat, mantle, waistcoat, apron, stockings, and shoes. He admired, and perhaps even tried, native footwear, which "being excellently tann'd by them, is excellent for to travell in wet and snow; for it is so well tempered with oyle, that the water cleane wrings out; and being hang'd up in their chimney, they presently driee without hurt as myself have often proved." He differentiated the aprons or breechcloths that adults of both sexes wore and the loose wrappings that they picked up and put down as required. William Wood referred to women's wrappings as "beaver petticoats."[31] When Daniel Gookin wrote that the "Indians' clothing in former times was of the same matter as Adam's was," he wasn't referring to the nakedness of the first couple or to the aprons of fig leaves they constructed for themselves but to the "coats of skins" God gave them when he banished them from the Garden of Eden.[32]

The English wanted these coats. The makers of high-style hats eagerly sought American beaver since it was the only fiber that when felted was both strong and supple enough to sustain its shape when wet. Thomas Morton reported that in the 1630s beaver sold for ten shillings a pound. Presumably that was the price given to the English broker, not the Algonkian supplier, but at ten shillings, a single pound of beaver would have purchased two and a half pounds of broadcloth, the most expensive of the English fabrics. Algonkians gave up Adam's clothing not because it was inferior to English cloth but because it had become too valuable to wear. The half-naked Indian on the Massachusetts seal obscures the interconnectedness of Adam's and Adam Smith's clothing.[33]

Indians did not exchange their beaver mantles for broadcloth but for duffels, or "trucking cloth," a kind of blanketing woven about sixty inches wide and dyed in deep colors. Plot said the Witney manufactories dyed most pieces "Red or Blue, which are the Colours that best please the Indians of Virginia and New England."[34] He believed the Indians tore duffels into "Gowns of about two Yards long, thrusting their Arms through two Holes made for that Purpose, and so wrapping the rest about them as we our Loose coats." No other seventeenth-century source mentions the armholes, though New England writers agreed about the length. The earliest writers used the terms *duffels* and *blankets* interchangeably. By midcentury, the common term for a two-yard length of trucking cloth was "Indian Coat." William Wood described customers at English trading posts choosing "a good coarse blanket, through which they cannot see, interposing it between the sun and them" to make sure it was of the proper weight and thickness. This they used for "a double end, making it a coat by day and a covering by night."[35]

His description displayed both arrogance and grudging admiration: "They love not to be imprisoned in our English fashion. They love their own dog fashion better (of shaking their ears and being ready in a moment)." Like other seventeenth-century writers Wood saw the Indian preference for loose wrappings from a stance of cultural superiority: Indians wore blankets because they were animal-like and because they didn't know better.[36] Some twentieth-century scholars have been almost as ethnocentric, arguing that because "Indians had no woven cloth before the arrival of European traders and settlers," it took time for their women "to learn sewing skills." Others assume that Indians were attracted to woven fabrics because they "were lighter and more colorful than animal skins and nearly as warm," as though the replacement of one form of clothing for another were a simple matter of consumer choice.[37]

What these explanations miss are the asymmetries between European and Algonkian textiles. Indians didn't adopt English blankets because they were superior to their traditional clothing but because furs and hides purchased new products like iron pots, knives, and guns. It is hardly surprising that the wearers chose to use their new clothing very much as they had the old. Nor did Indian women have any reason to take up English textile tasks when they were so fully occupied with their own. A trucking-cloth blanket might replace a mantle of skins, but it could not roof or furnish a wigwam. Trade with Europeans had a profound impact on male hunting and on the trading and manufacture of wampum, which became a kind of currency in the fur trade, but it had little effect on women's other textile work.[38] A hundred years after contact, Algonkian women were still weaving mats for wigwams and baskets to store and carry food.

Unlike wampum, baskets had only a minor role in English-Algonkian exchange. In a letter forwarding "30 fathom of Beades" to Governor John Winthrop of Massachusetts, Roger Williams offhandedly mentioned that he had sent a basket, "a present from Miantunnomues wife to your deare Companion Mrs Winthrop." To the Narraganset sachem and his wife Wawaloam the basket may have had as much diplomatic meaning as the beads, but to Williams it seemed a mere gratuity.[39] Wood also described exchanges between Indian and English women as "gifts." "These women resort often to the English houses," he wrote, adding that they usually brought with them "something that is either rare or desired, as strawberries, hurtleberries, raspberries, gooseberries, cherries, plums, fish, and other such gifts."[40] Mats and baskets must have entered into these exchanges, though evidence of their presence survives only by accident. A Springfield court record, for example, mentions "a double Indian mat compassing the bed." A Salisbury, Massachusetts, witch trial told of "a little Indian basket" that wouldn't stay in the loft where it was kept. (That an ordinary English brick had the same propensity shows that Indian goods had no monopoly on enchantment.)[41]

Baskets are hard to find in early records because they resisted commodification. As manufactured products they were less valuable to the English than furs and skins, nor were the materials of which they were made of particular interest to colonists. Where Indian women found abundant fibers for weaving, the English saw only dark forests, waste fields, and dismal swamps. But baskets were there, and they, like blankets, were essential props in the unfolding events that led to misunderstanding and war.

So far we have spoken of the native peoples of the Northeast collectively, but in fact there was no single "Algonkian" response to English colonization, no unified "Indian" point of view. The Wampanoags under their leader Massasoit welcomed early settlers at Plymouth in 1620 in part because they saw them as potential allies against their traditional enemies, the Narragansets. In Connecticut the Mohegans eventually joined a Puritan alliance against their feared neighbors the Pequots. Epidemics introduced by transient fishermen and voyagers had weakened coastal Indians even before the arrival of English settlers. Pious New Englanders saw God's hand in their destruction. When smallpox struck southern New England in 1633, William Bradford thought that lack of proper bedding may have contributed to the suffering. "They die," he wrote, "like rotten sheep." Running sores stuck to the mats they lay on. "When they turn them, a whole side will flay off at once as it were, and they will be all of a gore blood, most fearful to behold."[42]

War followed disease. In 1637, an English attempt to intercept Dutch control of the fur trade of the upper Connecticut River Valley led to the first of the region's fratricidal conflicts. Images of basketry appear in English descriptions of an attack on a fortified Pequot village on the western side of the Mystic River. Some soldiers grappled hand to hand while others went into wigwams "and brought out fire and set them on fire, which soon took in their Mats, and their houses standing close together, with the wind all was soon on a flame, and thereby more were burnt to death than were otherwise slain."[43] The victorious Puritans sold the survivors as slaves to Bermuda or divided them among their own people or their Indian allies. From a shipment of Pequot children sent to Massachusetts, one Englishman claimed "the fairest and the largest that I saw amongst them, to whom I have given a coat to cloathe her."[44]

In the decades that followed, the English colonies used coats to purchase land and to control Indians they wanted to remain friendly. At New Haven in 1638, colonial leaders offered the Quinnipiacs twelve coats of English trading cloth, among other goods. At Guilford the next year, the "sunk squaw" Shaumpishuh received twelve Indian and two English coats on behalf of the fourteen men, six women, and fourteen children who accompanied her. In 1658, another female leader, Namumpum, later known as Weetamoo, relinquished her claim to land for "20 yards blew trading cloth, 2 yards red cotton, 2 paire of shooes, 2 paire stockings, 67 broade hoes and 1 axe."[45] In 1660, Connecticut officials offered Robin Cassasinamon six coats for his services "in governing the Pequots." Parents who promised to indenture their children to "godly English" received a coat a year.[46]

One can read the history of seventeenth-century New England as a series of such exchanges. "Coats" or blankets bought furs first, then land, loyalty, and other Indians' heads. The cataclysmic war that Eleanor Field knew as "Churche's War" and that most people called "King Philip's War" began in a quarrel over a coat. When a southern New England Indian came to Plymouth in 1675 and accused three other Pokanokets of murdering a Christian Indian named John Sassamon, he showed officials "a Coat that he said thay gave him to Conseall them." When the accused men were called to account for their behavior they retorted that the informer was lying, that he had gambled away his coat and then refused to pay for the one they provided: "he not to pay so acused them."[47] This presumed argument over a blanket led to one of the worst wars in American history. Plymouth officials tried and executed the Pokanoket men, provoking attacks later that month on Plymouth Colony towns near the Rhode Island border. For a time it looked as if King Philip and his Narraganset ally Canonchet would succeed in pushing the English back to the Atlantic. Through English diplomatic efforts and with the help of Mohegans and other native allies, the colonists eventually prevailed. One chronicler claimed that when the English negotiated a treaty with the Niantic sachem Ninigret, they promised that "for every Indians Head-Skin they brought, they should have a Coat . . . and for every one they bring alive two Coats; for King Philips Head, Twenty Coats, and if taken alive, Forty Coats."[48]

Both English and Algonkian fabrics are central to the famous captivity narrative of Mary Rowlandson, a Massachusetts women captured in a combined Nipmuck, Narraganset, and Wampanoag attack on the town of Lancaster, Massachusetts, where her husband was minister. Rowlandson performed various textile chores for her captors, sewing shirts and an apron and knitting several pairs of stockings. Rowlandson's mistress during her captivity was Weetamoo, squaw sachem of the Pocassets, a woman she described as a "severe and proud dame," who spent as much time every day in dressing herself as "any of the gentry of the land." Weetamoo's "work," Rowlandson said, "was to make girdles of wampum and beads," ornaments that appear again in a richly detailed passage describing a dance in which Weetamoo and the Narraganset leader Quinnapin participated. "He was dressed in his Holland shirt with great laces sewed at the tail of it; he had his silver buttons, his white stockings, his garters were hung round with shillings, and he had girdles of wampum upon his head and shoulders."[49] Quinnapin had altered a standard English shirt into an impressive dancing costume. Instead of wrapping the long tail between his legs to form an undergarment, as the English did, he let it hang behind, the better to expose the "great laces sewed at the tail of it."

These "laces" may have been narrow tapes or "points" attached vertically to create a fringe, or bands of bobbin or bone lace sewn flat as on an English petticoat or pillow covering. Either way, the Narraganset sachem had appropriated—and transformed—powerful emblems of English gentility. Massachusetts law forbade "men or women of mean condition" to wear "gold or silver lace, or buttons, or points at their knees" or "bone lace above two shillings per yard." Weetamoo, too, had reinterpreted English clothing. Wearing a petticoat of kersey, a wool fabric often used in England for outdoor clothing, she was "covered with girdles of wampum from the loins upward; her arms from her elbows to her hands were covered with bracelets; there were handfuls of necklaces about her neck and several sorts of jewels in her ears." On her legs and feet were "fine red stockings and white shoes." All the dancers, Rowlandson wrote, were dressed "after the same manner."[50] Rowlandson was both fascinated and repelled by Weetamoo's apparel.

Despite their delight in English clothing, Weetamoo's people had not abandoned native textiles. Rowlandson was impressed with the handicraft she saw displayed all around her in the Nipmuck and Wampanoag camps. Like earlier observers, she commented on the warmth and tightness of Indian shelters. "It rained, but they quickly got up a bark wigwam where I lay dry that night." On another occasion, she was grateful for the kind woman who invited her into her dwelling and "laid a mat under me and a good rug over me." The mat was surely like those the first English settlers saw in Indian wigwams fifty years before; the "rug" was probably a shaggy bed covering of English origin. Although Rowlandson began her trek wearing an English "pocket," a detachable pouch attached to her waist with long strings, she too eventually acquired a back basket made from twined or plaited fiber. "We took up our packs and along we went, but a wearisome day I had of it," she wrote in describing her eighteenth "remove." She, like the warrior who told her he had a Bible in his basket or the young woman who walked "three weeks into the Narraganset country to fetch corn they had stored up," probably wore a twined or plaited burden basket, perhaps one much like these still being made by Wampanoags in the late nineteenth century (see page 416).[51]

Rowlandson's ethnographic descriptions were created amid the horror of war. In eighteen months, twenty-five hundred English soldiers and noncombatants were killed (about 5 percent of the colonial population). Five thousand Indians, as much as 40 percent of the estimated population, were killed. As in the Pequot War, survivors were enslaved.[52] In several chronicles written after the war, the Indian defeat was symbolized as a reversion to nakedness. In an unpublished letter to an English correspondent, Dinah Fenner's grandfather William Harris described the Narraganset leader Canonchet throwing off his clothing as he fled Connecticut troops. Harris assumed that he intended not only to lighten his load but to divert his pursuers. First came his silver-laced English coat, "but the captain would not stop for the coat. Then Canonchet threw away his great belt of wampum, but the captain was interested only in the chief himself who, when he came to the river, leaped into it, thereby wetting his gun." Another account adds an Indian coat to the story. Canonchet "first cast off his blanket, then his silver-laced coat, and lastly his belt of peag."[53]

The most dramatic account of such a capture was by Benjamin Church, the man whose chronicle helped date Dinah's basket. Church had the glory of capturing Philip, but the climax of his narrative is not Philip's death, however, but the melodramatic capture a few days later of the man Church considered to be the last great Wampanoag warrior, Annawon. Two members of Annawon's band, an old man and his daughter, led Church after dark to Annawon's fortress set in the declivity of a great rock. From above they could see how Annawon had set up a row of birch bushes against the rock, "where he himself and his son and some of his chiefs had taken up their lodging, and made great fires without them, and had their pots and kettles boiling and spits roasting." Annawon's son, wrapped in a blanket, lay with his head near the guns, which were "lodged in two crotches, and a mat placed over them, to keep them from the wet or dew." The camp was visible, but the cliff so steep it was impossible to reach it except by lowering oneself down "by the boughs and the bushes that grew in the cracks of the rock." "Captain Church then ordered the old man and his daughter to go down foremost, with their baskets at their backs, so that, when Annawon saw them with their baskets he should not mistrust the intrigue. Captain Church and his handful of soldiers crept down also under the shadow of these two and their baskets."[54] When Annawon's son realized he had been tricked, he "whipped his blanket over his head and shrunk up in a heap."[55]

In contrast, Annawon surrendered nobly. His final act was to cast a bundle at Church's feet. Inside were belts of wampum, two horns of powder, and a red cloth blanket. These, he said, "were Philip's royalties."[56]

We return then to our mystery and to the story Eleanor Field gave to the Rhode Island Historical Society. Read literally it points to an exchange of a basket for milk at a garrison in the Pawtuxet section of Providence (now Cranston) sometime in the eighteen-month period between June 1675, when the first shots in King Philip's War were fired, and December 1676, when the last of the Indian captives was sold. But a literal reading would turn an eleven-year-old girl into "Mrs. Fenner."[57] If the basket was indeed made in 1675–1676, it stayed in private hands 166 years, plenty of time for even the most reliable of family traditions to have lost or acquired detail. Field's allusion to "Churche's War" betrays the common antiquarian practice of dating artifacts through association with well-known public events. Benjamin Church's *Entertaining Passages Relating to Philip's War,* first published in 1716, was reprinted in 1842, the year Field gave her relic to the Rhode Island Historical Society.[58] Furthermore, the description of the basket maker as a "native of the forest" echoes popular writers of the time, as in Lydia Sigourney's lament for the vanishing "forest-tribes" or her description of a Mohegan woman gathering whortleberries "in a little basket of green leaves."[59]

Yet beneath the chronological confusions, the self-serving patriotism, and the fluttering romanticisms in Field's account are hints of something older, a story—or group of stories—long told. Measured in lifespans rather than years, the distance between her and her great-great-grandmother is shorter than it first appears. Dinah Fenner lived until 1761, dying in her ninety-eighth year. Field's mother could actually have known her as a child and perhaps listened to her stories. Dinah Fenner did experience King Philip's War. Her future husband was among the soldiers who defended Providence. She did eventually live in one of the old-

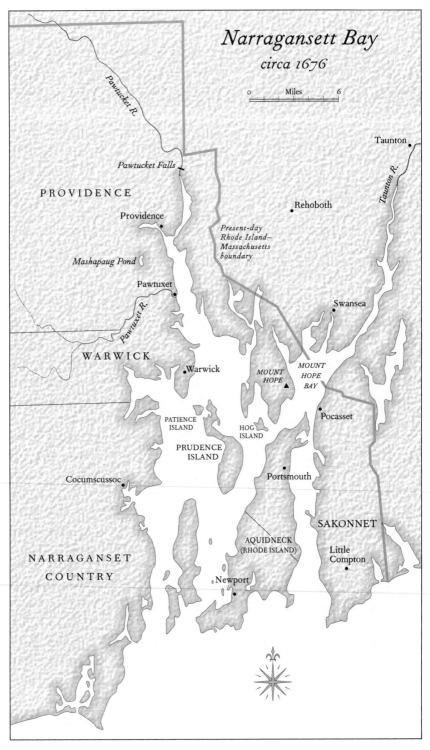

*Narragansett Bay*
*circa 1676*

Miles

Pawtucket R.

Taunton

Pawtucket Falls

PROVIDENCE

Rehoboth

Providence

*Present-day*
*Rhode Island—*
*Massachusetts*
*boundary*

Mashapaug Pond

Pawtuxet

Swansea

Pawtuxet R.

WARWICK

Warwick

*MOUNT*
*HOPE*

*MOUNT*
*HOPE*
*BAY*

Pocasset

PATIENCE
ISLAND

HOG
ISLAND

PRUDENCE
ISLAND

Cocumscussoc

Portsmouth

SAKONNET

NARRAGANSET
COUNTRY

AQUIDNECK
(RHODE ISLAND)

Little
Compton

Newport

est houses in Cranston, a Fenner house if not the Fenner garrison, and for many years she had Indian neighbors. Filtered through memory, this complex history might well have become an archetypal exchange of milk for a basket.

Opened out, the story becomes both longer and darker. It begins with Fenner's grandparents. Like most early English inhabitants of Rhode Island, they were dissenters from Puritan Massachusetts. Her maternal grandparents, William and Susanna Harris, came into Narraganset country in 1636 with Roger Williams who was banished from Massachusetts for "divers new and dangerous opinions." Her paternal grandparents, Joan and Richard Borden, arrived three years later with the visionary Anne Hutchinson; they eventually became Quakers. Rejected by the orthodox Puritan colonies, men like William Harris and Richard Borden scattered their dreams over the landscape, naming their children and their towns for principles they often defied in practice.[60]

Dinah's grandfather Harris was one of the most colorful and contentious of Rhode Island's early leaders. Thrown out of a town meeting for assault in 1641, he was charged with high treason in 1657 for claiming that Roger Williams had no more authority than any other man. Most of Harris's troubles came from his passionate quest for land. He named one of his sons "Toleration" and called his youngest daughter "Howlong," a name with multiple biblical references, the most apt of which, given his own propensities, was: "How long are ye slack to go to possess the land, which the Lord God of your fathers hath given you?"[61] In 1659, when the Rhode Island Assembly gave the town "liberty to buy out and cleare off Indians" in 3,000 acres near its core settlement, Harris interpreted the original deed in a way that would have given him and a small group of associates at Pawtuxet 300,000.[62] To support his allegations, he produced deeds he said had been confirmed by the heirs of the Narraganset leaders Canonicus and Miantonomo.

"Can any rationall man thinke that the Kings Majestie will approve or take it well that William Harris &c shall bee allowed to swallow up whole Townes & Plantations?" an opponent asked. Yet in two separate journeys to England, Harris secured legal claim to the grants. Abutters resisted, marshals and magistrates delayed, but he persisted, often siding with Quaker leaders in Newport to win allies.[63] When Harris defended a visiting Quaker in a public debate, Roger Williams told the crowd, "W. H. loved the Quakers (whom now he fawn'd upon) no more than he did the Baptists (whom he till now fawn'd on) but would love any, as a Dog for his Bone, for Land."[64] In Harris's own writings, it isn't easy to separate his passion for property from an almost Abrahamic vision of perpetuity through progeny. In a will he executed before one of his journeys to London, he entailed his lands at Pawtuxet to the fourth generation, "& my prayer now to God is that the great Grand children then may be so ffatherly wise as to intayle the said lands to theire fourth Genneration also." He seemed willing to make any sacrifice to plant his own offspring in soil he could claim as his own.[65]

Dinah's paternal grandfather, Richard Borden (or Burden), was a more peaceful man. Frequently asked to lay out lots in the new town of Portsmouth, he served on juries and as an arbitrator in local disputes. He entered court himself only twice, in cases that did not go to trial. Designated "Goodman Burden" in the 1640s, he was "Mr. Richard Burden" by 1655, when he was elected an assistant and then general treasurer of the colony.[66] He died in 1671, rich in cattle, land, and wampumpeag, and was buried in the Quaker burying ground. He left his widow an ample maintenance that included the profit and increase of thirty ewe sheep, "thirty fruit trees in the orchard that she may choose, liberty to keep fowls about the house not exceeding forty, and all household goods at her disposal." His piety had not prevented him from acquiring five slaves, listed in his inventory as a "negro man and woman" and "3 negro children."[67]

When Dinah's parents, Mary Harris and Thomas Borden, married in 1663, they united two of Rhode Island's wealthiest families. Dinah, born in 1665, was their second child.[68] There was no war in New England in the year she was born, but the name her parents gave her recalled one of Israel's first wars, a story told in the Book of Genesis about a Canaanite named Shechem who raped Jacob's daughter Dinah and then tried to marry her by promising to give her brothers any dowry they wished. The brothers asked only one thing—that Shechem and all his men be circumcised. Shechem foolishly agreed. While he and his soldiers were still sore from the operation, Jacob's sons killed them and "took their sheep, and their oxen, and their asses, and that which was in the city, and that which was in the field, And all their wealth, and all their little ones, and their wives took they captive, and spoiled even all that was in the house."[69]

When Dinah's grandfather Harris wrote associates in London in 1675 with news of King Philip's War, he too had a story about the destruction of sheep and cattle, and about the way in which combatants took their revenge on one another's bodies. He explained that in the initial skirmish at Swansea, Massachusetts, the Indians flayed off the skin and hair of their victims' heads "as Sure signes of whome they have kild of both cects [sexes]; as formerlly foreskins of males." The allusion might have been to the story of Dinah and Shechem or to an equally grisly story in another part of the Old Testament, this one too involving a bargain over a woman. When the young David asked for the daughter of Saul, the king said he could have her if he brought him "an hundred foreskins of the Philistines," a feat that he accomplished.[70] Although Harris didn't draw out the meaning of his biblical reference, he seemed to be saying that the Wampanoags, unlike the early Israelites, were willing to kill females as well as males. His own life makes clear, however, that the struggle for land in early New England, as in the land of Canaan, was a struggle for patriarchal dominion.

Bearing the name of Israel's first daughter, Dinah Borden grew up knowing that God's promise to Abraham, Isaac, and Jacob required righteous women willing to bear children. She was seven years old when her mother, near term with her fifth pregnancy, experienced a marvelous and terrifying manifestation of God's power. During a heavy rainstorm, Mary Borden was seated at an open window when a flash of lightning entered the room, killed the cat at her feet, but left her and her unborn child unharmed. In gratitude, she vowed to name the baby "Mercy"— regardless of its sex. When a son was born an hour later, she kept her promise, giving him a name more commonly assigned to girls and a story to explain it.

There is no explanation in the family history for the name she gave the next baby—Experience. The meaning behind the last daughter's christening is not difficult to find. Meribah was born on December 19, 1676, nine months after Providence was burned by Indians and one month after Thomas Borden died in an epidemic that swept through Aquidnek Island, where the family had taken refuge during the war. The name comes from the story in the Book of Exodus where Moses brought water from a rock after the children of Israel murmured in the desert: "And he called the name of the place Massah, and Meribah, because of the chiding of the children of Israel, and because they tempted the Lord, saying, Is the Lord among us, or not?" In the Old Testament, Meribah is both a place of contention and a place of deliverance: "Thou calledst in trouble, and I delivered thee; I answered thee in the secret place of thunder: I proved thee at the waters of Meribah."[71]

Dinah's mother had reason to rejoice and to mourn. She had a new child but had lost a husband; the war against the Indians had ended, but

her home in Providence had been burned, her brother Toleration had
been killed, and her father's flocks of cattle at Pawtuxet wasted. Her
father had returned from London in the early winter of 1676 with orders
from the Committee for Plantations that he hoped would resolve his land
claims. Instead he had found the country at war, the messages coming
into Providence "one after another, like the news to Job: of his sorrowes,
and our enemyes boasting: that god was departed from us, and was with
them." Writing from the safety of Aquidneck Island in early August
1676, he told an English correspondent that he lived in "the moste dangerous place (by the Indeans) in the country." Meribah's birth seems to
have been a witness to her mother, if not to the rest of the family, that
God was still with them, that he answered his children when they called to
him in trouble.[72]

At this distance, it is easy to forget how personal the war could be.
Harris probably knew Metacomet if only slightly. "I have told phillip," he
informed his London correspondent, "that he above all other Indeans
should love the English & be true to them, for, had it not bin for the
plimoth old plantors (now dead) the narrangasets had then cutt of his
fathers head." Metacomet understood the same history differently. He
told the Newport Quaker John Easton that Massasoit had kept other Indians from harming the Plymouth settlers, had given them corn, and shown
them how to plant. Massasoit had been "a great man and the English as a
litell Child." He had let the English have a hundred times more land than
his descendants now had for themselves. The Indians "had bine the first
in doing good to the English, and the English the first in doing rong."
Harris had told his English correspondents that the Wampanoags were as
"barbarous" as the Narragansets and as a little capable of "obedience to
good Law" as a "brute beast." Metacomet told Easton that the English
corrupted their own courts. If the worst of Indians testified against the
best, the English believed him, but if twenty Wampanoags asserted "that
a Englishman had dun them rong, it was as nothing."[73]

John Easton's meeting with Metacomet was a rare and ultimately
unsuccessful attempt to mediate the conflict. In his written account, Easton lamented that "the English dear not trust the indians promises nether
the indians . . . the Englishes." He blamed the leaders of Massachusetts
and Connecticut, men he called "prists" and "hyerlings," but he warned
Metacomet that when "English blud was spilt" every Englishman would
respond, for unlike their Indian neighbors, they "wear to be all under one
king."[74] So it happened. Officially Rhode Island remained neutral, but as

the conflict accelerated, its government first allowed Massachusetts and Connecticut forces to camp on colony lands, then marshaled its own troops and armed the entrance to Portsmouth harbor. In the end even Roger Williams participated in the sale of Indian slaves. For the English, it had become a question of survival. In Harris's view, if the Mohegans and other friendly Indians had not come to the colonists' aid, the Indians "might have forced us to Som Island: & there to have planted a litle Corne, & fished for our liveings."[75]

Harris's account of the destruction of cattle in Pawtuxet is especially revealing given the reference to milk in Eleanor Field's story. Losses of cattle and hay are in fact central themes in all the narratives of the war. The earliest Pokanoket attacks were on cows rather than people.[76] Indians attacked cattle with a fury that is inexplicable unless one understands a long-standing pattern of conflict that associated cattle-keeping with subordination to English ways. Roger Williams had hoped that Christian Indians would move "from Barbarism to Civilitie, in forsaking their filthy nakednes, in keeping some kind of Cattell." Although Metacomet and his people began to raise hogs, cows were less desirable. Hogs could forage in the woods, but cows required milking and feeding. They tied a family to one place and disrupted a division of labor that assigned hunting to males and cultivation to females. Since milk had not been part of the diet of Indians, dairying may not only have been inconvenient but useless. Furthermore, in relations with the English, cattle were a constant source of friction. In his interview with John Easton, Metacomet complained that Englishmen and cattle had increased so greatly that though his people "removed 30 mill [miles] from wher English had anithing to do, thay Could not kepe ther coren from being spoyled." When an English captive begged an Indian to spare his cows, the man replied sardonically, "What will Cattell now doe you good?"[77]

To William Harris's dismay, the Indians who attacked Providence killed nearly a hundred cattle, seemingly for sport, letting them lie where they fell, neither eating them nor carrying them away.[78] His description of the attack on Pawtuxet moves from mourning for the death of his son Toleration (with barely a pause to note the death of his African slave) toward an almost biblical lamentation for the loss of his flocks: "I have lost a deer son: a dillegent engenious Just man: temperate in all things, whom the Indeans lay in waite for by the way syd & killd him, and a negro man, and burnt our houses, and drove away aboute fifty head of Cowkind cattell, and fourscore horskinde of ours & carryed away some goods, and burnt above fifty loade of hay, and have put us out of our way of liveing."[79] The assaults on the Rhode Island settlements were about terror, but they were also about the destruction of livelihood. Without cattle, there was no meat or milk.[80] In such a setting, a gift of milk would have been truly miraculous, like the water that rushed forth from the rock at Meribah.

At the end of the war, it would not have been unthinkable for an Indian woman to approach an English house and ask for food. In a remarkable passage at the end of her captivity narrative, Mary Rowlandson described her own daughter's journey to Providence at the end of the war. Rhode Island's official neutrality (and proximity to the Wampanoag homeland) made it an obvious destination. "Her coming in was after this manner: She was travelling one day with the Indians, with her basket at her back; the company of Indians were got before her, and gone out of sight, all except one Squaw; she followed the Squaw till night, and then both of them lay down, having nothing over them but the heavens, and under them but the earth. Thus she travelled three dayes together, not knowing whither she was going; having nothing to eat or drink but water, and green Hirtleberries. At last they came into Providence, where she was kindly entertained by several of that Town."[81] Rowlandson does not tell us what happened to the woman who guided her child to freedom. The shift in pronouns in the last sentence is striking—"they" came into the town, but only "she," the English child, was "kindly entertained." In this telling, the "Squaw" simply disappears.

The kind of reception Indians received in Providence depended on who recognized them and under what circumstances. Authorities showed no mercy when a man named Chuff came into town in August 1676 with stinking wounds. They called out the drums and executed him on the spot. But two weeks later they allowed eight Indians, whom they described as the "old Crooked Woman & ye old Woman Peter ye Smiths mother" and "Titus (calld Kewashinit)" and their families to put up a shed near a well in the town center. One of Roger Williams's letters includes a poignant description of two children who came to an English farm in Pawtuxet in the fall of 1676. Although the farmhouse had been burned, the master "was in his Orchard and 2 Indian children came boldly to him, the boy being about 7 or 8: and the guirle (his sister) 3 or 4 yeare old." The boy said that an older boy had brought them to the sight of the English house "and bid them goe to that man and he would give them bread." The child said that "his Father and Mother were taken by the

Pequts and Monhiggins above 10 weeks agoe as they were clamming (with many more Indians) at Cowwesit."[82] Rhode Islanders gave refuge at first to Indians who seemed not to have engaged in the war. Such clemency did not last long. Toleration Williams soon arrived with his sloop and "cleard ye Towne by his vessel of all ye Indians to ye great peace & Content of all ye Inhabitants." Known combatants were executed. Others were sold as servants or slaves.[83]

Dinah Fenner was probably not in Providence during the war. Under Quaker leadership, the Rhode Island Assembly had refused to pay for fortifications on the mainland, suggesting instead that families move to Aquidneck Island.[84] The Bordens seem to have done so. Dinah's father was not on the list of twenty-four men who stayed behind to defend Providence, though he participated in the court-martial at Newport that condemned the Narraganset leader Quinnapin and seven others to death. His will, made in Portsmouth, asked that one son and a daughter remain with relatives there.[85] Dinah's mother eventually returned to Providence with her children. In January 1680, she petitioned for "Sattisfaction" for a barrel of gunpowder colonial troops had taken from her husband during the war. She asked the town fathers to "remember the widdow and fatherless."[86]

Thomas Borden's death and the losses of war weren't the only trials the family faced during this period. In 1679, Dinah's grandfather William Harris, en route to England to plead for his land claims, was captured by Barbary pirates. For the next two years, he languished in captivity while friends in London and Connecticut scrambled for the means to relieve him. Writing from prison in Algiers to "his very Loving Wife Susana Harris at patuxet in New England," he begged his family not to "weepe shed teare nor for me Cry," assuring them that within a very short time, "wee in heaven should bee / Where there an end of slavery shall see."[87]

Harris's allusions to slavery are interesting given recent developments in Rhode Island. In October 1676, the assembly had ruled that Indians without written passes "would be liable to be sold into service as captives."[88] Since long-standing laws forbade Indian slavery, Rhode Island officials forced captives to sign indentures. In one exchange, "an Indian Woman late of Pocasett" named Meequapew and her son Peter bound themselves to an English master in exchange for food, clothing, and lodging appropriate to their status, the mother to receive her freedom in two years, the son in ten or when he arrived at the age of twenty-four.[89] Those who could not establish their status as noncombatants went to the West

Indies with cargoes of pipe staves and pork. When Barbados and Jamaica objected to the importation of New England Indians "of too subtle, bloody and dangerous inclination," some were taken to Tangier on the north coast of Africa, not far from where Harris was imprisoned.[90] The proceeds from these sales were distributed to the men who had stayed behind to defend Providence. Dinah Borden's future husband, Thomas Fenner, was among them. A cryptic document among the town's papers suggests that the men were paid in bags of wool and yards of cloth as well as maize and specie. An Indian slave was worth one or two pounds in cash or from forty to a hundredweight in wool. In the final accounting, the cloth was subdivided into "a quarter and a half quarter of a yard to Each whole shaire."[91]

Dinah Borden married Thomas Fenner in July of 1682. She was not yet seventeen years old; it was his second marriage. Whether or not it was a love match, it surely represented a strategic effort on the part of the Widow Borden to ensure her family's security. The years following the war had brought one crisis after another—first her husband's death, then her father's capture by pirates, and finally her sister Howlong's scandalous behavior. While William Harris languished in an Algerian prison, Howlong became involved in an affair a Boston friend warned might bring more "Sorrow to her affectionate father Than his Turkish Slavery." Witnesses testified that she had behaved in a very peculiar manner at a neighbor's house, staying up all night, writing secret letters to her lover by candlelight, and drinking rum with the servants before breakfast. Although she was acquitted in court of the charge of "carnal copulation," the affair complicated her already difficult relationship with her mother, who frantically petitioned town officials not to allow Howlong to marry until her father returned. William Harris was finally ransomed in the autumn of 1681, but he died three days after arriving in London, leaving his affairs in Rhode Island unsettled. Ironically, it was Howlong who took on the task of settling his estate. In 1686, she became the second wife of old Arthur Fenner, moving into the house that nineteenth-century Rhode Islanders referred to as the "Fenner Garrison." Her niece Dinah and Arthur Fenner's son Thomas lived in a second Fenner house half a mile away.[92]

A one-page account in Howlong's papers listing "bever & small furs," "1 wolf 1 fox 1 Rakoone," and "2 Reekoane skins" hints that there were still Indians in the neighborhood.[93] Local Indians who survived the wars were both an annoyance and a resource for English families. A whole series of regulations governed their behavior. They couldn't cut wood on Sundays or at night or bring strangers into the town boundaries to hunt and fish.[94] Some, like the "Indian Girle" appraised at one pound ten shillings in Steven Hawking's estate, were clearly servants. The woman "Margret" who once pounded corn in Richard Arnold's cellar in Providence is known to history only because she took a leaky canoe over the river and drowned. The river plays a role in many stories. An "Indian called Sam" took up a hat in the bay and brought it to the nearest house. A while later a man "called Thomas Bradford" found the body that went with the hat as he was crossing over from the old Wampanoag side of the river. Men and women like these maintained a wary independence.[95]

In 1697, frightened by attacks in northern New England during King William's War, Providence appointed Thomas Fenner and others to search "beyound the outmost of our plantations" for strange Indians and "indevour to Resest Expulse Kill and Distroy them." When they didn't find any hostile Indians in the neighborhood, they disarmed four who lived nearby.[96] In 1709 Rhode Island attempted to contain the native people who still lived among them by setting apart sixty-four square miles of land as a reservation. To solidify their hold on land claimed by Connecticut, they designated a young man named Ninigret "prince of the Narragansets." Trustees appointed by the colony watched over the young monarch's affairs. Not surprisingly, when the colony cast up accounts, the trustees found that the costs to the government for its military and legal expenses in managing the Indians equaled nearly the value of their remaining land. The small reservation was all that was left.[97]

Town records for these years capture only the unusual, the violent, or the tragic, like the account of an unknown male whose body washed ashore in Portsmouth, with "A blackish stocking on one Leg And A whitish Stockin on the other," or the suicide of the "indian Lad of widow fish" who apparently hung himself with a rope of his own fashioning, being "found upon the ground with a walnut pealling hanging over him upon A lim of A tree."[98] But for every one of these events, there must have been hundreds of ordinary encounters, perhaps even an exchange of milk for a basket. Dinah's youngest son recalled that "when as a young man he traveled from his home in what is now Cranston to the center of Providence, it was usual to pass more Indians than white people on the way." In the early eighteenth century, he said, there was "a populous Indian village near Mashapaug pond."[99] By then Dinah Fenner had milk to spare. The inventory of her husband's estate taken in February 1718 lists fifteen cows complete with bells. In the bedroom with a new bedstead and a pair of bellows were some "wooden dishes and baskets." Perhaps one of these was made by a person her great-great-granddaughter would call "a woman of the forest."[100]

Dating Dinah Fenner's basket to the period of King Philip's War perpetuates the notion that New England Indians disappeared after 1676. Extending the chronology reduces the mythic but enlarges the historical significance of the basket, shifting the focus from English benevolence and Indian gratitude to the hard work of cultural survival.

The physical evidence in the basket itself is consistent with a somewhat later date. Field said that the woman made the basket by mingling shreds from her own blanket with "the inner bark from the Wikup tree." The minuscule fragments of wool still clinging to the interior of the basket may have come from a blanket, but under microscopic analysis they appear finer than the wool typically found in seventeenth-century archaeological sites. The wool does appear to have been unraveled from a woven object, however, since the scales typically found on wool filaments have been worn away. The object from which they were taken had at least some colored strands, since the original colors of red, blue, and black can still be seen.[101] Though the word *wikup* does not appear in Roger Williams's phrase book nor in the vocabulary of twentieth-century Narragansetts, it does show up in a Providence, Rhode Island, deed for July 25, 1704, which describes "two trees growing out of one Roote Called Wickupp trees." The description of the woman looking for her materials "by the side of the river" also rings true. The basswood or American linden does in fact grow near riverbanks. Also called the "Bee-Tree" because of its fragrant cream-colored flowers, it frequently has two or more trunks, just as the Providence deed says.[102]

While it is more dramatic to think of two women practicing peace in the midst of war, it is more credible to imagine Dinah Fenner's basket as an artifact in a less visible but far more enduring stream of trade, one that stretches backward to the "gifts" of fish and berries William Wood wrote about in the 1620s and forward to the Indian basket-makers who peddled their wares all over New England in the late eighteenth century. There is nothing qualitatively different between the exchange Eleanor Field described and the exchange the Maine midwife Martha Ballard wrote about in 1809 when she described a "little indien girl" who came to her house several times, bringing the gift of a basket and receiving potatoes in return. The baskets, however, changed. By the middle of the eighteenth

century, twined basketry declined as Algonkian families began to manufacture and sell woodsplint baskets, brooms, ax handles, and other forest
products adapted to English tastes. During this transition, some basket
makers surely continued to work in more traditional forms, making
twined baskets for their own use or for gift-giving.[103]

Although we cannot know who made the basket, archaeological evidence read alongside oral tradition tells us a great deal about the basket-
making tradition to which the maker was heir. Algonkian women found
materials for weaving in places that seemed wild and unproductive to
English colonists. Taught by her elders, a skilled basket maker would
know where wild hemp grew and in what marshes to find narrow-leaved
cattails for mats and hangings. In moist uplands, she would look for but-
terfly weed, spreading dogbane, and milkweeds growing as tall as a person. She could distinguish bog nettles, useful for weaving, from the more
common stinging nettle, and she would know the difference between
ordinary red cedar and the tall white swamp cedar whose inner bark when
beaten produced fibers soft as cotton. She would have learned long ago
that cornhusks gathered green and dried in a wind on a hot day could be
woven into a fabric tight enough to hold water.

A woman offering the gift of a basket would work carefully. She would
know how to peel and soak the inner fibers of basswood and how to
accentuate and define a pattern with brightly colored yarn. She would
know from experience that new yarn, unless spun tightly, was difficult to
work with because it stretched, but that ravelings from old cloths or a
blanket would hold their shape. She would use this wool sparingly, however, not only because it was valuable, but because it was fragile. She
could not know that more than two centuries later light would spill
through the spaces eaten by moths.[104]

The Rhode Island Historical Society began adding Indian relics to its collections in 1835. It accessioned, among other things, several sets of arrow-
heads, an "original deed from King Philip," a "String of Beads washed
out from an Indian Grave" in Tiverton, and "Indian remains dug up on
the Rail Road near the SW corner of the State," including a thigh bone
and hair.[105] The registrar neatly wrote the nature of each acquisition on
the right side of the page and the name of each donor in the ruled column
to the left. But when he came to Eleanor Field's contribution, he left the
name column blank. She was the society's first female donor, or at least

the first woman to contribute something without the cover of a husband's name. He copied her description of the basket with its coy allusion to herself but did not identify her further. Later, in pencil, another person wrote "Eleanor Field" in the margin, drawing a small hand with a finger pointing to the right.[106]

Field was seventy years old in 1842. In the previous two decades she had buried four sisters, each unmarried like herself. She herself lived another twenty-two years, dying in 1864 at the age of ninety-two. The obituary published in the *Providence Evening Bulletin* described her as a woman of "great strength of intellect, uncommon self-reliance, lofty independence, and a pride and dignity of bearing and of manner which would have befitted the Virgin Queen herself." In earlier years, she had "personally appeared before the General Assembly to oppose the grant of a charter to the Pawtuxet Turnpike Company, whose road had been laid out through her farm." One of her most prominent characteristics, the obituary said, was "an unspeakable repugnance to all 'progress,' as it is called." Although "change, under any form, distressed and annoyed her," she was liberal in spirit, a "Jeffersonian in her politics," a supporter of the Union side in the Civil War, and a generous benefactor to the families of soldiers.[107] Having no descendants of her own, she bequeathed her grandmother's basket and a powerful story to future generations.

# Two Spinning Wheels in an Old Log House

DOVER, NEW HAMPSHIRE, DATE UNKNOWN

*The spinning-wheels of wool and flax . . .*
*will be heard no more for ever; seen no more,*
*in fact, save in the halls of the Antiquarian*
*Societies, where the delicate daughters will*
*be asking, what these strange machines are,*
*and how they were made to go?*

Horace Bushnell, *"The Age of Homespun"*

The two spinning wheels that sit in the garret of the William Damm Garrison in Dover, New Hampshire, have lost their story. They could be exchanged for similar pairs in dozens of period houses in New England and no one would know. It is their setting that gives them resonance. The old garrison is one of the treasures of northern New England. Built sometime before 1695 on a narrow point of land thrusting into New Hampshire's Great Bay, it is a rare example of a form of log construction once common to the area. Unlike the chinked cabins of later frontiers, it was made of massive timbers squared in a waterpowered sawmill until they lay one atop the other like quarried stone. Their weight attests not only to the size of the trees that once covered coastal New England but to the violence that accompanied English attempts to turn those trees into lumber, ships, and fortunes.

When Ellen Rounds discovered the garrison in 1887, it was a derelict outbuilding open to wasps and weather. She repaired its roof and sashes, patched its plaster, and over the next thirty years filled its three rooms and garret with eight hundred "precious mementoes of ye olden time." In 1915, she donated the house and its contents to a new museum endowed by Annie Woodman "for the promotion of Education and Science and Art and the increase and dissemination of general and especially historical knowledge." The trustees put the house on rollers and pulled it three miles to the center of town, siting it on a broad back lawn between two brick mansions provided in Woodman's will. To shelter it from weather and protect visitors from the jarring sight of its rough, unpainted facade, they encased it in a trellised gazebo connected to the other houses by a columned walkway that reached across the grass in a graceful semicircle. The garrison became the connecting link between the natural history exhibits and Indian relics in the first of the museum's buildings and the decorative arts galleries in the second.[1]

The columned walkway is gone, but the gazebo, lined with wire mesh to protect it from nesting pigeons, is freshly painted and

*Above: William Damm Garrison, as restored by Ellen
Rounds, c. 1890. Below: William Damm Garrison after
removal to the Woodman Institute, 1916.*

PHOTOGRAPHS COURTESY THOM HINDLE

inviting. Entering its trellised shade, visitors confront the weathered timbers of the old house and the historical pieties of the nineteenth century.
Guns protrude from portholes on either side of the battened door. Inside,
a glass case displays a bit of charcoal, an iron key, the piece of a hoe, an ox
shoe, and the bolt from a lintel excavated from a house burned in a French
and Abenaki attack of 1689. Nearby are gentler mementos of colonial
life, a wooden bowl on a rough pine table, a clutter of trivets and iron
pots, and, in a little room beyond the parlor, spinning wheels and a cradle.
There are more wheels in the garret.

Ascending on treads worn almost to rungs, visitors emerge into the
speckled light of an imagined age of homespun. Under the eaves are the

two spinning wheels, one for flax and one for wool. Beside them is an old loom, partly rigged. A pile of weaver's reeds, or slays, sits on the breast of the loom. Three niddy-noddies, strange-looking implements once used for winding yarn into skeins, hang behind it. A framing post displays four hetchels, fierce-looking combs used for processing flax. In the sloping space beside them, a mane of brittle straw spills from the arm of a flax brake. On the opposite side of the garret, crammed in among farm tools, barrels, and an ancient rope bed, is a more obscure set of tools—a broken quill winder, a homemade skein winder, and the inner workings of a click reel.

The clutter of tools in the old garrison brings together two stories that at first glance seem separate, one about cloth-making, the other about war. New Hampshire colonists coexisted peacefully with their Indian neighbors during the first fifty years. But population growth in the Puritan colonies to the south, a disastrous betrayal at the end of King Philip's War, and almost constant conflict between England and France on the northern frontier changed things. Between 1689 and 1725, the fragile English enclaves in northern New England were under almost constant threat. Some English families fled the region. More resolute men, like William Damm, persisted. To stay put, to raise flax, to pasture sheep, and to establish sons and daughters on nearby farms were as essential to English victory as sending troops up the Cocheco River to Winnepesauki or over the mountains to Norridgewock.

The Algonkians whose land became New England buried material objects with their dead. Layering graves with woven mats and bark, they folded their loved ones into fetal position, arranging wampum, hoes, thimbles, tobacco pipes, glass bottles, baskets, and iron kettles at their heads and feet.[2] The English insisted on the poverty of the grave ("dust thou art, and to dust shalt thou return") while obsessively counting every spoon, sow, and plowshare left to the living. When William Damm died in 1718, inventory-takers appointed by a probate court moved through his house, yard, and barn, meticulously accounting for every possession, even the bed he died in and the last tools he touched, in pounds, shillings, and pence. The record they created tells us that toward the end of his life—and probably much earlier—he owned two "spinning wheels," a "Lining wheel," wool cards, a hetchel, and two looms.

The tools now in the house probably looked different from those Damm owned, but he would have understood their use. Textile equipment changed little from the late Middle Ages to the early nineteenth century. But the same tool used in much the same way can have different meanings in different settings. That is why the display in the garrison is so compelling. Ellen Rounds inadvertently connected Horace Bushnell's idealized age of homespun with the brutality and violence of colonial war. Murals painted about the time of Damm's death in the stairway of a grand house in Portsmouth, New Hampshire, the provincial capital, enlarge the connection by juxtaposing images of an Irish spinner, two Indian "kings," and an English monarch. The story of cloth-making in colonial New England is a story about empire as well as rural economy, about Atlantic trade as well as household production, and about Irish migration as well as English expansion.

English colonists planted their first permanent settlements in New Hampshire in 1623, three years after English separatists founded Plymouth and seven years before John Winthrop and his Puritans arrived in Boston. These early enclaves, many of them fishing stations, took on a new character in the 1630s when migration from Puritan Massachusetts began. Like the founders of Rhode Island, some newcomers had been cast out of Massachusetts for religious heterodoxy. Others were simply following the arc of opportunity toward the rich fishing grounds and massive forests of the Piscataqua. John Damm (spelled variously Dam, Damme, and Dame) was one of these. Born in Cheshire, England, he arrived in Salem in 1633 with a group carrying a patent to settle on New Hampshire's Great Bay. He was one of forty-two inhabitants who in 1640 formed themselves into a "Body Politique" in what is now Dover. His five youngest children, including the second son, William, were born there. On the town's tax list for 1648, he stood eighth on a list of fifty-seven. A farmer and skilled carpenter, or joiner, he was also part owner of a sawmill.[3]

Sawmills were the engines of colonial expansion. In 1660, a London cartographer pictured fifteen sawmills on the streams emptying into New Hampshire's Great Bay. The map also portrayed in schematic form the Abenaki stronghold in the interior at Penacook where Dover's richest man, Richard Waldron, had a trading post. Waldron's treatment of the Penacook indelibly shaped Dover's later history. Because English settlers were few and northern furs abundant, New Hampshire Indians remained neutral during King Philip's War, but when refugees fled across the border at the end of the war, Massachusetts authorities wanted them returned. In an act bitterly remembered among the western Abenaki well

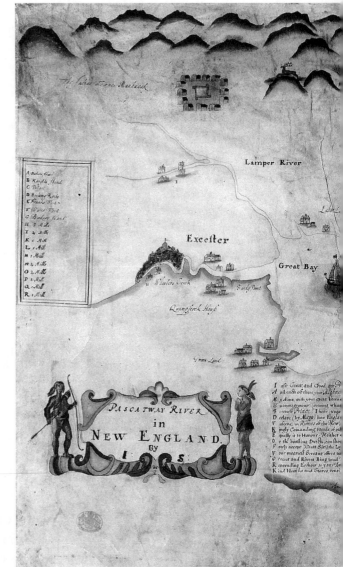

*John Seller.* Pascatway
River in New England,
*c. 1660. Penacook is in the
upper left. Damm built his
garrison above Dover near
Back River. Waldron was
at Cocheco.*

COURTESY BRITISH LIBRARY

into the eighteenth century, Waldron tricked his Penacook trading part-
ners into gathering with the so-called stranger Indians at Dover in September 1676. Inveigling them into giving up their arms, he allowed
colonial troops to surround the refugees and herd them back to Massachusetts, where most were hung or sold into slavery. The Penacook
leader Kancamagus never forgave him. Thirteen years later, he and his
allies joined a French-supported expedition in exacting a terrible
revenge.[4]

The attack came on June 28, 1689. Earlier that day Waldron had reassured his neighbors about rumors of war, telling them "to go and plant their pumpkins, saying that he would tell them when the Indians would break out."[5] He was so confident that he allowed an Abenaki woman to sleep in his stockaded house. She apparently unlatched the gate and let the assailants through. The details of the attack, as recounted by survivors, suggest that the double cross thirteen years before was only one factor. Falling prices for furs, increased indebtedness, and resentment of English law were reshaping relations in northern New England as they had done earlier in the Puritan colonies. The invaders dragged Waldron into the main room of his house, seated him "in an elbow chair, on a long table," and "insultingly asked him, 'Who shall judge Indians now?' " Then they slashed him "across the breast and belly with knives, each one with a stroke, saying, 'I cross out my account.' "[6]

That was only the beginning. With support from French Canada, the Abenaki hammered the northern frontier for more than fifty years in a powerful but ultimately losing attempt to preserve their homelands. English colonists in turn sent their fiercest warriors to raid Abenaki villages in the interior. The log garrisons of coastal Maine and New Hampshire are relics of these wars. William Damm's garrison first appears in provincial records in the winter of 1695 when the New Hampshire council voted to station two soldiers there. Erected on a high point of land about a quarter of a mile from Back River, it was a potential rallying point for the neighborhood. Although only half its present size, the house was a neighborhood refuge and a home for William and Martha Damm and five children, ranging in age from thirteen to three. Another child, Leah, was born in 1696.[7]

Although there is no record of an attack on Damm's garrison, there were enough assaults on nearby places to justify its existence. The diary of Dover's pastor, John Pike, shows the limitations of fortresses in a war pursued primarily through small raids. He recorded not only the massive attacks, the ones that have gotten into the history books, but the small strikes that caught people as they went about their work. Pike described people and places he knew. One man was killed "as he travelled the path near the west corner of Thomas Downs' field." Another was "slain by the Indians, as he travelled to seek his horse, up a little hill betwixt Cochecho and Tole-end." Terror struck even when there was no enemy to be seen. On December 25, 1692, "A doleful and tremendous noise was affirmed to be heard in the air nigh Capt. Gerrish's garrison, which continued with a little intermission near half an hour." Was it the cracking of frozen trees, the approach of Indians, or a Providential warning?[8] The good pastor recorded English folly as well as enemy treachery. In a garrisoned house in one of the newer settlements, a complacent captain sat down to dinner without posting a sentinel, allowing the enemy to decoy a family to their death by turning sheep into the corn. In another, the town's minister "coming down from the watch-box in the night, in a darkish colored gown, was mistaken for an Indian, and solemnly slain by a sorry soldier belonging to the garrison."[9]

Inadvertently, Pike also revealed the devastation visited on Abenaki villages. In October 1703, soldiers returning from "their second expedition towards Pequawket" brought in "six Indian scalps and five captives, all squaws and children except one old man." In a separate account, Dover's commander said that when troops reached Pigwacket, they found a palisade of timbers "and about one hundred wigwams therein, but had been deserted about six weekes, as we judged." He was certain the inhabitants had left in haste because there was corn scattered around the mouth of their storage pits. In another foray Dover men "surprised an Indian Wigwam in the woods," where they "killed two stout men, and one old squaw. Brought a young squaw and two children away."[10] The Abenaki survived by breaking up into small family bands and disappearing into the woods. Dover farmers could not do that. Mistress Ursula Cutt and three workmen were slain "as they were busy about hay upon her plantation near Boiling Rock." An ambush "laid between Capt. Gove's field and Tobias Hanson's orchard" caught people as they returned from church. "Thamsin Mesarvey, Mr. Waldron's maid-servant, was taken by 4 Indians, betwixt sunset and dark, at a spring in the Major's pasture, between his house (formerly burnt) and barn."[11] Then, on July 8, 1707, two Dover men were killed by Indians as they were "going with a cart from Lt. Zachariah Field's garrison to James Bunker's for a loom."[12]

That tell-tale loom shows that cloth-making had become part of New England life. It had not always been so. When John Damm arrived in Massachusetts in 1633, spinning wheels and looms were rare. When trade with England was disrupted in the 1640s by the English civil war, the Massachusetts General Court passed legislation encouraging colonists to sow flax and enlarge their small flocks of sheep, but it was commerce, not agriculture, that rescued them. As one writer explained, "when one hand was shut by way of supply from England, another was opened by way of traffic . . . to the West Indies . . . whereby among other goods much cotton-wool was brought into the country . . . which the inhabitants learned to spin." West Indian cotton remained part of household production throughout the colonial period.[13] For some Englishmen, the prevalence of cotton accentuated the marginality of New World production. One official dismissed the coarse druggets and serges made in New England, arguing that "these, as well as their homespun linen, which is generally half cotton, serve only for the use of the meanest sort of people."[14]

Probate records from Plymouth Colony show the gradual development of household production in southern New England. Before 1649, only 15 percent of estates listed spinning wheels. By 1660 that had risen to 40 percent as entries like "two Blanketts being homemade" began to appear alongside English textiles, some inventions even finding it necessary to distinguish "Inglish ticken" (English ticking). The reference in one man's inventory to "homade Cloth which the family hath needed to have worne before now had it bine Got Reddy" shows the difficulties of cloth-making in a still undeveloped economy. Some families solved the problem by pooling resources. Josiah Winslow of Marshfield owned just "the half of 23 yards and an halfe of homspun cloth at the Fullers." This reference to homespun cloth at the fullers is intriguing, since in English usage homespun was usually defined as a coarsely woven, *unmilled* fabric. In America, the words *homespun* and *homemade* were used interchangeably.[15]

Every writer who described the New England economy at the end of the seventeenth century—including Dinah Fenner's grandfather—mentioned small-scale textile production. In his letters to England in 1676, William Harris praised the "Tammyes" or worsteds of Rhode Island. Even Edmund Andros, the much-despised governor of the short-lived Dominion of New England, admitted that local wool was "much of it not inferior to English," adding that families made "their own ordinary clothing and covering for beds, and some good serges." Both men recognized that this was petty production. Large-scale manufacturing required specialized sorting, combing, bleaching, dyeing, pressing, and glazing, and middlemen capable of organizing work. Even if commercial manufacturing had been profitable, English policy forbade it. A law of 1699 prohibited the export by ship of raw wool, yarn, or finished fabrics from any of "the English plantations, upon any pretence whatsoever." Nor could any of these products be loaded upon a horse, cart, or carriage and carried from one colony to another. The objective of such regulation was not to keep a paltry American production out of England, but to protect sales of English cloth in America. Law as well as local circumstances ensured that colonists made cloth for household use or local exchange.[16]

The colonial official who asserted that only the "meanest sort of people" *wore* homespun may have been correct, but well-to-do families were just as likely to produce it. John Reyner, pastor of the Congregational

Church in Dover, New Hampshire, and a graduate of Magdalen College, Cambridge, owned six spinning wheels at his death in 1669. His estate also included, in addition to imported fabrics, twenty pounds of yarn and thirty-one yards of "homemade cloth." Dover's ruling elder, a man with the fearsome name of Hatevil Nutter, was also well equipped with wheels, wool, and cotton. Such families not only had the raw materials but the labor necessary for cloth-making. In 1694, Richard Martyn, a wealthy merchant and member of the New Hampshire Council, bequeathed his wife "that web of cloth which is now Spining in the house & Hannah Harriss her time till said web be Spun." The servant wasn't spinning the cloth, of course, but the yarn to make it. Once that was done, Martyn could take it to a local weaver, a man like John Fabes of Portsmouth, whose own estate contained forty yards of "homspun cloth," six yards of "very course Carsy," and five yards of serge.[17]

William Damm's inventory suggests that he, too, was a weaver. When the inventory was taken in 1718, the "backroom" of his garrison contained "2 pr looms." A pair of looms, like a pair of scissors or a pair of pants, was one object rather than two, but the presence of *two* pairs is quite unusual. There is further evidence of cloth-making in the inventories of Damm's relatives.[18] When Martha Damm's father, James Nute, died in 1691, his inventory contained wheels, cards, thirty pounds of cotton wool, ninety-five pounds of yarn, and forty-six yards of cloth. Ninety-five pounds of yarn could have produced as much as two hundred yards of cloth, not much by English standards but a hefty supply for this time and place. The 1700 inventory of Martha's brother-in-law also contained wheels, yarn, wool, and unspun cotton. One can imagine a small industry here with production extending from one household to another, Nute and his sons-in-law paying for West Indian cotton with lumber cut and sawed on their own land, the women cleaning, carding, and spinning it, and William Damm or an apprentice making it into fabric.[19]

The importance of cloth-making to Damm's household is confirmed in a complaint filed by the oldest son, Pomfret, claiming that before the inventory was taken his siblings had "taken away & concealed . . . a great weeb of wolling Cloath and a great deall of sheps woll & flacks [flax]."[20] But if Damm was a weaver, he was also a farmer, lumberman, and miller. His inventory lists "neat cattle," oxen, sheep, swine, and horses, a "breaking plough," a "horse plough," a dung fork, a harrow, scythes, sickles, saws, axes, chisels, wedges, gouges, a draw knife, a grinding stone, a cooper's adze, a gun, a carbine, and part-interest in two sawmills. This combination of implements was not unusual. Even in Damm's native Cheshire, rough cloth was often made by farmer-weavers.[21]

The 1707 diary of a Connecticut weaver helps us to understand how a man might combine cloth-making and farming. In the early spring, Manasseh Minor cut wood, mended fences, trapped a fox, and turned cattle out of his fields and into the woods. Soon he was washing and shearing sheep and preparing for planting. On a May day in his capacity as deacon he went to town to buy wine for the sacrament. Two days later, he "warped a peece of cloth." In June, he hilled corn and carried thirty-nine pounds of candles to market. In July, he carted hay, reaped wheat, and pulled flax. In August, he paid a hired girl for spinning. In September, he hooped barrels, harvested beans, and began "to gathar corn in the uper feild." In October, he made cider, killed a bull, and observed a public fast. He spent a day in November fishing, then shipped his beef out of the port of New London. In December he wove a coverlet and began weaving a rug, which he finished in January before beginning to winnow oats and cart boards for a new meetinghouse. Obviously weaving was a part-time occupation in which even a single "weeb" of cloth could be significant.[22]

Because Minor's farm was in Connecticut, there is more farming and less lumbering in his accounts than there would have been had Damm kept the diary, but the range of activities was similar. Everywhere in New England, weaving had to be fitted into the larger work of producing food and cash crops for export. Early diaries, all kept by men, give little sense of the female side of textile production. Lydia Minor and her female helpers must have spun the flax and wool Minor wove for family use and dipped the thirty-nine pounds of candles he carried to town. Frequent references in the diary to women being "brought on bed" suggest that his wife was also a midwife. Damm's inventory hints at a similar mix of female activities. It lists two churns and "Chees fatts" for dairying, three "powdering tubbs" for salting meat, cards for processing wool, a hetchel for combing flax, two "spinning wheels," and a "Lining wheel."

The spinning wheels now in the garret of the garrison can help us visualize one part of Martha Damm's work.


Although most Americans can recognize a spinning wheel when they see one, few understand how it works. A spinning wheel doesn't operate the way a coffee mill or a meat grinder might. That is, one doesn't feed wool or flax into one end and take yarn out the other. The basic operation takes place outside the machine between the spinner's thumb and fingers.

To demystify the process it helps to experiment with a bit of fiber. The wad of cotton from the top of a medicine bottle will do. Flatten it out, then tear a strip about an eighth of an inch wide. Gently pull on one end so that it grows longer and thinner. This step is called "drawing." As you draw, twist the tip of the extended fiber until it forms the beginning of a tiny thread. Spinning is nothing more than a continuous process of drawing and twisting. Keeping both things going at once is the difficult part. As Elizabeth Barber has observed, a spinner needs four hands—one to hold the fiber, another to draw it out, a third to twist it, and a fourth to hold on to the new thread, since letting it go while spinning allows it to "ball up in a snarl like an angry rubber band and then start coming apart." Because humans weren't made with four hands, somebody invented the spindle. A spindle is a weighted stick that can be spun like a top. Attaching a leader of yarn to the shaft, a spinner gave the spindle a quick turn, then dropped it, letting it twist the yarn as it fell. When the spindle stopped, she wound the newly spun yarn onto the shaft and started the process over again.[23]

A spinning wheel is a mechanical device for keeping a spindle in motion. Spinning on a large wheel like the one in the garrison was much like spinning with a drop spindle. The spindle was attached horizontally to the post, then connected by a single cord to the drive wheel. Using one hand to give the wheel an occasional turn, the spinner drew out her fiber with the other. As the thread lengthened, she stepped backward inch by inch until she had gone as far as her arm could reach. Then she reversed the action of the wheel, winding the yarn onto the spindle as she moved toward it. This back-and-forth motion explains why some people called the spindle wheel a "walking wheel." Wheels like this developed from those used in cotton manufacturing in Italy in the late Middle Ages, though in northern Europe and the British Isles they were adapted for spinning wool. Some spinners used a wooden peg called a "wheel finger" to turn the wheel, as the owner of the wheel in the garret must have done. Still visible is a worn spot where she hit the same spoke over and over again.[24] The wool wheel displayed on the main floor of the garrison has been fitted with an "accelerating head," a device invented in the early nineteenth century, but it is otherwise identical to those made in Europe since the Middle Ages.

With a spindle wheel as with a drop spindle, a worker had to pause frequently to wind her yarn. Bobbin-flyer wheels solved that problem. First
used in the Italian silk industry, they traveled in the late fifteenth century
to southern Germany where they were used in flax production. A spinner
using a flax wheel like those in the garrison threaded a leader of yarn
through the tip of a hollow bobbin and out onto one or more of the metal
hooks attached to a U-shaped device called a flyer. As the bobbin turned,
it automatically wound the newly spun yarn onto the shaft. By the early
seventeenth century many flyer wheels also had foot treadles that allowed
a spinner to sit as she worked, using both hands to draw. Some writers call

*Wool wheel and "wheel fingers" from
the William Damm Garrison,
Woodman Institute.*

PHOTOGRAPH COURTESY THOM HINDLE

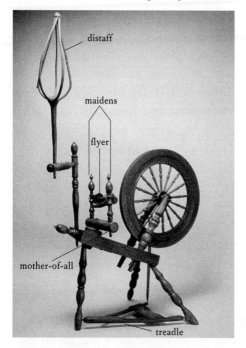

distaff

maidens

flyer

mother-of-all

treadle

*New Hampshire flax wheel.*
COURTESY MUSEUM OF AMERICAN
TEXTILE HISTORY, LOWELL,
MASSACHUSETTS

these "Saxony wheels." The name does not appear in New England inventories.

Treadle wheels were so convenient that one wonders why they didn't replace walking wheels. The reason is that different fibers required different handling. Although wool for home production was spun much finer than the bulky yarn used today in craft-weaving, it was generally spun thicker than flax. More important, the long drawing out that was characteristic of the walking wheel helped compensate for the short fibers and natural curliness of wool. Conversely, fuzzy wool might clog a bobbin. Combed flax, on the other hand, was straight and stiff, individual filaments sometimes measuring more than fifteen inches. The flax was usually combed into a cone-shaped bundle supported by a distaff. The distaff arm on the wheel in the garrison is broken, though someone has fitted it with a distaff made from the branch of a chokecherry bush. An intact wheel now at the American Museum of Textile History shows how it may once have looked.[25]

The drive wheel on the wool wheel has slender spokes set into a rim bent by steaming. In contrast, the rim of the flax wheel is composed of four short planks joined together and turned on a lathe. Weight rather than size gives it momentum. Its legs, posts, and spokes are also more decorative than those on the wool wheel. In England and the Continent, the turnings on flax wheels became so elaborate that one English writer dubbed them "Gentle Woman's Wheels," arguing that their busy posts and spindles were better adapted to "shew the Art of the Turner, then to add any goodness to the working."[26] The most expressive feature was usually the U-shaped frame that held the flyer. The horizontal section, called the "mother of all," supported two upright posts called "maidens" that ended in elaborate finials. Our flax wheel stops short of gentility, but it is more decorative than the wool wheel.

The "lining wheels" William Damm owned may have looked much like the flax wheel now in the garrison. There is one much like it in a 1659 Dutch painting that shows an old woman winding yarn with a niddy-noddy. But there are other possibilities. The range of wheels in seventeenth- and early-eighteenth-century English and Continental pictures is much wider than in American collections, suggesting that some designs dropped out over time. There is no known New England wheel, for example, like the low flax wheels with bent-wood rims that appear in both Dutch and English illustrations of the seventeenth century. Although they were fitted with a bobbin-flyer, their drive wheels were constructed in much the same way as the wool wheel in the Damm Garrison, only smaller, allow-

*Abraham de Pape.* Tobit and Anna, *seventeenth century.*

COURTESY NATIONAL GALLERY, LONDON

*From Iohannis de Brunes,*
Emblemata of Zinne-werck,
*Amsterdam, 1661.*

DEPARTMENT OF PRINTING AND
GRAPHIC ARTS, HOUGHTON
LIBRARY OF HARVARD COLLEGE
LIBRARY

*Frontispiece, Thomas Firmin,*
Proposals for the
Imployment of the Poor,
*London, 1681.*

COURTESY FOLGER SHAKESPEARE
LIBRARY

ing the spinner to turn them with a hand crank while seated. On the Continent, spinners used wheels like these to produce the gossamer-like yarns needed for lace or fine lawns.[27] Double-flyer wheels were designed for the opposite purpose. Used in poorhouses and factories, they allowed fast production of coarse linens. Fitting the two flyer assemblages above rather than beside the drive wheel saved space as well as labor, though as Karl Marx observed, "adepts in spinning who could spin two threads at once were almost as scarce as two-headed men."[28]

Some writers refer to spinning as unskilled work. They have obviously never tried it. A good spinning wheel helped, but a spinner's ability to draw evenly, maintain the right tension on the yarn, and control the speed of twisting was what really determined the quality of the finished prod-

uct.[29] Flax, hemp, cotton, worsted, and wool demanded different techniques, as did yarns destined for warping, weaving, knitting, lace-making,
shoe-binding, or embroidery. Some fabrics required loose, almost hollow
spinning, others smooth, tightly twisted thread. A fleece that had been
scoured to remove the natural lanolin handled differently than one spun
"in the grease." English sources tell us that kerseys were spun "thick by
great spinning," while wool destined for jersey was "wasshed out of his
oile and spun cleane."[30] Even the weather added complications. Too
much humidity caused wool to frizz and axles to stick; too little produced
static in the fiber and a wobbling wheel. The spindle wheel in the attic of
the garrison, made with a wooden, rather than an iron, axle and without
any device for adjusting tension, was probably especially vulnerable to
changes in the weather.[31] The word *homespun* is itself evidence that spinning was an important determinant of the quality of a fabric.

The other tools in the garrison remind us that spinning was one operation among many. Spun yarn had to be wound and measured into skeins,
using a hand-cranked reel or a simple niddy-noddy. After winding, skeins
were washed or dyed, then placed on an adjustable yarn-winder or
"swift" from which they could be wound into balls for knitting, onto
spools for warping, or onto the tiny bobbins called "quills" that were fitted into the weaver's shuttle. Weaving was the final process. A children's
puzzle published in England around 1800 illustrates these steps. In one
scene a woman spins wool on a walking wheel while another uses a "quill
wheel" and "swift" much like those in the garrison.

Some New England looms were built like the one in the puzzle, with
cantilevered beams extending from a single set of uprights. More commonly they were constructed with two identical frames (hence the phrase
"pair of looms") joined at the ends with crossbars. Although the loom in
the garrison was made in the early nineteenth century, its construction is
little different from looms made in Europe in the late Middle Ages. Built
like a house with its joints mortised and pegged, it was designed to with-
stand the constant motion of the swinging bar used to beat in the weft. It
was used at least some of the time for weaving linen. One can still see tiny
ridges on the beater bar where the taut threads rubbed against the wood.
The weaver warped such a loom by threading hundreds of warp threads
or "ends" through a slotted frame called a "sley," then through heddles,
finally winding them around a warp beam at the far end of the loom.
Near the weaver's feet a second beam took up the finished cloth as it was

*J. Wallis. Children's puzzle.*
*London, c. 1808.*

COURTESY MAINE HISTORICAL
SOCIETY, PORTLAND, MAINE

woven. The width of the loom was determined by the reach of the weaver's arms.
Throwing the shuttle through the raised warp
with one hand, he caught it with the other,
then pressed down the treadles to reverse the
position of the threads. English broadlooms were constructed in much
the same way but because they were twice as wide, they required two
weavers.[32]

As D. C. Coleman has explained, the English woolen industry did not
succeed through technical innovation—it "was one of the more techno-
logically stagnant and conservative industries in European economic history"—but through a capacity to organize household labor. Because
cloth-making involved so many steps, the work could be subdivided
again and again "yet remain, in respect of its central processes, capable of
being carried on in the home," or, more accurately, in hundreds of homes
linked by the entrepreneurial energies of clothiers.[33] As commercial production expanded, sorting, carding, spinning, dyeing, and weaving not
only took place in different workshops but in different parts of the country. Spinning was the most time-consuming task. Since it typically took
eight to ten spinners to keep one weaver supplied with thread, jobbers
sought workers wherever they could find them, in depressed agricultural
areas, in the more mountainous parts of Ireland, and even in poorhouses
and orphanages.[34]

Yet celebrations of spinning almost always portrayed a good housewife
who worked to clothe her family. The favorite spinning text was Proverbs
31, which described a "virtuous woman," presumably Solomon's mother,
who "seeketh wool, and flax, and worketh willingly with her hands." This
idealized vision of cloth-making influenced a poem by Edward Taylor, an

*Four-harness loom used in the Francis Grimes House, Deering, New Hampshire.*

English immigrant who became pastor at Westfield, Massachusetts, in the late seventeenth century. In the opening lines, he imagined himself as a bobbin-flyer wheel.

> *Make me, O Lord, thy Spin[n]ing Wheele compleat;*
> *Thy Holy Worde my Distaff make for mee.*
> *Make mine Affections thy Swift Flyers neate,*
> *And make my Soule thy holy Spoole to bee.*
> *My Conversation make to be thy Reele,*
> *And reele the yarn thereon spun of thy Wheele.*

In Taylor's version of Puritan theology, God's word held by the distaff of Scripture was spun into the soul through the action of the heart, then made useful through the reel of conversation. In the next stanza of the poem, he became a loom. God was the weaver; the holy spirit the helpful assistant; the church and its ordinances the fuller and finisher. The fabric they produced, "pinkt with Varnisht' Flowers of Paradise," recalled the heavily glazed and embossed worsteds made in the poet's native Coventry. Yet despite the clear allusions to commercial manufacturing, Taylor called his poem "Huswifery."[35]

The English divine John Dod argued that if a king's mother could spin, surely ordinary women should not think such labor beneath them.

When the promoters of spinning schools and workhouses employed the same verses, they mystified the underpaid labor that kept the engine of production going. In the same way, Dutch portraits of bourgeois women spinning in fine white aprons and ermine-trimmed gowns obscured the often frightful conditions in commercial linen production. In the hemp-hackling halls of Gouda, laborers were not allowed to open windows lest dust and lint fly onto the street. In the bleaching fields of Haarlem, women worked in the hot sun spreading and turning heavy webs of linen drenched in buttermilk.[36] German folktales captured the darker side of expanding outwork in stories about grotesque workers with thumbs grown to gigantic size from drawing flax and lips licked away from moistening the raw fiber with their own spit.[37]

In such a context, the spinning wheels and the "great weeb of wolling Cloath" in William Damm's inventory seem like a fantasy come true. In America, no man was forced to bend his back over another man's cloth nor employ his wife and daughters in market spinning. In a world where any man might own land, cloth-making was an extension of farming.

The rough walls of the garrison show the price paid for that dream.


In 1713, Massachusetts and New Hampshire officials traveled to Casco Bay near present-day Portland, Maine, to ratify "Articles of Pacification" signed by representatives of several Abenaki groups. Offering lawful subjection to Queen Anne, the Abenaki ostensibly promised colonists free liberty of hunting, fishing, and development in the "Eastern parts." At a conference held at Portsmouth in July 1714, officials from both colonies ratified the articles of peace with gifts of blankets, "fine white shirts," gunpowder, lead, rum, tobacco, and biscuits. Land speculators rejoiced. These new lands were opening at the very time Protestants in northern Ireland were struggling under burdens of taxation, uncertain land tenure, and falling prices.[38]

In Portsmouth, Archibald Macpheadris, an ambitious young merchant newly arrived from Ireland, would soon take advantage of these opportunities. In 1716, he married Sarah Wentworth, the teenage daughter of one of the key participants in the treaty conferences, and began to erect an impressive new house on Portsmouth harbor that was a radical contrast to Damm's log fortress and unlike anything New Hampshire had seen before. Hiring a builder fresh from London, he built in brick in the latest Palladian style. In a 1717 letter to Irish associates, he outlined a plan to

*Stairway murals.*
*Macpheadris-Warner*
*House, Portsmouth,*
*New Hampshire.*
PHOTOGRAPH GARY
SAMSON

send vessels to Cork, Belfast, Dublin, and Waterford to bring over "Servants & Good farmers" for the new plantations. The rivers had "more Salmon & all manner of fish than in any place in the World," he wrote, "& plenty of Good Middow & timber of all Sorts." A man who knew the business might cure a thousand tons of salmon in season, creating a good estate for himself in two years' time. Such a scheme would not only benefit New England; it would provide new sales for Irish linen.[39]

The murals in the grand central stairway of Macpheadris's house document his background and his ambition. As a newcomer and an Irishman, he wanted everyone who came to his house to know that he was both Protestant and pious, and that he understood the colonial cause. The presumed painter of the murals, Nehemiah Partridge, though a New Hampshire native, had apprenticed in Boston and had recently done work with the Dutch elite at Albany. The seemingly unrelated scenes he painted in Macpheadris's stairwell are united by a common theme of danger averted.[40] At the base of the stair, a woman sitting beside a flax wheel claps her hands as a spotted dog lunges at an eagle decimating her flock of chickens. Farther up the wall, an immense angel interrupts Abraham as he is about to sacrifice Isaac. On either side of the window on the landing are two immense Indians. The final panel portrays a mounted horseman with a full white wig and a *P* with a small crown above it on his saddle.

The spinner surely represents Ireland, known even in this period for its linen. The eagle that threatens her peace may be the papacy, a danger too in North America. The story of Abraham and Isaac has obvious religious connotations, but it could also allude to public events important to Mac-pheadris or his painter. The remaining panels suggest this. The Indians are two of the four Mohawk sachems who visited London in 1710 with men from the very families the painter knew in Albany. Mistakenly thought to possess the diplomatic authority that would secure Iroquois support in England's fight against the French and Abenaki, they were feted at the court of Queen Anne and paraded through the streets of London. Partridge based his wall paintings on engravings of their official portraits.[41]

The mounted horseman with the crowned *P* on his saddle is probably William III, *prince* of Orange before he defeated the Catholic James II in 1690 to become king of England. The spired town in the background appears to be Donaghal, the Irish market town on the River Boyne near where William's troops achieved the final victory. A long epic poem from the region recalls that in the battle at Pennyburn Bridge:

> . . . *brave Cornet Brown was slain*
> *MacPhetris died upon the purple plain*
> *Lieutenant Mackay fell upon the spot*
> *M'Cleland' son was wounded with a shot.*[42]

Family memory as well as Protestant pride may lie behind this image. Macpheadris's mural seems to say that those who inherit the Abrahamic covenant are often asked to sacrifice their children, but God will in the end send a ram into the thicket.

Two hundred families from northern Ireland arrived in Boston in 1718 and 1719. One group spent a miserable winter on Casco Bay before seeking grants on the Merrimack River in New Hampshire. They named their new town Londonderry for the Irish city where thirty years before Protestants had held back Catholic troops supporting James II. They, like Macpheadris, believed that Protestant courage in northern Ireland had assured a victory for William of Orange. Now Irish men would help secure a Protestant victory in North America. In his inaugural sermon, their pastor borrowed the words of the Old Testament prophet Ezekiel: "Moreover, I will make a covenant of peace with them; it shall be an everlasting covenant with them; and I will place them, and multiply them, and will set my sanctuary in the midst of them for evermore."[43]

Because the Penacook had withdrawn into the lake country of northern New Hampshire, Irish settlers at Londonderry thrived. Those in

*Nee Yeath Taw No Row,*
*engraving of London portrait.*
*An apparent prototype for the*
*Macpheadris mural.*
AMERICAN ANTIQUARIAN SOCIETY

Maine did not. Irish migration had hardly begun when Indians living on the upper Saco complained to Samuel Jordan, the proprietor of the Massachusetts truck house, that the new colonists were using hanging nets or seines to catch "all sorts of fish," destroying their own catch. Men from Ulster did indeed know how to catch and cure salmon, but they were unprepared for Abenaki resistance.[44]

A tense conference at Georgetown in 1720 turned into a festival of incomprehension. The Abenaki complained about the establishment of a settlement called Cork on the east of the Kennebec River. The commissioners were outraged about "insults" offered the new planters. When the English tried to talk about procedure, asking if the Indian leaders were actually authorized to speak for their people, the Abenaki spokesman deflected the question: "We desire that the people may be removed from Merry Meeting," the bay on the Kennebac where the Irish had settled. "That's no answer," the commissioners retorted. Mugg held up a string of wampum and asked again that the settlers be removed. The commissioners weren't interested in his complaint; they wanted reparations for dead cattle and for threats made to peaceful colonists. They told the Abenaki leaders that if they couldn't govern their young men, the settlers would be forced to take their own satisfaction. If the Abenaki wanted back the four men the English had already taken, they must bring in two hundred skins within twenty-five days. The English had good title to these lands going back seventy years.[45]

The colonial negotiators concluded the conference with a threat. "If you will constrain us, by your repeat'd Insults, to any Violent proceedings, we have force Enough; & wil pursue you to your Headquarters (which we are well acquainted with, & can Easily take Possession of) & will not leave you till we have cut you off Root and Branch from the Face of the Earth." The language was biblical, the speech itself a direct allusion to the last chapter of Malachi in the Old Testament: "For behold, the day cometh, that shall burn as an oven; and all the proud, yea, and all that do wickedly, shall be stubble: and the day that cometh shall burn them up, saith the Lord of hosts, that it shall leave them neither root nor branch."[46]

In 1722, Massachusetts once again declared war, calling the Abenaki "Robbers, Traitors and Enemies to his Majesty King George." Two years later provincial troops pushed to the presumed headquarters of the Kennebec Indians at Norridgewock, where they burned buildings, killed the French priest, and slaughtered more than eighty people, a third of the village. The remaining inhabitants fled, bleeding, to the French mission at St. Francis where they gathered strength for new attacks. A Massachusetts commander lamented that though his troops had accomplished "such a slaughter of them at Norridgewock as has not been known in any of the late wars," the depredations continued.[47] It took almost forty years for the English to subdue the Abenaki. Not until the final victory over French Canada would Maine's river valleys be safe for settlement.

Northern New Hampshire, too, remained Abenaki territory, but on the lower Merrimack, the Irish flourished. For a time, they even imagined establishing a linen industry. In 1728, Londonderry's town fathers appointed a sealer of "weights, measures, leather and all sorts of Good sufficient linen Cloth." A resolution in the New Hampshire legislature in 1731 confirmed the necessity for such an office when it deplored the "deceit practiced by persons travelling in this Province by selling of Foreign Linnens under pretence they were made at Londonderry." Although production was never very large, the reputation for quality persisted for several decades.[48]

New Hampshire's Irish were as adept at spinning stories as they were at making cloth. In the nineteenth century, people loved to tell about "Ocean-born Mary," who was born on a ship taken by pirates during her family's passage from Ireland. According to family lore, the pirate captain was so moved by the sight of the new baby that he gave her a length of silk that she eventually had made into a wedding gown. Framed fragments said to have been part of this gown spread among descendants as far away as Illinois. The part about the pirates can be documented. In August 1720, Captain Robert Peat of Salem told a maritime court he had left Londonderry, Ireland, on June 16 with a hundred immigrants on board. On July 17, when he was about sixty leagues east of Newfoundland banks, a pirate ship accompanied by a sloop with 140 men under the command of the notorious Thomas Roberts assailed him, boarding his ship and plundering the passengers of "all that was worth taking Even their very wearing apparell & put them in great Terrour of their lives by holding a pistol at their breasts & Telling them they should have no quarter." Even worse, they "tooke away most of their Saylers Rifled their Cabin Stateroom & Hold & damnifyed their vessel considerably." On July 28, 1720, while the ship was limping toward Boston, Mary Wilson Wallace was born. There could have been a length of silk, but it is more plausible to think the pirates robbed the pregnant mother rather than bestowed a gift upon her.[49]

A fragment of linen once owned by Wallace's daughter carries a more credible story. According to the inscription attached to it in the late nineteenth century, it was part of a web of toweling made for the daughter's marriage. Ocean-born Mary spun the warp, her daughter the weft, and the future father-in-law, Peter Patterson, did the weaving. It is a charming story, made even more interesting because the woman who preserved it had it notarized in 1890 by her husband, a Justice of the Peace, then photographed by the best photographer in Manchester, New Hampshire. By then Ocean-born Mary relics had spread across the United States and into Canada. They are part of a larger body of folklore about New Hampshire's Scots-Irish. The state's first historian, Jeremy Belknap, claimed that "spinning wheels, turned by the foot, were a novelty in the country" before the arrival of settlers from Ulster in the 1720s. Since the English introduced Dutch treadle wheels into Ireland in the seventeenth century as a way of stimulating linen manufacturing, his claim cannot be taken at face value.[50]

There is, however, a curious shift in nomenclature in New England probate inventories beginning about 1730. Earlier inventories differentiated spinning wheels by size or intended use. There were "large" and "small" wheels, "great" and "little" wheels, "wool" and "linen" (or more commonly "wooling" and "lining") wheels. Although eighteenth-century inventory-takers continued to use these terms, "Dutch wheel" gradually edged out "linen wheel" in western Connecticut and some parts of Massachusetts. In central Connecticut, the new term was "foot wheel."

Coastal Massachusetts and New Hampshire inventories showed an occasional "Irish wheel." While this is too broad a change to attribute to a small group of settlers in a corner of New Hampshire, it suggests that treadle wheels may have become more common in the eighteenth century and that in areas bordering New York, people attributed the new design to the Dutch rather than the Irish. The difference between a Dutch wheel and an Irish wheel was probably primarily aesthetic. An Irishman traveling in Holland in the 1720s said that the spinning wheels he found there were "much after the same form with ours in Ireland, called Dutch Wheels, only they are made firmer and the rims heavier."[51]

All of which adds new interest to the spinning wheel in Macpheadris's mural. Since it has a treadle, it could plausibly be called a "foot wheel." Since the presumed painter of the murals had strong alliances to Albany, it could also be a "Dutch" wheel. Since Macpheadris was an Irish merchant involved in bringing immigrants from Ulster to America, it could just as well be an "Irish" wheel. Whatever it was, it does not look a bit like wheels made in Londonderry in the late eighteenth century. Its legs are too stubby, its rim too heavy, the spokes on the drive wheel too bumpy. Perhaps it is an imaginary wheel, an artist's representation of something he poorly understood. The Londonderry wheels do, however, look much like the wheel in Dover's garrison. Interestingly, the inventory of Damm's son-in-law Samuel Hayes, taken in 1777, included an "Irish wheel."[52]

It was probably Hayes who sometime in the middle of the eighteenth century enlarged the narrow windows in the old garrison and gave them double-hung sashes like those that survive today. He may also have improved the interior woodwork, though he seems not to have changed the basic plan. There is surprisingly little difference between his inventory, taken in 1777, and that taken at Damm's death sixty years before. In 1718, Damm owned twenty-three ewes and seventeen lambs; sixty years later, Hayes had fifteen sheep and twelve lambs. Both men owned unspun sheep's wool, a comb or "hatchell" for processing flax, two kinds of spinning wheels, and unfinished "webs" of cloth.[53] Yet in the half century between the two inventories, the nature of New England cloth-making had changed.[54] This change cannot be discerned in the fabric of Damm's house or in the design of the spinning wheels now in it. It is a broad change, visible all over New England and in some other parts of North America as well, in the relationship between spinning wheels and looms in household inventories.

In Essex County, Massachusetts, almost half of households had spinning wheels by 1700, but only 6 percent had looms. That is exactly what one would expect to find in an artisan production system where families spun their own yarn and had it woven by a skilled neighbor. But between 1700 and 1730 loom ownership tripled while wheel ownership stayed about the same. The same thing occurred a bit earlier in western Massachusetts. When Edward Taylor arrived in Hampshire County in 1671, barely 35 percent of inventories listed spinning wheels, and looms were so rare as to be virtually invisible. By the time he died in 1729, two-thirds of households had wheels and an astonishing 20 percent had looms. Samples of other probate districts show even higher ratios of looms to wheels. In East Greenwich, Rhode Island, and Woodbury, Connecticut, in the 1730s there was one household with a loom for every two households with wheels. The same thing occurred in New Hampshire by 1750. If this were the West of England or the linen precincts of Ulster, one would suspect that yarn was being gathered from miles around by merchant clothiers. But New England in this period had no markets in yarn, and its very few clothiers were fullers and dressers of finished cloth. In New England, a high ratio of looms to wheels meant dispersed household production. Women had begun to weave.[55]

The account book of John Gould of Topsfield, Massachusetts, shows how this happened. Gould was a master weaver, the descendant of English artisans who came to Ipswich in 1640, but in the early eighteenth century he was unable to pass the craft on to his sons. His account book notes the employment of only two journeymen or apprentices between 1697 and 1724. Neither stayed long. Random entries suggest that his steadiest helper was his daughter Mary, who at the age of twelve wove a coverlet that took "a fortnight" to make. Later entries mention a daughter Phebe and two nieces. The wives and daughters of weavers had probably always done some work at the loom, but that practice accelerated in the early eighteenth century and then spread beyond artisan families.[56]

Scattered evidence of female weavers appears even in Manasseh Minor's diary. On January 5, 1718, he reported dryly, "bety ford Cam to weav." Whether she was working for him or only using his loom, we do not know. Farmers' and weavers' account books from other parts of New England have similar entries. In Providence, Rhode Island, two unmarried sisters, Tabitha and Joanna Inman, appear to have had a cooperative enterprise. One sister owned a wool wheel, the other a flax wheel and a loom. There are even references to female weavers among Christian

Indians. When Josiah Cotton traveled through southern New England in 1726, he stayed at the Bridgewater home of Hannah James, a woman who used to attend his Indian church at "Mattakees." In Cotton's view one mark of James's civility was that her children could read. Another was that she lived in "a high House of the English Fashion" with "2 Looms in it."[57]

Because William Damm died just on the cusp of this change, it is tempting to think that the second weaver in his household may have been his daughter Leah, the only child still unmarried at his death. Leah continued to live in the garrison after her marriage to Samuel Hayes, but she was dead by 1754 when Hayes, and his second wife, Joanna Critchet, signed a contract with a Dover man for the services of his daughter. The girl was to serve faithfully for seven years. In return Hayes and his wife promised to "learn her [to] read, & to knit, & to weave if Capable & also other household work." That weaving was listed alongside "other household work" tells the story.[58] Cloth-making lost its artisan identity as it became a female occupation.

In New Hampshire weaving passed into the female domain in exactly the same period that the colony's woodworking economy was maturing. Between 1715 and 1768, shipments of pine boards from the port of Portsmouth increased from one million to twelve million board feet. Men clearing land for new townships rafted timber down the tributaries of the Piscataqua, supplying raw materials for a shipbuilding industry that by 1740 was the second or third largest in New England. Specialized woodworking trades also expanded. Portsmouth merchants were exporting house frames to Lisbon as early as 1715. In the 1720s, they added chairs to the cargoes of foodstuffs and lumber they sent to the West Indies. In 1752, a Portsmouth ship bound for Newfoundland carried eight desks carefully packed in cases. By 1768, Portsmouth stood just behind Boston as an exporter of household furniture. As farmers brought more land under cultivation, opportunities for craft work expanded. Barrel makers supplied casks for salted meat, cordwainers turned the hides that were a by-product of the meat trade into shoes sold at market. Although some men continued to weave, especially in the Scots-Irish towns, there too weaving gradually slipped into the female domain as wood crafts became dominant. In Bedford, John Dunlap, son of a Scots-Irish weaver, became a skilled furniture maker. In Londonderry, Samuel Gregg came home from fighting the French to "learn to make foot wheels." In Newington, a man named William Damm, nephew of the builder of the garrison, became a skilled turner and chair maker.[59]

New Hampshire's story fits well into new scholarship in economic history. Historians are less disposed than they once were to describe a linear transformation from subsistence agriculture to market production. As economic historian Jan deVries has observed, the expanding commerce of the eighteenth century affected different regions in different ways. In some parts of Europe, putting-out industries captured child and female labor, simultaneously creating new goods and new markets for those goods. In other parts of the Atlantic world, farmers and their sons concentrated on market production, while children and women produced less saleable commodities for family use. The end result was an "industrious revolution" that transformed the Western world.[60] The New England story is intriguing because it contrasts so markedly with Pennsylvania, where continuing immigration of artisan weavers from the British Isles and continental Europe kept weaving in the male domain into the nineteenth century. In the Chesapeake, however, women began to weave almost as early as in New England and for much the same reason. Weaving had little commercial value and was designed to supplement rather than replace foreign imports. In later chapters, we will see what women did with their seemingly marginal occupation. Here it is enough to note that they took up weaving in the second quarter of the eighteenth century as an extension of household work.[61]

Perhaps someday the scholars who have taught us so much about the development of furniture trades in colonial New Hampshire will turn their attention to anonymous wheels like those in the garrison. No one knows who made them, but they do have a story. It begins with the transfer of textile technology from the continent to the British Isles in the sixteenth and seventeenth centuries and from Britain to America in successive waves of immigration. It is a story about conquest as well as settlement, about imperial objectives and Protestant vision, and about the distribution of work in colonial households. These old spinning wheels not only symbolize women's household labor but the shaping of male identity in market production.

In the half century after William Damm's death, new towns and parishes were carved out of Dover's original land grant and the center of the town moved from the neck to the falls of the Cocheco. Dover's inhabitants survived the war of the 1720s, joined in the assault on the French fortress at Louisbourg in 1745, and rejoiced in the final triumph over French Canada in 1763. They lived through the "Awful Earthquake" of 1727 and the "exceeding shock" of another in 1755 and endured the epidemic of "throat distemper" that struck the province in 1735. They suffered wind, hail, snow, drought, and political conflict with England, supporting the neighboring province of Massachusetts in its boycotts of British goods in 1769 and its open rebellion in the decade that followed.[62] Yet viewed through the lens of Samuel Hayes's inventory, the old garrison seems frozen in time, linked to the repetitive cycles of the seasons rather than to the clang of historical events. But that view is deceptive. In 1718, Damm was one of a handful of weavers in a colony with no more than four thousand English inhabitants settled in a few coastal towns. By the time Hayes and his wife contracted to teach a young woman weaving, there were forty thousand inhabitants in forty townships, and wheels and looms were everywhere.[63]

As English and Irish colonists moved up the Merrimac and into the Connecticut River Valley, the native inhabitants of these areas retreated to refugee villages at the head of Lake Champlain or into the borderlands between Maine and Canada until they were known only as deadly antagonists in war.[64] While there is no way to fully recover their story, the accidental survival of a piece of weaving offers a glimpse of a life beyond the reach of English settlement. In 1763, an eighteen-year-old girl named Rachel Meloon, captured nine years before from her parents' homestead in central New Hampshire, returned from Canada with new skills and a song. The New Hampshire Historical Society now owns a colorful strap she twined for her neighbor Peter Kimball from linen yarn and porcupine quills. Colorful patterns, no two alike, surround Kimball's name and the maker's initials.

One can imagine Meloon spinning the thread on her mother's wheel, singing a sorrowful song she had learned in an Indian village.

*She dokina wen to markit*
*Asoo sa sika me a saw*
*Sa waka catawunka naw*
*Chicka way sa catawunka naw*

*[She does not wake, Marguerite,*
*Cover her, do not cry for her,*

*Stretch the hide, it is not prepared,*
*Start the fire, it is not prepared.]*

It is a mourning song, a lament for a lost sister or friend. But it is also a song about work. When a woman dies, someone else must pick up the tasks she left. Someone else must prepare the skins brought back from the hunt, must tend the fire that warms the wigwam. The song ended with syllables that sounded to its twentieth-century translator like the Abenaki words for mill or river, followed by the repetitious refrain "departing, departing."[65]

*Rachel Meloon. Twined linen strap*
*ornamented with porcupine quills,*
*c. 1765–1773.*
COURTESY NEW HAMPSHIRE HISTORICAL SOCIETY

# 3

### ✦

# *Hannah Barnard's Cupboard*

HADLEY, MASSACHUSETTS, 1715

*Who they are by name we cannot tell—no
matter who they are—we should be
none the wiser if we could name them, they
themselves none the more
honourable.*

Horace Bushnell, *"The Age of Homespun"*

Hannah Barnard's cupboard was the most engaging, if not the most elegant, object in a furniture show mounted in Hartford, Connecticut; Deerfield, Massachusetts; and New York City in the spring of 1993. Describing the New York installation, one of the curators told a reporter, "No doubt about it. It was the dominant object of the show. I set up the other chests like so many little pews leading up to the cupboard, which sat there like a kind of throne or altar at the end of the line." *Altar* seems like the right word to describe this exuberant cupboard with its electric blue columns. But who or what did it celebrate? Could it have been Hannah Barnard herself? A reporter for the *Hartford Courant* thought so. Expressing amazement that in "this rigidly patriarchal period," a woman could emblazon her name on an article of furniture, he pronounced it "a remarkable cupboard with a proto-feminist message." A Hartford furniture collector offered a softer interpretation. Surely the cupboard must have been a gift from Barnard's future husband. It was "a Valentine in furniture."[1]

The authors of the exhibit catalog were more circumspect. While acknowledging that the woman's name made a strong statement about her role "as keeper of the household and a major portion of its assets: valued textiles and silver," they concentrated on stylistic analysis ("The Barnard cupboard was a stage for new Baroque concepts conveyed through traditional Hampshire County ornament") and on details that could be empirically affirmed (under polarized light microscopy the paint on the columns turned out to be a mixture of white lead and Prussian blue, an artificial pigment first synthesized in Berlin in 1704).[2]

Hannah's cupboard exemplifies both the enticements and the difficulties of historical interpretation based on physical evidence alone. Unlike Dinah Fenner's basket, it had no accompanying story when it turned up in the antiques market in 1934. We now know that Hannah Barnard was born in Hadley,

Massachusetts, in 1684, married John Marsh in 1715, and gave birth to a daughter the next year. None of these details, however, explains the flamboyant decoration on her cupboard. Are the bold Roman letters, the flat roses, the vines and flowers, and the insectlike flourishes assertions of self, emblems of love, symbols of fertility, markers of one woman's command of her household goods, or signs of everywoman's subordination to domestic duty? Or are they mere design conventions with no larger significance at all?

Fortunately, Hannah's cupboard belongs to one of the best-documented traditions in American decorative arts. Her hometown entered the annals of furniture history in 1883 when a Hartford banker began to speak of an antique chest he found there as his "Hadley chest." The name stuck. Scholars have now identified 250 related items made in Hadley and nearby Hampshire County towns between 1680 and 1740. Although early collectors thought of the Hadley chest as a folk form, furniture scholars today emphasize its dynamic origins in the period of rebuilding that followed King Philip's War. The first appearance of the famous Hadley motif—a two-petaled tulip joined to a single large leaf— was on the pulpit of the meetinghouse in Springfield, Massachusetts, a town long dominated by the fur trader and merchant William Pynchon and his sons. Hannah's cupboard has many of the qualities of this early furniture, though coming at the end of the period it incorporates new ideas as well, including the lavish use of paint.[3]

Hadley chests were status symbols commissioned by prosperous families in a world torn—and retorn—by war. The English towns of western Massachusetts, like those in coastal New Hampshire, experienced a disproportionate number of raids during the long conflict with French Canada. There were at least thirteen attacks during King William's War. Two hit Hadley directly. Queen Anne's War brought the massive assault on Deerfield in the winter of 1704 that resulted in the death or captivity of three-fifths of the town's population. Among the 109 captives taken to Canada were Hannah's future husband, John Marsh, and her father's sister, a woman also born with the name Hannah Barnard.[4] In the aftermath of such events, the cupboard seems not only a marker of status but an assertion of life and order.

But Hannah's cupboard can also be interpreted in the light of textile history. A cupboard was not only a decorative object. It was a container for other goods. Table linens and sheets filled its drawers or shelves; a richly decorated "cupboard cloth" embellished its top. These textiles, too, were marked with the owner's initials if not her full name. Furthermore, the floral imagery on chests and cupboards mimicked the imagery on luxury textiles. Cupboards and textiles belonged to a category of household goods called "movables." Unlike real estate, which was typically transmitted from father to son, movables formed the core of a female inheritance.

Passed on from generation to generation, Hannah's cupboard became her memorial. For more than a century, it preserved her name. Its history teaches us that material objects were not only markers of wealth but devices for building relationships and lineages over time, and it helps us to understand the cultural framework within which ordinary women became creators as well as custodians of household goods.[5]

Chests, boxes, cabinets, and cupboards were to the English what baskets were to the Algonkians. Made from local materials in a wide range of sizes, they had aesthetic as well as practical value. Ordinary chests were constructed from six pine boards nailed together at the corners and fitted with hinges at the top. Nearly every household had at least one. More expensive chests and cupboards were built like a house, with heavy rails and stiles fitted with panels and held together with mortise and tenon joints, hence the name *joined* furniture. A New England furniture scholar once joked that you could put wheels on a joined oak cupboard, hook it to the back of your car, and drive it to Virginia, and when you got there the cupboard would be in better shape than the car. Joined chests and cupboards asserted permanency, stability, and power in a world where Indians, witches, and illness lurked.[6]

In the seventeenth century, joined cupboards were largely confined to the parlors of ministers, merchants, and magistrates. Mary Rowlandson, author of the famous captivity narrative, inherited one when her husband died in Wethersfield, Connecticut, in 1678. Carved with tulips and gillyflowers, it was made by Wethersfield's most fashionable joiner. Busy trimmings, painted black to imitate the ebony on high-style London pieces, march up the stiles and across the drawer and rails, turning the flat panels into a busy argument between points and curves. The overhanging shelf with its supporting pilasters betrays the original sense of a cupboard as a *cup board,* a flat space for displaying silver or ceramic vessels. The

*Mary Rowlandson cupboard.*
LANCASTER PUBLIC LIBRARY, LANCASTER, MASSACHUSETTS

locked compartments below reveal the form's other function—to pre-serve precious household goods from greedy hands.[7] Rowlandson's weeks in the wilderness had taught her "the extreme vanity of this World," but they had not made her indifferent to material things.

A cupboard was a little castle, an edifice for preserving and displaying family wealth. Edward Taylor, the pastor-poet of Westfield, Massachu-setts, imagined Christ pulling a sinful soul from a trash pit, marveling that God could "Crown his shelfe, / Or Dress his golden Cupboard with such ware." In another meditation, he imagined himself as a cupboard. Jesus, the good housewife, came with dangling keys to open the door, finding "Love crincht in a Corner."[8] Most cupboards were less valuable than the linens stored inside. The eight tablecloths and twenty-eight towels and napkins in Joseph Rowlandson's cupboard were appraised at five pounds, the cupboard at two. Springfield's John Pynchon owned a parlor cup-board valued at three pounds and cupboard cloths and table linens worth more than thirteen. A single "wrought napkin" of Pynchon's was appraised at three shillings at a time when most of his land was valued at four shillings an acre.[9]

The cost of linen was not only in the fabric. Sewing and laundry both multiplied when diners began using hemmed squares of linen to wipe their greasy chins and fingers. Tablecloths and napkins demanded soap, hot water, bleaching ground, "smoothing irons," and the inclination to use them. In the first generation in New England, the Puritan gentry worried that too much investment in housekeeping could endanger the soul. John Winthrop's journal tells the story of a godly woman of Boston who brought with her from London, "a parcel of very fine linen of great value, which she set her heart too much upon." One evening, having "been at charge to have it all newly washed, and curiously folded and pressed," she left it in her parlor. Her "negro maid went into the room very late, and let fall some snuff of the candle upon the line." By morning the linen was tinder, and a part of the wainscot was scorched. "But it pleased God that the loss of this linen did her much good, both in taking off her heart from worldly comforts, and in preparing her for a far greater affliction by the untimely death of her husband." Puritans learned to mistrust the things they loved, but they did not abandon the markers of gentility.[10]

The most prosperous among them draped their cupboards in damask, diaper, satin, or lace-trimmed linen and filled their chests with fine tablecloths. Dutch genre paintings of the seventeenth century help us visualize the link between luxury textiles and cupboards. In a portrait by Gortzius Geldorp, a cupboard much like Rowlandson's stands sentry over a linen-covered table where the numerous members of a pious family fold their hands for grace. Though seemingly realistic, every detail in the painting is metaphorical. The upper shelf of the cupboard, swathed in a lace-trimmed cloth, simultaneously displays the family's wealth and recalls the chalice of the Lord's Supper. The tiny branches springing out of the tile floor beside the children, like the vine creeping along the door frame, recall Psalms 128:3—"Thy wife shall be as a fruitful vine by the sides of thine house: thy children like olive plants round about thy table." The orderly group at the table, their folded hands mirroring the folded napkins and neatly pressed linen, contrasts with the puppy licking a bowl in the foreground, an allusion perhaps to uncouth houses where people still ate out of common trenchers.[11]

The diary of the Bostonian Sarah Kemble Knight betrays the core values of an elite culture that, on both sides of the Atlantic, linked civility with fine linen. Traveling south toward Connecticut in October 1703,

*Gortzius Geldorp.* Portrait of
a Family Saying Grace, *1602.*

Knight stopped at a house where "the woman bro't in a Twisted thing like a cable, but something whiter; and laying it on the bord, tugg'd for life to bring it into a capacity to spread." The slovenly housewife knew that she should lay a cloth for her genteel visitor, but she hadn't mastered the art of keeping one in readiness. Her dinner was no better. Knight thought she had boiled the pork and cabbage in her dye kettle; the "sauce was of a deep Purple."[12]

The sardonic allusion to the woman's dye kettle should not mislead us. In New England, gentility was fully compatible with household production. Probate inventories suggest that spinning was as essential to the households of country clergymen as devotional tracts. Mary Rowlandson owned a spinning wheel, as did Westfield's Edward Taylor.[13] When the Boston diarist Samuel Sewall visited Northampton in 1716, he spent several hours with Solomon Stoddard at his parsonage, noting that old "Madam Stoddard, who is lame of the Sciatica . . . yet spins at the Linen-wheel." Esther Stoddard was a woman of impeccable Puritan credentials, the daughter of the first minister of Windsor, Connecticut, and the widow of Eleazar Mather, the less-famous brother of Increase Mather of

Boston. Her husband's inventories exemplify both gentility and industry. Stoddard's, taken in 1731, listed a flax wheel as well as "Needle Wrought Cushions" and a cupboard with its lace-trimmed cloth. To maintain twenty tablecloths and 125 napkins, Madame Stoddard had both a "New fashioned" and an old-fashioned "Ironing box."[14]

Although none of her linens have survived, napkins marked by her daughter-in-law are in the collections of the Northampton Historical Society. The cross-stitched initials *PC* show that Prudence Chester acquired them before her marriage in 1731. The damask napkin, woven with the insignia of King George I, was likely made in Germany for the English market sometime between 1714 and 1727. (The mounted monarch looks much like

*Damask napkin. Probably Germany, 1714–1727.*

NORTHAMPTON HISTORICAL SOCIETY, NORTHAMPTON, MASSACHUSETTS

*Linen napkin or towel, c. 1730–1731. The embroidered initials "PC" were probably worked by Prudence Chester before her marriage to John Stoddard in 1731. Later owners added their names in ink.*

NORTHAMPTON HISTORICAL SOCIETY, NORTHAMPTON, MASSACHUSETTS

the horseman in Archibald Malpheadris's murals.) A second napkin woven with a complex pattern of overlapping circles is more difficult to date since fabrics with similar patterns were made from the seventeenth century onward, but it too was likely imported. Napkins like these were purchased as yardage. A woman made them her own by cutting and hemming them and by marking them with her initials.[15]

Marking was an art acquired through an education that typically included the completion of an embroidered sampler. The earliest samplers were true patterns, elongated pieces of linen worked with a succession of motifs. By the early eighteenth century, many were made to be framed, and most had verses. Almost all were inscribed with the maker's name. Samplers displayed the wealth of an embroiderer's family as well as her literacy and her future role as custodian of fine textiles. Some sampler verses gave thanks for an education; others gave glory to God. Many explicitly addressed persons yet unborn.

*When I am dead and in my grave,*
*And all my bones are rotten.*
*When this you see remember me,*
*That I won't be forgotten.*[16]

To inscribe one's name on a material object assured some sort of immortality.

One hundred fifteen of 126 documented Hadley chests are marked. The vast majority—102 of the 115—have two initials, most of which have been identified with the maiden names of women. Six represent married couples, with the first initial of the husband's name on the right, that of the wife on the left, and the first letter of their surname in the middle. Seven, including Hannah's cupboard, have full names.[17] Since barely a third of women in late-seventeenth-century Massachusetts could sign their own names, these names asserted both ownership and literacy.[18]

The floral imagery on Hadley chests also links them to textiles. Most carvers used tulips in some form, though the treatment varied. The creator of the *MS* chest attached tulips to the reverse curves that border the rails and stiles, tucking the owner's initials into tight lozenges on the right and left panels. The center panel can be read as well as a fertility symbol. The designer of the *SH* chest, in contrast, splashed flowers and leaves over the entire ground, highlighting the shallow carving in red paint over a stippled background. The initials on this chest stand out boldly because they occupy the only plain field on the surface. The carving on the seven named chests is different still. Esther Cook's has leaves and tulips like those on the *SH* chest, but it also has a row of fleurs-de-lis, a motif found on several related chests. The fleur-de-lis, like the tulip, was associated in Christian iconography with life and immortality, though in this period it also appeared on mass-marketed objects like Staffordshire pottery.[19] Although the details vary, the echoes reflect a design vocabulary also employed on textiles. The leafy pattern of the *SH* chests echoes those on embroidered bed hangings, the reverse curves on the *MS* chest the banded flowers on samplers.

Hannah Barnard's cupboard shows a mixture of influences. Like Rowlandson's cupboard, it has heavy posts supporting a corniced upper shelf. Like chests made in Hadley and nearby towns, it is marked with the owner's name and covered all over with flowers, yet it is painted rather than carved. Its maker also experimented with form. The upper part is

*Mary Hollingsworth sampler,*
*c. 1665–1670.*
COURTESY PEABODY-ESSEX
MUSEUM, SALEM, MASSACHUSETTS

MS *chest with drawers.*
*Hartfield, Massachusetts,*
*area, c. 1715. Wadsworth*
*Atheneum, Hartford.*
WALLACE NUTTING COLLECTION.
GIFT OF J. PIERPONT MORGAN,
BY EXCHANGE, AND THE EVELYN
BONAR STORRS TRUST FUND

*Embroidered hanging.*
*English.*

WADSWORTH ATHENEUM,
HARTFORD, CONNECTICUT.
THE WILLIAM B. AND MARY
ARABELLA GOODWIN
COLLECTION. BEQUEST OF
WILLIAM B. GOODWIN

SH *chest, owned by Sarah*
*Hawks (1701–1783),*
*Hadley or Hatfield,*
*Massachusetts, c. 1710.*

POCUMTUCK VALLEY
MEMORIAL ASSOCIATION,
MEMORIAL HALL MUSEUM,
DEERFIELD, MASSACHUSETTS.
GIFT OF GEORGE SHELDON,
BEFORE 1886

*SW chest with
drawers. Hadley,
Massachusetts, area,
c. 1718.*
POCUMTUCK VALLEY
MEMORIAL ASSOCIATION,
MEMORIAL HALL
MUSEUM, DEERFIELD,
MASSACHUSETTS. GIFT OF
GEORGE SHELDON, 1892

built like cupboards made in Wethersfield forty years before, but the
lower section is entirely fitted with drawers, allowing easier access to the
objects inside. The lower half is in fact almost identical to a chest of
drawers now owned by Historic Deerfield that seems to have been made
by the same joiner. The flat Tudor roses that march across the drawers
link it, however, to three pieces made by different joiners but decorated in
a similar style.[20] The painting could have been added by the man who
made the cupboard, by one of the joiners who built the other chests decorated like it, or by a different person entirely, perhaps even Hannah herself. The character of the painting suggests a person used to working with

*Plate, tin-glazed
earthenware. England,
early eighteenth century.*
POCUMTUCK VALLEY
MEMORIAL ASSOCIATION,
MEMORIAL HALL MUSEUM,
DEERFIELD, MASSACHUSETTS.
GIFT OF MRS. BESSIE
GAMONS, 1954

wood, however. The designs were laid out with a straightedge and compass, the outlines incised into the wood, then filled in with pigment.[21]

Hannah's cupboard has undulating vines like the *MS* chest, curling letters and inverted hearts like the *SH* chest, leaf and diamond constructions and a row of half circles like those on other Hadley chests, and painted drawer "moldings" like the actual moldings on early cupboards.[22] Glorying in paint, its creator bent tradition in yet another way. The turned posts of seventeenth-century cupboards were painted black. The flamboyant blue on Hannah's shows off a vibrant new tint unavailable even in Europe before 1704. An awareness of European imports is also evident in the segmented roses that march across the drawers, which look very much like the roses on a tin-glazed plate owned by Esther Williams of Deerfield, who married in the same year as Hannah. In English delftware, flat "roses" were sometimes combined with checkered "thistles." The upright blossom in the central panel of Hannah's cupboard is in fact a thistle. The plump fruits on either side of the central panel are pomegranates, another widely used motif in English decorative arts.[23]

The unknown designer brought all of these elements together in a unified and powerful composition. Hannah's name is integral to the design, yet its placement sets it apart from the chests with full names in part because a cupboard required hinged doors. A chest with a lidded top had several unbroken surfaces for decoration, whereas a cupboard with drawers was broken in many places. Unless the designer wanted to string the name across a drawer, he (or she) had to fit it into one of the panels on the top, easy to do with an initial, hard to accomplish with a full name. The solution was brilliant. The name *Hannah* is a palindrome, a word that reads the same backward or forward. The composition takes advantage of this repetition, allowing the three letters *H, A,* and *N* to form two strong columns. *Barnard,* despite its tantalizing internal rhyme, was more difficult, since seven letters required four rows rather than three. Again the painter allowed *A* and *N* to dominate, keeping the curved letters *B, R,* and *D* somewhat narrower, filling in the extra space with a square. Since the Barnards, like other seventeenth-century families, spelled their name in various ways, sometimes writing Barnard, sometimes Bernard, the choice of an initial *A* was deliberate. When the cupboard was restored in 1994, the conservator discovered faint marks of an *E* beneath it.[24]

Inside the columns created by Hannah's name are two bold towers formed of seemingly unrelated things—paired leaves, pomegranates,

*Tapestry cushion cover, made at the Sheldon family tapestry workshop, England, c. 1610–1615.*

POCUMTUCK VALLEY MEMORIAL ASSOCIATION, MEMORIAL HALL
MUSEUM, DEERFIELD, MASSACHUSETTS. GIFT OF THE REVEREND
JOHN TAYLOR TO DEERFIELD ACADEMY MUSEUM, BEFORE 1806,
TRANSFERRED TO PVMA IN 1877

hearts, and diamonds. Nothing on the cupboard seems more "folk"-like, yet the composition is probably an abstracted version of the borders often used in late Renaissance tapestries and engravings. A cushion cover owned by Edward Taylor shows a central vase of flowers bordered by pillared constructions of fruit, flowers, leaves, urns, and masks, the massing strikingly similar to the borders on the Barnard cupboard. The busy turnings on seventeenth-century cupboards are, of course, a three-dimensional version of the same thing.

In a poem written about the time the first Hadley chests were being built, Taylor used imagery from gardening to celebrate marriage and the establishment of a new household. His poem puns on the word *knot*, which in seventeenth-century usage connoted, among other things, an embroidery motif, a calligraphic flourish, a little knob or bud on a plant, a decorative flower bed, or a marriage (as in "tying the knot").

> *A Curious Knot God made in Paradise,*
> *And drew it out inamled neatly Fresh.*
> *It was the True-Love Knot, more sweet than spice,*
> *And set with all the flowres of Graces dress.*
>
> *When in this Knot I planted was, my Stock*
> *Soon knitted, and a manly flower out brake.*
> *And after it my branch again did knot:*
> *Brought out another Flowre; its sweet breath'd mate.*[25]

Taylor's description of reproduction is lush, yet curiously asexual, almost parthenogenetic. Despite its allusion to a "True-Love Knot," there is no female presence, unless it is the earth itself. His image may in fact reflect the ancient notion of the womb as a passive receptacle for male seed.

A cupboard, too, is a container. Yet framed with a woman's name, Hannah Barnard's cupboard laid claim both to the garden and the branching flower.

Hannah Barnard was born in 1684 in a valley that had moved through the optimism of the early fur trade into a long era of contention and war. Hannah's maternal grandfather, George Colton, was an early settler at Springfield and a trusted military commander and courier under Colonel

John Pynchon, son and successor to the immensely powerful merchant, magistrate, and fur trader William Pynchon.[26] Her paternal grandfather, Francis Barnard, was typical of the discontented Puritans who left divided congregations in Wethersfield, Windsor, and Hartford, Connecticut, in the 1660s to establish new towns upriver from Springfield. By all accounts, Hannah's male progenitors were sober and industrious men, but in the 1670s, several of their children, including Hannah's future parents, were charged in Hampshire County Court with affronts to authority and good order. Their crimes—selling liquor to Indians, violating sumptuary laws, and breaking the peace—were symptoms of the economic stresses and the generational tensions that were reshaping the region.[27]

The exchange of English textiles for Algonkian furs had enriched the Pynchons and their allies, but it had also transformed the Pocumtuck villages on whose labor the fur trade depended. Disease, declining fur stocks, wars among Iroquois allies who supplied furs, falling prices for wampum, and growing dependence on alcohol put enormous stresses on village middlemen. By midcentury, they were making up shortfalls in store accounts by selling land. A small English trader who sold liquor threatened both sides—outraging the authority of the big merchants who controlled the county courts and offending Pocumtuck leaders who worried about the disintegration of their communities.[28] So it was that Francis Barnard's son-in-law, Dr. John Westcarr, found himself in Hampshire County Court in 1670 charged with selling liquor to Indians contrary to law. His accusers were Pocumtucks.

Nusco testified that Indians made drunk on Westcarr's rum had broken into his wigwam and spoiled it, though he admitted that he himself "had 6 qts & ½ of liquors of John Westcar & paid him a great beaver skin of my wives." Westcarr denied the charges, arguing that as a physician he needed large quantities of rum to prepare medicines. A second accuser, Wequamunko, retorted that he too had purchased liquor from Westcarr, and that as an old man he could not lie. "That which I Say is true . . . I paid for it in wampam after 2 fathoms a quart; I paid in black wampam." With John Pynchon presiding, the court fined Westcarr forty pounds. He appealed their decision to the court of assistants in Boston, but when that body, putting the case to jury, could not agree, Hampshire officials agreed to accept five pounds and dismiss the case, "considering he hath been at much expense & trouble."[29]

Meanwhile, his wife, Hannah, was having her own troubles with civil authority. In 1673, she was charged with the crime of wearing silk "contrary to law." The accusation, based on a Massachusetts act of 1651 restricting the wearing of gold or silver buttons or lace, expensive bone lace, or silk hoods and scarves to persons whose net worth exceeded two hundred pounds, was not unrelated to her husband's crime. Like him she was pushing against the limitations of an inherited social order. Although she was acquitted on her first appearance, she was presented again in 1675 and once more in 1677, after the death of her husband, when she was admonished "for wearing silk in a flaunting garb, to the great offence of several sober persons in Hadley." She was not alone in her rebellion. In the midst of King Philip's War, the court charged "38 wives and maids and 30 young men . . . some for wearing silk and that in a flaunting manner, and others for long hair and other extravagancies." Especially outrageous was the behavior of a sixteen-year-old girl from Northampton who wore silk "in an offensive way and garb, not only before, but when she stood presented." Hannah Westcarr's brother Joseph Barnard and his wife, Sarah, were among the offenders, as were "Goody Colton" of Springfield and her daughters, Mary and Sarah. In the eyes of the court, their behavior was "not Becomeing a Wilderness State." To defy civil authority was to defy God.[30]

The crimes of another brother were greater. In March 1676, Samuel Barnard was charged with taking part in a riotous assembly, "being there present with his Clubb where authority was Publiquely Affronted." He was already in trouble with the law for "Privately Plotting" with some of the garrison soldiers then in Hadley who were "conceiving a Disorderly designe of going to Narregansett" after Massachusetts forces withdrew from the river towns during a brief lull in King Philip's War. The men apparently hoped to join Connecticut forces who were attempting to cut off Philip's access to food supplies near Narragansett Bay. The death of Samuel's brother John during the fall campaign may have had something to do with his second rebellion. Although he was sentenced to be whipped twelve stripes on his naked body, through the mediation of his father the court remanded the punishment to a five-pound fine. The father pleaded "his wives illness & weakness of Body," suggesting that since she had already lost one son this "Affliction might be to[o] hard for her."[31]

The war seems to have unleashed many forms of misbehavior. Across the river in Hatfield in 1678, two men were found guilty of breaking into a weaver's cellar and behaving offensively, "in playing at Cards and other foule and Shamful abuses of the Cellar and implements . . . by their excrements." As a witness delicately explained, they had "layd their Tailes" on the weaver's cloth beam. The court ordered them whipped seven lashes apiece on the naked body, one man's seven stripes "to be added to the 18 stripes he is to receive for fornication."[32]

More disturbing were mysterious assaults from an unseen world that came in the decade after the war. As town selectmen, Francis Barnard and his brother-in-law Deacon Phillip Smith were responsible for "Relieving the Indigencies" of a troublesome widow named Mary Webster who lived at the end of the Middle Road near the meadow. She had started out well enough, marrying the son of a Connecticut magistrate in 1670, perhaps as a second wife, but by 1683 she was living alone in Hadley and terrifying her neighbors. Teams balked when they passed her door. Under the power of her glance, hay racks tipped, then mysteriously righted themselves, babies rose from their cradles, and hens fell down chimneys. Searching her body, good women found extra teats where the Devil and his imps "in the shape of a warraneage" or black fisher had sucked. Remanded to Boston in April, she was tried for witchcraft in September, found not guilty, and returned home to face her neighbors' scrutiny. When Smith, a member of the court that had sent her to Boston, fell ill, he was certain she had worked a malevolent design. "Be sure . . . to have a care of me," he told his family, "for you shall see strange things. There shall be a wonder in Hadley."[33]

Unable to pursue legal action, the selectmen looked the other way when the young men of the town "did three or four times in one Night, go and give Disturbance to the Woman." As long as they distracted her, Smith slept, but when the harassment stopped his agony resumed. Although the town's youth rolled and buried Goody Webster in snow and forced her to endure a mock hanging, she thrived while the deacon worsened. Fire danced on his bed. Pots of medicine emptied themselves. The bed shook. Strange things scratched under the sheets. A heavy smell, like musk, permeated the room until even an apple roasting in the fire was spoiled. Smith's body grew so heavy that the strongest man in town couldn't turn him. Seemingly dead on Saturday at sunrise, he was still warm on Sunday afternoon. On Monday morning his attendants found his face discolored and bruised and fresh blood running down his hair. His body was so distorted that even his sex was reversed. The jury that viewed the corpse found "a Swelling on one Breast, which rendered it like a Womans. His Privities were wounded or burned. On his back, besides Bruises, were several pricks, or holes, as if done with Awls or Pins."[34]

Smith was the richest man in Hadley. The inventory taken after his death showed a clear estate of 1,280 pounds, including sheep, cattle, wine, honey, sugar, tobacco, barley, codfish, Indian corn, and the income from a ship. He left his daughter Rebecca one hundred pounds, twenty to be paid "in the Negro girle I now have," unless she preferred other goods, her portion to be reduced to eighty pounds "in case she goe Cross to her Mother's minde in her marriage." Smith's wealth gave him status in the community and power to shape his daughter's and his servant's lives after his death, but it did not give him strength to resist his fear of Mary Webster. Although Smith's story convinced Cotton Mather that the man had been "murdered with an hideous witchcraft," Webster was not indicted. She stayed in her little house for another decade, dying of natural causes in June 1696. Among the small cache of goods she left were a Psalm book, a Bible, and a single tablecloth.[35]

In these same years, the Barnard children moved from rebellion to respectability. The occupations they chose—preaching, teaching, and keeping public records—demonstrated a better than common education. Joseph overcame his presentments for wearing flaunting apparel and selling liquor to Indians to become clerk of the Deerfield town meeting. Samuel followed a similar trajectory: in 1678 he married Mary Colton of silk-wearing fame and settled down as a householder in Hadley, where he became clerk of writs, a member of the school committee, and eventually town selectman. His second daughter, the Hannah of the cupboard, was born on June 8, 1684.[36]

Hannah Westcarr too became a sober citizen. A year after her last presentation in court for outraging "sober persons" with her flashy apparel, she acquired a very serious book, Richard Baxter's *The Reformed Pastor*. The inscription on the flyleaf survives, somewhat obscured by the effort of a later hand to copy it.

Hanah Wescar

Ejus Liber

1678

[Hannah Wescar, Her Book.][37]

The ornamentation imperfectly captures the "knotted" endings in baroque calligraphy; its tendrils curl outward from letters that have the stiffness of

an inexperienced but determined hand. The flourished letters on Hadley chests are a woodworker's rendition of a similar style. Sometime after her marriage to Simon Beaman in 1680, Hannah gave the book to her brother Thomas, pastor of the church at Andover, Massachusetts. In a more practiced hand, he added his own name and a tiny inscription in Latin, "Ex dono charissimae sororis, H.B." (a gift from my dear sister, H.B.). By then, Hannah had become Deerfield's schoolmistress.[38] It is not farfetched to think that Hannah Beaman was Hannah Barnard's first teacher. The invisible work of some schoolmistress or master surely lies behind the alphabetic assertiveness of the cupboard. But it is the cupboard's flamboyance, its unabashed claim for attention, that most recalls the upstart Barnards.[39]

Hannah was ten when her aunt saved Deerfield's schoolchildren by rushing them into the fort during an attack by French and Indians, eleven when her uncle Joseph was killed in a convoy of men carrying grain to the mill. She was twelve when her father's two hunting companions were shot in a seemingly random assault by supposedly friendly Indians. She was not quite twenty when Deerfield was burned and sacked and 109 captives, including Hannah Beaman, were taken to Canada. She married late, perhaps because her own mother's death in 1709 made her keeper of her father's house, though she too may have become a teacher, as did her cousin Bridget Barnard in Deerfield. In 1715, at the age of thirty-one, Hannah wed John Marsh, a Hadley soldier who had been among the captives taken to Canada. She died a year later after giving birth to a daughter.[40] Born too late to join in the rebellions of the 1670s, she left her mark on history on the front of a flamboyant cupboard.

Hannah's cupboard was a product of regional craft, a container for other goods, and a marker of the independence and ambition of an assertive frontier family, but in law it was a "movable." Anthropologist Annette Weiner has suggested that the contrast between "movable property" and "real property" is the Western version of the world's most pervasive economic classification, the distinction between alienable and inalienable possessions. Alienable possessions can be freely traded or given away. Inalienable possessions are so "imbued with the intrinsic and ineffable identities of their owners" that they can only be passed on to those who perpetuate the identity of the original owner. In early modern Europe and America, real property—land and buildings—was typically transmitted by inheritance from father to son. Daughters received their portions in household goods and cattle, which could be easily moved from one dwelling to another.[41]

Hampshire County probate records offer abundant evidence of this distinction. When John Billings of Hatfield died unmarried, the court divided his worldly possessions among his siblings "in Equall & proportion, the said Brothers to have all the Lands Equallie divided to them & the said Sarah to have her share in the Moveable goods." The court used similar language when it ordered that Joseph Barnard's sons were "to injoy all the lands in Equall proportions . . . & the daughters to be payd out of the moveable Estate so farr as they will Extend." When another Hampshire County man willed his lands to his sons and brother but neglected to provide for his daughters, the court added "that the daughters of the said deceased shall have their portions Out of the Movables."[42]

The association of males with land and females with movables was not a neutral division of resources. The possession of "real" property secured male authority. In such a system, women themselves became "movables," changing their names and presumably their identities as they moved from one male-headed household to another. But what if some portion of a woman's goods retained her name even as she lost it? That is the puzzle presented by Hannah Barnard's cupboard.

Hannah was John Marsh's second wife. The first wife had died young, leaving a son who did not survive long. After Hannah's death, Marsh married again. He was only in his forties when he died in 1725, but he was already a wealthy man, in part because of the goods brought to marriage by three wives, all daughters of substantial families. He owned parcels of "meadow," "woodland," "upland," and "outland" in addition to his homestead with its buildings and orchard. He owned horses, two yoke of "fat oxen," tools for farming and lumbering, and implements for household production—a cheese press, two spinning wheels, and a reel. He also owned an "Indian Boy Sippey about 14 Years Old." Since the name *Scipio* was commonly used for Africans, it is possible Marsh's slave came from the West Indies, though he could also have been a local Indian bound to pay his parents' debts.[43]

Marsh had five minor children at the time of his death, including Hannah's daughter Abigail. The will gave the only son, then two years old, all of the real estate. Abigail received 120 pounds "to be paid in what was her own Mothers," plus "her Mothers Wearing Cloaths . . . to be given her free." The younger girls received portions worth 100 pounds. Presumably these bequests, too, were to come from property their mother brought to marriage. The inventory divided Marsh's movables into a general list and into two subcategories labeled "3d Wives Goods" and "2d Wives Goods."[44] The general list contained "A Carved Work Chest" valued at thirty shillings, presumably the contribution of the first wife. Hannah's list included "a floward Chest" valued at thirty-two shillings and another "ditto" at ten. The "3d Wives Goods" listed a more modern (and expensive) piece of furniture, "A case of drawers" valued at four pounds.[45] Presumably the more valuable of the flowered chests was the cupboard that survives today. At thirty-two shillings it was certainly worth as much as most cupboards. Hannah's list also included eighteen sheets, eleven pillowcases or "beers," four tablecloths, eighteen napkins, a silver cup, a needle case, a ring for a muff, and two cupboard cloths. All of this would become part of Abigail's portion.[46]

In the Marsh family, demographic accidents—the early deaths of two wives and the husband's own premature demise—exposed female property. More commonly, the formulaic dispersal of movables, as in "one-third of my household goods," concealed the customs if not the individual voices that directed their disposal. Because daughters customarily received their portions at marriage rather than at the death of their father, wills and inventories often miss much of what moved from one generation to another. Land can be traced in deeds, but movables, by definition, flowed outside the constraints of law. That is why object-centered research is so useful. Probate records can tell us what sorts of possessions people had at the end of life and what kinds of things fathers (and occasionally mothers) willed to their children, but well-documented histories of surviving objects can tell us how certain objects were actually transmitted—or lost—over time.

Abigail Marsh married Waitstill Hastings and in 1742 had a daughter of her own. She named her not just Hannah, but Hannah *Barnard* Hastings. Since the use of middle names was extraordinarily rare in Hadley (or anywhere else in New England) in this period, this was a purposeful choice. Not surprisingly, this Hannah inherited the cupboard. The name persisted for two more generations. In 1769, Hannah Barnard Hastings married Nathaniel Kellogg, and the following August she produced a daughter whom she named for her long dead grandmother and herself. The third Hannah died in 1787, but in 1817 her brother honored both his sister and his mother by naming a daughter Hannah Barnard Hastings Kellogg. This Hannah's migration to California broke the link between the cupboard and its history. When its discovery was announced in *Antiques* magazine in 1934, the author said only that the name on the front belonged to an "ancestress of a later owner, Hannah Barnard Hastings of Hatfield, Massachusetts" and that at her death it had "passed to collateral heirs."[47] The cupboard helped to preserve the name, but the name also transformed the cupboard. Marked with the first owner's name, it became less portable, less exchangeable. It had become an inalienable possession.

In scholarly as well as common usage we speak of the "Marsh family," the "Barnard family," or the "Hastings family." Biologically, of course, there is no such thing. One can speak of a particular family through time only by ignoring the fundamental basis of reproduction, that every child requires both a mother and father. Barring sibling incest, in each generation, half of the genes must come from outside the original group. But law, culture, and convenience conspire to make us forget that. The pedigree of Hannah Barnard Hastings illustrates the fragility—and complexity—of female lineage. Notice how easy it is to trace the "Hastings" line, reading along the top of the chart from Hannah to her father, Waitstill Hastings, then to Waitstill's father, grandfather, and great-grandfather, all named Thomas Hastings. Everywhere on the chart, going from child to father to grandfather is simple—from Abigail Marsh to John Marsh to Daniel Marsh to John Marsh, for example, or from Hannah Barnard to her father and grandfather. But to trace daughter-mother lineages is more

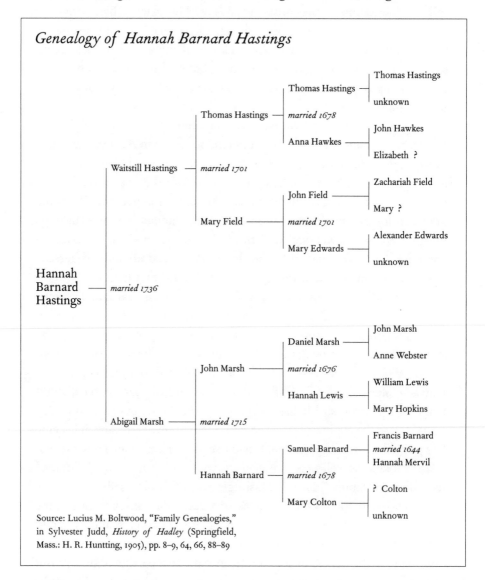

## Genealogy of Hannah Barnard Hastings

Source: Lucius M. Boltwood, "Family Genealogies,"
in Sylvester Judd, *History of Hadley* (Springfield,
Mass.: H. R. Huntting, 1905), pp. 8–9, 64, 66, 88–89

difficult. The names of all eight of Hannah's great-great-grandfathers survive, but only three of her great-great-grandmothers have complete names; two are simply "unknown."

Even though biologically the notion of descent from mother to daughter makes every bit as much sense as from father to son, it is extraordinarily hard to define such a "line" within Western genealogical conventions. To enfold a female lineage in a patrilineal line of descent, a girl would have to carry a chain of surnames that grew heavier with each generation. Abigail and Waitstill Hastings acknowledged just one link in that chain when they named their daughter for her maternal grandmother. Was it Hannah's memory or the cupboard that perpetuated her name for more than a century after her death? Probably it was both. In their passionate quest for land, signing deeds, enumerating probated wealth, registering cattle marks, parading militia titles, and hundreds of other acts, New England patriarchs perpetuated their names. Creating lineages, they asserted their ownership of things and sometimes of other people as well. But women too used property to assert identities, build alliances, and reweave family bonds torn by marriage, death, or migration.

Decorative arts scholars have discovered hundreds of examples of this phenomenon as they have gone about the work of establishing the provenance of museum objects. Challenging the attribution of a Hadley chest, one researcher demonstrated lineal descent from mother to daughter, with a slight detour to include a stepdaughter, in an unbroken line stretching from 1700 to the early twentieth century.[48] The persons involved may or may not have been conscious of a "female line." All that was required was a belief in each generation that certain objects ought to pass from mother to daughter. In a world where women's names changed with each marriage, labeling helped, but it was not essential. In the story of Dinah Fenner's basket, we have seen how an unmarked object with a compelling story moved from mother to daughter to granddaughter to sister over more than a century.

Establishing provenance is seldom easy, however, nor is direct transmission from mother to daughter the only alternative to patrilineal descent. The mystery of the *SW* chest, the painted twin of Hannah's cupboard, suggests the complexity of the problem. The chest was one of the earliest items collected by Memorial Hall at Deerfield. The first accession records listed it as an "Ancient oak cabinet—not carved but painted— bought of Jonathan A. Saxton about 1870." The inscription continued

with an incomplete sentence that seemed to imply the chest was "Long in
the Saxton—[family?]." By 1908, the custodian of the museum had come
up with a new attribution. The "Oak chest, marked SW . . . came down
in the White family." In keeping with a colonial revival propensity to
assign English origins to every ancient-looking object, a printed catalog
published at the time attributed it to Susanna White, who came to New
England on the *Mayflower*.[49]

Understandably, a recent catalog of Hadley chests dismissed the
*Mayflower* connection, yet it, too, proposed a rather fanciful attribution.
Noting that Jonathan Saxton had been administrator of the estate of
Charles Williams, it suggested that the chest was a "Williams family heir-
loom" and that it, like Hannah Barnard's cupboard, had once belonged to
John Marsh, whose third wife was named Sarah Williams. Since there
were two "flowered" chests in Marsh's inventory, the catalog suggested
that Hannah's cupboard and the *SW* chest were "successively brought
into the Marsh household" in 1715 and 1718. It did not explain why an
object ostensibly belonging to the third wife was listed with the second
wife's goods, nor did it attempt to show how a piece of furniture belonging to a woman married successively to a Marsh and a Grey ended up, six
generations later, in the Williams family.

Working with the same set of documents but with different assumptions about family history produces several alternative explanations. One
of these connects to a Sarah Williams who died in Deerfield in 1720. This
Sarah was a second cousin of John Marsh's wife and a first cousin of the
Esther Williams who owned the tin-glazed plate with the rose that looks
so much like those on Hannah's cupboard and the *SW* chest. Born in Roxbury, this Sarah married Hannah's cousin, Samuel Barnard of Deerfield,
in 1718. Like Hannah, Sarah died giving birth to an only child, though her
infant did not survive. Her husband left Deerfield, and though he remarried twice, he had no more children. When he died in Salem in 1762 he left
land and property to his Deerfield nephews and bequests to be paid "out
of my household goods" to his nieces, one of whom became the grandmother of the Jonathan Saxton who gave the *SW* chest to Memorial Hall
in Deerfield. Since Saxton's sister married Charles Williams, the *SW*
chest could easily have been both a Saxton and a Williams "family heir-
loom."[50]

It could also have come down "in the White family" either as an heir-
loom or as a piece of junk left behind in one of the many family migra-

tions. Jonathan Saxton's mother-in-law, Mercy White, was the daughter of Salmon White, a *male* with the initials "S.W." Although Salmon was too young to have been the original owner of the chest, his aunt Susannah Wells, who became Susannah White at marriage, may have been the "Susannah White" who inspired the *Mayflower* legend. But this trail, too, leads back to Hannah Barnard's cousin Samuel and his wife Sarah Williams. Samuel Barnard's sister Sarah Wells raised Susannah White. One can imagine the initials directing the chest from Sarah Williams to Sarah Wells to Susannah White and then by some forgotten path, perhaps through Salmon White, to Jonathan Saxton.[51] By then the chest may have been less a treasure than a burden. The first Hadley chests were often discovered on back porches, in barns, or in slaughterhouses. One even traveled to the Midwest as a shipping crate.[52]

Barring the discovery of a forgotten will, inventory, account book, or letter with an explicit reference to the chest, there is no way of knowing how it reached Jonathan Saxton or whether the "S" stands for Sarah, Susannah, or Salmon, or the "W" for White, Wells, Williams, Wright, Wait, or any other of the ubiquitous "W's" in Hadley or Deerfield. The first families of Deerfield and Hadley are so intertwined that it is almost impossible to trace one line of descent without encountering another. The very difficulty of establishing provenance reinforces the central point, however. Families are social constructions, made and remade over time. Family identities, like personal identities, are built from selective fragments of the past—names, stories, and material possessions. They can be lost or re-created, abandoned or invented.

Two pieces of silver in the collections of Historic Deerfield help us see some of the ways in which women used movable objects to define family. A tankard made between 1700 and 1710 bears its genealogy on its handle. The first set of initials belonged to Mary Williams Cook, who at death bequeathed it to her nephew, Dr. Thomas Williams of Deerfield. It then descended to several generations of Williamses, each heir adding his or her initials in turn. In this case, a lineage obscured in marriage returned to the paternal line in a gift from a woman to her brother's son. The inscription on the second piece of silver did the opposite, creating a complex web of lineages in a gift from one woman to another. The inscription reads: "This Cann Is Presented to Mrs: Anna Williams/ By her Uncle and Aunt Hinsdale/ 1754." Aunt Hinsdale, born Abigail Williams, was Anna Williams's paternal aunt. (Anna was about to marry Jacob

Cushing; the "Mrs." before her name denoted social rather than marital status.) The silver, which symbolized a familial relationship between two women whose maiden names were Williams, bore the Hinsdale coat of arms and descended in the Cushing family. Meanwhile, "Aunt Hinsdale" was widowed twice, becoming first Madame Hall and then Madame Silliman.[53]

When she died in 1783, Abigail Williams Hinsdale Hall Silliman, who had no children of her own, left more silver with the Hinsdale arms to the church at Deerfield and to a second niece, Sarah Williams. She also manumitted her slaves, honoring gendered notions of property by giving her male servant, Jockton, one hundred acres of New Hampshire land, and her female servant, Chloe, "a Bible a cow, a feather bed, a brass kettle, a pot, 2 tramels, chests, hand irons, chairs, and pewter things." In addition, she gave clothing, jewelry, and other valuables to seven female relatives including nieces Abigail Norton and Abigail Woodword and stepgranddaughters Frances Silliman and Abigail Williams Hall.[54] Such bequests assert an expansive, almost fluid, notion of family that undercuts simple notions of patrilineal *or* matrilineal descent. It also suggests how a woman, particularly a much-married woman, might accumulate multiple lineages. Identity for such a person derived less from membership in a particular lineage group than from the ability to move between and among them.

In eighteenth-century New England a few women—Abigail Silliman's older sister Eunice among them—crossed national, religious, and racial boundaries as well. Eunice was captured as a child during the Deerfield raid of 1704 and grew up a Catholic in the Mohawk village of Kahnawake. Her mother, also named Eunice, died on the journey that had taken her to Canada. Although her father repeatedly tried to redeem her, Eunice refused all contact, telling one negotiator through her Iroquois husband that "had her ffather not Married againe, She would have gone and Seen him long Ere this time." After her father's death, Eunice visited New England, eventually sending her younger brother Warham a silver cup purportedly taken as plunder in the Deerfield raid. Warham, believing it had belonged to their mother, had it engraved with cryptic initials that marked both the mother's death and the gift of the cup from his sister: "E.W. Obt., 1st March, 1703–4. June 20, 1732, E.W. to W.W." The inscription symbolically resurrected the first Eunice by reestablishing a bond with the second. The following year, Warham named a daughter Eunice. (Warham's own name was a legacy from his mother, whose maternal grandfather was the Reverend John Warham of Windsor, Connecticut.)[55]

In a legal system that required the subordination of women, one might imagine a female identity that was inherently fragile and derivative, shaped through attachment to others rather than by assertion of self. Yet, ironically, the force of patriarchy may have encouraged certain women to develop a more complex and in some ways more autonomous sense of self than their brothers. Never able to step into a ready-made identity, they learned to mediate between a family of origin and one or more families of marriage. Surely, for men as well as women, *family* meant brothers and sisters, aunts, uncles, and cousins, as well as husbands, wives, parents, and children, but for women, lived relationships almost always cut across patrilineal markers. In Annette Weiner's words, "To draw on other social identities, to enhance one's history, and to secure the appropriate transmission of inalienable possessions for the next generation involve voluminous exchanges, elaborate strategies, and productive efforts." The bequests of Abigail Hinsdale and Eunice Williams point to one of the central themes in Weiner's work—exchanges between brothers and sisters and their offspring.[56]

In 1742, Abigail Hastings took the first step in establishing a female lineage when she named her daughter for the mother she had never known. But that same year, she may also have had a role in creating a quite different memorial to her mother, a mammoth table stone in Hadley's burying ground that symbolically returned Hannah to her family of origin. Hannah's last remaining brother, Samuel Barnard, had died the year before. Although he was past fifty, he had never married. As executors of his estate, Abigail and her aunt Mary Cook were surely responsible for erecting the resolutely patriarchal monument that bears his name, his sister's name, and those of their parents. The father dominates the stone.

CAPTAIN SAMUEL

BERNARD DYED ON

[     ] 1728

AGE 74 YEAR

MARY HIS WIFE DYED

MARCH YE 5 1709 AGE

58 YEAR

HANNAH HIS DAUGHT

DYED ON SEPT YE 31ST 1716

AGED 32 YEAR

MR SAMUEL BERNARD

SON TO CAPT SM

BERNARD DYED ON

NOV YE 5 1741

AGED 58 YEAR

There is no evidence that "Mary his wife" had ever been a Colton or that "Hannah his Daught" had once been married to John Marsh. The men's names—Captain Samuel Bernard, Mr. Samuel Bernard—create a closed circle. The father kept his name by giving it away, but his son failed to forge a new link in the chain. Ironically, it was a daughter, dead at thirty-two, whose progeny preserved the Barnard name.[57]

The stone made Hannah Barnard an appendage of her father. The cupboard perpetuated her identity as a literate person, an heir to the material wealth of an ambitious family, and the future mistress of a household. The hearts, vines, pinwheels, thistles, and roses that embellished it were relics of regional English craft, symbols of fertility, and emblems of an expanding Atlantic commerce. The name on the cupboard affirmed both her literacy and her possession of property. The cupboard teaches us that in a world where most forms of wealth were controlled by male heads of household, certain objects were informally owned by women. Possession of durable goods not only offered the power to shape a material environment but the ability to build lineages and alliances over time.

Although few families in rural New England owned cupboards or fine carved chests, the stock of household goods in the Connecticut River Valley and elsewhere in New England was growing in the second quarter of the eighteenth century. This was not just a consequence of the expansion of English commerce and the maturing of the regional economy, but of the elaboration of household production. In the 1690s, only half of household inventories in Hampshire County listed spinning wheels. By 1750, more than 80 percent did. During that same period, the number of families with table linen grew from 22 percent to over half.[58] Obviously, few of these textiles have survived. Over time, sheets, tablecloths, towels, and napkins became bandages, menstrual rags, patches on shirts, filling for rag coverlets, or raw material for paper. But as material possessions expanded, so did literacy and the habit of possession.

Probate records occasionally capture the creation of female property. Recording "2 pair of sheets markt EC," "New Sheets markt MC," and a "pr of sheets called Hannahs," the clerk who recorded the records of a Hampshire County man named John Cowles briefly abandoned his secretarial hand to form large capital letters that looked for all the world like embroidery. Declared dependents in law, Hannah, Mary, and Esther Cowles used their needles to claim ownership of objects they used, maintained, and hoped to inherit.[59] Inventories are seldom that explicit. The person who took Ann Rosseter's inventory in Litchfield, Connecticut, identified "1 pr sheets not mark'd" presumably because her other seven sheets were, but he did not list the initials. The occasional lists that do specify initials show female inheritance at work. On the surface there is no reason why a man named Ephraim Colton would own a bed rug marked *H* or Joseph Warner a blanket marked *E*. Nor does the blanket marked *S:H* in John Scott's inventory or the one marked *W:T* in the household of Thomas Richards make immediate sense unless one recognizes the ways in which material goods entered male-headed households through female hands.[60]

Given the fragility of textiles, it is hardly surprising that the few surviving linens from the early eighteenth century belonged to elite families, those with several dozen rather than a single napkin, or many pairs of sheets. One would hardly expect, however, to find such a relic in the papers of a famous theologian. Yet neatly folded in box 36, folder 1655, in the Jonathan Edwards Papers in Yale University's Beinecke Library is an eighteenth-century linen bedsheet. It is made of two strips of fabric seamed down the center, hemmed, and marked in blue cross-stitch with the letters $T^E E$. A handwritten note stitched to the sheet explains, "This was spun by the Mother of President Edwards who was born in 1703—It is probably now 155 years old—Nov 1846." It was, of course, "President Edwards," not his mother, who was born in 1703. The great-granddaughter who wrote the note assumed that Esther Edwards had spun her sheet about the time of her marriage to Timothy Edwards in 1694. That is possible. She came from a famously industrious family. Her mother, Esther Stoddard, was the spinner Samuel Sewall saw at the parsonage in Northampton in 1716. Still, the impressive thing is that among the many sheets that must have been worn out by this family, one survived to become an artifact of the age of homespun.[61]

Esther Edwards's sheet, like Hannah Barnard's cupboard, passed from mother to daughter for three generations, its meaning growing richer as it aged. In 1840, the last owner of the sheet, Hannah Whittlesey, gave two quite different artifacts to the Connecticut Historical Society: a pair of silk shoes "worked by Miss Hannah Edwards daughter of Rev Timothy Edwards, of East Windsor, sister of President Edwards, and wife of Seth Wetmore, Esq of Middletown," and a fragment of crewel embroidery "wrought by Miss Molly Edwards, daughter of Rev. Timothy Edwards." Unlike the sheet, these were luxury goods, but Whittlesey claimed that Molly had not only spun the crewel in her embroidery but had dyed it "with the juice expressed from native plants."[62] The mystique of homespun had erased all evidence of her ancestors' investment in imported luxuries. Identifying artifacts, Hannah Whittlesey provided two paths to distinction for her female progenitors, one through their attachment to distinguished men ("President Edwards," "Rev Timothy Edwards," "Seth Westmore, Esq.") and another through their labor. They had been spinners, dyers, and embroiderers, never merely owners of goods.

The writings of Hannah Edwards Wetmore, owner of the shoes, suggest that for at least one of these women the business of creating and maintaining textiles was a burden. About 1736, Hannah recorded her religious conversion explaining that, during a period when she was "in a great hurry" about making stays (the boned waistcoats that functioned as corsets in this period), she went walking in her father's orchard. Thinking that there would probably never be another time in her life when she would be better able to determine what she should make of herself, she instantly "saw a Bible open Before me (or at Least I had as Lively and sensible an image of it on my mind as if I had seen it with Eyes)." She tried to read, but as she attempted to do so she was stopped "by a piece of stays intercepting and covering the pages," causing her "to Reflect what a vast hindrance the cares, and Business of the World, is to our making progress in Religion."[63] Like the seventeenth-century Boston woman who believed the fire in her linen cupboard was a judgment from God, Hannah Edwards feared the enticements of gentility and the distractions of household industry, but she could hardly escape them. Her grandfather, father, and brother made God's business their business by entering the ministry. She had no such choice. Contemplating mansions on high, she created property on earth that her descendants used to honor her memory. She probably would have been shocked to know that a hundred years after her death people cherished the stitchery she considered a "vast hindrance" to her salvation.

Hannah Barnard left no written record to explain the meaning she attached to her cupboard. Over time, however, it became her memorial and a link between generations of women who bore her name. Hannah's cupboard helps us see that the nineteenth-century Americans who attached labels to old shoes, spinning wheels, sheets, towels, tablecloths, and cupboards were not only memorializing their families. They were creating them.

# 4

# A Chimneypiece

BOSTON, MASSACHUSETTS, 1753

*Our fathers and mothers of the century past
had, in truth, no dejected classes,
no disability, only here and there a drone of
idleness, or a sporadic case of vice
and poverty.*

Horace Bushnell, *"The Age of Homespun"*

Displayed in one of the decorative arts galleries in the Museum of Fine Arts in Boston, Eunice Bourne's embroidery carries us to a world of wealth and taste far removed from Hannah Barnard's Hadley. In eighteenth-century parlance it is a "chimneypiece," a framed picture meant to be hung above a fireplace. The pattern, drawn by a Boston teacher in imitation of London designs derived from French and English engravings of aristocratic paintings, idealized country life. Lambs browse on the green, harvesters return from their work, and a woman seated on a rock spins with a drop spindle. Interpreted in the context of her own and her family's history, Eunice's embroidery raises two of the most difficult questions in social history: How does the seemingly private life of households relate to the public worlds of commerce and politics? And what, if anything, do women of different classes and races have in common?

*Eunice Bourne. Chimneypiece.*
*Wool, silk, metallic threads, and*
*beads on canvas.*

Born in Barnstable, Massachusetts, in 1733, Eunice was the ninth child and youngest daughter of Sylvanus and Mercy (Gorham) Bourne. Her father was a merchant, judge of the county probate court, and a member of the Governor's Council. He was also an Indian "guardian," a role to which inheritance as well as political privilege entitled him. His great-grandfather, Richard Bourne, a contemporary of Roger Williams, was the first missionary to the Cape Cod Indians and patron of the Wampanoag "praying town" of Mashpee. Eunice Bourne's maternal ancestors were equally prominent, though they were known less for religious zeal than for a capacity to triple their wealth in each generation. Her grandfather John Gorham was the second richest man in Yarmouth, after his brother James. Her grandmother was an Otis from Barnstable, daughter of the John Otis who built the town's first warehouse and founded the political dynasty that included the Revolutionary leader James Otis, Jr., and his sister, the poet and historian Mercy Otis Warren. With a few other families, the Bournes, the Gorhams, and the Otises dominated commerce and politics on Cape Cod in the middle of the eighteenth century, their wealth allowing them to send their sons and daughters to be educated in Boston.[1]

The Atlantic commerce that enriched the Bournes contributed both to the opulence and to the poverty of New England's first city. Boston in 1753 was a paradise and a charnel house, a site of pageantry, wealth, indigence, and despair. Here the poorest men in New England rigged ships while the richest toasted the king, the governor, and the "fair sex" in the new Faneuil Hall. Then as now, the city offered the affluent a plethora of schools and shops. In the neighborhood where Paul Revere made silver and John Singleton Copley's mother kept a tobacco shop, there were goldsmiths, cabinetmakers, clock makers, engravers, printers, wig makers, dressmakers, tailors, upholsterers, and teachers of dancing, drawing, needlework, and French. In Row's Lane, the organist of the Anglican church taught vocal and instrumental music. Not far away a private school for "Reading, Writing, and Cyphering" welcomed girls on off hours, from five to seven in the morning, during the midday break, and again from late afternoon until evening, reserving the regular schedule for their brothers.[2]

The same newspapers that advertised needlework schools and tailors carried stories of urban misery. In May 1753, a would-be prostitute named Hannah Dilley "stood one Hour on a Scaffold above five Feet high, below the Town-House, with a Paper notifying her Crimes, in large Capitals, fixed on her Brest." In November, a five-year-old child fell into a kettle of boiling wort in a South End brewhouse and died, while in a bricklayer's house not far away, a fifteen-year-old slave named Boney put on his sheepskin wig, buttoned an old patched jacket over his coat of blue serge, and plotted his escape. Boston had more deaths and fewer births per capita than the countryside that fed it and ten times as many slaves.[3]

Eunice Bourne's embroidery is meaningful precisely because it evades its own time and place. Under the tutelage of her Boston teacher, she created a landlocked kingdom safe from the fish smells of Barnstable or the misery of Boston. Her chimneypiece is a document in the history of female education, a marker of gender and social inequality, and a repository of powerful ideas about the nature of human happiness. Closed in on itself, it opens a window on three seemingly unrelated stories—the transfer of pastoral imagery from Europe to America, the efforts of the newly organized Society for Encouraging Industry and Employing the Poor to open a spinning factory, and the crusade of the Indians of Mashpee to free themselves from the guardianship of her father.

European historians have exposed the economic underpinnings of the pastoral ideal, showing how in England the aristocratic celebration of country life coexisted with the enclosure of common lands and the rise of rural manufacturing. These themes may seem less relevant to America, where manufacturing was undeveloped and most white men could aspire to own land. But America also had its dark underside, not only in the South, where slavery sustained commercial agriculture, but in New England, where men like Sylvanus Bourne kept a sharp eye on the Maine Indians whose alliances with Canada threatened their timberlands and fisheries, even as they monitored the Christianized Indians closer to home whose lands provided pasturage for sheep. The economic development that elevated the Bournes and the Otises to the provincial elite left urban poverty and economic unrest in its wake.

The Bournes were country gentry with urban aspirations. The father's papers betray the provincial origins of the family wealth and the Cape Cod twang of their neighbors in spellings like "wolling" for woolen, "curting" for curtain, and "reasons" for raisins. In order to pay for his children's fancy education, Bourne packed his whale boats and small schooners with oil, mackerel, tin teapots, and the rough cloth the family accounts called "humspun." The one surviving letter from Eunice's father to her mother captures a practical partnership typical of maritime families. "My dear," Sylvanus began, "if you have so much money in the Desk pay Mr. John Bursley Twenty two pounds which I owe him for oxen and let him signe the back of the order."[4]

Copley's portrait of Mercy Bourne, painted in 1766 when she was sixty years old, shows a resolute woman leaning lightly against the silk damask of a fashionable chair. Her own letters to her son Melatiah portray a practical matron worried about cabbage seeds, invoices for Boston goods, and the doings at Barnstable court. Outraged that a "vile Creature who took Goods by a ficticious Name" had been allowed to break jail, she wondered "whether the Sherif or any body Else takes any Care about him." She probably had no sense of the ways in which an expanding Atlantic economy—and her own family's success—would remove Eunice from the active partnership she and Sylvanus had experienced.[5]

While Eunice embroidered woolly lambs on her chimneypiece, her father carefully recorded in his big books the value of the real sheep that grazed on the scruffy land of Cape Cod. As judge of probate for Barnstable County, Sylvanus filed dozens of household inventories with references to wheels, swifts, hetchels, reels, cards, and dye tubs. Notations like "flax in the sheaf" or "cloth part woven" allow us to visualize textile production in southern Massachusetts.[6] Although sheep owned by prominent men fed on so-called surplus land taken from the Wampanoags, most sheep owners were small farmers with flocks of only five or six. Some of the cloth their wives and daughters produced for family use trickled into the Bourne and Otis accounts. Surplus homespun found a ready market in the new settlements of coastal Maine where little land was yet in cultivation. As Samuel Otis told his brother Joseph, a man willing to accept country cloth as payment could mark up his store goods as high as he wished. "This Homespun purchases Lumber, employs people that owe you, whose Labor turns out cheap also. Your own vessell freights the Lumber, your own carts dragg it. In short all these matters are so within yourself, without advancing a farthing cash."[7]

Fortunate marriages as well as good business sense sustained the Bourne wealth. One of Eunice's sisters married Samuel Jordan, a coastal Maine merchant whose father was a sometime translater for the Penobscot. Her brother Melatiah became a merchant in Boston; her brother William settled in Marblehead. At some point most of the male members of the family served in the colonial government, Sylvanus on the Governor's Council, and his sons and sons-in-law as military commanders or members of the General Court.[8]

Families like the Bournes helped sustain the silversmiths, portrait painters, and needlework teachers of Boston. Two embroidery teachers advertised in Boston papers in 1753. Still under thirty, Elizabeth Murray had arrived from Scotland four years earlier with a stock of millinery and a repertoire of skills. She mended lace; cleaned gloves; sold bone lace, netting, silk handkerchiefs, ribbons, tapes, fringes, spangles, ruffles, tippets, stomachers, earrings, and fans; taught "Dresden and Embroidery on Gauze, tenth Stitch, and all sorts of coloured Work"; took in young ladies to board; and in the depths of winter sold "clogs and Goloshoes."[9] Abigail Hiller, an older woman and native of Boston, taught in the north end of the town near the Baptist Meeting House. She had fled the city during the smallpox epidemic of the previous year, but in April 1753 advertised the reopening of a boarding school where she would teach "Wax-Work, Transparent and Filligree, Painting upon Glass, Japanning, Quill-Work, Feather-Work and embroidering with Gold and Silver, and several other sorts of Work not here enumerated." For the entertainment of the public, she offered an exhibit of wax figures of "Kings, & Queens, etc."[10]

Sales of expensive materials sustained both schools. Ten-year-old Faith Trumbull, who came from Lebanon, Connecticut, to study with Murray in the summer of 1753, accumulated charges of more than sixty pounds over a four-month period. Instruction represented only 10 percent of the total. The largest expenditures were for silk and silver-wrapped thread and for the black satin that formed the ground of her embroidery "The Death of Absalom." Rufus Green's payments for the education of his daughter Caty fell into the same proportions. Four months' instruction with Mr. Deblois amounted to only eight pounds, while a pair of sconces Caty worked under Abigail Hiller's predecessor cost her father thirty-nine pounds.[11]

Needlework education was a form of consumption, but it was not frivolous. Bending over their embroidery frames, little girls added value to themselves as well as to the silk their parents purchased. "I must be as dilegent as a bee," Faith Trumbull assured her parents. A series of letters from Jonathan Edwards's daughter Esther Burr to her friend Sarah Prince shows the continuing importance of needlework in female education. Burr was a highly intelligent and articulate woman who wanted to be respected for her mind. In 1757, she wrote Prince about "a smart Combat" she had had with one of the tutors at the college in Princeton, where her husband was president. The man insisted he had never known a woman with a little more learning than common who hadn't become "proud to such degree that she was disgustfull [to] all her acquaintance." Burr "talked him quite silent." Yet her fingers were as nimble as her tongue. In another missive, she thanked Prince for sending a pound of "cruels" (crewels), a worsted embroidery yarn.[12]

Faced with the responsibility of educating a twelve-year-old Philadelphia girl, Burr began with needlework. "I shall be very prowd if I can

make a Clever Girl of her, for she was realy a Baby when she came here—
she grows very notable. She has Worked one Chair for me in about three
weeks." The second chair took only two weeks. Burr herself completed
the largest in what must have been a set of covers for dining room chairs,
stitching "at odd times when I could spare the time. I recon if I could have
sat stedy at it I could have done it easily in five days." The relative quick-
ness of the project suggests that she and her pupil were using Irish stitch, a
technique taught in Boston schools and often employed for chair and table
coverings, pocketbooks, Bible covers, and other small objects.[13]

Needlework was work in a double sense. It resulted in an opus, and it
offered an antidote to idleness. Both values are reflected in the common
sampler verse:

> This needlework of mine can tell
> When I was young I learned well
> And by my elders I was taught
> Not to spend my time in naught.[14]

On linen, however, the verse would have looked more like this:

> ThISNeedLeWORKeOFMIneCAnTeLWhenIWA
> SYOUnGILeArnedWeLLAndBYMYeLderSIW
> ASTAUGHTnoTTOSPendMYTIMeInNauGht.

Changing the color of thread with each word only partly compensated
for the embroiderer's erratic use of upper and lower case letters or the
haphazard spacing of the sampler verses. Perfection in stitchery was more
important than mastery of language, which is why letters like those of
Esther Burr are so rare and Irish-stitched pocketbooks so common.

Yet for all its deficiencies, female education nourished sensibilities
ignored in the classical education offered to elite males. Faith Trumbull's
brother, the Revolutionary painter John Trumbull, understood this. "It is
common to talk of natural genius," he wrote,

> but I am disposed to doubt the existence of such a principle in the
> human mind; at least, in my own case, I can clearly trace it to mere
> imitation. My two sisters, Faith and Mary, had completed their edu-
> cation at an excellent school in Boston, where they both had been
> taught embroidery; and the eldest, Faith, had acquired some knowl-

edge of drawing, and had even painted in oil, two heads and a landscape. These wonders were hung in my mother's parlor, and were
among the first objects that caught my infant eye. I endeavored to
imitate them, and for several years the nicely sanded floors, (for carpets were then unknown in Lebanon,) were constantly scrawled
with my rude attempts at drawing.[15]

Of course, it was John rather than Faith who became a professional artist,
his works rather than hers that embellished the rotunda of the Capitol.
Faith hanged herself in 1775, becoming an American version of Virginia
Woolf's fantasy about "Shakespeare's sister," a tragic figure born both
an artist and a woman.[16]

A comparison between Eunice Bourne and her brother William offers
a more cheerful scenario. William graduated from Harvard College in
1743; Eunice attended an unknown Boston school and learned to embroider. His name and works are long forgotten; hers hang in the Museum of
Fine Arts in Boston. That would not be so, however, if her descendants
hadn't cherished her chimneypiece. When Cordelia Phinney gave it to
the museum in 1921, she thought it had been made by her third great-
grandmother, Mercy Bourne, but Mercy's will of 1781 attributes the
chimneypiece to Eunice.[17]

Eunice worked her chimneypiece in a technique she would have called
"tent-stitch" and that craftpersons today would call "needlepoint" on a
linen canvas with twenty-four warp ends and twenty-six wefts per square
inch. (In comparison, the typical needlepoint canvas sold today has eighteen threads per inch.) Her picture, which measures 20½ by 43½ inches, has
more than 500,000 stitches. The fineness of the fabric allowed the delicate
shading that gives the picture its richness and texture. The folds in the
women's dresses, for example, are delineated through subtle gradations
of color, as in a painting. The greens in the landscape have faded toward
blue, but the reds and pinks are still vivid. Most of the thread is either
silk or the fine two-ply worsted that Esther Burr called "cruels." A few
embellishments are worked in silver-wrapped thread with a silk core. All
of the materials would have been purchased from her teacher's shop.[18]

We don't know where Eunice Bourne studied, though her work
belongs to a cluster of embroideries dubbed "fishing woman pictures"
because of their frequent use of the same image of a female angler. Most
needlework scholars believe the patterns for these pictures originated
with Abigail Hiller's sister-in-law Susanna Condy, who advertised in

Boston papers in 1738 "Patterns from London, but drawn much cheaper than English drawing." Variations in execution suggest they were used in more than one school. Not long after Condy's death, Hiller advertised a "Variety of very beautiful Patterns to draw by, of the late Mrs. Susannah Condy, deceas'd." She may have been Eunice's teacher.[19]

Most needlework teachers offered a variety of designs. A young embroiderer could work a single vignette into a modest-sized picture or combine several designs into a broad landscape, as Eunice did. The outline was sketched on the canvas by her teacher, but she was free to select colors and add small details of her own choosing. Such a work required both industry and ingenuity. In Eunice's picture, French knots gave texture to the lichen on the rock, the horses' manes, the centers of flowers, and the lambs under the tree. A slightly different knot crisped the gentleman's hair, while tiny beads made a pearl choker for the spinner and a necklace of a different sort for the fishing lady. Metallic thread simulated buttons on a coat or a floral ornament in a lady's hair. Although Eunice worked most of her canvas in tent stitch, she used an astonishing variety of shades, outlining bricks and latticework in white, leaves and flowers in deeper shades of pink or green, and the scales of fish, feathers on ducks, and the flutter of insect wings in browns and blacks.

One of the most interesting details is the basket on the arm of the woman on the right. Its checkered surface suggests the woodsplint baskets sold by New England Indians, though the shape is clearly European. The woman and her partner are in fact derived from a French source, a crowded harvest scene in Claudine Bouzonnet Stella's series *Les Pastorales*, a set of engravings based on paintings by the artist's uncle, Jacques Stella.[20] Stella's harvester, who carries a wicker basket, links Eunice's embroidery to an aristocratic genre that over the course of two centuries became a stylized language for talking about politics, art, and love. Although the forms and tropes of English and Continental pastoral began in Renaissance readings of Virgil's *Eclogues*, they acquired multiple and sometimes ironic local referents. In the sixteenth century, England's monarch became "Eliza, Queene of shepeardes." In royal progresses around the countryside, courtiers in the guise of shepherds presented her with gifts. In a pageant at Sudeley in 1591, for example, Elizabeth received a "lock of wool, Cotsholdes best fruite," its whiteness symbolizing "virginities colour."[21]

In the era of James I, the idealized shepherd of Elizabethan pastoral was replaced by the good husbandman. Even poets adopted the language

Eunice Bourne.
Detail from chimneypiece.
COURTESY MUSEUM OF FINE ARTS,
BOSTON. SETH K. SWEETSER FUND

Claudine Bouzonnet Stella.
*"Return from the Harvest,"*
*from* Les Pastorales.
DEPARTMENT OF PRINTING AND
GRAPHIC ARTS, HOUGHTON LIBRARY
OF HARVARD COLLEGE LIBRARY

of agricultural improvement in homilies addressed to the landed gentry, advising them to:

> *Take knowledge of your sheepe, your corne your cowe*
> *And thinke it noe disparagement or taxe*
> *To acquaint your fingers with the wooll & flaxe.*

In one version, the phrase "Take knowledge of your sheepe" became "make mony of your sheepe."[22] Eunice Bourne's father would have understood that.

Despite its innocent exterior, pastoral almost always has political content. As Raymond Williams long ago observed, images of an abundant landscape yielding its fruits without struggle obscured the labor of rural tenants, many of whom were forced into outwork spinning and weaving in order to feed their families. The poet George Crabbe anticipated that argument:

> *I grant indeed that fields and flocks have charms*
> *For him that grazes or for him that farms;*
> *But when amid such pleasing scenes I trace*
> *The poor laborious natives of the place,*
> *And see the mid-day sun, with fervid ray,*
> *On their bare heads and dewy temples play . . .*
> *Then shall I dare these real ills to hide*
> *In tinsel trappings of poetic pride.*[23]

At its worst, pastoral covered the wolf of commercialization in sheep's clothing. At its best, it ignored the disappointments and uncertainties of rural life.

As Alexander Pope, the most prominent eighteenth-century theorist, wrote, "pastoral is an image of what they call the Golden age. So that we are not to describe our shepherds as shepherds as this day really are, but as they may be conceiv'd then to have been; when the best of men follow'd the employment."[24] The class assumptions of this configuration are transparent. Less visible are the sexual implications of the genre. New England school mistresses would have been horrified to read in Renaissance theory that the shepherd, having leisure, and "being well-fed with milk and meat, encouraged by the clement season and solitude, and having no experience of sorrow, fear, or hate, very easily enters upon sexual intercourse." Although the politeness of eighteenth-century embroidery contained the impulse, the deliberate pairing of male and female figures created a landscape animated by sex. The woman in the center of Eunice's picture angles. The gentleman beside her stands patiently, hat in hand, gesturing toward nothing in particular. Is he inviting her to walk? Or pointing out that other maidens willingly link arms with a lover?[25]

The courtesans who masqueraded as shepherdesses at London balls in the middle of the eighteenth century played on this trope. That did not prevent respectable ladies from donning the same garb. When Copley painted the daughter of a Boston merchant with a shepherd's crook in one hand and a young lamb nibbling leaves out of the other, he was imitating the work of an itinerant Englishman named Joseph Blackburn, who in turn copied the fashionable London painter Thomas Hudson.[26]

Researchers have not found the source of the fisherwoman motif in Boston needlework. The closest anyone has come is an illustration on an eighteenth-century playing card that itself must have been borrowed from another engraving. Scholars have, however, discovered the source of the tiny figures in the foreground—the man on horseback, the dogs, and the little person with a pole. They come from hare-hunting scenes painted by the English artist John Wootton and engraved in 1726 by "generous subscription from a great number of Nobles and Gentlemen." In the real world, of course, hunting and grazing didn't mix. The incongruity did not bother Eunice's teacher, who gathered morsels of country life from every direction, combining fish ponds and pastures, spinners and hunters, butterflies and deer in blissful indifference to logic or visual perspective. In a marvelously seductive and perhaps inadvertent move, she miniaturized the male world of guns and horses, subordinating the masculine energy of Wootton's hunting scenes to the softer world of courtship.

Eunice Bourne's embroidery is not a personal document, but it is a cultural artifact. It helps us to see some of the assumptions, hopes, dreams, and evasions available to her generation. Stitching in silk and worsted, she and the other young ladies who created Boston's fishing-woman pictures had the opportunity to indulge their love of clothes, joy in color, dreams of abundance, and fantasies about sex, all the while demonstrating the diligence and polished deportment expected of young gentlewomen. Eunice's embroidery is a female "work," a fantasy of thread and cloth, but it is not a celebration of a separate sphere. Men are everywhere present on this canvas, though they have been tamed by love.

The embroidery also tamed the workaday world Eunice knew in Barnstable. There is no hint here of the hard work of household production. Spinning is a decorative activity, pursued with an anachronistic implement, the drop spindle. No one has yet identified the exact prototype of the woman on the rock, which appears in at least three other Boston embroideries, though similar images appear in Stella's engravings.[27] In both old and New England, drop-spinning—or what some Englishman

*Susannah Heath.*
*Needlework picture,*
*c. 1774. Wool and mica*
*on linen.*
MUSEUM OF FINE ARTS,
BOSTON. GIFT OF MRS.
ANNA GODDARD PIERCE

called "spinning on the rock"—was a thing of the past. Whoever drew the pattern did, however, capture the action. The woman's distaff is awkwardly placed, but her posture is basically correct. She has reached as far as her arm can stretch and will soon have to release the hitch on the spindle and wind the spun yarn around the shaft. It is unlikely that Eunice Bourne had ever spun in this way, however. Indeed, one of her fellow embroiderers revised the same image, placing a posy rather than a spindle in the figure's outstretched hand.[28] Other Boston embroideries link the male in Eunice's spinning vignette with a reclining shepherdess rather than a spinner. In one version, the man's game bag has been replaced with a shepherd's crook. The woman languishes under a tree, cheek in hand, paying scant attention to the sheep around her.[29] For the daughters of the gentry, the ability to embroider rural work was a mark of their having escaped it.

Pastoral always implies an opposite. In Virgil, the counterpoint to rural tranquillity was a corrupt and contentious Rome. In a poem addressed to her husband, James, who was serving in the General Court, Eunice's cousin Mercy Otis Warren contrasted the peace of rural life with the tumult of political Boston.

> *Come leave the noisy smoky town*
> *Where vice and folly reign,*
> *The vain pursuits of busy men*
> *We wisely will disdain.*

*Eunice Bourne. Detail from chimneypiece.*

COURTESY MUSEUM OF FINE ARTS, BOSTON. SETH K. SWEETSER FUND

At one level, her invocation is an artful plea from a lonely wife—James was spending too much time in the city, and she wished he would come home. At another, it is a symbolic invocation of republican principles, an argument about the virtues of a middle landscape that simultaneously avoids the temptations of city life and the degradation of the wilderness.

> *The solemn shades, the sylvan scene*
> *All nature bright array,*
> *Secure and guard the wandering mind*
> *From errors baneful way.*[30]

In Mercy's poem, as in her cousin's embroidery, sylvan scenes united men and women in happy harmony.

These themes are realized visually in Boston's most famous eighteenth-century chimneypiece, the so-called Boston Common embroidery completed by another of Eunice's cousins, Mercy Warren's younger sister, Hannah Otis. It has the same oversized birds and berries as other Boston embroideries of the period, but it also has explicit local references. The house in the center is Thomas Hancock's mansion overlooking Boston Common. Even more telling is the way Hannah lined up the steeple of the West Church with the tripod and flare on Beacon Hill, the latter now faded but still discernible. In Hannah's lifetime, navigators used this alignment as a guide into the harbor.[31] Yet for all its specificity, Hannah's picture too operates through exclusion. A lamb worked in French knots grazes on the

*Hannah Otis. Chimneypiece, about 1750.*

green by the pond, but there is no clue at all to the city of twenty thousand spread beyond the garden, no hint of the urban crisis that in August 1753 brought three hundred spinners onto the common a few hundred feet from Hancock's fence.

The day before the spinning demonstration on Boston Common, Governor William Shirley returned to Massachusetts from a journey to London. His ship came to anchor against Spectacle Island about 5:00 p.m. on August 11, a Tuesday. An hour later, seventeen cannons saluted his barge as it arrived at Castle William, but instead of continuing on to Boston, he stayed at the castle that night, through the next day, and into Thursday. Finally, at noon on August 13, 1753, his barge moved toward Long Wharf while the guns on the batteries and in the ships on the harbor fired in welcome. Two mounted companies and a regiment of the town's militia were at the wharf when he arrived. They formed a double line down King Street as he and his entourage paraded to the courthouse where they greeted the clergy and other gentlemen of the town, then moved on to Faneuil Hall, where there were more gun salutes and an elegant dinner. That night fireworks and a bonfire on Fort Hill gave common people an

opportunity to express their joy at "his Excellency's Return to his Government."

Was he too exhausted from his journey to take the short trip by water to Boston on Tuesday? Did it take an extra day to prepare the dinner, gather a crowd, and give him the welcome he expected? Or was it an unfortunate accident that his ship arrived on the eve of an event too long planned to be postponed, a public spectacle that would engage the very men expected to welcome the governor?

On Wednesday, while the governor rested at Castle William, three hundred girls, some as young as seven or eight, carried spinning wheels to Boston Common where they demonstrated their skill for the milling throng. There were no military salutes or fireworks, yet one newspaper thought as many as five thousand people observed the demonstration. The day had begun at the South Meeting House, where the Reverend Mr. Samuel Cooper, preaching from 1 Corinthians 13:5, "Charity seeketh not its own," raised 453 pounds to support the spinning factory being built on Tremont Street by the Boston Society for Encouraging Industry and Employing the Poor. In the afternoon the members of the society "and a long Train of other Gentlemen of Note, both of Town and Country," walked in procession to the common led by a group of weavers, with one

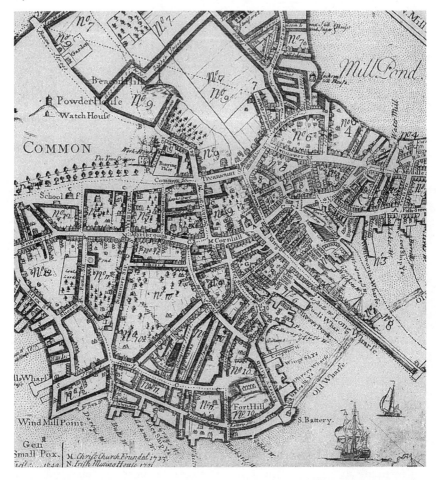

*William Price.* A New Plan of ye Great Town of Boston, *1743. Hancock's house is No. 7.*

COURTESY MASSACHUSETTS
HISTORICAL SOCIETY, BOSTON

young man at work on a stage "attended by Musick." The spinners sat in three neat rows, their wheels at attention, as their benefactors passed by, inspecting them as if they had been a company of militia.[32]

This curious conjunction during one August week of official pomp and entrepreneurial spectacle reflected the state of the urban economy in 1753. Governor Shirley's glory had been the successful assault on the seemingly impenetrable French fortress at Louisbourg in what is now Nova Scotia. In 1745, three thousand men in fishing boats (with a little help from English warships) conquered the Gibraltar of North America, signifying to pious New Englanders that God supported their efforts to overcome papist power and heathen treachery. This monumental victory meant nothing to the English, who gave Louisbourg back to the French in the Treaty of Aix-la-Chapelle. In the aftermath of war, William Shirley's problem was how to hold together a coalition of merchant supporters without government contracts.[33] In 1752, Eunice Bourne's brother Melatiah begged the Boston town meeting for a tax abatement. He had spent two and a half years "at the reduction of Louisbourgh where I was obliged to spend the Chief of what I then had." His health had been bad, and now all he had was half interest in a brig gone to Carolina, half of "an old sloop sailed ten days past loaded with lumber for Barbadoes," a few unsold store goods, and the cash and household furniture his wife had brought to marriage.[34]

He was not alone. While Boston's wealthiest men pleaded for relief, the selectmen petitioned the General Court, begging help for their "Once flourishing but now sinking Town." The provincial tax assessment was too high. Boston had once been "almost the sole Seat of Foreign Trade, receiving and exporting almost all the Commoditys produced by this and the neighbouring Governments," but in recent years shipbuilding, distilling, butchering, and tanning had thinned while the poor rate soared— "the most Observing and best Acquainted are very positive, that the Poor's Tax in Boston, is double (if not more) to what it is, in any Town of its bigness, upon the face of the whole Earth."[35] In response to the crisis, the Society for Encouraging Industry and Employing the Poor was born. Boston had always accepted responsibility for the poor as a Christian duty, but new circumstances demanded new solutions.

The society began by reprinting a pamphlet that described the miraculous rebirth of an Irish town through the opening of a linen factory. Ireland was in fact experiencing something of an economic revolution. Its linen industry had begun as a widely dispersed system of household production in which small farmer-weavers produced cloth from their own flax with the help of their wives, children, and servants. By the middle of the eighteenth century specialized markets for unbleached linen were feeding cloth to large linen-drapers, or bleachers, who sold their cloth through the Linen Hall in Dublin. The Linen Bounty Act of 1743 provided a subsidy for the exportation of low-priced linens to colonial ports. The destined markets were the sugar plantations of the West Indies and slaveholding societies of the mainland South. The Irish Linen Board supplemented the parliamentary bounty by offering "very high Premiums upon Linen Cloth, made fit for the Use of Servants and Negroes in the British Colonies."[36]

Although Parliament restricted American manufacturing, Bostonians

*François Morellon La Cave,*
*after William Hogarth,* The
Foundlings, *detail.*
R. A. NICHOLS AND F. A. WRAY,
*HISTORY OF THE FOUNDLING*
*HOSPITAL* (LONDON: OXFORD
UNIVERSITY PRESS, 1935), 279.

thought there was something to learn from the Irish situation. In 1750, the
*Boston Evening Post* reprinted a story from county Kildare about a
remarkable orphanage where children as young as eight years old produced most of the clothing they wore. The boys "pulled, rippled, and
bleached an Acre and half of Flax, and scutched a great Part of it." The
girls spun "120 Yards of good Linen for Shirting, 20 yards of Huckaback,
and 60 Yards of Cheque for Aprons; and made all the Shirts, Shifts, and
Aprons, Bands, and Caps, for the School," in addition to spinning wool
for a hundred pair of stockings knitted by the boys. This was a provincial
version of the great Foundling Hospital in Dublin, a place best known
today as the setting for a benefit performance of George Frederick Han-
del's oratorio *Messiah* in 1750. Lesser known is that poor children in such
places were expected to contribute to their own keep. The heading of the
London Foundling Hospital's subscription roll shows a woman kissing a
small child good-bye while a little girl carries her spinning wheel to the
front steps.[37]

Surely the poor women and children of Boston could do as well. Decrying "the Swarms of Children of both Sexes, that are continually strolling and playing about the Streets of our Metropolis, cloathed in Rags and brought up in Idleness and Ignorance," the gentlemen of the Society for Encouraging Industry went to work. Opening free spinning schools in various parts of the town, they advertised abroad for skilled weavers. Soon the town's poor would earn their bread in a linen factory.[38] The town already had an almshouse where the very young or the very old might be cared for and a workhouse for enforcing laws against vagrancy, but the poverty that plagued Boston at midcentury was of a different sort. Once respectable women were devastated by the same slump in trade that reduced the income of merchants like Melatiah Bourne. As sailors, rope-makers, and truckmen faced unemployment, so did the widows who kept taverns, ran boardinghouses, and took in washing. A spinning factory would relieve the decent poor, the working poor, without forcing them into the almshouse—or worse. In an article published in February 1753, a man who styled himself "Chronus" pleaded for support for the factory. "It is certain, that unless our numberous Poor, especially of the Female kind, are asisted in this or some such Way to get their own Living, they must not only lie as a heavy Burden upon the Publick, but will soon sink into a deplorable Corruption of Manners, and perhaps plead their Vices as a kind of necessary Recourse for a Livelihood."[39]

Women with capital and marketable skills might earn a living in Boston by shopkeeping or teaching, but success in the marriage market was even more important. When she married a wealthy Boston distiller in 1760, Elizabeth Murray passed her shop on to a fellow Scotswoman. Married three times and widowed twice, Murray improved her wealth with each venture.[40] A boardinghouse keeper named Mary Arthur was less fortunate. For years, her husband humiliated her in front of her guests, using a horsewhip to beat her down the stairs in public and doing worse in private. He wasted her goods and so annoyed her tenants that her once "thriving business" went to ruins. Although granted a divorce from his "bed and board," she was forced to petition the Governor's Council for the return of the movables that were rightfully hers. With four beds and a small stock of furniture, ten pairs of sheets, six pillowcases, a dozen towels, six tablecloths, and a "Negroe girl of 3 years," she was prepared to start over.[41] Women who lacked movables had only their bodies as capital. A woman advertising in the *Boston Gazette* in November 1753 offered "a good Breast of Milk." Having just buried her two-week-old baby, she was free to "go into a Family to suckle a Child, or take one into her own."[42]

However unappealing to modern tastes, the spinning schools offered poor women and their daughters opportunities they could get nowhere else. Boys indentured by the overseers of the poor were almost always offered some kind of vocational training; girls were bound out only as household servants. Private indentures discriminated in the same way. When her father died and her mother remarried, twelve-year-old Lucy Camp was indentured to a Boston inn-holder "as a menial servant." Though the master was required to provide food, washing, and lodging, and "two suits of cloaths, one suit for Sundays & another suit for working days and to learn the said Lucy to Read," he had no obligation to provide any other instruction. The phrase *art, trade, and mystery* was crossed out on the printed form.[43] A girl who could spin well had a potentially marketable skill. For their mothers, too, factory work might have been more attractive than having their offspring taken by the town overseers. As a charitable enterprise, the spinning factory was an innovative solution.

However, if the purpose was to bring down the cost of poor relief, the town fathers picked an expensive way to do so. In order to employ a few hundred spinners, they had to organize and sustain a complex operation that required technical and managerial expertise and a significant investment. The public pronouncements of the Society for Encouraging Industry and Employing the Poor made the task seem easy. All they had to do was open the factory and the poor would flock to its doors, transforming indigence into industry, unused time into cloth. Their own records reveal the frustrating realities behind that dream. The managers had to recruit and train spinners, purchase raw materials from outside the city, buy tools and implements, pay able-bodied men to perform other essential tasks in production such as hetcheling, bleaching, dyeing, and weaving, all the while generating enough income to pay for fund-raising, administration, rent, fuel, and housing.

An anonymous correspondent to a Boston newspaper argued that the spinning factory would contribute to the good of society "by taking away all pretence from a Number of idle Beggars, who are a Scandal to every Community, pointing out the Way in which they have it in their Power to get an honest Livelihood for themselves and their Families, and obliging them to enter upon it." This could only be accomplished, of course, "by witholding that injudicious Relief, which is distributed at our Doors, and which by a very mistaken Apellation, is usually term'd *Charity*."[44] Yet the factory itself was an even more conspicuous recipient of charity. Although detailed accounts of income and expenditures for manufacturing do not survive, a summary of auxiliary credits and debits for the period 1751–1759 is revealing. "Coating, hankerchiefs, Linning & other Manufactures" produced by the factory yielded profits of only £165.13.6, or 2 percent of the recorded income during that period. Contributions from subscribers totaled more than £1,200. Other gifts, including a "Ladies Donation" of £87.16.4, brought the total on the credit side to £1,845.17, barely enough to match debits for wood, rent, printers' bills, clerical fees, wages for a schoolmistress, and payments to the master weaver, Elisha Brown. These totals do not include the £1,800 the society spent on its handsome brick building, an enterprise financed by government loans and subsidies.

The society was able to raise all this money because for a time it convinced people that the project would soon be self-sustaining. In February 1753, the promoters reported that in the previous three months, they had made "four hundred eighty nine Yards of Cloth, on Account of the Company, and three hundred and forty Yards on Account of private People." The spinning school had already supplied "a great many excellent Spinners," and there were hopes of many more. Surely Boston was about to solve its poor relief problem. Poor children would no longer go hungry or be clothed in rags. Poor labourers would be relieved of part of their burden of supporting their families. Even the fishery would be assisted "as the Women and Children might get a Living for themselves, while the Men were upon their Voyages." The province as a whole would also be blessed. If farmers in Massachusetts could be encouraged to raise more flax, the factory would no longer have to import "the greatest Part of what we use from the neighboring Governments."[45]

This was an amazing prospect indeed since it was based on an output that could only have provided work over the three months reported for a single weaver and about ten spinners working full-time.[46] Production no doubt accelerated. "Mr Brown says he can gett 100 Spinners this Winter," an unsigned document in the company papers asserts, adding that "21 Looms have been Employed for a year or two & no want of spinners." But by 1759 the company was so deeply in debt that the General Court ordered its building sold at auction. Over the ten years it was in operation, the factory produced 17,221 yards of cloth "on account of the Company" and another 35,441 for "Private persons," barely enough cloth to keep one loom working full-time. It is hardly surprising that the society (and its public benefactors) eventually gave up trying to keep it going.[47]

From a purely economic point of view, Boston offered only one advantage to a would-be manufacturer—a supply of poor women and children. Training and managing this troop of workers cannot have been easy. According to the 1767 report, the 23,757 pounds of flax the society purchased "should have made at least as many yards of cloth, whereas only 17,221 yards were made." Somehow 25 percent of the company's projected output simply disappeared. Furthermore, the male weavers hired by the factory brought with them from Ireland clear ideas about the rights and prerogatives of their craft. Since they were paid by the yard rather than the hour, they wanted compensation for the extra time and trouble required to warp and weave poorly spun yarn, and they insisted on being paid an extra day's work for every piece of linen under twenty yards. Even without this extra pay, they were paid up to ten times as much as the spinners who supplied them with yarn. (Company records note that "1 Loom will Employ 10 Spinners"; for most fabrics the projected costs for spinning almost exactly matched the costs for weaving.)[48]

The spinning factory died because it cost the town too much money for too small a result. During the nonimportation crises of the 1760s, a group of merchants that included Melatiah Bourne tried to revive it. A report to the Boston town meeting on December 2, 1767, offered a clear-eyed assessment of the difficulties, concluding that linen manufacturing could be undertaken once again "if the Government would give encouragement," that is, if the old game of subsidies and subscriptions could be renewed.[49] By this time, the town knew that there was little hope of selling cloth in country towns. Learning "from the surest advices they have obtained from many parts of this Province . . . that a very great part of the Inhabitants in most Towns supply themselves with their own Cloathing," the committee suggested that Boston attempt to manufacture sail cloth for outfitting ships. Duck was "less liable to so many accidents as the Linnen." It could be made from either flax or hemp, and since hemp could be gotten from Russia, the manufactory would not be so "liable to fail by reason of a drought."[50]

What is intriguing about the 1753 experiment is not that it collapsed, but that it was tried. It is hard not to conclude that it offered Boston's mercantile community and their liberal supporters something even more important than a potential reduction in taxes—an opportunity to promote a social vision. The old notion that poverty was simply part of the human condition, something to be dealt with by charity and forbearance, was giving way to optimistic notions about human progress. A society constructed on principles of enlightened self-interest might eliminate the begging poor, but only if they could be made to work.

In the sermon he preached on the day of the spinning demonstration, Samuel Cooper explained that even if it were possible for a rational creature to "extinguish the Principle of Self-Love," this would be no virtue, for all human progress rested on the ability to balance concern for others with care for the self. Having banished the specter of selfishness, he launched into his larger task—to convince his audience that commercial expansion was a form of benevolence. While good men should always be willing to visit "*helpless* poverty, in her retired Abodes," they should take care "that these Bounties do not become the Wages of Idleness."

To banish poverty, a society needed to replace Idleness with Industry. Idleness would sit still and starve amid "Means of Plenty, neither sucking of the Abundance of the Seas, nor digging for the Treasures hid in the Land." Industry would grasp the opportunities nature provided, reaping comforts as well as necessities. "When we mention this Vertue, we cannot but immediately reflect upon the Blessings, which under the Smiles of Providence, it has procured to Mankind;—the Fields it has planted and reaped;—the Flocks and Herds it has raised;—the Cities it has founded and supported;—the Navies it has built; and the Commerce it has sustained. Industry, turns even the Wilderness into a fruitful Field, and the barren Rock into a luxurious Soil."[51]

In a country such as Italy where tyranny robbed men of "the Fruits of honest Diligence," indolence was understandable, but in a place where "every Man may *sit under his own Vine, and under his own Fig-Tree; and* enjoy with Security, what he has earned with the Sweat of his Face," there was no excuse for idleness. Spinning was a work "peculiarly adapted to prevent idleness." It could be fitted into "those little Vacancies of Time, that necessarily intervene between other Kinds of Business." It gave work to the poor "who perhaps would be glad to work at a cheaper Rate," and it trained "the Children of the Town, and especially those of the lower Sort" in habits of industry. Having visited the spinning schools, he had seen for himself that "Industry adds something, even to the innocent Gaiety and Sprightliness of Childhood."[52]

Cooper's vision was as idealized—and as selective—as any pastoral embroidery. By reducing his actors to two allegorical figures, Industry and Idleness, he avoided confronting differences between those who owned and those who labored in ships, fields, and industries. He did not seem to notice that Boston's poor women and children were forced to work at "a cheaper Rate" precisely because they had neither vines nor fig trees. The same was not true for New England Indians—and that was the problem.

When Barnstable's James Otis entered the Massachusetts house in 1745, the colony was at war with French Canada. His first act was to propose a scalp bounty of a hundred pounds for male Indians and fifty pounds for females. Men like Otis and his cousin Sylvanus Bourne knew what to do with hostile Indians. They also knew what to do with Indians who *might* be hostile. When the Penobscots of Maine refused either to take sides or to submit to the colonists' "protection" when war began again in 1755, Bourne joined Thomas Hutchinson and three others of the Governor's Council in warning "that it will not be Possible for the Forces in the Service of this Province to distinguish between that Tribe and any other Tribes with whom we are at War, and that if any of their People are killed by our Forces when in pursuit of the Enemy they must attribute it to their refusal to comply with the proposals made by this Government out of regard to their Safety."[53]

Dealing with Indian neighbors on Cape Cod was more difficult. Jealous colonists believed that the Wampanoags at Mashpee lived in a natural paradise. Situated on Long Island Sound in sight of Martha's Vineyard, their town had two saltwater bays stocked with seafowl, shellfish, lobsters, and fish of every description. Even the brooks yielded wealth. During the spring herring run, an enterprising man might take four hundred barrels in a season. The woods yielded deer; the rivers and ponds provided otters, minks, and other fur-bearing animals. And if these failed there were whales close to shore. Although the land was heavily wooded, it offered natural planting grounds and meadows. For two hundred years, English guardians wondered why the Mashpee, faced with such resources, seemed so poor. Why did they continue to live in wigwams? Where were their farms and fences, their ships, countinghouses, and herds?[54]

In 1753, this undeveloped Eden was Sylvanus Bourne's problem. He must have thought often of his great-grandfather, Richard Bourne, who had negotiated the deed for a twenty-thousand-acre reserve at Mashpee.

Bourne had not only converted a people, he had envisioned their gradual assimilation. He was succeeded in 1685 by a Wampanoag minister, Simon Popmonit. But when Popmonit died in 1720, the London-based New England Company, which provided support for the church, appointed Bourne's great-grandson, a graduate of Harvard College, to the post. The Mashpees responded by threatening to boycott the church if the new minister preached to them in English. Joseph Bourne took up the challenge and in 1729 preached his ordination sermon in Wampanoag. But colonial officials mistrusted white men who identified too closely with natives. Bourne's career ended in 1740 when he gave three Indians a pint of rum. Although he insisted the alcohol was for medicinal use, the General Court fined him, gave him a brief jail sentence, and relieved him of his position.[55]

Bourne's successor was Solomon Briant, a Wampanoag who had headed a nearby Indian church since the mid-1720s. Briant had begun his career as a missionary supported none too well by the New England Company. The benevolent gentlemen who supported the Indian mission were committed to employing native pastors, to whom they supplied primers, Bibles, inkhorns, paper, and even spectacles when needed, but they paid Briant one-tenth of what a full-time English missionary received. His pay improved when he took over the Mashpee church but at its peak was still only half of Joseph Bourne's. He was constantly in debt, and in 1751 vacated his pulpit for an entire year to go on a whaling expedition. Though the New England Company tried to replace him, he recaptured his position, continuing to preach at Mashpee until 1758.[56]

Meanwhile, Massachusetts moved to tighten its control over remaining Indian lands throughout the colony. Instead of responding directly to native complaints about English incursions, they appointed three guardians for each Indian town, giving them the power "to take into their hands the said Indians' lands, and allot to the several Indians of the several plantations such parts of the said lands and meadows as shall be sufficient for their particular improvement." Surplus land could be rented and the proceeds used to support the poor. The Mashpee fought the arrangement almost from the beginning, repeatedly petitioning the General Court to ask for a restoration of their rights. Their earliest petition begged the General Court to remove "the Honorable Colonel Bourn, Jeams Otis Esq., and Mr Crocker From being our Guardians, for we are more hirt since they have intermeddled about our lands and medows, for we are now destitute, and likely to starve to death with hunger or for want, for they stop our money, and we lived better before they come."[57] James Otis and Sylvanus Bourne kept their jobs.

Mashpee leaders petitioned again in 1753, assuring the General Court with somewhat more tact that though their guardians were "Good Honest men," they had leased land that the town needed for its own use. They also complained about being forced to meet with their guardians at a tavern: "There we go and some of us gitt too much liquor and lately there was fighting and quarreling there, and some of us abused by English men and we know not what to do." At the end of a long list of complaints, Mashpee's leaders reminded the court of their service in King George's War. Surely they had earned the right "to have Injoyed our lands as English men do theirs."[58]

In the long report they submitted to the General Court on December 27, 1753, Sylvanus Bourne and James Otis demonstrated firmness, rationality, and a total inability to comprehend the Indians' point of view. They hadn't rented out property the Indians needed for improvement—"each Family of Indians were fully accomodated with Land before any part was hired out to the English." If the Indians had been willing to improve what they had, they would have been able to raise more than enough corn for their own use. Besides, the guardians had let out only a small part of upland used by people who had died and left no children. Obviously, the guardians measured the Mashpee need for land according to their own notions of appropriate use, and they ignored communal rights of inheritance. In managing meadow, they gave each Indian proprietor his share "in case he had sufficient stock to eat the hay," claiming there was always a surplus left that no one needed. To the Mashpee complaint that the guardians lived too far away from them to respond to their needs, Bourne and Otis countered that "Food & Raiment is what the Indians ordinarily want," and they had always supplied those from the nearest sources. "Moreover tis seldom that two days pass in a year but that some of the Indians are passing by one or more of the Guardians house by whom they send frequently for what they want."

If non-Indians had moved onto the land, that was very difficult to prevent. One of the two English inhabitants "bought a house of an Indian & thereby saved him from going to Goal." Yes, the guardians had scheduled meetings in a tavern, but "there is no other house near the Mashpee Indians that will admit about a hundred Indians." There was only one complaint in the Indian petition that seemed to have merit—an Englishman had cut some wood in a remote area seemingly with the permission of a single Indian—but the guardians were looking into that trespass. Three days after Bourne and Otis submitted their report, the Governor's Council and the Massachusetts House of Representatives dismissed the Mashpee petition. After careful investigation, they concluded that "the Guardians have Discharged their Trust with great Fidelity."[59]

The accounts that Sylvanus Bourne and others prepared for the legislature during the Mashpee's long struggle for self-government show that 18 percent of the funds expended went to the guardians themselves. By their own standards, Bourne and Otis probably received small compensation, barely enough to meet the expenses of what they considered a form of public service, but the idea of paying for a guardianship they did not want infuriated the Mashpee. In 1757, they angrily petitioned the General Court. "We Desire no more Guardians to manage as they doe. They do us more hurt than good, we chuse to be as we were before they were set up."[60]

The next year, the New England Company appointed Gideon Hawley as pastor at Mashpee. Briant stayed on as his assistant at much reduced pay. Having spent several years as a missionary to the Iroquois, Hawley was stunned by the contrast between the two groups. Surely a half-naked savage was better than an Indian who had lost his independence. "Every Indian had his master and even old Solomon Briant their pastor was as abject as any of them. Their children were sold or bound as security for the payment of their fathers' debts as soon as they were seven or eight years old which two Justices of the peace with consent of parents, which was easily obtained, were authorized to do at the desire of their creditors. These Indians and their children were transferred from one to another master like slaves." Hawley's assertion can be fully documented in public records. As justices of the peace, Bourne and Otis themselves had facilitated many of these transactions, and Otis himself had at least three indentured Indians as well as African slaves. Although no crew lists survive, the whaling ships they sent out of Barnstable were surely manned in part by Native Americans, including perhaps Solomon Briant himself. Daniel Vickers's study of the whaling industry in nearby Nantucket shows that debt peonage achieved what legal slavery could not, forcing Native American men to leave their homes to work for other men rather than give up the one resource they had, their land.[61]

But in the light of Mashpee attempts to resist guardianship, Hawley's dreary story of dependency can be cast in another way. The fact that one

out of ten Mashpee dwellings in this period was a wigwam suggests cultural persistence as well as poverty. The Indian church's continued use of
the Eliot translation of the Bible, like their insistence on having a pastor
who spoke Wampanoag, reveals their determination to honor a cultural
heritage that was both Indian and Christian. Sending their sons to fight in
wars not of their making, they not only brought much-needed cash into
their community; they earned the right to speak the English language of
liberty. As the allusion to fights in the tavern suggests, there were no
doubt internal divisions in the community, men who wanted to reform
their hard-drinking brethren as well as cast off English guardians. By
reclaiming control of their land, Mashpee leaders hoped to stop the cycle
of dependency that had forced families to indenture their children and
send their young men on whaling ships or to war.[62]

To Gideon Hawley, old Widow Pease, who died in 1763 at the age of
ninety years, represented Mashpee resilience. A few years before her
death, a snow squall carried away the roof of her wigwam. She covered
herself with blankets and lay still. The next day, one of her neighbors,
coming to see how she had weathered the storm, "found a bank of snow
where she expected to find the squaw. The neighbour called and the other
answered under the snow with the voice of vigor & cheerfulness."[63] Having weathered many storms in her ninety years, the old woman was determined to live under her own vine and fig tree.

In 1760, in a daring transatlantic venture, the Mashpee were finally
able to outwit their would-be guardians by sending one of their men to
London to petition the king. To the document he presented, Reuben
Cognehew added the story of his amazing journey to London, a tale
designed to capture attention, exploit the long-standing English fascination with Indian character, and substantiate the benign character of royal
authority. Cognehew said that he had embarked from Rhode Island on a
ship supposedly bound for England only to find that the master had
tricked him, "basely and inhumanly" attempting to carry him to the West
Indies. Though the petition didn't make the charge explicit, the shipmas-
ter surely intended to sell Cognehew as a slave, a not unusual practice.
Fortunately, "the Almighty was pleased to frustrate his wicked designs by
causing the vessel to be shipwrecked on the Coast of Hispaniola."
Although the crew managed to get on shore, they were "soon after taken
off by one of your Majestys Ships of War, the Captain of which
impressed your Petitioner and the rest of the crew to serve on board your
Majestys Fleet at Jamaica." Somehow Cognehew managed to make his

case known to the admiral in Jamaica, "obtained his discharge and soon after took his Pasage to England in a Merchant Ship."[64]

His petition was artfully prepared. After laying out the precise bounds of the seventeenth-century grant to the Mashpee or "South Shore" Indians, it explained that the English inhabitants of Massachusetts Bay had "of late years unjustly encroached upon the said Lands." The Mashpee were loyal subjects and law-abiding citizens who had attempted to obtain legal redress, but all their efforts had been "frustrated by the Art and Deceit of such Agents as they have been obliged to employ in the Affair." They therefore laid their case "at the footsteps of your Majesty's Sacred Throne, where alone they could hope from your Majesty's known Justice and Equity to find that redress which your Majesty is at all times so ready to give to the just Complaints of all that live under your Royal patronage & Protection."[65]

In August 1760, the Royal Council on the recommendation of the lords of Plantation ordered the governor of the Bay Colony "to see that Justice be in all cases done to the several Tribes of Indians within the Province." In 1763, Cognehew, Solomon Briant, and Gideon Hawley met with officials in Boston to ratify an act giving the Mashpee the closest thing they had ever had to self-government. They could now elect their own constables, clerk, and a board of five overseers, only two of whom had to be English.[66]

Buried in the Massachusetts Archives for generations, Cognehew's odyssey—like that of Paul Revere—is a story about liberty. That Reuben Cognehew spread his alarm in Kensington rather than to "every Middlesex village and farm," that it led to a bureaucratic defeat for the Massachusetts government rather than the birth of a new nation, and that it concerned a small native enclave rather than the Anglo-Americans who surrounded it assured the story's disappearance from history.

Yet in their own struggle for self-government, Massachusetts leaders happily appropriated Indian identity. On May 24, 1766, Boston celebrated the repeal of the Stamp Act. The Hancock house was brilliantly lit for the occasion, a pipe of madiera opened on the lawn for "the populace," while the "genteel Part of the Town" dined inside. On the Common, the Sons of Liberty erected a wooden pyramid embellished with engravings and illuminated with 280 lamps. At the top was a box of rockets set to go off at the climactic moment in the demonstration when fireworks on a stage near the workhouse would be answered by those at Hancock's house.[67] Paul Revere's engraving of the pyramid survives. On the broad lower

*Paul Revere. Engraving of the obelisk erected on Boston Common, 1766.*

panels is an allegory of liberty that offers an Americanized pastoral. In the first scene, the reclining shepherdess of Boston embroidery has been replaced by the female version of the naked Indian from the Massachusetts seal. She has the familiar skirt of leaves, the headdress of feathers, and the curved bow, but the supplication to "Come Over and Help Us" has been updated. In the second frame she kneels before England's righteous ministers and pleads: "Oh save us, shield us from impending Woes / The foes of Britain only are our Foes." Apparently no one saw any irony in imagining America as both an Indian and a shepherdess. By 11:00 p.m., the "Air was fill'd with Rockets—the Ground with Bee-hives and Serpents—and the two stages with Wheels of Fireworks." At the prescribed moment the rockets on the pyramid went off, "ending in the Discharge of sixteen Dozen of Serpents in the Air."

Eunice Bourne's embroidery is a specimen of colonial needlework, a document in the history of female education, and an exemplar of eighteenth-century pastoral. Portraying an archaic form of spinning at a time when Boston leaders were contemplating the opening of a factory, it obscures the discrepancy between idealized visions of women's work and the often harsh circumstances under which they lived. Like all pastoral, it celebrates equality while ignoring difference. Imagining work as a joyful enterprise rather than a divine curse, it places love at the center of human relations, erasing all other dependencies of age, wealth, race, or class.

The history that surrounds it exposes its contradictions. Derived from aristocratic pastoral, it was paid for in whale oil and homespun. Both pretentious and naive, it foreshadowed a vision of America as a middle landscape carved out of a native wilderness and secure from European corruption. Eunice Bourne's own history reminds us once again that the affectations of gentility were no protection against the terrors of illness, death, and war. In 1754 she married Captain John Gallison of Marblehead. In the next seventeen years she gave birth to fourteen children. Shortly after the birth of her last child she suffered the first of a series of paralytic strokes. In the spring of 1778, at the age of forty-six, she died.[68] By then, the household production that in her embroidery had been a pretty fantasy had become an instrument of revolution.

# Willie-Nillie, Niddy-Noddy

NEWBURYPORT, MASSACHUSETTS, AND NEW ENGLAND, 1769

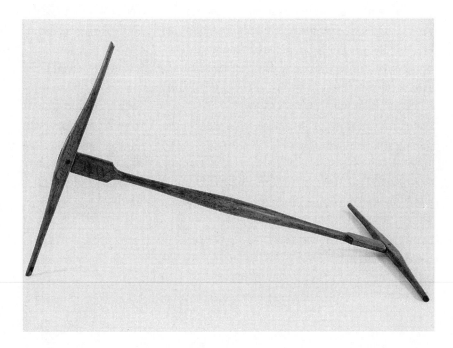

*Indeed, we say of history, and say rightly,*
*that it is a record of events; that is,*
*of turnings out, points where the silence*
*is broken.*

Horace Bushnell, "The Age of Homespun"

The Newburyport woman who inherited a cross reel owned by her grandmother called it a "Willie-Nillie" when she wrote down its history in the 1920s. Most antiquarians used the term *niddy-noddy*, as in the rhyme: "Niddy-noddy; Niddy-noddy, / Two heads, one body!" In broader usage, a niddy-noddy was an object that bobbed about, like a little toy man with his head on a spring. A willie-nillie displayed the same instability, as in the phrase "will ye, nill ye?"[1] A person using such a device to wind and measure yarn tipped it back and forth as she wound. Hence the nicknames.[2]

Neither term appears in probate records. Niddy-noddies and willie-nillies were either too small and insignificant to be recorded, or they were listed under the generic term *reel*. They do, however, have a small place in New England folklore. The donor of a Memorial Hall niddy-noddy claimed that it had been "taken to pieces and smuggled in under a woman's garments" when an ancestor came to Massachusetts from Ireland in 1733. If so, the smuggler found hundreds just like it when she got there. Cross reels can be found in virtually every colonial museum in New England. In the Damm Garrison three of them hang on nails in the garret, and two more sit on an exhibit case in a lower room. The American Museum of Textile History in Lowell, Massachusetts, has more than forty. Two of the more decorative ones are on permanent exhibit. The rest are lined up on a bank of shelves, row by row, looking like discombobulated chair stretchers, with one endpiece on each reel pointed toward the ceiling, the other toward the wall.[3]

The Newburyport willie-nillie, marked *P.W* for Polly Woodwell, was handed down from mother to daughter for more than two centuries. A later descendant scratched *MWH 1783* on the endpiece, acknowledging Polly's given name, "Mary," and her marriage to Enoch Hale, who was known in Newburyport history for the courageous capture of the British ship *Friends* in 1776.[4] Although the cross reel survived as a memento of family history, in its time it too had political significance.

*Polly Woodwell hand reel. Newbury, Massachusetts, last quarter of eighteenth century.*

COURTESY BETTY KNIGHT.

PHOTOGRAPH PETER BENES

In the 1760s the effort to force the repeal of parliamentary taxes by boycotting English goods gave household production a new significance. In March 1766, eighteen "daughters of liberty" met at the house of Ephraim Bowen in Providence, Rhode Island, to spin, dine without the pleasure of tea, and declare as a body that the Stamp Act was unconstitutional, that they would purchase no more British manufactures until it was

repealed, and that they would spurn any suitor who refused to oppose it.[5] Although Parliament repealed the Stamp Act, they replaced it with the odious Townsend Duties. Suddenly clergymen, militia captains, printers, politicians, and urban gentlewomen who had never before touched a spinning wheel took a new interest in household production. In the wisest nations, the *Essex Gazette* argued, women "determined the Condition of Men, by means of their Spinning Wheels: And Virgil intimates, that the Golden Age advanced slower, or faster, as they spun."[6]

Between March 1768 and October 1770, New England newspapers reported more than sixty spinning meetings held all along the coast from Harpswell, Maine, to Huntington, Long Island. One of the earliest was near Polly Woodwell's home in Newburyport. Unlike the little girls who spun on Boston Common in 1753, these spinners were dispensers rather than recipients of charity. Most spinners gathered at a minister's house and gave the yarn to their pastor for the support of his family or the poor. In the act of spinning, they asserted their commitment to their country, to God, and to a new version of an old ethic of productivity.[7]

Polly Woodwell's cross reel gives visible form to the language of knots and skeins in the newspaper stories of 1769–1770. The initials on the shaft raise a more complex question. Did the women who spun in public meetings and private households in 1769 own the yarn they reeled? What claim did they have on their own labor and its product? The newspapers describe the exemplary behavior of public-spirited women, depicting them as autonomous actors in a new political economy. New England diaries from the same period expose the petty quarrels and the occasional violence of ordinary life, showing more complex relationships between husbands and wives, parents and children, and mistresses, servants, and slaves.

Polly Woodwell's reel is not only a family relic. It is a historical sign-post. One end points straight up to the politics of boycotts, the other crosswise to the small politics of everyday life.

The nonimportation movement of the 1760s gave cloth-making a signifi-cance it had never had before. In Boston, patriotic merchants revived the spinning schools. In Hartford, members of a society for promoting arts, agriculture, and commerce offered a bounty of twelve pounds to the per-son who manufactured the most yards of woolen cloth in a year. In New-port, the editor of the *Mercury* displayed at his printing office "a Sample of Cloth, made by a Young Lady in this Town, which is equal in Width, Fineness and Goodness, to an English Plain."[8]

Newspapers trumpeted even the smallest success. In Newport, Rhode Island, a seventy-year-old woman who had "never spun a thread in her life before" became a very good spinner. In Windham, Connecticut, one woman raised six thousand silk balls from a single mulberry tree. In Sutherland, Massachusetts, a lady of fashion made and quilted a petticoat from remnants in her scrapbag, patching together forty-five pieces for the outside and ninety-two for the lining. With such efforts, surely Parlia-ment would relent.[9] In February 1769, several newspapers reported a seemingly spontaneous contest between two Connecticut women. "On the 16th Instant, the Wife of Mr. John Vaughan of Lebanon agreed upon a spinning Match with a neighbouring young woman; they began their work three Quarters of an Hour after Sunrise, and left off at Nine O'Clock in the Evening of the same Day." The winner had spun seven skeins and two knots of fine linen yarn and her competitor almost the same.[10]

Soon there were reports of large gatherings all along the coast of Massachusetts and into Rhode Island. For urban elites, spinning was a novelty. One writer described the Daughters of Liberty at Newport, Rhode Island, "laudably employed in playing on a musical Instrument called a Spinning Wheel, the Melody of whose Music, and the beauty of the Prospect, transcending for Delight, all the Entertainment of my Life."[11] Another assured readers that the young women who met at Daniel Weeden's house in Jamestown, Rhode Island, were "of good Fashion and unexceptionable Reputation."[12] Those at Taunton, Massa-chusetts, were "young Blooming Virgins . . . With all their Native Beau-ties of Sixteen." After their hard day's work the "Young Gentlemen" of the town regaled them with refreshments. How could the men resist? "Beauty when join'd with such superior Charms, / Might draw the Desart Hermit to their Arms."[13] A writer styling himself "The American Watchman" admitted that spinning was not an entirely decorous work. Since flax had to be spun wet, he cautioned the fair sex not to wet their thread with their "sweet, lovely Lips (which ought to be far *otherwise* employed)."[14] A Rhode Island bachelor wrote the *Newport Mercury* that as soon as he found the swiftest spinner in the country he intended to marry her, "provided her other accomplishments be agreeable (provided likewise, she will have me)."[15]

Some of these gatherings were spinning *matches,* contests in which a few women spun a great deal of yarn. Others were spinning *demonstrations,* public events attracting large numbers of spectators. Most were what rural Americans would have called *frolics,* work parties to benefit a single household. Of the 1,839 women known to have participated in a spinning meeting, 1,635, or 89 percent, gathered at a clergyman's house. He or his wife was the usual recipient of the yarn. This fact was not lost on Loyalist Peter Oliver who reprehended the gospel of manufactures. He thought the clergymen who kept the yarn made a "much better Profit than the other Spinners. . . . This was a new Species of Enthusiasm & might be justly termed, the Enthusiasm of the Spinning Wheel." In this period, *enthusiasm* was a derogatory term for religious excess. To call a minister "enthusiastical" was a little bit like calling him deranged. "The female spinners kept on spinning for 6 Days of the Week; & on the seventh, the Parsons took their Turns, & spun out their Prayers & Sermons to a long Thread of Politicks," he wrote.[16]

Oliver might have been describing an event reported in the *Boston Gazette* in May 1768. At Newburyport a few days before, "the young women of the Presbyterian Congregation, and some others, assembled at the Minister's House and generously gave Mrs. Parsons the spinning of two Hundred and Seventy skeins of good Yarn. They took *Labrador Tea* and coffee for their support and finished their work so long before night that Rev. Mr. Parsons gave them an Exhortation from Prov. 31:19, and concluded his Exercise by Daylight." Jonathan Parsons was without question "enthusiastical." A disciple of the British evangelist George Whitfield, he had been an itinerant preacher himself before accepting a call from a "New Light" congregation in Newbury in 1746. Organized as a Presbyterian society to circumvent a Massachusetts law allowing only one

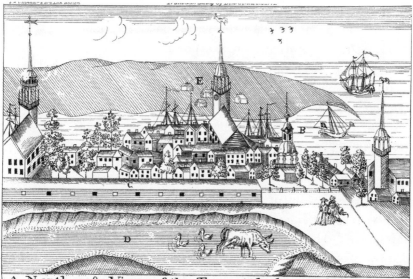

A North-eaſt View of the Town & harbour of NewburyPort

*View of Newburyport, 1771.*
REPRINTED IN EUPHEMIA VALE
SMITH, *History of Newburyport*
(NEWBURYPORT, MASS.: 1854)

Congregational church in a parish, Parsons's church was immensely popular among seafaring families. Polly Woodwell's father, a Newburyport shipwright, owned a pew in its meetinghouse. Polly and her younger siblings were baptized there. Although nobody kept a list of the women and girls who attended the spinning meeting, these are the sort of people who would have been there.[17]

The towering steeples in a view of Newburyport taken in 1774 suggest the religious diversity as well as the piety of the town. Parsons's church, once the largest wooden meetinghouse in New England, is portrayed in somewhat skewed perspective on the right. On the far left is the North Congregational Church, organized in 1768 by disaffected members of the First Congregational Church, which is pictured in the center between its two evangelical rivals. Although Parsons was the only Newburyport pastor to organize a spinning meeting, the new North Society acknowledged its support for the boycotts by serving a tea substitute grown in Maine at the ordination of their first pastor. In contrast, the pastors of the First Congregational Church avoided public pronouncements on politics, though one of them raged in his diary against the Stamp Act demonstrations, deploring mobs he thought composed of "Sailors Negroes the very Refuse of the People."[18]

The history of the Newburyport churches confirms the link between political and religious enthusiasm. Yet the politics of spinning, like Polly Woodwell's reel, turned in more than one direction.

Only six newspaper stories explicitly described the spinners as "Daughters of Liberty." "Young women" was the usual designation, though terms like "Daughters of Industry," "the fair sex," and even "noble-hearted Nymphs" also appeared.[19] Reports from Roxbury and Chebacco alluded to public events, referring to the "intolerable Burdens now Laid upon us" and to the necessity of recovering "our rights, properties and privileges," but the story from Harpswell cautioned that "the Ladies are impressed with such a nice Sense of their Liberties derived from their Maker, as not to be very fond of the tyrannic Restraints or the scheming Partisans of any Party."[20] The correspondent from Beverly, Massachusetts, insisted that his "Young Gentlewomen were not moved in the least by political Principles" and that they were "cordial Lovers of Liberty, particularly of the Liberty of drinking Tea with their Bread and Butter, to which their Pastor consents."[21]

On the surface ministers seemed primarily interested in promoting the conventional female virtues of industry and charity. In choosing texts for their sermons, they understandably avoided the famous passage from the Sermon on the Mount: "And why take ye thought for raiment? Consider the lilies of the field, how they grow; they toil not, neither do they spin" (Matthew 6:28). Nor did they consider the story of Mary and Martha in the Book of Luke. Martha was the industrious housewife, Mary a contemplative believer who sat at Jesus' feet. Jesus said that Mary had "chosen that good part which shall not be taken away from her" (Luke 10:38–42). Instead, they added to the familiar verses from Proverbs 31 and other Old Testament passages—"the women that were wise hearted did spin," and "Go to the ant thou sluggard," as well as less familiar texts from the New Testament alluding to "the coats and garments which Dorcas made," and describing primitive Christians as "Not slothful in business."[22] Preaching a gospel of work, they emphasized the spinners' benevolence. These women didn't spin to enrich themselves, but to clothe others.

The diary of Ezra Stiles of Newport, who benefited from five spinning meetings between 1769 and 1775, shows that his parishioners not only provided labor but food. On April 26, 1769, they brought more than enough tea, coffee, sugar, veal, pork, flour, bread, and rice to feed the participants, leaving the surplus for the family. Stiles downplayed any element of competition. Although his diary admits that almost six hundred spectators observed the work, he described it in the *Newport Mercury* as little more than a friendly gathering. The women "agreed to have no Trial who should spin most, but to spin good fine Yarn, and as much as they could without fatiguing themselves: And accordingly they spent the Day in a very agreeable industrious Manner."[23]

The placid surface of these stories obscures a deeper meaning. Women in Congregational churches had an eminent but equivocal position; they predominated among the covenanted members who made up an inner elite in each congregation, but unlike Baptist or Quaker women they neither voted nor spoke in public. In the spinning meetings, however, they showed both a capacity for organization and a desire to make a difference in the world. Many of these women had long been working around the edges of formal organization, evangelizing their sisters and sometimes influencing their ministers as well. Newport spinners may have been paying neighborly debts to Elizabeth Stiles, who was revered in her community for her medical skills and who was in declining health during this period.[24] Similar concerns were important in other towns. When the spinning bee was held in Chebacco, Massachusetts, John Cleaveland was a new widower with seven children between the ages of six and twenty. The wives of Amos Adams of Roxbury and John Chipman of Beverly also died in 1769; Samuel Eaton of Harpswell, whose fair followers presented him with wool for a suit, was not yet married.[25]

In Essex County, Massachusetts, the spinning meetings followed within a couple of years a religious revival in which young women had taken a central part. According to John Cleaveland, the minister at Chebacco, the revival there began at a "Conference Meeting" attended by "a considerable Number of the Youth, chiefly Females." The first of the converts, a young woman, had been brought "under great Concern" through private conversations with her mother. In a seven- or eight-month period, ninety persons were added to Cleaveland's church, two-thirds of them female. The revival spread to other towns as ministers exchanged pulpits and converts testified to the redeeming work. Samuel Chandler of Gloucester, Jedidiah Jewett of Rowley, and George Leslie of Linebrook, all of whom were later involved in spinning meetings, preached in Cleaveland's church, as did Polly Woodwell's pastor, Jonathan Parsons.[26]

The complex mixture of piety and patriotism in the spinning meetings is captured in the words of a song performed at Bridgewater. The poet, who was probably the local minister, began with an obvious allusion to the woman of Proverbs whose price was above rubies, then went on to the virtues of nonimportation:

> *Foreign productions she rejects*
> *With nobleness of Mind,*
> *For Home commodities, to which*
> *She's prudently inclin'd.*

He then returned to the immediate objective, the support of the ministry, ending with more general praise of female charity:

> *She works, she lends, she gives away*
> *The labors of her Hand.*
> *The priest, the poor, the people all,*
> *Do find in her the Friend.*
> *She cloaths herself and family,*
> *And all the Sons of need;*
> *Were all thus virtuous, soon we'd find*
> *Our Land from Slav'ry free'd.*[27]

These lines can be read in several ways. For the ardent supporter of the boycotts, they probably meant that if all the women of New England refused to purchase English goods, Parliament would be forced to relent. But in religious terms, they conveyed a much more traditional message: If more New Englanders would cultivate Christian virtues and uphold the churches and their neighbors, God would give us peace and prosperity in the land.

Stories about spinning meetings contrast with those about male gatherings. On August 14, 1769, Boston's Sons of Liberty celebrated the anniversary of the first Stamp Act demonstrations by meeting at the Liberty Tree in South Boston where "fourteen Toasts were drunk; After which they proceeded in Carriages to Mr. Robinson's at the Sign of Liberty-Tree in Dorchester; where three large Piggs barbicued and a Variety of other Provisions were prepared for dinner. . . . After dinner 45 patriotic Toasts were drank, and the Company spent the afternoon in social Mirth," returning to Boston about six, passing "in Procession thro' the Main Street." Considering the riots that accompanied the original

Stamp Act demonstrations, the author was probably wise to add, "The whole was conducted with the greatest Decency and good Order."[28]

That same month many papers carried the story of the spinning meeting at Brookfield, Massachusetts. The ladies assembled at their minister's house at 5:00 a.m., spinning until evening when they went out of the house into the front yard and continued their work until seven. "The young lady that excelled at the linen wheel, spun 70 knots," the minister reported, while "among the matrons there was one, who did the morning work of a large family, made her cheese, etc., and then rode more than two miles, and carried her own wheel, and sat down to spin at nine in the morning, and by seven in the evening spun 53 knots, and went home to milking." While New England's Sons of Liberty indulged in rum, rhetoric, and roast pig, her Daughters worked from sunup to sundown to prove their commitment to "the cause of liberty and industry."[29]

While the contrasting accounts surely illustrate a differing standard of male and female behavior, they also suggest a potential conflict within the culture itself between a commitment to liberty and a fear of anarchy. Perhaps New England ministers eagerly embraced the Daughters of Liberty because they could not unequivocally defend her Sons. In publicizing the spinning bees, they promoted a form of political resistance built upon sacrifice, self-discipline, and personal piety rather than on street action, drinking, and flamboyant self-assertion.[30] During the Stamp Act crisis, Ezra Stiles was horrified when Anglicans accused Congregationalists of fomenting riots. "I have uniformly persisted from the beginning to this Time in declaring for myself my own Resolution of not opposing this or any other Act of Parliament however grievous," he wrote Benjamin Franklin.[31] Amos Adams, another of the spinning ministers, rejoiced in the repeal of the Stamp Act, though he gave the credit not to political demonstrations but to God acting on the hearts of men. In the midst of the new crisis he urged patience, obedience, and moral reformation. "Perhaps by the suppression of extravagance, and the improvement of trades and manufactures; by the practice of frugality and industry, what was designed to bring us to a more absolute dependence may turn out, in its consequences, to be a blessing."[32]

There was less contradiction than we might suppose between John Chipman's assertion that "the young women were not moved in the least by political principles" and John Cleaveland's claim that "women might recover to this country the full and free enjoyment of all our rights, properties and privileges (which is more than the men have been able to do):

And so have the honour of building not only for their own, but the houses of many thousands, and, perhaps, prevent the ruin of the whole British Empire." The spinning bees were less an attempt to politicize the household than to feminize the body politic, to build public policy upon the example of New England's industrious daughters.

A writer using the pseudonym "Deborah Meanwell" made an explicit contrast between male and female behavior, asking why amid all the accounts of female industry, no one had reported on male diligence— "alas! we hear nothing of their working matches, nothing of their concern for the honor of their King, or for the safety or liberties of their country." Every morning brought news of their "nocturnal Carousals and Exploits; of their drinking, gaming, & whoring matches; and how they disturb the quiet of honest people, from street to street, until intoxication, and the morning Light, dazzle, and shut up their owls eyes." Young women should shun such rakes as they would the Devil.[33]

In the spinning meetings, then, we have an early example of an alliance between clergymen and women in an attempt to influence public policy. On the ground, however, the spinning meetings had a more prosaic meaning. Clergymen not only reported on their parishioners' benevolence, they profited from it, as Peter Oliver knew. The papers of Jeremy Belknap of Dover, New Hampshire, allow us to see the place of spinning in the material life of the New England ministry, providing another context for interpreting Polly Woodwell's reel.

Jeremy Belknap was just twenty-one years old when he arrived in Dover, New Hampshire, in 1765 as assistant to Pastor John Cushing. The son of a Boston leather-dresser, he had fulfilled his mother's dream of raising one son to the ministry. Although destined for the church since childhood, he had hestitated before accepting a call. Like most future clerics, he spent his first years after college keeping school, working first in Milton, Massachusetts, then in 1764 moving to coastal New Hampshire. He taught for a time in Portsmouth, where he studied theology with one of the local ministers—and cultivated a disdain for the Anglican services conducted at Queen's Chapel. Agonizing over the state of his soul, he contemplated joining Eleazar Wheelock at his Indian Charity School in Lebanon, Connecticut, believing that "a great load of guilt lies heavy on this land" because of its neglect of native conversion. But after receiving spiritual assurance of his own conversion (and word that Pastor Wheelock had a full supply of teachers), he accepted the call from the Dover church.[34]

His probation was short. Gracious manners and a ready wit won the allegiance of the local gentry. He was ordained on February 18, 1767, and on June 15 he married Ruth Eliot, daughter of a Boston bookseller, and brought her home to Dover on a horse borrowed from the town's most eminent inhabitant, Thomas Westbrook Waldron. When Belknap heard that the horse had died a few days after the journey, he wrote to offer his own less valuable horse and cash to make up the difference. Waldron responded by assuring his pastor that the horse had "slipped his wind" under the care of a local farrier, and that if "some unconcerned, officious gabbler had not blabbed the secret, I trust a jubilee year from that Hegira would have passed, without its reaching your ears." He had not the slightest thought of demanding satisfaction for the loss of the horse, signing himself the good pastor's "Most respectful, humble servant." Polished deportment had been rewarded in kind.[35]

Belknap was just as successful in securing the hearts of ordinary parishioners. In two years he brought more members into full communion than his predecessor had done in twenty. Even more remarkable in a period when church membership was becoming a female affair, he welcomed almost as many men as women. Part of his success may have been the restraint he showed in negotiating his settlement. He told the parish committee that he would forbear asking for an annual supply of wood, knowing that they still had the burden of supporting their aged pastor, John Cushing. He hoped that when the resources became available, they might voluntarily add wood to his annual compensation.[36] The spinning bee reported in several newspapers in 1769 may have been a response to that arrangement, an effort on the part of Belknap's parishioners to add to his income, but though it might have happened even without the boycotts, it was the boycotts that made it a fit subject for the "public prints."

Belknap's private papers show that he was the author of the story that eventually appeared in the newspapers. There are only tiny differences between the published version and the draft in his minuscule handwriting:

> After ye laudable Example of ye Ladies in divers Towns of this & neighboring Provinces, on Tuesday last about 40 Ladies met at yr ministers house in Dover, some of whom brought with ym Flax & Cotton to spin & others ye yarn ready spun—& after spending ye Day in a very industrious and agreeable manner [words crossed out]

generously presented to Mrs Belknap the fruits of their Labor
[words crossed out] wch amounted to 242 skeins of 7 knots each
beside ye surplus of their materials wch time did not allow to spin.
They behaved with ye utmost order & decency & were entertained
with the best Refreshments which ye Season afford wch were kindly
& plentifully supplied by those who were well wishers to Industry.[37]

The published version substituted "sisters to Industry" for "well wishers
to Industry," a shift that made clear that women supplied food as well as
labor.

Belknap's reference to "242 skeins of 7 knots" tells us there were reels
as well as wheels in his parlor. Without them it would have been impossible to report the amount of yarn produced. Skeins were made—and
measured—by reeling yarn off the spindle of the wheel onto a device of
some kind. A hand-cranked "click reel" from Newburyport and a niddy-
noddy from Dover show the range of implements used. Typically, one
loop of yarn around a wheel made a "thread" and forty threads a "knot."
To keep track of the counting, some reelers chanted a verse that required
her to repeat each number four times, once at each point of the niddy-
noddy: "One, 'taint one, 'twill be one, 'tis one. / Two, 'taint two, 'twill be
two, 'tis two," and so on. Once she reached forty, she marked the spot
with a different color or kind of yarn, twisting it around the forty strands
in a loose figure eight, then went on reeling. In the system used at Dover,
seven knots made a skein.[38]

A second scrap in Belknap's papers shows how he tallied the results. In
two neat columns, he meticulously recorded the amount of yarn spun or
contributed by each participant, labeling one column "Nots" (knots), the
other "Skeins," with thirty-eight entries under each. Though the entries
range from a low of 7 to a high of 224, the majority of participants produced between 30 and 50 knots.[39] This was typical of productivity elsewhere. At Linebrook, Massachusetts, for example, one carder and twelve
spinners produced 47 knots per person of good strong yarn. At Brookfield, Massachusetts, the winner of the spinning match spun 70 knots, a
woman who came late and went home early spun 53 knots, and those who
couldn't come at all sent 40 knots each.[40]

A recent experiment shows that with a niddy-noddy, an experienced
person could wind a seven-knot skein in about nineteen minutes. A hand-
cranked reel would reduce the time somewhat—from nine to fourteen
minutes depending on the reel used. There were probably several reels at

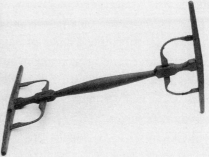

*Abraham de Pape.* Tobit and
Anna, *seventeenth century, detail.*
COURTESY NATIONAL GALLERY, LONDON

*Hand reel, or "niddy-noddy."*
WILLIAM DAMM GARRISON, WOODMAN
INSTITUTE, DOVER, NEW HAMPSHIRE.
PHOTOGRAPH THOM HINDLE

*William Hincks.* Views of the Irish
Linen Industry *(London, 1783),*
plate 6, *detail.*
MUSEUM OF AMERICAN TEXTILE HISTORY

*Rotary "click reel." Newbury,
Massachusetts, mid-eighteenth century.*
OLD NEWBURY HISTORICAL SOCIETY.
PHOTOGRAPH JAY WILLIAMSON

Belknap's house on the day of the spinning match, including a niddy-
noddy or two. If it took, on average, ten to twenty minutes to wind a skein
of yarn, it would have required five to ten women just to reel the 240
skeins. Thus at any one time a quarter of the women in the house could
have been occupied in reeling.[41] Stiles's descriptions of the 1769 meeting
at his house are intriguing in this regard. In the diary he said that there
were thirty-seven wheels and that the spinners included "two Quakers,

six Baptists, twenty-nine of my own Society," adding that there were also "fourteen Reelers," but in the published account he mentioned only "Thirty-seven Young Ladies of this Town." Was the omission of the reelers inadvertent, or were they somehow in a different category? They could have been men, especially ardent young men attracted by the presence of so many young ladies. But they also could have been children, servants, or slaves.[42]

Belknap's rough calculations show that the reelers counted knots rather than skeins. After he listed the knots, he divided each number by seven, then totaled both columns, dividing the total number of skeins by seven to check his arithmetic. The rounding error was small. The numbering system Belknap used was common but not universal. The skeins produced at Chebacco, Massachusetts, and Huntington, Long Island, contained ten knots rather than seven. The "double skeins" wound at Byfield contained fourteen knots, suggesting that seven was the base there too, but fifteen-knot skeins were common in Rhode Island; and at Brookline and Dedham, near Boston, each skein contained twenty knots.[43]

The total yardage obviously depended not only on the number of knots in a skein and the number of threads in a knot but on the size of the reel. The three spinning stories that took notice of that problem all said that forty revolutions made a knot, but in one place the reel measured two yards around and in another "two yards and one eighth." Seven-knot skeins in those places would have varied by a thousand yards, a variation that was unavoidable in a world without standardized measurements. The circumferences of thirty-five niddy-noddies now at the Museum of American Textile History in Lowell range from thirty-six to eighty-five inches, with most ranging between seventy-six and eighty-one inches. In England, reel sizes, like yardage, were usually based on multiples of nine inches (also referred to as "a quarter"), but there was nothing systematic about these differences. The makers could just as well have used the housewife's measure of a yard—from the tip of her nose to the end of an outstretched arm.[44]

Some spinning stories accounted for yarn in "runs" rather than skeins. That variation probably originated in England. In Dorset, a thread of linen contained two and a quarter yards (the same measure used at Huntington, Long Island), a knot forty threads, and a run twenty knots. In Gloucestershire, forty threads of woolen yarn made a "snap," and twenty snaps a "run." In Wiltshire, forty snaps made a skein, and five skeins a run. If the thirty-eight spinners at Wenham, Massachusetts, used the

Dorset method, their seventy-five runs amounted to just under two skeins per person, a rather modest amount of yarn, but since we don't know how big the reels were, the number of threads in a knot, or the number of knots or snaps in a run, there is no way of telling how much they actually spun. It is even more difficult to assess the meaning of the "49 runs of well-wrought yarn" made at East Windsor, Connecticut, since the writer didn't include the number of spinners. All we can know is that the women at both of these events produced quite a lot of yarn and that it pleased their minister.[45]

That, of course, was the point. The purpose of measuring yarn was not to achieve an exact measure but to impress readers with how much yarn a group of women were capable of spinning. Given the variation in the British Isles, the nomenclature in the New England stories is surprisingly consistent. In Ireland and much of England, linen was wound on a fifty-four-inch reel with 110 revolutions making a "lea," ten leas a "hank," and forty hanks a "bundle." The Dublin-inspired "Table to Regulate the Spinners" used at the Boston spinning factory in 1753 referred to hanks and "spangles." English worsted towns referred to "wraps" rather than "knots." Eighty revolutions around a thirty-six-inch reel produced a "wrap," and seven wraps a "skein," a system that is actually quite close to the forty revolutions around a two-yard reel used in many parts of New England.[46]

In the British Isles, the variations in terminology derived from long traditions of specialized production. In commercial cloth-making, the fineness or gauge of the yarn was measured by considering weight in relation to length. Only two New England stories did that. At Jamestown, Rhode Island, part of the yarn was spun at 90 knots per pound. A Milton, Massachusetts, woman did even better, spinning 140 knots to the pound.[47] New Englanders were more likely to describe production in terms of the objects it would make—"½ dozen shirts" in one place, eighty yards of three-quarter-width cloth in another, 178 knots for a coverlet in Braintree, or 10 knots for a pair of stockings.[48]

No minister placed a monetary value on the yarn contributed by his parishioners, but for Belknap we can make an educated guess. If the seven-knot skeins were of similar quality to the yarn listed in the inventory of one of his parishioners, the spinners gave their young pastor the equivalent of a full month's salary. No wonder he was so careful about his numbers and so eager to praise the women's industry.[49]

Belknap's church records read alongside Dover probate inventories allow us to guess the identities of some of the persons who gathered in his parlor. Mary, Hannah, Sarah, and Lydia Watson, ages nine to nineteen, were the daughters of a church member who owned three wheels, a loom, warping bars, and fifteen sheep. They were perfect candidates for a spinning bee.[50] Perhaps Colonel John Gage's two slaves, Phebe and Dinah, were there too. The inventory taken when he died in 1773 shows that the two women slept near the kitchen in a room behind the chimney. A male slave, Mobbo, slept in a garret packed with a pair of looms, a swift, quill wheel, reel, and four spinning wheels. All this equipment explains Gage's obituary, which described him as a "Gentleman . . . who had the Interest of his country truly at Heart." His personal clothing included a new pair of homespun stockings and a brown homespun suit as well as a brocaded jacket, two wigs, and a scarlet suit. In addition, he left 178 skeins and eight "balls" of tow, linen, and woolen yarn, plus unspun wool and flax and eighteen sheep and lambs.[51]

The detail in Gage's inventory allows us to estimate the value of flax in various stages of production. A pound "from the break" was worth a quarter of a shilling, combed flax two, and a pound spun as "fine warp" almost eight. Since forty-six skeins of this fine warp weighed six pounds (or fifty-three knots to the pound), it was considerably coarser than the yarn spun at the two spinning bees where newspapers reported weight— unless of course the reels and measurements used in New Hampshire were different than those in southern Massachusetts or Rhode Island. The variety of measures used makes it almost impossible to draw strict comparisons. Because most yarn was destined for family use, the important thing was that the person doing the measurement had a self-consistent system. In 1769, of course, the crucial measure was politics.[52]

Belknap's patron, Thomas Westbrook Waldron, understood the politics of homespun. His inventory, taken in 1785, does not include a loom, but it does list a clock reel, an old great wheel in the "out kitchen," homespun blankets on two of the beds, and a "large homespun table cloth" alongside the damask stored in a large trunk on the second floor. Among the silver knee buckles, scarlet great coat, and new Holland shirts in his wardrobe were four pairs of homespun stockings, a homespun cloak, and a homespun jacket and breeches.[53]

Pastor Belknap's preaching had something to do with the prominence of homespun in the estates of his parishioners, but it is worth recalling that most Dover families had been making cloth for years. Belknap's spinning story gave these fabrics new importance, but it didn't create the economy that produced them.

The emphasis in the newspaper stories on the generosity of New England women suggests that they not only owned their own labor but the wool, cotton, and flax they spun. Legally, of course, they did not. Male heads of household were responsible for family support and the disposition of family property. A woman might spend a day in spinning without her husband's or father's permission, but without his cooperation she could not have given away the family's flax and wool. Polly Woodwell's reel suggests the paradox of female autonomy in eighteenth-century New England. Her initials mark it as personal rather than family property, but its simple yet graceful design shows the hand of a skilled craftsman like her father, Gideon Woodwell, or her future husband, Enoch Hale.

Gideon Woodwell was a self-made man. Born in Charlestown, Massachusetts, in 1720, he was orphaned at the age of two, then bound out to a Newbury family when he was eight. He married sometime before 1740, but like many men of modest means was forced to supplement his income through military service. He was with the army that captured the French fort at Louisbourg in 1745. During the Seven Years' War, he commanded ship carpenters who built sloops and whale boats for transporting troops. At the end of the war, he opened his own shipyard at Joppa, on the road between the new town of Newburyport and Plum Island. By then he and his wife, Hannah, had twelve children, eight girls and four boys. Mary, the seventh daughter, was baptized in Jonathan Parsons's church on February 19, 1758. She would have been just the right age to have helped wind yarn at the spinning meeting in April 1768. Surely some of her sisters were among the girls who produced 270 skeins of yarn at the minister's house. When their mother died in 1772, Hannah, Alice, Sarah, Esther, Abigail, Mary, and Lydia were still at home. Little wonder that their father remained unmarried for almost a decade. He or his apprentices, including Enoch Hale, may have produced half a dozen willie-nillies during these years.[54]

Gideon Woodwell did not leave an account book, nor did his daughters keep diaries, but family papers from other parts of New England suggest the larger context in which they worked. The papers of two New Hampshire men, Samuel Lane and Matthew Patten, portray household production from a male perspective, highlighting the centrality of daughters' portions to the economy of households. The short and semiliterate account book of Deborah Sylvester of Scituate, Massachusetts, hints at the intersection of religion, work, and politics in the lives of unmarried women. The diary of Mary Cooper of Oyster Bay, Long Island, alludes to the rural frolics that may have been the model for the spinning meetings described in the papers, and it shows how important male cooperation was to a woman's ability to participate in such events. Finally, the diary of Elizabeth Porter Phelps of Hadley, Massachusetts, carries the story to the rural gentry, showing how wage workers, slaves, and farm tenants contributed to household production. These documents both complicate and confirm the centrality of cloth-making in the culture and economy of pre-Revolutionary New England.

The diaries and account books of Samuel Lane of Stratham, New Hampshire, show a man in command of his life. Lane was a shoemaker, tanner, surveyor, trader, farmer, public official, and record keeper extraordinaire. His wife, Mary James, the daughter of a Hampton, New Hampshire, weaver, brought a good supply of coverlets, fulled blankets, and bedsheets to their marriage in 1744. That Lane listed a "boughten Linen Sheet" and "1 pair boughten Linen pillow Cases" in his accounting of her portion suggests that everything else was made at home. Mary's father may have taught his daughter to weave; her mother surely taught her to spin. From the earliest years of their marriage, Lane raised flax and wool, but though he sometimes paid others to weave, he seldom entered debits for spinning.

Between 1744 and 1785, he credited twenty persons—nine men and eleven women—for weaving more than 1,260 yards of cloth. Significantly, he attributed all twelve of the coverlets to male weavers and 92 percent of the yard goods to women, more than half of it to two widows, Sarah Leavit and Sarah Jenness. The number of yards produced each year varied from 11½ yards of "fine cloth" in 1751 to 159 yards of varied fabrics in 1768, the biggest year. Agitation over the Stamp Act may have had something to do with the jump in production, but Mary's illness and death was a more important factor, as was the impending marriage of the second daughter.[55] In May 1770, Lane added to a collection of memorable events listed in his diary: "My Daughters Learned to Weave." He had reason to rejoice. In 1762, he had spent 1,298 pounds old tenor to provide his first daughter's portion. Textiles accounted for 42 percent of that expenditure. The girls had always done much of the spinning that went into their clothing and bedding; now they could complete the process with a little help from skilled neighbors. In July 1770, the Widow Jenness came to the house to help warp the loom. Thereafter, the number of accounts with outside weavers fell dramatically.[56]

Lane kept careful accounts of the goods each daughter received at marriage, standardizing the value of each item in old tenor and bestowing an occasional bonus on the older children if the younger received something they did not get. Accounts with the two oldest daughters, Mary Crocket, who married in 1762, and Susanna Clark, who married in 1773, are especially revealing. Although most of the textiles on both lists were made locally, Mary received an expensive quilt made from imported fabric. For the top of the quilt, Lane purchased a worsted fabric called "shalloon." The lining, too, may have been imported, but the wool for the filling came from Lane's own sheep. A Stratham seamstress, Moll Haley, did the quilting. Lane debited the shalloon at twenty-seven pounds, the lining at twenty, and the wool at four. The quilting cost fourteen pounds, or 22 percent of the total value of the quilt. When Susanna married, he simply listed "a homespun quilt I judge worth about 60." Since so much of the labor in this quilt, both for the fabric and presumably the quilting, was done at home, it was difficult to break down the costs. He nevertheless attached nearly the same monetary value to the homespun quilt as to the one made with store-bought goods.

Lane's method of accounting leaves no doubt that he considered his daughters' labor not as their own, but as part of a larger pool of family resources under his control. His aim in life was to ensure that each child got a fair portion, the sons in land, the daughters in movables. Mary and Susanna both went to marriage with homemade and store-bought goods. Each received coverlets woven by Sergeant Allen, rag coverlets made at home, a woolen wheel, a flax or "foot wheel," churns, washtubs, and iron pots. But they also received bed curtains of imported "China" or cheney, "cream colour'd tea dishes," "blue and white plates," and two or three bowls for punch. These were respectable but not luxurious fittings. A quarter of Mary's bedding and linens, including some of the feathers in her bed, came from Portsmouth stores. The expenditure for imported cloth dropped more than half by the time Susanna married. The escalating conflict with Britain reduced the reliance on imports, but since three-quarters of the textiles in Mary's portion had also been made locally, the transition was subtle. In both cases, the women's own hard work as well as their father's generosity produced their portions. By spinning their own towels and coverlets, they freed store credits for crockery and a few luxury textiles.[57]

Lane's accounts with Sarah Leavit help to explain the feminization of weaving. From 1749 to 1760 she wove plain and striped wool, plain and checked linen and tow, shirting, and many yards of undefined "cloth." Lane paid her, as he did others who traded with him, in shoes for herself and her children. In June 1753, she canceled a debt for making her daughter Sarah's "cloth pumps" by weaving fifteen yards. Lane valued that work at 9 shillings 6 pence. If she wove at the same rate as Anne Veazey, who took six and a half days to weave twenty-eight yards of linen and tow, she earned 3 shillings 2 pence per day. During the same period, Lane paid his male hands 4 shillings 6 pence for hauling timber, splitting stakes, and making fence. In February 1759, Lane credited her with six yards of shirting at 4 shillings per yard "to Ballance that part of the account which is Set at that Rate," then switched to 5 shillings for the "Remaining part of said Webb." She had apparently woven two different kinds of fabric on the same warp, a not unusual practice. Although her rate of pay increased over time, so did the cost of nearly everything else. Over the years she worked for Lane, her compensation went from .63 shilling to 5 shillings per yard, an eightfold increase. During the same period the value of a calfskin went from 4 to 40 shillings, a bushel of corn from 6 to 60 shillings, and the cost of women's shoes from 10 to 110 shillings.[58]

The quality of the work and the complexity of the fabric affected price. While Leavit was earning .63 shilling per yard for common fabrics, Patty Cate was getting a full shilling for "fine cloth" and Jonathan Veasey the same amount for woolen cloth of forty-five inches or an "ell" wide. In the 1760s, when Unis Kelley was getting 6 shillings per yard for what might have been narrow linen, Lydia Nokes was earning 11 shillings for ticking, and the wife of Daniel Allen 12 shillings for blanketing. In general the nature of the fabric rather than the sex of the weaver determined prices. Lane paid less for the blanketing the Widow Jenness wove in 1779 because it was "very narrow & mean," but he had the same complaint about Jonathan Veasey, who wove thirty-eight yards of "mean" cloth in 1751. This leveling of compensation is not a sign of equality, however, but of the low status of weaving as an artisan occupation. The few men who remained in the business specialized. Samuel Allen wove six coverlets for Lane between 1762 and 1769. Since coverlet-weaving required a multishaft loom and more complex warping than ordinary fabrics, it is not surprising that he received the highest compensation among the twenty weavers. If his coverlets were of standard length, he earned as much as 16 shillings per yard at a time when ordinary cloth yielded 6.[59]

Almost identical patterns of cloth-making can be found in the diary of Matthew Patten, a Scots-Irish farmer who lived in Bedford, New Hampshire. Male and female weavers appear in Patten's accounts as in Lane's, but since Patten usually settled with male heads of household, it is sometimes difficult to know who actually did the work. There is no question that Adam Weir was the person responsible for filling "2 yds of Double Dimaty with Cotton" or that Mary Burns wove the twenty-one yards she "brought home," but when Patten paid Moses Wells 44 shillings for weaving ten yards of striped cloth was he paying for the man's work or that of his wife or daughters? The ambiguity in his accounts occasionally takes comic form, as in the entry for November 6, 1760: "I went to John Smiths in Goffes town and got 7 yards of pleided Cloath *she* wove for us" (emphasis added). There is no question about the identity of the weaver, however, in his entry for July 13, 1781: "I went to Robert Spears in Goffstown and lent him 237 Dollars of Continental old money for which he is to pay me New money when he sells the fine cloath his wife is now makeing." Presumably that cloth would show up in somebody's else accounts as Robert Spears's work.[60]

Eventually it was not neighbors, however, but Patten's daughter Susanna who did most of the weaving. In the summer of 1768, Patten went into the woods and "hewed a poplar tree for a Cloath and yearn beam four our loom." His daughter was then in her teens. "I made 4 single pullys for to weave our fustine and Hannah McFarland and Susey put it in the loom," he wrote on May 2, 1770. Thereafter most weaving entries refer to Susey, or more fondly, "our Susey." By 1771, the father was reserving a certain spot of ground "for Susanna's flax seed." Susanna was probably seeking instruction, if not a better loom, when she "went to Hugh Greggs in New boston to Weave a piece of cloath for ourselves." After this, Patten had less to say about Susanna's weaving, presumably because it was now her business rather than his. In November 1775, however, he mentioned going "to Major Tolfords with some cloath that Susey wove for William Morrow." In June 1778, one of the sons went to New Boston to bring home "a Loom that Susey got Ensn Gregg to make for her." A few weeks later, Patten "set up Suseys new Loom and moved the old one to the back part of the Cellar."[61]

Susanna Patten is a more active and visible figure in her father's diary than Mary and Susanna Lane in theirs. The difference may be in the nature of the records or in the attitudes of the two fathers. Patten's references to "Susanna's flax seed" or "Susey's loom" suggest that she had graduated from a helper in her father's household into a semi-independent worker. It wasn't Patten who contracted with Ensign Gregg for the new loom, but Susey herself. She was not alone. Larger studies of the New England economy in this period show a subtle shifting of responsibility within households from parents to children.[62] Daniel Vickers has argued that "the tight generational interdependency that had once served the purposes of frontier development began to relax as the New England economy matured." As fathers became unable to employ all their sons in clearing land and building farms, they encouraged temporary engagement in crafts such as shoemaking, joinery, and coopering. That process took different forms in different parts of New England. In Connecticut, cattle and grain dominated; in Rhode Island, a triangular trade in molasses, rum, and slaves. In coastal Massachusetts and southern New Hampshire, men began to turn hides into shoes destined for export. Lumbering and auxiliary wood crafts, alongside fishing, were the mainstay in New Hampshire and elsewhere.[63]

In a period when men were sending their sons to sea or to war, apprenticing them to joiners, coopers, cordwainers, and silversmiths, their daughters were learning to weave. Some worked for wages, but most worked within the anonymity of the household production system. In the aggregate, household production allowed New Englanders to spend less on British goods than did people in other parts of North America, or, to put it another way, to keep themselves in bedding and clothing when they had less to spend. Household production was sustained not only by agriculture but by commerce. In the 1760s, 70 percent of cotton shipped into the mainland colonies from the West Indies went to New England, which helps to explain why wheels and looms were found in coastal towns like Newburyport as well as in the interior.[64]

A daughter who could work on her own, in or out of the house, no longer had to rely on her father to settle accounts with a storekeeper or with local craftsmen, though she also had less claim on her father's resources. The locus of responsibility had shifted ever so subtly from familial to individual enterprise, a transition marked in the appearance of women's initials on textile tools and names on fragmentary account books

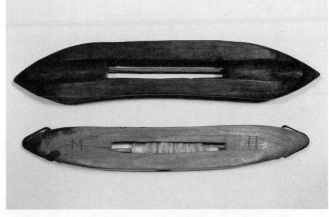

*Weavers' shuttles.*
*Newbury,*
*Massachusetts,*
*c. 1760–1810.*
OLD NEWBURY
HISTORICAL SOCIETY.
PHOTOGRAPH JAY
WILLIAMSON

and diaries. This is the broader meaning of the initials on Polly Wood-well's reel.

The few women's diaries that survive from this period offer suggestive glimpses of the way in which the ability to claim one's own labor shaped female consciousness. The dominant themes of the spinning meetings—religion, politics, and textiles—are entwined in Deborah Sylvester's diary. The early pages are nothing but a succession of sermon texts. Then, in the middle of the fifth page she adapted a verse commonly used in schoolgirl samplers:

> *Deborah Silvester Is my nam*
> *nu Ingland is mu nesian*
> *Scituate is my dweling place*
> *and Christ is my Salvasaon.*

A few pages later, she signed her name in a manner more typical of account books or diaries:

> *Deborah Silvester*
> *Har Book*
> *Setcuat the Jenury the 7*
> *1770.*

Gradually, she began to add notations of the work she had done for others. She combed wool, bleached yarn, made bonnets, cut out gowns and trousers, and made at least one "peteykot," but mostly she wove. She

produced "cotten and Lining," "woosted,"
"Chect," "linse woolse," "Camblet," "han-
kerchefs," "Dubbel woork," and "ems and
os," as well as coverlets. Toward the end of
her little book, she added a few entries for
"Skouling" her neighbors' children.

Religion is the unifying theme in the diary. In the winter of 1774, there
seems to have been a kind of revival in Scituate—or perhaps only a burning in Sylvester's soul, for on February 11 she began to write out complete
verses from the Bible as well as references. A visiting preacher she identifies as "Mr Theairs" began with "how can ye ascape the damnation of
hell," then moved on to more hopeful themes. Christ would "deliver
them who through fear of death were all their lifetime subject to
bondage." But those who "dispise this word and trust in oppression and
purvarsenes" would surely fall. This preaching gave her not only a
framework for understanding spiritual bondage but also a perspective on
contemporary politics. The longest entry tells the story of the Battle of
Lexington and Concord and the muster of Scituate's troops: "April the 19
ye 1775. the Regulers march out of Bouston and march to Lexington
whare the massekre furst begun and killd Six men taking ouer peopel at
unawers but thay murstard and drove them back to Charlston thay killd
41 whits one black and Sum Report thar was 500 of the Enemy wonded

and Slian. April the 20 all the touns mustard and march the 21 two Scituate Kompanis march for Mashfeld as men turnd back one kammpeanes the other march thaer but the Regglars wor goon for Boston and 40 or 50 tores with them." There is no doubt here about Sylvester's political views. The encounter at Lexington was a "massekre." Those who followed the "Regglars" to Boston were Tories. But her focus is local. She is careful to note that one of Scituate's companies came back but that the other marched toward Boston. At the end of the page she added another cryptic entry about a muster "whare thay wor ageting Elisha." Elisha Gross, Deborah's future husband, served at least five terms with the Massachusetts militia and the Continental Army; Deborah was past thirty and a citizen of a new nation when they married. At that point, her accounts stop.[65]

Deborah Sylvester's accounts are typical of those left by eighteenth-century women. Abigail Fearing began to enter credits in a small book in the 1760s, noting debts due for weaving checked shirting, drugget, worsted, "plain cloth," camblet, toweling, cotton and linen, cotton and tow, and "yard wide Linning and tow." Hannah Matthews's account book from the 1790s was more ambitious, reflecting perhaps the better education she had received. Recording debits on the left and credits on the right, she balanced her own labor in spinning, weaving, and combing worsted with corn, flax, mutton, hogs, lard, and occasional cash received from neighbors. Above the alphabetical index to her homemade book, she wrote, "The Property of Hannah Matthews Yarmouth June the 11th 1790." These records document the opportunity some women had to reap cash income in the years before marriage and the economic self-consciousness that may have accompanied it, but they also show the continuing power of coverture. It was probably Fearing's husband who, shortly after their marriage, turned the book over and began a different set of records in which he listed debits and credits for "Inglish hay," hemlock timber, and "oald Ceder Poasts us hoald." Matthews's records also diminished after marriage.[66] The newspaper stories about spinning bees were not far wrong: Women worked in order to marry.

Mary Cooper was fifty-four years old when she began her diary in October 1768. Although raised an Anglican, she had married a Quaker and was now attracted to a New Light Baptist congregation at Oyster Bay. Mostly she craved some sort of assurance that her life mattered. Like many of her contemporaries, she was something of a seeker. "We all went to the Quaker meeten where a multitude were geathred to here a woman preach that lately came from England," she wrote on June 1, 1769, adding "a most amebel woman she is." At the New Light meeting one Sabbath, she said it was "a good day. The Lord seemes near to many while we are waiteing on him of his appointments." But succeeding quarrels over the appointment of a minister distressed her. She could not understand why the Lord seemed to have forsaken a congregation that a few weeks before seemed a "greate and a florishing peopel."[67]

There was little more peace at home. Mary had given birth to six children, but only two daughters lived past childhood. When the older girl married without her parents' permission, Mary refused to speak to her, then repented when the daughter died four years later. Sorrowfully, she had the coffin carried into the house by the same window through which the daughter had exited. She was determined to do better by her younger daughter, Esther, who married her first cousin Simon Cooper but then, thinking better of her bargain, came home to weep and wail her circumstance. Esther and her husband both appear in the diary, though their occasional attempts at reconciliation all seem to have failed.[68] Esther was moody, but she was both a companion and a source of household help for her mother. In one of the earliest entries in the diary, Mary reported that Esther had "gon to Huntan Town to carry my coverleds to the weaver." Esther made the same trip in August 1773, but on neither occasion does the diary name the person who received the yarn. Mary's concern was not the cloth, but her daughter's presence or absence.[69]

Unhappy though she was, Esther constantly sought social outlets, among them the spinning frolics held in the neighborhood. She attended two, at different houses, in February, and another in March. This was the part of Long Island where in 1769, Boston newspapers reported a spinning match that produced 107 ten-knot skeins. But Mary's terse entries give no sense of the amounts of yarn spun at these gatherings and some indication that they were less decorous than those that got written up in the papers. They were part of a larger repertoire of rural work parties. On September 19, 1769, Simon proposed holding a wood-chopping frolic at the Cooper house. Mary's husband apparently agreed, for the next day the women were "very busie cooking for the work men." Most went away in the evening, Mary wrote, but "Some stay to dance, very greately against my will. Some anger about the dancing." A later entry suggests that it wasn't just Mary who was distressed by the dancing. On the Sabbath, Simon and Esther quarreled over "Ester dancing." Was the problem that she danced or refused to do so? Or perhaps that she danced with other men? "He got in an unexpresabel rage and struck her." Undaunted, Esther went off to a quilting frolic in mid-November.[70]

Esther's troubles with Simon were mirrored in Mary's own life. On her wedding anniversary in 1769, she wrote, "This day is forty years sinc I left my father's house and come here, and here have i seene littel els but harde labour and sorrow, crosses of every kind. I think in every repect the state of my affairs is more than forty time worse then when I came here first, except that I am nearer the desierered haven." It was hard work, not poverty, she railed against. Her husband owned a large farm and four slaves but he was tightfisted, willing to humiliate her before her friends by refusing to give her a turkey to roast for her guests. She didn't say how he responded when a man came to the house "and beged to sell a wheele to pay his house rent." There were probably religious conflicts as well. Mary warred against dirt and sin, constantly reassuring the unseen readers of her diary and God himself that she was not responsible when members of her household trespassed God's laws. "An old Indian come here to day that lets fortans and ueses charmes to cure tooth ach and drive away rats," she wrote on one such occasion. Somebody in the house was apparently enticed by the Indian visitor. "O Lord, though knowest that my soul abhors these abominations. Lay not this sin to my charge."[71] There was no joy in work nor happiness in marriage for Mary Cooper, but there must have been some satisfaction in spilling out her troubles in her diary.

The diary of Elizabeth Porter Phelps is more expressive than the others, going beyond mere accounting to tell stories. Phelps's family was among the wealthiest in western Massachusetts; the house she lived in as a girl and later as a married woman was one of the grandest in eighteenth-century Hadley. Yet even in 1757, when her father died, it contained a great wheel, a foot wheel, a reel, and more than 100 "runs" of homespun yarn. The family owned sheep, shears, and a great iron comb for combing worsted.[72] Two stories in Phelps's diary reveal a darker side of New England's rural economy, exposing tensions between a maidservant and her mistress and highlighting the significance of spinning as a fallback job for girls with few options.

The first story returns us to the street where Hannah Barnard was born, though no one named Barnard lived there. Elisha Cook, the son of Hannah's sister Mary, now owned his grandfather's homestead. His sister,

Hannah, and her husband, Moses Marsh, kept the tavern next door. It must have been a frantic place. The Marshes had lost five children to illness in the twenty years of their marriage, and the remaining four children were all under twelve. In January 1767, the tavern caught fire.[73]

Reporting the event in her diary, nineteen-year-old Elizabeth Porter expressed relief that "some few things was saved and blessed be God, all their Lives." She thought of the fire as a providence, an unexpected reminder of the fragility of life, much like the conflagration at the home of Hadley's minister ten months before. The week after that fire, Mr. Hopley had ascended the pulpit and preached from Job 2:21—"Naked came I out of my Mothers womb and naked shall I return thither: the Lord Gave and the Lord hath taken away; blessed be Name of the Lord." Unfortunately, this fire was no accident. On February 22, Elizabeth penned the astonishing news that "Sarah Bartlet that Lived with Captain marsh was brought to own that she wilfully set his house on fire . . . to burn some yarn that she had been discovered to make false ties in. She is now at Springfield jail."[74]

The indictment offers a few more details. Sarah Bartlet of Hadley, "spinster," had at midnight on January 20 taken a lighted candle in her right hand and voluntarily and with malice aforethought ignited "a Certain Bundle of Linnen Yarn and also a certain Bundle of Flax & Tow." Sarah first pleaded not guilty and then, no doubt with the help of an attorney, withdrew the plea and moved "that the Indictment may be quashed for the insufficiency thereof." The strategy worked. There is no further mention of the case in Elizabeth's diary. Yet together the court record and the diary take us inside a troubled household. Since spinners were paid by the run rather than the day, everything depended upon careful measurement—and trust between the spinner and her mistress. Obviously there was intense hostility, even fear, in this case. Flax is extremely flammable. That Sarah was even near the unspun flax and tow with her candle suggests carelessness, whether or not she deliberately set the fire. That she was wandering around the house at midnight further incriminated her.[75]

Whether the indictment represented actual behavior or a mistress's fantasy we do not know. What the story can reveal is the value of yarn in a rural economy. Raw flax was a kind of currency used to purchase the labor to spin it, as the account book of Joseph Barnard of Deerfield shows. When Mary Cary "went away" after twenty-three weeks' work, she was in debt to her employer for a mixture of homemade and store-bought cloth, including some wool and eleven knots of thread, probably of her own spinning.[76] Most farm girls did a little work for neighbors. Poor girls left home for longer periods, often returning with little to show for their labor. Over a period of years, they would accumulate enough to help set up a household when they married, but they would not have the worsted bed hangings or pattern-woven coverlets considered essential for the daughters of men like Samuel Lane or Matthew Patten.

A second, equally dramatic story in Elizabeth Porter Phelps's diary describes any working girl's worst nightmare. On September 11, 1768, the family was interrupted by a seemingly unexpected visit from two sisters. "Monday about 9 o'clock at night came here Sarah Goodrich with her sister Betty Daughters of Josiah Goodrich. Betty being with child had no setled place of abode therefore my mother was a going to set her spinning for her a week or two she not expecting to lie in this three months." Elizabeth went on to explain that since it was late, everyone went to bed including Sarah Goodrich, who intended to return home in the morning. "But we had not been a bed long before Sarah was obliged to get up Betty was so poorly." The family's hired hand went into town "after Aunt Porter then turned straight about after Mrs. Dickingson a midwife tho the child was born a half hour before she came . . . it Lived not an hour." The bald narrative conceals the family circumstances that may have lain behind Betty Goodrich's search for a home. A few months before, Sally's father, Josiah Goodrich, had moved "from Pittsfield up to Cowas about 100 and 30 mile." He had left his daughter Sarah with Elizabeth's "Aunt Porter," presumably as a servant. That Betty had "no setled place of abode" suggests that she supported herself by working a few weeks here and a few weeks there doing housework or spinning. Perhaps some employer had thrown her out when the pregnancy was discovered and she fled to her sister for help.[77]

When the baby died, it was the sister's employer, "Aunt Porter," who with her husband "Rode up in a Chaise and carried the Corps into town." Elizabeth went to the funeral. The next night she and her friend Penelope Williams sat up with the mother. That Sunday Mr. Hopkins preached "two rousing sermons" in which he "reproved all inquity but specially the sin of lying." There had been "two illegittimate children born the year past—one of Mary Cook the latter part of February confidently denied by the person she Fathered it upon and Likewise the person Betty

Goodrich charged with hers proffesses not to own it; these persons being all present but Betty, did hear a good earnest Sermon—may the Spirit of God set it home upon their hearts." Interestingly, the sermon was not about sexual sin but about lying, and it was directed not at the young women who gave birth out of marriage but at the men who refused to acknowledge paternity even when charged. A week later, the town had another case to ponder when on September 25, "the wife of one Trainer was delivered of a large child still born." The size of the child was significant, since the couple had been married just eight months before.[78]

Premarital pregnancy was common throughout New England in this period. Although it was still taken seriously in churches, courts had begun to look the other way. Two years before, Hadley churchgoers had witnessed a dramatic example of repentance occasioned by the terrifying death of a woman in childbed. When Elizabeth arrived at the meetinghouse on October 26, 1766, she heard that Submit Dickinson, who had married Samuel Gaylord seven months before, had died after giving birth to a stillborn child. The next Sunday, the bereaved husband "made a very humble confession for being guilty of the sin of fornacation." Perhaps he thought his wife's death was a judgment upon him. The minister read his confession aloud "so that this malloncolly instance might be a warning to all." Four years later, Gaylord married Elizabeth's friend Penelope Williams. They named their first daughter Submit Dickinson.[79]

Other references to textiles in Elizabeth's diary are more mundane. Both before and after her marriage to Charles Phelps, she reported the arrival and departure of part-time workers, women who came for several days or a week at a time to spin, weave, or tailor. Eunice Pomeroy came at least once a year from Amherst, other workers from nearby farms. In 1774 the Phelpses installed a tenant couple "at the Mountain Lot in a house newly built." The wife sometimes worked for Elizabeth, sometimes used the Phelps's loom to weave for herself.[80] The family also owned slaves—a woman named Peg and her daughters, Rosanna, age six, and Phillis, age two. Elizabeth was willing to share this wealth. In October 1767, she reported that "Peg our Negro woman went from here to Capt Marshes to live." The tavern was still short of help. Peg was back on November 1. The next autumn, she again left for three weeks, this time to help out at Colonel Partridges—"his Negros wife being lain in they wanted help a little while."[81] In a lull before slaughtering, the Phelpses were willing to get along without her, though one wonders who cared for her two children while she was gone.

Elizabeth imagined herself a benevolent mistress. Responsible for the spiritual as well as the physical welfare of slaves, she prayed for little Phillis when she was ill, worried when their new slave Caesar froze his finger, and used her own dressmaker, Rebecca Dickinson, to make Rose a gown. This did not mean she questioned her family's right to own them or their duty to work and obey.[82] She probably would have agreed with pastor Jonathan Ashley, who in a sermon to Deerfield's African Americans took two propositions from the Bible, first "that Christianity allows of the relation of master and servants," and second "that such as are by divine providence placed in the state of servant are not excluded from salvation but may become the Lord's freemen." Salvation did not mean freedom in this life but in the next. Elizabeth could take satisfaction, then, when "the wife of one Ralph Way a free Negro was taken into the Church" at Hadley or when "Esq. Porter and wife Desired Gods name might be praised for Smardin, their Negros Deliverance," and on the next page of her diary report that "Mr. Phelps set out with Cesar to sell him" or that in a summer when temperatures rose precipitously, "a Negro man melted himself Dead with the Violent Heat."[83]

Peg, however, was restless. In August 1771 she left with her mistress's permission to work for a time "for herself." On March 28, 1772, Elizabeth reported, "this Day our Peg who has Lived with us near 18 years of her own Choice Left us and two Children and was sold to one Capt Fay of Benington with a Negro man from this town all for the sake of being his wife." This was, of course, what most household helpers in New England did. Daughters spun and wove, then took both the textiles and themselves to new households. Hired girls came and went and eventually disappeared. Slaves were different. They weren't supposed to marry—or if they did they should find someone nearby. Elizabeth had hoped that the children might induce Peg to remain. Perhaps Peg hoped that someday she might purchase both her own and their freedom; there were examples of that among the blacks of Deerfield.[84] But it was not to be. In 1775, on an April morning, Elizabeth wrote, "a Little after eight our poor little Phillis left this world." A week later, Phillis's older sister, Rose, now fourteen, gave birth to a daughter. Elizabeth borrowed a neighbor's slave to do Rose's work for a few weeks until the girl became used to caring for a newborn. One Sunday she cared for the baby herself, sending Rose off to meeting. She no doubt hoped that Mr. Hopkins's sermon would teach the slave her duty.[85]

Elizabeth Phelps's stories alert us to the contradictory meanings attached to salvation in this period, to the simultaneous celebration and denial of family bonds, and to the double bonds of servitude amd marriage for African American women. Slaves were an anomaly in rural New England but common enough in port towns that they must have been present at most of the spinning bees reported in 1769–1770. Phelps's diary helps us to imagine the ways in which Jeremy Belknap's wealthy parishioner, John Gage, may have loaned his slaves Phebe and Dinah, though it tells us nothing about the revolutionary ideas they may have absorbed as they spun or reeled yarn in their pastor's parlor. Beneath the thunder of the political boycotts lay the subdued hum of unseen labor.

Jeremy Belknap, Mary Cooper, Samuel Lane, Matthew Patten, Deborah Sylvester, and Elizabeth Porter Phelps all wrote about spinning and weaving, but what they wrote differed. For Belknap, a spinning meeting was a material manifestation of spiritual energy, for Mary Cooper a temptation to frivolity. Samuel Lane kept tight control on his daughter's portions; Matthew Patten encouraged his daughter's autonomy. When Deborah Sylvester wrote her name on her account book she accepted responsibility for her own support. Elizabeth Porter Phelps, on the other hand, assumed a duty to care for others, to manage their work and their lives, and to pray for their souls. Household manufacturing is the thread that binds these stories together.

Some of the niddy-noddies in New England museums are marked with names. Most are not. They sit on bureaus, hang from nails on the wall, or march, neatly tagged, across a bank of shelves. They remind us of the ubiquity and the invisibility of common labor.

The newspaper stories of 1769 described New England cloth production at its most buoyant. Turning to their wheels, young women won the hearts of young gentlemen and the gratitude of their country. There was little sense in these stories of how much work it took to raise flax, shear sheep, clean wool, comb worsted, spin, reel, bleach, dye, and weave yarn, nor of the often difficult circumstances in which these tasks were completed. But late in 1769, the *Essex Gazette* carried the story of a "very melancholy Occurrence" at Windsor, Connecticut: "Four young Women went over the River in the Morning to pull Flax, in their Return towards Evening they went to wash their Feet, but the Bank being slippery, they slipt off into deep Water, and were all drowned. Their Bodies were taken up and buried a Day or two after."[86] Who were these mysterious women?

Did the flax field belong to their father or to a master with farms in more than one place? Did they cross the river alone or with the help of a male servant or brother? And why did all four women drown? Did one go after another—and another—when the first one slipped?

Behind the stories of patriotic production were many such stories, most of them long forgotten.

# A Bed Rug and
# a Silk Embroidery

COLCHESTER AND PRESTON, CONNECTICUT, 1775

*No mode of life was ever more expensive;*
*it was life at the expense of labour too*
*stringent to allow the highest culture.*

Horace Bushnell, *"The Age of Homespun"*

Betty Foot and Prudence Punderson are among a small group of New England women who left both written texts and textiles. Betty worked in wool, Prudence in silk. Betty's father was a patriot, Prudence's a loyalist. Betty spread her homespun flowers over an expansive bed covering; Prudence stitched her genteel scene onto a piece of silk measuring less than two feet square. Yet their lives and works, though different, speak to each other and to the larger themes of their time. Although they stood on opposite sides of the Revolution, they had a common understanding of independence. For them, liberty meant avoiding the snares of seduction and the temptations of idleness.

Elisabeth Foot, known to her family and friends as "Betty," was born in Colchester, Connecticut, in 1750, the oldest of the four children of Israel and Elisabeth Kimberly Foot. In 1775, she and her sisters Mary and Abigail ("Molly" and "Nabby" in her diary) kept house with their brother, Israel, in Colchester, while their parents spent much of their time on a second farm a few miles away. Betty's diary covers only ten months, from January to October 1775. A similar account left by Nabby continues a bit longer and picks up again in 1779. Neither describes the landmark day—November 5, 1778—when the three oldest Foot children, Betty, Molly, and Israel, married. The three handsome bed rugs attributed to their household mark that event. One rug bears the inscription "Mary Foot 1778." Another is marked *E.F.* The third rug has neither a mark nor a history, but it is so much like the others—and so unlike other Connecticut coverlets made in the same period—that it must have originated in the same neighborhood, if not in the same house. It was probably made by Israel's wife-to-be, Hannah Otis. Although neither Betty's nor Nabby's diary lasted long enough to record the making of the rugs, both amply document the skills that produced them. These bed rugs are masterworks of homespun and documents in the history of the American Revolution.[1]

Prudence Punderson's diminutive embroidery *The First, Second, and Last Scenes of Mortality* comes from the same part of Connecticut but from a different social realm. Stitched with crinkled floss on yellow silk, it portrays a comfortable parlor outfitted with curtains, a gilt mirror, and a tilt-top table where a young woman in a fashionable gown sits before a silver inkwell sketching. To her left is a slave tending a child in a cradle, to her right a coffin inscribed with the initials *P.P.*, a prophecy, as it turned out, of Prudence's own early death. Born in Preston, Connecticut, in 1758, she married Timothy Rosseter in 1783 and died a year later, shortly after giving birth to a daughter. Prudence may have learned embroidery in some now forgotten school in Norwich, perhaps one conducted by her mother, Prudence Geer Punderson, an accomplished needlewoman. Her father, Ebenezer Punderson, a Yale graduate and sometime schoolmaster, probably taught his daughter to write. Prudence was twenty-two when her father, stigmatized as a Tory, rowed into New London harbor to board an English man-of-war. For three years Prudence, her mother, and her sisters managed the household and the dwindling reserves in the store. In November 1778, they sailed for Long Island, where Ebenezer was serving as commissary of the British army. Prudence's brief journal dates from this period.[2]

Prudence Punderson was a self-conscious narrator, an organizer of small dramas. In her stitchery as well as her writing, she exploited the emotional potential of her subject. Betty was more matter-of-fact. Her diary, like dozens of others kept in rural New England in the eighteenth and nineteenth centuries, created stories through the accretion of small details, the diarist's voice breaking through only occasionally, and then often with irony and humor. She produced her bed rug in much the same way, producing a bold pattern, stitch by stitch, through subtle variation in repetitive details. Prudence's theme—the cycle of mortality—is the thread that links them. Their embroideries, like their journals, describe the length and width of young womanhood in Revolutionary New England.

In her study of New England account books, the historian Gloria Main has argued that improved literacy and an ability to earn money gave women of the pre-Revolutionary generation "greater control over their own lives."[3] In contrast, Cornelia Dayton, a legal historian, sees a decline in women's participation in Connecticut's courts during the same period. Especially disturbing was the rise of a double standard of sexual morality. Early colonial laws were repressive, but they had operated relatively evenhandedly, holding accountable men as well as women for children born out of wedlock. By the eve of the American Revolution, legal as well as social values had changed. Fornication had become a woman's crime.[4] Main's and Dayton's studies are based on massive amounts of quantifiable data. The writings and embroideries of Betty Foot and Prudence Punderson help us see how a changing economy and legal culture affected women whose names do not appear in account books and whose lives did not reach the courts. Together their words and works help us penetrate that fateful period of life Prudence called the "second scene of mortality," the age of young adulthood when women confronted the interlocking meanings of work and courtship.

Betty Foot was feeling sorry for herself. It was ten o'clock at night and her sister Molly "hant got home yet." Her cousin Ellen had been "sparked" the night before at a neighbor's house, and here she was without any excitement in her life. "I have been a knitting all day as stiddy as a Priest and so has Nab too." She and her sister Abigail were captives in the house, prisoners to work.

"Stiddy as a Priest" described her labor. After a slow start in early February, she knitted constantly from February 22 to March 17, producing worsted stockings for herself, Molly, and their mother. "I did Houswork & knit & at Night went over to Mr Otis's to beg emptens to put in the blue dye," she wrote on March 9. "I am knitting yet," she wrote a week later. On March 17 another cycle of work began. "Spun linen" was the new refrain. Through the end of March and into April, she sat at her wheel at least some part of every day except Sunday. In early May, after a week filling quills for her sister's weaving, she began to tackle last year's flax. "Carded tow," she wrote on May 10 and on the next nine days except Sunday.[5]

Textile work dominated her diary perhaps even more than her life. One might imagine her chained to her spinning wheel, like the maiden in Rumpelstiltskin, the pile of flax growing at night as she slept. She was captive at home, a hostage to textile production. Yet running across the steadiness of the diary are the comings and goings of other people. Betty knitted at home, at least most days, but her long cycle of spinning took place at a neighbor's house and was part of an exchange of work with her best friend, Hannah Otis. From March 16 until April 9, she lived at her friend's house, and though she didn't admit to it in the diary, she probably did a bit of "sparking" too. On March 20, after spinning all day, she wrote, "T Caples was here." The next day she "recievd a verry elegant piece of writing from Mr Caples." At night six young men showed up at the Otis house. Betty added dryly that "Hannah & I work'd on a Cheese Basket which we began last Night but I forgot to wright that."[6]

Betty's homespun pastoral gives no hint of the engines of war careening around her. Since January, the town militia had been mustering once a week. A network of correspondents kept Colchester's leaders apprised of developments in Boston, where British troops sustained a parliamentary embargo that enflamed a growing revolutionary movement.[7] News of fighting at Lexington and Concord reached Colchester on April 21, 1775: "In the morning we heard they had began to fight at Boston," Betty wrote, her breathless entry continuing under the next day's date, "I just got the work done up and the Quills filled when Jonah came & tell'd me I must go to making Biscuit for to carry to fight the regulars which I did and bak'd a pudding & you may guess the rest." Who was this "you" she addressed? Was her diary intended for a friend? For her unborn progeny? Or for some imagined reader in the sky who would understand the "rage militaire" that had seized Connecticut in the spring of 1775.[8]

There was no room for explanations or for detailed descriptions of the dough-making, mending, and kissing that filled that day. All Betty could offer her diary was a tumble of names: "at night David came to take his farewell of Ellen & hannah & nat & sarah Otis all came over here a little while." There were in fact three potential brides on the scene, though only Ellen had been sparked. Sarah Otis and Betty's brother, Israel, would eventually wed, as would Molly Foot and Sarah's brother "Nat." For the moment, Betty could only look on with sisterly condescension and perhaps a shade of jealousy. "Ellen & david lay abed till Sun about 3 hours high when they got up and he went home I suppose," she wrote on April 23, a Sunday.[9]

On Monday and Tuesday, Betty threw herself into milking, churning, and baking, pausing only to spool yarn for Ellen's weaving and to dispense supplies to Captain Eliphalet Baker of the Colchester militia, who "had 4 lb of butter on Elisabeth Wells' account," and to Jonah Cleaveland and a Mr. Wilds who had bacon, beef tongue, pork, and cheese "on the towns cost." Accountable to her parents, who were away at their farm in Marlborough, she took careful notes of the things she sent out of the house.

Baker's and Wells's companies marched toward Boston on April 25, joining other Connecticut troops near Lebanon. Within ten days two-thirds of Connecticut's militiamen had turned back, discouraged by reports of scanty supplies in Boston.[10] David Wilds may have been among them. On May 11, Betty noted that Ellen had gotten out of bed when her lover came to see her at night, then got back in with him at her side. The next morning, clearly annoyed, Betty wrote: "'Tis now 8 o'clock & Ellen & David a'nt up & I am a going to carding Tow." That night another militiaman came to the house for "a Coverlid & knapsack which we recon'd to be about worth 17s." A third and larger Colchester company was preparing to leave for Boston.[11]

The saga of David and Ellen continued as Nabby too began keeping a diary. Both sisters reported that the couple's wedding intentions were "published" (made public) at the Colchester church on June 11, but they got the news secondhand, since they missed meeting, being seriously engaged with a swarm of bees that wouldn't stay put. Nabby's account is the more descriptive: "I stayed at home and the Bees swarmed and Asa Bigelow was here and hived them th[ey] left the hive in the Afternoon and went down to captain Champion Wright's lot and setled on a tree as high as Haman." (Haman was the villain in the Old Testament whom Esther's uncle Mordecai tricked into building his own gallows.) Nabby was so absorbed by the bees she "had like to forgot to write that Ellen & David was cry'd of yesterday."

Ellen and David were married on June 22 while Nabby was doing her stint of work at the Otis house. She came home for the ceremony, but neither she nor Betty made much of the event. In a manner typical of rural diarists, they sandwiched their brief notations of the wedding between other seemingly unrelated incidents, making no effort to assign one thing more significance than another. "I went to Sally Well's funeral & at night Ellen was married to David Wilds & Margaret Foot came here to work." Work, marriage, and death—Betty had compressed all three scenes of mortality into one short entry, making no effort to exploit the romance or the sorrow of any. She could have said more about death. The Sally Wells whose funeral she attended was only seven years old. Although the Wells family was not as close to the Foots as the Otises, they were friends and neighbors. In April, Betty had spent two and a half days at the Wells house, some of it making gowns for the "little Girls." Sally was the third child to die in that family in five years.[12]

Like most New England brides, Ellen delayed "going to housekeeping." Nabby acknowledged the marriage by writing on July 1 that she had gone "a Rosberrying with David Wiles's Wife," but in nearly every other

entry in the weeks following the wedding, she remained plain "Ellen."
She and Nabby went strawberrying, then cherrying, and toward the end
of the month Betty reported that she and Ellen "went to pick whortel-
berrys & got some ripe apples." Most of the time, however, Ellen
remained at her loom with one or the other of the Foot girls helping with
the quilling and spooling. She wove swanskin for herself and bed ticking
for the family and handkerchiefs for no one in particular. On August 10,
Nabby spooled and warped a piece for Dr. Scott, and Ellen drew it into
the loom. There are subtle hints, however, that she was preparing to
leave. On August 22, Nabby borrowed a mare for Ellen from Thomas
Wells, and Ellen and Molly went "to Norwich to Buy earthen ware." On
October 10, 1775, she reported that she had done the work and helped
Betty "put on Ellen's Bed-quilt." This was the first quilt done in the
house that year. It did not, however, make much of an impact on Betty
who, writing retrospective entries for early October, said under the date
of the quilting, "I forgot what I did."[13] Ellen was still in the house when
Betty's diary ended on the last day of October. On November 4, Nabby
reported that Ellen had "moved over to Noah Foots." Curiously absent
from both diaries after the wedding, David may have been serving in the
militia, though neither Betty nor Nabby mentioned it.[14]

In their diaries, both sisters ignored the ongoing war. Although Colchester men participated in the Battle of Bunker Hill and the siege of
Dorchester Heights, the diaries do not mention either event. One could
argue, of course, that Betty's relentless labor was itself part of the Revolutionary movement, an assertion of her family's independence from
imported baubles, high taxes, and English assaults on American liberty.
Betty surely alluded to politics when she noted in the autumn of 1775 that
a hired spinner named Alice Welch had spun ten knots "& felt Nationaly
into the bargain." But since Alice, on a good day, was capable of producing thirty knots or more, the comment was sardonic. Betty had hovered
over the girl for most of the week, keeping her steadily at work, but on
Sunday Alice had a stomachache and on Monday she went home, coming
back at night to produce her mere ten knots. Betty confronted her own as
well as Alice's shortcomings when she wrote under the next day's date, "I
lay abed till sun an hour high. Got up and carded a little while & then Writ
Journal for 5 week back & Alice went home Sick after she had spun 4
knots. Procrastination is surely the Thief of Time."[15]

Betty was enlisted in her own war. She would not let life, like the diary,
slide away. Her journal had begun on January 1, 1775, a Sunday, with

what at first glance appears a peculiar notation for a woman who was already twenty-five years old: "I stay'd at home & Learnt to read and cypher." Over the next few weeks, the diary traced her progress in cyphering. On January 4, "I washed & went to School & cypher'd in Compound multiplication," then "went to school and began Reduction." On January 11, she "began the Rule of 3." By February 4, she had "finish'd the third case in Practice." Betty was doing more than improving her mind. She was preparing to teach. For a month she not only attended the night school but observed the day school as well. Even after she reckoned with her teacher (she owed "2 S for the Night Schooling"), she continued to work on her own. On February 17, she "went over to hear the Scholars examin'd in Arithmetic."

On January 2 she devoted her evening to writing letters. This wasn't her first effort. The drafts of letters written four years before to Peggy Smith and Jerusha Olcott survive among her miscellaneous papers. In contrast to the matter-of-fact style of the diary, they are pretentiously formal, mixing genteel greetings with biblical allusions, snippets of poetry with Connecticut idioms, and country punctuation with calligraphic flourishes. The letter to Smith begins: "Most Worthy and Exquisite Lady. It afford me no small pleasure and satisfaction when I take pen in hand to write to a person of your genius and talents. I wish health wealth and prosperity to all our friends who are friends indeed O that they might have in theire right hand length of days and in their left riches and honour I long to hear how affairs go on in my absence but I remain between the two extreams of hope and fear what the event will be but it does not deprive me of any rest." She continued that she had nothing special to write about, that all their friends were well and sent their compliments, and that they looked forward to hearing from her in writing "if we are deprived of the same by word of mouth." But before the letter was finished, she did have news, "melancholy news" to convey. Her uncle's wife had died while on a visit to Marlborough. "She had rid out for her health and an afternoon visit and never Returnd home again." Betty concluded by "Suscribing myself Madam your Most affectionate friend And well wisher." At the bottom of the page, she scribbled four rows of alphabets as though she were practicing her handwriting.[16]

Less of the letter to Jerusha Olcott survives. Betty drafted it on the blank spaces of a sheet containing the transcription of a ballad. Again there is a mixture of biblical and literary language. She borrowed from Proverbs 31 in her tribute to Jerusha: "Many daughters have done virtuously, but [thou] excellest them all. The number of those women who have noted worthyly, who had advanced their families, and nobly served the generations in which they leived, is not small. They are well entitled to applause, and I give it them with pleasure; but there was never any comparable to the merits, that best of women, and most beloved, thy merits far, far transcend them all!" She closed this not quite grammatical peroration with a flourish: "In the mean while, I remain with due respect to your Spouse, Your affectionate Kinswoman & humble Servant." In the space remaining, she practiced her signature: "Elisabeth Foot of Colchester in hartford County—Colchester april 3d 1772 Elisabeth Foot."[17]

Fortunately, the diary avoided such affectations. Although happy to acknowledge the "elegance" of one T. Caples, she limited her own literary excursions to gentle satire directed at her siblings, Israel and Molly, who apparently had less of a commitment to learning than she. When Israel went to the Otis house on his way to school, he found it "too hard for him for he could not go to School he was so out of Breath." On another day, Molly "took a trip to school having a fair wind . . . but at Night having contrary winds was drove back to Dr Scot's from thence to Mr. Otis's." Molly's future husband, Nathaniel Otis, was obviously far more interesting than cyphering. Two days later "Mol came home having weather'd out the Storm & made a pretty good Voyage for Nat come home with her."[18] Obviously, the winds that propelled or impeded Molly had nothing to do with the weather.

Betty's diary shows the seeming permissiveness of rural New Englanders as courts pulled away from the old Puritan laws against fornication. Should a girl become pregnant, she had only one protection: her lover's concern for his own reputation. If he chose to deny paternity, she had little hope of pursuing her case in the county court. In such a setting, girls needed to stand up to their would-be seducers.

The ballad Betty carefully wrote out (perhaps enclosing a copy in her letter to Jerusha) introduces a seeming hero:

> *O hark o hark a little while*
> *I'll Sing a ditty shall make you Smile*
> *Tis of a merchants son of late*
> *As he came Sailing up the straight*

But the second verse rebukes him, as though in the voice of a lover:

*Avaunt thou false Deceiver man*
*in vain you tempt my Soul to Sin,*
*My Virtues Proof say all you can,*
*Your artful Snares are spread in vain.*

*In vain you tell me of my Charms,*
*In vain bestow on Angels face;*
*A noble Scorn my bosom warms,*
*I See, and hate your forced Grimace.*

*My Beauty is beyond Compare*
*Wit Superlatively fine,*
*You say; and yet your Schemes prepare*
*To rob this Dimond sparkling mine.*

*Fond of your own imagined Sense,*
*You fancy Women Can have none;*
*But you shall see by my Defence*
*I dare assert our Rights alone;*

This was a different discourse of rights than the one being promoted in Boston. The spunky heroine resisted her false suitor because of her confidence in God's "watchful Eye." The next few verses again allude to Proverbs 31, "the sweet blush of Modesty / More beauteous than the ruby seems." But it is self-assertion, more than modesty, that allowed her to stand up to her lover. Betty's ballad shows how, in a setting where young people pretty much managed their own behavior, some women were beginning to internalize an ethic of restraint.[19]

When school ended, Betty's diary settled into a spare record of daily work, with textile production at its center. Although the coming of war gave new impetus to their work, the Foot sisters labored within a long-established system. In Colchester as in other parts of New England in the pre-Revolutionary period, almost three-quarters of households had spinning wheels and over 20 percent had looms.[20] For the Foots and their helper Ellen, spinning and weaving were merely two tasks in a regimen that included carding, dyeing, sewing, quilting, knitting, and even, on occasion, basket-making. Betty did most of the sewing and all of the knitting. Nabby and Ellen did the weaving, with a little help from Molly. Molly's work is the hardest to categorize since, unlike her sisters, she left no record of her own. She seems to have helped with the weaving and the bonnet-making, but for much of the time she appears to have been mainly responsible for housework. In a typical entry, Nabby wrote: "I wove and helpd mol do the work." The parents are even less apparent, the father hardly appearing at all and the mother coming across as a distant manager, moving back and forth from the house in Colchester to the farm at Marlborough, though she did enjoy frolicking. On September 26, 1775, Betty "went to Goshen with Mother after we had dug up a little Joy."[21]

For Betty and Nabby the word *work* had multiple meanings. When Nabby wrote that she "did the work," she meant housework, the largely invisible but essential everyday tasks a wife or daughter did for her family. When she wrote "Prudence Otis come here to work" or "Betty went to Mr Pomroy to work," she meant work for pay. A third use for the word appears in her entry for July 12, 1775: "I went to Mr Otis's and spooled some of Mrs Wrights yarn and come home about noon and got my piece to work and Eliza Wells was here and I helped Israel pole hay a little." That single entry records both paid labor (Nabby is weaving cloth for Mrs. Wright) and family labor (she is helping her brother with the hay), but it also refers to informal exchanges between households (the use of the Otises' spooling equipment) and the skill that allowed one woman to get a particular piece of weaving "to work."[22]

Betty's diary shows the same range. She records paid work ("I went to Mr Abner Hill's to work & fix'd two Gowns at 6d per Gown"), family work ("I did Hous Work bak'd & knit"), and something in between, the reciprocal labor that New Englanders referred to as "changing works."[23] Nabby's and Betty's diaries are filled with such exchanges. "I came home to work & Sarah otis with me & they owed me 3 weeks & 2 days work," Betty wrote. Working cooperatively relieved the tedium of repetitive tasks like carding or spinning. Exchanging labor also allowed families to enlarge their own productivity without expending cash for wage labor. Debts could be measured in the time expended or in the product produced, as on April 30 when Betty wrote that she had again been "to Mr. Otis's to work & they ow'd me 2 Run of Linnen towards changing works." "They" were the Otis daughters—Prudence, Mercy, and Sarah. On June 10, 1775, Nabby "beamed" a piece of cloth and "drawed it through the harness" while Mercy Otis "handed ends." Three days later Nabby went to the Otis house to card tow. By June 16 she had "finished paying Sal [Sarah]," but she continued to card, the debt now shifting in Sarah's direction. Nabby carded tow steadily for ten days, weighing out four pounds a day except on Sunday, when she did only a pound and a half. By June 24, she had Sarah and "finsh'd their Toe."[24]

Gloria Main's argument about the place of women in an expanding wage economy looks different when we incorporate changing works into the argument. Her study of New England account books does indeed show an increase in the number of references to female laborers—from 3.8 percent in the period before 1764 to 11.4 between 1765 and 1774, but what is striking is how few female names appear in either period. Even at the end of the colonial era, nearly nine out of ten entries were for male workers. The diaries help us to see that though women's work was fundamentally "domestic," it was not confined to a single household. Although Betty and Nabby assigned only a small fraction of their labor a monetary value, there are very few entries in either diary that do not involve some sort of an exchange with another person, usually a female friend or neighbor. Textiles dominate these exchanges.[25]

From January to the end of May, seventy-nine of the ninety-three work entries in Betty's diary describe some form of textile activity. Spinning appeared on twenty-three days, knitting on twenty-three, sewing fifteen, carding thirteen, and a cluster of other activities—quilting, hatcheling, spooling, and quilling—on five. Betty mentioned her own weaving only once, on March 7, 1775, when "I stay'd at home & finish'd Molly's Worsted Stockings and fix'd two Gowns for Welch's Girls which came to 1s 6d and I wove while Nabby went to Milking." Her fifteen sewing entries included nine occasions on which she "fix'd" gowns for other people. Although gown-making consumed only a fraction of her time, she almost always assigned it a monetary value, whether or not any cash was exchanged. The one exception was on February 3, 1775, when she "fix'd a Gown for Prude just to clear my teeth." Typically, however, she charged sixpence per gown or one shilling per day, with some variation to account for size and complexity.

In Betty's diary, changing works, work for pay, and simple neighborliness blended one into the other, as two consecutive entries for the spring of 1775 show:

> April 11: I went to Mr Amos Wells's to work & Mrs Wells & I made two Gowns for her little Girls & at night went to Mr Fosers & Mr Otis's
>
> April 12: I went from Mr Otis's to Mr Wells's before sunrise & it rained like a Thunder shower I made a Gown for Nab Fox & I made

a gown for Mrs Wells & about noon went to Mr Fosers from thence
to Mr Otis's & hannah came home with me to work & we fix'd our
wheels to spin linnen & Mr Wells's ow'd me 2s 6d for my work being
1s per day.

It is clear enough that Betty was attributing cash value to her work at
Amos Wells's house, even though Lydia Wells helped her do it, and that
her overnight stay at the Otis house was part of a long history of friendship, but when Hannah Otis came home with her that was a different sort
of exchange, the beginning of an exchange of spinning. The labor system
at the Wells house was equally complex. Betty not only made gowns for
Mrs. Wells and her daughters but for Nab Fox, who lived and worked
there. Ultimately, some part of Betty's work would be charged against
Nab, when she and her employer settled accounts.

Betty could also act as an employer, subcontracting part of her own
work to others. Once in this period, she invited Hannah Otis to join her
when she was called to a neighbor's house to sew. "I work'd at Mr Hall's
& Hannah Otis with me which came to 1s 8p I pay hannah."[26] On other
occasions, Betty hired teen-aged girls or women to help with the spinning. Eliza and Tiphosa Edes came to the house; "Mrs. Fox," who spun
"fine filler," worked at home. Alice Welch arrived on October 18 and was
soon joined by Eunice Wells and Eunice Dodge. Because the diary stops
at the end of October, we do not know what project motivated all this
energy.

Nabby's diary, which picks up again in 1776, tells us, however, that
Betty accomplished her goal of becoming a teacher. On April 13, 1776,
Nabby wrote, "I did work about house and helped betty fix & She set out
for gilead to keep School." Betty left no record of that labor, but her bed
rug tells us that her dialogue between steadiness and elegance, practicality
and refinement continued.

In a semifictional account published in 1824, the Connecticut writer Lydia
Sigourney told an amusing story about the visit of a tenant farmer to his
landlord's "lady." Seeing a rug on the floor, he picked his way around
until a large table stopped him. Since he couldn't move the table, he
exclaimed apologetically, "I *must* tread on the kiverlid." When the good
lady assured him that the "coverlid" was actually a floor rug, he took two
or three steps on tiptoe. "I ha'nt been used to seeing kiverlids spread on

the floor to walk on. We are glad to get 'em to kiver us up a nights." The old farmer's consternation was understandable. Until the end of the eighteenth century, a rug was a heavy covering for a bed, as in the old rhyme, "Snug as a bug in a rug." The typical English bed rug was loom woven, the weaver having knotted short lengths of coarse woolen yarn onto the warp as he wove, creating a shaggy surface. By the end of the seventeenth century, rug weaving was a local industry in Norwich and Colchester, England, towns that gave their names to two Connecticut towns known for rugs of a different kind. These were made with a needle, several strands of homespun yarn being looped through the surface of an existing blanket or other heavy fabric.[27]

Specialists have identified at least twelve related bed rugs made in Colchester, Norwich, or Lebanon, Connecticut, between 1778 and 1809. Most have five oversized flowers emanating from a two-handled pot. Similar flowers fit within the undulating leaves or vines of the border. Although they clearly reflect a common design source—a teacher, pattern book, or string of imitators—there cannot have been a single manufacturer. The actual construction, the number and size of flowers, and the yarns used differ markedly. Some embroiderers turned vines into full leaves. Others abandoned the pot. All used flowers with both scalloped and pointed edges, but only a few, including the Foots, used the flat Tudor rose. The rugs vary randomly in width and length. Yarns cover a spectrum of household dyes from deep indigo through shades of olive green, brown, red, and gold.[28]

Within this corpus, the three rugs associated with the Foot family are unique. Mary's rug is the only one with a date, but that date is significant. That three of the Foot children married on November 5, 1778, suggests that three brides cooperated in producing three astonishingly similar bed coverings. The logical owner of the unmarked rug is not, therefore, Abigail Foot, the younger sister, but Israel's bride, Sarah Otis. As we have seen she was constantly in and out of the house, "changing works" and socializing. Nabby surely participated in the process as did various hired helpers.

The three rugs use the same design vocabulary as the other Norwich-Colchester rugs but a different needlework technique. Instead of looping the thread to create a pile, as all of the others did, the makers of these rugs covered the entire surface with a flat darning stitch. The result is crisper and more geometric, almost like the blackwork embroidery of Elizabethan England, though its immediate source appears to be the filling stitches used in high-style crewel embroidery, including bed hangings worked by Prudence Punderson's mother. The scale and materials are, of course, radically different. The yarn in the Foot bed rugs is homespun, home-dyed wool, quite unlike the imported yarns used in crewelwork. The base fabric gives us some sense of the plain cloth Betty Foot and her sisters were weaving. It is homely fabric, woven in a simple tabby. The two panels, a little less than forty inches wide, have been joined down the center with the same thread used in weaving.

New England bed rugs are a perfect example of the marriage of industry and refinement. A writer in *Antiques* in the 1930s doubted that her "ancestresses ... were particularly enthusiastic over the ornamental quality of their weavings. If they had been, their recourse to hand-embroidered embellishments would have been far less frequent than was evidently the case. To many a pent-up woman's soul the swift and willing needle, plumed with bright thread, came as a shining deliverer from the tyrannous restrictions of the loom."[29] To a skilled weaver, the loom was no tyrant. The dazzling coverlets produced by Pennsylvania's male artisans show what an apprentice-trained weaver could do. The Foot sisters used skill with a needle to compensate for a less developed talent at warping and weaving. Needlework was "freer" in the sense that the design could be developed as it was worked, but its apparent ease disguised the artistry in conception or the weeks of work that went into carding, spinning, and dyeing the materials.

Their father's probate inventory, taken in 1785, lists a dye tub; Betty's diary refers both to blue and red dyes "set" in the house in 1775. The rugs themselves tell us that the sisters used indigo in various baths to produce three shades of blue. The browns probably came from the hulls of butternuts or black walnuts. It took only a few dozen hulls to dye several ounces of wool, and the process was fairly simple—soaking the hulls overnight, then simmering them for an hour or more, the time determining the depth of color. Indigo dyeing was more difficult. In the typical technique, a small cake of indigo purchased at the store was dissolved in stale urine, then steeped over low heat and allowed to ferment for about two weeks. A covered pot helped to control the stench; indigo smelled like putrifying flesh or feces even before it was added to urine. The "emptens" Betty begged for at the Otis house were part of the mix. Yeast left over from brewing speeded fermentation. Through a complex chemical process, the bacteria in this mixture liberated hydrogen from the urea, changing the color as well as the chemical composition of the mixture. The liquid was ready for dyeing when it had turned yellow or tan. In a process that must have seemed magical, yarn immersed in the pot became blue when exposed to the air. Dyers alternately dipped and aired their yarn for an hour or more at a time until the blue was dark enough to suit. Once dry, it could be washed in soapy water until the smell went away. Though unpleasant to process, indigo dye was remarkably stable: it didn't fade in sunlight, it wasn't destroyed by boiling, and it didn't react with other substances in the air to produce unexpected hues.[30]

Although all of the yarns on the decorative surface of the three rugs are homespun, there are variations among them, suggesting different grades of wool as well as different hands in spinning. In Mary's rug, there are two brown yarns, both z-spun, but one has a warmer dye and is not quite as tightly twisted. The dominant color is indigo, but the dyeing was obviously done in different stages. The fringe on Mary's rug came later. Made on a tape loom, it was constructed of a different wool, more loosely spun, and dyed in a different bath. Some was applied over repairs made with cotton thread, suggesting that it was taken off at some point and reattached. There are also small repairs to the blue motifs done with brown plied thread. They are worked so carefully, however, that they are barely noticeable.

Some unknown person may have contributed the design, though Betty could have drawn it. On September 8, 1775, she wrote that she "drew a Quilt Border for Mrs Brush."

*Quilted calimanco petticoat, c. 1760–1790.*

COURTESY OLD STURBRIDGE VILLAGE

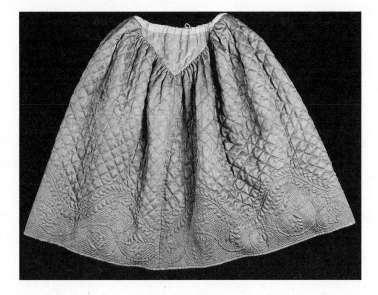

*Mary Foot bed rug, 1778.*
HENRY FRANCIS DU PONT
WINTERTHUR MUSEUM. BEQUEST OF
H. F. DU PONT

*Bed rug.*
HISTORIC DEERFIELD,
PHOTOGRAPH BY PENNY LEVERITT

Bed quilts in this period were usually "whole cloth" rather than pieced or appliquéd. That is, two lengths of a fine fabric were joined down the middle to make a bed-sized spread, then put together in a kind of sandwich, with the decorative fabric on the top, carded wool or tow in the middle, and a less valuable fabric, often yellow homespun, as backing. Since Betty drew only the border of Mrs. Brush's quilt, it is possible that it already had some kind of center design. But it is just as likely that the quilt she referred to was not a bedcovering but a petticoat, which was also called a "quilt" in letters and inventories of this period. Surviving petticoats usually have simple crosshatched quilting over most of the surface combined with more decorative designs for the borders. One Connecticut petticoat even has a full-masted ship flanked by a mermaid. Others have undulating ferns, leaves, or flowers much like those on the Foot bed rugs.[31]

All the motifs in the rugs can be found on other objects made in the

*Above:* E.F. *(Elisabeth Foot) bed rug.*
*Right: Close-up of pattern stitches*
*used in* E.F. *bed rug.*
CONNECTICUT HISTORICAL SOCIETY,
HARTFORD, CONNECTICUT

same period or earlier. Reverse curves like those on the borders appear in seventeenth-century band samplers (see Mary Hollingsworth's on page 118) and in schoolgirl embroidery made in Norwich, Connecticut, as late as the 1790s. Flat flowers with geometric "filling" also appear on ceramics as we saw in the chapter on Hannah Barnard's cupboard. Interestingly, Hannah Barnard's daughter, Abigail, lived in Colchester in 1775. Having been widowed twice, she was now the wife of the town's pastor,

Ephraim Little. Her daughter, Hannah Barnard Hastings Kellogg, may have been the "Mrs Kellog" Betty worked for in April 1775. Later that month, Betty noted that they owed her for three weeks and two days' work.[32]

The design of the rugs was apparently sketched directly onto the blanket, then carefully outlined in three rows of running stitches in variant shades of blue. Once that was done, details were filled in with a technique called "pattern darning." This is counted-thread embroidery, with each stitch entering and leaving on a precisely determined thread of the warp or weft. Varying the length and placement of stitches produced checks, chevrons, crosshatching, zigzags, and other geometric configurations. Such a technique required careful planning if not formal cyphering. The women who did it were "stiddy as a Priest." They were also inventive. Although there are only three basic flower shapes—a lobed flower, a jagged-edged carnation, and a flat-petaled rose—none is worked in exactly the same way. Using the same wool, the same stitches, and the same basic patterns, they came up with amazing variations.

Among the three, Mary's rug is the most original. Instead of embroidering five flowers in a pot as the others did, she attached six large flowers and three oversized leaves to a flowing vine. A delicate inner border defines the flat part of the bed, covering the larger border, the part that would have draped over the side, with a less rigid version of the curving vine used in the others. Betty's rug is the least varied. Unlike Mary and Sarah, who subdivided all but one flower on their rugs, she covered the entire surface of two serrated and two lobed flowers with a single filling stitch and used only one pattern on all five petals of one of the roses. She was also less ambitious than Sarah in stitching the stems of the central bouquet, resting content with a single line of stitching, where Sarah used three, and extending only two stems as far as the pot, where Sarah did four. Although her work is impressive, there was obviously a limit to her patience.

Although bed rugs were relatively common in colonial Connecticut, elaborately embroidered ones were not. About a quarter of inventories taken between 1730 and 1790 list rugs, but most were probably quite plain. Color was the most frequent modifier and green the most popular color, confirming Florence Montgomery's statement that "tufted green wool" rugs were a common import to the colonies in the eighteenth century. A "shag rug" from Litchfield described as "not finished" tells us that some rugs were home produced. A shag rug need not have been dec-

*Above: Prudence Geer Punderson.*
*Crewel bed valance, c. 1770.*
*Right: Close-up of filling stitches.*
CONNECTICUT HISTORICAL SOCIETY,
HARTFORD, CONNECTICUT

orative, however, as a surviving example now at Historic Deerfield reminds us. Its maker used the same running stitch and the same indigo dye as more ambitious embroiderers, but could manage only a simple stripe, working up one panel of the background at a time so that when joined the center seam was quite visible. In the Connecticut inventories, only one reference among forty suggested an elaborate design—a Norwich inventory of 1788 that listed a "flowered rug" in a household that also had "2 Work'd Chairs."[33]

The diaries tell us that the Foot sisters and Sarah Otis had the basic skills needed to make the rugs, not only spinning, weaving, and sewing, but dyeing and drawing patterns. But they also had the resources. As daughters of prosperous farmers, they had the ability to *use* wool rather than sell it and even occasionally to hire help. Betty's income from teaching, though undoubtedly small, may have given her even more opportunity to pay for spinning or dyeing, though it surely cut into her time. Just as important to our understanding of the rugs are the values described in the diary—the ethic of productivity that Betty called "steadiness," the collective labor she referred to as "changing works," the yearning for refinement revealed in her response to an "elegant" piece of writing from a would-be lover, and perhaps most of all the focus in early adulthood on courtship and marriage.

Only hindsight allows us to attach significance to Betty's entry for October 1, 1775: "I went to meeting to Town Mr Huntington Preach'd Hebrews 4 & 3 how can we escape if we neglect so great salvation." The visiting minister was David Huntington, the man Betty Foot married on November 5, 1778. A native of Lebanon, Connecticut, the site of Eleazar Wheelock's earliest efforts to educate New England Indians, Huntington apparently followed Wheelock to New Hampshire, graduating from Dartmouth College in 1773. After a period studying theology with his home pastor, Solomon Williams, he was installed over the church in Marlborough, Connecticut. Nabby attended his ordination on May 28, 1776. Betty was probably there, too, since she was teaching school at Gilead, the next town over.[34]

Because the Foot diaries end so soon, there is little evidence of the stresses of war or of the constant calls for shirts, stockings, and blankets to supply the army. As inflation outstripped the ability of towns to pay, colonial officials fixed prices for stockings, tow cloth, flannel, and blankets, using patriotism to motivate home manufacturers. By 1779, some towns were asking citizens to "loan" clothing to the effort, promising to repay them at the end of the war. Enthusiasm for the cause was waning in 1781 when Benedict Arnold, once the pride of the American army, led a British raid on New London that ended in the burning of the town and the massacre of Connecticut soldiers at Fort Griswold.[35] But none of this could have been predicted on April 21, 1775, when Betty Foot and her sisters stayed up baking biscuit for men to carry to go fight the regulars. The struggle had deepened when they began their bed rugs, but despite the violence and the uncertainties of the future, they spun wool, steeped their reeking pots of indigo, spooled, quilled, and warped their yarn, then built their elaborate designs stitch by stitch. This was their way of running up a flag. War or no war, they intended to go to housekeeping in style.

Prudence Punderson's needlework gives us a darker view of the war and a more complex story about courtship.

Prudence and her father were both storytellers, though they did not begin to write until the Revolution disrupted their lives. Ebenezer published two versions of his story in London during the war. Prudence told hers in the privacy of the letter-journal she kept on Long Island after her family fled Connecticut in 1778. Their lives before the war are documented in more prosaic sources, stacks of daybooks from Ebenezer's store, a few inventories and family papers, and public records. Prudence's embroideries bring these materials together, showing the intersections of agriculture and commerce, religion and politics, literature and life in one corner of Connecticut.

In addition to *The First, Second, and Last Scenes of Mortality,* Prudence's extant needlework includes two fan-shaped "fire screens," a set of framed pictures of the Twelve Apostles, and a small scene, on black silk, of a young woman seated on a Queen Anne chair, purportedly a portrait of Prudence Geer Punderson as a girl. There is also a tiny thimble marked *PP* in the collection. Ebenezer's store provided the materials with which his daughter worked. He typically sold silk in quarter-yard pieces and thread in "needles full," suggesting that someone in the neighborhood if not in the Punderson household was teaching needlework. As a former schoolmaster, Ebenezer surely had some part in his daughter's education. Occasional charges in his account book for "schooling" young girls indicate that his wife, too, may have offered instruction. After the war, the family opened a school on Long Island. In this period, however, Prudence, Sr., was probably too absorbed with child-rearing to have done much else. Prudence, born in 1758, was the oldest of eight children. The youngest was born in 1774.[36]

Among Prudence's papers is a list of "Days Observed by the Church" and "Dayes kept in memory of the Saints." Her embroideries of the Twelve Apostles confirm the family's commitment to the Anglican faith.

Prudence's grandfather, another Ebenezer, was famous among Connecticut Anglicans—and perhaps infamous in Groton—for having resigned his position as Congregational pastor there in order to take Anglican orders. In 1734, he returned from London as "Itinerant Missionary of the Venerable Society of New England" with an annual salary of seventy pounds. In more than thirty years as an Anglican missionary, he helped establish eleven new churches, served for many years as rector at Groton, and was the first preacher at Trinity Church in New Haven. During his tenure at New Haven, Connecticut's most prominent layman complained

*Prudence Punderson's thimble, engraved* PP.
CONNECTICUT HISTORICAL
SOCIETY, HARTFORD,
CONNECTICUT

*Prudence Punderson.*
*Silk embroidery of girl with*
*Queen Anne chairs.*
COURTESY ZEKE LIVERENT
ANTIQUES, COLCHESTER,
CONNECTICUT

*Prudence Punderson.*
*"St. Peter: He was Crucified*
*at Rome with his head*
*downward."*
CONNECTICUT HISTORICAL
SOCIETY, HARTFORD,
CONNECTICUT

that though "Mr. Punderson seems a very honest and laborious man," the church was actually declining. The problem he believed was partly "his want of politeness, and partly by his being absent so much, having five or six places under his care. I wish he was again at Groton and some politer person in his place." Punderson ended his days in Rye, New York, where he died in 1764, having seen both of his sons acquire whatever politeness Yale College had to offer. His greatest contribution to the Anglican cause may have been his children. Three of his daughters married priests; his son Ebenezer, though a merchant, became a champion of orthodoxy.[37]

Prudence's *Twelve Apostles* exemplify both piety and politeness. Surrounded by symbols of martyrdom, they are dressed in the garb of eighteenth-century clerics and surrounded by Connecticut's best furniture. Saint Matthew dips his pen into an inkwell just like the one in *The First, Second, and Last Scenes of Mortality.* Saint Peter, barefoot and dangling his keys, sits beside a Queen Anne chair identical to those in Prudence's portrait of her mother. Prudence's fascination with furniture is understandable. Her mother's younger brother, John Wheeler Geer, was an accomplished cabinetmaker. Almost twenty years younger than his oldest sister, he was closer in age to Prudence than to her mother. His artistry reinforced hers.[38] Fragments in her letter-journal show that she practiced drawing, and she seems to have owned or had access to a manual called *The Artist's Vade Mecum.* Although her drafting is awkward, her needlework is exquisite. A talented miniaturist, she meticulously delineated the smallest detail—fingers, eyebrows and lashes, bird feathers, fish scales, sheep's wool, apple blossoms, and the configurations of stiles and stretchers on high-style chairs. The largest of her pictures, *The First, Second, and Last Scenes of Mortality,* measures 12 by 17 inches. (In comparison, the elegant but more derivative silk embroideries of Faith Trumbull, daughter of Connecticut's governor, are both over 50 inches wide. Eunice Bourne's chimneypiece is 20½ by 43½ inches.)

The Punderson parlor was an oasis of politeness in a predominantly rural but increasingly multicultural world. New London County had among the highest population of African Americans in New England, and the Punderson store, situated at Poquotonic Neck in Norwich, was accessible to nearby Pequot and Mohegan families. The Thames River was a conduit for grain, livestock, salt meat, and timber products shipped out of the port of New London.[39] Punderson's customers brought in cheese, hops, feathers, honey, beeswax, potatoes, and beans, which they exchanged for kettles, frying pans, teapots, crockery, dictionaries, spectacles, West Indian tamarinds, English tammy, soap, razors, and thimbles. The most important local commodities were the bushels of flaxseed that Ebenezer shipped to New York for eventual export to Ireland, and the pork, oats, shingles, and barrel staves that he sent to the West Indies. In 1775, he had 720 gallons of molasses and 110 gallons of rum in his warehouse at Poquotonic, and cheese, codfish, oats, bacon, a thousand feet of pine boards, three thousand hogshead staves, and "thirty Sets of Shaky Hogsheds" at his warehouse and wharf in Groton.[40]

Textiles appeared on both sides of his ledgers. Since most farm families in the area owned spinning wheels, looms, and sheep, they were already weaving for household use. The Punderson store gave them an opportunity to trade extra fabric, especially the unfulled woolen they called "flannel," for printed calico, lace, broadcloth, "Tafety," and other imported goods. Two shillings a yard was the standard payment for flannel, though Robert Park got less because his was "but Little Blue & only ¾ yard wide."[41] Captain Asa Avery traded 20 yards of homemade cloth for 22 yards of "Chek." Mary Meech bought a teapot with her flannel. The Widow Commen was more productive than they, and also more restrained in her purchases. On the day she brought in 112 yards flannel, she spent less than a quarter of its value on cheap cloth and indigo. Lucy Smith had more expensive tastes. She used the 9 yards of flannel she brought into the store as a down payment on copperplate bed curtains that put her more than four pounds in debt. Other women paid directly in labor. Mary Spicer got 2¾ yards of lace and "12 nedles full of silk" for nine days' work spinning worsted. Mercy Chapman turned a credit for weaving 25 yards of linen toward 5 yards of chintz. The enticements of luxury goods kept women like these at their looms.[42]

Their work helped to enrich Ebenezer Punderson. According to his published narrative, he owned "three large Farms, as well as Dwelling-houses, and Stores" before the war and had an annual income, exclusive of his family's support, of more than three hundred pounds sterling. "Myself and Family being beloved and esteemed by all that knew us, we enjoyed every blessing that this world could bestow."[43] The ordinary folks who came into the store had less, but they valued the small luxuries he provided.

In one two-week period, the daybook recorded transactions with seventy-nine persons from fifty-four families, including Sampson Poquiantup, a Pequot, and Cato, a freed black or slave.[44] Among the Indian customers, there were two who modeled the dependency and drunkenness that reformers disdained. On October 26, 1772, "An Indian fellow Pawn'd 2 Silver Rings for 5 pts Rum and a Squa a Piece of Cloth for 3 quarts Rum, To be Redeem'd Saterday Next." Most entries for Pequot and Mohegan customers, however, look very much like those for English farmers. Joseph Charles "alias Scodoab," paid for "12 pains Glass" with rye.[45] The Sunsiman family used rye and beans to pay for yard goods, molasses, and a scythe. Samson Pauguanup, a pious Mohegan farmer, showed his support for education by paying for two yards of tape delivered to the "Indian School Master."[46]

Joseph Johnson, later to become a leader with Samson Occum in the movement to establish a Christian Indian town called Brotherton in Iroquois territory in New York, was one of Punderson's customers. His diary gives us a glimpse of the life of an educated Mohegan in this period. A graduate of Eleazar Wheelock's school at Lebanon, he had nevertheless been forced to go to sea as a common sailor. In 1771–1772, he was living with relatives on a farm at Mohegan, worrying over the state of his soul, planting, harvesting, and shelling corn, cutting shingles, clearing brush, dressing flax, boiling pumpkin for his uncle's hogs, and gathering and covering barrels of apples with hay. As a sailor, he had learned to mend his own clothing, but his writing also shows the aesthetic interests he had acquired at school. In most respects, it would be difficult to differentiate his diary from that of any other introspective and lovesick man of his age. "Moon Shined very bright this last Even," he wrote. "Played on my flute." But scattered entries reveal his mastery of crafts long associated with his people. While cutting firewood for his uncle in January, he harvested birch logs from which he carved ladles and "Pudden spoons." He also found work weaving rush bottoms for chairs. Like Betty Foot, he was choring about at home while preparing to be a teacher. For that work he needed proper clothing, which is why on February 3, 1772, he stopped at the Punderson store and bought eight pence's worth of buttons for a jacket.[47]

Johnson's public writing shows he was acutely aware of his dual identity as a Mohegan and an educated man. In a letter to Connecticut's governor, he played on white stereotypes of his people. "I am an Indian. I am of a Nation little respected in these days, and for good reason," he began. Criticizing his own people, he explained that when Englishmen had "in a brotherly manner" tried to convert them to Christianity, they had "walked, every one according to the Imagination of their own wicked & unchristianized hearts; and lived in Intemperance, Excess, rioting, and other desolate Practices." Johnson may have believed all these things, but he also knew that to plead his case, he needed to identify with white values. He ended with a powerful argument for his own cause. "If an Indian is Capable, is faithfull, & is Serviceable as an English man" in his business as a schoolmaster, why might he not "meet with the same Encouragement?" In other words, shouldn't persons with the same qualifications receive the same salary and have the same opportunity to teach? Johnson did eventually get work teaching at an Indian school in western Connecticut, though he was soon deeply involved with Occom in planning for a new community where Christianized Indians could be both Indians and "men."[48]

Joseph Johnson's dreams, like Ebenezer Punderson's, were disrupted by war. He died somewhere in Iroquois territory during the tense early months of the Revolution. By then, the prosperity and good esteem that once surrounded the store at Poquotonic had turned into jealousy and revenge. The day Betty Foot heard about the fighting "at Boston," Ebenezer was attending a court at Stonington, Connecticut. He was in a vulnerable position. Earlier that month, he had refused to appear before Revolutionary authorities in Norwich—he called it the mob's committee—to answer charges of tea drinking and of saying that the Continental Congress "was an illegal body, and that their petition to the king was haughty, insolent, and rascally." When news of the fight at Lexington and Concord reached Stonington, his life was in jeopardy, or so he believed. In his published narrative, he said that a "mob instantly gathered and were very fierce to take me, but were dissuaded by several justices of the peace then present. Word was carried to the militia, who called their God to witness, that I should be instantly drawn in quarters before the Liberty Pole. They joined the mob; and, for three hours, it was with the utmost difficulty that the said authority could keep them from violence."[49]

In Lebanon, Connecticut, Governor Jonathan Trumbull refused to offer him protection. Heading for New York on a road not much traveled, he "was soon taken up in the town of Colchester, where was instantly a mob of three or four hundred people." Hauled before a committee of safety in which one of the local justices of the peace was sitting, he was asked if he would join the militia and go to Boston. No, he said, he would "suffer any death rather than take up arms against my king." When a soldier threatened to shoot him, he begged for his life. He was finally allowed to sign a more moderate covenant and continue home, but in Norwich the harassment continued. On May 28, a Sunday, he embarked in an open boat out of New London, caught a coaster that took him to Newport, then boarded "his majesty's ship Rose."[50]

On shipboard, waiting for passage to England, he wrote a series of affectionate and admonitory letters to his family. In one, he described his last meeting with his wife, mother, and children. With tears "dropping from every eye, each express'd a willingness to die with me, if the cause required it, rather than desert either their religion or their king."

Although he feared their wealth would be confiscated, he believed it better to live together "in some lonely peaceful cottage, labouring with our own hands for the plain or coarser necessaries of life" than accept the governance of a deluded mob. This "horrid rebellion" began in greed and in a false religion. The wicked notion that God elected men to salvation regardless of their deeds led men to believe they could "with a quiet conscience run counter to divine and civil laws." His heart bled for the "poor, well-meaning, deluded wretches . . . raised to this pitch of enthusiasm by the rich and great, who keep them from the truth, and fill their weak but innocent understandings with innumerable falsehoods." He asked his "honoured mother" to assist his wife in instructing the children in "the dreadful consequences attending the great rebellion in the reign of king Charles the first. Let them know how many great and good men lost their lives for being loyal to their king."[51]

His mother did more than teach history. In August, with the help of a sympathetic justice of the peace, she dragged up an old promissory note and in a friendly suit for debt attached part of his estate, preserving some of his store goods and much of his household furniture from immediate confiscation. Meanwhile, Prudence, Sr., and the girls were managing the store, coping with dwindling stocks and disappearing customers. In September there was a new crisis, the death of baby Ephraim just a month before his first birthday.[52]

Ebenezer was still in Newport Harbor, on board the *Rose,* when an American prisoner from Colchester made his escape from a tender belonging to the ship. He was Hannah Barnard's grandson, Charles Bulkeley, who had been taken prisoner when the British captured a West Indian sloop bound for New London.[53] In Ebenezer's view, men like Bulkeley were little more than brigands. He thought the war itself had been made by pious smugglers posing as merchants; privateering was only the next step. As for ordinary men, they were simply deluded. His own motives were, of course, pure. In February he wrote from London that he was about to return to America to join the king's forces. He had used his last money to pay the debt for his board, intending to go "moneyless, and by that means friendless," into the war. With typical extravagance, he concluded, "My dear, most likely I shall not live to see you again: if I do not, put our children in mind that their father seal'd the truth of the principles he would inculcate in them, with his own blood."[54]

In his work helping supply troops on Long Island, Ebenezer faced harassment but not death, but it was almost three years before he could arrange for his family to join him. Prudence's *The First, Second, and Last Scenes of Mortality* was probably completed during this period. Her education had been disrupted by the war, her health was not good, and her little brother's death reinforced her sense of life's transience. Some have called her embroidery a mourning picture, but it is much more than that. It is a celebration of her family's wealth, a moral allegory, and a self-portrait.

The inventory taken at the time of her grandmother's lawsuit documents the family wealth. It lists, among other household furnishings, "four Duzon of Cheres & four Round tables & four Squar tables and two Round Stands . . . and Seven Looking Glasses," as well as "one Negro Woman and one Negro Gal." The tables, chairs, mirror, and diminutive slave in Prudence's embroidery are all on this list. The Connecticut Historical Society now owns the little inkstand on the table as well as a similar though not identical table and looking glass. At one level, the composition of the embroidery may be a tribute to Prudence's uncle. Cabinetmakers' shop signs were sometimes arranged in exactly the same way. Sequential images of a cradle, a table, and a coffin made a visual argument for the flexibility of a craftsman who could provide all the needs of a family from birth to death. John Wheeler Geer's account book does include charges for coffins, desks, tables, chairs, and cradles.[55]

The carpet, curtains, and slave are evidence of the Punderson wealth. Fewer than 1 percent of Norwich households in this period had any sort of floor covering, and only 10 percent had window curtains. In inventories, luxury textiles and slaves often appeared together, as in the estate of Ebenezer Backus, who owned an easy chair and a floor carpet as well as a slave named Frank. Captain Samuel Johnson had a set of "green baize window Curtains" as well as four slaves. If the "gal" in Ebenezer's inventory is the girl in Prudence's embroidery, she was both a servant and an object of display. Dressed in a neat striped apron with a string of beads at her neck, she helped furnish the room.[56]

As much a marker of the Punderson wealth as the carpet, the curtains, and the African child is the framed picture on the wall. Only 3 of 130 Norwich inventories listed pictures. Captain John Pollard of Preston owned a series of framed engravings portraying the life of the Old Testament Joseph. He also had "6 Pictures emblematical of the Prodigal Son." The inventory-takers wrote down the individual titles: "Receiving his patrimony, leaving his Father, Reveling with Harlots, Feeding with Swine,

*Prudence Punderson.*
The First, Second, and Last
Scenes of Mortality.
CONNECTICUT HISTORICAL
SOCIETY, HARTFORD, CONNECTICUT

*Edward Hicks (att.).*
*Henry Van Horn shop sign.*
COURTESY ABBY ALDRICH
ROCKEFELLER FOLK ART MUSEUM,
WILLIAMSBURG, VIRGINIA

Returned to his Father, Feasted on his return." Although the topics are different from those Prudence embroidered, they display a common interest in biblical characters, in groupings of related pictures, and in narrative.

*The First, Second, and Last Scenes of Mortality* is also "emblematical," though its meanings are less obvious. The coffin and the fabric draped over the mirror surely signify death, but it is not a mourning picture. It is a meditation on life's transience. The title indicates that it is meant to be read

sequentially. The child in the cradle is in the first stage of mortality, the woman at the table in the second, and the unseen person in the coffin has just completed the last. Since Western culture usually posited at least four and sometimes as many as seven stages of mortality, there is little question but that Prudence intended to signify a life cut short. The flowerless stem in the sketch on the table accentuates the theme, as do the empty chairs. Unlike conventional schoolgirl embroidery, there is no celebration of courtship here. The only male in the embroidery is in the tiny picture above the cradle. Dressed in what looks like a theatrical costume, he stands, spear in hand, just outside an enclosed space where a sorrowful woman turns her face to a brick wall. The identity of the woman is obscure but her circumstance is clear enough. She is both confined and grieving. Perhaps Grandmother Punderson's history lessons included the  story of some tragic figure, like Mary, Queen of Scots, persecuted for her religion, yet even more unfortunate in love.[57]

Other elements in the picture are more easily read. The woman at the table faces a straightedge and compass, symbols not only of freemasonry but of personal rectitude. Eighteenth-century engravings admonished young people to "Keep Within the Compass." In one, a virtuous woman stands within the triangle, while around the border smaller pictures tell the story of a prodigal woman who succumbs to drink, neglects her baby, turns to streetwalking, and ends up in prison pounding hemp. A reference to Proverbs 31 is updated in a cheerful couplet: "How blest the Maid whose bosom no headstrong passion knows, / Her days in Joy she Passes, her nights in soft repose" (see page 240).

Prudence's embroidery is not only a meditation on mortality but on female virtue. That notion is reinforced by the presence of the coffin in the parlor. Most educated people in 1775 would have recognized the allusion to Samuel Richardson's novel *Clarissa*. Faced with a tyrannical father who wanted her to marry a man she could not respect, Clarissa ran away with the villainous Lovelace, who, when he failed to seduce her, imprisoned her in a brothel and then raped her. Clarissa chose to die alone and impoverished rather than accept his support. When she was in her last illness, a friend of Lovelace's visited the lodging room where she lay dying. He heard "a sort of lumbering noise upon the stairs, as if a large trunk

*Tilt-top tea table, c. 1760,
owned by Punderson family.*
CONNECTICUT HISTORICAL SOCIETY,
HARTFORD, CONNECTICUT

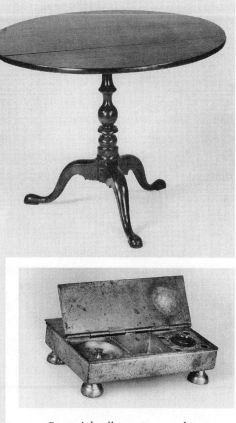

*Looking glass, c. 1765,
owned by Punderson family.*
CONNECTICUT HISTORICAL SOCIETY,
HARTFORD, CONNECTICUT

*Pewter inkwell, c. 1760, owned
by Punderson family.*
CONNECTICUT HISTORICAL SOCIETY,
HARTFORD, CONNECTICUT

were bringing up between two people." Through the door came two attendants with a coffin, bearing allegorial devices and the name *Clarissa Harlowe.* Clarissa, "being used to draw for her needle-works," had executed the design herself. Since she did not know "what her *closing-day* would be," she had given as the date of her death "the fatal day of her leaving her father's house." Over a passage from the Book of Job, she had drawn the head of a white lily, "snapt short off."[58]

Prudence's embroidery incorporated both the coffin and the notion of a broken stem, but the initials on the coffin, *P.P,* are clearly her own. Her picture is both "emblematical" and a self-portrait. Among her papers is an undated writing seemingly cut from the letter-journal. There may once have been other identifying marks, including the name of the person to whom she sent it. Internal evidence dates it from just before her departure for Long Island. Entitled "Please for Changeing my situation for Life," it begins by praising an unnamed suitor: "My Friend leaves me no room to doubt his affections, he is of an honorable Family, & of a religious turn of mind a man of sence & well educated which cannot but render him very agreable in conversation, is comely & of a handsome size & stature & I believe knows enough of the world not to Think too lightly of domestick cares." Then in a calm and rational tone it outlines the "Obsticles that forbid, which outways the above & Calls me from New England to attend the best of Parents within the Kings Lines." The first obstacle was their "different Principles in Religion." The second was that she would be "chusing for myself without a possibility of haveing my Papas approbation." Third, there were overwhelming differences between them in politics. As if that weren't enough, "from the tumultous jarring times of Civil War I think may be raised many objections against settling for Life."

Keep Within the Compass, *English engraving.* COURTESY WINTERTHUR MUSEUM

> *Please for Changeing my situation for Life.*
>
> My Friend leaves me no room to doubt his affections; he is of an honorable Family, & of a religious turn of mind a man of sence & well educated which cannot but render him very agreable in conversation; & comely & of a handsome sise & stature & I believe, knows enough of the world not to think too lightly of domestick Cares.
>
> Obsticles that forbid, which outways the above & Calls me from New-England to attend the best of Parents within the Kings Lines. Our different Principles in Religion are first to be mentioned which are no less thought of by him; but are esteemed by himself then by the writer, next chusing for my self without a possibility of haveing my Papas approbation, thirdly the states Confine his Publick Principles, & from the tumultous jaring times of Civil war I think may be raised many objections against settling for Life & my ill state of Health which looks but too proboble to end only with my Breath makes me unwilling to bestow on my Friend or go to my Parens under their present situation such a helpless Burthen

*Above: Prudence Punderson. "Please for Changeing my situation for Life."*
*Right: Sketch from Prudence Punderson letter journal.*

Finally, her "ill state of Health which looks but too probably to end only with my Breath makes me unwilling to bestow on my Friend or go to my Parens under their Present situation such a helpless Burthen."[59]

In this little discourse, Prudence appears obediently composed, but her struggle cannot have been easy. She was apparently attracted to this unnamed man. In one of the earliest letters written from Long Island, she thanked her "Kind Uncle" David Gere for "the Care & Concern you shew'd for us, & in Peticular of your kind & tender Cautions, when you immagined I was going under the paw of the Bare." The bear was a moral rather than a mortal enemy. "Oh my Friend," she continued, "I daily see & hear of those poor deluded creatures, you picter'd out of our Deceived & Ruined sex, many of them very Prety Girls & of good family & fortune." Such misguided girls might "with Dear Olivia say":

> *When lovely Woman Stoops to folly,*
> *And finds too late that men betray,*
> *What charm can sooth her melancholy*
> *What art can wash her guilt away,*
> *The only art her guilt to cover,*
> *To hide her shame from every eye,*
> *To give repentance to her lover,*
> *And Wring his bosom—is to die.*

The song is from another English novel, *The Vicar of Wakefield* by Oliver Goldsmith. Olivia, like Clarissa, had run away with a false lover, though her parents proved more forgiving.[60] Olivia's song contrasts with Betty Foot's ballad. Betty's song focused on a woman's ability to resist the wiles of a duplicitous lover. Olivia assumes, like her fictional counterpart in *Clarissa*, that death must follow seduction. Her extravagant commitment to virtue recalls Ebenezer Punderson's equally melodramatic promise to die rather than violate his duty to his sovereign. In his view the "wretches" who supported the Revolution were no wiser, and a good deal less sympathetic, than women who gave in to seduction.[61]

On November 20, 1778, Mrs. Punderson and the seven surviving children left Connecticut for Long Island, where they were reunited with Ebenezer after more than three years. After a short time together, the family was again separated. The mother and younger children set up housekeeping at East Hampton. Prudence, Ebenezer, Jr., and eventually a younger sister, Hannah, joined their father at the other end of the island, the two girls living "at different Lodgings, Papa & my Bror too & fro." The early letters Prudence copied into the pages of her journal were alternately whimsical and sentimental. On a horseback ride to the end of the island, she was "mounted in the fassion of the He without a Pillion, & behind my Papa." The workers at the British fort were merry despite their fatigue, and in the solitary cedars were "feather'd warbling musissions, whose sweetly inchanting notes answers every silant reflection." Much later, she described her family crowded into a

little horse cart for their first journey to "Public workship since the declaration of independance." Although they looked like "the shatered
remains of Prosperity," she playfully predicted that "this splendid
Carage," which they called "our Coach & two," was likely "to become a
general fassion."[62]

She could also tell a rousing story. In a letter ironically titled "The
treasures of Poverty, Protecks our peace," she told her friend Sally Ros-
setter about a rebel attack on the house she, her father, and her sister Hannah were sharing. It is worth quoting in full because it shows both the
roughness of Prudence's prose and her capacity for narrative:

> last Evening, about 9 some Body taped at our door, thinking no
> harm I open'd it, & instantly rushed in too men with blacked faces
> who snach'd the Candle from my hand & were well armed, each a
> gun & pistol, without the least stop they rushed into Papas Bead-
> room not with standing (Sister Hannah seeing where they were
> going) started before them & held the first door—we find Dear
> Sally a nesessaty of our mimicing the amisons, which we will
> according to our abilitie Papa is still senseless & wild not wake'd
> from his sleep, tho rassed on his elbow & they enter'd the room one
> Cockt his Gun at Papaas breast Cry'd you are a dead man, I
> instantly seiz'd it & forst him without the door Sister encountered
> with the other one, who once pointed his gun at her, but she being
> not frightened from her affections stood her ground, seeing them
> both without the door & finding it necessary Papa should be in a
> position for his own defence; I steped back got his Pistols & puting
> them under my apron slipt them by those fends unpreceiv'd, handed
> them to Papa who was but just come to himself, the one had enter'd
> the second time with his Gun Cockt in the former position, I
> grasped & wave'd it out of mischeifs way till by a sudden spring
> thirst him without the door & half acrost the next room, the other
> now fearing to stand his ground alone, not knowing the bad State of
> Papas Pistols, one with out primeing & the other lain loaded more
> then 6 Months & not knowing my want of strength believe he
> feared I Should disarm his mate for he followed close my elbow, Sis-
> ter fasten'd the door after us while Papa escape'd in his shirt, they
> knowing he were gone set on their business one stood sentry while
> the other pillage'd us of 20 worth of apparel beside many Papours
> of valew in three or four minutes time & exit the House.[63]

She had another opportunity to behave as an amazon when she and her brother Ebenezer, in attempting to cross to Westchester, were interrupted by a sentry who told them that "the Greatest part of Washingtons Army" was nearby. They walked across Throgs Neck in the boiling sun "just 2 hours after the Rebels had left the ground." Prudence was less stalwart this time. Leaning on her brother and his friend for support, she saw "guns shivered to peices . . . & green Boughs cut & cover'd with human gore (of their wounded) Oh it is horror to behold such a sene." Terrified that the French were about to come upon them, her brother "immediately set out for n York & leave me to get a passage in the first Boat." They seem to have believed, probably correctly, that women were in greater danger of harassment with their men present.[64]

Prudence copied a letter from her father, written in August 1779, that suggests she and Hannah were supporting themselves by doing some sort of piecework. "Be good Girls lively & Airy not giving way to Malan-cholly," he wrote. "I desire that Prudy will not send any more Flowers to New York untill I come, & by all Means not to be Anxious about doing any sort of Work." Among his recommendations, he started to write the word *study,* then crossed it out, thinking perhaps that too much attention to books might threaten Prudence's delicate health. Instead he urged both daughters to "take all agreeble pastime." Their "Affectionate Unkle Doc-tor" added a postscript offering medical advice.[65]

Alarmed at his family's deteriorating health, Ebenezer once again set sail for London, hoping to secure a more lucrative appointment. In a nar-rative composed at Westminster in 1780, he described his family's "Sick-ness and Poverty." His wife was "frequently bereaved of her senses" and threatened to fall into a permanent delirium. "And my eldest Child, a young woman of great sensibility, is thrown into a nervus disorder called the *St. Vitus's Dance.*" Today physicians describe St. Vitus Dance as a temporary spasmodic condition caused by an untreated streptococcal infection, but in the eighteenth century it was associated with a mechani-cal dysfunction of the nerves, perhaps caused by too great a capacity for feeling. Under ordinary circumstances, "sensibility" was a positive qual-ity, a sign of delicacy and refinement, but under extreme misfortune it could become a disability. In her own letters Prudence assumed a noble posture. When her sister Hannah went to live with their father's sister, Clarina Bartow, in Westchester, New York, Prudence remained behind. She wrote her mother that while she could earn her own living, she had no mind "to sacrafise my Pride to the Gratifycation of another tho a kind

Near & Dear Aunt." Still she could not resist a tear. "I think, Dear Mama
with the Psalmist I may say—

> *Bereived Bereft of all am I,*
> *As dead & out of mind;*
> *& like a skaterd vesel lie,*
> *Whose parts can ner be joind."*

Acting nobly did not preclude displaying one's "sensibility."[66]

By December she was seriously ill. For five weeks she suffered with a
severe pain in her right arm and "a swelling just above my right Breast."
The doctor had "endeavoured to scatter it but to no purpose . . . the Cav-
ity of matter lay so deep in my stomock that he was obliged to cut 3 times
down with his launcet before he could reach it." Although two doctors
told her that the bone was "defected" and that she would be "long
desabled from the use of my nedle," she trespassed their limits to write
her sister an account of her illness. Then the letters stopped.[67]

When they resumed in January 1782, Prudence seemed vigorous and
happy. As the war wound down, she and Hannah were finally able to
leave Great Neck to meet their dear "Mama Brothers & Sisters whom
Adverse Fortune has not permited us to behold for these three years
Past." Back in East Hampton, she threw herself into a new family enterprise. Their house had become a "Beehive." They had "Three Schools in
it, besides Boarders & a large Family of our Selves, which leaves no one
room, but what is sufficiently Improved." Prudence herself had become a
teacher. She broke off a letter to Sally Rosseter, because the family clock
(she called it "our Hourly Monitor") summoned her to her classroom, "to
attend my little Companions who are all ready asembled, & waight my
approach."[68]

There are no more entries in the journal. On October 14, 1783, the
Anglican pastor at East Hampton married Prudence to Timothy Rosseter, the brother of her friend Sally. He may well have been the suitor she
left behind in Connecticut five years before. His father was the Congregational pastor at Preston. He himself had served as a physician in the
Continental Army. Yet somehow in the trials of war, these obstacles had
been removed. In the end, however, Prudence's embroidery proved
prophetic. On August 17, 1784, a month after giving birth to a daughter,
she died. She had named the baby Sophia for the virtuous sister in *The
Vicar of Wakefield*.[69]

Within a few months the remaining members of the Punderson family were back in Connecticut. In a letter to a friend still in London, the Anglican pastor at Norwich rejoiced that the "vindictive Spirit of the Country" had almost disappeared. As evidence, he offered the fact that "Our Friend Ebenezer Punderson, is returned to Pamutanoc with his Family, and our general Assembly have returned to him all his Estate; and he is well received,—and not a Mouth opened against him."[70] The war was at last over.

There are two footnotes to the story. One concerns Prudence's younger brother Ebenezer, who had spent part of the war with their father on Long Island and part in school in England. He was, according to family tradition, "a very gay blade," the sort of person the novels warned girls about. One day a young woman came to Ebenezer Sr., and told him that "her young sister, seventeen years old, who was teaching school in a little nearby village, was in trouble and that his son Ebenezer was responsible for it." In fiction this would have been the signal for the father to buy off the girl or disinherit the son, but this story ended differently. Ebenezer listened to the woman, asked a few questions, then summoned his son. Could he vouch for the girl's integrity up to the time of her encounter with him? He could. Then he asked him what he intended to do. "Young Ebbie had made no plans, for he did not suppose that his father would ever consent to his marrying the girl. Her family was very plain and in humble circumstances, but they were perfectly respectable, and the girl was pretty and very much in love with gay Ebbie. The old man said to him, 'If she is good enough to be your mistress, she is good enough to be your wife. You will marry her this week.' And he did." Reportedly, there never was a more devoted married couple.[71] To the end, Ebenezer remained a benevolent patriarch, using his authority as a father to enforce morality and protect a defenseless girl from the consequences of misguided love.

The second afternote concerns another dependent in the Punderson family, a person who may have appeared in Prudence's *Scenes of Mortality*. In the will he composed in 1805, Ebenezer made his bequests to his two sons conditional on their paying to their "Honoured Mother" a half dollar a week "for the support of my Negro Wench Jenny." If Jenny is the slave child in Prudence's embroidery, the person described as a "negro gal" in the inventory taken in 1775, she had spent the war with Ebenezer's mother. By 1805, however, slavery was becoming an anachronism in Connecticut. Although a handful of slaves remained with their masters until the end of their lives, Jenny did not. In 1807, as Jane Punderson, she married Neptune Jones, a New London mariner. He died at sea three years later. Undaunted, she married Sampson Cato in 1815, in New London's First Congregational Church, and was soon widowed. Just before her own death she did something unusual. Although she could neither read nor write, she composed a will. It is hard not to see this as an act of independence. "I Jane Cato," it began, continuing, "Whereas I have few debts if any & but little property in the whole I forbear to appoint an Executor but recommend my friend Caesar Anderson to take administration on my estate." She left her few possessions including her clothing to Caesar's wife, Susan.[72] In claiming the right to dispose of her own property, Jane asserted her personhood.

Prudence Punderson worked in silk, Betty Foot in wool. Though different, their words and works expose the dilemmas of white womanhood in eighteenth-century New England. Both women for a time lived by their needles. For Betty sewing was a temporary occupation on the path to teaching, for Prudence the only escape from wartime poverty and dependence. For both, self-support was an ideal, the aid of friends and family a necessity. Prudence's writing was effusive, Betty's economical. Yet both wrote of the treachery of men and the foolishness of lovers. Prudence's melodramatic warnings about seduction and Betty's casual descriptions of bundling suggest that for women at every social level sex was an insistent presence. Negotiating the "second scene of mortality" required a wary independence and a willingness to work. A woman could be ruined by indolence as well as by an untrue lover.

Prudence learned that women sometimes had to play the part of "amisons," though, for her, illness proved more dangerous than war. Betty lived until 1849, dying in her ninety-sixth year "full of faith, and with an unshaken hope of a blessed immortality." Her obituary added that she was "naturally possessed of a strong mind and very retentive memory, both of which had been strengthened by culture." Prudence and Betty were both strong women. Their memories survive because they had ego enough to sign their work and because their descendants cherished the fragmentary writing and the stitchery they produced in their youth.[73]

# *Molly Ocket's Pocketbook*

BETHEL, MAINE, 1785

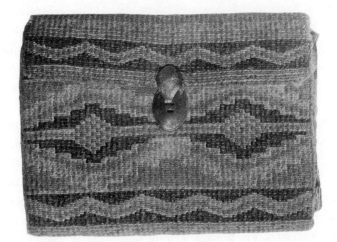

*Here lie the sturdy kings of Homespun, who climbed
among these hills, with their axes, to cut away room for
their cabins and for family prayers, and so for
the good future to come.*

Horace Bushnell, "The Age of Homespun"

In the accessions book of the Maine Historical Society, under the date September 15, 1863, following the notation for a fragment of Spanish cedar taken from the windowsill of the John Hancock Mansion in Boston, is the acknowledgment of the gift of "a pocket book made by Mollocket, the last of the Pequawkets." Mrs. Lucia Kimball of Bethel, Maine, gave it to the society through Dr. Nathaniel True, editor of the *Bethel Courier*, principal of Gould Academy, and collector of local history. The jingling rhyme of "pocket," "Mollocket," and "Pequawket" was not lost on the organizers of the society's exhibits. A faded label, still in the files of the museum, improved on the theme:

> *Old Mollocket*
> *Made this Pocket*
> *She was a Pequawket*
> *And last on the Docket*[1]

Straining for a closing rhyme, the would-be poet made Molly the last of a dying race, transforming her pocketbook into an antiquarian curiosity.

In the twentieth century it acquired more dignity. The first to discover its importance was Charles Willoughby, a self-taught anthropologist who began his career in Maine and went on to become director of the Peabody Museum at Harvard University. His *Antiquities of the New England Indians*, published in 1935, included a full-page photograph of the pocketbook, a diagram of its weave structure, and a technical discussion based on comparison with other twined textiles. His carefully documented discussion laid the groundwork for the inclusion of Molly's pocketbook in an archaeological exhibit that opened sixty years later at the Maine State Museum in Augusta, where the pocketbook is now on permanent loan.[2]

In this setting, Molly's pocketbook belongs to prehistory. Visitors to "12,000

*Preceding page:*
*Marie Agathe (Molly Ocket).*
*Twined pocketbook.*
COURTESY MAINE HISTORICAL
SOCIETY, ON LOAN TO MAINE STATE
MUSEUM, AUGUSTA, MAINE

Years in Maine" move up a carpeted ramp from 10,000 B.C. to the dawn of European exploration, learning how pottery shards, spear points, stone weights from fishnets, seeds, fruit pits, and pollen counts illuminate ancient lifeways. Using a technique that archaeologists called "upstreaming," the exhibit uses artifacts from later centuries to illustrate techniques developed in prehistoric times. Beyond a reconstructed shell heap or "midden" in a section devoted to technologies from the so-called Ceramic Period three thousand to five hundred years ago is Molly's little pocketbook. In the background of the exhibit case are screen prints of moose petroglyphs and in the foreground harpoons and spear points made from bone and antler. The label on the pocketbook acknowledges that it was made "in 1778 by Molly Ocket (Mary Agatha), an Abenaki woman who lived in the Rumford area," but justifies its inclusion in an exhibit on prehistory by observing that it is "the only surviving twined textile artifact from Maine."

Molly Ocket's pocketbook does document the persistence of ancient twining techniques, but it reveals as well the complex history of a people living in the violent borderland between New England and New France. The pocketbook is both an Abenaki and a colonial artifact. In the eighteenth century a pocketbook was a wallet, a place for keeping cash, receipts, and notes of hand—small slips of paper that fulfilled the same need as bank checks or a credit card would today. Molly made the fabric in the pocketbook, if not the pocketbook itself, for Eli Twitchell, a Bethel gunsmith who with his father and brothers helped to transform the site of an old Pigwacket village into an American town. The moose hair used to create its design not only illuminates Abenaki and New England lifeways but the embroidery traditions of French Canada. The wallet leads us, then, into a story about cultural exchange as well as conquest.

Molly Ocket was not "the last on the docket." She was a clever woman who knew how to survive in new circumstances, and she was a storyteller among storytellers. Because her people demanded attention from the Massachusetts government, sometimes as enemies, often as friends, much of her early life can be reconstructed from official documents. Because she was a powerful personality, her neighbors remembered her, preserving in their stories some evidence of her later life. The same people who told tales about Molly also told stories about themselves. Their stories document the ways in which memory transformed the violence of colonial conquest into a frontier pastoral.

· · ·

By 1770, central Maine was a patchwork of overlapping grants, some given to companies of merchants who promised to develop the land, others to descendants of men who had fought in the colonial wars. The country didn't yield easily to English domination. The landscape was too forbidding, the territory too great, and the French too accessible to those who considered the river valleys and intervales their homeland. Their Algonkian neighbors called them the "Wabenaki," or "people of the dawn." They lived in small family bands, moving with the seasons. Molly Ocket's people were named for a valley on the Saco River called Pigwacket—"the cleared place."[3]

This was the place Dover's minister John Pike described in 1703 when he told of soldiers bringing back six scalps, five captives, and a story about an abandoned fort at "Pequawket."[4] Pigwacket acquired a larger place in New England lore in April 1725, when a company under Captain John Lovewell headed up the Merrimac River and across the lake country of New Hampshire toward the peaceful valley they considered to be the headquarters of a dangerous enemy. Although Lovewell's father had served with Benjamin Church during King Philip's War, he was a mercenary, working for the scalp bounties offered by the Massachusetts government. He and his men paused at Ossipee to build a small fort, leaving seven men to guard supplies, then tramped toward the Saco. The route was well known. Lovewell himself had collected scalps in the area more than once, but this time he was on an official expedition with thirty-four of the best men he could find. On the morning of May 8, camped near a gentle pond scooped out of the mountains, they rose from prayers to spot an Indian on an opposite shore. Fearing they had been seen, they dropped their packs and raced toward him, little knowing that a larger force was already moving toward them from the opposite direction. In the battle that followed, Lovewell died almost immediately, but the rest of his men fought on, exchanging taunts and gunfire with Indians they had met before. At nightfall, the Pigwacket withdrew. Around midnight, the fifteen colonial soldiers remaining began the long journey back through the woods to Ossipee. When they got there, they found their impromptu fort deserted. Scrawling a message on birchbark, the rest of the company had fled.[5]

Lovewell's raid looms larger in New England folklore than in history. Less than three weeks after the battle, the *New England Courant* announced the publication of an "excellent new song" giving a full account of "the

bloody fight." The story was engaging because it described an open battle, not a series of skirmishes with a half-hidden enemy. In the words of
the balladeer, "the Indians were so thick, / A man could scarcely fire a
gun, and not some of them hit." It also provided heroes to mourn. Fourteen-year-old Susanna Rogers, daughter of the minister in Boxford,
Massachusetts, composed "A Mournful Elegy on Mr. Jonathan Frye," a
young man who purportedly prayed as the bullets flew around him, and
when wounded chose to die alone in the woods rather than impede the
retreat of his comrades. The mystique of Pigwacket survived into the
nineteenth century, forming the center of a tale by Nathaniel Hawthorne
and a poem by the young Henry Wadsworth Longfellow, who on the centennial of the fight in 1825 composed a "Commemoration Ode" that not
only honored the heroism of Massachusetts soldiers but acknowledged
the ancient woods where a "holier faith" replaced the "dark, mysterious
rite" of the red man.[6]

Molly Ocket too told stories about Lovewell's fight. Hers were so
vivid that some thought she had been there, but she was reporting things
she had heard from others.[7] Her modern biographers believe she was
born fifteen years after the battle at a site farther downriver. When she
was three or four years old, a tenuous peace between the Abenaki and the
English was once again broken. Colonists called the new conflagration
"King George's War" for their monarch, but to Molly's family it must
have seemed much like the others. Unwilling to endure another series of
raids, her parents and a few other families approached the truck master at
Saco, Captain Ammi Ruhamah Cutter, pledged their allegiance to the
English cause, and asked for protection.[8] Cutter didn't know how to handle their unexpected petition. He rushed off a letter to General William
Pepperrell at Kittery explaining that twenty Pigwackets had arrived at his
truck house, including an ailing woman who had died that morning. The
men were willing to fight with the English but "are loth to go & leave the
women & children—& I can't think it advisable to leave any of the men
behind—the People also of Beddeford are very averse to having any of
them tarry at the Falls—& ye Indians will by no means consent to go back
into the Woods for Fear of the French Indians." Pepperrell shot back a
reply. If the Pigwackets could be sent to Boston, the women and children
might be kept at government expense while men served as "pilates with
Our Scouts."[9]

Molly and her relatives sailed to Boston, where Governor Shirley was
happy to see them. Since this was the first instance of the so-called east-

ern Indians quitting the French in time of war, he wanted all measures taken "to convince them and others of those Tribes, how much they will find their Advantage in our Friendship and Protection." At the same time he hoped the legislature would consider how best to dispose of them "to save Charge to the Province, and to make them in some Measure useful to us."[10] On July 28, 1744, the Pigwacket leaders met with the Governor's Council to ask for a safe place to settle during the war. The minutes of that meeting show what it meant to come under the protection of Massachusetts. Shirley proposed settling them at Weymouth, south of Boston. The Pigwackets said they would rather live "at Saco River our Native Place where all our Friends lived." The governor said Weymouth was a better choice. It was only fifteen miles from Boston and three miles from the sea, and it "would be a great advantage to you to be so nigh me, that you may make your Application to me at any time." The legislature confirmed the governor's decision. The Pigwackets were to become wards of the state, semi-hostages living on a small reserve. As refugees, they could either accept the place offered or go home and face scalping parties from both sides.[11]

It wasn't as easy as Shirley thought to find a town in southern Massachusetts willing to accept them. The Pigwacket languished on Castle Island while a legislative committee considered their disposition. In December, the house agreed to supply corn, pork, molasses, and rum to "the Families of the three Pigwacket Indians now scouting with Capt. Jordan" in exchange for their making ten pairs of snowshoes per week. Jordan was to supply the materials and "inspect their Work as to the Sufficiency of the Bows and Strength and Form of filling them." He was also to bring down from the truck master at Saco "a Number of Snow Shoes in Part made, also sundry Bows and Materials for making others." The bows (or rackets) of snowshoes were typically made from bent ash, then filled in with rawhide strips woven hexagonally using a wood or bone needle. The instructions to Jordan suggest that even before the war, truck masters were serving as middlemen, collecting rawhide from one source and rackets from another, then putting them out to weavers. He was to set "an equitable Price on each Pair of Snow Shoes so made," subtracting the value of the materials and giving the Indians "the Benefit of the Overplus, if any there be."[12]

In February, a Pigwacket soldier who had already served with provincial troops at Annapolis-Royal asked the government for permission "to leave his Sister and his little Son in some Place that he shall chuse near

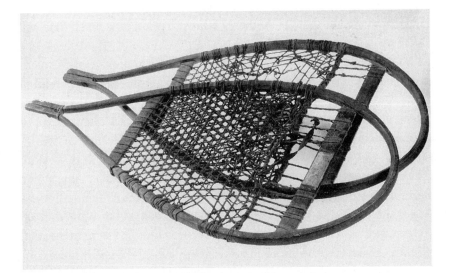

*Snowshoes purchased by Artemas Ward in 1758.*

ARTEMAS WARD HOUSE, SHREWSBURY,
MASSACHUSETTS, OWNED BY HARVARD UNIVERSITY.
PHOTOGRAPH BY HILLEL BURGER, PEABODY MUSEUM,
HARVARD UNIVERSITY

Boston, and enter himself a Voluntier." The government agreed, promising him arms, ammunition, provision, clothing, and his share of scalp money if he found a company willing to take him. Meanwhile, a committee empowered to investigate the situation on Castle Island recommended "the Remainder of the Pigwacket Indians (at least the young People that may consent to it) be disposed of in such English Families, as shall be willing on reasonable Conditions to receive them for a term of Years." If that didn't meet with the approval of the Indians, the government should try to find them someplace more agreeable to their way of life than Castle Island, where they could earn their keep by making snowshoes.[13]

Where the Pigwackets spent the next year is uncertain, but by June 1746 they were camped together on a neck of land in the town of Rochester, Plymouth County. Like Christian Indians elsewhere in Massachusetts, they had been given local guardians. The early plan to set them to work making snowshoes seems to have failed. In the account he submitted to the legislature, their guardian Noah Sprague charged the province ten pounds for the "ash & maple Timbers Cut in my Swamp to make Dishes & baskets being there Winter work." He also charged for the "cedar shingles they cut and rived out for their wigwams," for the green apples "no bigger than walnuts" they had picked, and for "a poor old Cow that Fell on the Ice & hurt her self which we kild for the Indians who complaind for want of Provision who Eat her Flesh & made Mogesins of her hide." He added thirty pounds (reduced to twenty-five) for his own "extraordinary Travlle & care."[14]

The Pigwackets were unhappy in their confining and poorly furnished reservation. Their English neighbors were also displeased. In August 1747, a Rochester resident petitioned the General Court, charging that "the Pigwacket Indians, placed in that Town by the Government, are very insolent and surly, and strike a great Dread to the Women and Children there: They therefore pray the said Indians may be removed from thence." The investigating committee blamed those who had sold them liquor and urged better supervision by the guardians. The Pigwackets were both exiles and visible representatives of a hated enemy. On the very day the petition charging them with insolence was presented to the legislature, a Northfield, Massachusetts, man turned an Abenaki scalp in to the assembly and asked for his bounty. Any Indian, including one willing to fight with the English, probably struck dread in the hearts of white children. (As late as 1900, residents of Rochester used the name *Pigwacket* for a rough tract of land at Assonomock Neck mostly unoccupied "and given up to woods and huckleberry pastures," though no one could remember where the name came from.)[15]

When the war ended in 1748, most of the Pigwackets went home, but a few children, including Molly Ocket, remained behind with white families. Were they refugees or hostages? In negotiations at Falmouth in 1749, the Abenaki spokesman asked for the return of a child living at Richmond's Island. When the commissioners answered, "That Boy was given to Capt. Jordan before the War, by his Father, who is since dead," one of the Pigwackets who had been in Boston retorted, "That boy was taken at Saco at the Same Time we were." The implication, of course, was that the Pigwackets who had spent the war in Massachusetts had been coerced into leaving their homeland. The assertion seems to have taken the commissioners by surprise, and they didn't respond until afternoon, when a Penobscot negotiator politely asked that three girls then at Plymouth—Ooneez, Mareuso, and Mareagit—be returned to "their native Land."[16]

The commissioners were indignant. "We suppose these are Pigwacket Indians. We shall force none of that Tribe to remain among the English, but they shall all be returned home. There was in the Morning something said by one of the Pigwackets, as if they were forced away from home. This is the first Time any such Thing has been publickly suggested. Capt. Cutter brought them up, and declared they desired to come and live with the English; and when the Government ask'd them if it was so, they declared that it was so. Soon after the treaty was appointed, the Government told them they might attend it if they would, and you now see them here with your own Eyes, at Liberty to return. And the Children were not kept back by the Government, but it was their own Choice, and they shall be sent down immediately." The Abenaki spokesman responded, as if setting an example for how to handle recalcitrant children, that they would gladly return the English boy still in Canada. If he said he didn't want to go home, they would "take him out a Hunting and return him." They obviously expected the English to do likewise.[17]

Molly Ocket had spent five years among the English, part of it among her own people at Castle Island and at Rochester, but some of it alone in an unknown English family. Perhaps she returned reluctantly. The English official who delivered the three girls said the Abenaki "carried them into the Woods, tho much against their Inclinations." Molly had learned many things while in Massachusetts, not the least of which was English.[18] She next appears in Catholic mission records at St. Francis, Quebec, where in 1764 her daughter Molly Susup, listed in mission records as Marie Marguerite Joseph, daughter of Marie Agathe and Pierre Joseph, was baptized.[19]

By then English colonists had begun to move into the old Pigwacket homeland. In 1761, Colonel Joseph Frye of Andover, Massachusetts, petitioned the General Court for permission to lay out a township between the lower settlement on the Saco River and the "Mountains above Pigwacket." A member of the force that had captured Louisbourg in 1755, Frye fled Fort William Henry when it was conquered by the French, killing an Abenaki pursuer with his bare hands, then wandering through the woods "subsisting only on whortleberries" until he reached the safety of another English outpost. Having "spent the prime of his life in the defence of his Country," he believed he deserved a new start. By paying a hundred pounds and promising to settle his land with sixty good families, he won the right to lay out and name his town.[20]

He was not the only one who had found the Pigwacket country attractive. Like the Abenaki, the first Englishmen who wintered in the north country relied on meat, shooting what they could find and dragging it out of the woods before the wolves came, but their objective was to replace wild animals with their own herds. In 1762, two Massachusetts men and an African slave drove a hundred head of cattle and eleven horses from Gorham, Maine, cutting wild hay near Lovewell's Pond to feed their animals through the winter. In stories told long after the fact, some described feasting in the spring on hasty pudding, partridge eggs, cream, and maple sugar. The milk was so plentiful, they said, that it ran down the hills. Others remembered thin cattle huddled against the wind and the faint sweetness of cornmeal boiled in sap as thin as when it came from the tree.[21] Maine was both a forbidding and an appealing land.

Soon hopeful settlers from southern Massachusetts came up the Saco in canoes or overland in ox teams to Fryeburg. Some followed the old military route from Ossipee. A half dozen families arrived in 1763, and a few more the following year. Caleb Swan, a Harvard graduate and classmate of John Adams, took up land in 1766. A dozen more families arrived in 1767. By then, Fryeburg residents had established a small trade in beaver and sable skins, buying them from local Indians, then carrying them down the Saco to Biddeford to trade for grain.[22] North of Fryeburg on the Androscoggin River, another group of settlers was carving out the township that became Bethel. Its original name was "Sudbury-Canada" because the land grant was based on a long overdue promise to heirs of Sudbury, Massachusetts, men who participated in a 1690 expedition to Canada. The defeat of France in the Seven Years' War finally allowed their heirs to take up the land.[23] Molly Ocket and her people moved in and out of the area, sometimes trading at Fryeburg, sometimes at Bethel, but retaining strong ties to Quebec.

In 1772, a sometime soldier, thief, and common laborer named Henry Tufts heard of an Indian healer living near Sudbury-Canada. He had been wounded in a drunken frolic, and somebody told him the Indian might help him. Limping toward what seemed to him the outer limits of civilization, he found the Pigwacket village. At first he was put off by the ragged wigwams and the strange language, but a few Indians who spoke English, "though broken," soon appeared. Among them was Molly Ocket, "the great Indian doctress," who agreed to take on his case. She visited him daily on his bed of bearskins, and though her potions "ill accorded with the gust of an Englishman," they worked. Tufts was soon joining Molly's kinsmen in hunting. He stayed with Molly's band almost two years, bribing his hosts with rum to get them to teach him the secrets of their medicine. Tufts thought the larger confederation of which Molly's village was a part "was in number about seven hundred of both sexes, and extended their settlements, in a scattering, desultory manner, from Lake Memphremagog to lake Umbagog, covering an extent of some eighty miles." In one village, he visited "with old king Tumkin Hagen, who was at the head of the whole tribe."[24]

Tufts said Molly went to Quebec every spring for Catholic rites, but though he acknowledged that she sold her furs for cash and sometimes had as much as forty dollars on hand, he did not mention any intercourse with the new English settlements nearby. In his account, the Abenaki villages exist in a world far beyond whites. Yet Molly and her kin were already connected to traders at Fryeburg and Bethel. Some said she was living with the Indian guide Sabbatus in these years. Others noted her connection to James and Mary Swan, who were in Fryeburg by 1766 and in Bethel a decade later.[25]

By 1770 there were fifty families in Fryeburg. As town founder and would-be benefactor, Colonel Frye alternated between poetic rhapsody and officious meddling. His "Memorandum Book of the Loan of Tools," begun in 1773, annoyed some of his neighbors who thought borrowing was a rite of friendship and resented having to sign a promissory note, but he had lost too many tools, he said, to indulge in sentimentality. In a more contented mood, he composed an ode to the "verdant groves" and "sylvan songsters" of his new home:

> *I would not change these rural scenes*
> *For what in Court is to be found,*
> *Nor quit these groves and purling streams*
> *For highest rank on hostile ground.*[26]

There was no memory here of the blood spilled in these groves and streams during a half century of war. The land was now blessedly free of hostile Indians—or so men thought.

The American Revolution led to one more skirmish between the Pigwackets and their white neighbors. Like other Abenaki bands, they were involved on both sides, never formally or in mass, but in small raids emanating from St. Francis or one of the American forts. According to an Abenaki woman who, like Molly, lived near the Androscoggin, the pressure to join one side or the other was so intense that the men in her band were unable to hunt or provide for their families. She could understand the old battles between men of different nations, but this war was unexplainable. "O, strange *Englishmen* kill one another," she said. "I think the world is coming to an end." She knew only one thing, that the land she stood on was her country. "Why should we fight for t'other country, for we never see t'other country; our hunting is in this country."[27] Most of the new inhabitants of interior Maine agreed. What they wanted was a chance to feed their own families in the Abenaki land of milk and maple sugar.

On August 3, 1781, Nathaniel Segar and two companions were working in a small clearing in Sudbury-Canada when six Indians "came running out of the woods, and told us that we were their prisoners." Segar was surprised as well as frightened. He knew one of them, "named Tomhegan, for he had been often at my house." This was no doubt the man Tufts had called Tumkin Hagen. Now engaged in mercenary work for the British, he and the others were painted and armed with guns, tomahawks, and scalping knives. Raiding isolated cabins as they made their progress upriver, they were alternately merciful and unfeeling. They let one man go because he didn't have any shoes, then had second thoughts and went back and scalped him. They were gentle with women, even those who talked back, but on the trail terrorized their captives by pulling bloody scalps from their packs, clasping the hair in their teeth, then shaking their heads as they jumped from rock to rock, whooping and singing. They cracked lice with their teeth and in one frontier cabin dumped maple sugar into a tub of cream, slurping it up like hogs. They seemed to operate according to an unspoken quota. If they found a prisoner they liked better, like the African named Plato who was working with his master in the woods, they let others go, leaving them to perish or find their way home.[28]

Tomhegan and his men delivered their prisoners to the British command at St. Francis, collected their bounty, and went back to hunting. Nathaniel Segar and his companions spent the rest of the war in a prison camp at Montreal, where their treatment, they said, was worse than what they had received from their Abenaki captors. Many years later, a Bethel woman recalled visiting Segar as a child, hearing him tell his story, and seeing the watch case he had carved with a pocketknife during his imprisonment. He was now a revered hero of the American Revolution.[29]

Molly Ocket's pocketbook preserves a different story, a story of intercultural exchange rather than war. The weave structure is Algonkian, the form European. Combining native hemp and moose hair with a commercially woven wool lining, it shows the complex intertwining of cultures in this period. It is particularly interesting in the light of Noah Sprague's comments about the work performed by the Pigwackets who lived in Massachusetts in 1747. His reference to "ash & maple Timbers Cut in my Swamp to make Dishes & baskets" suggests two familiar Native American technologies—the creation of deep bowls burned and chiseled out of hardwoods and baskets woven from rived ash splints. Molly's twining is quite unlike these products.

Like Dinah Fenner's basket, it employs techniques thousands of years old, but it also relates to a newer traffic in moose hair emanating from the French mission schools. Sisters at the Ursuline convent in Quebec began experimenting with moose-hair embroidery in the early eighteenth century, during a period when imported threads were scarce. By 1714, nuns at Trois-Rivières were already skilled in working embroidered flowers on birch bark, using the long hairs of the moose as a substitute for silk. This was painstaking work. Even the longest hairs on the moose, those found on the mane, cheeks, and rump, were much shorter than embroidery threads.[30] In 1792, Mrs. John Graves Simcoe, wife of the English governor of the newly established province of Upper Canada, saw birch-bark boxes and pincushions worked at Montreal that used dyed moose hair to create naturalistic roses and forget-me-nots. "It is so short that it must be put through the Needle for every stitch," Simcoe marveled. The same kind of work was done at Trois-Rivières, where pocketbooks, work baskets, and dressing boxes were produced for sale to white colonists and visitors.[31]

The anthropologist and art historian Ruth Phillips argues that the persistence of this sort of work after supplies of more conventional materials became available shows the significance of indigenous art in an emerging white identity. "As the largest of the deer family the moose conveyed an idea of the grandeur of the northeastern forests and the heroic strength Aboriginal hunters need to do battle with them." After the conquest of French Canada, the English picked up these themes. By 1790, young ladies' schools in New Brunswick were teaching birch-bark embroidery as well as conventional needlework.[32] Using moose hair to embroider garden flowers on bark, they imagined a marriage between the American landscape and European art. Some white women carried the affectation even further. In 1791, a New Brunswick woman gave Margaret Shippen Arnold, wife of the American turncoat Benedict Arnold, an elaborate workbox embroidered with moose-hair forget-me-nots and roses. Inside it is a poem ostensibly written by "Elasaba of the Micmac Tribe."

> *When more pleasing scenes engage*
> *And you in polished circles shine*
> *Then let this wild, savage page*
> *Declare that gratitude is mine*
> *October 7th 1791.*

The poet may have been an assimilated Micmac, but it is just as likely she was a white women who had discovered the power of moose-hair embroidery as "an exotic signifier of North America."[33]

Molly, too, worked in moose hair, but her technique was radically different. She created her design as she twined, wrapping the outer thread in each weft with three twists of moose hair, alternating colors. There was no need for a needle since the ground fabric and the embroidery devel-

*Commonplace book with moose-hair—embroidered birch-bark covers, probably Quebec convent work.*
PEABODY MUSEUM, HARVARD UNIVERSITY. PHOTOGRAPH BY HILLEL BURGER

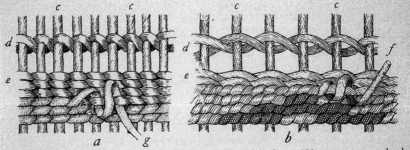

Figure 137. a, Method of weaving the bag illustrated in figure 136: c, c, warp cords; d, double woof cord; e, woof cords pressed close together; g, method of applying the porcupine quills. b, Technique of the weave of wallet shown in figure 138: c, c, warp cords; d, double woof cord; e, woof cords pressed close together; f, way of applying the moose hair which is wrapped three times around each twist of the woof strand instead of once as in the quill, g. (Enlarged.)

*From Charles Willoughby,* Antiquities of the New England Indians. *The figure on the left is the Yohicake bag pictured on page 49. The figure on the right is Molly Ocket's pocketbook.*

COURTESY PEABODY MUSEUM, HARVARD UNIVERSITY

oped together. Like most twined textiles from the northern woodlands, her design was geometric, diagonal in its individual elements, and arranged in broad bands.[34] She used the natural white underhairs of the moose together with dyed fibers in red, green, blue, or yellow. No one has yet attempted to identify the source of her dyes. Seventeenth-century coastal Indians used bloodroot, red bedstraw, and various barks to dye the porcupine quills they used to ornament their clothing, and other sources suggest that native dyers supplied moose hair to the convents, but until someone attempts to analyze the pigments in the moose hair, there is no way of knowing for sure how Molly's pocketbook was colored. As Charles Willoughby observed, the twining itself is "an illustration of the highest development of the native textile industry." The pocketbook is small, the outer fabric measuring only 4¾ by 11 inches, but the gauge is so fine that it must have taken many hours to complete. Although the colors have faded, the fabric is still beautiful, delicate in conception and execution.[35]

Molly's design sense confirms the backhanded evidence in Tufts's narrative about her people's love of ornament. He said that the interior of Tomhegan's wigwam was ornamented with "rude drafts and pictures" representing animals, people, and implements of war, and that his wife's clothing was "somewhat gaudy." She wore "nose and ear jewels, and bracelets on her arms; besides a variety of trinkets and gewgaws decorating the other parts of her body." Later accounts allude to Molly's jewelry and describe her as a "pretty, genteel squaw." According to one Maine traveler, Penobscots in this period wore a combination of European and indigenous clothing. Women, like men, covered their legs and feet with embroidered stockings made from trade cloth. Their deerskin moccasins were "elegantly fashioned and ornamented with porcupine quills," sometimes having "little tassels made of a tin cylinder packed with deer hair colored red" that created a "pleasing rustle" as they walked.[36] In 1817, an unknown artist painted a Passamaquoddy girl at a British fort. She had large hoops in her ears, a string of beads and a cross at her neck, and silver medallions on her breast. Her pointed cap was embellished with bands of ribbon or embroidery much like those on Molly's pocketbook. Although there are few references to Molly's clothing, settlers did remember her jewelry. A Gilead woman who knew her well recalled a "pointed cap."[37]

Pocketbooks were European in conception. They were useful accessories, designed to hold important papers and cash, but also to make a statement when lifted from a pocket. A Boston shop in the 1750s displayed them with French necklaces, wig ribbons, Merry Andrew cards, hoop petticoats, and walking canes with ends shaped like "Negro Heads."[38] The Abenaki understood their function. In July 1727, a committee of the Massachusetts House heard complaints that Captain William Woodside of Fort George had been overcharging Indians for goods. Among the exorbitantly priced items were a silk checked shirt, ruffles of striped muslin, a "pocket book," and "a housewife."[39] A "housewife" was a narrow pouch stitched into small compartments for needles, pins, and thread. Like a pocketbook, it was meant to be folded and placed in a pocket.

Pocketbooks could be used by either sex, but the pockets that held them were different. Men's coats had built-in pockets as early as 1550. Women's pockets were detachable pouches tied to a cord that went around the waist.[40] Newspaper advertisements for lost property suggest that then as now there were not only differences in the possessions the two sexes acquired, but in the way they carried them. In 1763 a man's lost *pocketbook* had pieces of silver, paper money, invoices of goods, lottery tickets, and several receipts. In contrast, a woman's lost *pocket* had earrings, buttons, a silver thimble, and a stay hook in the shape of a heart.[41]

*Watercolor portrait of Denny*
*Sockabasin, daughter of a*
*Passamaquoddy chief, at a*
*British Fort, 1817.*
COURTESY ABBY ALDRICH
ROCKEFELLER FOLK ART MUSEUM,
WILLIAMSBURG, VIRGINIA

*The outside of Molly Ocket's*
*pocketbook, open.*
COURTESY MAINE HISTORICAL SOCIETY,
ON LOAN TO MAINE STATE MUSEUM,
AUGUSTA, MAINE

Women were more likely to embroider than to own a pocketbook. Ebenezer Punderson owned a tent-stitch pocketbook worked by his wife or daughter. Matthew Patten received "a purse workt in holes with Creall [crewel]" from the wife of a friend. He didn't have the vocabulary to identify the technique she used, but it was surely queen stitch, which was worked on a canvas and did indeed produce small perforations like tiny buttonholes.[42] Eli Twitchell would have been perfectly comfortable, then, putting his cash in an ornamental wallet. Whether Molly or some other person transformed the twining into its present form, we do not know. Twitchell's is a "double pocket-book" like Punderson's, though its two side-pleated pouches were sewn into a lining made from green wool. Twitchell used his pocketbook. The binding on the edges is almost worn through, exposing the blue wool used to baste it.[43]

Twitchell's father, fourth in an unbroken succession of Joseph Twitchells, was one of the original grantees of Sudbury-Canada. Born in Sherburne, Massachusetts, he became captain of the militia, town clerk, representative, judge, and sometime guardian to the Christian Indians at

*Embroidered pocket. Made by a "Miss Lambert of Salem, who married Samuel Woodkin, Soldier in the French War."*

*Ebenezer Punderson pocketbook, showing inside pouches.*

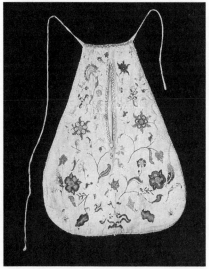

nearby Natick. According to Twitchell family lore, Indians came to the old homestead long after their father's death "to see if there was not something still due them." That is probably true. During Twitchell's lifetime, Natick Indians had control over their own affairs. As land sales whittled away their original grants, the remaining Indian inhabitants were increasingly dependent on the white men who employed them as farm laborers, surveyed their land, indentured their children, and administered their estates. By then most of his descendants were in Bethel. The population growth that hounded Indians out of Natick took the descendants of Englishmen to Maine. In the 1760s, Twitchell bought up the best mill lots and nearly all the land on which the compact part of Bethel now stands. Although he remained in Sherburne, four of his sons became Bethel residents.[44]

Eli Twitchell marched with Middlesex militia to Bunker Hill in 1775, but he was no military hero. He thought that carrying a heavy pack when he was still a young boy led to the disease that later required cutting away part of the bone in his arm. His injury prevented him from engaging in heavy labor, but he became a gunsmith and sometime jeweler. Old-timers recalled that in the early years at Bethel, groups of Abenaki came down the Androscoggin in canoes to have their guns and jewelry repaired. Molly Ocket may have been among them.[45]

The label Twitchell's daughter Lucia Kimball attached to the pocketbook when she gave it to the Maine Historical Society said it was made "about the year 1785," yet the silver clasp she attributed to her father is clearly dated 1778.[46] Since the inscription also misidentified the materials, saying the pocketbook was made from "HedgeHog Quills," the label may simply be in error. But it is also possible the clasp was recycled from another object. Seven years was time enough to wear out a pocketbook, especially one that was cheap or poorly made. If so, the original pocketbook may have provided the dimensions of the fabric Molly twined.

Molly surely understood the power of money. According to Tufts she kept a cache of coins in her wigwam. A poor white man who knew this came begging for cash one winter to buy corn for his starving family. "She rallied him on the score of his coming to borrow of the poor Indians, who (she said) were generally despised by the white people." Still she gave him the money and told him to come back the next year and trap furs with her to pay the debt. He kept his word. Tufts's Molly is a savvy trader as well as a skilled healer, a woman used to bargaining for furs and dispensing cash. On one of her trips to Quebec, he said, she gave the priest money to pray her dead husband out of purgatory. When he responded to her insistent questions by telling her that his prayers had been efficacious, she scraped "the money off the table into the corner of her blanket," tied it up, and left. Molly may or may not have had a pocketbook, but she knew about money.[47]

In the nineteenth century, stories about Molly's money grew into legends. Some people thought she had coins buried in a teakettle on the side of a hill. They tried for years to find where her pot was. Finally someone discovered an effigy of an arrow on a stone in the woods. He and his friends continued in that direction until they came to a larger stone marked with a cross. Unfortunately, just as they began to dig, they remembered that it was the Sabbath. Returning on Monday morning, they saw two men leaving with something that looked like a kettle hanging on a pole between their shoulders. They never did see Molly's money.[48] Sylvanus Poor, who knew Molly well in the last years of her life, told a different story. He said she had "a large supply of bracelets, jewelry, &c," but that she gave most of it away before her death.[49] Most stories about Molly emphasize her generosity, and they may have been true. Unlike Joseph Frye, she was comfortable borrowing and lending, trusting that what she gave would return to her in some form. But figuring Molly in this way allowed people to believe that their possession of Pigwacket land was benign, that they were the natural successors rather than the conquerors of the Abenaki. The story about Molly's pot of coins may have been more honest. In their hunger for Indian land, sabbath breakers and the pious went after the same pot of gold.

The pocketbook Molly made for Eli Twitchell shows the contradictory impulses that characterized economic life in the mountain valleys of northern New England. Cash mattered, but survival depended on maintaining a web of relationships that transcended market values. Molly was both an outsider and a participant in that world. To understand her story, we need to know the stories white settlers told about themselves.

Bethel's first settlers told contradictory stories about the olden time. Some of these survive only in family papers; others appeared in town histories in the nineteenth century. Alternating between nostalgia and humor, they figured a past strangely attractive yet irreversibly lost.

The landscape was a "royal hunting ground," a land that gave its gifts unbidden and without labor. Yet danger lurked in the woods, not just the threat of Indians or marauding wolves, but the temptations of indolence, intemperance, and rage. Men and women who moved to such a place needed to be stronger and braver than folks in more settled places. In subduing a wild landscape, they subdued themselves, becoming a people worthy of the name *Bethel,* the place where God appeared to Abraham and said, "Unto thy seed will I give this land," and where Jacob took a stone for a pillow and dreamed a dream that his seed would be "as the dust of the earth, and . . . spread abroad to the west, and to the east, and to the north, and to the south." The town's first pastor, Eliphaz Chapman, suggested the name. Like many others, he had traveled from Massachusetts to Sudbury-Canada in the 1780s, trudging overland to York, then across to Saco, up the river to Fryeburg, and along the old Indian trail where he built a log house for his family. His children eventually spread out, helping to found the town of Gilead, near Bear Mountain to the west.[50]

Settlers arrived with their kin. By 1790, there were almost sixty families in Bethel. All but twelve shared a surname with someone else. Four of Joseph Twitchell's sons—Eleazar, Eli, Joseph, Jr., and Peter—took up land laid out by their father. Six of the ten children of Moses Mason of Dublin, New Hampshire, settled in Bethel, but because three of them were daughters their names were not Mason but Twitchell, Marshall, and Clark. The town had five households headed by a Bartlett and five more by a Russel, four families named Bean, and three each named Abbott, Grover, Kilgore, Powers, and Swan. Settlers came from towns all over Massachusetts, from interior New Hampshire, and from older towns in Maine, and because they were young the town kept growing. In 1790, half the population of Bethel was under the age of sixteen.[51]

Like farmers all over New England, Bethel pioneers uncovered ancient relics as they plowed, but because the Abenaki had only recently departed, they occasionally uncovered strangely familiar things, old cellar holes that once held corn, the skeleton of a girl Molly Ocket said had been killed in a drunken frolic, and, in one old camping ground, a cache of guns. Oliver Fenno, the town blacksmith, decided the barrels would make good shovel handles. One day, "as he was heating a barrel at his forge, an unseen charge of powder exploded sending the ball through the workbench on the opposite side of his shop."[52]

There were still Indians around when the first families came. Some, like Molly, became local fixtures. Others came down the river in their canoes once a year, camping for several weeks at a time, making moccasins, baskets, and birch-bark boxes to trade for tobacco, alcohol, cloth, and food. They "used to speak of the happy people that formerly dwelt there, away from the incursions of the whites," and they insisted that their people had never sold the land above Lewiston Falls.[53] Molly, too, claimed the valley where Bethel sat as her homeland, boasting of her noble descent and "the bravery of her father and grandfather who, she said, were prominent chiefs in their tribe, and who had passed through all the exciting scenes of warfare between the French and English during the 17th and 18th centuries."[54]

White folks, too, told stories about the war, but they muted the violence. Maybe it was close acquaintance with Abenaki children, including Molly's daughter, that led one man to talk about how the raid on St. Francis with Roger's Rangers had sickened him. He said they had been ordered to kill all the women and children, but when a "papoose" looked up at him, he couldn't make himself do it. Seeing his hesitation, his commander snapped, "Nits will be lice," and killed her himself. The raid on Bethel in 1783 left fear and bitter feelings, but some Abenaki, too, thought Tomhegan was a rogue. Sabbatus led the party that went after him.[55]

After the Revolution, war gave way to friendly contests of skill. Bethel folks remembered wrestling matches with visiting Abenaki, recalling with pleasure the time Jonathan Barker defeated a string of braves camped on the Alder River. Nobody could wrestle like Eli Twitchell's brother Pete, who had wit as well as muscle. One day he told a companion he was strong enough to throw him over the house. When the fellow took the challenge, Twitchell picked him up and clambered up a long-sloping roof that reached almost to the ground. He was just ready to throw his opponent off the peak when he yelled "Enough!"[56] People also said that Molly's daughter, Molly Susup, who went to school with Bethel children, used to "engage in sports with the boys, with whom she was frequently more than a match."[57]

Women who told stories about Tomhegan's raid were as likely to focus on their own fright and foolishness as on the danger. Abigail Bean's descendants said that when their grandmother heard that Indians were ransacking Bethel, she packed her children into a canoe and crossed the

Androscoggin River to her brother's house. "*There* said she I have forgotten to feed my little pig it will starve." He brother "jumped into the boat and paddled acrossed the river, and to his surprise little piggie had a peck of Corn Meal dough in its trough. Grandma was so excited she did not know what she was doing."[58] Lucy Marshall's story is more somber, but it too focuses on the small details of frontier life. When a neighbor ran to their house to tell them that Nathaniel Segar and his companions had been taken, they threw some provisions in a sack, gathered up their children, and rushed away, hoping to find shelter at a homestead several miles away. When they finally sat down to rest, Lucy was dismayed at her lack of clothing, "for during the morning I had slipped off my shoes, having nothing on except a thin skirt and a handkerchief over my shoulders." Like many rural women, she didn't bother in summer with the layers of clothing propriety required. Throwing a kerchief and simple skirt over the linen shift she had slept in, she plaited her hair in a long braid, dispensing with a cap.[59]

Jonathan Clark's wife, on the other hand, was all dressed up when Tomhegan and his party found her. While they rifled her house, she quickly hid her husband's silver watch in the ashes. They tried to take her gold necklace from her neck, "but the string broke and the beads were scattered about the room." After they left, she was able to find almost all the beads. Segar said that when the Indians tried to take the silver buckles from her shoes, "she asked them what business they had with her feet, and they finally left them." He was afraid they would kill her for her boldness, but she "shewed no fear."[60]

Other stories celebrated frontier abundance and the adventure that came with it. Men remembered Sudbury-Canada as a hunter's paradise. There were trout, salmon, sturgeon, otter, beaver, mink, sable, and muskrat in the creeks and rivers, and moose and deer in the woods. One year, three men alone killed sixty moose. "They tried out the tallow for candles, cut off and carried away the best portions for food, and left the remainder to be devoured by wolves." It was also a birdhunter's dream. In 1791, thousands of wild pigeons nested west of Bethel Hill. For weeks, settlers feasted on the young squabs, which were easy to catch and fat and tender just before they were able to fly.[61] Molly's friend Sabbatus used to bring home the lip of a moose as a special treat for his employer, Nathaniel Swan. Molly too "would go into the woods, shoot a moose, and then come out to the settlement for assistance to bring in her game." So abundant were ducks in these years that she "shot and saved feathers sufficient to make a good bed for her friend, Mrs. Swan."[62]

Memories of winter hunting expeditions surely contributed to old Jonathan Bean's fantasy that he could walk on water. As an old man he lost his reason and one summer day strapped on his snowshoes and started to cross the Androscoggin. Fortunately, someone in the family rescued him as he sank.[63] In her own old age, his granddaughter Lucy Smith remembered every detail of this wild landscape. She and her siblings used to go into the woods to find the cows in their pasture a mile or more away, walking through "two swamps of Firs Hemlock and Basswood," and then what seemed like an immense journey through "Poplars Willows Alders Elms and Maple" until they could sit down in the little clearing and tell Rover to go get the cows. One night near dusk, he refused to move. No matter how they tried, he would "curl his tail between his legs and look up and whine." The next day their father found bear tracks on the hill. Another time Lucy's mother chastised her for running through the wheat field when she thought she saw a bear, but when her two brothers, coming home by the pasture road, got a sight of him, she forgave her. The littlest brother had a hard time running since he was wearing a pair of his father's old boots.[64]

Bears were a nuisance—killing sheep, robbing beehives, and rifling corn—but they seldom attacked humans, except in stories. Enoch Foster liked to tell how he raced up a tree, shaking the trunk furiously to dislodge the snarling animal creeping up the trunk toward him. When it fell, it continued to circle the tree. Certain he was doomed, he punctured a vessel in his arm and using a pointed stick wrote in blood on his handkerchief, "killed by a bear." Fortunately, the bear got bored and went home.[65]

That story wasn't as good as the one told in Fryeburg about Hugh Stirling's wife, Isabel. Like Molly Ocket, she could handle a gun. When her husband was laid up with rheumatism, he craved the taste of venison steak. She, knowing there had been several white frosts and that the acorns were falling fast, knew where to look. Taking her gun, she went before sunset to a nearby grove. Sure enough deer soon came to feed. She felled a fine buck and was reloading her gun when she heard "the snarls of a catamount." The cat sprang at a bear that was just coming out of the woods, "fastened his teeth in its throat, and tore it. But the bear was not idle. It held the cat by the neck, and with the claws of its hind feet tore the body of the cat." It was a duel to the death. Isabel sat quietly in her perch until both animals were dead, then went home and cooked her husband a venison steak. Isabel Stirling had her equal in Mrs. Samuel Osgood, who drove off wolves from her sheep "armed only with her broom."[66]

These stalwart housewives were prodigies of production. During the "great freshet" of 1785, Joseph Swan's wife sat at her loom until the water rose to the sills, finally escaping out of an upstairs chamber, lamenting the web she had left. A Fryeburg woman was so industrious that one day after cooking the noon meal, she spent the afternoon spinning, washing, and scouring yarn. After her children were in bed, she "knit a pair of breeches, bound and finished them, so that her brother could wear them the next morning." Mary Stirling, the daughter of the woman who shot her own steak, was also devoted to cloth-making. She walked home from a neighbor's house on snowshoes, carrying the flax they had given her for a stint at nursing, combed and dressed it herself, spun the yarn, wove and whitened it, then sent her father on horseback to the coast to sell it.[67] No wonder an eccentric farmer complained about his feeble wife. He had been cheated, he said. When they were courting, "her friends had collected all the yarn in the neighborhood and hung it up around her room and made me think it was her own spinning." After marriage he was forced to take care of her.[68]

In the stories the fringes of woods and pastures offered both food and danger. Lucy Smith recalled that in her childhood, blackberries, blueberries, and raspberries were never far from the cabin. One day when her parents were out picking and she was left in the care of her older sister, she decided to go find some berries for herself, but when she tried to go home she could not find the way. She wandered from one seeming path to another looking for the window in the back of the cabin, until, hopelessly lost, she sat down "in the midst of windfalls in the shape of a house" and started to cry. Fortunately, her parents heard her as they were returning with their own berries. In old age, she could still remember the comfort of her father's arms and the taste of berries on her tongue. "Father stood me on one of the logs, I clasped my arms around his neck and he carried me home, they gave me some Blackberries, calling me their little lost girl. I can recollect all this perfectly, but how I got over the two booming high brooks, I never could tell, nor the too high log fences." Her parents said some "evil Genius" had carried her there.[69] In or out of the woods, in the sunlight of the pasture on a summer day, or under the heavy coverlets of winter, there were unseen forces. Life was a struggle between the angels of light and darkness.

Lucia Kimball remembered gathering blueberries as a child with Molly, but it was the minister's wife who told about the time Molly brought a pailful of blueberries to the house early on a Monday morning. They were so fresh Mrs. Chapman suspected they had been picked on Sunday, and she scolded her for violating the Sabbath. Molly was offended and stayed away for weeks. When she came back, she refused to sit down to dinner, saying it would choke her. She had been right "picking those blueberries on Sunday, it was so pleasant, and I was so happy that the Great Spirit had provided them for me." According to Nathaniel True, the woman "felt more than half condemned for reproving her as she did. Who could possibly judge this child of nature by the same law that would condemn those more enlightened."[70] In this telling, Molly, like the wolves and the berries, belonged to the landscape.

Maine pioneers were both attracted to and repelled by wilderness life. They admired Indian resilience yet feared Indian hunger. A Vermont family remembered meeting Molly near the Connecticut River in the dead of winter. Finding "she was scantily supplied with provisions, having nothing but a little bread," they gave her a large piece of pork from the barrel in their sleigh. Molly reciprocated by sharing one of her medicinal secrets. In the nineteenth century stories of her medical prowess spread from the mountains of Vermont to the coast of Maine, growing more elaborate with each telling. People said she cured families in Troy and Potton, Vermont, of a virulent dysentery "with a decoction of the inner bark of the spruce" and salved the bruises of a man wounded in a drunken frolic with "an application of warm milk punch." She taught a little girl in Newry how to count in "Indian," then shared secrets of roots and dyes. She treated an infected hand with the pounded roots of Solomon's seal, which she gathered on Jockey Cap Ridge near a depression now named "Molly Ockett's Cave." She delivered the first white child born in Andover, Maine, and she knew the powers of the mineral waters at Poland Spring. Somebody even claimed that in Paris Hill in 1809, she treated the infant Hannibal Hamlin, later to become vice president under Abraham Lincoln.[71]

The stories about Molly grew larger over time. A Vermont minister who met her for the first time in 1785 said that if her statement that her husband and son had died in Lovewell's War were correct, "she was then more than 100 years old. . . . I saw and conversed with her frequently, from 1812 to 1816 and have no doubt that she was born earlier than 1685, and that her statements were generally to be credited."[72] Imagining Molly as a witness to Lovewell's fight provided a peaceful ending to a frightening story. Men gave their lives to subdue the wilderness, but in the end the descendants of the Abenaki became their friends. Combining stories about frontier abundance with stories of Indian hunger performed a similar function, making the disappearance of Molly's people seem as inevitable as the disappearance of wild pigeons. Tales about pioneer women as courageous and powerful as Molly gave white settlers a claim on the land. When there were too few ducks to provide feathers for bed ticks, dooryard geese would fill the need. Beside the prodigious production of household looms, Molly's pocketbook seemed almost frivolous.

Molly Ocket may have lived close to nature, but she was no child. She was an intelligent and resourceful woman who learned how to walk between two worlds without losing her way. As her biographers Bunny McBride and Harold Prins have observed, she learned early that whether she liked it or not, she "had to befriend settlers to survive." But she refused to become "a small bead on someone else's dress." The five years she spent in Massachusetts prepared her to interact with English-speaking families, but she did not lose her sense of history or her commitment to her own people. The persistence of Abenaki enclaves along the border between New England and Quebec gave her the freedom to move in and out of the Yankee settlements, offering or withdrawing her services as she chose. She was sometimes hungry, but she maintained her self-sufficiency almost to the end. She died in a "camp of sweet-smelling cedar" near Andover, Maine, in a wigwam built by white neighbors who visited her daily to tend to her needs, then auctioned off her few possessions to pay for her care.[73]

In *The History of the District of Maine,* published in 1795, James Sullivan portrayed the region's Indians as attractive and clever but uncultivated. They lacked both intellectual achievement and true religion. As a lawyer specializing in land titles, he felt entitled to point out that they had never possessed a legal right to the land. Surely they had been entitled to use it, in their own way, for a time, but since they had not used it efficiently or with any idea of "improvement of the soil," their day had passed. With proper cultivation "five hundred of rational animals may enjoy life in plenty, and comfort, where only one Savage drags out a hungry existence." Thus, human progress required their decline. "The earth was made for man." Though it began as a "rude mass of matter," it was destined to advance to "the highest state of elegance to which the noblest refinement of human reason can bring it." In successive stages, Maine had been the "habitation of beasts, and birds; then the haunt of roaming and unsocial barbarism; then the dwelling of savage tribes; and finally the high cultivated, and beautifully decorated soil of civilized nations."[74]

Sullivan was born in 1744 in a small settlement on the Salmon Falls River marking the boundary between Maine and New Hampshire. When he first began his political career, an opponent suggested in print that he himself might have been a bit of a savage.

> *The dews of education ne'er refined*
> *Thy MOHAWK manners, and thy rustic mind.*
> *On thee fair Science never deign'd to smile*
> *Nor rubb'd thee polish'd with her smoothing file.*
> *For thee nor Learning rais'd her classic flame,*
> *Rough as the savage wilds from whence you came.*[75]

Sullivan apologized for the false libel that inspired this attack, but he did not apologize for his origins. He believed that the District of Maine was an ideal setting in which to raise a virtuous, republican yeomanry.

The Sullivans are an American success story. James served as an agent for John Hancock in Biddeford, Maine, before the Revolution, became a member of the Continental Congress, and finally governor of Massachusetts. His brother John led the American army that vanquished the Iroquois from upstate New York at the end of the war, then became the chief executive of New Hampshire. But the expansion of northern New England was achieved not just by military conquest, political leadership, and careful laying out of land. It was accomplished by ordinary families with modest dreams. One Maine man observed that his pioneer parents "built no castles in the air. They had no trade or profession but to get a living in the same way their fathers and mothers did." Their vision extended no further than their immediate needs, complained one man of his Fryeburg neighbors. If they "wished to remove Stark's Hill and could do it in a day—the Hill would be removed; otherwise, it would not!"[76] But modest dreams, multiplied many times over, transformed New England's landscape.

On the eve of the American Revolution there were fewer than 30,000

# 8

# A Linen Tablecloth

NEW ENGLAND IN THE EARLY REPUBLIC

*The long strips of linen, bleaching on the grass,*
*and tended by a sturdy maiden, sprinkling them,*
*each hour, from her water-can, under a broiling*
*sun—thus to prepare the Sunday linen for her*
*brothers and her own wedding outfit—will have*
*disappeared, save as they return to fill a picture in*
*some novel or ballad of the old time.*

Horace Bushnell, "The Age of Homespun"

A coastal New Hampshire dealer purchased the tablecloth at an estate sale in the central part of the state. One can imagine the scene—old crockery, carpenter's tools, glassware, and children's games on folding tables beneath a striped tent, and arranged along the margin of the auctioneer's carpet, wrought-iron chairs, a broken spinning wheel, and a Maytag. The stack of old linens went as a lot. When the dealer got them home most were so moldy they had to be burned. The tablecloth was worth saving. She plunged it into water as hot as she could stand, stirred in a cup of detergent and half a cup of bleach, then let it steep for several days. It came out whiter than it had ever been. She ironed it, admiring the way the light picked up the subtle pattern, added a cardboard tag on a string, and stacked it with the other linens on shelves under the stairway in her shop. When the engineer came looking for a Christmas gift for his wife, it was ready. To her, it was not just a beautiful object; it was a historical document.

The tablecloth is made from two panels of patterned linen joined in the middle to form a square. The weave structure is what experts call "overshot." The fishnet trimming is made from the same thread. Together, the fiber, the pattern, and the trim characterize household production in New England in the first decades after the American Revolution. Sheets, towels, and tablecloths were still made at home in narrow webs that required seaming in the middle for larger objects. Overshot, a weave easily accomplished with four harnesses, was common not only on coverlets but on table linens and clothing. Edgings, tassels, and fringes exemplified an emerging neoclassicism and the spread of rural refinement. Everything about the tablecloth suggests the period 1790–1820, a time when factory-spun cotton was just becoming available. It invites us to think about New England's industrial beginning as contemporaries might have experienced it, not as a dramatic departure from old patterns of production but as a modest addition to what they already knew.

*Preceding page:*
*Linen tablecloth, privately owned, photographed in Chase House, Strawbery Banke Museum, Portsmouth, New Hampshire.*

Travelers' accounts, memoirs, and diaries describe the social circumstances in which fabrics like this were made. Most cloth was made in the cooperative, neighborhood-centered networks we have already seen in Betty and Nabby Foot's diaries. Exchanging tools and labor, weavers worked primarily for household use, mixing homemade and store-bought fabrics in clothing and household furnishings. Surviving pattern drafts show the variety they achieved even with simple equipment. Probate inventories document an increase in the possession of table linen, forks, and ceramics, but the emerging gentility in rural households was fragile and constantly threatened by dirt, fatigue, and the often competing values of men and women.

The typical textbook account of the industrial revolution in America begins with two innovations—Samuel Slater's adaptation of British technology to waterpower spinning at Pawtucket, Rhode Island, in 1790 and Eli Whitney's introduction of a cotton gin on a Georgia plantation in 1793. These two inventions presumably triggered a new industrial economy by allowing the expansion of plantation agriculture in the South and mechanized cloth-making in the North. Jefferson's embargo of 1807, followed by the War of 1812, completed the process, diverting capital from shipping to manufacturing. In this radically condensed version of history, household production appears only as a backdrop to change.[1] Contemporaries saw it differently.

In the summer of 1794, a Wiltshire clothier named Henry Wansey traveled through New England assessing the region's manufacturing potential. He wasn't impressed. He saw a kerseylike homespun in Waltham, Massachusetts, that was stout and serviceable, but since no one could fix a price for it he didn't think it had much commercial promise. He acknowledged the many small enterprises in the region, including a bone-lace industry in Ipswich that employed "near an hundred cushions," but these he believed were "rather the seeds of manufactures, than any large or permanent establishments." The woolen factory at Hartford, established during the Revolution, was "much on the decay, and hardly able to maintain itself." The factory near New Haven was in even worse condition. There were no windows on the north side of the building; the millstream was insufficient; and the two carding engines were warped and cracked, having been made of unseasoned wood. Nor did he think the cotton mills at Paterson, New Jersey, or at Hell Gate near New York City were going to amount to much. Americans, he believed, paid too much to hire foreign workmen, who, having no personal investment in the business, promised more than they could perform. He didn't bother to visit Rhode Island. Had he done so, he would have found a single, tiny factory at Pawtucket employing nine children.[2]

Wansey saw more hope for industries that supported household production. At Spencer, Massachusetts, he found "a neat house, with a water-mill adjoining . . . inhabited by a clothier, that is, one who mills and dresses home-spun woollen cloth for the housewives of the neighbour-hood." He also thought an establishment in Charlestown, Massachusetts, that manufactured wool cards might well succeed since "every housewife keeps a quantity of these cards by her, to employ her family in the evenings, when they have nothing to do out of doors." Americans, he believed, took a peculiar pride in homemade fabrics. A man he met on the stage claimed his linen breeches were "stouter and better than any he got from Europe." A woman told him her check window curtains and all her bed furniture had been made of flax "raised, dressed, and spun by herself and sister." There were probably many families like these, but since the population of the United States was expanding faster than its manufacturing capacity, he was certain there would be good markets for British goods for many years to come.[3]

Most Americans hoped so. They wanted the neatest fabrics Europe had to offer without the inequalities they saw inherent in industrial development. With few exceptions, political theorists argued that the success of representative government depended on maintaining an agricultural economy in which most white men owned land, and livelihood depended neither on wage labor nor patronage. When Congress instructed Alexander Hamilton to prepare a report on manufactures in 1790, most had in mind devices that would encourage household production and provide essential military supplies, not advanced economic development. James Madison wasn't the only one who recoiled at the idea of manufacturers "planting a Birmingham and Manchester, amongst us." British industrialization was the nightmare against which they measured the American dream.[4]

Writing from Philadelphia in November 1791, Connecticut Congressman James Hillhouse told his wife, "It is [a] matter of Curiosity here to know what progress and improvements are made in the Manufactures of our Country—and I have a Mind you should send a small piece of your homespun I believe it to be the best that has been made."[5] That a wife's homespun should be a source of family pride is not surprising. That it should be a measure of the progress of American manufacturing shows how determined Americans were to retain their rural republic. In practical terms that meant letting other countries produce the complex manufactures they needed or craved. Americans would concentrate on producing raw materials for home consumption and export. The prosperity of the 1790s confirmed this vision. As agricultural products flowed out of American ports, English manufactures poured in. Imports compensated for the deprivations of war without displacing long-ingrained habits of household production. Country girls wore calico gowns on Sunday and home-woven "tyers" over homemade gowns during the week. Knitting their brothers' stockings from homespun wool, they wove sheets, towels, and tablecloths for their trousseaus, imagining a day when they might arrange English teacups and sugar dishes on a tastefully trimmed cloth of their own manufacture.

New England diaries describe this world. Matthew Patten, a New Hampshire farmer, and Martha Ballard, a Maine midwife, wrote of sowing, weeding, harrowing, raking, pulling, spreading, stacking, breaking, and swingling flax. Rhode Island's Thomas Hazard, a blacksmith, reported making hetchels and spindles. Married women like Sarah Bryant of Cummington, Massachusetts; single women like Ruth Henshaw of Leicester, Massachusetts; and a Kennebunkport ship captain's wife, Elizabeth Wildes, described combing, spinning, and twisting linen; making harness, spooling, winding, warping, "putting in" and "getting out" their webs of linen; then bleaching, boiling, scouring, dyeing, and dressing the finished cloth. Although no one person did all of this work alone, the division of labor in domestic production was more fluid than in commercial manufacturing. Because work was unspecialized, each worker knew a little bit about a great many tasks. Within households, husbands and wives managed different steps in linen production, but even the simplest piece of fabric usually represented exchanges of tools and labor among neighbors.

Behind the labor of households was the work of rural craftsmen—blacksmiths, turners, and wheelwrights. "Isaac Huston made a new Crank for my wifes foot wheel," Matthew Patten wrote on July 23, 1778. Four years later, he reported a new upgrade: "I got my wifes heck new teethed and a new end on a spool and a new foot wheel from james Gorman toward my laying off land he sold in Derryfield this faull for taxes." (The heck was the part of the flyer that guided the yarn to the reel.) Samuel Lane provided each of his daughters with a great wheel and a flax wheel at marriage. Martha Ballard paid for her own spinning wheel with credits from midwifery. Investing in textile equipment was wise economy in households with growing daughters.[6]

Men began the flax-production system in the spring, as Patten did on May 18, 1787, when he reported to his diary, "I sowed about ¾ of a bushel of flax seed and I suppose near as many pease." The very same day, 150 miles away in Hallowell, Maine, Ballard's husband was engaged in similar work. "Clear . . . Mr. Ballard ploughd flax in," she wrote. Farmers sowed flax broadcast, like grain. Since the seed was light, it took skill to distribute it evenly and well. In the month of flax planting, the Pattens dined on shad and eels from the Merrimack, the Ballards ate salmon from the Kennebec. Both families interrupted their work to attend a funeral.[7]

"I wed flax," Ballard wrote on June 16, 1788, a month after her husband completed sowing.[8] Her patch of flax was an extension of her garden. Patten's crop was larger. With three-quarters of a bushel he could have seeded half an acre. Getting the seed was the biggest problem. One year he went to a neighbor's house and got what the man's wife "guesed to be a peck of flax seed," but when he got it home he found it was very dirty and when cleaned yielded much less. That year he gathered twelve quarts of seed from various families.[9]

The harvest began the last week in July or first week of August and lasted three or four days. "Finished pooling Flax," Patten wrote, his spelling betraying his Scots-Irish brogue.[10] Ballard and her daughters usually did their own pulling, lifting the plants carefully by the roots, holding the stems as straight as possible to avoid tangling, then stacking them in neat bundles for later processing. Sometimes they were spreading cloth made from last year's crop on the grass to bleach while they were harvesting the new one.[11]

The seasonal rhythms were similar for the Rhode Island blacksmith Thomas Hazard, who lived farther south than Ballard and Patten, and so began a bit earlier, sowing oats in one field, flax in another, in eel season. On August 8, 1786, he went clamming with his brother in the daytime, then "in the Evining helpt him Stack his Flax." In another year, he interrupted haying to go after "Rose Dyer to coum and help Rake & pull Flax." She got pork from the Hazards' barrel for her trouble. Women who hired out for fieldwork were often both physically strong and poor. They were the kind of women who did other people's washing, as Dyer sometimes did. "Put the Flax in the Barn & Crib . . . Rose Dyer washt here— and I paid her so we are Eaven," Hazard wrote in another season.[12]

Once the ripe stalks were out of the ground, some farmers used a flail to knock off the seed, as Samuel Lane of Stratham, New Hampshire, may have done when he referred to "faning" flaxseed. More effective was drawing the stalk through an iron comb. In some places this process was called "rippling," though New England diarists didn't use that term. In December 1783, Hazard wrote that he had used iron from an old scythe to make a comb for his cousin "to Hachel Seed ends of Flax." A rippling comb and a hetchel looked much alike. The seed Hazard carried "to John Franklins Feary" in 1783 may have ended up on the other side of the Atlantic. In Ireland commercial linen-growers preferred to harvest their flax before it was ripe, importing their seed from America. In one Connecticut town, merchants exported more than four thousand bushels of flaxseed in a single year. That kind of yield was more common in the Middle Atlantic states than in New England, where most farmers produced primarily for local use.[13]

After the seeds were off the stems, retting began. In Europe this was often done by submerging the flax in a quiet pool or stream; New Englanders more commonly spread it on the ground, letting it absorb moisture from dew, ground fog, or rain until the outer shell broke down, releasing the strong inner fibers or "line." Agricultural manuals warned against attempting either process in July or August, when "every drop after a shower, becomes a burning-glass and literally scorches the fibres." Matthew Patten's daughters violated these instructions when they spread flax "to Dew Rott" on August 21, 1781. Martha Ballard was more patient, perhaps because she had learned by experience that in hot weather fermentation produced a dark stain that was difficult to remove in bleaching. In 1796, the Ballards spread their flax on September 12 and "housed" it on October 1. Lane referred to this work—and almost any other associated with linen production—as "flaxing," sometimes hiring a neighbor's son to help.[14]

The next task was pounding the stems to loosen the woody residue still clinging to the line. This was usually done in two steps, "braking" with a heavy plank then "swingling" or beating the fibers with a wooden paddle until the remaining husk and the short fibers called "tow" fell to the ground.[15] A Windham, New Hampshire, farmer named John Campbell stacked his flax so carefully that each bundle yielded roughly a pound after breaking and swingling. In March 1796, for example, a helper named John Cochran "Breaked 19 Bundles," which when swingled yielded 19¼ pounds. The next day Cochran broke 20 pounds and Campbell swingled

*William Hincks.* Views of the
Irish Linen Industry *(London,
1783), plates 4 and 6.*
MUSEUM OF AMERICAN TEXTILE
HISTORY

20½. They didn't do so well the next week, only 15 bundles for Cochran and 15¼ pounds for Campbell, but in early April they were back at it again, interrupting their labor only to "go to George Davidsons to frolic."[16] Prosperous families hired out the dirtiest, most backbreaking, and most tedious work when they could. Women were probably paid in cash less frequently than men. Moses Rodman and his wife, Miriam, arrived at the Hazard house together, he to break flax, she to help with the slaughtering. Hazard gave the husband cash for processing 25 pounds of flax; his wife gave Rodman's wife "the Cows Tripe to pay her."[17]

Ebenezer Parkman of Westfield, Massachusetts, worried when a hired hand brought swingled flax into the house to dry, knowing that a dwelling in a neighboring town had burned down when the bundles caught fire. Fortunately, it was daytime when a coal snapped out of the fire, and the family caught it before any damage was done. Parkman was both relieved and chastened; "had it occurred last night, while we Slept, what would have been ye Event!"[18] The iron combs or "hetchels" used in the next step of processing could also be dangerous if left unattended, which is why Hazard made boxes for the hetchels he forged.[19]

Hetcheling, like wool carding, was women's work. A skilled worker

drew the flax through successive hetchels until it was smooth and ready for spinning. Ballard began combing as early as January, continuing the work in odd moments through July, sometimes continuing to comb one crop while weeding another. In late winter, she alternated combing with other indoor tasks. "I Combd 9 lb flax and knitt 40 Purls on my stocken," she wrote on March 11, 1799. A month later, she was "hatcheling flax and makeing soap." Combing was an antecedent to spinning, and in most houses spinning had no season. Between 1789 and 1793, Ruth Henshaw recorded at least one round of spinning in every month of the year.[20]

Work exchanges, or in New England parlance "changing works," relieved the tedium. "Spun and sang songs," Henshaw wrote on December 23, 1789, two days after her friend Sally arrived to help with the work. Later, Ruth would go to Sally's house to repay the favor.[21] Isolation as much as the work itself provoked Elizabeth Fuller's sardonic account of her labors. "I spun," she wrote on February 8, 1794. "I should think I might have spun up all the Swingling tow in America by this time." On another day she celebrated taking the last of her cloth out of the loom by mocking the political rhetoric of the day: "Welcome sweet Liberty, once more to me. How have I longed to meet again with thee."[22] Her situation was unusual. Most diaries record a constant stream of people in and out of each other's houses. When Julia Cowles stopped at a neighbor's house and found her friends spinning, they persuaded her to remain awhile and read to them from an improving work called "Haller to His Daughter."[23]

The spinning meetings that had been so visible before the Revolution continued into the early republic. In Pittsfield, Massachusetts, in July 1788, forty-five "young ladies . . . met at the house of Rev. Mr. Allen, and presented his consort with fifty-five runs of yarn spun in the best manner, as a sample of their industry, generosity and amity." In October, twenty-four "married ladies" repeated the favor, producing twenty-six runs of woolen yarn. Allen was an ardent patriot who had spent much of his time during the war preaching the gospel of revolution. His parishioners also embraced the gospel of spinning, as did the hundred members of "the fair sex" who carried their wheels to Samuel Deane's house in Portland, Maine, in May of that year, presenting Mrs. Deane at the end of the day with "TWO HUNDRED AND THIRTY SIX seven knotted skeins of excellent cotton and linnen. . . . Some had spun six, and many not less than five skeins apiece."[24] The spinning frolics Henshaw attended in the autumn of 1789 may have been spontaneous gatherings like the wool breaks, twisting parties, and quilting bees that also enliven her diary, but when she and her friends "with 30 other ladies made Mrs Morse a visit & presented her with about 130 Skeins yarns of our own manufacture," they were engaged in a more formal act. Henshaw's description lists the number of participants, the precise quantity of yarn, and the formal presentation in language very close to the newspaper stories.[25]

Spinning frolics gave textile work a public meaning, but in their private notations most women measured yarn according to its intended use rather than against some abstract standard of productivity. "I spun one Black stocking Cleane my West room and Scoure the Pewter," Elizabeth Wildes wrote on October 5, 1789. Obviously she wasn't spinning the stocking, but the yarn she would use to knit it. Her way of describing her work shows how she saw it. She didn't speak of yards produced but of objects imagined: "I spoold my aprons at Night," or "wove some on the Children coats."[26] Henshaw recorded her work in a similar way. She didn't spin yarn but filling for a gown, linen for curtains, and blue wool for surtouts. She warped shirting, wove aprons, and carded wool for a wrapper.[27] Both women occasionally measured their work in the time expended. "I spun linnin in the forenoon," Wildes wrote. But only on days of unusual productivity did they use the language of knots and skeins. Six or seven skeins was the typical notation, a pretty good day's work at a spinning bee, though Wildes was proud of having spun two skeins on a wash day.[28]

Still, recording work was in itself a form of measurement. When Bal-lard wrote that she had twisted eighteen knots of thread or that her daughter Hannah had taken four coverlets out of the loom, she not only created a blueprint for future production, she affirmed her identity as an industrious worker. The least expressive of New England diaries reflect this ethic. When Wildes wrote, "I fixt my Cap and made some minxpye and wove some," or Bryant hastily scrawled "spun a mop warpt a piece," they defined their lives through labor. Sarah Weeks did the same when she reduced a week in February 1805 to a bare list: "Monday, Tuesday, Wednesday, Thursday, Friday, Saturday, 20 run linnen."[29] Rural produc-ers measured their days not in coffee spoons, but in knots and skeins.

"This day I am 20 years of age Spun 3 skains linning. Wove 3 yards all wool," Ruth Henshaw wrote on December 15, 1792. That combination of tasks was characteristic of New England households. By the end of the eighteenth century, the vast majority of weavers were women. Connecti-cut's occupational tax list of 1798 listed only thirty-nine male weavers at a time when thousands of households owned looms. All but two lived in the southwestern part of Fairfield County, near the New York border. If male artisans were still active in other parts of the state, they were not producing enough cloth to merit notice.[30] That was also true in Essex County, Massachusetts. In a study of probate records, Gail Mohanty identified eighty-three self-described male weavers between 1691 and 1820, but she found exactly the same number in 1790—five—as in 1700, despite the radical expansion in population.[31]

In a memoir written in old age, an Essex County woman named Sarah Ann Emery remembered her uncle Thurrill, a weaver who kept a large flock of sheep, which he "fatted" in winter, then slaughtered and sent to market. A hired girl spun the wool from the fleeces "into yarn which the old gentleman (he was a weaver by trade) wove into cloth, which met with a ready sale. After a hard day's work out of doors, it was no infre-quent thing to hear his loom till twelve or one o'clock at night." The uncle was a production weaver, producing a specialized, but probably rather crude, product for market. In contrast, the back chamber in Emery's parents' house in Newburyport was "fitted up with looms, woolen, linen and spooling wheels, swifts, reels, cards and warping bars" used for household manufacturing. Emery remembered cloth-making as an orderly process regulated by the seasons. In autumn, "the lengthening evenings began to be enlivened by the busy click of knitting needles," as the women of the family, excluding a somewhat idle grandmother, worked up the yarn they had carded and spun. The weaving was either "put out to some neighboring woman" or done by somebody "hired to weave at the house for a few weeks." If wool, the finished fabric was carried to the mill in Byfield "where it was fulled, colored and pressed in time to be made up before Thanskgiving."[32]

The diaries show a mixture of production methods. Even skilled weavers like Bryant or Wildes sent specialized fabrics to neighbors, and young women relied on more experienced weavers for help with setting up their looms. On April 12, 1790, Henshaw noted that a Mrs. Wheeler had come to her house "in forenoon to warp web," adding "I went up there PM to weave out her peace [piece]." Wheeler was not doing the weaving but the warping, the difficult preliminary threading of the loom. Once that task was done, a less skilled person could throw the shuttle, as Ruth did a few hours later with a different web of cloth already set up at the Wheeler house.[33] The same process was at work in Cummington, Massachusetts, when Bryant "warpt a piece for Mrs. Snell," or in Hallowell, Maine, when Merriam Pollard came to Martha Ballard's house "to instruct Dolly about her weaving." These encounters were both economic and social, as Hazard noted in his entry for February 19, 1808: "Renued Carpinter dind and drank Tea here she helpt my daughter worp a Pease to weave."[34]

Neighbors also shared equipment, a practice that helps explain the missing items in some probate inventories. Inventories listing "half a hetchell" or "half a dye pot" formalized joint use of implements that, like the baby in Solomon's court, could not be divided. Flax combs (also called hackles or hetchels) came in varied sizes. "I hetchel'd 43 lbs & ½ of flax & then went after the fine hatchel to Mr Otis's," Elisabeth Foot wrote on April 10, 1775.[35] A shortage of equipment encouraged egalitarian exchanges like those in Abner Sanger's diary: "I go to Daniel Gleason's. Get my wife's weaving slay and said Gleason's wife's harness to weave with." The weaver at Sanger's house was a hired girl named Polly Mead, who went to a second neighbor's house two days later to borrow another harness, then a few days later spooled and warped her web at a third location.[36] The "slay" (sley) and the "harness" were detachable implements used to adapt a loom for weaving different kinds of fabric.[37] Pennsylvania's artisan weavers sometimes owned as many as sixteen sleys in different sizes. An occasional New England inventory mentions five; most had only two or three, which is why Martha Ballard borrowed a "40 sleigh of the widdow Coburn" to weave one kind of cloth and a "64 twenty slay" from Merriam Pollard to weave another.[38]

Later generations were often amazed at all this coming and going. A New Hampshire storyteller told about the time her grandmother needed "a certain reed and harness which could not be obtained nearer than the west part of the town." She mounted a smart colt, and "with a baby in her arms and another child on a pillion behind her . . . started on her ride of five miles over some of the worst hills in town." But as she started home with the reed and harness "at least four feet long . . . bound to the colt," she discerned signs of a coming storm. "My great, great uncle Cate said that when she passed his house she was going like the wind, the sky was black with the coming storm, and the thunder and lightning were terrible. As soon as it cleared off he saddled his horse and followed, 'expecting,' he said, 'to find Tabitha and the children dead in the road. But I went *clean* over, and there she was, getting supper and singing as lively as a cricket.'" She had stayed ahead of the storm and reached the house without even getting wet.[39]

Though male heads of household formally controlled the means of production, the management of cloth-making was a female responsibility, and neighborhood exchange as well as family labor was essential. Wansey was right in thinking that the most successful businesses would support rather than compete with this system. When John Scholfield, the son of a Yorkshire clothier, set up a wool-carding mill half a mile from the meetinghouse in Pittsfield, Massachusetts, in 1801, local housewives were skeptical. They soon discovered they could spin twice as much wool in a day by starting with the soft rolls produced by machine carding. Although Scholfield imagined turning his carding operation into a full-fledged factory that would spin and weave as well as card, he eventually succeeded not as a cloth maker but as a manufacturer of carding machines for other towns.[40] Thomas Hazard took his wife "to see the Carding Machine" opened by his cousin in Peace Dale, Rhode Island, in 1804, though he was dismayed to hear a few weeks later that "Deborah Rodman hurt hur Hand very much yeasterday with the Carding Machine." As long as they didn't have to work in a mill, most women appreciated the convenience of machine carding. Martha Ballard increased her wool production after the opening of the carding mill at Winthrop, Maine. She called it the "masheen." In 1810, Sarah Bryant began taking wool to a mill near her home in Cummington, Massachusetts, listing small batches ranging from four pounds to forty on the inside cover of her diary.[41]

New Englanders also spun cotton, though they were ambivalent about the region that produced it. Matthew Patten's grandson Isaac Tolford, writing from New Orleans Territory in 1801, described the emerging cotton kingdom in disdainful terms.

> There is great talk about Jeffersons rivers of Rum and mountains of sugar in this country but for my part I have seen none as yet nor nothing else that is verry attracting as far as I have been I see nothing but Barrennes & Indolence. . . . New Orleans to be sure is a place of great trade but its commodities which consists of Cotton wooll Flour And Lumber Logwood & some sugar is not the produce of this territory (Lumber excepted) it is brought down the river in square flat boats From Kentucky Tenisee And the Ohio which is the distance of 3500 miles back to the Ohio (the other places on the side of it) The town itself is the highest land that I have yet seen here and might be made as convenient for shipping as any Port in the United States but the indolence of the people which are principaly Spanish will not allow them to make it so their whole aim is money there are no sort of manufactorys here & very few Mechanuks.[42]

Tolford reflected contemporary politics in attributing prosperity to the combination of raw materials, mechanical genius, and industrious habits. That he dismissed the Spanish for being interested only in money suggests that he considered commerce inferior to manufacturing. When he wrote of "manufactorys," he was no doubt thinking of the small enterprises that were beginning to appear all over New England.

New England diarists also noticed the appearance of tiny factories. In September 1809, Hazard purchased fifteen pounds of yarn at "the Cotton Facktory" a few miles from his farm. It was only a supplement to his homegrown wool and flax. A few days after his visit to the factory, he carried home tow cloth from the weavers, and in early October, he spread his flax for retting, turned his sheep into the cow pasture, and settled accounts with neighbors for the wool spindles he had made them. Martha Ballard occasionally added "facktory filling yarn" or "factory warp" to the webs she sent her daughter for weaving. The small amount of cotton Sarah Bryant used, however, was still hand-carded and -spun. In all three households, the dominant fiber was flax.[43]

Neither diary-keeping not cloth-making was unique to New England. When Aletta Clowes Clark of Sussex County, Delaware, wrote of going to her neighbors', the Russells, "to worp" or to her sister's house "to help about sizing a webb" she documented the neighborly work exchanges that sustained subsistence production everywhere. On an April day in 1791, she penned religious sentiments that might have come from Martha Ballard—"a fine rain this afternoon, thanks be to the Great Providence." Her allusions to wheat harvest, slaves, and "Camp Meeting" differentiate her world from much of New England, but her references to "frolicks" could have come from Henshaw or Sanger. Another Sussex County weaver, Hannah Wolfe Burton was wealthier than Clark but exemplified a similar commitment to household production. Although an undefined group of slaves she referred to as "our people" planted and harvested her flax, she helped with the hetcheling and took personal responsibility for weaving, overseeing the work of her daughter and a hired helper. Like Ballard, she preferred family help to paid help. "I am very much tried with Betsy for weaving my peace so bad," she complained, adding that her daughter Matilda "weaves hers so much better."[44]

Everywhere that cloth-making was an extension of agriculture and wives and daughters the major source of labor, similar stories could be told.


Diaries, memoirs, probate inventories, and travel narratives describe the methods of production and the settings in which homemade textiles were used. Surviving fabrics, like our tablecloth, exhibit the techniques favored by household manufacturers and the range of their skill.

Connecting written documents to artifacts is never easy, especially when the nomenclature is inconsistent, as in a New Hampshire weaving draft labeled "Barlecorn Dimaty Hucabuc."[45] In most weaving books, barleycorn, dimity, and huckaback are considered separate weaves. Weavers who have attempted to use pattern drafts like these have discovered little correspondence between colonial and modern usage. One century's huckaback is another's "Ems and Os."[46] When Martha Ballard noted that she had spent part of the day "whitening diaper," or Ruth Henshaw that she had taken a "diaper web" to Widow J. Southgate, or Eliza Wildes wrote that she had "put in a piece of diaper," what kind of fabric did they mean? True diaper was a pattern-woven linen of high quality characterized by an overall configuration of fine triangles or lozenges. Homemade "diaper" may have been something quite different. A collection of Vermont weaving drafts includes both "Federal Diaper" and "Diaper M's and O's." It is easy enough to know what Wildes was doing

*Overshot tablecloth, detail.*

*"Ms and Os," detail.*

*Plain linen, detail.*
PRIVATE COLLECTION.
PHOTOGRAPHS GARY SAMSON

on April 2, 1791, when she reported spun "great threads" for dimity—a corded fabric made by alternating thick and thin wefts—but when she wrote of weaving "Friesye" or "freesy," her meaning is difficult to decipher. Henshaw's references to "shepperdie" or "sheppurde" are even more mysterious. In English usage, "shepherd's" gray, "shepherd's plaid," and "shepherd's velvet" all denoted a gray or subtly checked fabric, sometimes made of mixed black and white wool, but Henshaw was spinning "*tow* for sheppurde." Perhaps she was alternating unbleached and bleached linen to create a subtle check.[47]

There is no doubt, however, about the importance of a weave structure known as "overshot." A New York coverlet dated 1773 is the earliest documented overshot fabric in America, though the term appears in probate inventories a bit earlier. A Woodbury, Connecticut, inventory of 1769 lists an overshot "blanket"; one from Litchfield County the next year a black, white, and blue overshot coverlet. When Elizabeth Porter Phelps invited her neighbor to help her warp a piece of "overshot" in June 1778, she may have been making a coverlet, but more likely she or her helper was weaving linen, not because overshot was particularly appropriate for linen—most weaving experts would not have recommended it—but because it was easy to do. A Hillsborough County, New Hampshire, inventory of the 1790s even included "1 overshot cotton & linnen gown."[48]

Household linens found in the same shop as our tablecloth show the range of weave structures common in the period. A sheet with an inked inscription is in a simple tabby-weave; a towel in what modern weavers would call "Ms and Os." The small all-over pattern was created by threading the loom so that alternating cells of plain weave were surrounded by corded columns created by allowing the weft threads to cross several warps at a time in a regular pattern. Overshot allowed more variety, but it was better adapted to mixtures of wool and cotton or linen than to linen alone. In overshot, every other shot was in tabby; in alternate rows the weft yarns shot over the wefts to create a pattern. Hundreds of combinations were possible. The New Hampshire tablecloth displays a simple pattern of alternating squares and ovals that is attractive but clearly homemade and a sharp contrast to the intricately woven patterns in imported linens, like those owned by Prudence Stoddard in the mid-eighteenth century. (See page 116.) Although the weaving is neatly done, the pattern cannot be made to match in the middle.[49]

Hundreds of patterns or "drafts" used by household weavers have survived. Usually written on narrow strips of paper cut from the back of old accounts or letters, they are often pocked with pinholes where the weaver marked the progress of her work. Among the earliest are those left by the semiliterate Scituate weaver Deborah Sylvester, whose papers include one labeled simply "The Draft of a Civerled" as well as more poetic notations like "Inden [Indian] moon" and "Rial [Royal] Rib."[50] References to monarchy gradually disappeared after the Revolution. In a collection of weaving drafts by an otherwise unknown woman named Hannah Davis, there is one called "The Royal Beauty or the Federal Constitution." All but four of the fifteen drafts in her collection were written for a four-shaft loom, and all but two—"Diaper M's and O's" and "Federal Diaper"—

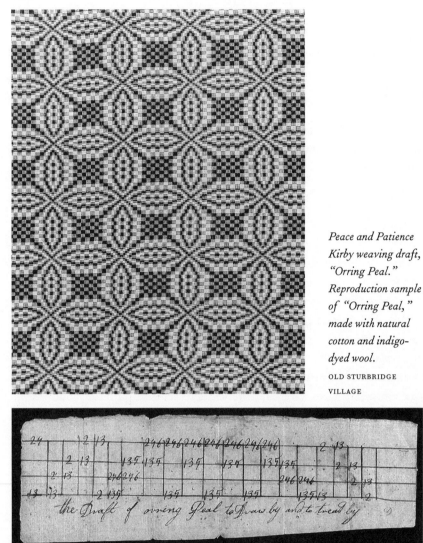

*Peace and Patience Kirby weaving draft, "Orring Peal." Reproduction sample of "Orring Peal," made with natural cotton and indigo-dyed wool.*

OLD STURBRIDGE VILLAGE

were overshot. One specifies colors: twenty-five knots of green, twenty of red, twenty of black, and five of yellow. The few instructions included were no doubt intelligible to her but probably not to anyone else—"begin at the tip and go through and begin back and go through again and continue to go through." The drafts are undated, but the handwriting is uneven, written in the half-printing, half-cursive style of partially educated persons in the eighteenth century, and she uses the old-fashioned long *s*.[51]

In contrast, "Mary Palmers Draught New England Glory, North Ston-

ington" displays the elegant handwriting taught in young ladies' academies. A draft called "Polly's Delight," now in a Vermont collection, is
also gracefully written, quite unlike the awkward writing on "Nine
Snoballs" in the same collection.[52] Woven white on white, overshot patterns were subtle. When enlarged into coverlets made with indigo-dyed
wool combined with factory-spun cotton, they became quite dramatic.
The names attached to the patterns in Peace Kirby's records add a color
of their own: Rose in the Garden, Heart's Delight, Flowers of Eddin
Burg, Irish Beauty, Sixteen Blossoms, Wagon Wheels, Blazing Star,
Prussian Leaf, Orring Peal. Some of these names echo folk songs and
dances performed at quilting bees or spinning frolics in the New England
countryside.[53]

Eighteenth-century women exchanged weaving drafts the way later
generations exchanged recipes, using a language intelligible only to them.
In a 1793 letter, a New Hampshire woman named Sarah Kendrick wrote,
"Dear Sister after my love to you I would inform you that we are all well
as comon you desiered me to write to you about weaveing waile. alowing
14 nots to one yard you may Skip one half your gears and as to diaper you
must mark your shaves by your slay and strike eleven gears in a beer."
Before marriage she and her sister had probably collaborated on many
weaving projects, so there was no need to send complete instructions.
The sister knew exactly what she meant by marking her "shaves" by her
"slay" or striking eleven "gears in a beer." In both cases she was describing the process of warping a loom. Her instructions suggest that for wale,
a ridged fabric somewhat like modern corduroy, she used a rather open
warp, skipping some of the heddles or gears as she threaded. In contrast,
diaper required a denser threading. She used her slay as her guide and
made sure she used eleven heddles (an uneven number) for each section,
or "beer," of the warp. Sending weaving instructions, she reinforced her
bond with her sister. She concluded, "as to news I have but little to write,"
signing herself "your affectionate sister," then adding, "I have not got a
name for my little daughter yet."[54]

Linen tablecloths were often finished with a simple turned edge. Ours
has a fancy trimming called "netting." As early as 1770, the *Boston News-
Letter* advertised a "suit of Nett Curtains for a Bed." Netting became
more common in the late eighteenth and early nineteenth centuries. It not
only fit well with neoclassical fashion but made good use of readily available cotton thread. Fancy coverlets might be finished with ten or twelve
inches of netting, simpler curtains or tablecloths with a few soft tassels.[55]

Writing to a friend in Virginia, a friend of Martha Washington said, "Her netting is a source of great amusement to her and is so neatly done that all the younger part of the family are proud of having their dresses trimmed with it."[56] The delicate netting used on clothing and household textiles was a refined version of the fishnet Matthew Patten used for his seines on the Merrimack. Like knitting and crocheting, netting was made from a single continuous thread rather than interlocking warps and wefts. It is a kind of macramé worked with a needle of steel or ivory, open at both ends, and a second implement called a "mesh."[57]

Ruth Henshaw recorded her experiments with fringes as early as 1794. During a visit to Norfolk, Virginia, in 1801, Henshaw was very busy making fringes, perhaps because her spinning wheel and loom were far away in Massachusetts, but she also continued this work in odd hours after her arrival home. She noted making a "triming for Phebe Denny's Cloak, of netting & Knoting," and alluded to "tufting fringe," "cotton fringe for chair & counterpin," a "festoon fringe" for a skirt, and "yellow trims" with balls of cotton. Some of the fringes may have been simple edgings made by unraveling the weft from a few inches of fabric, as on the day she "finished fringing & marking diaper." But the "netting" she worked on in the spring and summer of 1802 must have looked much like that on our tablecloth.[58] Netting appears on an embroidered coverlet, a bed valance, and a fancy table cover owned by the Copp family of Stonington, Connecticut. The family also saved several lengths of unused fringes. Like the unknown maker of our tablecloth, they mixed linen and cotton in their work, adding two-ply linen theads to three-ply cotton in the tassels on the tablecloth and adding cotton netting to a tabby-woven linen valance.[59]

There are dozens of other examples in New England collections. A very fine bird's-eye towel with a netted fringe has the cross-stitched initials *ERP* and a note stitched to it that says, "This was the style of Towel that [torn] when your Grandmother went to housekeeping," that is, when she was married in 1809. A twill-woven towel attributed to Betsy Alexander of Bow, New Hampshire, c. 1819, has a similar fringe, though the netting is made from cotton rather than linen.[60] Sarah Hodgdon of Sanbornville, New Hampshire, added netting to a pair of curtains made from a semisheer fabric, probably woven at home, that added heavier threads of cotton to homespun linen to create a textured check.[61] Fanny Kimball made her tablecloth of plain linen, embroidering flowers in the corners. There are many tablecloths with netted fringe in New England

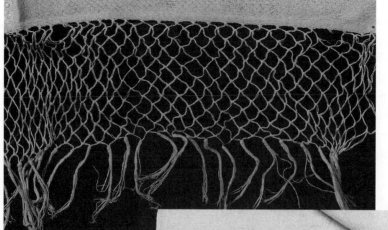

*Patterson family. Linen
towel with netted edging.
Bedford, New Hampshire.*
ROYAL ONTARIO MUSEUM,
TORONTO

*Clara Philbrick. Linen
towel with netted edging.*
COURTESY OF THE SOCIETY FOR
THE PRESERVATION OF NEW
ENGLAND ANTIQUITIES. GIFT
OF GEORGE O. SWASEY AND
CLARA S. WOODBERRY, 1949.
PHOTOGRAPH BY DANA SALVO

collections, though few with netting as evenly made and delicate as that
on our cloth. The maker of a cloth now at the Maine State Museum seemingly ran out of trimming, perhaps because the cotton shrank after she
washed it. The edging almost reached around three sides, then had to be
pieced. The plied cotton gives it a heavy look.[62]

New England home weavers were poorly trained but ambitious. In
museums and historical collections, the region's textiles really do have a
distinctive look. More sophisticated than fabrics from the rural South,
their weaving is less complex than that left by Pennsylvania's apprentice-
trained male artisans. New England fabrics often display mismatched

seams, weft skips, and broken twill, sure marks of ambitious but imperfectly trained weavers. A tablecloth woven in Lenox, Massachusetts,
about 1800, for example, was made from two lengths of fabric in which a
threading error produced an awkward stripe about two inches from the
selvage. The maker of the tablecloth flaunted her mistake by sewing the
two strips of fabric together so the stripes were right in the middle, then
added a fringe to the edge. She may not have been a perfect weaver, but
she would make no apologies for her work. In this era, possessing any sort
of tablecloth was an achievement.

Rural diaries sustain Horace Bushnell's description of sturdy maidens
bleaching linen for their wedding "outfits," though they modify his notion
that they spun and wove their Sunday clothing. The same families who
manufactured cloth bought cloth. In the months before her daughter Hannah married, Martha Ballard made frequent trips to the stores in Hallowell,
Maine, purchasing crockery, knives and forks, and imported fabric. Her
girls wove diaper for towels and linen for sheets, but they also made bed
quilts of store-bought calico. Similar combinations appear in other
diaries.[63] On a day when Ruth Henshaw and her sisters were busy weaving
woolen shirting, their parents returned from Boston bringing "fabric for
gowns" and "fashionable hats, purple sattin lined with straw color." The
shirting the girls were weaving helped to pay for the satin, though it never
appeared in the credit column under their father's name at the store.[64]

The diary of Elizabeth Perkins Wildes vividly describes the range of
fabrics and fibers used in one household. Wildes lived on a rocky half-
acre in Kennebunkport, Maine, but her father, a prosperous farmer, supplied her with flax, worsted, and wool.[65] Her husband, who was engaged
in the West India trade, brought home raw cotton, which she stored in the
cellar, bringing it up a little at a time for spinning. "We Spun Salt water
coten all Day," she wrote on a March day in 1792. She may have been
spinning a silky, long staple fiber developed in the late eighteenth century
by crossing South American and Caribbean varieties. Usually called "Sea
Island cotton," it got its name from the plantations along the coast of
South Carolina and Georgia where it was grown. Eliza's reference suggests that her husband's ship may have picked up cargoes in the lower
South, though "salt water cotton" could also have been grown on one of
the islands. (There were many varieties of cotton in this period, including
the short-staple kind with the bristly green seeds that grew well in the

interior but didn't become commercially successful until the invention of the cotton gin.)[66]

Eliza knitted stockings, hose, and mittens, wove tow for towels, and made at least one tablecloth, but the bulk of the fabric made during the period of the diary went into ordinary clothing. She made gowns for her little girls and a "loose" gown (perhaps a maternity dress) and "white" gown for herself. She wove lots of handkerchiefs, both the pocket kind and bigger ones to be tucked into the bodice of a low-necked gown. Some of the red yarn she dyed may have gone into handkerchiefs or the workaday jackets she and her sisters spun and wove.[67] She integrated homespun with store-bought goods, sewing gowns of muslin and chintz and a "yellow Base Coat" for her sister Suky and a gown of calico, a grogram skirt, and a new green cloak for herself. She took good care of these materials because they were precious, mending silk stockings and washing, ripping apart, and remaking an old camblet gown. Eliza was a dress and bonnet maker who produced many items of apparel for her neighbors. On July 13, 1792, she wrote, "Phebe Stone came here to get a pocket book made." On March 2, 1790, she "made Sukey a pin bal." Sewing and cloth-making intersected. She could spin part of the day, then turn to stitching a delicate cap of store-bought lawn an hour later. On August 31, 1789, she "wove out my piece and begun to make Mrs Cartice a bonnet."[68]

In the Wildes household, maritime enterprise and household labor produced a measure of gentility and a standard of cleanliness far beyond the capacity of ordinary families. Israel Wildes was a well-dressed man. The inventory taken after his death lists six pairs of breeches and six coats, four waistcoats, five jackets, seventeen shirts, two pairs of old trousers, and thirty-one pairs of stockings as well as shoes, boots, silver shoe and knee buckles, and two "elastic surtuits." A surtout was an overcoat. An *elastic* surtout was an overcoat made from a fabric interlined or impregnated with "gum elastic," the eighteenth-century term for rubber.[69] At thirty-four shillings, his best elastic surtout was the most expensive item in his wardrobe. It was followed by a red broadcloth coat and one of silk, each valued at twenty-four shillings. But the next most valuable item was a coat of green homespun, a symbol of Israel's patriotism and his wife's industry.

Eliza's labor is everywhere present in this list. Among the five jackets, valued from three to six shillings, was surely the one she mended on June 1, 1790. The most valuable of the shirts displayed the ruffles she had stitched, and though his expensive "plated" stockings were surely imported, the diary makes clear that most of the others were her work. Taken together, the shirts and stockings account for almost half of the value of his clothing. The inventory lists seven tablecloths, eighteen towels, and a single napkin. Eliza probably brought most of this linen with her when she married, some of it woven at home, some of it made from imported fabric. The most valuable tablecloth was appraised at nine shillings; the maple table on which it was spread was worth only six.

In the early colonial period the possession of any sort of table linen set a woman apart from the crowd. That was less true by the end of the eighteenth century, but though middle-class standards of behavior were spreading, genteel dining was still beyond the reach of most families. In northern New England, travelers didn't have to go far from market towns to find "wretched cabins" where families subsisted on rye and corn bread, salt pork, and spruce beer. In the new settlements, one traveler reported, farmers lived "in little cabins made of tree trunks still covered with bark and mortised at the corners, the chinks filled in with clay to stop the wind and rain. These wretched huts are no more than 14 to 16 feet high at the center and 8 to 10 at the walls, and covered with a roof made of large pieces of bark of that fir tree called hemlock fir by the English." These cabins had only one room with a garret above, a few loosely fastened boards serving for the ceiling of one and the floor of another. In summer, settlers kept a fire burning in front of the door to drive away mosquitoes.[70]

Even in older towns there was little scope for amenities. Seth Sprague of Duxbury, Massachusetts, described the typical mode of eating breakfast during his childhood. His father would get up early, make a large fire, "hang on a pot with bean *porrage* in it and then go to the barn to feed the cattle." The bean porridge, like the pease porridge in the nursery rhyme, could have been freshly made the day before or "nine days old." While his father was in the barn, his mother crumbled bread into two pewter basins. When the children appeared for breakfast and the father returned from the barn, the mother ladled porridge into each dish. "My father and mother would eat out of one bason, myself and two sisters, out of the other. My mother would then put the porrage pot away, wash the two basons, then go to weaving or spinning."[71] John Weeks, who grew up in Salisbury, Vermont, in the late eighteenth century, wrote that he had been "both a witness and a participator in the custom of setting the large six-quart dish in the centre of the table, while half a dozen or more children stood around it, each with a spoon, partaking of this homely but healthful repast of samp and milk."[72]

By 1800, however, new standards of behavior had developed in coastal towns and in the houses of the rural gentry. Ann Smith, the wife of a Portland, Maine, shopkeeper, described a quite different breakfast in her diary entry for June 8, 1807: "I was up this Morn before the (Lazy) sun, baked a Large loaf of bread in a Duch oven (our usual mode of baking in Summer) which I mixed & sit to rising last night) put on the tea kittle—while I was thus imployed our boy Ben harnessed the horse, & put him to the Chaise—My husband and self steped in, & had a charming ride and returned at Seven o-clock & took our breakfast." The casual aside to the reader ("our usual mode of baking in Summer") as well as the parentheses around "Lazy" (did she question the appropriateness of the adjective?) mark this as a composition, a self-conscious attempt to capture a moment and mood. The breakfast too was a performance, as much about atmosphere and gesture as about food.[73]

Tablecloths, knives and forks, and ceramic tablewares were essential props in these domestic dramas, though Americans had difficulty getting the arrangement right. As in the Wildes house, napkins were in short supply. A European nobleman whose visits encompassed only respectable houses complained that "one has to wipe one's mouth on the tablecloth, which in consequence suffers in appearance."[74] The late introduction of table forks added to the awkwardness of the American performance. As late as 1827, European visitors still observed people shoveling food into their mouths from the round end of knives. An etiquette book of the 1830s still defended the practice, advising young ladies that if they wished to imitate the French or the English, they could "put every mouthful into your mouth with your fork; but if you think as I do that Americans have as good a right to their own fashions as the inhabitants of any other country, you may choose the convenience of feeding yourself with your right hand armed with a steel blade; and provided you do it neatly and do not put in large mouthfuls, or close your lips tight over the blade, you ought not to be considered as eating ungenteely."[75]

In Norwich and Stamford, Connecticut, almost two-thirds of probate inventories listed table linens by 1810, but only half of New Hampshire households did. John Crommet of Durham had six "homespun diaper table Cloths," Captain Daniel Reynolds a fine dimity tablecloth and six towels on rollers, but hardly anybody had napkins. Only three of fifty inventories from Hillsborough County in the 1790s listed napkins. Jonathan Parker, a physician, had seven old diaper napkins, three old diaper tablecloths, and two old coarse tablecloths, but his household was

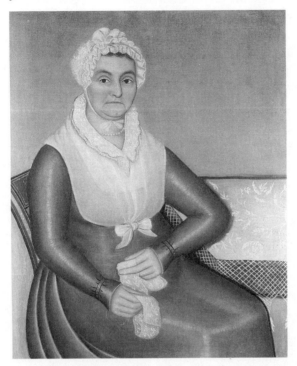

*Ammi Phillips.*
*Alsa Slade, 1816.*
NATIONAL GALLERY OF ART.
GIFT OF EDGAR WILLIAM
AND BERNICE CHRYSLER
GARBISCH

unusual. Knives and forks were also rare, though teapots were common. Hannah Hopkins of Amherst, Massachusetts, had a fine tablecloth and two coarse ones, plus a "tea table cloth," a description that would fit our fringed cloth.[76] Too small for a large dinner table and too fancy to be used for wiping greasy fingers, it was probably used on ceremonial occasions only.

An 1816 portrait by Ammi Phillips, a Berkshire County, Massachusetts, artist, shows a netted edging much like that on our tablecloth, though the mesh is deeper and the tassels come to deep drops or points. The subject, Alsa Slade, looks sturdy enough to milk a cow or beat in the weft on a loom, but there is no evidence of plebian production in her portrait. She is very much a lady. She holds a different kind of lace in her hand, perhaps machine-made mesh or bobbinet that she is embellishing with hand-embroidered flowers. More lace trims her cap and collar.[77] Her tablecloth was a mark of her respectability and her cleverness. It was also a measure of her capacity to direct household resources toward ornamental as well as practical ends.

Ornamentation had its dangers. In the early republic, the attempt to define an American character reinforced long-standing religious con-

*Fanny Kimball.*
*Linen tablecloth.*
NEW HAMPSHIRE
HISTORICAL SOCIETY

cerns about luxury. Even so industrious a woman as Sarah Bryant sometimes worried about the temptations of refinement. Could an interest in
pattern and design lead to an obsession with surfaces? Bryant sometimes
used the pages of her journal to make small sketches that might have been
quilting patterns or designs for coverlets. On December 12, 1795, she
sketched a flower, surrounding it with fragments of verse: "vain woman
foolish pleasures bent / Prepares for his own punishment," and below the
flower: "Each pleasure hath its poison, too / And every sweet a snare."
New Englanders struggled between the desire for refinement and a fear
of pride. Too much investment in worldly things might threaten the soul.

Yet small refinements added to the peace and orderliness of life.
Martha Ballard savored the oases of gentility she found in rural Maine,
where most socializing was still organized around some sort of work,
such as husking, quilting, or barn-raising, occasions for drinking as well
as dancing. The gathering at a neighbor's house in July 1790 was different. The invited couples had "what cherries and currants we wisht for and
other handsome entertainment." She was also pleased with the "Elligant
supper" served after a delivery in Hallowell in 1793, but the later behavior

of the father might have given her pause. As a sea captain, John Molloy
could afford the trappings of gentility, but within a few years his wife
divorced him for committing "divers acts of Adultery" in Boston and the
West Indies. Ostentatious entertainment did not compensate for shallowness of character. In Ballard's own household, an orderly dinner was a
hard-won pleasure. Memories of meals disrupted by her son's drunken
rages accelerated the pleasure she took in a peaceful dinner at his house in
May 1808: "We had Beautiful rice puding and Calvs head and harslett."
This was a rural feast. Cows "freshened" when their calves were born,
supplying milk for the pudding and meat for the table. But this was also
the season when the hard work of flax production began. Sowing and
weeding the young plants, Martha Ballard and her family sowed the seeds
of rural refinement.[78]


In a long poem entitled "Greenfield Hill," a Connecticut clergyman and
writer, Timothy Dwight, imagined a rural society that repudiated the
affectations of aristocratic Europe yet aspired to civility and order.
"Refinement hence even humblest life improves," he wrote. Europe, he
believed, was caught between enormous wealth and enormous want. In
America, every man had the opportunity to achieve competency, yet none
had the opportunity for ostentation. Dwight's poem refurbished the evasions of eighteenth-century pastoral. As Richard Bushman has observed,
his celebration of rural simplicity was written in exactly the same period
that New England elites were building elegant new mansions filled with
mahogany tables and glittering mirrors. By carving out an imagined
space between European affectation and frontier rudeness, he and other
writers of the period actually protected the growth of gentility. Displacing their criticism onto imagined Europeans or local fops, they "cleared
the way to construct costlier houses according to standards of ever more
refined taste, thinking of themselves not as effete aristocrats but merely
as republican gentlemen."[79]

Idealizing the "simple life" was a way of assuaging anxiety over one's
privileges. On September 10, 1808, a privileged schoolgirl named Sarah
Connell took a walk with female friends. Her diary entry might have
described an engraved or embroidered pastoral rather than a real day in
an actual New England village, though the rustic repast she described
sounds much like the "handsome entertainment" of Martha Ballard's
diary.

We pursued our way through the woods till we arrived at the great Pear tree, where we all stopped and hung up our bonnets. We then passed through the little gate, and entered the little cottage, which is not visible till within a yard of the door, and it then discovers itself peeping through the foliage. The old Woman was ironing, but our abrupt visit did not seem to disturb her. Her daughter, Mrs. Fish, was nursing her little infant, while her little boy, apparently four years old, was expressing his delight at our visit. We were recived with unfeigned hospitality. Pears and Cyder were set before us, with the recommndation of a hearty welcome. How much superior is the sweet cheerfulness of the honest rustics, and their friendly repast, to all the parade of ceremony, and the insincerity of the Great. Tenderness supplies the place of refinement. . . . They are happy, they are all the World to each other.[80]

Eliza Southgate, the well-educated daughter of a wealthy coastal Maine family, was less sure about the "honest rustics." In a letter to her cousin Moses Porter, she complained, "Our novelists have worn the pleasures of rural life threadbare. . . . Yet let us judg for ourselves,—we all have seen what the pleasures of rural life are, and whatever Poets may have ascribed to it, we must know there is as much depravity and consequently as much disconent in the inhabitants of a country village as in the most populous city. They are generally ignorant, illiterate, without knowledge to discover the real blessings they enjoy by comparing them with others, continually looking to those above them with envy and discontent and imagine their share of happiness is proportioned to their rank and power." By this time, the "rustics" in central Maine were engaged in open rebellion against the nonresident land-proprietors who claimed to own their farms.[81]

Eliza was less idealistic than Sarah, but she too showed little ability to understand her neighbors on their own terms, nor did she see any irony in the decorations constructed in 1803 for a New York dinner in honor of her uncle, Rufus King. Down the center of each table, she wrote, was "an enclosure about 2 feet wide, filled with earth, and railed in with a little white fence and little gates every yard or two . . . some places flocks of sheep, some cows laying down, beautiful little arches and arbors covered with green." In the world of fantasy one could enjoy the pleasures without the labors, the inconveniences, or the tumults of country life.[82]

# 9

## *A Counterpane and a Rose Blanket*

*The house was a factory on the farm, the
farm a grower and producer for the house.*

Horace Bushnell, *"The Age of Homespun"*

When a volunteer from the Brick Store Museum in Kennebunk, Maine, carried the cotton counterpane to the textile museum for analysis, the curator told her it was English. She said it might have been used in Maine, but it could hardly have been made there. The weaving was expertly done, and there was no center seam, the usual tip-off to home weaving. Furthermore, it looked almost exactly like coverlets manufactured in Bolton, Lancashire, in the early nineteenth century. Fortunately, the Brick Store Museum had in its files an 1811 newspaper story, a nineteenth-century memoir, and a letter from Dolley Madison documenting Eliza Bourne's counterpane "manufactory." A few weeks later, the curator traveled to Maine, where she joined the director of the museum in an expedition to the old Bourne house. In the barn out back, they found the treadle piece and cloth beam from Eliza's broadloom.[1] Without written documents, the story of Bourne's enterprise would be lost. But without physical evidence, it would be less interesting. Her counterpane documents the materials she used, her weaving skill, and her relationship to a Lancashire prototype.

A homespun blanket, now at the Royal Ontario Museum in Toronto, provides an instructive contrast. The dealer who sold it to the museum in 1966 said it came from New England, but she had no idea when or where it was made. It is a humble blanket, tabby-woven of undyed wool with a center seam and stripes of indigo at each end and along the sides. It could have been woven anywhere there were sheep, looms, and household weavers. Only the roses in the corners set it apart. At first glance they seem entirely innocent, an earnest if somewhat awkward attempt to refine a homely household textile. But adding a rose to a blanket created a pun that anyone in the early nineteenth century would have recognized. In contemporary usage, a "rose blanket" was an English broadloom blanket milled to a high loft and ornamented in the corners with geometric embroidery that imitated the compass roses on early maps. This blanket, like Bourne's

*Elizabeth Perkins Wildes Bourne and daughters. "Mary Wise" counterpane, 1810, center detail.*

*Anonymous. Embroidered
blanket.*
ROYAL ONTARIO MUSEUM, TORONTO

coverlets, is an adaptation of a commercial
product, but it is so obviously homemade
that no one would confuse it with its model.

    Together, the counterpane and the blan-
ket show the intersection of household production and commerce in the
first decades of the nineteenth century. They also show how household
industry sustained republican virtue in the public culture of the time.
Read alongside the federal census of 1810, Eliza Bourne's story shows
how in the years of renewed conflict with Great Britain mechanized spinning and family need transformed an anonymous weaver into a skilled
*"artizan."* The rose blanket tells a different story. Although it too evolved
from an English import, it belonged to a larger body of home weaving
that played freely with the forms and motifs of English models, until

innovation rather than imitation became the dominant value. In the agricultural fairs of the early republic, rose blankets straddled the line between household manufacture and "fancy work." The counterpane and the rose blanket provide different visions of the political economy of the early republic.

During Thomas Jefferson's administration, English harassment of American shipping provoked a new attempt at boycotts. The Embargo of 1807 and the Nonintercourse Act that followed revived the rhetoric of the Revolution. From Maine to Virginia, partisans toasted domestic manufactures, spinning wheels, and the "American Fair."[2] In the autumn of 1810, there was even a vicarious spinning match among women in different parts of the Northeast. It began in New York State, when newspapers reported that a Miss Triphosa Butler had spun and reeled eleven skeins of woolen yarn of ten knots of forty threads each in fifteen hours and ten minutes. The challenge spread to Massachusetts, where "two young ladies, Miss *Lois* and Miss *Maryamny* [sic] daughters of Mr. Jonathan Nye of New-Braintree, upon trying their skill at the Spindle and in 15 hours they produced on common wheels and reels 33 skeins of excellent woolen yarn of seven knots of forty threads each, which outdoes Miss *Triphosa* five knots and a half each, in less time by ten minutes." Two weeks later, an "Eye Witness" from Winthrop, Maine, responded that a pair of spinners in his neighborhood, Miss Sarah Keen and Miss Zilpha Cummings, had "upon trial of their skill," produced "forty skeins and twenty threads in sixteen hours and fifteen minutes, which they spun reeled, and put up in order, all with their own hands." The newspapers insisted that if the American "yeomanry" would imitate these families, "they would be relieved from the odious dun of the shop keeper, and the curse of foreign gew gaws and fashions, and their Country become emphatically Independent."[3]

Republican newspapers assailed their opponents. "Poor effeminate slaves! who would sacrifice every thing to the enjoyment of luxury! Ye are blots upon the country," screamed an essay in the *New Hampshire Gazette.* For these writers the dangers of luxury were even greater than the threat of savagery. "Go among the substantial farmers of our country, and ask them which they would prefer; to live free in a cottage, upon Indian bread, or to live slaves in a splendid house, richly furnished, feeding on luxuries?" In this period, as during the Revolution, slavery was the specter that allowed white men to define themselves as free. Some writers less anxious about factory production argued that national independence depended upon the integration of southern agriculture and northern enterpise. One Fourth of July toast put it succinctly: "May our Manufactories and Fisheries of the North, with the Sugar cane and Cotton tree of the South open to us such a sour[c]e of local independence, that we shall not need the aid of foreign Despots."[4]

In 1809, Congress expressed its faith in household manufacturing by commissioning a national census that not only counted iron foundries, mills, and factories, but the produce of household looms. In his preface to the summary statistics from the census of 1810, Tench Coxe praised the "sagacity and energy" that had given Rhode Island "the first comparative importance in cotton mills and establishments," but he emphasized that the key to national productivity lay in expanded household manufacturing. Cloth-making not only contributed "to the comfort and happiness" of women, it left men free "for the duties of the farm, and other employments, requiring exposure and strength." It might also provide an outlet for what he called "our redundant southern cotton." Such a material, he wrote, might "render every industrious female *an artiȝan,* whenever her household duties do not require her time." He could have been describing Eliza Perkins Wildes Bourne.[5]

Elizabeth Perkins was born in Arundel, now Kennebunkport, Maine, in 1765. She married Captain Israel Wildes in 1785 and was widowed eight years later. In 1795, she married John Bourne, a Kennebunkport shipbuilder, adding her three children to his six. Eventually there were fifteen children in the family—his, hers, and theirs.[6] The diary Eliza kept before her first husband's death conveys textile production in its most conventional form, with spinning and weaving interspersed with dressmaking, visiting, child care, and housework (see pages 298–300). A family history written by her son Edward Bourne describes her life after her second marriage and explains how she transformed subsistence production into a commercial enterprise.

John Bourne was a shipbuilder as well as a merchant, and for much of the year, Eliza boarded a crew of carpenters from the shipyard next to the house. She also "kept the store, employing herself, in moments when customers did not require attention, in bonnet making and kindred appointments." On one such occasion, little Edward was playing about the shop while his mother was engaged in her work. He had seen his older brother

*John Brewster, Jr. Elizabeth
Perkins Wildes Bourne, c. 1797.
Between 1797 and 1809, Brewster
painted at least fifteen portraits of
Kennebunk and Kennebunkport
families, including Eliza's sisters
Abiel and Susannah ("Sukey")
Perkins.*

THE BRICK STORE MUSEUM,
KENNEBUNK, MAINE

set fire to bits of gunpowder spilled on the street, and when he saw a keg
of the magical powder behind the counter, he thought he would try it
himself. Just as he reached for a coal from the fire, Eliza caught his hand,
saving them both from oblivion.[7]

Edward later insisted that he didn't have anything but a homespun coat
until he had been in college for two years, but he surely exaggerated his
family's reliance on homemade cloth. John Bourne was a successful busi-
nessman and a leader in town affairs. There was money enough to send
the older girls to Susanna Rowson's fashionable academy in Newton,
Massachusetts. Although a slump in trade and the impending marriage of
the oldest daughters provided the motive for enhanced manufacturing,
the form the new enterprise took—the production of stylish counterpanes modeled after English imports—shows Eliza's ambition. As
Edward explained, the coverlet business allowed his mother "to furnish
for most of the children, the means for their necessary fashionable
apparel, and in other respects, to make such a show, as was appropriate to
the social standing of the family." He added that Abigail, the youngest of
the Wildes daughters, "was the most skillful cooperator on this new
engine of physical labour."[8]

In February 1811, the *Kennebunk Weekly Visitor* published a description of the counterpane business. "Amongst the household manufacturers in this division, none have as yet been discovered who appear to have excelled a Mrs. Bourn of Kennebunk." She had three looms, one of which was fitted with a fly shuttle, and within eight months had "woven two hundred and twenty-two yards of cloth of different kinds in this loom, which at the lowest value is worth one hundred and twenty-three dollars and ninety cents. The other two looms are constructed to weave Cotton Counterpanes, the whole width." One broadloom had produced twenty counterpanes worth seventeen dollars each, the other ten valued at ten dollars each. "The labor expended is thought not to exceed the constant labor of three women with the assistance of children."[9]

Without question, Eliza was an industrious woman. Edward admitted that he had sometimes heard her address her girls as "lazy drabs," but "such occasional interjections were only a part of the regimen, instituted for the purpose of fireing up the spirit, and rooting and grounding them in habits of industry." She understood the importance of a proper appearance, but when it came to other niceties, she was sometimes surprisingly indifferent. "Without doubt, she could have sat down with Dr. Franklin, and made a comfortable repast on his sawdust pudding." On one memorable morning, she almost made a meal out of lampblack. The boys had tried grinding it in an old coffee mill, and when the maid came to make breakfast by candlelight, she took it by mistake. "What is the matter with this coffee?" the children complained. "It is good enough," the mother replied, "only a little oily, strange you can't be satisfied." Not until the mistake was discovered was she willing to admit defeat. "But probably, had she been alone, she would have taken her usual portion in Christian resignation and trust."[10]

Bourne's industriousness as well as her concern with making an appropriate "show" are both displayed in the counterpanes she and her daughter constructed. Like the Lancashire coverlets, they were made from factory-spun cotton in several weights, the thick weft being raised with small rods during weaving to create a tufted pattern. Although the weave structure is a simple one, the execution of the pattern required a meticulousness that few New England weavers possessed. Eliza and her daughter probably worked with a paper draft of the pattern, counting out each tuft as they worked. Edward said his mother initially tried weaving her counterpanes on a standard household loom, joining two strips in the center as was customary for sheets, blankets, and the vast majority of pat-

*Elizabeth Perkins Wildes Bourne and daughters. Cotton counterpane labeled "Mary Wise 1810."*

THE BRICK STORE MUSEUM. GIFT OF MRS. JOHN B. CORNING

terned coverlets in America. But the result "did not satisfy her tastes; and she had a loom made of sufficient width to complete them in one piece."[11]

In 1809, Abigail Wildes wove a poem into one of her coverlets and sent it to Dolley Madison.

> *Beneath this bed illustrious pair repose*
> *Secure from foreign and domestic foes.*
> *May white plumed seraphs watch around this bed,*
> *And heaven its kindlier influences shed.*[12]

The sentiment is peculiar given the fact that John Bourne was a Federalist and ostensibly among James Madison's "domestic foes." The petition he helped compose that year called the continuing restrictions on shipping "highly oppressive and against the manifest spirit of the national constitution."[13] He surely would have agreed with another local man who, in the Fourth of July celebration, sarcastically toasted the "Embargo Policy.

It cuts down the tree to kill the caterpillars." In other towns, Federalists were ready to say that the Commonwealth of Massachusetts, once "strong like Samson," now had her head in the "lap of Delilah."[14]

As nonparticipants in active politics, women could transcend party politics and at the same time achieve political ends. The coverlet was a nonpartisan appeal with local ramifications. Dolley Madison's sister, Anna Payne, was married to Congressman Richard Cutts of Saco, Maine. Perhaps the coverlet was part of a complex strategy designed to remind Cutts of his obligation to his neighbors. Anna Cutts herself commented on the capacity of New England women to cross party lines. Writing to Dolley from Boston in 1804, she described endless games of chess with "Madame Knox," wife of a Federalist landowner, and playing a card game called "Loo with Sarah Apthorp Morton," the queen of the city's literati. "The Federal party in Boston prevails," she reported, adding that "in spite of my connections, I find much civility among them." Dolley Madison made a point of following the same practice. "By her deportment in her own house you cannot discover who is her husband's friends or foes," one Congressman wrote.[15]

Abigail Wildes had grown up with—and perhaps even participated in—public ceremonials that figured women in this way. In 1800, the second parish of Wells included little girls in the commemoration of the death of Washington. Dressed "in white, with a black belt round the waist, on which was inscribed in large letters, 'Washington,'" they marched in procession to the meetinghouse, "where an eulogy was pronounced."[16] Federalists may have been even more zealous than Republicans in introducing females into such events. In 1799, Zilpah Wadsworth (the future mother of the poet Henry Wadsworth Longfellow) presented a flag to the Federal Volunteers of Portland, Maine, on behalf of the young ladies who had contributed the money to buy it. Since the band continued playing all through her speech, it didn't really matter "whether or not anything was said," but that was fine with Zilpah. She was happy to perform a service for the young men, who seemed inspired by receiving their flag "from the ladies in person." She also liked the fact that the men responded with a ball, which "gave us all a very agreeable evening." Still, the notoriety disturbed her: "to have one's name handed about so publicly & in the newspapers it was too much. I was mortified & distressed."[17]

Abigail Wildes might not have been so coy. According to her brother, she "was fond of out-door exercise, and enjoyed, very much riding on horse back. . . . I have seen her put her horse on his utmost speed, and go through a race skillfully, as one of the opposite sex." Her mother didn't object to having her name in the newspapers, and Abigail herself surely valued the approbation of powerful people.[18] The motto on her coverlet was consistent with the apolitical stance expected of genteel women in this period, but the fact that she had made it herself played into an older image of women as economic producers. The renewed emphasis on household manufactures in this period offered an alternative to the abstract iconography of republican virtue.

The first lady responded in her own hand in a letter dated January 20, 1810. "I have just now had the pleasure to receive the valuable and beautiful counterpane from Miss Wildes which does so much credit to her Ingenuity and Industry. I beg she will receive my sincere thanks for the singular favor, as it is greatly augmented by her expressions of kindness for an unknown friend who can never forget her. I hope she will add to my obligation by accepting from me some token of my regard. D. P. Madison."[19] The "token" was a necklace and earrings delivered by Anna Cutts. Though Dolley Madison alluded to Abigail's "Ingenuity and Industry," she responded as one lady to another, cementing a friendship through a seemingly frivolous item of jewelry.

The formality of Abigail's answer, written from Kennebunk in August 1810, would have pleased her Boston teachers: "Your sister, Mrs. Cutts, has, in the most obliging manner, delivered me the very elegant gold chain & earings, which you have had the kindness to send me. I pray you Madam, to accept my best thanks for a present, in itself of so much value, but greatly enhanced by the honor it does me, and the pleasure which must ever accompany the recollection, that it is from Mrs. Madison to her / very obedient / Abigail Wildes."[20] Thanks to a dual education in industry and refinement, Abigail was both a manufacturer and a lady.

Eliza Bourne simultaneously upheld her family's social position and inculcated habits of self-reliance in her daughters. Her manufactory was limited as well as sustained by its family setting, however. The oldest daughter married in August 1810, the second in November, and Abigail in January 1811. In Edward's words, the three helpers "on whom the mother had relied for carrying on the works of the household, and the various branches of domestic manufacture, had within six months all flown away, on the wings of love and left her in a somewhat helpless condition, without foreign aid." The manufactory languished for a time until

Julia Bourne was able to learn her mother's craft, but as Edward observed, times had changed and the mother had no need to press her youngest daughters "into such severe service, as was demanded of the others."[21]

If Dolley Madison kept Abigail's coverlet, it was burned in the British assault on Washington in 1813. By then, Abigail's father and other voters in coastal Maine had resoundingly rejected James Madison, Richard Cutts, and all they stood for. In the congressional election of 1812, the Federalist candidate got 622 votes, Cutts 41.[22] As the nation's capital prepared for a British invasion, the poem on the coverlet took on an ironic meaning. The first couple were no longer secure from either foreign or domestic foes. On December 20, 1811, Dolley wrote her sister from Washington with news of the two ships dispatched by the navy. "No Constitution heard of yet; the Hornet went to take despatches and to let them know our determination to fight for our rights," she wrote. Politics was not so important, however, that it prevented her from attending to her sister's wardrobe. "I wrote by the Hornet to Mrs. Barlow, and begged her to send me anything she thought suitable in the way of millinery. I fear I cannot obtain a new-fashioned pattern for you, but will make you a cap such as is much worn."[23] On May 12, 1813, she reported from Washington that the town expected an invasion at any minute, that the fort was being prepared, and that five hundred militia and almost as many regulars had been mustered. "The twenty tents already look well in my eyes, who have always been an advocate for fighting when assailed, though a Quaker. I therefore keep the old Tunisian sabre within reach."[24]

In August 1814, the president left Washington to join federal troops defending the city. When it became clear that the British force was advancing, Dolley gathered up her own and the president's papers and the portrait of George Washington that hung in the state dining room and fled. When she and her husband returned, they met a scene of desolation. Despite the damage, the Madisons were determined that Washington would remain the nation's capital and that Dolley's legendary entertainments would continue. In her substitute White House, she made up for the loss of damask curtains and upholstery by dressing herself regally. At one dinner, she compensated for the lost mirrors and chandeliers by arranging her slaves around the house with pine torches.[25]

Eliza Bourne asserted the independence of household manufacturers; Dolley Madison, the liberty to consume. Both women believed that it was necessary "to make such a show, as was appropriate to the social standing of the family." In that sense, there wasn't a great deal of difference between the manufactures of a Federalist household and the entertainments of a Republican presidency.

An examination of New England data from the census of 1810 shows that Bourne's manufactory was both unusual and in important respects representative of its time. Her fly shuttle and broadlooms set her apart, as did her almost total reliance on machine-spun cotton, but, as a household manufacturer, she was typical in being female, in producing about two hundred yards of "different kinds" of fabric in a season, and in relying on the labor of her grown daughters and younger children. The anonymous rose blanket is more representative, however, of the kinds of fabrics being made on household looms.

Most references to the census rely on aggregate data for states and counties published in Coxe's report, but for some places, including parts of Maine, Vermont, New Hampshire, and Massachusetts, manuscript totals for towns as well as counties survive, and in a few districts, where census takers took manufacturing data on the same pages as population, there are house-by-house counts.[26] These data provide an astonishing close-up of New England production on the eve of industrialization. Edward McCarron's work in linking house-by-house counts for Topsham, Maine, with occupational information derived from deeds, probate records, and town histories shows that in coastal Maine cloth-making took place in artisan as well as agricultural households.[27] The heads of Topsham's weaving families included forty-five yeoman, ten mariners, three housewrights, four blacksmiths, three shipwrights, two tanners, a joiner, a mason, a millman, five "gentlemen," three men called "Esquire," and a man identified in local records as a clothier. In every occupational category, more men owned looms than did not. The only group for whom weaving was not the norm were transient or marginal persons; of the twenty persons listed on the census but found nowhere else in local records, nineteen were without looms.

Since 88 percent of Topsham households claimed cloth-making while just over half had looms, some loom-owning families were obviously weaving for their neighbors. At six yards a day, the 4,593 yards credited to nonweaving families would have provided work for three full-time artisans or thirty domestic weavers working two or three days each month. There may have been an artisan weaver in Topsham. The local history identifies James Fulton as the son of a "journeyman weaver of linen" from county Derry, Ireland. When he died in 1812, he left his "weaver's loom" to his son. Whether his son continued his father's occupation we do not know, but it is unlikely that Fulton or any other weaver in Topsham worked full-time. There were simply too many weavers doing their own work to make that possible. That 76 percent of Topsham's widows owned looms versus only 56 percent of the general population argues that here, as elsewhere in New England, most weaving was done by women. Furthermore, loom owners were distinguished from non–loom owners by having a larger number of females in the ten to fifteen and sixteen to twenty-five age groups, substantiating diary evidence linking household production with the coming of age of daughters.

Census records from other parts of New England confirm these patterns. They also provide rich detail on the sorts of fabrics being made, though strict comparisons are impossible because of variations in terminology. In Essex and Middlesex County, Massachusetts, census takers reduced everything to the generic term *cloth*. Those in Orange County, Vermont, took the opposite approach, constructing nine categories— woolen, linen, cotton, tow, cotton and linen, cotton and wool, cotton and tow, tow and wool, and worsted, giving some sense of the variety that lay behind the common category "mixed." In most places, census takers used three categories: linen (or "flaxen"), wool (including worsted), and cotton, a category that often included mixed-fiber materials.[28] These detailed counts tell us that 80 to 90 percent of rural New Englanders produced cloth, that 40 to 50 percent did their own weaving, and that most produced little more than could comfortably be consumed at home. The census further confirms Henry Wansey's prediction that the most successful rural enterprises sustained rather than competed with household manufacturers. The most important were the 671 wool-carding mills listed in the federal census. Connecticut had a carding mill for every 1,424 persons. Even Maine, which still had many backcountry settlements, listed one for every 3,049 inhabitants.[29] There were few home producers who could not get their wool carded by machine.

The 112 cotton-spinning factories were concentrated in southern New England, with a quarter in Rhode Island, others along rivers in Norfolk, Worcester, and Essex Counties, Massachusetts, and a few in southern New Hampshire and Maine. Although the number of spindles in active operation had increased almost tenfold between 1808 and 1811, most of the yarn was still woven "in private families, mostly for their own use, and partly for sale."[30] The Rhode Island mills sold both yarn and instructions for weaving, offering to buy back cloth once it was woven. This had an appreciable effect on census returns from tiny Kent County, which recorded a whopping seventy yards of cloth per capita, but little impact on overall totals elsewhere. In Thomas Hazard's part of Rhode Island, 57 percent of reported cloth was still flaxen and 21 percent woolen. In Martha Ballard's Kennebec County the corresponding numbers were 45 percent linen, 38 percent woolen, and 17 percent cotton, and in Sarah Bryant's Hampshire County, 46 percent linen, 29 percent wool, and 25 percent cotton, the latter category, as in Maine, including mixed-fiber goods.[31]

The memoirs of two women whose towns are documented in detail show how weaving and nonweaving families interacted. Mary Palmer Tyler, wife of Vermont superior court justice and early American playwright Royall Tyler, lived in Brattleboro, Vermont. Minerva Mayo, the daughter of a poor but respectable farmer, lived in Orange, Massachusetts. Brattleboro was a trading town, Orange an area of subsistence farms, yet the per capita cloth production in the two places was similar. Orange averaged sixteen yards per household, Brattleboro fourteen. The memoirs give us some sense of the varying circumstances in which that cloth was made.

Raised in Boston, Tyler first encountered the economy of homespun in the 1790s when her father's business failure forced the family to move from the city to rural Framingham, Massachusetts.

> We learned to spin, borrowing wheels of our good-natured neighbors, who seemed pleased to teach the city ladies their craft. We learned, while we lived there, to spin flax, on a little foot wheel, and wool, tow and cotton, on a large wheel. There was a plump rosy faced girl whose name was Zerniah Price, who was one of our nearest neighbors and who seemed to take great interest in teaching us. She taught us how to card wool, cotton and tow, and how to hatchel flax, some of which was raised upon the farm; and my mother would change work with Zerniah's mother and other women, knitting and sewing for them while they would weave cotton and flax into cloth which we would get dressed into fustian at the mill for the boys and also for Father's summer working dress.[32]

Twenty years later, finding herself on a farm near Brattleboro with her husband frequently away at court, Tyler took up textile production in earnest.

The 1810 census for Brattleboro credits no loom to Royall Tyler but lists 98 yards of wool, 69 of linen, and 49 of mixed-fiber cloth. "All this time my dairy and spinning wheels were busily attended, in your father's absence, by myself, with the assistance of one and at times two girls," Mary recalled. The census counted fifteen persons in the house, including four children under ten and three women over sixteen, one of whom may have been Mary's younger sister Sophia, and two who could have been the "girls" Mary hired to spin flax for "sheets and common table linen." The memoir tells us she turned her weaving over to a Mrs. Peck until that weaver left town, then to a Mrs. Fisher, who may have been the wife of the Ebinizer Fisher, listed in the census with a family of twelve (including three females over ten). The Fisher loom produced 155 yards for family use and perhaps some part of the 98 yards attributed to the Tyler household as well. Despite her husband's status as a professional, Mary Tyler was a thrifty housewife, and she soon suggested another arrangement, as her memoir records. "[H]aving to give nine pence a yard for weaving, I suggested to your father the expediency of getting a loom, and having our flax and wool wove in the house. Ever ready to comply with my wishes, he got one immediately, and for twelve or fifteen years we made the children's clothes summer and winter for common wear."[33]

Mary's allusion to having cloth woven "in the house" leaves the identity of the weaver (or weavers) hidden. Presumably Sophia or one of the unnamed "spinning girls" did the work with some assistance from neighbors. Their inexperience showed. At one point, Tyler tried to make blankets, having them woven "a yard and a half quarter wide, being the capacity of our loom, intending to have them fulled at the mill and dressed so as to have two breadths in a blanket for the width." Unfortunately, when the blankets came home, the fuller had shrunk them so much she had to give up one full blanket in order to match the lengths in the other two, "spoiling the look of them" by requiring an extra seam. Though they were "very thick, white, and a fine nap upon them," she "was sadly disappointed," and apparently never tried the experiment again, though she and her helpers did continue to make simpler fabrics.

Minerva Mayo's strange little memoir offers a quite different picture of the rural economy. Copied into a school exercise book by her cousins after her death in 1824, "The Life and Writings of Minerva Mayo by Herself" consists of a handful of poems and letters and a short auto-biography written as she was about to run away from home. She intended to "march for the Ohio," for it was "riveted into my mind that I can never rest satisfied until I have tried my fortune." She helped herself to a little money from the family tavern, took her brother's greatcoat and hat to protect and perhaps disguise herself, but apparently didn't get far. She may have been ill when she sat down to compose an apologia for her life. It began with her earliest childhood, the period covered in the census.

In 1810 Calvin and Sally Mayo and three children lived on a rough farm under the shadow of Big Tully mountain. Minerva was then seven years old. In Orange, as in a few other places in Hampshire County, the census taker chose to record the amount of cloth woven on each loom rather than the amount of cloth produced by each household. Since Calvin Mayo did not own a loom, he was listed as a nonproducer, though his wife could well have been using the loom at her father's house. The census credited Edward Ward with a hundred yards of wool, a hundred yards of cotton, and two hundred yards of linen.

Minerva's memoir doesn't focus on her mother's productivity, how-ever, but on her own misbehavior. "I was born a rogue," she wrote. Though she often felt "the rod of correction," for burning and breaking things and eating without permission, she persisted in her naughtiness, until her desperate mother arrived at the perfect solution. "Very many hours, I have been kept tied to my Mother loom as it prevent my running away." Now, at the age of eighteen, Minerva was ready to try again. Whether she managed to leave home we do not know. She died three months after completing her memoir. Minerva's temperament may have been unusual, but other mothers must also have struggled to tend both a loom and a child. There was always too much work to do, never enough hands to do it. Some no doubt responded with harshness.[34]

Calvin Mayo was a marginal farmer, but because he owned land and had the support of kin, he was never forced into wage work. Other men were not so fortunate. Hiram Munger, who was born in Monson, Massa-chusetts, was driven by his family's poverty to work in a small cotton fac-tory as a child. Built over a gristmill, it had only twelve or fifteen workers, most of them children. "Here was where I was first made acquainted with American slavery in the *second degree*," he wrote. "The treatment of the help in those days was cruel, especially to poor children of whom I was one." Other families found respite, and perhaps kinder employers, in the mills. William Davis was living on his farm in 1812 when he began working irregularly at one of Samuel Slater's mills to pay off debts at the company-owned store. In 1815, he moved his family into a mill-owned tenement house and he and his three oldest children, ages seven to twelve, signed on for steady employment. The Davises continued to work for Slater until 1827, taking their pay in store goods as well as cash. When the younger children turned seven, they, too, went into the factory, their work being credited to their father's account until they turned eighteen.[35]

The work of families like these—and the southern slaves who produced the cotton—sustained Eliza Bourne's coverlet manufactory, but this combination of factory and artisan production was rare in New England in 1810. Most home weavers used only a little factory-spun cotton to supplement their own flax and wool. Some mills attempted to manufacture common fabrics, like shirting, checks, or ticking, by selling the yarn to local weavers, then buying back the finished cloth when it was done. This informal system of outwork was never very successful. Weavers might return the cloth to the mill where they bought it or sell it elsewhere if the price was right, and the quality was frustratingly uneven. After 1810, some Rhode Island mills established a more conventional system of "putting-out," placing yarn with country storekeepers as far away as New Hampshire. But most weavers worked only when and how they wished. In 1815, one manufacturer wrote in exasperation to his New Hampshire middleman: "I did not expect but that your weavers would take from you such yarn as you had to put out. You will on a little reflection see, that if the weavers are to weave just such kind of goods as they chuse and those only, that we are in but a sorry way, what advantage shall we derive from putting out yarn in large quantities, if it is to be selected by the weavers & that which they do not like is to be returned unwoven."[36] Rural weavers could afford to be independent because outwork was merely a supplement to their own household weaving. In Chatham, Connecticut, for example, Sally White wove about one hundred yards a year for a local storekeeper, taking her pay in black lustring, cotton lace, a breast pin, a comb, and skeins of yarn that she no doubt turned into fabrics for herself and her family.[37]

As long as farming remained viable, most New England weavers continued to work for themselves. The anonymous rose blanket shows what some of them did with their homespun wool.

. . .

The bright pink roses on the blanket at the Royal Ontario Museum introduce three stories—one about the export of English blankets to North America, another about the expansion of female education in the early republic, and the third about the celebration of household production at the agricultural fairs that developed in the region after 1810.

No one knows when the Oxfordshire firms that shipped blankets and Indian "coats" to North America in the early seventeenth century began ornamenting the corners of their best-quality blankets with embroidery. This stitchery, produced quickly in London workshops, probably by poor women and children, was a crude but colorful representation of a compass rose. Some historians believe these "rosings," as they were sometimes called, originated in small motifs used to mark the places where individual blankets were cut from long webs of cloth. Since all extant rose blankets have end stripes, a device designed for the very same purpose, that explanation pushes the origins of the motif far back in time. As early as 1711 the bylaws of the blanket-makers' guild of Witney, Oxfordshire, required every member to "shoot and weave or cause to be Shott and Weaved at each end of every Blankett . . . two shoots at the least of Colloured yarn to show the length of such Blankett." In some, the "shoots" of black or brown wool extended the full width of the blanket to form a narrow stripe at each end. The famous "point blankets" used in the Indian trade had several short stripes in the corners to mark length and value.[38]

In its mature form the embroidery seems to have been a kind of trademark for a mass-produced but highly desirable blanket. The "38 prs. rose blanketts" ordered by a New York merchant in 1746 probably looked much like the fluffy Oxfordshire blankets that survive in American collections today. Whether found in the Shelburne Museum in Vermont, at Colonial Williamsburg, or in the American Fur Trade Museum in Nebraska, these blankets all have the same distinctive loft, the same natural brown or black stripe at the ends, and the same flamboyant embroidery in the corners. The "white Blanket flowerd at the Corner" in Solomon Stoddard's inventory of 1729 was probably also an English specimen, as were those advertised alongside India cottons and Irish linens in Vermont newspapers of the early 1800s. Rose blankets remained popular into the nineteenth century, spreading west with the new nation. In 1828, an advertiser in the *Missouri Republican* offered rose blankets in various sizes, just as his predecessors in Connecticut had done forty years before.[39]

*Detail of English rose
blanket.*
WINTERTHUR MUSEUM

*John Neagle.*
*Red Jacket, 1824.*
GILCREASE MUSEUM, TULSA,
OKLAHOMA

Perhaps the compass motifs had something to do with maritime pride; the black crosshatching surrounding the compass motif echoes the navigational lines on early maps. In 1815, the Early Blanket Company was exporting rose blankets in widths ranging from forty-five to ninety-nine inches. Common ones sold for twenty shillings and the really large ones

Samuel Lane's compass,
made by Joseph Halsy,
Boston, 1747.
NEW HAMPSHIRE HISTORICAL
SOCIETY

for sixty-six shillings at a time when "Negro blankets" were nine shillings a pair. Company accounts also list Hudsons, Yorks, shaggs, super, light, and common blankets, both "cornered and uncornered," and red, blue, green, white, and striped kerseys and duffels.[40] The motifs in surviving blankets vary, but all seem to have been worked in a similar rough worsted, much like rug yarn, in various combinations of red, coral, green, yellow, and black. The embroidery was added after the blanket was fulled, and probably after it was cut since many surviving examples have been finished on the cut edges with a loose blanket stitch in the same yarn as the embroidery.

People seeing such blankets for the first time sometimes wonder if they are "Indian blankets." The patterns do have the geometric quality associated with indigenous art, and in fact the same blanket makers who sold "duffels" to coastal Indians in the seventeenth century and "point blankets" to the Hudson's Bay Company in the eighteenth and nineteenth centuries also produced rose blankets for commandants at English forts. Four rose blankets went to Detroit in 1781, and forty-four to the Piankashaws in 1797. In 1823, the Philadelphia Academy of Art hung a sketch in oils of the Seneca orator Red Jacket wearing a rose blanket across his shoulder, its star mirroring the star on his silver medal.[41] But this is simply another example of the way popular English exports crossed ethnic lines.

Rose blankets may have been among the products needed when in

*Homespun blanket found in
Maine, corner detail.*
PRIVATE COLLECTION.
PHOTOGRAPH BY GARY SAMSON

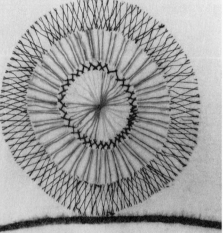

*English rose blanket,
corner detail.*
NORTHAMPTON HISTORICAL
SOCIETY, NORTHAMPTON,
MASSACHUSETTS

*Child-sized English
blanket, corner detail.*
OLD STURBRIDGE VILLAGE

1810, someone proposed that Congress break its nonintercourse with England in order "to buy blankets and nick-nacks for the Indians." In Pittsfield, Massachusetts, a probably male writer who signed himself "DOROTHY DISTAFF" responded that Massachusetts women were not only capable of producing bedding and clothing for their own households but for the interior trade.

> What sort of nick-nacks he wants I don't know—but as to blankets and all sorts of cloths that an Indian, squaw or papoose need wear, unless they are more whimsical and extravagant than our white gentlefolks—I know we can make enough for the Six Nations in our town.—Instead of going cap-in-hand to Old England, and telling them that our women are all a set of do-nothings and know-nothings, like too many of our men, let him . . . tell us what he wants in our line; and we will *put our hands to the distaff*, and pledge our spinning wheels (of ten times more value than all the wheels within wheels at Washington) that he shall have, much sooner, cheaper, and better, than he could get from England, enough of every article of clothing, from head to foot, for the Indians.

Adopting the voice of a female rustic, the writer not only satirized the "wheels" of Washington, but the ideas of elite Bostonians.[42]

Whether household weavers ever produced blankets for the Indian trade, we do not know, but long before 1810 they had begun to imitate English rose blankets. The New England versions look very different from English blankets. Woven in twill or tabby on narrow looms, they have the telltale center seams, unsorted wool, and warping errors common to household production. The embroidery is tighter and more varied than in the English examples and typically worked in indigo and in various shades of pink or gold rather than in the brighter English colors. The blankets themselves range from sturdy twill to true disasters. The maker of a blanket now at Sturbridge persisted in embroidering five compasslike rings, one for each corner and the middle, on a blanket so warped that it simply could not be made to lie flat. Home weavers probably began making their own rose blankets long before 1790, the date on a crudely worked example at Historic Deerfield. The "green and red starr blanket" listed in a Woodbury, Connecticut, inventory of 1759 could have been a local product. References to "star" blankets, "flowered" blankets, "compass" blankets, and "rose" blankets continued into the nineteenth century.[43]

*Detail of embroidery.*
ROYAL ONTARIO MUSEUM, TORONTO

*Reverse side of embroidery.*
ROYAL ONTARIO MUSEUM, TORONTO

The flowered blanket at the Royal Ontario Museum is another takeoff on the English blankets, but it is also an adaptation of the floral embroidery taught in young ladies' schools. Naturalistic roses often appear on samplers in this period, reflecting the age's interest in gardening. The female department of Vermont's Chester Academy, for example, offered instruction in "Drawing, Painting and Ornamental Needle Work" alongside "Courses of Lectures on Natural Philosophy, Chemistry, and Botany."[44] Botany had its practical application in the garlands of roses, worked in silk, that often appeared on samplers in this period. In most, successive layers of satin stitch define the interfolded petals of each rose.[45]

The person who embroidered our blanket had surely seen works like these. She began with a rough outline loosely stitched in pale blue linen thread, sketching her flower freehand. Although the blanket itself is made from the rough wool typical of early American production, that in the roses has the silken sheen and soft texture of merino, a wool derived from sheep imported into America from Spain and promoted by agricultural innovators. Like the indigo stripes that run across all four sides of the blanket, the wool in the embroidery was probably home dyed. A second bath of the imported dye called "cochineal" would have produced the pink; the green (now faded to brown) may have begun with a mixture of

Family register "wrought by Dolly Pollard, Augusta, July 18, 1820." Dolly's grandmother was the midwife Martha Moore Ballard.

MAINE HISTORICAL SOCIETY, PORTLAND, MAINE

fustic and sumac. The ends of the blanket have been finished in the pink wool, the embroiderer using it sparingly to make sure that it extended the full width.[46]

If the rose in the corners suggest school-girl embroideries and the wool in them the introduction of merino, their presence on a natural wool blanket points toward the textile exhibits that developed in New England cattle shows after 1810. The "cattle shows" began with a gentleman farmer named Elkanah Watson, who in the fall of 1807 displayed a pair of Merino sheep "under the great elm tree in the public square" in Pittsfield, Massachusetts. Born in Plymouth, Massachusetts, in 1758, Watson spent time in a British prison during the Revolution, served as an agent for a Rhode Island manufacturer in France and the Carolinas, tried southern agriculture for a time, then settled in Albany, New York, before coming to Pittsfield in 1807, ostensibly to retire. Inspired by the experiments of George Washington Custis in Virginia and Robert Livingston in New York, he was determined to educate his backward neighbors in the wonders of progressive agriculture. To his delight, a crowd gathered.[47]

In November 1808, newspapers as far away as Portsmouth, New Hampshire, picked up a story from the *Pittsfield Sun* about Watson's experiments with sheep. His Spanish ram and ewe had produced more than eight pounds of wool, which when cleaned and carded gave him six pounds eleven ounces of rolls, and some "tags and cuttings" left over. He had it spun and woven "in a superior style *by the Shakers*," who had a community in nearby Hancock, then sent it to a clothier for fulling, dyeing, and finishing. He ended up with 7½ yards of cloth "full thirty inches wide," arguing that since English broadcloth came in double-widths of fifty-six inches, measuring only twenty-eight inches "for the half," he had an advantage. Even by paying others to do the carding, spinning, and weaving, he realized substantial savings. Cloth that would have cost him $26.25 in a store was manufactured for only $7.92. Even if he counted the value of the wool at $1.50 a pound, he had a clear profit of 25 percent.[48]

Four years later, under Watson's tutelage, the Berkshire County Agricultural society launched its first exhibition. The day began with a parade led by the sheriff of the county and four marshals on gray horses. In Watson's recollection, it "extended at least half a mile." In the lead were sixty yoke of prime oxen, connected by chains, drawing a plow "held by two of the oldest men in the county." A band followed, then the members of the society, each wearing "a badge of wheat in his hat." Next came a stage drawn by oxen on which were a broadcloth loom and a spinning jenny, "both in operation by English artists," followed by a procession of "mechanics" and a stage filled with American manufactures—rolls of broadcloth, bolts of duck, rose blankets, muskets, anchors, and leather, with the flags of the United States and Massachusetts displayed above them. With characteristic enthusiasm, Watson pronounced this rural spectacle "splendid, novel, and imposing, beyond any thing of the kind, ever exhibited in America," adding that it had cost him a great deal of trouble and money.[49]

His crowning achievement came two years later when he devised a scheme for attracting the attention of Berkshire's women. The society had added manufactures to the exhibit in 1812, giving premiums for the best superfine broadcloth made from "the down" of Watson's merinos. In January 1813, they offered "seven valuable premiums of silver plate" exclusively for household manufactures. On the day of the exhibit, the hall was filled with homemade goods, but curiously, the women who had made them were nowhere to be seen. Watson installed his wife in a private room in the tavern, "then despatched messengers to the ladies of the village in every direction," telling them that Mrs. Watson waited to receive them at the cattle show. When the leading ladies responded, the farmers' wives, who had been "lying in wait to watch the movements of the waters," came too. Female spectators and candidates for premiums soon filled the hall, providing Watson "one of the most grateful moments of my life." They had another exhibition of cloth in October, securing the assembly room over the Female Academy for the Ladies.[50]

By this time, the United States was at war with Great Britain and Pittsfield was a rendezvous point for recruits. The government fitted up a house for the commandant of the post and laid out thirteen acres for a camp. Local carpenters quickly assembled three plain wooden buildings, three stories high and 130 feet long. Later, prisoners of war were kept there as well, and a hospital was built. The new camp gave the women of Pittsfield opportunities for patriotic service and socializing. On July 4, 1812, "the bountiful hand of female benevolence spread the table of festivity and enjoyment for the soldiers, who were regaled by the republican ladies in a style which reflected honor upon their patriotism." A few weeks later, the ladies of Cheshire, ten miles to the north, served a sumptuous dinner under "a bower erected for the occasion at the encampment." There was "beef, ham, lamb, pigs, turkeys, fowls, green-peas, string-beans, new potatoes, puddings, pies, and indeed everything requisite for an entertainment of the first order." There were officers' dinners at the tavern and balls organized by the men. There was even an exhibition of an elephant in the fall of 1813.[51]

The commissary for the regiment was Thomas Melville, Jr., who had just returned to New England after twenty-one years in France. In December 1812, he managed to collect 487 pairs of socks from Pittsfield and nearby towns, but by 1814, he was unable to meet his quota of a thousand blankets, coats, vests, and overalls for lack of public money.[52] Rescued by peace, he nevertheless continued to preach the gospel of manufactures. In his speech to the society in 1814, Watson exclaimed that "almost every woman in our country, not only understands manufacturing both woollen and linen," but would seize the opportunity to expand production. The only thing preventing them from contributing to the cause was the reluctance of farmers to expand sheep raising. "Some have apprehended we shall be over stocked with wool. To such I ask, if there were ten times the quantity raised in this County, and each female could have as much to manufacture as she wanted in the course of the year, would it not all be converted into cloths for market—give rise to new branches—add greatly to our wealth—and above all, confine the younger class of females to habitual industry?"[53]

In an equally enthusiastic speech two years later, his successor, Thomas Gold, trucked out the familiar scripture from Proverbs. "In fine, the ladies of Berkshire have reclaimed the properties, and merit that meed of praise, which Solomon, the wisest man of his time, awarded to the sex of that day—'They will do good and not evil all the days of their lives. They seek the wool and the flax, and work willingly with their hands. They make themselves coverings of tapestry. Their clothing is silk, and purple. Their husbands are known in the gates.' "[54] Thanks to the Berkshire County Agricultural Society, the women too would be known in the gates. In the published account of 1814, women received prizes for flannel, plaids, table linen, colored counterpanes, worsted and cotton shawls, carpeting, and white cotton counterpanes that must have been much like those of Eliza Bourne. Fourteen of the seventeen textile prizes went to women, the remaining three to a male clothier, a hatmaker, and a maker of "superfine broadcloth."

In 1820, William Cullen Bryant, a young lawyer living in Great Barrington, Massachusetts, delivered an ode to the Berkshire Cattle Show.

> *And here, while autumn wanders pale*
> *Beneath the fading forest shade,*
> *Gather'd from many a height and vale,*
> *The bounties of the year are laid.*[55]

The diary of his mother documents the "bounties" of one household weaver. With the help of her daughters, Sarah Bryant wove stripes, checks, and patterned coverlets, as well as plain cloth, using locally gathered peach leaves, goldenrod, butternut bark, smartweed, and hemlock, as well as imported madder, annatto, copperas, and indigo to dye her goods. In the 1820s, she wove a series of plaids for gowns, fine linen for shirts, and tablecloths with "double diamonds" requiring eight harnesses on her loom. She reached her limit in 1833 when she attempted "12 wing damask" in a number sixty reed, finally taking it out and starting over with a simpler pattern.[56]

The list of prizes in New England cattle shows in this period shows that there were dozens of women much like her. By 1823, the *New England Farmer* was announcing shows in Worcester, Brighton, Pittsfield, Plymouth, and Northampton, Massachusetts; Amherst, Concord, Exeter, and Acworth, New Hampshire; Burlington, Windsor, and Middlebury, Vermont; Pawtuxet, Rhode Island; and Hartford, Windham, and Granby, Connecticut; as well as giving occasional notion of fairs in other parts of the country.[57] The committee organizing the second "Cattle Show, Ploughing Match, and Exhibition of Manufactures" at Worcester "felt peculiar satisfaction in finding that the softer sex shared in the general zeal, and had contributed their full proportion towards this interesting exhibition." There as elsewhere the committee mixed mill-made with homemade fabrics. At Brighton in 1822, for example, the Woolcott Manufacturing Company received the first premium for "Superfine Cassimere" and a Mrs. Putnam the premium for "Diaper." Some of the prizes for household manufactures went to male heads of household, others to the women who made them. Single women were more likely than married women to receive prizes on their own. At Brighton in 1818, "Miss Boame, of Kennebunk" received an eight-dollar gratuity for a cotton counterpane. This was surely Julia Bourne, who at the age of fifteen was ready to take up the work her older sisters had left behind.[58]

Rose blankets were there from the beginning. Typically exhibited in pairs, they were often singled out as being better than the ones exhibited before. Most of the prizes went to women, but in 1830 the *Massachusetts Spy* reported that the prize for the best rose blankets at the Worcester Cattle Show had gone to John Hunter of New Braintree. A more detailed story appearing a week later gave the credit to *Mrs.* John Hunter, praising her for manufacturing blankets "greatly superior to the imported blankets of the same description." In 1825 she had received three dollars for "two Rose Bed Blankets, of a beautiful texture, and finely wrought." Her blankets were no doubt impressive, but since her husband was a member of an elite group of progressive farmers in New Braintree, a town that produced several presidents of the Worcester County Agricultural Society, her fame was solidified by her connections.[59]

Although newspaper reports never described the prizewinning blankets in detail, surviving examples give us some sense of the variety and

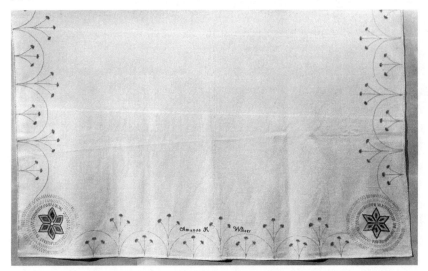

*Amanda K. Winters.*
*Pair of rose blankets.*
NEW HAMPSHIRE
HISTORICAL SOCIETY

range. Stimulated perhaps by the competition, home manufacturers began producing
their blankets in punning pairs. Amanda K.
Winters of Grantham, New Hampshire,
stayed close to the conventional compass
star on her first blanket, but on the other she arranged five-petaled flowers around each ring, adding an arched border to the ends. Sarah Prescott
of Westbrook, Massachusetts, worked a series of perfectly executed
motifs on blankets woven by her mother. On one she attached delicate
stems and leaves to a version of the pinwheels found on many geometric
compasses. On the other she embroidered a naturalistic rose and a more
complex version of a compass turned flower.[60] A pair marked with the initials *C.P.* (for Clara, Cleora, or Climena Philbrick of Weare, New Hampshire) has a neatly worked version of a compass star on one blanket and a
crosshatched rose on the other. These pairings suggest that our blanket,
too, may once have had a mate.

Other women scattered flowering compasses over the entire surface of
their blankets. Syrena Parmalee of Bristol, Vermont, went further. Like
the maker of our anonymous rose blanket, she framed natural wool with
stripes of indigo, but instead of stopping with flowers in the corners, she
splashed baskets of roses and two weeping willows down the center of her
blanket, and embroidered trailing curves much like those on the Foot bed
rugs along one side and the end. She was as practical as she was ambitious.
She disdained ornamenting the side of a coverlet that would be turned to

the wall, nor did she attempt to cover the entire surface, as the Foot sisters did. In the early republic, a homemade blanket was worth displaying.

These clever blankets transformed an English import into an American icon, simultaneously demonstrating household independence and rural pride. Like the Bourne coverlets, the Prescott rose blankets were produced by a mother and daughter who combined old-fashioned skills in spinning and weaving with the enticements of an elite education. Sarah Prescott attended Miss Beach's Academy in Dorchester, Massachusetts. Her samplers and those of her sister, now at the Peabody-Essex Museum and in the Westford Public Library, are delicately wrought in silk. Her mother, Olive Prescott, was a skilled weaver who received prizes for blankets, coverlets, and carpets at Middlesex County cattle shows in the 1830s, sometimes as "Mrs. Abram Prescott," sometimes as "Olive," and once as "Oliver Prescott."[61]

Although the Philbrick blankets are less sophisticated, they too emerged from a prosperous rural household blessed with a bevy of daughters. The father, Joseph Philbrick, was a judge of the Court of General Sessions and an active member of the Hillsborough County Agricultural Society. In 1831, the mother, identified as "Hannah Philbrick of Weare," received an award at the annual cattle show for "the best specimen of dressed woolen cloth not less than 10 yards." Her daughters Cleora and Climena won prizes for a counterpane and a "Wrought Lace Veil." The next year Hannah won fifty cents for "a carpet of great firmness and durability" and Climena for "a pair of blankets, of fine wool,

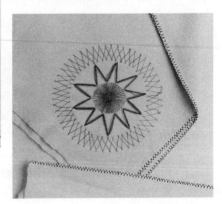

*Olive and Sarah Prescott. Embroidered blankets, corner details.*
PEABODY-ESSEX MUSEUM,
SALEM, MASSACHUSETTS

*Philbrick family. Embroidered blankets, corner details.*
SOCIETY FOR THE PRESERVATION OF NEW ENGLAND
ANTIQUITIES. GIFT OF GEORGE O. SWASEY
AND CLARA S. WOODBERRY, 1949.
PHOTOGRAPH BY DANA SALVO

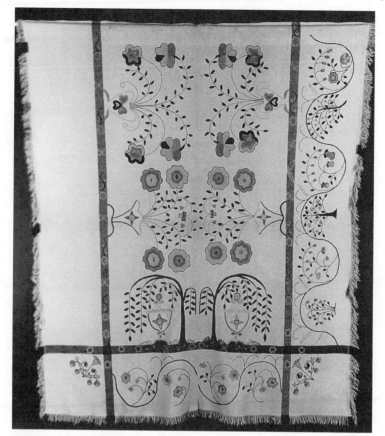

*Syrena Scott Parmelee.*
*Embroidered blanket, 1827.*
VERMONT HISTORICAL SOCIETY,
MONTPELIER, VERMONT

well made."[62] Joseph Philbrick's inventory, taken in 1831, shows the range of textile production in this household of girls. In addition to a pair of rose blankets, there were woven coverlets, fulled cloth for blankets, blue, green, and white undressed cloth, striped bed ticking, cotton and linen, tow and linen, striped and check fabrics, more than 50 yards of diaper, and 19½ yards of floor carpet. That several of the daughters were as yet unmarried partially explains this abundance.[63]

The counterpane and the rose blanket describe a moment in New England history when public events once again thrust home manufactur-

*Anonymous. Rose blanket, detail.*

ers into public view. In Eliza Bourne's case, economic privilege and a troop of daughters allowed her to produce coverlets that fully met the standards of English commercial production. The rose blanket is a cruder but more democratic object. Acknowledging the refinements of elite embroidery, it flaunts its independence. Simultaneously homemade and ornamental, it marries the conventions of English blanketry with the enticements of elite embroidery, in an object that is both practical and witty.

Eleanor Washburn Tracy, the sixteen-year-old bride of the principal of Vermont's Royalton Academy, captured the contradictory impulses that produced blankets like these when she wrote her brother, a student at Dartmouth College, in the early winter of 1819:

Dear Brother: I should be very happy to write you a few words, and should, if I hadn't been making pies and got some fatigued. I can't think of anything to write, and so I will tell you what I have been doing this fall. I have spun my husband a coat and myself a gown and seven or eight runs of stocking yarn, beside knitting and sewing.

Have learned the Hebrew letters, and how many parts of speech there are in Latin.

Perhaps I shall learn some Greek next. I don't think that what I have written is very good, but I hope you won't criticize it at all, from

your sister, Eleanor.[64]

Our rough wool blanket with its pretentious pink rose speaks a similar language. If it could talk, it would brag about the skeins of wool its maker had spun in a day. It would quote a few lines of poetry, perhaps an ode to a rose, then apologize for its lack of perfection.

# A Woodsplint Basket

## RUTLAND, VERMONT, AFTER 1821

*Their producing process took everything at a disadvantage; for they had no capital, no machinery, no distribution of labour, nothing but wild forest and rock; but they had mettle enough in their character to conquer their defects of outfit and advantage. They sucked honey out of the rock, and oil out of the flinty rock.*

Horace Bushnell, "The Age of Homespun"

Displayed in the "Hall of the North American Indian" at Harvard University's Peabody Museum, the basket looks like many others made in New England in the early nineteenth century. It is a lidded storage basket woven from ash splints that have been swabbed with dye then stamped on alternate wefts with simple designs cut from a potato or the top of a cork. The surprise is inside. Firmly pasted to the inner contours of the lid and across the bottom and up the sides of the body are overlapping pages from the *Rutland* (Vermont) *Herald* for the fall and winter of 1821–1822.[1] A name scrawled on the newspaper in the lid identifies the subscriber as "M Goodrich." If he was the Moses Goodrich listed in the 1820 census for Poultney, a town near Rutland, he was a typical Vermonter—a man passing through from one place to another. Unlisted in the census of 1810, he was gone by 1830, leaving his and his wife's names on an infant's gravestone but no other evidence of his identity.[2]

The basket too may have been a migrant. Its dominant characteristics—alternating wide and narrow splints and regularly spaced stamping—are typical of those made by Mahican and Schagticoke families along the borders between Massachusetts, Connecticut, and New York in the late eighteenth and early nineteenth centuries. The construction of the basket measures the distance Algonkian weavers traveled from the twined textiles of the early colonial period. Woodsplint basketry developed after wars and disease forced remnant groups to find new ways of making a living. Already skilled in using forest products, they adapted to an emerging market for inexpensive and lightweight containers. By the early nineteenth century, an "Indian" basket was almost by definition a woodsplint basket.[3] This one could have arrived in Vermont with the maker or an early owner—perhaps Moses Goodrich or someone close to him.

Vermont in the early republic was a ragged patchwork of farms set among mountains and wood, yet this seeming backwater had among the highest literacy rates in the Western world. Its leading citizens

built churches, schools, and lodges; founded newspapers, debating societies, and academies; and celebrated mechanical invention and household
industry in full confidence that aristocracy, superstition, and indolence
were about to vanish from the earth. "We have had considerable advantage of Schooling for our Children. Sence we have been hear the two girls
and Uriah can read a newspaper very well," an early settler assured his
Massachusetts relatives. Eight newspapers appeared in the Connecticut
River Valley before 1800. Across the mountains, the *Rutland Herald* was
founded in 1794 by the former Hollis professor of mathematics at Harvard College, a sometime minister who identified himself on the title
page of one of his books as a "Member of the Meteorological Society in
Germany, of the Philosophical Society in Philadelphia, and of the Academy of Arts and Sciences in Massachusetts." The second editor of the
*Herald*, William Fay, had a more modest education, but he too was committed to rational discourse.[4]

Lining a basket, Fay's papers became an instrument of good housekeeping. Woodsplints are silken on the outside but on the reverse can be
as rough in spots as a farmer's hands. The lining protected the contents
against dust, insects, and subtle abrasion. Smaller than a trunk but larger
than a workbox, a lidded basket was a convenient repository for extra
clothing, papers, bonnets, or other personal possessions. Displayed
beside a worktable or on top of a chest it would have added decorative
interest to a simple room. The person who lined this basket may or may
not have read the newspapers she used, but if she did she discovered competing ideas about women. Notices of the annual Cattle Show and Exhibition of Manufactures for Rutland County offered prizes for the best
woolen and linen cloth, butter, and cheese. But a front-page essay in the
papers lining the lid asked why women were "less courted" now than in
the medieval age when they were shut up in castles. Obviously, it was
because their too frequent appearance in public had made them common.
The pages of the *Rutland Herald* describe a world of persistent household
production and emerging gentility.[5]

The newspapers also acknowledge a darker underside of New
England life. On the reverse of one of the papers in the lid is a story about
the murder in Massachusetts of a woman described as "the last of the
Natick tribe of Indians," a respected healer shoved into the kitchen fire by
her own grandson. A tiny advertisement in the body of the basket offers
for sale a little pamphlet, published by the *Herald*, describing the trial of
Stephen and Jesse Boorn of Manchester, Vermont, for the supposed mur-

der of their brother-in-law Russel Colvin. This is a story about a deranged husband, a wayward wife, vindictive brothers, nightmares, ghosts, and mysterious fingernails found in the stump of a tree. It is also a story about bones carried to the river in a basket.

Our basket attests to the artistry and industry of New England's Indians and the neatness of an early owner. The newspapers that line it provide unexpected links to the mythology of "disappearing" Indians, and the order and disorder of households.


For many years, historians assumed that Vermont was empty of human inhabitants before the white man came, and that during the colonial period the few Indians found there were in transit from French Canada. Scholars now tell us that when the English arrived in North America, the people known as the western Abenaki inhabited a region bounded on the west by Lake Champlain, on the east by the White Mountains, and extending from southern Quebec to the present border with Massachusetts. Archaeological evidence reveals continuous occupation in the Champlain Valley for more than eleven thousand years. As Colin Calloway has observed, "Lake Champlain was not only an area rich in resources and a vital waterway, it was also a sacred center of the western Abenaki universe." After King Philip's War, refugees from southern New England, including Mahicans from the Hudson River Valley and Pocumtucks from western Massachusetts, quietly joined the Abenaki.[6]

During the colonial wars, Vermont Indians, like those in northern New Hampshire and Maine, developed religious and cultural links to French Canada, but the 1763 treaty that ended the French occupation of Canada cut off trade goods and military supplies from the north and threatened the Abenaki homeland by breaking the dike of migration from southern New England. Settlers from Massachusetts, Connecticut, and New Hampshire swarmed into areas that had once seemed hostile to white habitation. In 1761 alone, sixty townships were granted along the Connecticut River Valley in what is now Vermont. Soon there were colonial towns on the western side of the Green Mountains as well.[7]

By the time English authorities got around to granting Vermont's supposedly unoccupied land to New York in 1764, the government of New Hampshire had already assigned three million acres, nearly half of the present state, to land speculators and settlers, a situation that led to armed conflict between "Yorkers" and "Green Mountain Boys." Vermont fought two revolutions, one against the British and another against its neighbors. In 1777 it declared itself a republic. The white settlers who poured into the region from southern New England deplored tenancy, demanded popular government, and championed religious liberty, but they had little interest in the Abenaki whose ancient homeland they were claiming.[8]

Vermont's war against New York soon became a movement to occupy fertile lands around Missisquoi. The Onion River Land Company, founded by Revolutionary heroes Ira and Ethan Allen and their friend Remember Baker, fought rival claimants in court. In one suit Ira Allen challenged both New York grants and the rights of the Abenaki, insisting that the Indians had abandoned their land during the war "& have made no Claims by themselves or assigns till Lately."[9] But as Yankee settlers moved onto their land, the Abenaki did make claims, appearing unexpectedly at homesteads or newly cleared fields protesting that the land was theirs, and sometimes claiming "rent" in food and hay. Allen claimed that they also destroyed fences and threatened to burn barns or kill cattle, and he blamed the machinations of other white men for the disturbance.[10]

In October 1787, a group of Abenaki raised a British flag when they approached cabins at Swanton and Highgate on the Missisquoi River. A complaint sworn by the local justice of the peace, an ally of the Allens, said that the Abenaki threatened a family at knifepoint and extracted tribute of ten bushels of corn from one man and fifteen bushels of potatoes from another. The head of the Indian Department in Canada summoned the offending group, who admitted they had been at Missisquoi Bay "in search of their livelyhood by Fishing and Fowling." They were unhappy to find Yankee families occupying lands handed "down to them by their Predecessors, who were the proprietors of the same long before the French came to Canada," but they said they had threatened no one. They were hardly in a position to do so. Although there were twenty persons in their party, as the Vermont complaint had said, eleven of them were women and eight were nursing children.[11]

Although scattered groups continued to protest the white presence, there was little they could do. Not long after the Allens built a second sawmill at Swanton, the remaining Indians dismantled their church and carried the stones and bell by canoe to St. Hyacinthe in Canada. The Abenaki who remained in Vermont either dispersed into small family bands or learned to live on the edges of white communities, working as farmhands, lumberjacks, tanners, or household servants, invisible unless ill fortune or local whimsy exposed them.[12] In Bennington, on a Sunday evening in August 1802, two white farmhands crushed the skull of Stephen Gordon, a transient Indian who had worked with them through the day harvesting grain. Contemporary accounts describe Gordon either as a "dark Canadian" or an Indian from the former Mahican town of Scaticoke. Although the men were arrested and tried for murder, a local jury refused to convict them of a capital crime. They were local men, strongly allied with the Republican majority in town. Despite strict instructions from the Federalist judge, the jury returned a verdict of manslaughter, allowing the men to go free after paying a fine and spending three months in prison. Newspapers as far away at Stockbridge, Massachusetts, debated the verdict. Summarizing the argument for the defense, a New Hampshire newspaper suggested that Gordon had provoked the attack: "The threat of the deceased, accompanied with an Indian scalping hoop, &c., was perhaps more likely to excite the passions than any common threat."[13]

Vermont was in many respects a remarkably open society in the years after the American Revolution, in part because there were so few persons of color in the Yankee towns. But here, as elsewhere, attitudes hardened in the nineteenth century. For years, Lemuel Haynes, born the illegitimate son of a white woman and a Connecticut slave of "unmingled African extraction," presided over Rutland's west parish. Author during his youth of a powerful but unpublished essay "on the illegality of Slave-keeping," he served in the Continental Army, migrated to Vermont in the 1780s, and became a prolific writer, Federalist, and defender of religious orthodoxy. He was well regarded among the clergy, an original trustee of the Vermont Missionary Society, and a leader in clerical associations. In 1818 long-standing disagreements over doctrine led to Haynes's dismissal. His Calvinism was apparently too rigorous for his more liberal congregation, but concern about respectability was also a factor. According to a friend, Haynes "lived with the people of Rutland thirty year and they were so sagacious that at the end of that time they found out he was *a nigger,* and so turned him away."[14]

In contrast to Haynes, a Rutland potash and pearl-ash maker, soap boiler, indigo dyer, and sometime musician named Pearson Freeman deliberately exploited his African American identity. In an advertisement in the *Rutland Herald* he announced that he was ready for business "at his

*Lemuel Haynes, from Timothy Mather Cooley,* Sketches of the Life and Character of the Rev. Lemuel Haynes. (NEW YORK: HARPER, 1837).

old stand, In Rutland, where there is plenty and variety of *music,* notwithstanding some fairer complexioned people, who pretend to make *all blue,* may assume to know more of dark hues, still continues to Dye Cotton, Linen and Sheep's Woolen Yarn Blue; and from twenty years' experience thinks that he knows how to fix this colour, and would be happy in this; and with every musical instrument to aid his old customers." Freeman, a freed slave, had worked in the potash and soapboiling business in Connecticut before moving to Vermont in 1793. By 1795, he had worked himself up from hired hand to proprietor.

In 1819, he published a curious notice that could have been a tongue-in-cheek advertisement for his own product or a genuine complaint against unknown persons who were trying to ruin his reputation:

> FOUND
>
> In the subscriber's barn, near the potash, some time since, about 200 wt. of *something,* bearing the appearance of *Salts of Lye,* in a tub, under very singular circumstances. They were doubtlessly deposited there by some malicious person a view to injure the reputation of the chief of the *African Band.* But be it known to the villain, whoever he may be, that *he may fall into the pit he has attempted to prepare for another.* However, the owner is requested to prove his property, pay charges and take it away.

Freeman's racial consciousness led him to name a son for Toussaint L'Ouverture, the hero of the Haitian revolution. Ten years later, Freeman's son Pearson Toussaint Freeman posted a notice in the *Herald* that he was available to teach violin, bass viol, clarinet, or flute, and to play the violin or lute for dances.[15]

Haynes succeeded by being as much like a white man as possible, Freeman by broadcasting racial difference. Neither man could fully avoid the stigmatization of race. American Indians faced the same options. They could fade into the crowd or flaunt difference. There is a curious story from Springfield, Vermont, about "a half-breed Indian shoemaker" named Philip Cook who around 1820 divided the young men of the town into "Indians" and "soldiers" and organized a mock fight. He built a "wigwam of boughs" on the top of the hill, and gave the "young men serving as Indians hatcheled flax to wear as hair, with feathers sticking around the crown, and painted their faces to look as much like real warriors as possible." The other group drew an old Revolutionary cannon to the base of the hill. Old-timers feared that the game would grow serious, but the men all had a wonderful time and no one was hurt.[16]

Basket-selling offered another opportunity to assert an Indian identity. A town history from the eastern part of the state describes small groups of Abenaki coming down the Connecticut River "in birchbark canoes in summer." The men spent their time in fishing and hunting while the women "sold their wares from house to house." A more colorful story appeared in 1835 in the *Green Mountain Democrat*. A family group, identified as "part of the tribe of the Missisiques, who live a wandering life on the eastern shore of Lake Champlain," had camped near Windsor, where they subsisted by making and selling "Indian articles." They had supposedly been caught by bad weather while on their way to enroll a son at Dartmouth College in Hanover, New Hampshire. Though they were committed to securing a white man's education for one of their own, they knew that to sell crafts, they needed to acknowledge, even flaunt, difference.[17]

Unfortunately, there is no way of knowing what sort of "articles" these families were selling, nor is there any record of similar groups camping near Rutland. The town's Antiquarian Museum displayed boxes of sewn birch bark in the 1870s, but the only documented woodsplint baskets from the area date from much later in the nineteenth century, when "fancy baskets" developed at St. Francis in Quebec entered the tourist trade. There are no known woodsplint baskets made in Vermont in the early nineteenth century, unless we assume that a woodsplint basket lined with a Vermont newspaper was made there. Certainly there were materials for making such a basket at hand. The basket could also have come from the old Mahican territory along the Hudson River corridor. Although Mahicans at Scaticoke and Stockbridge ostensibly went west after the Revolution, some may have remained.[18]

Although its precise origin is unknown, the basket itself is full of information about its design and construction. To say that it is a "woodsplint" basket is to gloss over the hard work involved in preparing materials for weaving. The initial step was finding the right kind of tree, usually a sapling six to nine inches in diameter. Women and men both did this work. Experienced basket makers knew how to identify straight, unknotted trunks that were likely to produce good splints. Cutting the logs in convenient lengths, they carried them out of the woods on their shoulders, then began the hard work of making splints. White oak had to be worked green; ash was more forgiving. Using a sharp ax, the splint maker split each log, then used a crooked knife to cut and shape long sticks of equal size. Pounding the sticks along their length caused them to break apart along the annual growth rings, the individual splints opening out like a fan, ready to be separated and stacked for weaving. Pounding out splints took both skill and strength.[19]

Using the same technique, Yankee basket makers produced plain but sturdy baskets. Well-documented Indian baskets are almost always decorated, suggesting that customers liked buying baskets that to their eyes appeared "Indian." In central Massachusetts and northeastern Connecticut, freehand, almost whimsical designs were the norm, as in a round storage basket purchased near Framingham, Massachusetts, before 1839. In western New England tighter designs were more common. There is a similar range in checkered blankets made in Vermont and Connecticut during the same period. Embroiderers often filled the space formed by an open check with simple motifs, as Elizabeth Chittenden, the wife of Vermont's first governor, did in a blanket made for her daughter. Her designs are varied and playful. In contrast, the repetitive motifs and tripled stripes on a blanket made in the Goodwin family in Chelsea, Vermont, look more like baskets found in the old Mahican homeland between Vermont and New York. There is no point in asking where these ideas came from. Basket makers may or may not have influenced blanket makers, but they surely catered to their tastes.[20]

Decoration began with the preparation of stains and dyes. Early twentieth-century accounts emphasized the use of natural dyes—wild berries, bloodroot, onion skins, spruce root, gold thread, and barks. Experiments done at the American Indian Archaeological Institute in

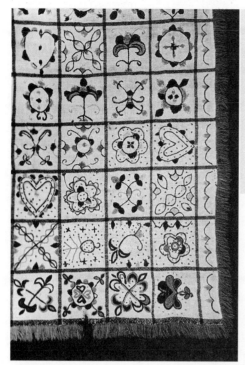

Covered storage basket purchased near
Framingham, Massachusetts, 1839.

PEABODY MUSEUM, HARVARD UNIVERSITY,
39-36-10. PHOTOGRAPH BY HILLEL BURGER

Left: Elizabeth Meigs Chittenden.
Embroidered blanket.

VERMONT HISTORICAL SOCIETY,
MONTPELIER, VERMONT, 41.11

Right: Goodwin family.
Embroidered blanket.

SHELBURNE MUSEUM, 1964-105

Covered storage basket, probably
Mahican, 1820–1840.

FROM THE HISTORY COLLECTION OF
THE NEW YORK STATE MUSEUM, 40.12.2

Connecticut determined that plant dyes of that sort produced only pale washes, not the strong colors that most surviving baskets display. When analyzed, the sources of basketry colors in their sample turned out to be no different from those used in contemporary signboard, furniture, or housepainting. The pigments came in a cake and were diluted with water and "size," a glue made from animal skins. The most popular pigment was indigo. Our basket is different. The bluish black that creates its checkered surface is not indigo, as in so many others, but a "flame carbon," a pigment made by burning some sort of fuel and collecting the sooty residue produced in the smoke. (Holding a table knife above a burning candle imitates the process.) Flame carbons could be made from oil, as in the "lamp black" used in John Bourne's shipyard in Kennebunk, but the pigment in our basket seems to have been made from wood. The ancestors of this basket maker had presumably been making black paint of this sort for centuries. The second color in the basket, a rusty red, has almost disappeared from the outer surface. The scientist who analyzed a tiny sample taken from an exposed spot on the underside of the lid could determine only that it was "organic in nature" and that its color was not produced by common dyestuffs used in European and American textiles.[21]

Our basket illustrates three different methods of applying color. The reddish splints were dyed, like fabric, by immersion in some sort of bath. The black wefts were swabbed after weaving, leaving color on the exposed surface alone. The geometric designs were stamped. The early-twentieth-century anthropologist Frank Speck thought that Indians learned stamping from printers, noting that there was a seventeenth-century Indian printer (appropriately named James Printer) at the Christian Indian town of Natick. A more obvious protoype was calico printing. In the late eighteenth century, rural New Englanders earned extra income by "stamping" cloth with woodblocks dipped in dye. But there is no reason to assume that Indian basket makers picked up the idea from anybody else. The technique is quite simple. Oral histories of later basket makers tell us that the stamps were homemade, carved out of corks, potatoes, or turnips.[22] Stamping was one way to create multiple designs with small effort. The bottom row on the front of this basket shows the progression of stamping from right to left. The motif on the far right is smudged; the ink got lighter with each application.

The imperfect stamping reflects the circumstances in which baskets like these were made. To survive, a basket maker needed to make attrac-

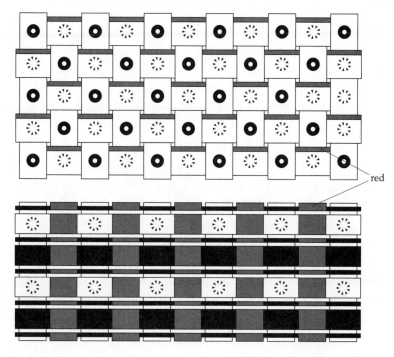

red

DRAWINGS BY MINDY CHIOU

*Covered storage basket with*
*swabbed and stamped decoration.*

PEABODY MUSEUM, HARVARD
UNIVERSITY, 18-03-10. PHOTOGRAPH
BY HILLEL BURGER

tive baskets, but she also needed to work quickly and perhaps engage less skilled persons in the work. This basket displays both artistry and haste. It has a definite back-front divide, with the stamping extending around only three sides, as though the back of the basket was supposed to stand against a wall. The part of the body that fits under the rim of the lid is also undecorated. But the overall design of the basket is both thoughtful and aesthetically pleasing. The weaver obviously saw the lid as an integral part of the design. Extending the alternating bands of dark and light onto the rim, she added a new rhythm by stamping the lighter wefts, creating a triangular line from body to rim that closes and completes the design. The effect was even stronger when the basket was new. The vertical pieces visible on the three decorated sides of the basket are actually supplemental warps, beige now but once red. They are purely decorative and were inserted after the weaving was completed. On the lid itself, stamped rings alternating with sunbursts march across the top, but again the weaver added complexity to her design. Slipping thin strips of red through every other weft, she reinforced the diagonal march of the circles. Although current scholarship downplays "tribal" characteristics in early-nineteenth-century baskets, looking instead at family traditions and individual styles, the use of red and black links this basket to known Mahican work. Perhaps additional research will turn up other baskets with its distinctive features. Market demand was surely one factor in its production, but artistry was another.

The newspapers were added by the person who purchased the basket. That practice was common. The earliest known example, a Mohegan basket now in a private collection, has an 1808 Hartford newspaper, but others were lined with religious publications like the *Gospel Palladium* published in Warren, Rhode Island, in 1820, or the *Christian Watchman* of 1834. Often only fragments of the papers survive. Over the years mice or insects nibbled at the paper to get at the wheat paste underneath.[23] When this basket came to the Peabody Museum in 1913, the newspapers were in fragile condition. Many years later, when it was slated for exhibition, a conservator went to work, using careful methods that not only improved the appearance of the interior of the basket but added years to its life.

She began by taking photographs of the interior to document the exact placement of the papers, then removed and replaced them, backing them with an acid-free lining. The most difficult task was to lift the paper from the basket without creating further damage. Working sheet by sheet, she applied a poultice designed to dissolve the paste underneath the paper without damaging the paper itself. Because early-nineteenth-century paper was made from rags rather than the wood pulp that became common later, it is remarkably tough. The conservator was able to tease the papers off the basket onto a fabric support and then wash them in several changes of hot water, reversing them onto a sheet of Mylar to scrape away any remaining residue. Finally, she lined them with a transparent tissue and reapplied them to the basket in their original order, using the photographs and carefully drawn "map" as her guide.[24]

For the museum conservator, the basket offered both a technical challenge and an opportunity to restore the integrity of an engaging artifact. Like the person who first lined the basket, she was more interested in the fabric of the newspapers than in their content. But in the course of her work, she exposed at least for a moment a fascinating story on the back of the sheet lining the lid. This story connects our basket with a central theme in New England history and folklore, the myth of the disappearing Indian.

Page two of the *Rutland Herald* for December 26, 1821, is no longer visible in the basket, but other extant copies of the same issue expose its gruesome story:

> In Natick, on the evening of the 6th inst. Hannah Dexter, a celebrated Indian doctress, was murdered in her own home, by her grandson, Joseph Purchase. The circumstances of her death are as follows—It seems from the evidence in the case that some Indians had met at her house for the purpose of a *frolic*, which terminated in drunkedness and fighting; that she reproved her grandson, for his misconduct, and was, in consequence, threatened by him with death. Also, that he drove his sister and brother-in-law from the house, and put his threat in execution, by knocking her into the fire, and burning her to death, while they were gone to alarm the neighbors. She was between 75 and 80 years of age, and maintained an unblemished character. She was the last of the Natick tribe of Indians. Her murderer was secured, tried and committed to the jail in this town to await the sentence of the law.

The story plays on the horror of a disrupted household order. Everything seems topsy-turvy. There is a man attacking his own grandmother, a sister and brother-in-law fleeing the house for help, and the terrible image of an old woman being knocked into her own fire. This is a story about drinking and violence, but it is also a story about Indians. Hannah Dexter was a person of "unblemished character," though curiously, even though she had two grandchildren in her house, the writer described her as "the last of the Natick tribe of Indians." The unspoken assumption is that the grandchildren were the product of a mixed racial alliance—perhaps, as was commonly the case, between an Indian and an African American.[25]

The theme of the disappearing Indian is laced through early-nineteenth-century literature. Its presence in this 1821 newspaper predates by five years the publication of James Fenimore Cooper's *The Last of the Mohicans*. Ironically, the maker of our basket may have been a Mahican, but unlike Cooper's savvy woodsmen, she or he lived by peddling baskets on the margins of settled towns. That was the common occupation of the "last Indians" in New England local history.[26] Massachusetts and Connecticut town chronicles tell about Molly Hatchet, the presumed last of the Paugussets; "Old Betty," the last of the Wangums; Mercy Nonsuch Mathews, the last of the Western Nehantic; and Tamer Sebastion and Eunice Mauwee, both of whom are described in various places as the last of the Pequots. Granny Sprague, who bottomed chairs in Natick, was ostensibly the last of the Nipmucks. Darkis Onerable earned a similar distinction on Nantucket. Like most of the others, she was both memorialized and consigned to the margins of her town. Though considered a "noble woman of her Tribe," she lived out her life as a servant to a white family and died in the town asylum.[27] Although these basket makers often had English names and worshiped in mainstream churches, they were marked by lineage and occupation as Indians.

The stories white writers told about Indian basket makers reflect both the racist assumptions of the tellers and the real-life circumstances of men and women forced to eke out a living outside the dominant culture. The persons who told these stories were often sympathetic to their subjects, who seemed to them both degraded and curiously attractive. They described basket makers who were often drunk, yet just as often endowed with a wit that endeared them to their neighbors. They wore outlandish costumes and behaved in outlandish ways, yet retained an innate pride in their own worth. They were wanderers who neverthless had an almost instinctual attachment to place. They were unambitious, yet trudged through Yankee towns carrying on their backs huge quantities of brooms and baskets and sometimes their children as well. They entertained as well as outraged their neighbors.

In northern New England, where wars with the Abenaki were only a generation away, the stories were fewer and less quaint. In Vermont town histories, "Old Joe" steps out of the woods, like Squanto in the pilgrim story, to welcome and assist white settlers. Like Cooper's Chingachgook, Joe was willing to fight beside white frontiersmen. When at a great age he became lost in the woods on a winter hunting trip, a search party found him and carried him home to die in his bed. The leading men of New-bury, Vermont, attended his funeral, and in honor "to an old soldier who had assisted them in war even against men of his own race they fired Joe's gun over his grave during the services." Joe has some of the characteristics of Molly Ocket, who was more independent and less marginal than the Indians in Massachusetts and Connecticut histories, and whose legends were extant in Vermont border towns as well as in Maine. Yet despite their greater autonomy, Joe and Molly shared many features with the semifictional characters of southern New England—they were wanderers, they were tipplers, and they were blessed with a droll wit.[28]

Stories about Indian basket makers describe women who defied white notions of appropriate gender behavior. They were towering figures, outsized in manner if not in body, and impossible to ignore. Molly Hatchet was six feet tall. Lydia Francis carried a large butcher's knife under her shawl and always traveled with "a big brindle dog, as ugly as his mistress." Tuggie Bannocks, who "was as much negro as Indian and was reputed to be a witch," had a "full set of double teeth all the way round, and an absolute refusal ever to sit on a chair, sofa, stool, or anything that was intended to be sat upon." In white eyes, these women often possessed male attributes, as of course did Molly Ocket, who was "a good huntress," and her daughter Molly Susup, who could outwrestle white boys her age.[29]

Sarah Boston, reputed to be "the last lineal descendant of King Philip," weighed nearly three hundred pounds and could work "in the fields like a man, taking her pay in cider." She loved to frighten troublesome boys. "One night a party of young men, out on a good time, were passing the old cemetery in Grafton. Their ideas of wit, somewhat confused by liquor, suggested their knocking loudly on the wooden gate, and calling out: 'Arise, ye dead, and come to judgment.' Slowly from one of the graves the immense form of Sarah Bostons stretched itself up. Saying,

'Yes, Lord; I am coming,' she started in their direction. The young men, well-nigh paralyzed with fear, stumbled into their wagon, and, lashing their horse into a furious run, did not look behind them until safe in their own homes." But Sarah had a softer side. When asked why she cut down a productive cherry tree in her yard, she said it shaded the house so that she couldn't see to read her Bible. Her biographer concluded, "At the dawning of the judgment day she may be among the first to answer, 'Yes, Lord; I am coming.' "[30]

Indian basket makers not only behaved in wild and unexpected ways, they lived in wild and hard-to-find places. In West Barnstable, folks remembered old Hagar at Hagar's Spring and old Mookis who lived on one of the trails beween Scorton and the ponds. Ruth Pomham, known to contemporaries as "Old Ruth," lived alone in the wilds of "Gungy" outside New London. A Litchfield basket maker dwelt at "hardscrabble." Simon Gigger lived "in a swamp towards Shrewsbury, in a hut built of stones, the walls being two feet thick at the base." He sat in his curious house "surrounded by his family, making baskets and drinking." Joseph Aron, a veteran of the Revolution, lived alone in a swamp near West-borough, "weaving baskets, wandering into the houses and barns of his white neighbors, and quoting scraps of Scripture, right, or oftener wrong." They were fleeting characters, men and women whose dwellings were destined to disappear, leaving only an impression in the ground or a bed of tangled tansy.[31]

They were also given to intemperance. Andrew Brown, like other Indians, made baskets, then drank up the profits from the sale of them. His wife was no better. Locals joked about the day she pointed to her husband lying under a tree and slurred, "Poor old Indian got dhrunk on schwamp water." The stories about Molly Ocket were kinder, but they too acknowledged her taste for alcohol. "When provided with a glass in any of the families which she visited, she would become very loquacious and entertain her company with stories and amusing anecdotes." When she couldn't get rum, she would make do with beer, drinking a pint "with the greatest relish." Connecticut's Molly Hatchet also had an "overfond-ness for 'uncupe' as she and earlier Indians called rum." Sarah Boston spoke for many when she said, "The more I drink, the drier I am." John Greenleaf Whittier immortalized the drunken Indian in a tale from his childhood about opening the door on a dark and stormy night to "a gigantic horseman" who seemed cut out of the blackness. At first the man tried to steer the horse through the door, but when that failed, he dis-

New England basket seller,
*from Sarah S. Jacobs,*
Nonantum and Natick
(BOSTON: MASSACHUSETTS
SABBATH SCHOOL SOCIETY, 1853)

*Cornelius Kreighoff.*
The Basket Seller, *c. 1850.*
COURTESY ART GALLERY OF
ONTARIO, TORONTO

mounted, identified himself "as the great Indian doctor," then dragged the young Whittier through the house in a vain search for rum. He finally collapsed in tears "and confessed that he was so drunk already that his horse was ashamed of him."[32]

In these moralistic stories by white writers, drink and the uncertain support acquired through basketry led to Indian poverty and sometimes violence. In Westborough, people told tales of Simon Gigger and his sister Sallie, "who escaped killing one of her white neighbors, only because the gun refused to go off." The worst violence, however, was inflicted on family members. Deb Brown was lame because her husband, in one of their many quarrels, broke her hip. Fights between Simon Gigger and his wife Bets Hendricks were legendary. "One time she got more than even with him by striking him with a scythe and cutting his thumb so that it fell over into his hand. But this quarrel, like all the others, was readily healed, and the cut thumb was cured by a generous application of balm of Gilead." Despite the violence, there was poetry in these lives. When Gigger left home, Bets usually followed a few steps behind, "she carrying a load of baskets, which they sold at the farm-houses, he, the violin. They often found work in rebottoming the chairs, and when the work was done, and the bread and cider disposed of, Gigger or Bets would delight the children by getting what music they could from the old fiddle." Their end came on a winter night, when they returned home drunk and lost their way in a snowstorm. The next day people found a bit of calico sticking up in the snow that proved to be a part of Bets's dress. "Farther on—as usual, a little ahead of his wife—they found Gigger's body,—both frozen to death within sight of their home."[33]

Most writers attributed such behavior to atavistic impulses that kept Indians from taking steady work. There was, for example, the curious case of Deb Browner, who lived a respectable and prosaic life most of the year, but in the autumn wrapped herself in a blanket, let her hair flow free, and headed north, "bearing by a metomp of bark around her forehead a heavy burden in a basket." There were others who worked in taverns or did odd jobs around the town in winter, but in late summer "seized with the spirit of their fathers or the influence of their early lives . . . wandered off for weeks and months, sometimes selling brooms and baskets, sometimes reseating chairs, oftener working not, simply tramping trustfully, sure of food whenever they asked for it."[34]

The Connecticut writer Lydia Sigourney thought that Mohegan women were "more easily initiated into the habits of civilized life" than their men. Yet even for them, "the distaff, the needle, and the loom were less congenial to their inclinations, than the manufacture of brooms, mats, and baskets." Wearing "a little round bonnet of blue cloth, in a shape peculiar to themselves," they wandered around the county, peddling their wares door to door. If they found no market, they begged "a morsel of bread for the infant at their back." When employed in the families of whites, repairing worn chairs or doing other work, they were "uniformly industrious, and grateful for any trifling favour." The same could not be said for their men, who retained the warlike spirit of their ancestors. Near New London, two men, one a Pequot, the other a Mohegan, died on the same day and were buried in a common cemetery. The women of the town stood crying, but the men insisted that the "accursed Pequot" should not be buried next to a man in whose veins flowed the blood of Mohegan royalty. "Such was the haughty spirit, which lurked in the bosom of an oppressed, a crushed people. They could not forget the throne that was overturned, though they grovelled among worms at its footstool."[35]

In such a setting, men like John Cooper, who through hard labor had acquired oxen, cows, swine, and "riches heretofore unknown among the unambitious sons of Mohegan," became objects of disdain. His brothers regarded him with suspicion, not out of envy, but because his manners "approximated too closely to the habits of white men. . . . They conceived poverty to be less degrading than daily toil, and thought *he* could not be a true Indian, who would not prefer the privations of one, to the slavery of the other."[36]

Near John Cooper lived Arrowhamet, or Zachary, and his wife, Martha, who though a descendant of Mohegan royalty was a model of Yankee housekeeping. Her motivation to neatness was enhanced when she and her husband took in an orphan, a sickly white girl who became like a daughter to them. Once this young woman arrived, there were no more rents in her clothing; "old Martha was arrayed every afternoon in a plain black silk gown, made in a very proper and becoming manner." Because she was now too old to go into the woods for herbs, she enlarged her garden, cultivating food and medicine that strengthened her patient. "The interiour of the humble house evinced the daily use of the broom, and near its door two bee-hives, ranged upon a rough bench, sent forth the cheerful hum of industry." The young white woman even improved Martha's baskets, which now "displayed the light touches of a pencil, to whose delicacy the natives laid no claim." This Mohegan household combined the best of both cultures, the virtue of industry and respect for nature. In summer, Martha sought out wild strawberries and whortleberries, bringing them to her young charge "in a little basket of green leaves, that their freshness and fragrance might tempt the sickening palate."[37]

Although most writers acknowledged the achievements of men like Samson Occom, the legendary Mohegan missionary, and recognized the existence of industrious Indians like Zachary and Martha, most doubted the power of education to transform what were increasingly seen as racial defects. They imagined Indians as in many ways superior to Africans, but lacking their steadiness and resilience. When a Massachusetts official asked a Natick man why so many of his race reverted to intemperate habits when removed from the influence of white masters or guardians, he replied, "Ducks will be ducks, notwithstanding they are hatched by the hen," or in the writer's rendition of the man's dialect, "Tucks will be tucks for all ole hen he hatch um."[38]

Yet the keepers of local memory remembered Indians not only as walkabouts and ne'er-do-wells but as objects of mystery and yearning. In Stowe, Vermont, settlers recalled the mysterious brook where Indian Joe and no one else could find nuggets of gold. In Rochester, Massachusetts, people told of an Indian healer appropriately named Nathan Hope, who in the time of a great epidemic brought a healing root. Molly Ocket was revered not only for her medical skills but for her connection to the past. So vivid were her accounts of Lovewell's raid on Pigwacket in 1725 that people were convinced she had been there and that she was nearly 140 years old when she died. In Rhode Island, people said the Narraganset witch Tuggie Bannocks could raise from the dead every person who had ever slept in the tumbledown tavern where she lived. Men and women who were the "last of" their people not only left memories but subtle marks on the landscape. In Marshfield, Vermont, when the waterfall named for Indian Molly roared from heavy rains, people imagined her descending it in her canoe.[39]

Most people believed that in spite of Yankee efforts to convert them, reform them, and govern them, Indians were destined to disappear. Some did. Intermarrying with non-Indians, white or black, many of the descendants of New England's earliest people gradually ceased to register in their neighbors' consciousness as "Indian." Hence the reference to Hannah Dexter, who had many descendants, as the last of the Naticks. Some scholars use the term *acculturation* to describe this process. Ann McMullen prefers the term *conversion*, because it suggests that disappearance was in some sense a choice. By restricting use of identifying symbols, people forced to live in a hostile environment avoided recognition and appeared "superficially, to be like non-natives."[40] As the Natick tribal historian Thomas Doughton has observed, the native peoples of central New England "were not, all of them, creatures of white imagination: intemperate, immoral, drunken, or childlike. On the contrary, many were rooted in area towns, stable residents, some of them property owners, woven into the region's social fabric." They were "farmers, plumbers, washerwomen, mariners, chair bottomers or chair caners, 'Indian herb doctors,' barbers, shoemakers, domestic servants, baggage masters, itinerant entertainers, day laborers, railroad engineers, mill operatives, specialty bakers, broom and basket makers, housewives, and stage coach drivers." On Cape Cod and the islands they were whalemen. Everywhere they were veterans of wars.[41]

If basket makers are more visible in fiction, memoirs, and town histories than others, it is in part because their work required them to remain visible. To earn a living without giving profits to a middleman, peddlers of brooms and baskets needed to travel, and some of them liked to. Furthermore, since basket-making stood outside both the agricultural and the new manufacturing economy, it offered a kind of independence not available to wage laborers. Successful basket makers learned to exploit Yankee prejudices, reinforcing the qualities that others saw in them. Read in this way, the stories about Sarah Boston rising up in the graveyard at Westborough or Deb Browner taking her annual journeys with a backpack take on new significance. The "quaintness" noted in town histories was also a mark of cultural survival.

Native folklore captures the spirit of defiance behind some basket makers' refusal to conform to white expectations. One tale transforms a besotted Indian into a trickster, celebrating cleverness rather than addiction. When the old man went to a Yankee house begging cider, the owner told him he could have as much as he could carry in his basket. Fortunately, it was a very cold day. The Indian went to the brook and dipped his basket in the water, taking it out and letting it freeze, then repeated the process again and again until it was lined with a thin coating of ice. Then he went back for the cider and carried it home. This story not only turned a drunk into a trickster, it transformed a basket into a pail. In older times, of course, such a trick would not have been necessary since weavers could produce twined vessels tight enough to hold water.[42]

A more powerful set of stories preserves outrage at the violence of English conquest. A Pequot legend identifies the red centers of rhododendrons that grow in a swamp in eastern Connecticut with the blood of ancestors massacred in 1639. A Narraganset legend tells of a settler in Rhode Island's South County who, when learning of a legend that spruces represented the souls of Indians killed by whites, vowed to chop down every one on his five hundred acres of land. He cut with such vengeance "that a stately spruce which he set out to destroy, fell upon him, and killed him." A story told by Gladys Tantaguidgeon recalled a later period when the killer was poverty rather than war. On a cold winter day an Indian woman and her baby "sought shelter for herself and child with the settlers. The white folks treated the Indians very badly so they refused to take her in." Spurned, she walked on until she came to a stream that was too deep to wade through and the ice too thin to cross. She and her baby were both found dead by its side the next day. Before this corn had always grown in a nearby field; afterward it would never grow again.[43] Such stories counter sentimental references to the Indian presence in the landscape.

Algonkian stories also counter the Yankee assumption that white settlers were universally generous to wandering basket makers, willing to feed and shelter them whenever they appeared. A story preserved in a Mohegan-Pequot dialect into the twentieth century tells of an old woman who went to an English settlement to sell brooms. When night fell, she approached a lighted house hoping the mistress would invite her to stay.

> I go rap! rap! on the door. A white woman comes and opens the door. I know her. She says, "Come in"; she smiles.
>
> I say, "Can I stay here tonight?"
>
> The white woman says, "Yes! Are you not hungry? I made some bread and cheese, can you eat some?"
>
> "I am not hungry tonight. I will eat if I live in the morning." The white woman says, "You must not say that you saw me here.' " (She did not wish it to be known that she was a witch.)
>
> Then I put down my back-basket, and then I lie down. I go to sleep. Early I arise. There is nothing (to be seen) of the house; it is all a great stone. Then I find my bread and cheese (to be) a great cold piece of cattle dung and a white bone. Horrors![44]

In this tale, the white woman's hospitality is double-edged. She is both welcoming and dangerous. The broom seller, though weary, wisely resists her food.

Stories like these have the doubleness often associated with people surviving in the shadow of oppression. Peddling baskets allowed a person to live close to the land, to draw sustenance from the things around her, and to move freely with the seasons. But in the emerging world of market production, basket-making was a tenuous mode of subsistence that exposed those dependent on it to poverty and despair. Trudie Lamb Richmond captures both of those elements in her discussion of basket-making on the Schagticoke reservation in western Connecticut. Memories of gathering plants with her own grandmother helped her recover the spirituality associated with basket-making, but interviews with old-timers reminded her of the cultural costs of marginality. One longtime resident remembered how a basket maker named Jim Pan enticed children to help him by promising candy. At the end of the week, he would gather up a load of baskets to sell in the town and at nearby farms. "We would wait all day for his return thinking about the sweets we were going to get and listening for the sounds of his horse. But if we heard the horse coming back slowly and Jim singing at the top of his lungs, our chins would sink to our chest, knowing full well there was no candy that day. Jim had spent it all on firewater."[45]

In this story, the only loss was candy. In other households, drinking could take away the spiritual and physical food that sustained life. The early-nineteenth-century writer William Apess (also spelled Apes) recalled with bitterness his grandmother's drinking. Born in Colrain, Massachusetts, in 1798 to parents of mixed African-Pequot descent, Apess lived for a time in Colchester, Connecticut, near the Mohegan reservation, but when he was three his parents separated, and he was sent to live with his maternal grandparents.

> At a certain time, when my grandmother had been out among the whites, with her baskets and brooms, and had fomented herself with the fiery waters of the earth, so that she had lost her reason and judgment and, in this fit of intoxication, raged most bitterly and in the meantime fell to beating me most cruelly; calling for whips, at the same time, of unnatural size, to beat me with; and asking me, at the same time, question after question, if I hated her. And I would say yes at every question; and the reason why was because I knew no other form of words. Thus I was beaten, until my poor little body was mangled and my little arm broken into three pieces, and in this horrible situation left for awhile. And had it not been for an uncle of mine, who lived in the other part of the old hut, I think that she would have finished my days; but through the goodness of God, I was snatched from an untimely grave.[46]

Apess knew that in publishing his story he would reinforce the stereotype of "the poor degraded Indians." He confronted the issue directly, blaming his suffering not only on his grandmother but on the white men who "brought spirituous liquors first among my people." He believed that whites brought something more dangerous than alcohol—"the burning curse and demon of despair."[47]

*Frontispiece of William Apes
from* A Son of the Forest:
The Experience of William
Apes . . . written by himself.
(NEW YORK, 1831)

Apess helps us to understand that the myth of the disappearing Indian covered a darker truth, that to make way for white farms, Indians *had* to disappear. In the seventeenth century, people believed that God brought illness to make way for his chosen remnant. In the early republic, writers more often appealed to the logic of the new political economy. The author of an 1801 Massachusetts report on the old praying town of Mashpee concluded that despite years of effort by Christian pastors and government officials, the inhabitants "have become neither a religious nor a virtuous people, nor have they been made happy." With "a hundredth part of the pains which have been bestowed on these savages" the state could have built a town with four times as many white inhabitants, all of whom would have enjoyed the benefits of civilization and contributed "by their industry to the welfare of the state, and by the taxes, which they pay, to the support of government." Mashpee had become a drain on the public coffers and an object lesson in bad management.

As if the point weren't clear enough, the author felt compelled to offer a parable:

> This plantation may be compared to a pasture, which is capable of feeding fifteen or sixteen hundred sheep; but into which several good-natured and visionary gentlemen have put three or four hundred wolves, foxes, and skunks, by way of experiment, with the hope that they might in time be tamed. A shepherd has been placed over them at high wages; and as the animals have been found to decrease, other wolves, foxes, and skunks have been allured to the pasture, to keep up their number. But the attempt has been in vain; the wild animals have worried the shepherd; have howled, and

yelped, and cast other indignities upon the gentlemen, who from time to time have visited them, for the sake of observing how the experiment went on; and have almost died with hunger, though they have been fed at an enormous expense.

Even though Indians were the racial equivalent of wild animals, "the pious and benevolent" should continue in their efforts, "however hopeless," to turn them into "good men and christians."[48]

William Apess was surely aware of such attitudes. In five books published between 1829 and 1833, he confronted white racism. In an essay entitled "An Indian's Looking-Glass for the White Man," he asked his readers to imagine that people of all colors stood before God with their nation's sins written on their skins; "which skin do you think would have the greatest?" Surely the Indian could not be charged with robbing a nation of its land, murdering its women and children, and "then depriving the remainder of their lawful rights, that nature and God require them to have"? Nor could they be charged with enslaving another nation "to till their grounds and welter out their days under the lash with hunger and fatigue."[49] In short, Apess was asking his white neighbors to measure their own behavior against the democratic values and Christian ethic they ostensibly embraced.

Soon after the publication of this essay, Apess turned rhetoric into action by helping to organize and lead a revolt at Mashpee. Working with the Wampanoag pastor Blind Joe Amos, he established a temperance association, then participated in the writing of an "Indian Declaration of Independence" submitted to the governor and council of Massachusetts. It proclaimed that after July 1, 1833, "we, as a tribe, will rule ourselves, and have the right to do so; for all men are born free and equal, says the Constitution of the country." To put their belief into practice, the Mashpee declared that from thenceforth no white man could take wood or cut hay on their land without permission. The effort to enforce that prohibition cost Apess and others thirty days in jail for "riot, assault, and trespass," but the publicity helped to rouse support for a petition to the legislature that eventually returned to the citizens of Mashpee the rights of town governance they had fought for in the years before the American Revolution.[50]

Apess's looking glass used American ideas to reveal American behavior. At Mashpee he invoked the resounding phrases of the Declaration of Independence (phrases that he like many others thought were in the Constitution) to challenge white hegemony. In his account of the religious conversion of basket maker Anne Wampy, he used dominant religious ideas to counter the stereotype of the unchangeable Indian. Each spring Wampy tramped twenty or thirty miles through the countryside carrying a load of baskets so large she was almost hidden from view and a burden of bitterness that few could see, but in Apess's narrative the wandering basket maker became a Christian heroine. Responding to the ministrations of converts among her own people, she passed through the terror of sinfulness to the joy of redemption, overcoming her craving for rum and acquiring a love for everyone around her. With tears "streaming down her furrowed cheeks" and "glory beaming in her countenance," she told Apess she felt so light she wanted to fly.[51]

Christianity offered solace to Anne Wampy but it did not alter the economic values expressed in the 1801 report. Americans had long imagined a world in which sheep replaced wolves, skunks, and forests. Nowhere did this transformation occur more rapidly than in the area served by the *Rutland Herald*. The quaint illustrations that embellish notices for "Estray Sheep" in the papers lining our basket give little hint of the ecological and social changes that in a few decades transformed the old Abenaki homeland. The human population of Vermont almost doubled between 1800 and 1830, but the sheep population grew even faster.[52] Thanks in part to duties on imported woolens passed in response to the "Report on Manufactures" advertised on a page in the lid of our basket, New England's nascent woolen industry took off after 1822. By the late 1830s most Vermont towns had a thousand sheep, some as many as five thousand. In Rutland County there were three hundred sheep per square mile, ten for every inhabitant. Addison County, on the shores of Lake Champlain, had even more. In less than twenty years Vermont had changed from an area of subsistence farms into the largest wool producer in the nation in proportion either to population or territory.[53] But in 1821, when the *Rutland Herald* published its story about the murder of Hannah Dexter, "the last of the Natick tribe of Indians," this process had barely begun.

Yankee writers said that Indian basket makers were wanderers who drank too much, had disorderly households, and preferred desultory work to constant labor. Stories in the *Rutland Herald* argue that among white families as well, there were violent families, men and women who rejected the norms of their society, who drank, fought with one another, and periodically disappeared. Some of the most vivid stories appear in notices from estranged husbands warning shopkeepers not to give credit to their wives. One such ad appears on the reverse of a page in the lid of our basket. "Whereas Cynthia, my wife, has left, without any just cause, my bed and board, these are to forbid all persons harbouring or trusting her on my account, as I will pay no debts of her contracting after this date." Advertising was a way of dealing with the economic implications of marital separation without going through a divorce.[54]

There were dozens of such ads published in the *Herald* and other Vermont newspapers in the early nineteenth century. Although some cited instances of adultery or desertion, a surprising number focused on the fundamental duty of a wife to contribute to household support. One husband's advertisement began, "whereas Hannah, my Wife, refuses to labour, and says she will run me into Debt, this is to forbid all Persons trusting her on my account, for I will not pay any debt of her contracting after this date." The accused wife was not only indolent, she flaunted her power to use her husband's credit. In a similar way, a Rutland man complained that his wife had been disposing of his property without his knowledge.[55]

A more creative man added this poem to his complaint against his wife, Sukey:

> For she will neither spin nor weave,
> But there she'll sit and take her ease;
> There she'll sit, and pout, and grin,
> As if the Devil had entered in;
> For she would neither knit nor sew,
> But all in rags I had to go:
> So, farewell Sukey! and farewell, wife!
> Till you can live a better life.[56]

If there were women who refused to spin and weave, there were others who sustained their families with little else. Among the few rejoinders from accused wives was one in which a wife claimed that the family had been kept from starvation "by the Fruit of my industry principally." Defending herself against the charge of having left her husband, one woman wrote, "I never left your house only to set up my loom at your son

Edgcoms to weave for you to pay a debt." Another responded that her husband had taken away her cloth, flax, wool, and provisions "& all my yarn that I had spinned."[57] Both sides in these controversies assumed that a good wife contributed to the family economy through manufacturing. What was at issue was control of resources. In a harmonious household, a husband honored his wife's debts, and a woman did her part to pay them. If he had ultimate responsibility, she had the right to manage the yarn she spun and the raw materials with which she worked.

Elopement notices had been a staple of colonial advertising. Although there were subtle changes in rhetoric in the early republic, the form of complaints remained remarkably stable. Husbands and wives recounted their spouses' failures and solicited the goodwill of neighbors. Casual readers no doubt read these ads much as people do the personal columns in newspapers today. As early as 1794, an aggrieved husband alluded to the entertainment value of the ads:

> Some of our Old-Fashioned Neighbors say, That it is a shame for us to Quarrel in our Old Age, and that we ought to bear in mind the covenant of our God and cleave fast to the guide of our youth (and all such stuff). But I think the jolly part of our Community, all the young sensible people, seem to agree that it is nonsense for two old Stocks to keep any longer together, 30 or 40 years is long enough! Besides, Neighbors want to have something to talk about, when they meet together in the long winter evenings. All our relations too, far and near, who take the Newspapers, will hear from us—and it is some honor to be in the newspapers; and as we are too old not to go far abroad to the wars, it is certainly best for people of spirit, to keep up something in imitation of it at home.[58]

Although the number of elopement notices eventually declined, an emerging genre of crime literature provided more sensational accounts of family deviance.

As Karen Halttunen has argued, writers in the early nineteenth century no longer assumed a common depravity from which all sin emerged, but began to explore the "mysteries" of marginality, the supposedly unfathomable darkness in some souls.[59] The murder of the Natick Indian Hannah Dexter offered an opportunity for that sort of treatment, but in Rutland in 1821, there was an even more dramatic case on readers' minds. A little advertisement visible on the rear wall of the basket announced the availability of a pamphlet on the "interesting trial" of Stephen and Jesse Boorn for the murder of Russel Colvin. The title of the pamphlet explains why this trial became the most sensational and written about in Vermont's history: "Trial of Stephen and Jesse Boorn, for the Murder of Russel Colvin Before An adjourned term of the Supreme Court of Vermont, begun and holden at Manchester, in the County of Bennington, Oct 26, A.D. 1819, To which is subjoined, The Particulars of the Wonderful Discovery Therafter, of the Said Colvin's Being Alive, and His Return to Manchester, Where it was Alledged The Murder Was Committed."[60] The African-American preacher, Lemuel Haynes, who became pastor at Manchester after leaving Rutland, published his own account of the trial with an appended sermon. His publisher may have been responsible for the title, which played on the current public fascination with Gothic narrative: *Mystery Developed; or, Russel Colvin, (Supposed to Be Murdered,) in Full Life: and Stephen and Jesse Boorn, (His Convicted Murderers,) Rescued from Ignominious Death by Wonderful Discoveries.* His text defended the respectable people of Manchester against the slander of superstition and at the same time drew religious lessons from the purported death and resurrection of Russel Colvin.[61]

Historians have read the Colvin trial for evidence of changing standards of jurisprudence, as a story about conflict between progressive villagers and superstitious farmers, and as an example of the obsession with deviance in the print culture of the early republic. Underlying these themes, however, is a story about family conflict that centers on work.[62] The husband and wife in this story are not unlike the debt-ridden husbands and wandering wives of the elopement advertisements, except that Colvin had no credit to preserve, and his wife no reputation to defend. When Colvin disappeared in May 1812, his neighbors hardly noticed. He had often been away, sometimes taking his son Rufus with him. His wife, Sally, told the court that her husband "used to get up, take the boy on his back, and go off and stay a day or two, without saying any thing about it. Once I understood he went off and staid 8 or 9 months—I was not then at home, and expect he was not in his right mind." Curiously, she learned about her husband's long absence only after she herself returned. Both spouses were wanderers.[63]

Sally was also away at the time of the incident that led to Colvin's disappearance—or murder. This time her son Lewis was her informant. "When I returned from over the mountain, about five days after the disappearance of my husband, I asked Lewis where Russell was; he answered gone to hell. I heard nothing at my father's what had become of my husband." Only later did the story begin to come out. On the day of Colvin's last disappearance he had been in the field with Lewis gathering stones, when a quarrel broke out with his brothers-in-law, Stephen and Jesse Boorn. As the pamphlet published by the editors of the *Herald* put it, Colvin "was not at all times enabled to provide for himself and family the necessaries of life, and was probably much dependent on the Boorns. Without doubt, this was what led to the quarrel alluded to by some of the witnesses."[64]

Maybe that quarrel did lead to blows and to Colvin's death. Or maybe it only led to the men leaving him behind in the field, wounded. Had he wandered off, or was his body buried somewhere in the sheep pasture between Boorn's house and that of their neighbor Thomas Johnson? The mystery would have remained a private puzzle if Sally Colvin hadn't become pregnant four or five years after her husband's disappearance. Perhaps her parents threatened to throw her out. In any case, she went to the local justice hoping to use an old colonial law that allowed a woman to seek child support from the father of her child. But the justice told her, "I could not swear my child on any person if my husband was living." Back at home, she "stood in the stoop" talking to her brothers, who told her she could seek child support for her baby since her husband was dead. She chose not to do so, perhaps because she didn't believe them, maybe because she did. Stephen Boorn once referred to his sister as "one of the devil's unaccountables."[65]

Not long after this, old man Boorn sold the field where the quarrel had taken place to his neighbor Johnson. Soon after, one of the Johnson children found an old hat in the field, partially decomposed but clearly recognizable as Colvin's. Bit by bit the suspicions spread. Somebody remembered that Stephen had said that he had put Colvin "where potatoes won't freeze." That made Johnson think about the four-by-four root cellar under the old house Boorn had used for a sheep shed. After the shed had burned, people began to gossip about what might be inside. An uncle dreamed that Colvin appeared to him, told him he had been murdered, and led him to the cellar hole. Stephen was furious when a pert hired girl at a nearby house said, "They are going to dig up Colvin for you, ain't they?"[66]

The Boorns were arrested and imprisoned. During the pretrial period, officials excavated the cellar hole on the farm and found buttons and a jacknife belonging to Colvin, but bones in a stump in the woods proved ambiguous. There appeared to be human toenails among them, but when an expert examined the bones, he doubted they were human. The court even ordered the exhumation of an amputated leg to compare with what they had found. Under intense pressure, first Jesse then Stephen confessed. Jesse's confession followed a night of terror when a being he could not identify came through the window of his cell and sat on his bed. Stephen's account, taken down by a magistrate, was more matter-of-fact but to his listeners even more chilling, because it laced the details of harvesting potatoes with the horrors of family violence.

Stephen said that on the fateful day in May he had stopped in the field by his father's farm and had quarreled with Colvin. "Russell told me how many dollars benefit he had been to father, and I told him he was a damned fool, and he was mad and jumped up, and we sat close together, and I told him to set down, you little tory, and there was a piece of a beech limb about two feet long, and he catched it up and struck at my head." They tussled. Stephen hit back. Colvin fell, opening a gash in the back of his head, near his hair. When Stephen realized his brother-in-law was dead, he dragged the corpse to a corner of the fence and covered it with briars, then went to the barn, got some boards, "and dug a grave as well as I could . . . and went home crying along, but I want afraid as I know." He told everybody that Colvin had gone away.

Later, when he was living at his uncle's house, he decided to find a better hiding place for the body. He had the use of his father's field to plant some potatoes, "and when I dug them I went there and something I thought had been there, and I took up his bones and put them in a basket, and took the boards, and put on my potatoe hole, and then it was night, took the basket and my hoe and went down and pulled a plank in the stable floor, and then dug a hole, and then covered him up, and went in the house and told them I had done with the basket and took back the shovel, and covered up my potatoes that evening." The next step in the disposal of the body came when Stephen lived at another farm "under the west mountain." When his nephew came to say that the old shed had burned down, he went there, found a few bones still in the rubble, and when the family "was to dinner I told them I did not want my dinner, and went and took them, and there want only a few of the biggest of the bones, and throwed them in the river above Wyman's, and then went back, and it was done quick too, and then was hungry by that time."[67]

Although the attorneys argued over the validity of the confessions, they were damning. The jury deliberated for "about an hour," returning with a double verdict of guilt. The legislature commuted Jesse's sentence to imprisonment, but as Stephen sat awaiting execution, telling his story to the Reverend Mr. Haynes, somebody thought of publishing a notice in the newspapers asking if anybody knew the whereabouts of Russel Colvin. Amazingly, word came from New Jersey that he had been found working there as a laborer. When a presumably deranged man claiming to be Colvin began his journey to Manchester, Vermont, in December 1819, crowds met him at every stop. This was like a man rising from the dead. Was he an imposter? Or had the real Russel Colvin returned in time to save his brother-in-law from the gallows? The man who claimed to be Colvin stayed only a short while in Vermont. His public interrogations in Manchester won Stephen a new trial and acquittal but did nothing to restore order to the Boorn household. Colvin—or his look-alike—was indifferent to Sally, seemed not to know his children, and eventually went back to the farm in New Jersey where he had found refuge. To this day, nobody knows whether he was an imposter or a madman.

Russel and Sally Colvin, like the husbands and wives in the elopement ads, defined the margins of respectability in a state proud of its newspapers, churches, and schools. Vermont in the 1820s was a land of settled farms and wanderers. The issue of the *Rutland Herald* pasted into the lid of our basket displays a tiny advertisement from Cyrus Beardsley of Poultney, Vermont, saying that he had found in the woods on his farm "twelve yards of tow cloth, partly whitened, one checked woolen blanket, one linnen shirt, partly worn, and one old shirt." He begged the owner "to prove property, pay charges, and take them away."[68] Where did these mysterious textiles come from? Had some thief snatched them from a clothesline, then dropped them as he fled through the woods? Or were they the possessions of a fleeing servant, a wandering wife, or a drunken husband? There was plenty of material in the *Herald* to feed that kind of speculation.

In his celebration of the "age of homespun" Horace Bushnell marveled that Yankee farmers could create farms in the granite cold of New England. "Their producing process took everything at a disadvantage," he wrote, "for they had no capital, no machinery, no distribution of labour, nothing but wild forest and rock." In his view, strength of character allowed early settlers to overcome the defects of geography. "They sucked honey out of the rock, and oil out of the flinty rock." New

England's inhospitable landscape appears as well in a poem printed on one of the newspapers curving across the bottom and up the sides of the woodsplint basket:

> *Thou art the firm, unshaken rock*
> *On which we rest;*
> *And rising from the hardy stock,*
> *Thy sons the tyrant's frown shall mock,*
> *And slavery's galling chains unlock,*
> *And free the oppress'd.*

Linking the American Revolution with the newer struggle over the expansion of slavery into the western territories, the poet ignored the two centuries of war with the Abenaki that preceded Yankee settlement in Vermont.[69]

In Vermont, as elsewhere in the new republic, ideals of freedom coexisted with indifference to indigenous claims. In the first decades of the nineteenth century, Vermonters cleared lands, fenced fields, sowed flax, and carried wool from their sheep to newly constructed carding mills, believing that as they did so they were creating both a virtuous and an industrious republic. Meanwhile, in the green land along their borders Indian basket makers struggled to preserve their own kind of liberty.

# II

--->->-<-+-

# An Unfinished Stocking

NEW ENGLAND, 1837

*This transition from mother and daughter power
to water and steam-power is a great one, greater
by far than many have as yet begun to conceive—
one that is to carry with it a complete revolution
of domestic life and social manners.*

Horace Bushnell, *"The Age of Homespun"*

An unfinished stocking in the collections of the New Hampshire Historical Society symbolizes the continuity of women's work in early New England. Fine steel knitting needles, or "pins," protrude from the fabric like crossed spears, though the ends are blunt rather than pointed. Only one millimeter in diameter, they are smaller than the oooo needles available to knitters today. On needles like these, New England knitters produced stockings for everyday use and Sunday wear; stockings of linen, wool, worsted, cotton, and silk; plain stockings, ribbed stockings, and stockings embellished with purled designs, and when those wore out they darned and "footed" them to make them new again.

Depending on one's perspective, an unfinished stocking shows work in motion or work arrested. That round balls of unbleached linen remained attached to a stocking that was never finished suggests that its value lay outside the thread. No one knows who began it or why it was saved. It might represent a life interrupted by death or some long forgotten woman's feckless vow to get back to her knitting when she could. Perhaps it was lost in the bottom of a trunk or basket, emerging at a time when factory production had transformed it into a curiosity. Whatever its origins, it looks back to the colonial period and forward to the age of domesticity, knitting together the complex strands of female life.

Although imported stockings, many of them made on an ingenious machine called a "knitting frame," were available from the seventeenth century on, hand knitting was ubiquitous throughout the colonial period and into the early republic. Mary Rowlandson unraveled and knitted stockings for her captors in a Nipmuck village in 1676. In 1769, seven "Ladies of the first Fashion" in Newport, Rhode Island, supported the cause of liberty by joining "in the laudable Business of KNITTING."[1] On a Colchester, Connecticut, farmstead a few years later, Betty Foot worked at her knitting as "stiddy as a Priest." In coastal Maine, Eliza Wildes packed hand-spun and hand-knitted stockings into her husband's sea chest, while

*Reuben Moulthrop.*
*Mrs. Ammi*
*Ruhamah Robbins,*
*1812.*

along the Kennebec, the midwife Martha Ballard knitted stockings duri-
ing lulls in her patients' labors.

As hand spinning declined, knitting increasingly defined female character. In 1812, the Connecticut painter Reuben Moulthrop painted Elizabeth Robbins with her knitting on a table beside her. Her lacy bonnet
signified her gentility, the book in her hands her piety and soberness, and
the knitting on the table her commitment to household industry. Like the
godly spinners of seventeenth-century England and Holland, this minister's wife was a Bathsheba who worked willingly with her hands.[2] The
Revolution and the War of 1812 reinforced these ideals. Patriotism continued to animate New England life in the early industrial era, as families
experimented with new forms of production, including the manufacture
of silk. Whether they labored in factories, performed outwork at home,
or carried their knitting needles to new homes in the West, New England
women defined their lives through work. Adapting their skills to new
opportunities and new settings, they complained about their burdens,
rejoiced in their successes, and once in a while, though not often enough,
stood up for their rights.

· · ·

In the collections of the Vermont Historical Society is a cluster of objects neatly wrapped in tissue paper that traces one woman's adventure in 1837 with a new form of household production. "Injured cocoons of Silk Worms picked apart to be used for weaving with other material," reads the label on the first packet. The label on the second, "Silk just as it is reeled from the Cocoons of the Silk worm," explains that it took at least fifty cocoons to make one thread and that "after the end is found by a little picking it will reel down to the mouth of the worm inside." The third packet contains spun silk and the fourth thread, prepared for knitting by doubling and twisting. Beside them is an unfinished stocking still on its tiny needles. The label reads: "Stocking commenced 50 years ago, unfinished for want of perseverance."[3]

This wrinkled display documents Laura Flint's youthful experiment in silk-making, her memorialization of that enterprise half a century later, and her acceptance of a work ethic that, even in its violation, shaped her generation. New England's silk craze was in part a response to the enticements of a wage economy. By developing new forms of household manufacture, some people hoped to keep their daughters on the farm. Although the experiment failed, it exemplifies the tensions in this period over the waning of household industry. Mrs. Flint didn't need her unfinished stocking, but she couldn't throw it away. For half a century it sat in a bottom drawer documenting her "want of perseverance."

Laura Riley was fifteen years old when she began her silk stocking. The baggy mate that survived along with her packets of thread and cocoons suggests she was probably wise to give up her task. She was not an accomplished knitter. Born in Lyndon, Vermont, in 1822, she was the daughter of a merchant and the granddaughter of a prominent Jeffersonian. Her future husband, Ephraim Flint of Baldwin, Maine, was a graduate and later trustee of the private military academy that became Norwich University. In a period when marginal farmers were fleeing Vermont for the West, sending their sons and daughters to seaports and mill towns to find work, substantial families like hers were experimenting with new forms of agriculture, improving their sheep breeds, investing in commerce, and joining Masonic lodges and temperance societies. Their experiments with sericulture were a manifestation of their optimism. They were part of a generation of Americans who believed that a free society offered unbounded opportunities for human progress.[4]

A few Connecticut towns had experimented with sericulture before the Revolution, but the real craze came in the 1820s and 1830s. Encouraged by enthusiastic reports in agricultural journals, government officials passed legislation encouraging the new enterprise. For a time Vermont's legislature offered twenty-five cents a pound for every pound of cocoons raised in the state; twenty-five cents for every pound of raw silk reeled from cocoons; and twenty-five cents for every pound of sewing silk manufactured therein. The governor of Massachusetts predicted that silk would become "the staple product of the country . . . second to no other branch of industry or source of wealth." In 1830, the legislature of New Hampshire sent a committee to Connecticut to observe the many steps in production.[5]

*Mr. Harper's Report to the Legislature of the State of New Hampshire on the Culture of Silk* explained that few skills were involved in sericulture that New England farmers and housewives did not already possess. Mulberry seed was sown like carrots and in similar light, loamy soil. Through successive transplanting, the young seedlings would develop into berry-producing orchards. Thrifty farmers gathered the mulberries when ripe, mashed them to a jelly, and separated the seeds by washing, being careful not to save them over for more than one year. Although it took thirty years for a mulberry tree to fully mature,

*Laura M. Riley Flint.*
*Unfinished stocking, 1837.*
VERMONT HISTORICAL SOCIETY,
MONTPELIER, VERMONT

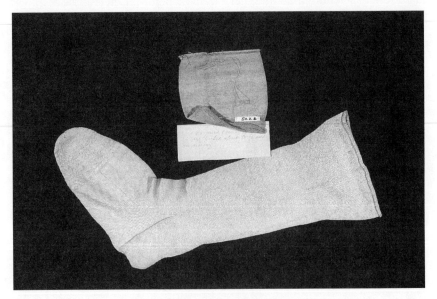

even tiny seedlings could produce food for silkworms.[6] The best incubator was a moderately cool room, where the eggs could be laid on paper until warm weather in the spring. Since warm weather caused the eggs to develop at about the same rate as the mulberry seedlings, there would be food for the larvae once they hatched. Fed on tender leaves, the larvae grew rapidly through successive moultings. Experienced sericulturalists arranged them on trays set on racks in an outbuilding, attic, or barn, carefully cleaning the trays after each moulting by enticing the worms onto branches, then returning them once the cleaning was done.[7]

When fully grown, the caterpillars would crawl onto the edges of trays or the supports of shelves, attach themselves, and begin to spin their cocoons: "In the first place they throw out some coarse silk, or floss, called by the Connecticut people 'tow-silk,' which constitutes the outer part of the cocoon when perfectly formed." Within this outer covering was the finer silk, spun out in a single filament that varied in length "from nine to twelve hundred feet." About twelve days after the caterpillars began their cocoons, the manufacturer needed to stop the process by killing the grubs inside; otherwise the silk would be ruined. Usually it was sufficient to lay them in a low oven or in the sun in the brightest part of the day.[8] Unlike flax or wool, silk came ready-spun. The trick was to unreel each thread from its cocoon. The first step was to strip the cocoon of its outer floss. The worker then sorted her cocoons according to quality, dropping each batch into a large kettle filled with water kept just at the boiling point, stirring them with a whisk made from a bunch of broom corn. "In this way, the ends are collected and attached to the brushy extremity." Lifting the threads as they unwound, the worker attached the ends to a common reel. If she did this carefully, the silk fibers would "run off about as fast and with as little difficulty as yarn from a spindle." When the reel was full, she tied the end pieces together, took it off the reel, and dried it. "In this situation it is called raw silk, and is ready for the market as such." To produce sewing thread, a housewife spun the raw silk on a common woolen wheel, twisting on new lengths as needed. A thrifty worker could also card and spin the fragments of "silk tow," leaving little waste.[9]

Lest women resist becoming custodians of larvae, the promoters of sericulture emphasized its royal origins. *Mr. Harper's Report* explained that silk cultivation began in China with the Empress Si-ling-chi, who "gathered the worms from the trees, and with the women attached to her household, endeavoured to attend them with much care in the Imperial apartments." Successive empresses not only attended to the cocoons but to spinning, weaving, and embroidering. As the culture spread, it continued to be attached to aristocratic households. "In Greece, noble ladies were the first to attend to the rearing of the worms." In America, sericulture was first suggested in the earliest years in Virginia, was revived under Charles II, spread to Georgia and South Carolina and eventually to Pennsylvania and New Jersey. Families in Mansfield, Connecticut, took up the work in 1760.[10] Silk was therefore an appropriate product for persons Horace Bushnell would later call "Queens and Kings of Homespun."

At the Worcester County Cattle Show in the fall of 1829, Pliny Earle of Leicester, Massachusetts, displayed raw silk made "from his own silk worms; also, some very nice manufactured silk, and a pair of stockings, knit by his daughter, Sarah Earle, from silk of her own culture." The reporter added that the stockings were of "close and even texture, and of a much more durable quality than those that are imported."[11] The promoters of sericulture said that mulberry trees were no harder to grow than apple trees and silkworms no more difficult to raise than chickens, and they insisted that children could do much of the work. They didn't anticipate the ingenuity of five-year-old Edmund Bullock of Guilford, Vermont, who disrupted his mother's experiments by taking worms and mulberry leaves from the attic to feed his pet chickens.[12]

Women who preserved mementos of their short-lived experiments in sericulture often associated them with children. A tiny skein of silk thread made by Mary Palmer Tyler, the Vermont housewife whose wool blankets came back from the fulling mill smaller than she had hoped, is accompanied by a little note in blue ink: "This silk is the first I made assisted by my beloved Winship the summer before he died—The worms egg given him by his cousin Amelia P. Curtis." Winship Tyler died in 1832 at the age of fourteen. The youngest of eleven children, he once wrote his older brother, "My amusements are few this spring, if I had more, it would be merrier, but I take what I can get and get more if I can." Experimenting with sericulture was apparently one of his "amusements."[13]

For most families it was little more. The New England climate was ill adapted to the enterprise and the results were often disappointing. That 95 percent of mulberry trees in western Massachusetts died during the harsh winter of 1839 did not discourage the promoters of the New England Silk Convention that met in Northampton in 1841. Their resolution proclaimed that "it is a manifest indication of Divine Providence, that this country, as well as China, was designed to be a great silk growing country."[14] But most farmers abandoned the experiment within a few years. Henry Stark of Dunbarton, New Hampshire, recorded the rise and fall of his mulberry plantation in a homemade journal that began in September 1828, when he set out eleven hundred trees on land given him by his father. By 1830, he had managed to manufacture a pound of sewing silk from his sixteen hundred caterpillars, but though he quadrupled the number of larvae he raised the next year, his yield merely doubled. That seems to have been the end of the matter. Succeeding pages in his journal are blank.[15] In most parts of the region, the experiment was over by 1840.

The cattle shows, however, continued to celebrate other forms of household production, though it became increasingly difficult to know where homespun ended and fancywork began. At Pawtucket in 1824, girls from a Providence academy displayed "net curtains," and at Worcester in 1829, "The young misses, belonging to the Mulberry-Grove School in Leicester, presented for examination a variety of fancy articles, principally wrought with beads—such as purses, reticules, needle books, &c &c. They discovered great neatness and ingenuity, as did, also, similar articles presented by the young misses of Miss Stearnes's School in New Worcester." Two years later, some among the all-male panel of judges regretted not having their wives along "to comfort and advise in the doubts and difficulties which occurred" when examining such "an immense collection of curious and cunning works of the needle."[16]

No wonder the judges were confused. The exhibits at the annual cattle shows ranged from fine shoe leather to down tippets. Hearth rugs, straw bonnets, and cotton counterpanes were constants, but rural women also displayed their ingenuity and artistic sense through artificial flowers, feather fans, and a curious array of ornamental objects made from castoffs and weeds. At Brighton there was a bonnet made from cornhusks, at Pawtucket "a vandyke of milk weed down," at Hartford floor carpets and window blinds of rushes, and at Exeter a "beautiful grass indispensable, and a handsome basket, made of musk-melon seeds."[17] There was a sense that almost anything a woman made was deserving of public exhibition.

At the same time, there was an assumption that what mattered most was perseverance. In a perhaps unconscious effort to shame those who still failed to engage in manufacturing, the organizers reached out to children, the aged, and the disabled. They celebrated a pair of "well-knit

Woollen Stockings" made by a blind woman as well as a patchwork quilt of 12,100 pieces made on her sickbed by a girl "racked with bodily pain and distress." A report from Worcester honored a woman who "though having met with the calamity of losing one of her arms by amputation . . . represented the Committee with a pair of large Drawers, and a pair of large Woollen Hose, which she knit, with one hand, in a style that would do credit to two good hands."[18] No wonder Laura Flint condemned herself for her unfinished stocking.

Yet through all this, there was an acute sense that something was passing, that all this fuss about productivity obscured a truth too disturbing to acknowledge. In the autumn of 1831, the *Massachusetts Spy* praised a Mrs. Bogue of Shutesbury who "on the anniversary of her birth day, at the completion of her ninety fifth year, spun fifty four knots of woollen yarn,

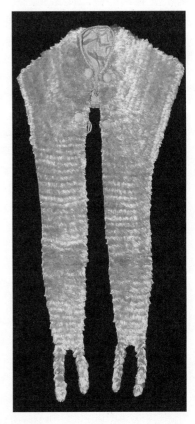

*Milkweed tippet.*
COURTESY OLD STURBRIDGE VILLAGE

of a superior quality," but assigned her contribution to the past: "Such women were our mothers! How many of the younger portion of their descendants at the present day can equal this performance?"[19]

Diaries, letters, and memoirs help us to see the many ways in which New England women experienced these changes. The letters and diaries of Sarah Weeks Sheldon of Salisbury, Vermont, show how one rural woman moved from a dutiful daughter in the early 1800s, through a stint as a country schoolmistress in the 1810s, into the dilemmas of the 1830s, when a new economy seemed to be pulling her sons away from her. Hard work was her mainstay through these years, but her most insistent concern was establishing a respectable Christian household in a world that seemed determined to prevent it.[20]

Like Betty Foot forty years before, she was determined to make something of herself through teaching, but her first job ended in dismissal.

"And behold I had nearly murdered a little girl two months ago," she explained in a sardonic letter to her brother. The school committee told her that they "in general do not approve of strangling as a punishment."[21] By 1810, Sarah could write from Pittsford, Vermont, that she had "found a society here like that I have always been wishing for." She thanked her mother for having prepared her for such a position by giving her a religious education. "If I had been educated like many in my native place, I should not dare to show my head here; but now I have, and hope to deserve that attention I could wish, from the worthy and deserving. The most desirable people in Pittsford are within the limits of my district." Sally's desire to be numbered among "the best people" was the driving force of her life, and the motive for her sometimes harsh treatment of her own children.[22]

She and her husband, Samuel Sheldon, whom she married in 1813, became the parents of four sons: Homer, Horace, Harmon, and Henry. In 1831, when the youngest was ten years old, Sarah began keeping small memoranda of textile production, eventually entering some of these records into blank pages of her manuscript "Dye Book." In a typical year she wove two hundred yards, keeping some for her own use, trading the rest for store goods. She wove sheets, shifts, diaper, dimity, and kersey; dyed factory cotton with madder, copperas, and indigo; and mixed white and black wool to create gray for her children's clothing. She also spun and knitted stockings. (She clearly had the resources and skill to produce stockings as sturdy as those in other New England collections, but among her textiles only a workaday linen shift survives.) Sarah was skilled enough at weaving to produce cloth for her neighbors as well as herself. After Thanksgiving in 1834, she wove two blankets for one family, taking her pay in dried apples, and twenty yards for another in exchange for "pine timber and shingle stuff." The lumber was apparently for the new house her husband was building. The family had shivered in an unfinished shell all fall, using a blanket for a door.[23]

The Sheldons weren't poor, but they were farmers in an era when prices fluctuated widely and cash was often scarce. Samuel was a decent man, but in Sarah's letters he appears cold and a bit tightfisted. She was constantly short of cash and none too happy about the kind of support, financial or emotional, she received from her husband. While her son Homer was clerking in a store in Middlebury, she wrote to ask if his employer would give her a new cloak in exchange for butter and stockings. She would "Pay when I git it. I do not ask him to trust." Her relent-

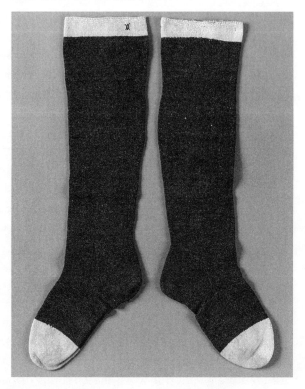

*Hand-knitted wool stockings owned by John Geer, Preston, Connecticut.*
LITCHFIELD HISTORICAL SOCIETY. GIFT OF WILLIAM WARREN

less production filled both a pecuniary and a psychological need. Because she felt deprived, both materially and emotionally, she resented the very work that she recorded so meticulously in her accounts. The respectability that she craved, for herself and her sons, cost her constant labor. After staying up all night spooling sixty-five runs of linen for sheets, she wove constantly for more than a week, coming out of her frenzy of productivity to do "an unaccountable washing—10 sheets, 5 flannel, 15 or 20 shirts, 11 pair stockings." After she had spread her clothes on the grass, she made four tablecloths and seven towels.[24]

In ten letters to Homer written between 1830 and 1834, she was alternately affectionate and controlling, bitter about her situation and determined to overcome her troubles through hard work. She defended herself against his unspoken accusations. "I think how you said once, that Mother had whipt learning into you—You would never have been where you now are if I had not—But I suspect you have forgotten how many times you have sit in my lap to read, when you were to[o] small to go to school." She was proud that Homer was working in a store, but worried lest he disappoint: "Homer, you cant tell how it makes the water come in my eyes, when Uncle Crook tells me that Mr.– – – says he has got the best clerk in Middlebury. . . . Now, my son, do always remember that one of the greatest comforts of your Parents, is to have you do well—And should you turn out a spend thrift, a licentious profligate, a gambler, or a trifler—We should be like a tree stript of all its leaves and branches. . . . Solomon says that a good name is better than great riches—When you are tempted to do any thing improper in any way—think of me." Homer did disappoint her—again and again. In the spring of 1833, he was in Boston, working for his board. "I have just received a letter from Mr. Case," she wrote him on April 7. "[H]e says tell Homer to buy Franklin's life and read it and read it. He says he found you chewing and smoking which you ought not to do—And Grandma has request me in particular manner to have you go to meeting on the sabbath, constantly."[25]

Homer was both a worry and a confidant. She even sent him messages in invisible ink. "If I send you a Newspaper with my name, you take it, I mean the envelope, and hold it by a hot fire, carefully, but let it almost burn, and then read it—but let no one know it," she wrote. In another letter, she confided that she had no friends. Her husband was "like a broken reed he seems to wilt at every trial keeps everything to himself—wants no ones advice, cares for no one, helps no one, dreads every thing, reads news, has the headache, and goes to bed." She knew how hard it was for Homer to support himself. She had had to do it herself even after marriage: "my father never bought me but one frock—and yours never but one—I have to worry thro' thick and thin to get all my clothes, crockery chairs clock, and so on."[26]

For all her piety, Sarah could not escape the attractions of consumption. She wanted a husband who bought her clothing and furniture. She wanted a son who clerked in a store. "I never could rest to have you on a par with mean, ignorant, low lived boys," she wrote. "Now, Homer, if you wish to convince me that you esteem education as a privilege, I say now Homer go on and be a man—a real man—a virtuous man—a dignified man—an honest man—a real business man." If he had any regard for his mother, he should never think of becoming "a nasty miserable sailor." He should avoid mixing with people "younger and inferior" to himself. He should go into his store and learn his trade and pattern himself after his superiors.

To nail the lesson down, she described the behavior of a man named Slade, reputed to be the best clerk in Middlebury. She observed him one day and saw how when his employers went to dinner, he opened drawer after drawer, took out "muslins, silks, laces &tc which Mr. Birge had put away in a hurry, folded them carefully and replaced them—and put every thing in order." Slade always treated her handsomely, giving her lemon in her sugar and water. On day as she was completing her shopping, he offered her some sugar paper, rolled up nicely. "This I will give you, said he, the Ladies all want to get it to colour with." This kind of work was much better than whaling.[27] After a stint in New Orleans, Homer did come home, eventually settling down as a clerk in his brother's store. That Sarah's letters survive tells us that at some level he listened.

Persis Sibley Andrews was younger and temperamentally more cheerful than Sarah. Born in Freedom, Maine, in 1813, she had studied at Coney Female Academy in Augusta, where she developed a talent for painting and drawing, but she had not neglected the lessons learned on her father's farm. She claimed to have brought fifty-five pairs of stockings to her marriage in 1842, all but two of her own manufacture. Eleven pairs were made from purchased yarn—three of silk, two of worsted, and six of cotton, the rest from materials spun at home. Half were "ribbed, seamed, or figured, and knit with much care and time." Two surviving pairs confirm her description. They are skillfully made of very fine thread with an attractive pattern along the leg that knitters might recognize as "Feather and Fan" or "Old Shale." One pair contains three kinds of cotton, medium weight for the welt and upper leg, a slightly finer one for the patterned section, and a heavier thread for toes and heels. The other pair is silk in the foot and leg and cotton in the upper margin where garters would have been tied.[28]

Persis was a skilled craftswoman who was eager to acquire new patterns wherever she could find them, even in the home of a poor woman living in a garret in Belfast, Maine. The woman "was born in the Highlands of Scotland—her father was Clan Leader—they moved to New Brunswick when she was a few years old and she is now the wife of a Yankee. . . . She show'd me some relics of antiquity that I covet more than anything I have seen since I have been in town. Viz. the hose and garters of her grandfather—they are of most beautiful manufacture,—curiously knit of worsted, in large diamonds of white and red, and come just below the knee where they are fastened with the beautiful garter of all the colors of the rainbow."[29]

Prosperous young women eagerly exchanged patterns in this period, sometimes carrying their knitting to afternoon tea parties that began with work, then, as suitors arrived, ended in games and dancing.[30] Marriage

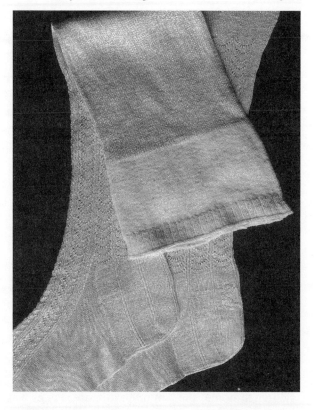

*Persis Sibley Andrews.*
*Hand-knitted stockings,*
*cotton and silk.*
MAINE STATE MUSEUM

brought greater responsibility and unwelcome isolation. Like Sarah Shel-don, Persis measured her husband's affection in part through his willing-ness to provide store-bought goods. Homebound with a small child in the winter of 1845, she complained, "I suffer for common Shoes suitable for the Season, & so does my child, & I am in great need of factory cloth—never having used an inch for myself since I kept house." She had been ill, and her husband, a young lawyer whose work demanded constant travel, seemed too busy to attend to her needs. "If I were a man I w'd not let my family suffer just for want of a little attention. Neglect is harder to bear than poverty."

Store cloth and a new venture in household manufacturing soon mended Persis's spirits. When her husband took three great spinning wheels in payment for legal work, she decided to keep one. She traded two newborn puppies for a reel, swift, wheel pin, and a patent wheel head, and, with wool from her father's farm, set to work. That was the begin-ning of an enterprise she memorialized a few years later in her diary, after a day doubling, twisting, and dyeing stocking yarn: "I . . . manufacture

all our worsted and yarn stockings every year. I venture to say that no
family is better supplied with handsome and comfortable."[31] In August
1845, she and her hired girl, Costella, tackled a bigger project. "We have
had a loom set up in our back kitchen & I am weaving my web of wool
flannel myself. Father gave me a bag of wool. Costella has spun the filling—I hired a woman to spin the warp, & I shall get 18 yds. of nice cloth
pretty cheap. . . . It is not common now to make cloth in families,
but . . . we have tho't to do a little something to convince the neighbors
that we sho'd be smart women if we were not nearly always sick."[32]

Persis continued to spin and weave because her father had wool to
spare, because she had acquired the skills in her youth, and because in a
small town there was little else she could do to contribute to the family's
support. Cloth-making was also a source of pride. It would remain a random activity, however, not only because her husband's prospects were
improving but because an inability to keep a hired girl left her with little
time to spare. After Costella left, she had to make do with a poor girl from
one of the backcountry towns, "thirteen years old—with only one suit of
clothes—*positively* without a change of linen or stockings." The mother
who sent her oldest daughter into household service no doubt assumed
that her daughter could now earn her own stockings. With eight other
children at home, she had none to spare. Persis was grateful for the girl,
however ragged, because the local high school had offered her a chance to
teach a drawing class, "w'h I c'd not do if I had not this Diantha, for girls
are scarce as gold dust. Costella is the fourth girl who has left me to go to
Mass. As soon as they get clothes up & a little money to bear expenses
they are sure to go, for there they are paid more."[33]

By the end of the year, Persis's textile production had been reduced to
a single, compelling project, the design and manufacture of a hearth rug,
a product made somewhat like the bed rugs Betty Foot and her sisters had
embroidered many years before. Persis spun and dyed the yarn, put the
background fabric in a frame, and went to work, stitching from a design
she had drawn herself. But the work went slowly. When an unexpected
move forced her to interrupt the work, she salved her disappointment
with bitter humor. "I may finish it before I move, but shall *not* at the
expense of duty to my husband or daughter, but for this latter I shall get
no great name, for the rug I shall be famous thro' out the County." Persis
aspired to more than sweeping and spinning.[34]

Women of ambition had been complaining about their helpers for a
hundred years, but in this period there were not only fewer Dianthas to

call upon, but more reasons why middle-class women might resent their lack of help. Persis Andrews had a small family, but she wanted to paint, and teach, and write, and she resented the political obligations that took her husband away from home and left her little scope for enlarging her own gifts. Unlike Samuel Sheldon, who was depressed by the pace of change, Persis's husband was determined to make his way in the world, and eventually he did serve in Congress, leaving his wife behind. For her as for Sarah Sheldon, education left cravings that a rural village could not supply.

New England women moved into the industrial age with trunks full of stockings and a heavy weight of history. Public speakers, writers, and their own consciences constantly reminded them that in comparison with their grandmothers, they had little work to do. In reality, there was plenty of work, some of it created by the labor-saving devices that had supposedly liberated them. An abundance of factory-made cloth expanded the standard of clothing a family required; new concepts of cleanliness required a greater investment in laundry, mopping, and cleaning; more varied foodstuffs, condiments, and table accessories encouraged more complex meals and entertainments; cookstoves, oil lamps, indoor pumps, and iceboxes added additional forms of maintenance. Even more important, idealized notions of child-rearing enlarged maternal responsibility for the character of children at the very time that schools and expanding wage work made children less accessible as household helpers and more susceptible to outside influence.[35]

Some women found outlets in church work, mothers' associations, and temperance societies. A few embraced abolition, a cause that achieved new visibility when two Southern abolitionists, Angelina and Sarah Grimké, toured the region. In the spring of 1837, as Laura Flint was feeding her silkworms, other women were circulating petitions. The 56,706 New England women who sent their signatures to Congress outnumbered male signatories three to one. In May the *Liberator* reported a conversation overheard between a female abolitionist and her neighbors. The second woman was skeptical that she could do anything about slavery. The other insisted that women had the power to change the world through their influence on men. "Perhaps some ladies can do so; but for my part I don't see how I can do anything," the first retorted. Overhearing the conversation, her daughter-in-law broke in, "Why, Mother, you can do something. You have great influence over Father; for a few days ago *when you told him to put the sheep into the other pasture,* HE WENT

RIGHT OFF AND DID IT." Such a trifling influence, the author believed, showed that a woman who understood the nature of her own power could assist the abolitionist cause.[36]

Significantly, this writer located female power in the household economy rather than in religion or moral sensibility. Women deserved to be heard because they were workers, not because they were morally superior to men. Persis Andrews and Sarah Sheldon lived by that ethic, as did their rural counterparts who went to the mills.


The first women to enter New England's textile mills thought of their work in much the same way as their counterparts who remained at home, but they soon learned that factory owners and machines were neither as flexible nor as forgiving as the housewives who had once managed their labor. Mechanized production exposed workers to the unfamiliar disciplines of clocks and bells, forcing them to adapt the motions of hands and eyes to the rhythms of machines.[37] "I tend a pair of looms and I think you [would] smile to see me trim and fold thirty yards of cloth in the breast beam of one of my looms and keep them both going," Jane Stevens of Bedford, New Hampshire, wrote home shortly after beginning work in Lowell.[38]

Although tiny factories with a handful of workers persisted in the 1830s, public attention was riveted on the tall brick buildings rising along major rivers. The growth of factories that integrated all the processes of cloth-making under one roof created cities out of fields and farms. There were only two hundred people in East Chelmsford, Massachusetts, in 1820. Six years later, when it was incorporated as the town of Lowell, the population had increased to twenty-five hundred. By 1836, there were eighteen thousand inhabitants in what many considered a model city. The six thousand women in the city's cotton mills outnumbered male employees six to one.[39]

Although Lowell was the most visible of the new industrial centers, the river power of New Hampshire also attracted capital. In Dover, New Hampshire, not far from William Damm's old garrison, was a handsome arrangement of new brick buildings that encompassed all the steps in the production of printed calico. Dover manufacturers, like their counterparts at Lowell, employed country girls between the ages of twelve and twenty-five. Some moved to town with their families; most came alone. As in Lowell, the company built boardinghouses, encouraged Sunday worship and weekday Bible classes, and attempted to control leisure time, assuring parents that factory life would not degrade the workers' morals. They issued contracts to boardinghouse managers requiring them "to close their house at 10 o'clock in the evening, and not to allow of any card playing or gambling in any form," nor "intemperate drinking" and "profane and improper language."

They were both patronizing and a bit afraid of the girls. In June 1825 a worried manager reported that eighty girls in one of the factories had purchased a flag that they intended to present to the local militia on the Fourth of July "without allowing all to participate. It is a piece of aristocracy with which I do not feel pleased & considerable unpleasant feeling is excited among the girls in No 2." To keep peace he invited the organizers to present the standard from his own lodging, where he would treat all the factory girls who attended to a glass of wine. "It will probably cost 20 or 30$ but I believe will be money well invested."[40]

Despite the manager's reference to "aristocracy," company officials were less worried about internal dissension than about the infection of radical ideas. Dover's John Williams proposed subsidizing the construction of a new meetinghouse by extracting annual pew rent from the operatives. "The Universalist Hall I do not consider a proper place for our females," he explained in his annual report to the corporation's board of directors. "You are aware that our establishment is collected from all quarters and countries and is indeed a most miscellaneous population. That but few attend church of any kind is a melancholy fact." Nor was he happy when an English worker employed in the printing works advertised himself as an agent for "the philosophical book publisher and persecuted writer Richard Carlisle of London." American manufacturers were well aware of labor unrest in Great Britain. "Some of our intelligent English workmen say the doctrines of Payne, Carlisle, and the French atheists have been one great cause of the distress in Manchester by producing immorality." No one wanted workingmen's organizations and strikes to emerge in Dover.[41]

They had reason to worry. Williams's skills as a negotiator stopped a small walkout of English printers in January 1827 and averted a crisis in August 1828, when workers threatened to boycott local merchants, who had decided to cut costs by closing their stores early two evenings a week and eliminating the practice of giving free patterns and trimming with each sale of fabric.[42] But the factory officials were unprepared for what happened in the early winter. As an anonymous eyewitness described it many years later, "there were exactions on the part of the corporation that the independent spirit of the fair spinners and weavers could not brook." The girls went on strike, parading through the town with a band at their head and bearing an American flag.[43] Unlike the patriotic spinners of 1769 or the young women who marched in Washington's Birthday processions in 1800, they were asserting their own rights, not abstractions like patriotism or household industry.

*The Mechanics Free Press,* a workingman's paper published in Philadelphia, complained that though "half the newspapers from Maine to Georgia" had noticed the strike, none had given a full account of its cause, a set of odious restrictions that not only demanded punctuality but promised to close the gate five minutes after the tolling of the bell and to fine workers each time it had to be opened. "What would the good people of this city say, to see 3 or 400 girls running, like hunted deer, on the ringing of a bell?" the writer asked. They might as well shut up the girls in a nunnery. Furthermore, a regulation forbidding talking while at work reduced the women "to the level of the State prisoners at Sing Sing." These were free women, and though the writer didn't say it, persons used to coming and going as they pleased in their own villages.[44]

Although Dover's 1828 strike was the first in the nation entirely by women, it was part of a larger cluster of labor actions that hit factories all over the Northeast in the late 1820s and early 1830s. New England elites wanted to dismiss the agitation as a consequence of foreign influence or radical infiltration. Because one of the earliest turnouts was in Paterson, mill managers referred to worker discontent as "New Jersey feelings."[45] When eight hundred women paraded the streets of Lowell in 1834 to protest a 25 percent wage reduction, the *Boston Evening Transcript* dismissed their behavior as "not altogether to the credit of Yankee Girls," adding that one of the leaders had "mounted a stump and made a flaming Mary Wollstonecraft speech on the rights of women and the iniquities of the 'monied aristocracy.' "[46]

But workers considered themselves both thoroughly American and demonstrably ladylike. The weavers who struck the Hopewell Mill in Taunton, Massachusetts, in 1829 marched through the streets in a solemn procession, wearing black silk dresses, red shawls, and matching green bonnets, their costume emphasizing their unity and their respectability.[47] Like the young women who marched in Washington's Birthday parades or presented banners to local militias, they claimed their rights as daughters of free men. During a second Dover strike in 1834, the workers accosted their agent in heartfelt but halting verse:

> *We will assert our liberty,*
> *While we are of a nation free;*
> *Though you may say we're a feeble band;*
> *Yet our designs we understand.*

They had internalized another familiar theme of the revolution. "Who among us can ever bear / The shocking fate of slaves to share?" they chanted.[48]

The same themes appeared at Lowell in 1836. As they marched the strikers sang:

> *Oh! isn't it a pity, such a pretty girl as I—*
> *Should be sent to the factory to pine away and die?*
> *Oh! I cannot be a slave,*
> *I will not be a slave,*
> *For I'm so fond of liberty,*
> *That I cannot be a slave.*

When more than a third of the employees joined the strike, a local storekeeper marveled that young women could "manage this whole affair with so much dexterity and correct judgement, that no power or skill, could be successfully employed against them." The strike succeeded because economic times were good, because the owners needed their labor, and because sympathetic bystanders understood their rhetoric of liberty. These girls had come from towns where female labor had always been collective and voluntary, where most women worked in the years before marriage, and where the social distance between workers and employers was thin. They were both producers and "pretty girls."[49]

Both supporters and opponents of the strikes invoked the old vision of a "middle landscape" that situated freeborn workers between aristocrats on the one hand and savages and slaves on the other. There was overt racism on both sides, a shared belief in the superiority of white labor. No one needed to tell Dover's citizens that their new factories had risen only a few feet from the garrison where Kancamagus and his troops killed Richard Waldron in 1689. In 1826, an orator in one of Dover's patriotic celebrations made explicit reference to the Indian wars. "How changed the scene!" he exclaimed. "Instead of the war whoop and savage yell along your river . . . the rattling of 10,000 spindles adds to the roar of your cataract." In 1832, a handbill promoting protective tariffs for American manufactures argued that without the mills "Dover would be a howling wilderness in comparison with what it now is."[50]

Other writers thought the mill towns encouraged savagery. In the middle of the Lowell troubles, the *Boston Evening Transcript* published a satirical piece, supposedly left on a stagecoach "by a celebrated foreigner," who reported that on arriving in Lowell he found "a large number of the males and females parading the streets," and that "not until the regular troops had shot twenty-seven of the ringleaders that harmony was restored in the city." The same writer reported the existence in the town of a hotel called "the American House," the keeper of which was "one of the aborigines, and has carried out his native wild propensities to a ludicrous extent," erecting a hotel in the manner of "a huge wigwam, without windows or chimnies, and those who go there eat their food off the ground, and sleep on buffalo skins." The only food served in this establishment was "venison, bear's flesh, coons, possums, and wild turkeys, and such other game as may be taken in the adjacent woods." Presumably industrialization was just another species of savagery.[51]

The twin themes of slavery and savagery reappeared in a rare broadside, now in the collections of Dover's Woodman Institute. Under a masthead proclaiming "Liberty, Independence, and Equal Rights," it reprinted an article from Dover's Jacksonian newspaper, the *Gazette*, defending the 1834 strikers against impropriety. They not only acted within their rights as "DAUGHTERS OF REPUBLICAN AMERICA," they did so with dignity and decorum: "Instead of forming processions and parading the streets to the amusement of a crowd of gaping idlers, they have confined themselves for the most part within their respective boarding-houses and seem impelled by no other motive than a firm determination, to maintain their just rights." A second article, signed by "A Watchman," took the argument even further, suggesting that self-sacrifice rather than self-assertion was the source of freedom. He believed in the strikers' cause but thought they should be prepared to give up their jobs if the mill owners refused their demands. "And shall the daughters of those mothers and grandmothers who wielded the battle axe to destroy the savages of the forest, hestitate a moment to deny themselves a few of the luxuries of life (should such denial become necessary,) in order not only that they may be free, but that posterity may continue to enjoy our present privileges."[52]

The "Watchman" assumed that Dover mill workers had choices, that they worked not to feed themselves but to provide consumer goods they could well do without. Like the women of 1769, they should deny themselves in order to save their country. Suppose the company followed through on its threats and closed down the mills. Then the workers should simply go home. If they submitted this time, there would soon be another reduction, until wages were so reduced that, like mill workers in England, they would become objects of charity. "Better would it be that Cocheco falls should again be the abode of the 'four-footed denizen' of the forest, and the haunt of savage nations, than that the 'Bell of No. 2' at each successive peal should call together hundreds of willing and obedient slaves." But the choice was not that grim. There were now movements afoot that might save the household economy of rural New England. "And who could not but admire amid the pure country air, free from the noise and bustle of settled villages, and the stench and danger of Cotton Mills, to pick the mulberry leaves and assist the untiring silk worm to wind his ball, and from it to reel the material for the most beautiful and durable fabric that female innocence can be attired in."[53] Through sericulture, the operatives of New England mills might become both manufacturers and ladies.

This was labor consciousness rooted in the household economy of an improving society, a vision of women's work that was simultaneously domestic and progressive. In fact, most factory workers did go home, not because mill owners refused to accede to their demands but because they had never seen their work as anything but a temporary expedient, a way of acquiring clothing and household goods in the years before marriage. Although tens of thousands of women moved from "farm to factory" in the antebellum period, few stayed long, on average less than three years even if they came from marginal families, and most did not. They worked primarily for themselves, rather than to supply family need, though the presence of kin in the mills encouraged them to stay longer.[54]

Worried relatives pondered the enticements and dangers of factory work. Persis Andrews saw only sorrow as she reported in her diary that her brother's daughter "Malvina, was brot home *dead* from Manchester, N.H., where she had been at work in a factory. She was sick of Typhoid fever only eight days. Her sister Columbia has also been very sick at the same place. . . . Seven years ago Amanda the sister next older was bro't home a corpse from Lowell."[55] But those who actually worked in the mills were usually more positive.

Jane Stevens was a granddaughter of Matthew Patten, the Scots-Irish farmer who built his daughter a loom in Bedford, New Hampshire, in the 1760s. She might have been a rural housewife like her mother and grandmother before her, but her husband's early death and her own ambition took her to Lowell in 1829. When her daughter, Sophia, whom she had left behind with relatives, proposed joining her there, she hardly knew what to say. "I should be glad to have her come here but she must make up her mind to be steady and give her whole attention to her work and abide by it if she will do that she may come here as soon as she can. . . . I think fifty two dollars a year ought not to be thrown away by a girl of fourteen for the sake of going idle." Sophia must, however, wash and mend her clothes and "not come dirty and ragged unless she wants me to disown her." A year later she reported that the girl was doing "better than I expected . . . she now packs filling and works verry well she packs from twenty six to forty two set in a day with two hundred twenty five bobbins to the set." The language of machines was new; the habit of counting yarn and cloth was familiar.[56]

Although the setting in which Jane worked was dramatically different from the farm in Bedford, the interweaving of autonomy and interdependence in her account is much like that in rural diaries from the late eighteenth century. She put her money in a bank, yet saved to take care of an aging relative. She left home for a factory, yet preferred homespun to factory-spun stockings. In a letter home, she begged her aunts to send her enough yarn "for 4 pr as I have but one for decent every day woolen stockings and I must have some if I have to buy my yarn here and do not want to do that for the yarn we get here is hardly worth kniting and when I buy anything I want that which is good." In exchange, she offered to send her aunt Sarah "a ball of yarn for thread which I wound off snarld bobins" in the factory. Eventually, she made peace with factory cotton, sending some home for Aunt Polly "to cloud," a form of tie-dying that produced a variegated yarn. Jane offered to supply the indigo.[57] Although Jane's stockings have not survived, earlier stockings made in Connecticut show what "clouded" stockings might look like.

Jane persisted in the mills, though like many factory workers, she changed locations frequently, working for a time in Nashua, New Hampshire, closer to her home, before returning to Lowell. In an undated letter she reported that the factory was having difficulty keeping girls, perhaps

*Stocking made with
variegated blue-and-white
yarn.*
LITCHFIELD HISTORICAL
SOCIETY

for good reason—"there has been four or five girls had their fingers taken off by cleaning when their looms were going and yesterday one had all her fingers in her right hand very badly cut." She stuck it out through wage cuts and shutdowns, proud not only of her ability to take care of herself but to contribute to her family's welfare. In 1847, she wrote home that no matter what it took she intended to pay funeral expenses for one of her beloved aunts "if it takes every cent I earn from now till the June payment is up, and I guess I shall have enough for I am making over three dollars per week." Her health was good. She had a will to work and sixty-five dollars in the bank, "and I have earnd it all since I came back last fall and have spent as much as I wanted to."[58] In widowhood, Jane had achieved her own kind of liberty.

Mill girls were the most visible female laborers in Massachusetts in 1837, but they were far outnumbered by women, who worked part-time in their own villages making straw and palm-leaf hats and bonnets.[59] Although hat makers were engaged in a classic form of outwork, nineteenth-century writers memorialized the industry as a domestic innovation. One author claimed that the hat industry began with fourteen-year-old Betsey Metcalf of Providence, Rhode Island, who in 1798 took some oat stubble from her father's field and commenced braiding a straw hat in imitation of a Dunstable bonnet she had seen in a Providence store. The historian of Framingham, Massachusetts, said it was the wife of Joseph Bennet and her daughter Betsey who first began braiding rye straw in 1799 or 1800. Another source says that "Miss Hitty Eames, the daughter of Henry Eames, and later the wife of Abel Eames," some years before her marriage in 1803, "took straw from 'the best bed' and after much patient industry made a straw bonnet." Henry Adams, in his *History of the United States during the Administration of Thomas Jefferson*, says a girl in Wrentham, Massachusetts, not far from Boston, introduced the industry into Massachusetts. Sarah Anna Emery of Newburyport, Massachusetts, claimed her aunt Sarah taught her to braid straw in the spring of 1800.[60]

A writer signing himself "A Friend to Agriculture, Commerce and Manufacturers," writing in the *New England Farmer* in 1824, urged support for a national tariff on imported straw bonnets, arguing that straw braiding was a commendable enterprise not only because it turned things of little value into profitable commodities, but because it employed "females and children, a class of people peculiarly deserving the fostering care of all governments, by reason of the influence which their labor may be made to have upon the wealth of the nation and the happiness, safety, and morality of society; and of their inability to avail themselves, as men do, of various other trades and employments, when the one by which they can support themselves is cut off." It was an appropriate domestic occupation because it had been introduced by enterprising Connecticut women who created a truly American bonnet by using a native grass called ticklemoth (*Agrostis alba*) to imitate English leghorn.[61]

The straw bonnets surviving in New England collections were sewn from yards and yards of braided fiber. Palm-leaf hats, on the other hand, were woven much like baskets, beginning at the center and moving outward. Storekeepers bought palm leaf wholesale from Boston merchants, who imported it from the West Indies and then distributed it to customers on credit, along with instructions for weaving. Thomas Dublin, who has linked surviving store accounts to other records, has shown that hat makers worked about a day and a half a week on average, that they came from families who owned their own land but were larger and poorer than their neighbors, and that they did most of their work in the winter months, between October and April. Some families turned in as many as fifteen hats at a time and were paid in goods from the store. Although most accounts were listed under the male head of household, girls over the age of fifteen often kept their own accounts. Their work supplemented the income of their fathers' farms and gave them a way of providing for themselves and their future households, much as spinning and weaving had done in earlier decades. Sixty-seven percent of hat-making credits went for cloth and sewing supplies.[62]

Although families who wove palm-leaf hats were doing work much like that done by Native American basket makers, it did not have the same social value. Because hat-making families cultivated their own land, they remained linked to an industrious rural economy. Basket makers, on the other hand, were suspiciously unattached to market values. The career of a New Hampshire coverlet weaver exposes this boundary.

At the Strafford County, New Hampshire, cattle show in 1825, a woman known at the time as Hannah Leathers received a premium of three dollars for the "best counterpane." In 1829, Hannah and her sister Mary petitioned the New Hampshire state legislature to change their name. They were among more than fifty persons by the name of Leathers who made the same request between 1822 and 1835. Only one, Elijah Leathers of Barnstead, New Hampshire, revealed his true motivation, explaining that "there is a strong prejudice against the name of Leathers."

And so there was. In Barrington, New Hampshire, a group of basket makers by the name of Leathers lived in an out-of-the-way place known as Leathers City. According to local lore, they traveled throughout the region peddling their wares, begging, and stealing. Hannah Leathers, who had given birth out of wedlock in 1810, had enough trouble without carrying a discredited name. She became Hannah Wilson, and as such wove more than 177 coverlets, carefully weaving each client's name and a number, but not her own name, into the margin. These are "raised-weft" coverlets like those Eliza Bourne made ten years earlier, though instead of using cotton alone, she highlighted the pattern in indigo-dyed wool. Whether this was her major form of income or a supplement to some other form of work, including perhaps factory weaving in one of the mills in Farmington and Milton, we do not know. The daughters of local mill owners were among her customers. By one means or another, she supported her son and eventually managed to purchase a house. Her latest surviving coverlet, dated 1860, included her initials (*HW*) as well as her client's name. It may have been the last she made. She died nine years later of consumption in the home of her married son.[63]

Hannah Wilson's story shows both persistence and change. The techniques she used were identical to those Eliza Bourne and her daughters perfected in Kennebunkport before 1810, but where Eliza was a privileged woman, the wife of a shipbuilder and merchant, Hannah was the breadwinner for a child and a solitary craft worker in an increasingly industrial economy. She is representative of weavers who subsisted on the margins of factory towns by specializing in products that could not yet be made by machine, things like patterned carpets, rag rugs, or figured bed coverings. In Providence, Rhode Island, in the 1830s, these so-called niche weavers included an African American widow named Ann Axtell, as well as several male weavers, a number of whom had emigrated from Ireland. In western Connecticut, two sisters, Samantha and Zeloda Barrett, supported themselves by working a small farm, knitting stockings, and spinning and weaving "flowered blankets" and coverlets.[64]

An industrializing economy gave a few weavers the capacity to persist in hand production by giving other families the cash to purchase their

*Hannah Wilson. Counterpane, cotton and wool. Inscription in border "Rhoda Ann Leighton no 75 1837."*

NEW HAMPSHIRE HISTORICAL SOCIETY

products. In other parts of the American continent, however, New England weavers continued older traditions of household production.

In the early nineteenth century, thousands of white families fled the rocky land their progenitors had settled, taking their textile skills with them. Daniel Knapp described his move from Bedford, New Hampshire, to Oil Creek, Pennsylvania, as "our journey from Egypt to the land of Canaan. First we landed safe at Keen and escaped out of the hands of Pharaoh from thence we hired teams to help us up the hills." He sold one of his horses for a pair of oxen; bought cows, sheep, swine, a loom, a quill wheel, and two good spinning wheels; and commenced clearing land. He wrote: "I like here very much better than I expected, I have Dryed 10 Bushels of Aples and can get any thing I want, I can have one pound of Pork, fat, Butter, or Sugar, for 1 yd weaving, I can have 3 lb flax for 1 yd Diaper, the surveyor says we have 489 acres of Land, with all sorts of good timber on it." In Bedford he had had "no Credit." In the new settlement he was in "good credit and have Been Town-Clerk this year." Knapp seemed happy to claim all this work for himself, but in a postscript he revealed the identity of the worker who paid for the butter and flax with her weaving: "Tell Polly my Wife wants if she can send on a small piece of paper a Draft of Birdseye Diaper."[65]

Almira Doty, who left her story in a memoir written long after the fact, was less positive about the "credit" one might achieve by moving. She had grown up in a family of wanderers. Born in Wilmington, Windsor County, Vermont, in 1790, she was five years old when her family packed up their few possessions and "crossed the Green Mts. to Bennington," where some of their relatives had already settled. Since opportunities seemed limited there, they moved in the spring to Adams, Massachusetts, where her father tried keeping a tavern. Sixty years later, Almira could still remember the shocking scenes of that year. In one drunken fight two men tore the clothes off each other: "one had his chin torn off, the other his nose bitten off," yet they sat down to another cup and "made up friends." When the Dotys returned to Bennington, where her father tried his hand at farming and then at blacksmithing, she was finally able, at age eleven, to attend the district school and learn to write. Her brief education was to her advantage, for when her family moved once again, this time to Pennsylvania, she stayed behind in Shaftsbury, Vermont, to teach school. She was seventeen years old.

She married Sylvester Stewart in December 1810, but like many rural brides delayed "going to housekeeping" for several months. "The day after marriage I sewed all day on a coat for a female friend of mine for which I received twenty-five cents." Three months after the wedding, Sylvester collected her and her household goods, a "bed, bedding & bedstead, two tables—a kitchen and tea table—one bureau, six chairs, one light stand, a good assortment of crockery and glass ware, spider, gridiron, toasting iron, chopping knife and one set of silver teaspoons to his fathers . . . eleven dresses, eleven pairs of stockings with every article of clothing necessary for my wear—all of which I had earned by the labor of my hands and made."

For a few months, the young couple lived with Sylvester's parents. Almira remembered this period with fondness. When her father-in-law offered to give her all the flax she could spin, she accepted "joyfully— took the flax, hatch[el]ed it, and then commenced spinning, and with my own hands spun yarn enough to make sixty-five yards of tow and linen cloth before it was time to begin to spin wool. My husband had sheep. I spun yarn to make 40 yards of cloth, stocking yarn for husband and myself, yarn for two coverlids, colored it and had it ready for the weaver by September." Sylvester was equally industrious. By March 1812 he had a farm ready for them a mile and half from his father's. They seemed settled for life, but in less than a year Sylvester returned from helping move a neighbor to New York State "all in raptures with the country." On February 15, 1813, "with three sleigh load of household goods . . . we left the home of our birth place to go among strangers." It took them five days to reach Locke, New York, on the southern end of Lake Owasco, where they purchased a log cabin from a family who took the sashes from the dwelling's two windows with them. So Almira's homespun became a substitute for glass. From March until October they lived "with nothing but a white towel hung at each window." No sooner had they built "a nice snug frame house" than Sylvester again got the urge to move. In 1815 they were off to Susquehanna. The new cabin had windows but no fireplace or door. Almira cooked outdoors on an open fire until October, hanging one of her homespun blankets for a door.

Perhaps it wasn't wanderlust but ambition, a desire to get ahead, that turned Sylvester into a wanderer, but he seems to have arrived at each new settlement in its moment of decline. In 1821, he moved his family to a rough area in the shadow of the Catskills, where he "launched on the business of carrying the mail." As Almira recalled, the experiment "proved bad business for us and here all we possessed was sold by the sheriff." Situating his family in a small log house, he went to work as a day laborer to support them. When Almira became ill, they had no other choice but to send some of their children home to family in Vermont. In 1827, Almira returned to Vermont for a visit, hoping to regain her health. Her brother offered Sylvester and all the children work in a factory in North Bennington, but to revert to wage labor was a terrible thing for a man who valued his independence. Sylvester's father rescued him from this indignity by offering him a share of his farm. He struggled along as best he could, carefully paying off legacies to the other children when the father died. But farming in Vermont had never been easy, and as commercial sheep farming expanded, small farmers like Sylvester had little chance of prospering. One Sabbath, he said to Almira, "I wish you were willing to go to Ohio to live. I could there buy me a farm with what we have got."

Ever the good wife, she agreed. In 1833 the Stewarts once again left Vermont. After Sylvester's death in 1846, Almira returned briefly to North Bennington. A visit one Sunday to the singing school brought back memories: "Forty years ago, I was there in all the buoyancy of youth when my morning was bright and my brow unclouded . . . but not so now. Years have gone by—I have seen affliction, my bosom has been wrung with agony and bitter tears have furrowed my cheeks." She would experience more sorrow, this time for her daughter, who by 1847 was living in a "miserable log cabin" in Ohio with six children, including an infant. "I was a witness on many occasion of the brutal & inhuman treatment she received from her husband." When she received word a few months later that the daughter had died, she could not shed a tear. "Poor Sufferer, I said, You have found that rest which you longed for." Almira made one last trip to Vermont before she followed her brother and sons to Wisconsin. She ended her life in a small city in Illinois, where in 1871 she described herself as "a prisoner of hope in this city of Irish & Dutch," adding that "the city is governed by Catholics, the mayor is Catholic."[66]

Like Almira Stewart, Patty Bartlett grew up in northern New England. Her parents, however, were more settled and prosperous than Almira's. They were among the oldest—and most prolific—families in Bethel, Maine, the town where Molly Ocket once practiced her healing arts. Patty completed grammar school, then began instruction in the unknown school where she began a large linen sampler marked with her name. After her marriage to David Sessions, she packed away the unfinished sampler and the silk thread her parents had bought her, turning to more practical things. When David bought an old loom from a family migrating west, Patty wove a tick for their bed, filling it with cattails since she had no feathers. Soon she had all the weaving she could do "fetched to me from ten to twelve miles." Her arthritic mother-in-law, a midwife, provided a different sort of training. One day when the old lady couldn't get to a delivery fast enough, Patty rushed ahead, performing the work so skillfully that the only doctor in the town encouraged her to continue.[67]

Patty had buried four of her seven children by the time Mormon missionaries came to her town in 1833, bringing news of an American prophet and a marvelous book translated from golden plates buried in a hill in upstate New York. David and Patty and their children eagerly embraced the new gospel, and by 1837 they were in the Mormon settlement of Far West, Missouri, where Patty's last child was born. When the Mormons were driven out of Missouri at gunpoint, David and Patty moved to the swampy river-bottoms along the Mississippi that became the Mormon city of Nauvoo, Illinois. Here their youngest child died, and here they were initiated into the strange new doctrine of "plural marriage."[68]

Patty suffered when David took a second wife, but she believed in the new gospel and remained with the Saints when they were driven from Nauvoo in 1846. She continued to practice midwifery and nursing during a year in Iowa, and in September 1848 she delivered the first male child born in the Salt Lake Valley. To her it was a fulfillment of prophecy: "it was said to me more than 5 months ago that my hands should be the first to handle the first born son in the place of rest for the saints even in the city of our God I have come more than one thousand miles to do it since it was spoken."[69]

Six months after arriving in the Rocky Mountains, she "commenced to finish my sampler that I began when I was a girl and went to school." Why Patty picked up her embroidery at this moment is difficult to say. Perhaps it was homesickness. Perhaps she was desperate for diversion from the hard work of establishing a new home. Although there was little time for fancywork, on the day she gathered the first lettuce and radishes from her first western garden, she added a few more stitches. On August 21, after staying up most of the night delivering a baby, then carrying "a web to sister Gustan to weave," she "finished my Sampler that I commenced when I was young."[70]

Although the school where Patty began her sampler has not been identified, the imagery, materials, and stitchery are representative of work done in New England from the colonial period into the nineteenth century. At the top are rows of alphabets in Roman and cursive letters, in the center a happy couple, joining hands, surrounded by fruit trees, flowering shrubs, a spotted dog, a swayback horse, a jaunty rooster, and an antlered deer. This is pastoral embroidery, a celebration of conjugal happiness and rural life. But it is also a memento of a life. On the top is the schoolgirl inscription, "Patty Bartlett is my name and with my needle I wrought the same. A.D. 1811," then beside it a notation: "in the 54th year of my age AD 1848."

*Patty Sessions. Sampler,*
*silk on linen.*

The young couple on the sampler join hands in happy innocence, an ironic commentary on Patty's own life. Two years after their arrival in Utah, David died, leaving her to care for his young second wife and their children. She struggled along as best she could, doing a man's work as well as a woman's. "I have to cut wood for two fires," she wrote on December 2, 1851. Seven days later, she was "almost wore out cuting wood." But on December 14, a little more than a year after David's death, she happily reported: "I was married to John Parry and I feel to thank the Lord that I have some one to cut my wood for me."[71]

The verse Patty stitched on her sampler, though hardly original, nevertheless reflects her values:

> *The mind should be inured to thought*
> *The hands in skillful labours taught.*
> *Let time be usefully employed*
> *That art and nature be enjoyed.*

With someone to cut her wood, she continued her textile work and her midwifery, eventually delivering more than four thousand babies. On June 24, 1863, after taking a web of cloth from her loom, she thought back on her Maine upbringing. "I do feel thankful to my heavenly Father that he gives me health and strength and a disposition to work and make cloth and other things for my comfort now in the sixty ninth year of my age. And I also feel thankful that I had a mother that put me to work when I was young and learned me how." Patty died in 1888 at the age of ninety-four. She insisted on knitting almost to the end. As her sight declined and her fingers grew feeble, she dropped stitches and made so many errors that her family secretly unraveled her work at night, then gave her the needles the next day as though nothing had happened.[72] Like the old women who exhibited at New England cattle shows, she deserved a prize for perseverance.

Like Patty Sessions, Lucy Meserve Smith was the child of early Maine immigrants, and she, like Patty, was part of the Mormon migration to Missouri, Illinois, and the Great Salt Lake. She had a more positive attitude toward polygamy, however, probably because she had never known anything else, and perhaps too because she had such a highly developed sense of female solidarity. Shortly after settling in Provo, south of Salt Lake City, she organized a spinning match. "Myself, Sister Eliza Terrel, Sister Rua Angeline Holden and Sister Hannah Maria Smith took our spinning wheels and went to a large room in the Seminary and tride our best to see who could reel of the greatest No. of Knots from sunrise to sunset." But this was more a social occasion than a contest. Lucy found joy in sisterhood. "On the whole we concluded we all beat." When her only baby died, she mothered the children of her husband's other wives, taking as much pride in their development as if they had been her own. This complex household provided an opportunity for specialization. Lucy sat at her loom month after month weaving while "Sister Hannah" did the household work. Since there were no daughters, she taught the boys to wind quills for her shuttle and hand ends while she warped. Her weaving brought in needed cash as well as providing clothing for the family. When she finally got a little house of her own, she wove twenty-two yards of carpeting in a pattern so complex it required fourteen shuttles. There were so many colors and shades she could only weave two yards a day, "but it was a beauty when done, and it lasted many years."[73]

During the winter months, the pioneers sometimes danced away the night, but in the spring "we did not need any more dancing for exercise, but we could play on the Whimmikie Whammikie two Standard Lillikie Strikiety Huffity Whirlimagig (Flax Wheel.)." Lucy and her friends even made a flag for the town's brass band, but when she proposed giving a speech "on behalf of the Ladies of Provo" at the presentation ceremony, the presiding authority "put his foot on it."[74] Mormon patriarchs, like Dover manufacturers, were wary of unofficial flag ceremonies, but they were enthusiastic about household production. Brigham Young preached a gospel of manufactures worthy of his native Vermont. He urged mothers to teach their daughters "to spin, color, weave and knit, as well as work embroidery." In doing so they would prove "helpmeets in every deed, not only in domestic relations but in building up the kingdom." In a typically droll sermon, he joked that the younger generation made stockings with "a leg six inches long while the foot is a foot or a foot and a half long; or the leg only big enough for a boy ten years old while the foot is big enough for any miner in the country . . . it is a fact that the art of knitting stockings is not near so generally understood among the ladies as it should be. I could tell you how it should be done had I time and knew how myself."[75]

Lucy Smith knew how to knit stockings. In the memoir she wrote in old age, she measured her life not so much through the suffering she experienced when the Latter-day Saints were driven from their homes in Nauvoo, nor through the privations of the early years in Utah, but through the work she had accomplished in a long and varied life.

> I can count up nearly 50 bed coverleds I have woven. I carded and spun the cotton and formed the draft, and wove one counterpin for myself which is yet good. If my friends could know of the great amount of spinning cotton flax tow and wool, and the many hundreds of yards of draft work such as diaper and carpets besides the white counterpins, and coverleds, besides six years work in the cotton factories, with the addition of being driven from my home in the winter, having scurvy for lack of vegatables, &c. They would wonder that I am alive say nothing about my helpless condition at the present time.

Then she went on, creating an encyclopedia of nineteenth-century textile production.

She had colored "many pounds of yarn with madder, Indigo, Logwood, Red-wood, Cochineal, Bagle wood, Tan Bark, cotten-wood bark, coperas, allum, sage-brush, yellow weed, Onion-peals, and Magenta."

She had "cut and made dresses cloaks coats pants and Temple suits with their aprons &c."

She had "cut torn and sewed hundreds of pounds of rags for carpets and rugs, also woven many rag carpets braided and sewed many mats and rugs . . . braided Palmleaf and straw hats and sewed the straw hats myself."

She had done "considerable nice quilting," cutting and piecing the tops and carding the batting for filling. She had knitted edgings and "netted a few yards."

And she had knitted nearly enough stockings, socks, and mittens "to fill a barrel."

She closed her recital with a wry admission: "I took a few lessons in drawing, and a few lessons in French."[76]

Her barrel's worth of stockings have disappeared, but an example of her "draft work" survives, a white linen tablecloth with a netted fringe, now at the Pioneer Memorial Museum in Salt Lake City. It confirms her claim that in pattern weaving she took special care to "get every figure right, and that I would have if I had to undo a half yard."[77] Lucy couldn't speak French but she understood the language of refinement.

The unfinished stocking at the New Hampshire Historical Society not only exemplifies old-fashioned techniques of household production; in its new setting in the exhibit "New Hampshire Through Many Eyes," it documents the memorialization of New England's preindustrial economy. Displayed near it is an impressive pair of white cotton stockings purportedly made by Mary Wilson Wallace, the "Ocean-born Mary" of Londonderry fame. Examples of Mary Wallace's linen and scraps from the silk purportedly given her mother by pirates in 1725 traveled west in the 1830s and eventually found their way to museums as far away as Toronto and Washington, D.C. The stockings returned to New Hampshire from California in 1964 with a story that they had been worn by Mary's son-in-law Thomas Patterson at his wedding in 1775 and by every male Patterson ever since. If so, they were made from slave-grown cotton brought from the West Indies on the eve of revolution. Spun and knitted by an Irish immigrant on a farm carved out of an Abenaki forest, they were passed on from father to son for seven generations. In a will signed in 1830, Thomas Patterson did indeed leave his wearing apparel to his five sons and "beds, beding, table cloths, towels, and linen" to his four daughters. Some of his children were still in New Hampshire; many had moved on to New York. That so many Patterson textiles survived the family migrations attests to the strength of the stories that came with them. Patterson's stockings, knitted with a purled thistle in each leg, exemplify family pride, skillful knitting, and the mythical power of New England's age of homespun.[78]

In an address published in the *New England Farmer* in 1832, the president of the Middlesex County Agricultural Society reassured those who worried about the social consequences of New England's transition from an agricultural society to one devoted to manufactures, arguing that their fears for the future were unjustified. People had complained in 1804, when water power was applied to the spinning of cotton, and again in 1816, when mechanized weaving began. Grandmothers thought the world would come to an end if the spinning wheels that had seen them through the Revolution were "packed away, neglected and forgotten, among the rubbish of old chairs, side saddles and panniers, in the garrets of our houses." But there was no reason for alarm. Anyone could see that "the sun rises and sets as usual—our elections, thanksgiving and new years' days, come and go just as they used to do twenty years ago," and "our attention is now to be directed to fine needlework, many beautiful specimens of which are annually exhibited at our Shows." In this man's view, fancywork would quietly take the place of homespun, becoming a source both of "pleasure and profit."[79] Whether he was thinking of embroidered hearth rugs or milkweed tippets we do not know.

Other men were more suspicious of fancywork. In 1831, the chairman of the Hillsborough (New Hampshire) Cattle Show and Fair celebrated household manufactures that were "of a durable and very useful nature. . . . We believe there has been a material reform within a few years past, and instead of the tinsel and flouncing furbelows that served only to flutter in the wind, we see an anxious desire for what is serviceable."[80] The following year, a new chairman turned the whole argument around, suggesting that fancywork ought to be less serviceable in a literal sense and more imaginative. The committee he chaired was pleased to see articles "which are of acknowledged utility in the common business of life. . . . But we wish for something more. We would see the efforts of ladies in other capacities than that of mere upholsterers." Any woman of

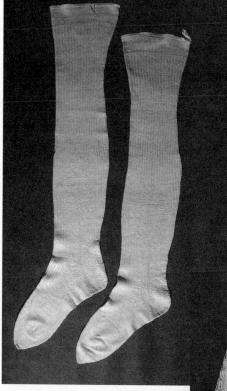

Mary Wilson Wallace.
Cotton stockings, c. 1775,
with a detail showing
the ornamental knitting
on the leg.
COURTESY NEW HAMPSHIRE
HISTORICAL SOCIETY

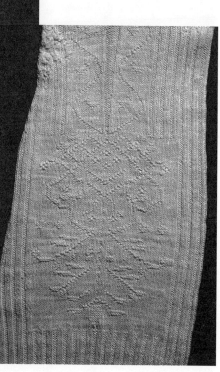

ordinary abilities could make a rug, and though some might ornament it with more taste than others, such articles offered little scope for true artistry. Surely there was room in the society's exhibits "for a *few exclusively Fancy Articles.*" Among these were "elegant specimens of painting, drawing and transferring," and even of literature. "Poetry is unquestionably a Fancy Article, and within the jurisdiction of this Committee."[81]

In fact, the transition that the chairman imagined was already under way as women like Horace Bushnell's favorite "poetess," Lydia Sigourney, began to contemplate the scraps of linen left behind by their mothers and grandmothers. In the next half century household textiles became the paper on which poets, novelists, centennial orators, and family chroniclers all over America wrote their stories of New England's past.

# AFTERWORD
-+->-<-+-

Urban fantasies about rural life are as old as the Greek eclogues and as American as the L. L. Bean catalog. Privileged people in many centuries have imagined the pleasures without the muck and labor of country living. Nineteenth-century Americans gave us the age of homespun. They taught us to believe in a time when families made almost all of the things they needed, relying on God and their own hands rather than distant markets.

In Horace Bushnell's version of this story, there were no dejected classes and only isolated cases of vice or poverty. Fathers who climbed the hills "with their axes, to cut away room for their cabins and for family prayers" were seldom tempted by the tavern nor their wives and daughters by the fripperies of commerce. The revolutions of the spinning wheel and the thwack of the loom sustained the rugged virtues of hard work, neighborliness, and unaffected piety. Yet hovering over Bushnell's sermon, unbidden and unseen, were the echoes of aristocratic pastoral. A hundred years before he gave his speech at Litchfield, New England girls were embroidering frolicking lambs and winsome shepherdesses on chimney pieces and samplers. Politics transformed pastoral affectation into a vision of an American republic sustained by rural virtue. The rhetoric of the Revolution and the War of 1812 emphasized household production, not only because it was an essential component of the nation's economy, but because images of industrious, self-sacrificing, and patriotic women domesticated and softened the often harsh realities of political conflict, economic uncertainty, and war.

The age of homespun provided an ideological haven from the artificiality of Europe and the rudeness of the American landscape. Americans situated their yeoman farmer between aristocrats and savages, seldom invoking one without acknowledging the other. In poems, sermons, and diaries, and in counterpanes, blankets, and tablecloths, they celebrated family solidarity and household industry, even as they spun slave-grown cotton and turned up Indian bones with their plows. Their ability to transform forests into farms seemed to them a literal fulfillment of the promise of the Old Testament prophet Micah that every man might sit under his own vine and fig tree and none would come to make afraid.

Their vision lives with us still. Inherited ideals of rural life survive in children's books, craft shows, and the names of suburban streets. The age of homespun haunts public discourse in debates over family farms, anxieties about the deterioration of family values, and invocations of lost community. When AIDS activists organize a national quilting bee, evangelical writers celebrate home schooling, or the First Lady proclaims that it takes a village to raise a child, they are creating new versions of the American pastoral. The mythology of homespun persists not only because it is adaptable to so many political persuasions, but because it allows us to forget that greed and war were so much a part of the American past. Horace Bushnell was surely correct in arguing that ordinary people make history through the smallest acts of everyday life. But people make history not only in the work they do and the choices they make, but in the things they choose to remember.

The history of textiles is fundamentally a story about international commerce in goods and ideas. It is therefore a story about exploitation as well as exchange, social disruption as well as entrepreneurship, violence as well as aesthetics. The objects nineteenth-century Americans collected tell us that. Dinah Fenner's little basket, with its basswood warp and wefts of moth-eaten wool, shows the integration of Algonkian and English fabrics in a transatlantic economy that transformed English blankets into Indian "coats." The textile tools in William Damm's garrison continue the story, showing how New England merchants exchanged timber for West Indian sugar and cotton while colonial troops defended newly cleared land against French and Abenaki soldiers. Over the course of the eighteenth century, men sawed boards, built barrels, rigged ships, and manned garrisons, while their wives and sisters learned to weave as well as spin.

In southern New England, the Algonkian survivors of King Philip's War settled into anonymity, constructing brooms, bottoming chairs, weaving woodsplint baskets, and carving pudding spoons that they traded in Yankee towns. In northern New England, Molly Ocket learned from her experience as a hostage during the colonial wars how to move in and out of the world of pocketbooks without surrendering to its power. Others were not so fortunate. Succumbing to poverty, alcohol, and hunger, they both confirmed and denied an emerging mythology about disappearing Indians. Some, like the maker of the woodsplint basket lined with the *Rutland Herald*, eluded Yankee scrutiny. Uncounted in Federal censuses, little seen in local histories, they moved along the sparsely settled towns of the upper Hudson Valley and Vermont, turning up occasionally as farmhands or wandering basket makers, seldom leaving a name. They marked the edges of Yankee fears about wanderers, violent men, and profligate women.

An oak cupboard painted with roses, inverted hearts, vines, and the letters of a woman's name shifts the focus of this history from the struggle for land and power to the inner politics of households. For Anglo-American families, bed furnishings, table linens, cupboard cloths, and napkins were forms of wealth, emblems of gentility, and the core of female inheritance. Over the course of the eighteenth century, more and more women became creators as well as custodians of such goods. Betty Foot's bed rug shows how women in one Connecticut town adapted the motifs of high-style embroidery to the exigencies of household production, insisting upon beauty and comfort even in the midst of war. Prudence Punderson's silk embroidery exposes the limits of that aspiration in its orderly arrangement of chairs, tables, a cradle, and a coffin, and its juxtaposition of a solitary embroiderer and her slave.

The desire for refinement spread with the expansion of household production. In the early nineteenth century, hundreds of rural families responded to a rhetoric of agricultural improvement and to the notion that in a republic women might be both manufacturers and ladies. Eliza Philbrick documented that era when she labeled the coverlets and household linens made on her grandfather's farm before 1816, but in the gown she made for a Daughters of the American Revolution party in the 1890s, she wrapped herself in an imagined gentility, embellishing New Hampshire wool with an embroidered bed valance worthy of an urban dame, then gathering around her shoulders a linen "kerchief" that may well have begun life as a netted tea cloth. Her dress falsified her family's past only in its details. Sixty years before she made her rust-colored gown, her mother and aunts—Clara, Cleora, and Climena Philbrick—were embroidering roses and starbursts on homespun blankets, and though their embroidery was unpolished in comparison with the fine crewelwork made in elite households, it asserted the impulse toward betterment that often lay beneath rural industry.

New England Indians were less likely to save material possessions than to pass on the skills used to make them. In the early twentieth century, anthropologists rediscovered New England Indians, paying particular

*Ella Amos, Mashpee, Massachusetts.*
NATIONAL MUSEUM OF THE
AMERICAN INDIAN.
PHOTOGRAPH BY FRANK SPECK

*Marjorie Mye and others. Woodsplint back baskets.*
PEABODY MUSEUM,
HARVARD UNIVERSITY

attention to workaday baskets like those used at Mashpee. Ella Amos looks out from a photo by Frank Speck as if to say, "We were here all along."[1] There is history as well as ethnography in the basket she wears. Although it was made about 1870 by her grandmother, Marjorie Mye, it has the lightness and practicality of the basket Mary Rowlandson wore during her captivity in the time of King Philip's War. Given the devastation of that war and the continuous assault on Christian Indian lands all over New England in the years that followed, it is a tribute to the political savvy and continuing resistance of Mashpee families that at the end of the nineteenth century Wampanoags were still weaving baskets and gather-

*Hannah Gove. Coverlet.*
SOCIETY FOR THE PRESERVATION
OF NEW ENGLAND ANTIQUITIES.
GIFT OF GEORGE O. SWASEY AND
CLARA S. WOODBERRY, 1949.
PHOTOGRAPH BY DANA SALVO

*Eliza Philbrick, 1911, with
coverlet by her grandmother,
Hannah Gove.*
PHILLIPS LIBRARY, PEABODY-
ESSEX MUSEUM, SALEM,
MASSACHUSETTS

ing corn on land cultivated by their ancestors. Woven into this basket are the petition Reuben Cognehew carried to London in 1760 and the essays William Apess wrote during the revolt of 1833.

Old baskets, twined bags, embroidered bed rugs and blankets, cotton counterpanes, painted chests and cupboards, spinning wheels, reels, pictorial embroideries, and ordinary stockings document forgotten forms of work, enduring habits of possession, and the mnemonic power of goods. Objects like these bob up from the depths of the American past like bottles on a wave, begging us to read their notes.

Somewhere in New Hampshire a real bottle sits on a shelf. It is filled with hair. A faded note, barely visible through the glass, explains, "The brown hair was cut from mother's head when she was a young woman; and the gray was cut off after she died. The *golden lock* was was [*sic*] spun from brother Josephs head as he sat on the front of her wheel. Mother was born Nov 20, 1801 Died May 3, 1857 Joseph was born May 3, 1828." Who was this mother? Who was brother Joseph? An earnest genealogist might answer those questions, but only history can explain why the person who corked this bottle memorialized both her loved ones and her mother's spinning wheel.

# Notes

## Prologue

1. Laurel Thatcher Ulrich, "Wheels, Looms, and the Gender Division of Labor in Eighteenth-Century New England," *William & Mary Quarterly,* 3d ser., 55 (1998): 3–38.
2. Essex Institute Accession Book, Essex Institute, Salem, Massachusetts, e.g., 793, 921; Accessions Book, 1835–1880, Rhode Island Historical Society, Providence; Suzanne L. Flynt, Susan McGowan, and Amelia F. Miller, *Gathered and Preserved* (Deerfield, Mass.: Memorial Hall Pocumtuck Valley Memorial Association, 1991), 12; *Catalogue of the Collection of Relics in Memorial Hall,* 3d ed. (Deerfield, Mass.: Pocumtuck Valley Memorial Association, 1920), 101–4.
3. Edward Taylor, *The Poetical Works of Edward Taylor,* ed. Thomas Johnson (New York: Rockland Editions, 1939), 98.

## Introduction: The Age of Homespun

1. William Butler, "Another City upon a Hill: Litchfield, Connecticut, and the Colonial Revival," in *The Colonial Revival in America,* ed. Alan Axelrod (New York and London: Norton, 1985), 18–34, 35.
2. "Litchfield County Celebration," *New Englander* 10 (1851): 77; *Litchfield County Centennial Celebration, Held at Litchfield, Conn., 13th and 14th of August, 1851* (Hartford: Hunt, 1851), 12–17, 144–47, 73, 101, 155, 172, 211–12; scrapbook of press clippings, Litchfield County Centennial, 1851, Litchfield Historical Society, Litchfield, Connecticut (hereafter cited as Centennial scrapbook).
3. *Litchfield County Centennial Celebration,* 8, 9, 211–12, 146–47, 145.
4. For the larger history of civic celebrations, see Mary Ryan, "The American Parade: Representations of the Nineteenth-Century Social Order," in *The New Cultural History,* ed. Lynn Hunt (Berkeley, Los Angeles, and London: Univ. of California Press, 1989), 137; Mary Ryan, *Women in Public: Between Banners and Ballots, 1825–1880* (Baltimore and London: Johns Hopkins Univ. Press, 1990), 22–23, 42; and David Glassberg, *American Historical Pageantry: The Uses of Tradition in the Early Twentieth Century* (Chapel Hill and London: Univ. of North Carolina Press, 1990), 11.
5. *Observer,* 21 Aug. 1851; Centennial scrapbook.
6. *Litchfield County Centennial Celebration,* 33, 66, 40, 49, 50, 64; "Litchfield County Celebration," 84.
7. *Litchfield Enquirer,* 21 Aug. 1851, and unidentified clipping, Centennial scrapbook, 5, 27, 92, 93; Thomas Dublin, *Transforming Women's Work: New England Lives in the Industrial Revolution* (Ithaca, N.Y., and London: Cornell Univ. Press, 1994), 53.
8. Robert L. Edwards, *Of Singular Genius, of Singular Grace: A Biography of Horace Bushnell* (Cleveland: Pilgrim, 1992), 113–15, 121–31; Mary Bushnell Cheney, *Life and Letters of Horace Bushnell* (New York: Harper, 1880), 93, 235, 248. Several of the newspaper accounts comment on Bushnell's appearance. The reference to his hair is in the clipping from the *Palladium,* Centennial scrapbook, 41. The silver does not appear in the portrait by Jared Bradley Flagg, done in 1847.

9. Horace Bushnell, "The Age of Homespun," in *Work and Play* (London: Strahan, 1864), 39, 40.

10. Ibid., 43–44.

11. On eighteenth-century versions of these ideas, see chaps. 4 and 5. Novels and stories by New England women that deal with New England domestic life and history include Catherine Maria Sedgwick, *A New England Tale* (1822); Sarah Josepha Buell Hale, *Northwood* (1827); Sally Wood, *Tales of the Night* (1827); and Lydia Maria Child, *Hobomok* (1824) and *The Rebels* (1825).

12. Bushnell, "Age of Homespun," 42, 44, 45–46.

13. Ibid., 47. Bushnell's speech builds upon the Christian notion that "the first shall be last and the last first" and on the democratic ethos of the early republic. As Michael Kammen has noted, the plain granite obelisks erected at Bunker Hill and at Fort Griswold in Groton, Connecticut, in the early nineteenth century reflected an American anxiety over hero worship. In the words of John Quincy Adams, "Democracy has no monuments. It strikes no medals. It bears the head of no man on a coin." Michael G. Kammen, *Mystic Chords of Memory: The Transformation of Tradition in American Culture* (New York: Knopf, 1991), 19.

14. Bushnell, "Age of Homespun," 50, 59, 65, 69, 52–53.

15. Ibid., 48, 49, 62.

16. Ibid., 62, 66, 67.

17. Centennial scrapbook, 28, 29; "Litchfield County Celebration," 88; Bushnell, "Age of Homespun," 39.

18. Christopher Monkhouse, "The Spinning Wheel as Artifact, Symbol, and Source of Design," in *Victorian Furniture: Essays from a Victorian Society Autumn Symposium*, ed. Kenneth L. Ames, special issue of *Nineteenth Century* 8 (1981): 159, 163, 166, 167, 168, and n. 62, 173; Flora Adams Darling, *Founding and Organization of the Daughters of the American Revolution and Daughters of the Revolution* (Philadelphia: Independence, 1901), 18–19; *Report of the Daughters of the American Revolution*, vol. 1 (Washington, D.C.: Government Printing Office, 1899), plates 3, 4, 5, opposite 40, 42, 46; *Second Report of the National Society of the Daughters of the American Revolution, October 11, 1897–October 11, 1898* (Washington, D.C.: Government Printing Office, 1900), 219–21; Eileen Boris, *Art and Labor: Ruskin, Morris, and the Craftsman Ideal in America* (Philadelphia: Temple Univ. Press, 1986), 116–18, 132–33; Eliza Calvert Hall, *A Book of Hand-Woven Coverlets* (Boston: Little, Brown, 1912); and Melody Graulich, "Piecing and Reconciling," in Eliza Calvert Hall, *Aunt Jane of Kentucky* (Albany, N.Y.: NCUP, 1992), xiii–xxiii.

19. Ann Douglas, *The Feminization of American Culture* (New York, 1978); Daniel Walker Howe, "The Social Science of Horace Bushnell," *Journal of American History* 70 (1983): 305–22 (quote on 322).

20. Nina Baym, *American Women Writers and the Work of History, 1790–1860* (New Brunswick, N.J.: Rutgers Univ. Press, 1995), 237.

21. William Allen, *An Address Delivered at Northampton, Mass., on the Evening of October 29, 1854* (Northampton, Mass.: Hopkins, Bridgman, 1855), 21, 22. At New Haven, James Kingsley defended his ancestors against suspicions of witch-hunting while confining all references to actual women to footnotes. James L. Kingsley, *Historical Discourse Delivered by Request before the Citizens of New Haven* (New Haven, Conn.: Noyes, 1838), 53, 100–2.

22. Oliver N. Bacon, *A History of Natick from its First Settlement in 1651 to the Present Time* (Boston: Damrell & Moore, 1856), 34–37. Stowe somewhat inconsistently urged his listeners both to abandon the theological absurdities of Catholic doctrine and to exer-

cise more charity toward other Christians. Although one of the commemorative hymns was composed by "Mrs. L. S. Goodwin, of Natick," she had nothing to say about Natick's women. She was more concerned with the apparent disappearance of the first inhabitants of Natick, Eliot's praying Indians: "'Tis no light thing—a nation built / Upon another's dust!"

23. The editor of Middletown's centennial history honored women only in metaphor. "Hereafter let it be remembered," he wrote, "that Middletown is a matron with the weight of Two Hundred Years upon her brow." David D. Field, *Centennial Address* (Middletown, Conn.: Casey, 1853), 12, 91, 50.

24. Joseph Willard, *An Address in Commemoration of the Two-Hundredth Anniversary of the Incorporation of Lancaster, Massachusetts* (Boston: Wilson, 1853), 111. Although Willard obviously borrowed from Rowlandson's narrative in his own discussion of King Philip's War, he mentioned her only in relation to her husband, the Lancaster pastor Joseph Rowlandson. "The heavy calamity that befell him, not only in the loss of his property, but in the death or captivity of his family and relations is sufficiently well known by those versed in your contemporaneous history, and the simple narrative penned by his excellent wife after her return from dreary bondage." Another speaker honored women of the past who were true "help-meets," quipping, "that God made *woman* in the beginning. *He* did not make *ladies;* they are made by *milliners.*"

25. *History of Bedford, New-Hampshire, Being Statistics, Compiled on the Occasion of the One Hundredth Annversary of the Incorporation of the Town* (Boston: Judge, 1851), 11–13, 14–15, 56. The poet noted that Bedford's housewives also knew how to make "Haggis" and "Brose," two Scots-Irish dishes.

26. *History of Bedford,* 75, 77–78. Divine approval was not enough for Mrs. E. Vale Smith of Newburyport, Massachusetts, one of the few female authors of an antebellum town history. Toward the end of her otherwise conventional narrative, she pondered the absence of women. One might expect men to dominate politics, but why were there so few women among the town's writers and poets? "We meet with evidence continually, of the existence of women whose natural talents evidently fitted them to take the first place in intellectual circles, but their minds were not so quickened by suitable instruction as to dare utterance. . . . And so, generation after generation of these 'mute, inglorious' Sapphos have passed away and left not a trace behind." Mrs. E. Vale Smith, *A History of Newburyport* (Newburyport, Mass.: n.p., 1854), 386.

27. Bushnell, "Age of Homespun," 72.

28. Lydia Huntley Sigourney, *Poems* (Philadelphia: Carey and Hart, 1849), 162. Sigourney's poem supports Mary Kelley's argument that the earliest women's historians in the United States were primarily interested in validating an intellectual role for themselves. See "Women Writing Women's History" (Wiggins Lecture, American Antiquarian Society, Worcester, Mass., 27 Oct. 1995).

29. Bushnell, "Age of Homespun," 48.

30. Charlotte Perkins Gilman, "Women and Economics," in *The Feminist Papers,* ed. Alice S. Rossi (New York: Bantam, 1973), 585. On the dilemmas of refinement for middle-class women, see Richard L. Bushman, *The Refinement of America: Persons, Houses, Cities* (New York: Knopf, 1992), 331, 440; and on Bushnell's social conservatism, Howe, "Social Science," 310, 321.

31. Cheney, *Life and Letters of Horace Bushnell,* 26.

32. Ibid., 28, 30.

33. Edwards, *Of Singular Genius,* 10, 55; "The Age of Homespun," manuscript, Litchfield Historical Society, Litchfield, Conn., 56.

34. Cheney, *Life and Letters of Horace Bushnell,* 93–94.

35. Edwards, *Of Singular Genius*, 260–67.

36. Ibid., 237, 255–60; Bushnell, "Age of Homespun," 41; John W. DeForest, *History of the Indians of Connecticut* (Hartford, Conn.: Hamersey, 1852; repr., Brighton, Mich.: Native American Book Publishers, n.d.), 43–44.

37. Donation Book, 3, 11 Sept. 1851, Connecticut Historical Society, Hartford; United States Census, 1850, Connecticut, microfilm 42, Connecticut State Library, Hartford; Litchfield County Superior Court Docket, 5 (Aug. 1848–Feb. 1855), 97; *Litchfield Enquirer*, 19 Sept. 1850; Ann McMullen and Russell G. Handsman, *A Key into the Language of Woodsplint Baskets* (Washington, Conn.: American Indian Archaeological Institute, 1987), 21.

38. Bushnell, "Age of Homespun," 44.

39. Daniel F. Secomb, *History of the Town of Amherst* (Concord, N.H.: Evans, Sleeper & Woodbury, 1883), 148.

40. Anne Farnam, "George Francis Dow: A Career of Bringing the 'picturesque traditions of sleeping generations' to Life in the Early Twentieth Century," *Essex Institute Historical Collections* 121 (1985): 80–88; Jane C. Nylander, *Our Own Snug Fireside: Images of the New England Home 1760–1860* (New York: Knopf, 1993), 18; Monkhouse, "Spinning Wheel," 155–72; "Boston Celebration of the Seventy-fourth Anniversary of American Independence," *Boston Daily Evening Transcript*, 5 July 1850 (hereafter cited as *BDET*).

41. Lemuel Gott, *History of the Town of Rockport* (Rockport, Mass.: Rockport Review, 1888), 97–100.

42. Nylander, *Our Own Snug Fireside*, 16, 17; *History of Amherst*, 166; Sylvester Judd, *The History of Hadley, Massachusetts* (Springfield, Mass.: Huntting, 1905), 437–38.

43. Rodris Roth, "The New England, or 'Olde Tyme,' Kitchen Exhibit at Nineteenth-Century Fairs," in *Colonial Revival*, ed. Axelrod, 159–83.

44. Edwin Emery, *History of Sanford, Maine* (Fall River, Mass., 1901), 381; W. R. Cochrane, *History of the Town of Antrim* (Manchester, N.H.: Mirror Steam, 1880), 114–19; Robert C. Mack, *Exercises on the 150th Anniversary of the Settlement of Old Nutfield* (Manchester, N.H.: Clarke, 1870), 3–5, 9–13, and passim; Charles Edward Banks, *History of York, Maine* (Boston, 1935) 2:429–32; *Proceedings at the Centennial Celebration of the Battle of Lexington* (Boston: Lockwood, Brooks, 1875), 120, 125, 128–30, and passim.

45. *Proceedings at the Celebration of the Two Hundred and Fiftieth Anniversary of the Incorporation of the Town of Dedham* (Cambridge, Mass.: University Press, 1887); Edward T. Fairbanks, *The Town of St Johnsbury Vt* (St. Johnsbury: Cowles, 1914), 398. Other towns took the new craze for floats to great heights. At Gloucester, Massachusetts, in 1892, a tableau of the age of homespun appeared alongside the Spirit of Cape Ann standing on a raised dais before a huge shell, her right hand on an anchor, her left upon an oar. In a "procession of fantastics" in Lee, Massachusetts, in 1878, a log cabin and "a collection of spinning wheels, worked by dames in the costumes of the past century" followed a "company of plantation darkies seated on a stupendous ox-cart, followed by a number of grotesque figures on horseback, among them the Father of his Country with his beloved Martha and the rotund Falstaff." "Descriptions of the School Tableaux," *Official Programme: 250th Anniversary Incorporation of the Town of Gloucester* (Gloucester, Mass.: Williams, 1892); Aaron B. Cole and J. L. M. Willis, *History of the Centennial of the Incorporation of the Town of Eliot, Maine* (Eliot: Caldwell, 1912), 109, 113; C. M. Hyde, *The Centennial Celebration, and Centennial History of the Town of Lee, Mass.* (Springfield, Mass.: Bryan, 1878), 40. Although the main focus is on a later period, there is a good introduction to late-nineteenth-century historical parades and pageants in Glassberg, *American Historical Pageantry*, 9–40.

46. *The Complete Poetrical Works of Longfellow* (Cambridge, Mass.: Riverside, 1893), 173, 177, 169, 171, 181, 182, 180.

47. James D. McCabe, *The Illustrated History of the Centennial Exhibition* (Philadelphia: National Publishing Company 1897; repr., 1975), 240; Monkhouse, "Spinning Wheel," 163; Nylander, *Our Own Snug Fireside*, 15 figure 12; *New York Times*, 10 May 1889, 5; *Boston Evening Transcript*, 9 May 1889, 8; *Woman's Journal* 20 (1889): 28, 76, 92, 100, 124, 133, 140; Harriet Spofford, *Three Heroines of Romance* (Cambridge, Mass.: University Press, 1894), 24, 28, and drawing on 14; Claudia L. Bushman, *America Discovers Columbus: How an Italian Explorer Became an American Hero* (Hanover, N.H., and London: Univ. Press of New England, 1992), 183.

48. Monkhouse, "Spinning Wheel," 168; Suzanne L. Flynt, Susan McGowan, and Amelia F. Miller, *Gathered and Preserved* (Deerfield, Mass.: Memorial Hall Pocumtuck Valley Memorial Association, 1991), 50; correspondence of Dr. Mary Forrester Hobart regarding presentation of the Martha Moore Ballard Diary, Maine State Library, Augusta; Jean Smith, "Linton Park, Pennsylvania Painter," *Antiques* 120 (1981): 1203–9; Karal Ann Marling, *George Washington Slept Here: Colonial Revivals and American Culture, 1876–1986* (Cambridge, Mass., and London: Harvard Univ. Press, 1988), 80–81; Photograph, 1965.29, and Towel Fragments, 1965.29.3 and 1965.29.4, New Hampshire Historical Society; Mack, *Exercises on the 150th Anniversary of the Settlement of Old Nutfield;* Boris, *Art and Labor*, 116–18, 132–33; Hall, *A Book of Hand-Woven Coverlets;* Graulich, "Piecing and Reconciling," xiii–xxiii; R. Fellow, "American History on the Stage," *Atlantic Monthly* 50 (1882): 309; Alice Morse Earle, *Home Life in Colonial Days* (New York: Grosset & Dunlap, 1898; repr., Stockbridge, Mass.: Berkshire Traveller, 1974), and other works; Susan Reynolds Williams, "In the Garden of New England: Alice Morse Earle and the History of Domestic Life," Ph.D. diss., University of Delaware, 1992; George Francis Dow, *Everyday Life in Colonial New England* (1935; repr., New York: Dover, 1988); Farnam, "George Francis Dow," 80–88; Charles Andrews, *Colonial Folkways: A Chronicle of American Life in the Reign of the Georges* (New Haven, Conn.: Yale Univ. Press, 1919). Despite the frontispiece, Andrews has little to say about women.

49. Erik Trump, "Primitive Woman—Domesticated Woman: The Image of the Primitive Woman at the 1893 World's Columbian Exposition," *Women's Studies* 27 (1998): 215–58, quotes on 220, 231–32.

50. Elizabeth C. Barney Buel, *The Tale of the Spinning-Wheel* (Litchfield, Conn., 1903), 3–4; Flynt, McGowan, and Miller, *Gathered and Preserved*, 53; Neltje Blanchan, "What the Basket Means to the Indian," in *How to Make Baskets*, ed. Mary White (New York: Doubleday Page, 1915), 181, 194, 182; Philip J. Deloria, *Playing Indian* (New Haven, Conn.: Yale Univ. Press, 1998), 113; Gary W. Hume, "Joseph Laurent's Intervale Camp: Post-Colonial Abenaki Adaptation and Revitalization in New Hampshire," in *Algonkians of New England: Past and Present*, ed. Peter Benes (Dublin Seminar for New England Folklife, Annual Proceedings, 1991), 101–13; Ann McMullen and Russell G. Handsman, " 'We Didn't Make Fancy Baskets until We Were Discovered': Fancy-Basket Making in Maine," in McMullen and Handsman, *A Key into the Language of Woodsplint Baskets*, 39–59.

51. Hume, "Joseph Laurent's Intervale Camp," 101–13.

52. Over the years, she, her mother, Clara, and her sister Helen contributed many objects to the Essex Institute, mixing conventional relics (a piece from the North Bridge at Concord, lava from Vesuvius, a shingle from a church where Washington once worshiped) with fabrics "woven at Judge Joseph Philbrick's Farm in Weare, N.H. before 1825." Eleven swatches of homespun accessioned in 1912 were still on exhibit in 1992. *Boston*

*Evening Transcript*, 27 Jan. 1905, 15 Mar. 1927; Essex Institute Accessions Book 1, 22 June 1889, and passim; according to Salem street directories, she lived at 26 Orne Street, Salem, from 1882 until her death. See, for example, *Naumkeag Directory* 27 (1920): 387, and 30 (1924): 422. A large collection of textiles went to the Society for the Preservation of New England Antiquities after her death. Other items, including the original of the embroidered panel and a scrapbook of clothing fabrics, are at the Beverly Historical Society.

53. Farnam, "George Francis Dow," 80–88; Essex Institute Accession Book, #2523, 22 June 1889; Eliza Philbrick, "Spinning in the Olden Time," *Essex Antiquarian* 1 (1897): 87–92; Francis H. Underwood, *Quabbin: The Story of a Small Town with Outlooks on Puritan Life* (1893; repr. Boston: Northeastern Univ. Press, 1986;), 20–24, quote on 24.

54. Ruth B. Phillips, *Trading Identities: The Souvenir in Native North American Art from the Northeast, 1700–1900* (Montreal and Kingston: McGill–Queen's Univ. Press, and Seattle and London: Univ. of Washington Press, 1998), 25, 33, 52–54, 101, and passim; McMullen and Handsman, *A Key into the Language of Woodsplint Baskets*, 161–63; Sarah Peabody Turnbaugh and William A. Turnbaugh, *Indian Baskets* (West Chester, Pa.: Schiffer, 1986), 86.

55. Buel, *Tale of the Spinning Wheel*, 30.

56. Ibid., 2; "Mrs. John L. Buel, Prominent Litchfield Citizen, Dies," *Litchfield Enquirer*, 4 Nov. 1943, 1, 6; Margaret Gibbs, *The DAR* (New York: Holt, Rinehart and Winston, 1969), 84–87, 91–93, 97–99, 102–3; Elizabeth C. Barney Buel, *Manual of the United States for the Information of Immigrants and Foreigners*, 4th ed. (Washington, D.C.: National Society Daughters of the American Revolution, 1926), 15. She also wrote *Socialist Propaganda in the United States* (Connecticut DAR, 1925).

57. Buel, *Manual for Immigrants and Foreigners*, 15; Gibbs, *DAR*, 102–3.

58. Judith Reiter Weissman and Wendy Lavitt, *Labors of Love: America's Textiles and Needlework, 1650–1930* (New York: Wings, 1987), 195; *Sybil Carter Indian Lace Association*, promotional pamphlet, Litchfield Historical Society. Aida Smith to "dear Miss Quincy," 9 Sept. 1920, and Conversation with Miss Gertrude Whiting, president of the Needle and Bobbin Club, 15 Mar. 1919, in Papers of Mary Perkins Quincy, Litchfield Historical Society.

59. Butler, "Another City," 36, 43, 49; Dorothy Bull, "Litchfield: An Historic Masque," printed program, Litchfield Historical Society, 4 August 1920.

60. David Herlihy, *Opera Muliebria: Women and Work in Medieval Europe* (Philadelphia: Temple Univ. Press, 1990), 33, 75–97, 176–80; Alice B. Clark, *Working Life of Women in the Seventeenth Century* (1919, repr. London: Routledge & Kegan Paul, 1982), 102–3; Joan Pong Linton, "Jack of Newbury and Drake in California: Narratives of English Cloth and Manhood," *ELH* 59 (1992): 31.

61. *Providence Gazette*, 12 Mar. 1766; *Boston Evening Post*, 21 Mar. 1768; *Essex Gazette*, 23–30 May 1769, reprinting material from the Boston papers for 30 Mar.

62. Bushnell, "Age of Homespun," 48.

63. Flynt, McGowan, and Miller, *Gathered and Preserved*, 9–18; *Catalogue of the Collection of Relics in Memorial Hall*, 3d ed. (Deerfield, Pocumtuck Valley Memorial Association, 1920) 29, 72–75, 78, 82.

64. Russell R. Menard and John J. McCusker, *The Economy of British America, 1607–1789* (Chapel Hill: Univ. of North Carolina Press, 1985), 96–97, 279–86, 296; James F. Shepherd and Gary M. Walton, *Shipping, Maritime Trade, and the Economic Development of Colonial North America* (Cambridge, U.K.: Cambridge Univ. Press, 1972), 106.

## Chapter 1: An Indian Basket

1. Basket with associated manuscript dated Field's Point, 1842, Rhode Island Historical Society, Providence, 1842.2.1; Dennis V. Piechota, Conservation Report, 30 Sept. 1977, Curatorial Files, Rhode Island Historical Society. The story of the basket's origins has been published repeatedly and uncritically. See H. M. Chapin, "Indian Implements Found in Rhode Island," *Rhode Island Historical Society Collections* 18 (1925): 23–25; Charles Willoughby, *Antiquities of the New England Indians* (Cambridge, Mass.: Peabody Museum, 1935), 251, 252, figure 135; Jonathan L. Fairbanks and Robert F. Trent, eds., *New England Begins: The Seventeenth Century* (Boston: Museum of Fine Arts, 1982), 1:77, figure 68; Sarah Peabody Turnbaugh and William A. Turnbaugh, *Indian Baskets* (West Chester, Pa.: Shiffer, 1986), 121.

2. Russell Bourne, *The Red King's Rebellion: Racial Politics in New England 1675–1678* (New York: Oxford Univ. Press, 1990), 38–39, finds in Field's story evidence that "fundamentally important dramas of reconciliation went on among the peoples" even as the war "was staggering toward a hateful, mutually ruinous halt."

3. Ibid., 39. A description of an early exhibit is in *Rhode Island Historical Society Museum Illustrating the History of the State* (Providence, 1916), 5–6.

4. Willoughby, *Antiquities,* 254; Piechota, Conservation Report; Cameron McDonald, a University of Connecticut archaeology student, personal communication, 30 July 1997.

5. William S. Simmons, *Spirit of the New England Tribes: Indian History and Folklore, 1620–1984* (Hanover, N.H., and London: Univ. Press of New England, 1986), 255–56.

6. Despite their seeming differences, both baskets and blankets are textiles. Both have warps and wefts, vertical and horizontal elements that intersect to form a continuous surface. I. Emery, *The Primary Structures of Fabrics: An Illustrated Classification* (Washington, D.C.: Textile Museum, 1966), 210; Turnbaugh and Turnbaugh, *Indian Baskets,* 70; James B. Petersen, "The Study of Native Fiber Industries from Eastern North America: Resume and Prospect," in *A Most Indispensable Art: Native Fiber Industries from Eastern North America,* ed. James B. Petersen (Knoxville: Univ. of Tenesee Press, 1996), 8–9. Emery divides fabrics into two primary groups, those that are felted (pressed or matted into coherence) and those that are produced by the interworking of previously prepared elements. Among the latter, one large group is composed of "two-or-more-sets-of-element structures" in which "a transverse set (the weft)" is interworked with "a longtitudinal set (the warp)" (17, 27). Blankets and many baskets fit the latter category.

7. E. Lipson, *The History of the Woollen and Worsted Industries* (London: Cass, 1965), 102–3; Francis Jennings, *The Invasion of America: Indians, Colonialism, and the Cant of Conquest* (Chapel Hill: Univ. of North Carolina Press, 1975), 98; Leon E. Cranmar, *Cushnoc: The History and Archaeology of Plymouth Colony Traders on the Kennebec* (Augusta, Maine: Maine Historic Preservation Commission, 1990), 97–98; Christina B. Johannsen, "European Trade Goods and Wampanoag Culture in the Seventeenth Century," in *Burr's Hill: A Seventeenth-Century Wampanoag Burial Ground in Warren, Rhode Island,* ed. Susan Gibson, (Providence: Haffenreffer Museum of Anthropology, Brown University, 1980), 30; D. C. Coleman, "Textile Growth," in *Textile History and Economic History,* ed. N. B. Harte and K. G. Ponting (Manchester, U.K.: Manchester Univ. Press, 1973), 1–12.

8. Roger Williams, "A Key into the Language of America" (1643), repr. *Rhode Island Historical Society Collections* 1 (1827): 91, 93; Daniel Gookin, "Historical Collections of the

Indians in New England," in *Collections of the Massachusetts Historical Society for the Year 1792* (Boston, 1806), 151.

9. Gookin, "Indians in New England," 151; William Wood, *New England's Prospect*, ed. Alden T. Vaughan (Amherst: Univ. of Massachusetts Press, 1977), 11 and n. 75; Thomas Morton, *New English Canaan* (New York and Amsterdam: Da Capo, 1969; facsimile of Amsterdam, 1637), 42.

10. Gookin, "Indians in North America," 150; Williams, "Key," 33.

11. Morton, *New English Canaan*, 25, 28–29; Wood, *New England's Prospect*, 108; *John Josselyn, Colonial Traveler: A Critical Edition of* Two Voyages to New-England, ed. Paul J. Lindholdt (Hanover, N.H., and London: Univ. Press of New England, 1988), 101–2, 93; Gookin, "Indians in New England," 152; Williams, "Key," 107. Williams said that their old men made the turkey feather mantles, which were "as velvet with us."

12. Fairbanks and Trent, eds., *New England Begins*, 1:78–79; "Morell's Poem on New-England," *Collections of the Massachusetts Historical Society* 1 (1806): 132; Williams, "Key," 47; Wood, *New England's Prospect*, 112–13; *John Josselyn*, 91. Nathaniel Morton, *New Englands Memoriall* (Cambridge, Mass., 1669; repr., New York: Scholars Facsimiles and Reprints, 1937), says that on their first landing on Cape Cod in November 1620 the pilgrims "found two of their Houses covered with Mats, and sundry of their Implements in them" (16). Gookin, "Indians in New England," distinguishes between the "best" houses, which were covered with bark, and the "meaner" houses covered with mats, but other writers do not make that distinction (151). Williams, "Key," says that they used "burching bark" and "chesnut barke which they dresse finely, and make a Summer-covering for their houses" (48).

13. Katherine Billings, "Beads of Shell and Glass," in *Burr's Hill*, ed. Gibson, 118–19; examination of wampum strips from the Mashantucket Pequot site with Professor Margaret Ordonez, Textile Laboratory, University of Rhode Island, 13 June 1991; Benjamin Church, *Diary of King Philip's War 1675–76*, ed. Alan Simpson and Mary Simpson (Chester, Conn.: Pequot, 1975), 170; *John Josselyn*, 101, 14.

14. Williams, "Key," 47; *John Josselyn*, 102.

15. "Morell's Poem," 135; Eric Kerridge, *Textile Manufactures in Early Modern England* (Manchester, U.K.: Manchester Univ. Press, 1985), 24; Margaret Swain, *Embroidered Stuart Pictures* (Haverfordwest, U.K.: Shire, 1990), passim.

16. "Morell's Poem," 135–36.

17. Williams, "Key," 92; cf. William Cronon, *Changes in the Land: Indians, Colonists, and the Ecology of New England* (New York: Hill and Wang, 1983), 92–93.

18. Turnbaugh and Turnbaugh, *Indian Baskets*, figures 4, 76, and Joanne Segal Brandford to Sarah Peabody Turnbaugh, 1974, copy provided by Turnbaugh.

19. R. L. Andrews and J. M. Adovasio, "The Origins of Fiber Perishables Production East of the Rockies," and Michael J. Heckenberger et al., "Fiber Industries from the Boucher Site: An Early Woodland Cemetery in Northwestern Vermont," in *A Most Indispensable Art*, ed. Petersen, 45, 57–67, and figures 3.2, 3.7, and 3.10; Tonya Barody Largy and Alan Leveille, "Earliest Evidence for Textiles from Millbury III," *Northeast Anthropology* 50 (1995): 31–33; Kathryn A. Jakes and Lucy R. Sibley, "A Comparative Collection for the Study of Fibres Used in Prehistoric Textiles from Eastern North America," *Journal of Archaeological Science* 21 (1994): 641–50; A. C. Whitford, "Textile Fibers Used in Eastern Aboriginal North America," *Anthropological Papers of the American Museum of Natural History* 38 (1941): 5–22. Willoughby, *Antiquities*, 243–48; Robert S. Grumet, *Historic Contact: Indian People and Colonists in Today's Northeastern United*

*States in the Sixteenth through Eighteenth Centuries* (Norman and London: Univ. of Oklahoma Press, 1995).

20. William C. Gilman, Esquire, Norwich, manuscript donor record; William C. Gilman and Eliza Gilman, family history, typescript, manuscripts, Connecticut Historical Society, Hartford, Conn.; Melissa Jayne Fawcett, *The Lasting of the Mohegans*, part 1 (Uncasville, Conn.: Mohegan Tribe, 1995), 21; Edward W. Hooker, ed., *Memoir of Mrs. Sarah Lanman Smith* (Boston: Perkins & Marvin, 1840), 106–26; Willoughby, *Antiquities*, 254; Fairbanks and Trent, *New England Begins*, 1:78; Ann McMullen and Russell G. Handsman, *A Key into the Language of Woodsplint Baskets* (Washington, Conn.: American Indian Archaeological Institute, 1987), 8, 86; Turnbaugh and Turnbaugh, *Indian Baskets*, 121. Some secondary sources substitute "two hundred years" for "three hundred years" in Cynthia's account, but the handwritten accession record is quite clear. Gilman was a missionary who helped reestablish a Mohegan church at Montville, Connecticut.

21. Alexandra van Dongen, ed., *"One Man's Trash Is Another Man's Treasure": The Metamorphosis of the European Utensil in the New World* (Rotterdam: Museum Boymans-Van Beuningen, 1996), 194; author's conversation with George Hamel, New York State Museum, 30 July 1997.

22. Ellen Rasmussen, "Rare Narraganset Basket Highlights Heritage Plantation Collection," *Northeast Basketmakers Guild Newsletter* (fall 1992): 1–2; and curatorial information supplied by Sunnee Spencer, Director of Education, Heritage Plantation of Sandwich, Sandwich, Massachusetts.

23. William Scranton Simmons, *Cautantowwit's House: An Indian Burial Ground on the Island of Conanicut in Narragansett Bay* (Providence: Brown Univ. Press, 1970), 87, 81, 97, 101, 44; Paul Robinson and Gail Gustafson, "Partially Disturbed Seventeenth-Century Indian Burial Ground in Rhode Island: Recovery, Preliminary Analysis, and Protection," *Bulletin of the Archaeological Society of Connecticut* 45 (1982): 41–50; Paul A. Robinson, Marc A. Kelley, and Patricia E. Rubertone, "Preliminary Biocultural Interpretations from a Seventeenth-Century Narraganset Indian Cemetery in Rhode Island," in *Cultures in Contact*, ed. William W. Fitzhugh (Washington, D.C., and London: Smithsonian Institution Press, 1985), 107–30; Kerridge, *Textile Manufactures*, 24; Phyllis Dillon, "Trade Fabrics," in *Burr's Hill*, ed. Gibson, 104 and figures 99, 105; Gibson, ed., *Burr's Hill*, catalog entries for accession numbers MAI 8/5237b, MAI 8/5234a, MAI 8/5209; MAI 8/5215, 142, 158, 160.

24. Susan Gibson, "Introduction," Beth Bower, "Aboriginal Textiles," and Dillon, "Trade Fabrics," 9–24, 89–91, 100–107, 155; figures 77, 79, 93, 145, 146, and catalog entries for MAI 8/5256a, HMA 77-230, MAI 8/5238, MAI 8/5233, MAI, 8/5253, MAI 8/5206d, HMA 77-241, HMA 77-247, GHFL 5, in *Burr's Hill*, ed. Gibson, 90, 91, 101, 141, 143, 151, 153, 154. The Burr's Hill site was discovered in 1851, when crews working for the Providence, Warren, and Bristol Railroad found human skeletons buried with hoes, knives, clay pipes, and an impressive nineteen-inch pestle. In 1913, Charles Read Carr of the George Hail Free Library in Warren undertook the first and to this date only systematic excavations, reburying the skeletons but gathering artifacts that were scattered among three repositories. The burial goods are now in the process of being returned to the Narraganset and Wampanoag peoples whose ancestors lived in the area.

25. Kerridge, *Textile Manufactures*, 1, 77, 124; Lipson, *Woollen and Worsted Industries*, 130.

26. In early usage, *cloth* designated fabrics made entirely of wool. Worsteds were called "stuffs" or "tammies." By law, cloth weighed from nineteen to twenty-three ounces per square yard. (In comparison, the heaviest such fabrics made today, used for men's over-

coats, weigh sixteen or seventeen ounces.) The Protestant Reformation gave English worsted manufacturing a boost when Huguenot refugees brought new weaving and finishing techniques and a new vocabulary to towns like Norwich in East Anglia. The English word *tammy* derives from the French *estame,* for worsted. J. de L. Mann, *The Cloth Industry in the West of England from 1640 to 1880* (Oxford: Clarendon, 1971), xv; Florence M. Montgomery, *Textiles in America 1650–1870* (New York: Norton, 1984), 242, 160; D. C. Coleman, "An Innovation and Its Diffusion: The 'New Draperies,'" and U. Priestley, "'The Fabric of Stuffs': The Norwich Textile Industry, c. 1650–1750," in *The Textile Industries,* ed. S. D. Chapman (London and New York: Tauris, 1997), 2:613–56; Kerridge, *Textile Manufactures,* 8, 11, 18, 19, 20, 29, 110, 138, index 427–28; J. Thirsk, "The Fantastical Folly of Fashion: The English Stocking Knitting Industry, 1500–1700," in *Textile Industries,* ed. Chapman, 3:115.

27. "England's Great Joy and Gratitude," in Lipson, *Woollen and Worsted Industries,* frontispiece. In some rural counties, farmer weavers produced a little linen or woolen cloth in what contemporaries called the "bumpkin trade," but serious manufacturing was increasingly organized by merchant clothiers who integrated elements in production that took place in different towns and sometimes in different regions. As Daniel Defoe expressed it, an English "Linzey-Woolsey" might be "made at Kidderminster, dy'd in the country, and painted, or water'd at London." Montgomery, *Textiles in America 1650–1870,* 279.

28. Robert Plot, *The Natural History of Oxford-shire,* 2d ed. (Oxford, 1705), 283–85; Kerridge, *Textile Manufactures,* 184–85, 214–15.

29. Adam Smith, *The Wealth of Nations* (1776; repr., London: Penguin, 1986), 104–5, 112–17. On the relation of Smith's ideas to the economic thought of New England Puritans, see Stephen Innes, *Creating the Commonwealth: The Economic Culture of Puritan New England* (New York and London: Norton, 1995), 39–63.

30. Acts 16:9; Matt B. Jones, "The Early Massachusetts-Bay Colony Seals," American Antiquarian Society *Proceedings,* 44 (1934): 13–44; John D. Cushing, "A Note Concerning the Massachusetts-Bay Colony Seal," American Antiquarian Society *Proceedings* 76 (1976) part 1, 171–77; William S. Simmons, "The Earliest Prints and Paintings of New England Indians," *Rhode Island History* 41 (1982): 75–76; Karen Ordahl Kupperman, "Presentment of Civility: English Reading of American Self-Presentation in the Early Years of Colonization," *William and Mary Quarterly,* 3d ser., 54 (1997): 199–204; Jill Lepore, *The Name of War: King Philip's War and the Origins of American Identity* (New York: Knopf, 1998), xvi–xvii, 79–83; Neal Salisbury, "Introduction: Mary Rowlandson and Her Removes," in Mary Rowlandson, *The Sovereignty and Goodness of God, Together with the Faithfulness of His Promises Displayed* (Boston: Bedford, 1997), 20; Morton, *New English Canaan,* 29, 30; Williams, "Key," 106, 107.

31. Morton, *New English Canaan,* 30; Wood, *New England's Prospect,* 115; Williams, "Key," 106.

32. Gookin, "Indians in New England," 152; Genesis 3:7, 21.

33. Morton, *New English Canaan,* 78; *Plymouth Colony Records,* C. H. Simmons, Jr. (Camden, Maine: Picton Press, 1996), 1:27, 59, 61, 69, 78. In this computation, I assumed that an average broadcloth would weigh twenty ounces per yard. The best English hats, called "beavers" or "casters," sold for from thirteen to twenty shillings in late-seventeenth-century Massachusetts. In the same accounts, blankets cost from three to ten shillings. Elspeth M. Veale, *The English Fur Trade in the Later Middle Ages* (Oxford: Clarendon, 1966), 175–76, 147; Kerridge, *Textile Manufactures,* 134, 138, 65; Montgomery, *Textiles in America,* 160; Emery, *Primary Structures of Fabrics,* 22; George Francis Dow, *Everyday Life in the Massachusetts Bay Colony* (1935; repr., New York: Dover, 1988), 5–6,

60–61; *John Josselyn*, 14; Thomas Willett Inventory, 25 Nov. 1674, typescript, Plimoth Plantation, Massachusetts.

34. Although Witney is the best documented center of duffel manufacturing, the fabric was also made in Norwich, East Dereham, Romsey, Downton, Devizes, Totnes, Holford, and elsewhere. Gookin, "Indians in New England," 152; Plot, *Natural History of Oxford-shire*, 284; Kerridge, *Textile Manufactures*, 33.

35. Plot, *Natural History of Oxford-shire*, 284; Gookin, "Indians in New England," 152; *John Josselyn*, 93; Wood, *New England's Prospect*, 84; "The Present State of New-England with Respect to the Indian War," in *Narratives of the Indian Wars, 1675–1699*, ed. Charles H. Lincoln (1913; repr. New York: Barnes & Noble, 1959), 34.

36. Wood, *New England's Prospect*, 84; Williams, "Key," 108, 137. Also see Linda Welters, "From Moccasins to Frock Coats and Back Again: Ethnic Identity and Native American Dress in Southern New England," in *Dress in American Culture*, ed. Patricia A. Cunningham and Susan Voso Lab (Bowling Green, Ohio: Bowling Green State University Press, 1993), 6–41.

37. Alden T. Vaughn and Edward W. Clark, ed., *Puritans among the Indians: Accounts of Captivity and Redemption, 1676–1724* (Cambridge, Mass.: Belknap Press, 1981), 47 n. 24; Cronon, *Changes in the Land*, 93.

38. Lynn Ceci, "Native Wampum as a Peripheral Resource in the Seventeenth-Century World-System," in *The Pequots of Southern New England*, ed. Laurence M. Hauptman and James D. Wherry (Norman and London: Univ. of Oklahoma Press, 1990), 48–63; Billings, "Beads of Shell and Glass," 118–19; Peter A. Thomas, "Cultural Change on the Southern New England Frontier, 1630–1665," in Fitzhugh, ed., *Cultures in Contact*, 146–48; Cronon, *Changes in the Land*, 102; "Inventory of the Estate of Edward Wharton," in George Francis Dow, *Everyday Life in Colonial New England* (1935; repr. New York: Dover, 1988), 262–67; John Pynchon to John Winthrop, Jr., in *The Pynchon Papers*, vol. 1 (Boston: Colonial Society of Massachustts, 1982), 102. On possible implications of these changes for male-female relations, see Kathleen Bragdon, "Gender as a Social Category in Native Southern New England," *Ethnohistory* 43 (1996): 573–92, and Ann Marie Plane, "Putting a Face on Colonization: Factionalism and Gender Politics in the Life History of Awashunkes, the 'Squaw Sachem' of Saconet," in *Northeastern Indian Lives, 1632–1816*, ed. Robert S. Grumet (Amherst: Univ. of Massachusetts Press, 1996), 140–65.

39. *The Correspondence of Roger Williams*, ed. Glenn W. LaFantasie (Hanover, N.H., and London: Univ. Press of New England, 1988), 1:196; Paul A. Robinson, "Lost Opportunities: Miantonomi and the English in Seventeenth-Century Narraganset Country," in *Northeastern Indian Lives*, ed. Grumet, 13–28.

40. Wood, *New England's Prospect*, 115–16; cf. my discussion of bartering and trade among colonial Englishwomen in *Good Wives: Image and Reality in Northern New England, 1650–1750* (New York: Knopf, 1982), 45–48.

41. David D. Hall, *Witch-Hunting in Seventeenth-Century New England: A Documentary History, 1638–1692* (Boston: Northeastern Univ. Press, 1991), 35, 233; original Pynchon Notebook, Rare Books and Manuscripts, New York Public Library, printed in Samuel G. Drake, *Annals of Witchcraft in New England* (Boston: W. E. Woodward, 1869; repr., New York, 1972), 219–58.

42. Cronon, *Changes in the Land*, 86–88.

43. N. Morton, *New Englands Memoriall*, 101; Bourne, *Red King's Rebellion*, 68–71; Kevin A. McBride, "The Historical Archaeology of the Mashantucket Pequots, 1637–1900: A Preliminary Analysis," in *The Pequots in Southern New England*, ed. Hauptman and Wherry, 96–105; Grumet, ed., *Northeastern Indian Lives*, 139–42.

44. Bourne, *Red King's Rebellion*, 76.

45. John W. DeForest, *History of the Indians of Connecticut* (Hartford, Conn.: Hamersley, 1852; repr., Brighton, Mich.: Native American Book Publishers, n.d.), 164–77; Samuel G. Drake, *The Book of the Indians; or, Biography and History of the Indians of North America* (Boston: Antiquarian Bookstore, 1841), 2:27–28, 3:3–4.

46. DeForest, *Indians of Connecticut*, 273; Kevin A. McBride, "The Legacy of Robin Cassacinamon: Mashantucket Pequot Leadership in the Historic Period," in *Northeastern Indian Lives*, ed. Grumet, 74–92.

47. "A Relacion of the Indyan Warre, By Mr. Easton, of Roade Isld., 1675," in *Narratives of the Indian Wars*, ed. Lincoln, 7–8.

48. Douglas Edward Leach, *Flintlock and Tomahawk: New England in King Philip's War* (New York: Norton, 1966), 113; "Present State of New-England," 34.

49. Weetamoo's first husband, Wamsutta, known to the English as Alexander, had died mysteriously in 1662 after being summoned to Plymouth to answer charges of conspiring against the colony. Early in the war, she fled to Rhode Island where she married Quinnapin, a Narraganset leader whom Rowlandson referred to as her "master." Rowlandson, *Sovereignty and Goodness of God*, 61, 66, 79, 83, 84, 87, 97; Salisbury, "Introduction," in Rowlandson, *Sovereignty and Goodness of God*, 25–26.

50. Montgomery, *Textiles in America*, 258, 272, 273; Dillon, "Trade Fabrics," 101.

51. Rowlandson, *Sovereignty and Goodness of God*, 50, 57, 61, 41, 48, 43, 56, 59.

52. Harris to Sir Joseph Williamson, "Harris Papers," 163; Leach, *Flintlock and Tomahawk*, 243–44; Salisbury, "Introduction," in Rowlandson, *Sovereignty and Goodness of God*, 1. Also see the introduction to Richard Slotkin and James K. Folsom, eds., *So Dreadfull a Judgement: Puritan Responses to King Philip's War, 1676–1677* (Middletown, Conn.: Wesleyan Univ. Press, 1978).

53. Lincoln, *Narratives of the Indian Wars*, 90–91; *A Rhode Islander Reports on King Philip's War: The Second William Harris Letter of August, 1676*, ed. Douglas Edward Leach (Providence: Rhode Island Historical Society, 1963); Drake, *Book of the Indians*, 3:49.

54. Church, *Diary of King Philip's War*, 162–67.

55. Ibid., 167–68.

56. Ibid., 170.

57. Howard M. Chapin, "The so-called 'Fenner Garrison House,'" *Rhode Island Historical Society Collections* 31 (1938): 46–48; Samuel Greene Arnold, *History of the State of Rhode Island and Providence Plantations*, vol. 1 (New York: Appleton, 1859), 414.

58. Church, *Diary of King Philip's War*, 181–83.

59. Felicia Hemans, "Edith, a Tale of the Woods," "The American Forest-Girl," and "The Last Wish," in *Records of Woman, 1828* (Oxford and New York: Woodstock, 1991), 69–82, 131–35, 314–17; [Mrs. Lydia Huntley Sigourney], *Sketch of Connecticut Forty Years Since* (Hartford, Conn.: Cooke, 1824), 58–59, and Lydia Huntley Sigourney, "Pocahontas," in *Poems* (Philadelphia: Carey and Hart, 1849), 207.

60. Carl Bridenbaugh, *Fat Mutton and Liberty of Conscience: Society in Rhode Island, 1636–1690* (Providence: Brown Univ. Press, 1974), 4–11; *Correspondence of Roger Williams*, map, 1:80; Clarence Brigham, ed., *The Early Records of the Town of Portsmouth* (Providence, 1901), 56; Howard M. Chapin, *Documentary History of Rhode Island* (Providence: Preston and Rounds, 1916), 60, 61, 66; John Russell Bartlett, *Records of Rhode Island and Providence Plantations, in New England*, vol. 1 (Providence: Green, 1856), 18, 127; Arnold, *History of the State of Rhode Island and Providence Plantations*, vol. 1, 37, 40, 51, 70, 264; and C. S. Brigham, "Map of Providence Plantations," insert, *Rhode Island Historical Society Collections* 10 (1902): 376–77. John Josselyn called Rhode

Island "a Harbour for . . . Saints Errant." *John Josselyn*, 110; Sydney James, *Colonial Rhode Island: A History* (New York: Charles Scribner's Sons, 1975), 37–38.

61. William Harris Papers, *Rhode Island Historical Society Collections* 10 (1902): 25, 78, 82; Irving B. Richman, "The Land Controversies of William Harris," *Rhode Island Historical Society Collections* 10 (1902): 11–22. Gloria Main, "Naming Children in Early New England," *Journal of Interdisciplinary History* 27, no. 1 (summer 1996): 17, has found so-called hortatory names, such as Hope, Mindwell, and Experience, "particularly popular among Mayflower and Rhode Island families." Joshua 18:3. The phrase "How long" appears more than sixty times in the Bible. There is no way of knowing which verse or concept prompted the name. Alternative explanations might include Psalms 13:2 ("How long shall mine enemy be exalted over me?"), 1 Kings 18:21 ("How long halt ye between two opinions?"), or, an even more intriguing possibility, Jeremiah 31:22 ("How long wilt thou go about, O thou backsliding daughter? for the Lord hath created a new thing in the earth, A woman shall compass a man").

62. Richman, "Land Controversies," 11–12, 16–21.

63. Ibid., 16–21.

64. Roger Williams, *George Fox Digg'd out of His Burrowes*, in *The Complete Writings of Roger Williams*, ed. J. Lewis Diman, vol. 5 (New York: Russell & Russell, 1963), 315, xlv–xlvi.

65. William Harris Will, *Early Records of the Town of Providence*, vol. 6 (Providence, R.I.: City Printers, 1894), 48–58.

66. Emery Battis, *Saints and Sectaries: Anne Hutchinson and the Antinomian Controversy in the Massachusetts Bay Colony* (Chapel Hill: Univ. of North Carolina Press, 1962), 318, puts Borden among the "peripheral supporters" of Anne Hutchinson. On his trajectory in Portsmouth, see Howard M. Chapin, *Documentary History of Rhode Island* (Providence: Preston and Rounds, 1916), 2:37, 38, 49, 96, 103–4, 117, 120, 132, 134, 137, 148, 153, 155, 156; Bartlett, *Records of Rhode Island*, 1:76, 80, 91, 111, 265, 273, 277, 281, 282, 299, 300, 345, 353, 354; and Brigham, ed., *Portsmouth*, e.g., 16, 29, 33, 169, 172.

67. John Osborne Austin, *Genealogical Dictionary of Rhode Island* (Albany, N.Y., 1887), 23–24; *Early Records of the Town of Providence*, vol. 15 (Providence, R.I., 1899) 135–36.

68. Austin, *Genealogical Dictionary of Rhode Island*, 23–24.

69. Dinah's birth is described in Genesis 30:21 and her defilement and the brothers' revenge are told in chap. 34.

70. *A Rhode Islander Reports*, 28. Harris may have believed, as Roger Williams did, that the Indians were in some sense Israelites, perhaps even a remnant of the lost Ten Tribes. Williams to Thomas Thorowgood, 20 Dec., 1635, *Correspondence of Roger Williams* 1:30.

71. Austin, *Genealogical Dictionary of Rhode Island*, 23; Hattie Borden Weld, *Historical and Genealogical Record of the Descendants as far as Known of Richard and Joan Borden* (Albany, N.Y.: Joel Munsell's Sons, 1899), 62–66; Exodus 17:7; Psalms 81:7. On the epidemic, see Austin, *Genealogical Dictionary of Rhode Island*, 424.

72. Harris to Sir Joseph Williamson, 12 Aug. 1676, *Rhode Island Historical Society Collections* 10 (1902): 162.

73. Ibid., 164; "John Easton's Relacion," 10, 11.

74. Harris to Williamson, 164; "John Easton's Relacion," 16, 17, 10.

75. *A Rhode Islander Reports*, 18; James, *Colonial Rhode Island*, 98–99.

76. At Swansea, a straggling settlement of a few dozen families dispersed around the tidal estuary at the head of Mount Hope Bay, an old man and a boy on guard duty looked into the field beyond their barn and saw men slitting the throats of cattle. The boy shot and killed one of the band, who in retaliation killed nine people returning from Fast Day

services. Leach, *Flintlock and Tomahawk*, 35–44; Bourne, *Red King's Rebellion*, 109–10.

77. Virginia Anderson, "King Philip's Herds: Indians, Colonists, and the Problem of Livestock in Early New England," *William and Mary Quarterly*, 3d ser., 51 (1994): 601–25; "John Easton's Relacion" in *Narratives of the Indian Wars*, ed. Lincoln, 11; *Correspondence of Roger Williams*, 2:711.

78. *A Rhode Islander Reports*, 44, 46.

79. Harris to Williamson, 162; *A Rhode Islander Reports*, 84–86.

80. Bridenbaugh, *Fat Mutton and Liberty of Conscience*, 42–48.

81. Salisbury, in Rowlandson, *Sovereignty and Goodness of God*, 110.

82. *Correspondence of Roger Williams*, 2:728.

83. *Early Records of the Town of Providence*, vol. 8 (Providence, R.I., 1895), 13–14.

84. Bartlett, *Records of Rhode Island*, 533, 534, 536, 537–38, 545–46; William Staples, *Annals of the Town of Providence* (Providence: Knowles and Vose, 1843), 169.

85. *Early Records of the Town of Providence*, 8:12; Austin, *Genealogical Dictionary of Rhode Island*, 23; Bartlett, *Records of Rhode Island*, 544.

86. *Early Records of the Town of Providence*, 15:183.

87. Harris Papers, 38–42, 324, 328, 329, 331.

88. Bartlett, *Records of Rhode Island*, 2:553; Brigham, *Portsmouth*, 188.

89. Brigham, *Portsmouth*, 430, 431, 433, 434.

90. Lepore, *Name of War*, 154–55, 170.

91. Staples, *Annals of the Town of Providence*, 169–70; Arnold, *History of the State of Rhode Island*, 1:425; *Early Records of the Town of Providence*, 15:157–58.

92. Richard Wharton to Susanna Harris, 29 May 1681, William Harris Papers, 41–42, 340; *Early Records of Providence*, 15:231–33; 6:75–85; 17:107–12; *Rhode Island Historical Society Collections* 10 (1902): 340, 343–44. Elaine Forman Crane, *Ebb Tide in New England: Women, Seaports, and Social Change, 1630–1800* (Boston: Northeastern Univ. Press, 1998), 197; Rhode Island Historical Society, Providence, manuscripts, I:34, 57; IX:10.

93. Howlong Harris to Mary and Ephraim Pray, manuscript, Rhode Island Historical Society, Providence, box 10:106. In January 1676, Roger Williams had reported that men out seeking cattle had seen "an Indian howse halfe a mile from where Capt. Fenners howse (now burned) did stand." William Harris gave his daughter Mary Borden a farm in the same general area—"on the Northern and Northeasterne part of the Hill Called Neotakeonconit Hill." On the Providence rate list for 1670, which may be organized geographically, Thomas Borden is listed next but one to Captain Arthur Fenner. On the 1679 rate list, the widow Mary Borden is listed next to Thomas Fenner. On the 1680 list, she is on the same page as Fenner but not so close. *The Early Records of the Town of Providence*, 15:135, 186, 225. *Correspondence of Roger Williams*, 2:705, 711, 713–14; Leach, *Flintlock and Tomahawk*, 123–35.

94. Brigham, *Portsmouth*, 205; *The Early Records of the Town of Providence*, vol. 17 (Providence, 1903), 18–19.

95. *The Early Records of the Town of Providence*, vol. 7 (Providence, 1894), 35, 52, 54, 154–55, 266; 15:239–40.

96. *The Early Records of the Town of Providence*, 17:146, 163, 176.

97. Ruth Wallis Herndon and Ella Wilcox Sekatau, "The Right to a Name: The Narraganset People and Rhode Island Officials in the Revolutionary Era," in *After King Philip's War: Presence and Persistence in Indian New England*, ed. Colin G. Calloway (Hanover, N.H.. and London: Univ. Press of New England, 1997), 114–15, 135; James, *Colonial Rhode Island*, 141–45, quote 142.

98. Brigham, *Portsmouth*, 294, 295, 297, 300, 305, 312. The index, p. 460, lists twelve inquests. Two are from the prewar period.

99. James Pierce Root, *Genealogy of the Fenner Family* (Newport, R.I., 1886), 40; Edwin M. Stone, *The Life and Recollections of John Howland* (Providence: Whitney, 1857), 293.

100. Root, *Fenner Genealogy*, 2:21, 26; *The Early Records of the Town of Providence,* vol. 16 (Providence, 1901), 53–59. "This ancient edifice is in a fine state of preservation, and has been occupied successively by Major Thomas Fenner, his son Hon. Joseph Fenner, James Fenner (who inherited it from his grandfather Joseph), and Thomas Fenner, his son in company with his step-father, Job Sheldon. Since then it has descended to the Joy and Hazard families who are in the Fenner line. This is 1887."

101. Communication from Margaret Ordonez, Textile Department, University of Rhode Island, 18 June 1998. At my request and with the cooperation of the Rhode Island Historical Society, Professor Ordonez kindly examined the basket, removed four tiny fibers of each color, and examined them under a light microscope at the conservation laborary at URI.

102. Williams's dictionary included only *Wekinash* for *reed* and *Mishquawtuck* for *cedar*. Later Indian dictionaries designed for the translation of the Bible reduced all fibrous plants to *hashap* for *flax*, the Old World version of the Indian's hemp, nettles, and milkweed. A New England dialect dictionary offers the related word *wicoby* for basswood, the term deriving perhaps from the Abenaki word *Wig-bi* meaning "stringy bark." Williams, "Key," 89, 90; *The Natick Dictionary,* 260; Mitford M. Mathew, *A Dictionary of Americanisms on Historical Principles* (Chicago: Univ. of Chicago Press, 1951), 2:1870; *The Early Records of the Town of Providence,* vol. 5 (Providence, 1894), 244; George B. Emerson, *A Report on the Trees and Shrubs Growing Naturally in the Forests of Massachusetts,* 4th ed. (Boston: Little, Brown, 1887 [1st ed. 1846]), 2:584–85. Emerson added that "Indians made ropes and woven mats from the tough fibrous inner bark."

103. Laurel Thatcher Ulrich, *A Midwife's Tale: The Life of Martha Ballard Based on Her Diary, 1785–1812* (New York: Knopf, 1990), 322; Ted Brasser, *A Basketful of Cultural Change* (Ottawa: National Museum of Man, 1975).

104. Jakes and Sibley, "Comparative Collection for the Study of Fibres," 641–50; Marilyn J. Dwelley, *Summer and Fall Wildflowers of New England* (Camden, Maine: Downeast Enterprise, 1977), 65, 66, 137, 138, 157, 247–49, 342; conversation with Ella Sekatau, Narraganset basket maker, Charlestown, Rhode Island, 8 Mar. 1998.

105. Accession Book, 1835–1880, Rhode Island Historical Society, Providence, entries for 1835, 1836, 1838, and 1843.

106. Ibid., entry for 1842.

107. Roscoe L. Whitman, *History and Genealogy of the Ancestors and Some Descendants of Stukely Westcott* (priv. pub., 1832), 206; George Taylor Paine, Manuscript Genealogy of the Fields of Fields Point, Rhode Island Historical Society, Providence; Eleanor Field obituary, Rhode Island Historical Society, Providence.

## Chapter 2: Two Spinning Wheels in an Old Log House

1. *Dedication Ceremonies on July 26, 1916, The Annie E. Woodman Institute at Dover, New Hampshire* (Concord, N.H.: Rumford, 1916), 3–7, 15–19, 31–32.

2. Susan Gibson, "Introduction," and Christina B. Johannsen, "European Trade Goods and Wampanoag Culture in the Seventeenth Century," in *Burr's Hill: A Seventeenth-Century Wampanoag Burial Ground in Warren, Rhode Island,* ed. Susan Gibson (Providence: Haffenreffer Museum of Anthropology, Brown University, 1980), 22, 23, 27.

3. George Wadleigh, *Notable Events in the History of Dover, New Hampshire* (Dover, 1913), 11, 18–20, 24, 32, 67, 68; John Scales, *Colonial Era History of Dover, New Hampshire* (Dover, 1923; repr., Heritage, 1989), 90, 91.

4. Colin G. Calloway, *The Western Abenaki of Vermont, 1600–1800* (Norman and London: Univ. of Oklahoma Press, 1990), 39, 79–81, 109; James Garvin, "That Little World, Portsmouth," in *Portsmouth Furniture: Masterworks from the New Hampshire Seacoast*, ed. Brock Jobe (Boston: Society for the Preservation of New England Antiquities, 1993), 15; Charles E. Clark, *The Eastern Frontier* (New York: Knopf, 1970), 11–115, 169–74; William G. Saltonstall, *Ports of Piscataqua* (Cambridge, Mass.: Harvard Univ. Press, 1941), 14; Jeremy Belknap, *History of New Hampshire* (Dover, N.H.: n.p., 1812), 1:75, 76; Colin G. Calloway, "Wanalancet and Kancamagus: Indian Strategy and Leadership on the New Hampshire Frontier," *Historical New Hampshire* 43 (winter 1988): 264–90. Waldron's act had repercussions far beyond New Hampshire: in 1704, a Jesuit at the French mission at St. Francis justified the attack on Deerfield by "rehearsing some things done by Major Waldron above thirty years ago." Evan Haefeli and Kevin Sweeney, "Revisiting *The Redeemed Captive:* New Perspectives on the 1704 Attack on Deerfield," *William and Mary Quarterly*, 3d ser., 52 (1995): 3–46.

5. Scales, *History of Dover*, 324, 325.

6. Belknap, *History of New Hampshire*, 1:126, 127.

7. Calloway, *Western Abenaki*, 88, 89, 90–112; Scales, *History of Dover*, 1:201–15; Richard McAlpin Candee, "Wooden Buildings in Early Maine and New Hampshire," Ph.D. diss., University of Pennsylvania, 1976, 284–93, and " 'Logg' Houses of the Piscataqua Region," in Sarah L. Giffen and Kevin D. Murphy, *"A Noble and Dignified Stream": The Piscataqua Region in the Colonial Revival, 1860–1930* (York, Maine: Old York Historical Society, 1992), 26–29.

8. Clark, *Eastern Frontier*, 67–72; Garvin, "That Little World," 15; "Journal of the Rev. John Pike," *Collections NHHS*, vol. 3 (1832; repr., 1870), 55–58, 43–52.

9. Ibid., 56, 54,

10. Ibid., 59, 60, 51, 58.

11. Ibid., 45, 54, 53, 60.

12. Ibid., 59; Sybil Noyes, Charles Thornton Libby, and Walter Goodwin Davis, *A Genealogical Dictionary of Maine and New Hampshire* (Portland, Maine.: Southworth-Anthoensen Press, 1928), 119, 232, 595.

13. At first, the English colonists considered cotton an inferior—even dangerous—fiber. The preamble of a Massachusetts law of 1643 encouraging wool production warned that children dressed in cotton had been "much scorched with fire, yea, divers burnt to death." There was little cotton manufacturing in England in this period, the word being more commonly applied to a cheap napped woolen. Rolla Milton Tryon, *Household Manufactures in the United States, 1640–1860* (1917; repr., New York: Augustus M. Kelley, 1966), 28–33, 44–46, 61–64; Eric Kerridge, *Textile Manufactures in Early Modern England* (Manchester, U.K.: Manchester Univ. Press, 1985), 24, 75, 124–25; Florence M. Montgomery, *Textiles in America 1650–1870*, New York: Norton, 1984), 206.

14. E. B. O'Callaghan and B. Fernow, eds., *Documents Relative to the Colonial History of New York*, vol. 5 (Albany, N.Y.: Weed Parsons and Company, 1855), 598, quoted in Tryon, *Household Manufactures*, 78.

15. Tryon, *Household Manufactures*, 25; William Harris Papers, *Collections of the Rhode Island Historical Society* 10 (Providence, 1902): 147; *Calendar of State Papers, Colonial Papers*, vol. 13 (London: Kraus Reprints, 1964), 255; Harris, 147; Public Record Office, Great Britain; *Calendar of State Papers, Colonial Papers* 13:255.

16. Plymouth Colony Inventories, typescript, Plimoth Plantation, Massachusetts, nos. 147, 145, 131, 127, 123. Montgomery, *Textiles in America,* 272. I found sixteen references to "homemade" or "homespun" fabrics in 152 inventories from Plymouth, Hampshire, and Providence in the 1660s through the 1680s. Also see John Talcott Estate, 4 June 1660, Hartford District Probate Records, Connecticut State Library, Hartford, Connecticut, microfilm 5380; *The Probate Records of Essex County* (Salem, Mass., 1916–1920), 2:432, 278 (hereafter cited as *ECPR*).

17. *New Hampshire Provincial and State Papers,* vol. 31 (Concord, N.H.: n.p., 1911), 376; New Hampshire Probate Records, New Hampshire State Archives, Concord, New Hampshire, nos. 43, 32, 198, and books 1:122, 10:32; Scales, *History of Dover,* 314; Noyes, Libby, and Davis, *A Genealogical Dictionary,* 516, 427; Collections of the Dover Historical Society, vol. 1 (1894), 53, 79, 152, 153, 156, 160.

18. The phrase "pair of looms" appears in a handful of inventories from New Hampshire and Plymouth County, Massachusetts. Even counting these "pairs" as two looms, only 8 percent of all loom-owning households in my New England study had more than one loom. John Graves, Sr., who died in Hatfield, Massachusetts, in 1731, was the only one among almost five hundred loom-owners who claimed more than two. His three looms are listed in his inventory unceremoniously as a "Great Loom & Its Irons" and "2 Ditto." Hampshire County Probate Records, 5:87–88, Hampshire County Courthouse, Northampton, Massachusetts.

19. New Hampshire Probate Records, nos. 212, 220; Noyes, Libby, and Davis, *A Genealogical Dictionary,* 181, 403, 515.

20. William Damm Estate, New Hampshire Probate Records, no. 437.

21. Kerridge, *Textile Manufactures,* 176–77.

22. *The Diary of Manasseh Minor,* ed. Frank Denison Miner (n. p., 1915), 98–106 and passim.

23. Elizabeth Wayland Barber, *Women's Work: The First 20,000 Years* (New York and London: Norton, 1994), 36–39, 90; Rachel Brown, *The Weaving, Spinning, and Dyeing Book,* 2d ed. (New York: Knopf, 1997), 225–28.

24. Brown, *Weaving,* 230–31; Maureen Fennell Mazzaoui, *The Italian Cotton Industry in the Later Middle Ages 1100–1600* (Cambridge: Cambridge Univ. Press, 1981), 78–79; Peter Kriedte, *Peasants, Landlords and Merchant Capitalists: Europe and the World Economy, 1500–1800* (Cambridge: Cambridge Univ. Press, 1983), 32–36; Charles Singer et al., *A History of Technology* (Oxford: Clarendon, 1956), 2:202–3; Kerridge, *Textile Manufactures,* 5–10. Most of what I have to say about the construction of the tools in the Damm Garrison is based on a visit I made there with the New Hampshire weaver and collector Craig Evans and the spinning wheel "sleuth" Florence Feldman-Wood. I am grateful for their generosity and absolve them of responsibility for my errors.

25. Brown, *Weaving,* 232–33; Patricia Baines, *Linen: Handspinning and Weaving* (London: Batsford Ltd., 1989), 28–30, 37–50; Museum of American Textile History, Lowell, Massachusetts, 1959.1.152.

26. Bud Kronenberg, *Spinning Wheel Building and Restoration* (New York: Van Nostrand Reinhold, 1981), 25–28; Randle Holme, *Academy of Armory, 1688* (Menston, England: Scholar, 1972), 3:286; photocopies made by Florence Feldman-Wood of wheels in the Museum of American Textile History.

27. Baines, *Linen,* 30; Wayne E. Franits, *Paragons of Virtue: Woman and Domesticity in Seventeenth-Century Dutch Art* (Cambridge: Cambridge Univ. Press, 1993), 184, 189.

28. Thomas Firmin, *Proposals for the Imployment of the Poor* (London, 1681); Baines, *Linen,* 32; Walter Endrei and Rachel P. Maines, "On Two-Handed Spinning," in *European Women and Preindustrial Craft,* ed. Daryl Hafter (Bloomington and Indianapolis: Indi-

ana Univ. Press, 1995), 37–39; Karl Marx, *Capital: A Critique of Political Economy,* vol. 1, trans. Ben Fowkes (London: Penguin, 1990), 495; Joan Whittaker Cummer, *A Book of Spinning Wheels* (Portsmouth, N.H.: Peter Randall, 1993), 219–37.

29. A Wethersfield, Connecticut, woman was actually tried for witchcraft partly for her spinning skill; a fellow servant testified that she spun more fine linen yarn than any woman could have spun "without some unlawful help: which yarn did not well prosper." Perhaps it was the woman's experience in some unknown spinning district of England that gave her such speed, but her reputation for telling fortunes and blighting other women's children made everything she did seem suspect. Sherman W. Adams and Henry R. Stiles, *The History of Ancient Wethersfield, Connecticut,* vol. 1 (1904; repr. Somersworth, N.H.: New Hampshire Publishing, 1974), 682–84; David D. Hall, *Witch-Hunting in Seventeenth-Century New England: A Documentary History, 1638–1692* (Boston: Northeastern Univ. Press, 1991), 174, 177–78; "The New York Cases of Hall and Harrison," in *Narratives of the Witchcraft Cases 1648–1706,* ed. George Lincoln Burr (1914; repr. New York: Barnes and Noble, 1972), 48–52.

30. Kerridge, *Textile Manufactures,* 5, 14–24; Baines, *Linen,* 50–59, 109. For a typical reference to spinning as unskilled work, see Jan de Vries and Ad van der Woude, *The First Modern Economy* (Cambridge: Cambridge Univ. Press, 1997), 597.

31. In surviving collections, wheels without wooden axles are extremely rare. Those in New England may in fact have come into the region from Canada in the nineteenth century. Since Dover had many Canadian immigrants, this is certainly possible, though most of the implements in the Damm Garrison seem to have come from long-settled farms in Dover and surrounding towns. Letter from Florence Feldman-Wood to the author, 19 Nov. 1998.

32. Kerridge, *Textile Manufactures,* 172.

33. D. C. Coleman, "Textile Growth," in N. B. Harte and K. G. Ponting, *Textile History and Economic History* (Manchester: Manchester Univ. Press, 1973), 1–10. Also see Peter Kriedte, Hans Medick, Jurgen Schlumbohm, *Industrialization before Industrialization: Rural Industry in the Genesis of Capitalism,* trans. Beate Schempp (Cambridge and New York: Cambridge Univ. Press, 1981), and Maxine Berg, *The Age of Manufactures: Industry, Innovation, and Work in Britain, 1700–1820* (Oxford, U.K.: Blackwell, 1985).

34. Kerridge, *Textile Manufactures,* 158–61, 194–96, 201–3; G. E. Fussell and K. R. Fussell, *The English Countrywoman: A Farmhouse Social History, A.D. 1500–1900* (New York: Blom, 1971), 45; Herbert Heaton, *The Yorkshire Woollen and Worsted Industries* (Oxford: Clarendon, 1965), 334–38, 345; G. D. Ramsay, *The Wiltshire Woollen Industry in the Sixteenth and Seventeenth Centuries* (New York: Kelley, 1943; repr., 1965), 12–15, 90–99; Jane Gray, "Gender and Uneven Working-Class Formation in the Irish Linen Industry," in *Gender and Class in Modern Europe,* ed. Laura L. Frader and Sonya O. Rose (Ithaca, N.Y., and London: Cornell Univ. Press, 1996), 36–46.

35. Edward Taylor, *The Poetical Works of Edward Taylor,* ed. Thomas Johnson (New York: Rockland Editions, 1939), 116. For background on textiles made in Taylor's hometown of Coventry, England, see Kerridge, *Textile Manufactures,* 13, 21, 29, 34–35, 79, 96, 134–35, 140, 147.

36. Ibid., 159; John Dod and William Hinde, *Bathshebaes Instructions to Her Son Lemuel* (London, 1614), e.g., 31–33, 45–46, 51; de Vries and van der Woude, *First Modern Economy,* 597; Linda Stone-Ferrier, "Spun Virtue, the Lacework of Folly, and the World Wound Upside-Down," in *Cloth and Human Experience,* ed. Annette B. Weiner and Jane Schneider (Washington, D.C., and London: Smithsonian Institution Press, 1991), 215–42. For additional images of Dutch spinners, see Franits, *Paragons of Virtue,* figures 54, 55, 56, 160, 161, 166, pp. 72–76, 184–89.

37. Jane Schneider, "Rumpelstiltskin's Bargain: Folklore and the Merchant Capitalist Intensification of Linen Manufacture in Early Modern Europe," in *Cloth and Human Experience*, ed. Weiner and Schneider, 177–213.

38. New Hampshire Provincial Papers, vol. 3 (Manchester, 1869), 542–46; Nicholas Canny, *Kingdom and Colony: Ireland in the Atlantic World 1560–1800* (Baltimore and London: Johns Hopkins Univ. Press, 1988), 129–30; Minutes of "A Meeting with the Delegates of the Eastern Indians," in Colonial Papers, Massachusetts State Archives, Boston, microfilm, roll 29:36–52.

39. Alexander Macpheadris Papers, Portsmouth Atheneum, Portsmouth, New Hampshire.

40. Richard McAlpin Candee, *Building Portsmouth: The Neighborhoods and Architecture of New Hampshire's Oldest City* (Portsmouth, N.H.: Portsmouth Advocates, Inc., 1992), 41–44; Mary Black, "Contributions toward a History of Early Eighteenth-Century New York Portraiture: Identification of the Aetatis Suae and Wendell Limners," *American Art Journal* 12, no. 4 (1980): 5–27; Garvin, "This Little World," 16–19; Clark, *Eastern Frontier*, 102–7; Alexander Macpheadris Inventory, and Alexander Macpheadris to Mr. James Callwell, Cork, 24 Dec. 1717, and Alexander Macpheadris to Mr. John Gault, undated, MS, Macpheadris-Warner Papers, Portsmouth Athenaeum, Portsmouth, New Hampshire. There are many candidates for the man on horseback. He could be Sir William Phips, the Maine frontiersman and Massachusetts governor knighted for his maritime prowess during King William's War, a man Cotton Mather called a "guardian angel" of New England. He could also be the duke of Portland, a hero in Ireland's struggle during the same period. Because the *P* appears beneath a crown, just as an *R* might do for a reigning king, I assume it represents William. Cotton Mather, *Magnalia Christi Americana*, ed. Kenneth B. Murdock (Cambridge, Mass: Harvard Univ. Press, 1977), 324–25; C. P. Hill, *Who's Who in History*, vol. 3 (Oxford: Blackwell, 1965), 348–49; Leslie Stephen and Sidney Lee, *Dictionary of National Biography* (Oxford: Oxford Univ. Pres, 1964), 285–92; Elizabeth Carroll Reilly, *A Dictionary of Colonial American Printers' Ornaments and Illustrations* (Worcester, Mass.: American Antiquarian Society, 1975), 187; Emerson W. Baker and John G. Reid, *The New England Knight: Sir William Phips, 1651–1695* (Toronto: Univ. of Toronto Press, 1998). I have profited from conversations on this matter with Richard Candee, Joyce Geary Volk, Emerson Baker, Eliga Gould, and especially Edward McCarren, though none should be blamed for my speculations.

41. Eric Hinderaker, "The 'Four Indian Kings' and the Imaginative Construction of the First British Empire," *William and Mary Quarterly*, 3d ser., 53 (1996): 487–526.

42. Patrick Macrory, *The Siege of Derry* (London: Hodder and Stoughton, 1980), 232.

43. Canny, *Kingdom and Colony*, 105; Edward L. Parker, *The History of Londonderry* (1851; repr., Londonderry, N.H.: Town of Londonderry, 1974), 1–29.

44. Bunny McBride and Harald E. L. Prins, "Walking the Medicine Line: Molly Ockett, a Pigwacket Doctor," in *Northeastern Indian Lives 1632–1816*, ed. Robert S. Grumet (Amherst: Univ. of Massachusetts Press, 1996), 321–26, 345 n. 8. Unlike the missionaries who served as go-betweens in seventeenth-century Massachusetts, Jordan was a military man as well as a longtime resident of the area. His father had settled early in Maine, pasturing sheep on Richmond Island at the mouth of the Kennebec until King William's War drove him away. Provincial Papers 43:718, 31:494, microfilm, Massachusetts State Archives, Boston.

45. "Council of Kennebeck Indians," Georgetown, 25 Nov. 1720, microfilm, Massachusetts Archives 29:68–74. The participants on the English side were Shadrach Walton, Samuel Moody, Johnson Harmon, and John Wainwright, and for the Abenaki, Warrocusot alias Mogg, Wowurna alias Captain Joseph, Muggus alias Moses, Obomacohawk, John Hogon, and Tuddebow'hunsevit.

46. Malachi 4:1.

47. Calloway, *Western Abenaki*, 123.

48. Martha Coons and Katherine Koob, *All Sorts of Good Sufficient Cloth: Linen-Making in New England 1640–1860* (North Andover, Mass.: Merrimack Valley Textile Museum, 1980), 12–18.

49. Parker, *History of Londonderry*, 292; Leander Winslow Cogswell, *History of the Town of Henniker, Merrimack County, New Hampshire* (1880; facsimile, Somersworth, N.H.: New Hampshire Pub., 1973), 757; "The Story of Mary Wilson," *New Hampshire Folklore*, 20; "Essex County Notarial Records," *EIHC* 44 (1908): 328; *Boston News-Letter*, 17–24 Oct. 1720. There are framed fragments of Mary's dress at the Henniker Public Library, the New Hampshire Historical Society, Concord, and the Daughters of the American Museum, Washington, D.C. Diane Dunckley kindly helped me trace the donor of the DAR fragment.

50. Belknap, *History of New Hampshire*, 2:37; Coons and Koob, *Good Sufficient Cloth*, 12, 14; Registration Files 1965.29, New Hampshire Historical Society, Concord.

51. John Horner, *The Linen Trade of Europe during the Spinning-Wheel Period* (Belfast: M'Caw, Stevenson & Orr, 1920), 17–18; G. B. Thompson, *Spinning Wheels* (Belfast: Ulster Folk Museum, 1966), 19–20, 31.

52. Strafford Country Probate Records, Strafford County Courthouse, Dover, New Hampshire, 4:222.

53. Ibid., 1:249–53.

54. On Londonderry wheels, see Coons and Koob, *Good Sufficient Cloth*, 51; Caleb Stark, *The History of the Town of Dunbarton, Merrimack County, New Hampshire* (1860), 248; Samuel Gregg, *Autobiography of Major Samuel Gregg* (n.p. 1806), photocopy, Textile Department, Museum of American Textile History, Lowell, Massachusetts.

55. Laurel Thatcher Ulrich, "Wheels, Looms, and the Gender Division of Labor in Eighteenth-Century New England," *William & Mary Quarterly*, 3d ser. 55 (1998): 3–38.

56. Benno M. Forman, "The Account Book of John Gould, Weaver, of Topsfield, Massachusetts, 1697–1724," *Essex Institute Historical Collections* 105 (1969): 36, 39; John Gould Account Books, 1697–1724, Essex Institute, Salem, Massachusetts, 91, 93.

57. *Diary of Manasseh Minor*, 144; *The Early Records of the Town of Providence* (Providence: 1894, 1901), 7:130–35, 16:236–42; Josiah Cotton, "Some Inquiries Made among ye. Indians in the General Visitation begun Septr. 4: 1726," Curwen Papers, American Antiquarian Society, Worcester, Massachusetts; Daniel R. Mandell, *Behind the Frontier: Indians in Eighteenth-Century Eastern Massachusetts* (Lincoln: Univ. of Nebraska Press, 1996), 200. (Doug Winiarski kindly shared the reference to Hannah James.) In March 1737, the Reverend Mr. Matthias Plant of Newbury, Massachusetts, noted that he had "payd to the Ilseys young women fifty shillings for weaving forty yards of woosted at fifteen pence pr yd." The Ilseys were presumably daughters of Jonathan Ilsey, identified as a Newbury weaver when his estate was probated in 1753. "The Diary of the Reverend Matthias Plant, Newbury, Mass.," typescript, Essex Institute, Salem, Massachusetts, 16 Mar. 1736/7; Jonathon Ilsey Estate, Essex County Probate Records, 14459, cited in Gail Mohanty, "Unnoticed Craftsmen Noted: Commercial Handloom Weavers and Weaving in Essex County, Massachusetts, 1690–1790," chart 1, unpublished paper provided by the author. Other references to female textile workers in Plant's memoranda include: 9 July 1739, "paid Mrs Brown for my wifes stuff wove at Wenham"; 18 Mar. 1736/7, "Then I payd Mr James wife for ye abovsd forty yards for pressing it, at two pence halpeny a yard." Also see Nicholas Perryman Ledger, typescript, New Hampshire Historical Society, Concord, 46a; Nathaniel Coffin Account Book 1:56, Coffin Papers, Society for the Preservation of New England Antiquities,

Boston; and additional Connecticut references in Gloria L. Main, "Gender, Work, and Wages in Colonial New England," *William and Mary Quarterly,* 3d ser., 51 (1994): n. 78.

58. Katharine F. Richmond, *John Hayes of Dover, New Hampshire* (Tyngsboro, Mass., 1936), 1:46; *Collections of the Dover, N.H., Historical Society* (Dover, N.H.: Scales and Quimby, 1894), 1:16, 39; New Hampshire Probate Records, 18:492–93.

59. Main, "Gender, Work, and Wages," 62–63, 65; Daniel Vickers, *Farmers and Fishermen: Two Centuries of Work in Essex County, Massachusetts, 1630–1830* (Chapel Hill: Univ. of North Carolina Press, 1994); Garvin, "That Little World," 15–21; Brock Jobe, "Furniture Making in Eighteenth-Century Portsmouth," in *Portsmouth Furniture,* ed. Jobe, 43, 46–49, 55, 285–91; Charles S. Parsons, *The Dunlaps and Their Furniture* (Manchester, N.H.: Currier Gallery of Art, 1970) 1–8; Gregg, *Autobiography,* 8.

60. Jan de Vries, "Between Purchasing Power and the World of Goods: Understanding the Household Economy in Early Modern Europe," in *Consumption and the World of Goods,* ed. John Brewer and Roy Porter (London and New York: Routledge, 1993), 107, 108; Main, "Gender, Work, and Wages," 62–65; Vickers, *Farmers and Fishermen,* 247–59. On the gender division of labor, see Merry Wiesner-Hanks, " 'A Learned Task and Given to Men Alone': The Gendering of Tasks in Early Modern German Cities," *Journal of Medieval and Renaissance Studies* 25 (1995): 89–106; and Judith M. Bennett, "Medieval Women, Modern Women: Across the Great Divide," in *Feminists Revision History,* ed. Ann-Louise Shapiro (New Brunswick, N.J.: Rutgers Univ. Press, 1994), 58–59.

61. Adrienne D. Hood, "The Gender Division of Labor in the Production of Textiles in Eighteenth-Century Rural Pennsylvania (Rethinking the New England Model):" *Journal of Social History* 27 (1994): 537–60, and "The Material World of Cloth: Production and Use in Eighteenth-Century Rural Pennsylvania," *William & Mary Quarterly,* 53 (1996): 43–67; and personal communication from Jean Elliott Russo, who has discovered several female weavers in colonial Maryland, and is now editing the Somerset County court records.

62. Scales, *History of Dover,* 224, 225, 130, 179–81; Wadleigh, *Notable Events,* 53, 54, 88, 98, 103, 129, 135, 136, 139–41, 142–43, 146, 150, 158–61.

63. Clark, *Eastern Frontier,* 336; *Historical Statistic of the United States,* part 2 (Washington, D.C.: Bureau of the Census, 1975), 1170.

64. Colin G. Calloway, "Introduction: Cultural Encounters in Early New Hampshire," *Historical New Hampshire* 53 (1998): 66–67; Calloway, *Western Abenakis,* 192–202 and passim.

65. The text of the song was published as early as 1824. Although the transcriber knew no Abenaki, she captured enough of the syllables to allow a twentieth-century collector of Abenaki songs, Jesse Bowman Bruchac, to recognize it as a mourning song and to create the translation printed here. Donna-Belle Garvin, "Conflict and Assimilation: The Story of Rachel Meloon," *Historical New Hampshire* 53 (1998): 101–14.

## Chapter 3: Hannah Barnard's Cupboard

1. Owen McNally, "Furniture from New England Towns: Window to the Past," *Hartford Courant,* 6 Feb. 1993, B1, B3.

2. Philip Zea and Suzanne L. Flynt, *Hadley Chests* (Deerfield, Mass.: Pocumtuck Valley Memorial Association, 1992), 20, 28.

3. Zea and Flynt, *Hadley Chests,* 5, 16; Clair Franklin Luther, *The Hadley Chest* (Hartford, Conn.: Case, Lockwood, and Brainard, 1935), xix–xxvi; Patricia E. Kane, "The Seventeenth-Century Furniture of the Connecticut Valley: The Hadley Chest Reap-

praised," in *Arts of the Anglo-American Community in the Seventeenth Century: Winterthur Conference Report, 1974*, ed. Ian M. Quimby (Charlottesville: Univ. Press of Virginia, 1975), 79–122; Philip Zea, "The Fruits of Oligarchy: Patronage and the Hadley Chest Tradition in Western Massachusetts," *Old-Time New England* 72 (1987): 1–65; Suzanne L. Flynt, Susan McGowan, and Amelia F. Miller, *Gathered and Preserved* (Deerfield, Mass.: Memorial Hall, 1991), 5–15; Kevin M. Sweeney, "From Wilderness to Arcadian Vale: Material Life in the Connecticut River Valley, 1635–1760," and Philip Zea, "Furniture," in *The Great River: Art and Society of the Connecticut Valley, 1635–1820*, ed. Gerald W. R. Ward and William N. Hosley (Hartford, Conn.: Wadsworth Atheneum, 1985), 17–21, 185 ff.; also see Brock Jobe and Myrna Kaye, *New England Furniture: The Colonial Era* (Boston: Houghton Mifflin, 1984), 130–31.

4. Richard I. Melvoin, *New England Outpost: War and Society in Colonial Deerfield* (New York: Norton, 1989), 191, 192, 19, 20.

5. Gloria L. Main, "The Distribution of Consumer Goods in Colonial New England: A Subregional Approach," in *Early American Probate Inventories*, ed. Peter Benes and Jane Benes (Dublin Seminar for New England Folklife, Annual Proceedings, 1987), 153–68, and "An Inquiry into When and Why Women Learned to Write in Colonial New England," *Journal of Social History* 24 (1990–1991): 579–89. In an effort to measure the distribution of consumer goods in early America, Main has created an "Index of Amenities" that includes some of the things we have been discussing here, particularly linens, earthenware, and silver. "In the Valley," she writes, "the only subregion for which we have a useful sample in the period 1725–1729, the index rose to an extraordinarily high level for householders in the lower and middling classes."

6. Victor Chinnery, *Oak Furniture: The British Tradition* (Woodbridge, Suffolk: Antique Collectors' Club, 1979), 501; Zea and Flynt, *Hadley Chests*, 12; Zea, "Furniture," 185–86, 196–98; William N. Hosley, Jr., talk at Antiques Forum, Colonial Williamsburg, 5 Feb. 1995.

7. Gerald W. R. Ward, "Some Thoughts on Connecticut Cupboards and Other Case Furniture," *Old Time New England* 72 (1987): 66–69; Chinnery, *Oak Furniture*, 210, 502–10; Mary Rowlandson, *The Sovereignty and Goodness of God*, ed. Neal Salisbury (Boston: Bedford, 1997), 111; David L. Greene, "New Light on Mary Rowlandson," *Early American Literature* 20 (1985): 29–31; Zea, "Furniture," 185–87, 198–200; Walter A. Dyer, "The Tulip-and-Sunflower Press Cupboard," *Antiques* 27 (1935): 140–43; Joseph Rowlandson Inventory, #4658, and Samuel Talcott, Will and Inventory, #5380, Hartford District Probate Records, Connecticut State Library, microfilm. On Mary Rowlandson's second marriage see Greene, "New Light on Mary Rowlandson," 24–38.

8. Edward Taylor, *The Poetical Works of Edward Taylor*, ed. Thomas Johnson (New York: Rockland Editions, 1939), 151–52, 148.

9. Estate Records, Hartford District Probate Court, #4658 and 5380; Hampshire County Probate Records, County Court House, Northampton, Massachusetts, 3:5, 14–15, 86; 5:15, 18–20; Linda R. Baumgarten, "The Textile Trade in Boston, 1650–1700," in *Arts*, ed. Quimby, 264. Rowlandson's second husband also owned a "great cupboard," which with a table listed in his inventory was valued at two pounds; his "sheets table linnen napkins & towells" were worth nineteen pounds and fifteen shillings. The "cupboard in the Parler" of the Reverend Mr. Solomon Stoddard of Northampton was less valuable but at ten shillings it was appraised at exactly the same amount as the "cupboard cloth" on its top.

10. *The Journal of John Winthrop*, ed. Richard S. Dunn, James Savage, and Laetitia Yeandle (Cambridge and London: Harvard Univ. Press, 1996), 352.

11. Wayne E. Franits, *Paragons of Virtue: Women and Domesticity in Seventeenth-Century Dutch Art* (Cambridge: Cambridge Univ. Press, 1993), 142–45.

12. "The Journal of Madam Knight," in *Colonial American Travel Narratives*, ed. Wendy Martin (New York: Penguin, 1994), 54. In contrast, Solomon Stoddard's well-regulated household had a "New fashioned Ironing box," valued at six shillings. Hampshire County Probate Records, 5:18–21.

13. The inventory of Pastor John Williams of Deerfield listed fifty pounds of wool in various grades with a "Great wheel" to spin it alongside "blue China curtains," a quilt and valances of Indian calico, a satin blanket, and a diaper tablecloth. Hampshire County Probate Records, 1:171, 3:19; 1:156, 5:51; Gloria Main, "Probate Records as a Source for Early American History," *William and Mary Quarterly*, 3d ser., 32 (1975): 89–99.

14. Jane C. Nylander, "Textiles," in *The Great River*, ed. Ward and Hosely, 380–81; James Russell Trumbull, *History of Northampton* (Northampton, Mass.: n.p., 1898), 1:204–5; 2:64.

15. Stoddard's inventory taken in 1748, which lists a "Best Damask Table Cloth" and "Six Napkins" plus three diaper tablecloths and nine diaper towels. Nylander, "Textiles," 374–75, 380–81; Hampshire County Probate Records, 7:194 ff.

16. Glee Krueger, *A Gallery of American Samplers* (New York: Dutton, 1978), 24. Also see Betty Ring, *American Needlework Treasures* (New York: Dutton, 1987), e.g., figure 5, Margret Palfrey sampler; 32, figure 51, Cordelia Bennet sampler. Computations based on Ethel Stanwood Bolton and Eva Johnston Coe, *American Samplers* (Boston: Massachusetts Society of the Colonial Dames of America, 1924), show that by 1730, 60 percent of New England samplers contained one or more verses.

17. Zea, "Fruits of Oligarchy," 1, 9–15, figure 12; Zea and Flynt, *Hadley Chests*, 13; William N. Hosley, Jr., and Philip Zea, "Decorated Board Chests of the Connecticut River Valley," *Antiques* 119 (1981): 1148–51; Kane, "Seventeenth-Century Furniture," 110–19. For English examples, see Chinnery, *Oak Furniture*, 60, 62, 369; David Knell, *English Country Furniture: The National and Regional Vernacular 1500–1900* (New York: Cross River, 1992), 49.

18. Main, "When and Why Women Learned to Write," 579–89. Note especially tables 4 and 5, which include Hampshire County.

19. "Ironback," cat. 211, in *The Great River*, ed. Ward and Hosely, 325; Robert F. Trent, "Joinery of Middlesex County," in *Arts*, ed. Quimby, 139; Leslie B. Grigsby, *English Slip-Decorated Earthenware at Williamsburg* (Williamsburg, Va.: Colonial Williamsburg Foundation, 1993), 40, 46.

20. There are two other related pieces, a chest of drawers at Winterthur made by a still different joiner, and a cheaper board chest with drawers painted less ambitiously but in a similar manner. Patricia E. Kane, "New Haven Colony Furniture: The Seventeenth-Century Style," *Antiques* 103 (May 1973): 950–62; William N. Hosley, Jr., "The Wallace Nutting Collection at the Wadsworth Atheneum, Hartford, Connecticut," *Antiques* 126 (Oct. 1984): 860–74; Ward, "Some Thoughts," 74–77; Dean A. Fales, Jr., *American Painted Furniture 1660–1880* (New York: Dutton, 1972): 16, 17, 20–23; Zea and Flynt, *Hadley Chests*, 19–23; Zea, "Furniture," 204–7. For early images and the provenance of the three pieces, see "The Editor's Attic," *Antiques* 10 (1926): 188–190; "Connecticut Valley Polychromed Press Cupboard," *Antiques* 25 (1934): 129; "The Editor's Attic," *Antiques* 26 (1934): 168; "The Editor's Attic," *Antiques* 29 (1936): 139–40. The *SW* chest has been heavily repainted.

21. The *SW* has been repainted but enough of the original work remains to demonstrate the technique. Although the Winterthur chest was stripped of a later coat of paint, the original paint, when exposed, was in excellent condition. The design, pigments, and methods of application are strikingly similar to the Hannah Barnard cupboard. I would like to thank Suzanne Flynt for looking at the Barnard cupboard and the *SW* chest with me and Brock Jobe for showing me related physical evidence in the Winterthur chest.

22. Fales, *American Painted Furniture*, 19, figure 16; Kane, "Seventeenth-Century Furniture," 94, 101, 102, figures 9, 10, 17, 19; Zea, "Furniture," 202, 206, figures 81, 84.

23. Fales, *American Painted Furniture*, 24–29, 39, 42–43, 367–8; Charles F. Montgomery, "Furniture Symposium," *Antiques* 43 (1988): 357–58, figures 3 and 3a; John Kirk, "The Tradition of English Painted Furniture," *Antiques* 67 (1980): 1082–83, figures 8, 8a, 8b; Elizabeth Carroll Reilly, *A Dictionary of Colonial American Printers' Ornaments and Illustrations* (Worcester, Mass.: American Antiquarian Society, 1975), 187; Grigsby, *English Slip-Decorated Earthenware*, 10, 41, figures 2, 46.

24. Conversation with Susan Buck, Society for the Preservation of New England Antiquities Conservation Center. Zea and Flynt, *Hadley Chests*, 28 n. 56. Variant spellings of names were common in this period. A piece of silver owned by one of Hannah's relatives was marked "Bernard"; Silver Beaker, "The Gift of Samuel Bernard to the Church in Deerfield 1723," c. 1723, Historic Deerfield, L-20-85.

25. Edward Taylor, "Upon Wedlock and Death of Children," in *Poetical Works,* ed. Johnson, 117.

26. Melvoin, *New England Outpost*, 85, 138, 150, 163, 167, 184, 199, 145, 171; George Sheldon, "Genealogies," *A History of Deerfield, Massachusetts* (1895–96; repr., Deerfield, Mass.: Pocumtuck Valley Memorial Association, 1983), 2:65; Joseph H. Smith, *Colonial Justice in Western Massachusetts, 1639–1702: The Pynchon Court Record* (Cambridge, Mass.: Harvard Univ. Press, 1961), 375, 380, 383, 384; Carl Bridenbaugh, ed., *The Pynchon Papers* (Boston: Colonial Society of Massachusetts, 1982–85), 69, 277–82, 293–97; Mason A. Green, *Springfield, 1636–1886: History of Town and City* (Springfield, Mass.: Nichols, 1888), 96, 125–27, 132, 135, 139, 154, 175, 176; John H. Lockwood, *Westfield and Its Historic Influences 1669–1919* (Springfield, Mass.: privately printed, 1922), 62–65.

27. Sylvester Judd, *The History of Hadley, Massachusetts* (Springfield, Mass.: Huntting, 1905), part 1, 10–14, 51, 70, 85, 283, 284, 447, part 2, 8; Thomas R. Lewis, "The Landscape and Environment of the Connecticut River Valley," in *The Great River*, 8–9.

28. Peter Thomas, "Cultural Change on the Southern New England Frontier, 1630–1665," in *Cultures in Contact*, ed. William W. Fitzhugh (Washington, D.C., and London: Smithsonian Institution Press, 1985), 146–55; Neal Salisbury, "Indians and Colonists in Southern New England after the Pequot War: An Uneasy Balance," in *The Pequots in Southern New England*, ed. Laurence M. Hauptman and James D. Wherry (Norman and London: Univ. of Oklahoma Press, 1990), 89–91.

29. Local Indians again accused him in 1674, but by the time the case reached the court, King Philip's War had begun. Westcarr died in September 1675. Judd, *History of Hadley*, 64; Hampshire County Court Records, Hampshire County Courthouse, Northampton, Massachusetts, 1:89, 99, 121–23, 133; Smith, *Colonial Justice*, 122.

30. Judd, *History of Hadley*, 91–92; Green, *Springfield*, 139; Melvoin, *New England Outpost*, 183–84.

31. Hampshire County Court Records, 1:169; microfilm, 0879184, LDS Family History Library, Salt Lake City, Utah; Smith, *Colonial Justice*, 286; Judd, *History of Hadley*, 90; Douglas Edward Leach, *Flintlock and Tomahawk: New England in King Philip's War* (New York: Norton, 1966), 171–79; Russell Bourne, *The Red King's Rebellion: Racial Politics in New England 1675–1678* (New York: Oxford Univ. Press, 1990), 181–84.

32. Smith, *Colonial Justice*, 289. For other references to weavers in court records, see *Records and Files of the Quarterly Courts of Essex County, Massachusetts*, vol. 3 (Salem: Essex Institute, 1911), 194; Middlesex County Court Records, book 3:286, folios 1679 86–4, Massachusetts State Archives, Boston. Jenny Pulsifer kindly supplied the Middlesex reference.

33. Judd, *History of Hadley*, 228–31. Smith's wife, Rebecca, and Francis Barnard's second wife, Frances Dickinson, were sisters. John Dickinson Estate, Hampshire County Probate, book 1:182; Abram W. Foote, *Foote Family* (Rutland, Vt.: Tuttle, 1907), 23–24; Judd, *Hadley*, 203; Pynchon Court Record, 316. In September 1677, a year after the death of King Philip and long after the few surviving Pocumtucks had apparently fled the valley, a small group of local and Canadian Indians attacked the neighboring towns of Deerfield and Hatfield, killing thirteen people and taking more than a dozen captives, including the new Mistress Barnard's married daughter and her children. The daughter returned from Canada eight months later with a baby girl she had named "Captivity." Melvoin, *New England Outpost*, 124–25; Foote, *Foote Family*, 23–24; Judd, *History of Hadley*, 175–78, part 2, 77–78.

34. Cotton Mather, "Memorable Providences, Relating to Witchcrafts and Possessions, 1689," in *Narratives of the Witchcraft Cases 1648–1706*, ed. George Lincoln Burr (New York: Barnes and Noble, 1972, orig. pub. 1914), 131–34; Judd, *History of Hadley*, 228–31; Pynchon Court Record, 69.

35. Hampshire County Probate Records, 2:244, 3:21–23.

36. Zea, "Fruits of Oligarchy," 23–24; Judd, *History of Hadley*, part 1, 283–84, 446–48; part 2, 8; Sheldon, "Genealogies," *Deerfield*, 2:65.

37. I am grateful to the Deerfield librarian George Proper for finding and photocopying this inscription. George Sheldon, "The Hannah Beaman Book and the Regicides," *History and Proceedings of the Pocumtuck Valley Memorial Association, 1912–1920* (Deerfield, Mass., 1921), 25–33, argues that Westcarr got the book from English Civil War general Edward Whalley, who got it from Baxter himself. The use of Latin led one Deerfield historian to conclude that Hannah could never have written it herself. Yet there is no reason why a literate woman of her generation couldn't have used a common Latin phrase. Minus the flourishes, the inscription is quite compatible with her later signature. Sheldon, "Hannah Beaman Book," 30. Sheldon was unable to connect the signature with that of any other educated contemporary but thought it looked a bit like three autographs of General William Goffe, the second of his "Regicides." It came to Sheldon's museum from a descendant of Samuel Williams, an associate and teacher of the third Thomas Barnard.

38. Hampshire County Probate Records, 5:66, 6:22, 58, 59, 77; Sheldon, *Deerfield*, 1:244, 272, 303, 308, 624, 2:840; Richard E. Birks, "Hannah Beaman, Deerfield's First School Mistress: Her Times and Her Experiences," *History and Proceedings of the Pocumtuck Valley Memorial Association, 1912–1920* (Deerfield, Mass., 1921), 496–513.

39. In 1728, a niece, Bridget Barnard, became the first female teacher to be paid out of Deerfield town funds. Judd, *History of Hadley*, 56–58, 418; Sheldon, *Deerfield*, 840. The town also enjoined farmers "to procure School Dames to teach their children."

40. Judd, *History of Hadley*, part 1, 255–57; part 2, 8, 91; Melvoin, *New England Outpost*, 19–20, 191–92, 198, 200; Sheldon, *Deerfield*, 1:298, 304, 305; 2:65.

41. Annette B. Weiner, *Inalienable Possessions: The Paradox of Keeping-While-Giving* (Berkeley: Univ. of California Press, 1992), 6, 154, 33, 32, 37, 42–43; Toby Ditz, *Property and Kinship: Inheritance in Early Connecticut, 1750–1820* (Princeton, N.J.: Princeton Univ. Press, 1986), 65, 69–70. Ditz argues that bequests of land to daughters were actually substitutes for personal property. Although the general distinction between movables and real property prevailed throughout western Europe, different economies and cultures produced variations on the theme. See, for example, Martha C. Howell, "Fixing Movables: Gifts by Testament in Late Medieval Douai," *Past and Present* 150 (1996): 3–45.

42. John Billing Distribution, 8 Sept. 1698; Joseph Barnard Distribution, n.d.; Charles Fierre Will and Distribution, 29 July 1699; Hampshire County Probate Records, 3:19, 47, 63, 1690–1700.

43. Of the 117 names in the Hadley valuation list of 1720, Marsh's father-in-law, Samuel Porter, ranked first; his father, Daniel Marsh, was fourth; and his second father-in-law, Samuel Barnard, was seventh. On the valuation list of 1731, "Heirs of John Marsh, and Widow Sarah Marsh" rank fifteenth out of eighty-seven. Sheldon, *Deerfield*, 2:298, 376–79; Judd, *History of Hadley*, 278, 283; Hampshire County Probate Records, 4:134, 5:51 ff. In this he was not alone. Deerfield's minister John Williams, whose book *The Redeemed Captive* describes his own and his neighbors' experiences in French Canada, owned a "Molatto boy Meseck" and a "black boy Redear" at his death. The ownership of Sippey confirmed Marsh's status as a man on the move. Less than 6 percent of Hampshire inventories in this period list bound servants or slaves.

44. John Marsh Will, 5 June 1725, Hampshire County Probate Records, 4:134, microfilm, LDS Family History Library, film number 0879184. As it turned out, little John never did come of age. He died on 3 July 1726 at age three. Lucius M. Boltwood, "Family Genealogies," in Judd, *History of Hadley*, 92.

45. John Marsh Inventory, Hampshire County Probate Records, 4:138–40. I thank Suzanne Flynt for the suggestion that the cupboard may have left the household.

46. Marsh's inventory has been known to furniture researchers since the 1930s, yet none has noted the importance of the separate listing of each wife's goods. When Hannah's cupboard surfaced in the antiques market in 1936, the Reverend Clair Franklin Luther, the first systematic cataloger of Hadley chests, was certain Marsh's inventory contained the clue to the identity of the similar *SW* chest. Marsh's third wife was named Sarah Williams. Surely the first flowered chest in the inventory was Hannah's cupboard and the second belonged to Sarah. It was an attractive notion, yet it ignored the structure of the document. Unless one assumes that Hannah Barnard conveniently anticipated the initials of her successor, the least likely place to find a chest marked *SW* was with her goods! For more on the provenance of this chest, see pages 133–35.

47. [Lydia Nelson Hastings, ed.], *The Hastings Memorial* (Boston: Samuel Drake, 1866), 7, 8, 11; Thomas Hopkins, *The Kelloggs in the Old World and the New*, vol. 1 (San Francisco: Sunset, 1903), 172, 369; Hampshire County Probate Records, 68:51; Donald Lines Jacobus, *The Bulkely Genealogy* (New Haven, Conn.: n.p., 1933), 172; *Antiques* 25 (Apr. 1934): 129; Henry Ford Museum and Greenfield Village Files, Court Cupboard, 36.178.1; "Connecticut Valley Polychromed Press Cupboard," 129; "The Editor's Attic: Which Hannah Barnard?" *Antiques* 26 (Nov. 1934): 168; "The Editor's Attic: The Vindication of Hannah," *Antiques* 27 (Apr. 1936): 139–40. I can find only three girls in colonial Hadley given a surname for a middle name, none before Hannah Barnard Hastings. Boltwood, "Family Genealogies," 8, 64, 91–92.

48. Marius B. Peladeau, "A Hadley Chest Reconsidered," *Antiques* 119 (1981): 1084–86.

49. Pocumtuck Valley Memorial Association Accession Book, 1:181, ms. PVMA Library, Deerfield, Massachusetts; *1908 Catalogue of Relics in Memorial Hall*, 94, MH 702; George Sheldon, *A Guide to Memorial Hall* (n.p., 1908), 38; Suzanne Flynt to Laurel Ulrich, 10 Mar. 1995; Zea and Flynt, *Hadley Chests*, 22. The entry in Sheldon's account book doesn't mention a chest.

50. Stephen W. Williams, *The Genealogy and History of the Family of Williams* (Greenfield, Mass.: Merriman & Mirick, 1847), 21, 33, 34; *Vital Records of Deerfield, Massachusetts* (Boston: 1920), 1:2, 264; *Vital Records of Roxbury Mass.* (Salem, Mass: The Essex Institute, 1925), 2:437; *Vital Records of Roxbury Mass.* (Salem, Mass.: The Essex Institute,

1926), 2:437; Sheldon, *Deerfield*, 2:66, 67, 279–80; Samuel Barnard Will, Essex County Probate, microfilm: 167–71, Massachusetts State Archives. (Sheldon incorrectly states on page 377 that Sarah, daughter of Samuel Williams, Jr., married John Polly.)

51. Sheldon, "Genealogies," 2:281, 393, 66, 67, 358. Sarah and Thomas Wells both left property to nieces and nephews: Thomas Wells Estate, Hampshire County Probate Records, 7:272–73; Sarah Wells Estate, Hampshire County Probate Files, box 9:25, Hampshire County Probate Court, Northampton, Massachusetts.

52. Zea and Flynt, *Hadley Chests*, 3–4.

53. Registration Records, Colonial Deerfield. In 1777, Madame Silliman occupied pew number one, next to the pulpit, in Deerfield Church. Sheldon, *Deerfield*, 1:479, 2:744, 904, "Genealogies," 2:204–5, 378, 380, 382.

54. Sheldon, "Genealogies," 2:204–5.

55. John Demos, *The Unredeemed Captive* (New York: Knopf, 1994), 231–32 and passim; Flynt, McGowan, and Miller, *Gathered and Preserved*, 16; Sheldon, *Deerfield*, 2:377–81.

56. Weiner, *Inalienable Possessions*, 67.

57. Judd, *History of Hadley*, part 2, 8; Samuel Barnard Estate Papers, box 10:9, Hampshire County Probate Court, Northampton, Massachusetts; Waitstill Hasting Estate Papers, box 68:51, Hampshire County Probate Court, Northampton, Massachusetts.

58. Hampshire County Probate Records, 5:37.

59. Sheldon, "Genealogies," 2:67; Hampshire County Probate Records, 3:249; the sheets and towel "markt E P" in the estate of a man named Joseph Post, like the "H rug" listed in the inventory of Ephraim Colton, hint at similar strategies. Hampshire County Probate Records 8:73; Norwich District Probate Records, book 1, microfilm, Connecticut State Library, Hartford.

60. Litchfield, 3 Dec. 1772; Middlesex County Probate Records, 24:233, microfilm 0521778, Family History Library, Salt Lake City; Hampshire County Probate Records, 8:73; Robert Stone, *Connecticut Blankets, Coverlids, and Bed Rugs* (Lee's Summit, Mo.: The Fat Little Pudding Boys Press, 1999), 17, 20, 38. Lieutenant John Smith of Hadley owned six pairs of sheets "as pr marks," Hampshire County Probate Records, 7:286, Dec. 1750.

61. Edwards Family Papers, Beinecke Rare Book and Manuscript Library, Yale University, New Haven, Conn.

62. Connecticut Historical Society, 1840.7.1, 1840.7.2, gift of Miss Hannah Whittlesey, Middletown. Whittlesey was the granddaughter of Hannah Edwards Wetmore.

63. Hannah Edwards Wetmore Diary, 1713–1773, Edwards Family Papers.

## Chapter 4: A Chimneypiece

1. Lydia B. (Phinney) Brownson and Maclean W. McLean, "The Rev. Richard Bourne of Sandwich, Mass.," *New England Historical and Genealogical Record* 118 (1964): 85, 86, 203, 204, 211; Russell M. Peters, *The Wampanoags of Mashpee* (Mashpee, Mass.: Indian Spiritual and Cultural Training Council, 1987), 16; Frederick Freeman, *The History of Cape Cod* (Boston: Piper, 1969), 677–80; Donald B. Trayner, *Barnstable: Three Centuries of a Cape Cod Town* (Hyannis, Mass.: F. B. & F. P. Goss, 1939), 390, 443; Daniel R. Mandell, *Behind the Frontier: Indians in Eighteenth-Century Eastern Massachusetts* (Lincoln and London: Univ. of Nebraska Press, 1996), 18–19; John J. Waters, Jr., *The Otis Family in Provincial and Revolutionary Massachusetts* (Chapel Hill: Univ. of North Carolina Press, 1968), 36, 38.

2. *Boston Gazette,* 27 Nov. and 12 June 1753; Lawrence A. Cremin, *American Education: The Colonial Experience, 1607–1783* (New York: Harper & Row, 1970), 400–1; Paul Staiti, "Accounting for Copley," in *John Singleton Copley in America,* ed. Carrie Rebora, Paul Staiti, et al. (New York: Metropolitan Museum of Art, 1995), 26–29; Betty Ring, *Girlhood Embroidery: American Samplers and Pictorial Needlework, 1650–1850* (New York: Knopf, 1993), 55.

3. William D. Pierson, *Black Yankees: The Development of an Afro-American Subculture in Eighteenth-Century New England* (Amherst: Univ. of Massachusetts Press, 1988), 6, 10–11, 15, 20; *Boston Gazette,* 1 and 8 May and 20 Nov. 1753, 1 Jan. 1754. The smallpox epidemic of 1752 took more than a thousand people; African servants, who contributed only 8 percent of the city's population, accounted for 16 percent of the deaths.

4. Brownson and McLean, "Richard Bourne," 118:282–83, 119 (1965): 32–35; Bourne Papers, Houghton Library, Harvard University, Cambridge, Massachusetts, 1:29, 72; 5:9; Silvenus Bourn, Promissory Notes, 1743–1748; Sloop *Plymouth,* Voyages to West Indies, 1764, Kingston, Jamaica, 1748; Ship *Two Friends Three Voyages:* 1749–1750, 1753–1759, 1766–1773, Bourne Papers, 3 and 4, Baker Library, Harvard Business School, Cambridge, Massachusetts.

5. Jules David Prown, *John Singleton Copley,* vol. 1 (Cambridge, Mass.: Harvard Univ. Press, 1966), cat. 179; *Copley,* ed. Rebora and Staiti, et al., 222–23, 307; Bourne Papers, Houghton Library, 1:128, 146; Elaine Forman Crane, *Ebb Tide in New England: Women, Seaports, and Social Change, 1630–1800* (Boston: Northeastern Univ. Press, 1998), 130–38.

6. Barnstable County Probate Records, Barnstable County Registry of Probate, Barnstable, Massachusetts, 9:41, 8:510, 9:28.

7. Samuel A. Otis to Joseph Otis, 12 June 1767, Gay-Otis Papers, Butler Library, Columbia University, New York; Sylvanus Bourn to Joseph Otis, 11 Apr. 1763, Otis Papers, Massachusetts Historical Society; Waters, *Otis Family,* 125 n. 61, 126, 128.

8. C. F. Swift, *Genealogical Notes of Barnstable Families* (Barnstable, Mass.: Goss, 1888), 116–21; Thomas Amory Lee, "The Gallisons of Marblehead," *Essex Institute Historical Collections* 58 (1922): 313–24; Sybil Noyes, Charles Thornton Libby, and Walter Goodwin Davis, *A Genealogical Dictionary of Maine and New Hampshire* (Portland, Maine: Southworth-Anthoensen Press, 1928).

9. *Boston Evening Post,* 15 and 29 Jan., 5 and 12 Feb., 26 Mar., and 31 Dec. 1753; Ring, *Girlhood Embroidery,* 1:54–57, and inside front cover; Susan Burrows Swan, *Plain and Fancy: American Women and Their Needlework, 1700–1850* (New York: Rutledge, 1977), 132–35.

10. Ring, *Girlhood Embroidery,* 1:38–49; *Boston Gazette,* 17 and 24 May, 25 and 31 June, and 6 and 13 Sept. 1736; *Boston Evening Post,* 17 and 29 Mar. 1742, 1 and 8 Feb. 1748, 9 Apr. 1753, and 24 May 1756.

11. Ring, *Girlhood Embroidery,* 52–53, 55–57; receipt from Elizabeth Murray to Jonathan Trumbull, John Trumbull Sr. Papers, box 6, Connecticut Historical Society, Hartford, Connecticut.

12. *The Journal of Esther Edwards Burr, 1754–1757,* ed. Carol F. Karlsen and Laurie Crumpacker (New Haven and London: Yale Univ. Press, 1984), 257.

13. *Journal of Burr,* ed. Karlsen and Crumpacker, 182, 73, 274; Susan Burrows Swan, *A Winterthur Guide to American Needlework* (New York: Crown, 1976), 45.

14. See, e.g., Sarah Taylor sampler, 1756, in Glee Krueger, *A Gallery of American Samplers* (New York: Museum of Folk Art, 1978), 25.

15. Ring, *Girlhood Embroidery,* 1:56; *The Autobiography of Colonel John Trumbull,* ed. Theodore Sizer (New Haven: Yale Univ. Press, 1953), 5.

16. Ann Brandwein, "An Eighteenth-Century Depression: The Sad Conclusion of Faith Trumbull Huntington," *Connecticut History* 26 (1985): 19–32.

17. Pamela Parmal to Michelle Jarrett, 14 July 1999; Howard Finney, Sr., *Finney-Phinney Families in America* (n.p., 1957), 53, 61, 100, 113. Cordelia was descended on one side from Melatiah Bourne, Eunice's brother.

18. I. Emery, *The Primary Structures of Fabrics, An Illustrated Classification* (Washington, D.C.: The Textile Museum, 1966), 246; Swan, *Plain and Fancy*, 228, 234. I would like to thank Elizabeth Creeden of Plymouth, Lauren Whitley of the Textile Department, Boston Museum of Fine Arts, and Michelle Jarrett for help with this analysis.

19. Helen Bowen, "The Fishing Lady and Boston Common," *Antiques* 4 (1923): 70–73; Nancy Graves Cabot, "The Fishing Lady and Boston Common," and "Engravings as Pattern Sources," *Antiques* 40 (1941): 28–31, 367–68. Ring, *Girlhood Embroidery*, 1:40, 42; Clifford K. Shipton, *Sibley's Harvard Graduates: Biographical Sketches of Those Who Attended Harvard College* (Boston: Massachusetts Historical Society, 1937, 1951), 5:163–65, 8:20–30.

20. *Sources of Design for Textiles and Decorative Arts* (Boston: Museum of Fine Arts, 1973), 33–35, figures 26, 27, 28; Swan, *A Winterthur Guide*, 34, plate 3, 40, figure 15; Ring, *Girlhood Embroidery*, 1:46, figure 43; Cabot, "Engravings," 40:367, figure 2.

21. Andrew McRae, *God Speed the Plough: The Representation of Agrarian England, 1500–1660* (Cambridge: Cambridge Univ. Press, 1996), 271, 273–74; Rebora and Staiti, *Copley*, 176–78. Also see Raymond Williams, *The Country and the City* (New York: Oxford Univ. Press, 1973); Louis Adrian Montrose, "Of Gentlemen and Shepherds: The Politics of Elizabethan Pastoral Form," *English Literary History* 50 (1983): 416; Don Wayne, *Penshurts: The Semiotics of Place and the Poetics of History* (London, 1984), 263. The literature on English pastoral is complex and contradictory. Obviously a genre that has survived for so many centuries takes many manifestations. Useful studies include James Turner, *The Politics of Landscape: Rural Scenery and Society in English Poetry 1630–1660* (Oxford, U.K.: B. Blackwell, 1979); Andrew V. Ettin, *Literature and the Pastoral* (New Haven and London: Yale Univ. Press, 1984); E. Kegel-Brinkgreve, *The Echoing Woods: Bucolic and Pastoral from Theocritus to Wordsworth* (Amsterdam: Gieben, 1990); and Roger Sales, *English Literature in History: 1780–1830 Pastoral and Politics* (New Haven and London: Yale Univ. Press, 1984).

22. From *The Poems of James VI of Scotland*, ed. James Craigie, 2 vols. (Edinburgh and London, 1955–1958), 2:180, 181, quoted in McCrae, *God Speed the Plough*, 281–82.

23. Kegel-Brinkgreve, *Echoing Woods*, 578.

24. Quoted in Ettin, *Literature and the Pastoral*, 6.

25. Kegel-Brinkgreve, *Echoing Woods*, 42.

26. Ring, *Girlhood Embroidery*, 1:268; Prown, *Copley*, 1:222, 231, figures 20, 38; Charles Coleman Sellers, "Mezzotint Protoypes of Colonial Portraiture," *Art Quarterly* 20 (winter 1957): 429–31; catalog entry 7, in *Copley*, 176.

27. Swan, *Plain and Fancy*, title page, 22; Anita Schorsch, *Pastoral Dreams* (New York: Main Street Press, 1977), 71; Phebe Hobart, needlepoint picture, Museum of Fine Arts, Boston, 50.3787; Hope Hanley, *Needlepoint in America* (New York: Charles Scribner's Sons, 1969), 58.

28. Eric Kerridge, *Textile Manufactures in Early Modern England* (Manchester, U.K.: Manchester Univ. Press, 1985), 154; Rachel Brown, *The Weaving, Spinning, and Dyeing Book*, 2d ed. (New York: Knopf, 1997), 225–28.

29. Ring, *Girlhood Embroidery*, 1:44–45; Swan, *Plain and Fancy*, 24.

30. Rosemarie Zagarri, *A Woman's Dilemma: Mercy Otis Warren and the American Revolution* (Wheeling, Ill., 1995), 45.

31. Ring, *Girlhood Embroidery*, 1:49, figure 47.

32. *Boston Evening Post*, 13 Aug. 1753; *Boston Gazette*, 14 Aug. 1753; M. A. DeWolfe Howe, *Boston Common: Scenes from Four Centuries* (Cambridge, Mass.: Riverside, 1910), 22–32.

33. Gary Nash, "The Failure of Female Factory Labor in Colonial Boston," *Labor History* 20 (1979): 165–88. Waters, *Otis Family*, 85–88, 94–95.

34. Bourne Papers, Houghton, 1:17.

35. *Report of the Record Commissioners of the City of Boston, Containing the Boston Town Records, 1742 to 1757* (Boston: Rockwell and Churchill, 1885), 238–40.

36. *A Letter from Sir Richard Cox* (Boston, 1750); Thomas M. Truxes, *Irish-American Trade, 1660–1783* (Cambridge: Cambridge Univ. Press, 1988), 175–78; W. H. Crawford, *The Handloom Weavers and the Ulster Linen Industry* (Belfast: Ulster Historical Foundation, 1994), 1–18.

37. *Boston Evening Post*, 18 June 1750; R. H. Nichols and F. A. Wray, *The History of the Foundling Hospital* (London: Oxford Univ. Press, 1935), 130–31, 138–40, and illustration facing page 278. Another print of this engraving can be found at Yale Center for British Art, Paul Mellon Collection, B1975.4.1259.

38. Nash, "Factory Labor," 180, 187, 188, 183–84.

39. Ibid., 181–83; *Boston Evening Post*, 26 Feb. 1753.

40. Ring, *Girlhood Embroidery*, 1:54–55; Mary Beth Norton, "A Cherished Spirit of Independence: The Life of an Eighteenth-Century Boston Businesswoman," in *Women of America: A History*, ed. Carol Berkin and Mary Beth Norton (Boston: Houghton Mifflin, 1979), 48–65.

41. *Mary Arthur v. George Arthur*, Suffolk Files, 129733, Massachusetts State Archives, Boston.

42. *Boston Gazette*, 20 Nov. 1753.

43. Bourne Family Papers, 5:165, Houghton.

44. "The present State of the Linen Manufacture in Boston represented, and its Support recommended." In "A Letter to a Friend," *Boston Evening Post*, 26 Feb. 1753.

45. Ibid., 19 Feb. 1753.

46. Ezekiel Price Papers, 361, Massachusetts Historical Society, Boston: "A good Workman may make 12 or 16 yds a day of ¾ wide or 10 or 12 of ⅞ or 8 or 10 yd wd."

47. The amount 52,662 yards in ten years amounts to 5,266 yards per year. At an average of 10 yards per day that is 526 days weaving. Only in a few peak years could the factory have employed many spinners. The ratio of company production to private production led Gary Nash to conclude that poor women withdrew their labor from the factory. Poor women may have disdained factory labor, but there is nothing in the sources to suggest that work for private persons in any way undermined the activities of the factory. In its first advertisement, the company solicited private business.

48. Price Papers, 318, 359; *A Report of the Record Commissioners of the City of Boston, Containing the Boston Town Records, 1758 to 1769* (Boston: Rockwell and Churchill, 1886), 231.

49. Ibid., 227.

50. Ibid., 236. A draft of the committee's proposal in Ezekiel Goldthwait's handwriting is in Price Papers, 301.

51. Samuel Cooper, *A Sermon Preached in Boston, New-England, before the Society for Encouraging Industry and Employing the Poor: August 8, 1753* (Boston, 1753), 7, 27–28.

52. Cooper, *Sermon*, 29, 32.

53. Massachusetts Archives, 32:683.

54. Mandell, *Behind the Frontier*, 108; *Extracts from the Itineraries and other Miscellanies of Ezra Stiles*, ed. Franklin Bowditch Dexter (New Haven: Yale Univ. Press, 1916),

159–60; Frederick Freeman, *History of Barnstable County: Annals of the Thirteen Towns of Cape Cod,* vol. 1 (Boston: Piper, 1869), quoting Hawley, 684–85.

55. Jack Campisi, *The Mashpee Indians: Tribe on Trial* (Syracuse, N.Y.: Syracuse Univ. Press, 1991), 80–81; Mandell, *Behind the Frontier,* 108–9, 127.

56. Jean F. Hankins, "Solomon Briant and Joseph Johnson: Indian Teachers and Preachers in Colonial New England," *Connecticut History* 33 (Nov. 1992): 40, 43, 45, 47, 48, 51.

57. Provincial Records, Massachusetts State Archives, Boston, 32:424–26, Mandell, *Behind the Frontier,* 156–58; Campisi, *Mashpee Indians,* 83.

58. Ibid., 83–84; Mandell, *Behind the Frontier,* 156.

59. Provincial Records, Massachusetts Archive, 32:447–51.

60. Ibid., 32:314, 33:34; Mandell, *Behind the Frontier,* 148, 157. There has not yet been a detailed study of guardianship records in the Massachusetts Archives. These would yield not only a great deal of information about the management of Indian affairs, but information of value to genealogists and social historians as well.

61. Quoted in Hankins, "Briant and Johnson," 49; Waters, *Otis Family,* 98–99.

62. Freeman, *History of Barnstable County,* 688; *Extracts from Stiles,* 16; Stiles's "Plan of Mashpee, and Indian Town" shows dispersed settlement around streams, ponds, and bays in 1762. Compare Jean M. O'Brien, "Divorced from the Land: Resistance and Survival of Indian Women in Eighteenth-Century New England," in *After King Philip's War: Presence and Persistence in Indian New England,* ed. Colin G. Calloway (Hanover, N.H., and London: Univ. Press of New England, 1997), 148–51.

63. *Extract from Stiles,* 500.

64. Provincial Records, Massachusetts Archives, 33:147–48.

65. Ibid., 33:146–47.

66. Ibid., 33:145; Mandell, *Behind the Frontier,* 157–58; Campisi, *Mashpee Indians,* 85.

67. Howe, *Boston Common,* 33–34.

68. Lee, "Gallisons of Marblehead," 313–24, and "Lee Family of Marblehead," *Essex Institute Historical Collections* 52 (1916): 154.

## Chapter 5: *Willie-Nillie, Niddy-Noddy*

1. Peter Benes, *Old-Town and the Waterside* (Newburyport, Mass.: Newburyport Historical Society, 1986), 61; relevant entries in the *Oxford English Dictionary.*

2. Joan Whittaker Cummer, *A Book of Spinning Wheels* (Portsmouth, N.H.: Peter Randall, 1993), 303.

3. *Catalog of the Collection of Relics in Memorial Hall* (Deerfield, Mass.: Pocumtuck Valley Memorial Association, 1920), 73, 75; Benes, *Old-Town,* 61, 143. For illustrations of British and continental cross reels see Wayne E. Franits, *Paragons of Virtue: Women and Domesticity in Seventeenth-Century Dutch Art* (Cambridge: Cambridge Univ. Press, 1993), 186, 187, 188; Alan Raistrick, "Extracts from the Academy of Armory by Randle Holme of Chester, 1688," *Spinning Wheel Sleuth* 21 (July 1998): 12–13; Edward H. Pinto, *Treen; or, Small Woodware throughout the Ages* (London: Batsford, 1949), 318; Patricia Baines, *Linen: Handspinning and Weaving* (London: Batsford Ltd., 1989), 67.

4. In the early twentieth century Polly's great-granddaughter, Alice Hale Knight, attached a handwritten label to the willie-nillie, claiming that the original owner was "Polley Woodwell mother / of Mary Woodwell who / married Enoch Hale." Since the vital records of Newbury and the published Woodwell genealogy list Mary's mother as "Hannah," and since Polly was a common nickname for Mary, the two inscriptions probably refer to the same person. The vital records give the marriage date as 1781

rather than 1783. William W. Woodwell, *Matthew Woodwell, of Salem, Mass., and His Descendants* (Salem, Mass.: The Essex Institute, 1910), 4–5, 9–10; *Vital Records of Newburyport, Massachusetts* (Salem, Mass.: The Essex Institute, 1911), 214.

5. *Providence Gazette,* 12 Mar. 1766. *Boston Evening Post* 21 Mar. 1768 (hereafter cited as *BEP*). *Essex Gazette,* 23–30 May 1769 (hereafter cited as *EG*), reprinting material from the Boston papers for 30 March. On Ephraim Bowen's political activities see William R. Staples, *Annals of the Town of Providence* (Providence, 1843), 201–26.

6. *EG,* 23–30 May 1769.

7. John J. Currier, *History of Newburyport, Mass., 1764–1905* (Newburyport, Mass.: by the author, 1906), 1:46, 48. *Boston Gazette,* 16 Oct. 1769 (hereafter cited as *BG*); Linda Kerber, *Women of the Republic: Intellect and Ideology in Revolutionary America* (Chapel Hill: Univ. of North Carolina Press, 1980), 39, 41; Mary Beth Norton, *Liberty's Daughters: The Revolutionary Experience of American Women, 1750–1800* (Boston: Little, Brown, 1980); Laurel Thatcher Ulrich, " 'Daughters of Liberty': Religious Women in Revolutionary New England," in *Women in the Age of the American Revolution,* ed. Ronald Hoffman and Peter J. Albert (Charlottesville: Univ. Press of Virginia, 1989), 211–28; Alfred Young, "The Women of Boston: 'Persons of Consequence' in the Making of the American Revolution, 1765–76," in *Women and Politics in the Age of the Democratic Revolution,* ed. Harriet B. Applewhite and Darline G. Levy (Ann Arbor: Univ. of Michigan Press, 1990).

8. *Newport Mercury,* June 1770 and 22 May 1769 (hereafter cited as *NM*); *BG,* 25 Dec. and 17 Apr. 1769.

9. *BEP,* 8 August 1768, 17 July 1769; *BG,* 13 March 1769.

10. *EG,* 7–14 Feb. 1769; *NM,* 6 Feb. 1769.

11. *EG,* 23–30 May 1769.

12. *NM,* 13 Feb. 1769, 17 Apr. 1769.

13. Some spinners were even younger. At Captain Goddard's house, near the liberty pole in Newport, eight "Eight little Misses, all under Twelve Years of Age" met to spin. *BG,* 16 Oct. 1769; *NM,* 1 May 1769.

14. Ibid., 8 May 1769.

15. Ibid., 15 May 1769.

16. *Peter Oliver's Origins and Progress of the American Rebellion,* ed. Douglass Adair and John A. Schutz (San Marino, Calif.: Huntington Library, 1961), 63–64, quoted in Young, "Women of Boston," 208–9.

17. *BG,* 9 May 1768; Mrs. E. Vale Smith, *History of Newburyport* (Newburyport, Mass.: n. p., 1854), 48–49; Joshua Coffin, *A Sketch of the History of Newbury, Newburyport, and West Newbury* (Boston: Samuel G. Drake, 1845), 234–35; Franklin Bowditch Dexter, *Biographical Sketches of the Graduates of Yale College* (New York: Henry Holt, 1885), 389–93; *Vital Records of Newburyport, Massachusetts,* 214; Estate of Captain Gideon Woodwell, 27 Jan. 1794, Essex County Probate Records, 363:154, microfilm, Massachusetts State Archives, Boston.

18. Smith, *History of Newburyport,* 61; Benes, *Old-Town and the Waterside,* 107, 149; Clifford K. Shipton, *Biographical Sketches of Those Who Attended Harvard College,* vol. 6 (Boston: Massachusetts Historical Society, 1942), 496–502, and vol. 15 (Boston: Massachusetts Historical Society, 1970), 29–33.

19. Three were in ministers' houses (4 Sept. 1769 in Providence, 16 Oct. 1769 in Bewick, and 27 Nov. 1769 in Pomfret) and three in other private homes (1 May 1769 in Newport and 2 May 1769 in Jamestown, in addition to the 1766 match in Providence discussed above).

20. *BEP,* 10 Oct. 1768; *EG,* 6 June 1769; *BEP,* 6 Nov. 1769; Franklin Bowditch Dexter, ed., *The Literary Diary of Ezra Stiles* (New York: Charles Scribner's Sons, 1901), 8–9.

21. *New Hampshire Gazette*, 16 Oct. 1769 (hereafter cited as *NHG*); *BEP*, 9 June 1769; *BG*, 16 Oct. 1769. The description was apparently too rustic for the *BG*, which left the carrot but added that "The young Gentlemen the Sons of Liberty, waited upon the young Ladies and treated them with Cake and other Necessaries."

22. Exodus 35:25; Proverbs 6:6–8; Acts 9:39; Romans 12:11. Another sermon used Proverbs 14:2: "Every wise woman buildeth her house."

23. Dexter, ed., *Diary of Stiles*, 8–9; the account for the next year similarly disdains competition: *NM*, 1 May 1769, 4 June 1770.

24. Richard Shiels, "Feminization of Congregationalism," *American Quarterly* 33 (1981): 46–62. Dexter, ed., *Diary of Stiles*, 563–65.

25. Christopher M. Jedrey, *The World of John Cleaveland* (New York: Norton, 1979), 105; Clifford K. Shipton, *Sibley's Harvard Graduates: Biographical Sketches of Those Who Attended Harvard College* (Boston: Massachusetts Historical Society, 1965), 13:178–86; *EG*, 11 July 1769; George Augustus Wheeler and Henry Warren Wheeler, *History of Brunswick, Topsham, and Harpswell, Maine* (1878; repr. Somersworth, N.H.: New Hampshire Publishing, 1974), 736. Samuel Chandler's wife may have been mentally ill (Shipton, *Sibley's Harvard Graduates*, 9:488).

26. John Cleaveland, *A Short and Plain Narrative of the Late Work of God's Spirit* (Boston, 1767), 4–16.

27. *BEP*, 11 Sept. 1769.

28. *NHG*, 25 Aug. 1769.

29. Ibid., 18 Aug. 1769.

30. *EG*, 10–17 Oct. 1769.

31. Edmund S. Morgan, *The Gentle Puritan: A Life of Ezra Stiles, 1727–1795* (New Haven: Yale Univ. Press, 1962), 231–33.

32. Amos Adams, *A Concise Historical View* (Boston, 1769), 48–50.

33. *NM*, 29 May 1769.

34. Belknap's mother was a granddaughter of Increase Mather; his uncle Mather Byles, a pastor and poet, was his lifelong mentor. [Jane Belknap Marcou], *Life of Jeremy Belknap* (New York: Harper and Brothers, 1847), 9–32; Shipton, *Biographical Sketches*, 15:175–78.

35. *Life of Jeremy Belknap*, 36.

36. By 1771, the brief revival at Dover had slowed to a stop. "I fear there is but little religion here," he wrote a friend. "People's attention turns more to the externals than the vital part." It took until 1786 to add another twenty-one members—seventeen women and four men. "Members of First Church, 1718–1850," *Collections of the Dover, N.H., Historical Society*, vol. 1 (Dover: Scales & Quimby, 1894), 210–12; George Benson Kirsch, *Jeremy Belknap: A Biography* (Ann Arbor, Mich.: University Microfilms, 1974), 30.

37. Jeremy Belknap Papers, MS, Massachusetts Historical Society, Boston.

38. Benes, *Old-Town*, 61; Cummer, *A Book of Spinning Wheels*, 303.

39. The second-highest entry was for 109 knots. The "Nots" column adds up to 1,695, which divided by 7 equals 242. The numbers on the right were produced by dividing individual totals by 7 and rounding them off. The totals of the two columns are close—only a difference of one skein despite the rounding error.

40. *BEP*, 11 Sept. 1769; *NHG*, 18 Aug. 1769.

41. Lara Friedenfelds, "The Niddy-Noddy: Education, Measurement, Standardization, and the History of the Mundane," unpublished term paper, Harvard University, 12 May 1997.

42. *Diary of Stiles*, 8–9.

43. *EG*, 2 May 1769, 16 Aug. 1768.

44. *NHG*, 18 Mar. 1768; *New London Gazette*, New London, Connecticut, 2 June 1769; *EG*, 16 Aug. 1768; David J. Jeremy, "British and American Yarn Count Systems: An Historical Analysis," *Business History Review* 45 (1971): 336–67; Friedenfelds measured several dozen reels at the American Museum of Textile History.

45. Jeremy, "Yarn Count Systems"; *EG*, 17 Apr. 1769; *BEP*, 23 June 1769.

46. Jeremy, "Yarn Count Systems." Randle Holme in *Academy of Armory, 1688* (Menston, U.K.: Scholar, 1972), 3:288, says that a hundred revolutions around a reel made a knot, halch, or hank that was tied up with a "Lay Band, (to keep it from ravalling or running into Snigsnarles)."

47. *EG*, 7 Feb. 1769, 2 May 1769; *BG*, 22 May 1769, 7 Aug. 1769, 16 Oct. 1769; *NM*, 17 Apr. 1769, 1 May 1769.

48. *EG*, 17 Apr. 1769; *BEP*, 23 June 1769, 2 Nov. 1769, 29 May 1769; *NM*, 8 May 1769; *BG*, 15 Nov. 1768; *BEP*, 12 June 1769, 30 Oct. 1769.

49. Strafford Probate Records, Strafford County Court House (hereafter SCPR), Dover, New Hampshire, 1:36–39. Based on John Gage inventory; see discussion below.

50. The Watson girls were granddaughters of Christine Otis, the celebrated Dover captive who returned from Canada in 1714 to marry Captain Thomas Baker. Although she tried, she was never able to retrieve the children by her first husband that she left behind in Canada. Christine Baker was still alive in 1769, but at the age of eighty-one she may have been too feeble to spin. SCPR, 21:419–20; John Scales, *Colonial Era History of Dover, New Hampshire* (Dover, N.H.: 1923), 226–32, 354; Laurel Thatcher Ulrich, *Good Wives: Image and Reality in Northern New England, 1650–1750* (New York: Knopf, 1982), 213–14.

51. SCPR, 1:36–39; Scales, 398; *NHG*, 2 and 9 July 1773.

52. Ibid., 9 July 1773.

53. SCPR, 12:76–84.

54. Woodwell, *Matthew Woodwell, of Salem, Mass.*, 4–5.

55. The Samuel Lane Papers are at the New Hampshire Historical Society. My computations are based on extracts from these papers kindly provided by Jerald Brown. For more on Lane and his family, see Jerald E. Brown, *The Years of the Life of Samuel Lane, 1718–1806* (Hanover, N.H. and London: Univ. Press of New England, 2000).

56. Also see Jane C. Nylander, *Our Own Snug Fireside: Images of the New England Home, 1760–1860* (New York: Knopf, 1993), 61–62, and "Provision for the Daughters: The Accounts of Samuel Lane," in *House and Home*, ed. Peter Benes (Dublin Seminar for New England Folklife, Annual Proceedings, 1988), 11–27. Brown, *Years of the Life of Samuel Lane*, 114–23.

57. Florence M. Montgomery, *Textiles in America 1650–1870* (New York: Norton, 1984), 199, 360.

58. New Hampshire's currency had stabilized by the time the Widow Jenness began working for Lane in 1766. Over two decades, she wove a variety of linens from "Bengall" (probably an imitation of a striped fabric imported from India) to bed ticking for the base price of six shillings per yard old tenor. Blankets, woolens, and a thick cloth called "bearskin" yielded from 50 to 75 percent more; Montgomery, *Textiles in America*, 160, 163.

59. Both the worst- and the best-paid weavers were male. In 1744, Morris Fling produced fourteen yards of cloth for Lane. Though he still called himself a weaver in a deed he gave Lane in 1756, he did no more work for the Lane family.

60. *The Diary of Matthew Patten of Bedford, N.H.* (1903; repr., Camden, Maine: Picton Press, 1993), 6, 7, 9, 19, 42, 54, 55, 86, 87, 101, 102, 133, 150, 434.

61. Ibid., 219, 244, 266, 274, 351, 384, 385. For other references to Patten's construction and maintenance of the loom, see 212, 213, 227, 228, 234.

62. Gloria L. Main, "Gender, Work, and Wages in Colonial New England," *William & Mary Quarterly*, 3d ser., 51 (1994): 62–63, 65.

63. Daniel Vickers, *Farmers and Fishermen: Two Centuries of Work in Essex County, Massachusetts, 1630–1830* (Chapel Hill and London: Univ. of North Carolina Press, 1994), 247–59; Main, "Gender and Wages," 62–63, 65; James Garvin, "That Little World, Portsmouth" in *Portsmouth Furniture: Masterworks from the New Hampshire Seacoast*, ed. Brock Jobe (Boston: Society for the Preservation of New England Antiquities, 1993), 15–21; Brock Jobe, "Furniture Making in Eighteenth-Century Portsmouth," in *Portsmouth Furniture*, 43, 46–49, 55, 285–91. Other studies that emphasize economic diversification include Jedrey, *John Cleaveland;* Edward S. Cooke, Jr., "The Social Economy of the Preindustrial Joiner in Western Connecticut, 1750–1800," in *American Furniture 1995*, ed. Luke Beckerdite and William N. Hosley (Hanover, N.H., and London: Chipstone Foundation and Univ. Press of New England, 1995); and in greater detail in Edward S. Cooke, Jr., "Social Economy in Pre-industrial America: The Furnituremakers of Newtown and Woodbury, Connecticut, 1760–1820" (Baltimore: Johns Hopkins Univ. Press), esp. 95–112.

64. Russell R. Menard and John J. McCusker, *The Economy of British America, 1607–1789* (Chapel Hill: Univ. of North Carolina Press, 1985), 96–97, 279–86, 296; James F. Shepherd and Gary M. Walton, *Shipping, Maritime Trade, and the Economic Development of Colonial North America* (Cambridge: Cambridge Univ. Press, 1972), 106.

65. *Massachusetts Soldiers and Sailors of the Revolutionary War* (Boston: State Printers, 1908), 6:909; Jacob Silvester Family Group Record and Deborah Silvester Individual Record, International Genealogical Index, Family History Library, Salt Lake City, available on FamilySearch.com.

66. Account Books of Abigail and John Fearing, Spaulding-Fearing Papers, 1747–1929, Massachusetts Historical Society, Boston, Massachusetts; Hannah Matthews Book, 1790–1813, Henry Francis DuPont Winterthur Museum and Library, Winterthur, Deleware.

67. Field Horne, ed., *The Diary of Mary Cooper: Life on a Long Island Farm, 1768–1773* (New York: Oyster Bay Historical Society, 1981), 13, 55.

68. Ibid., viii–ix.

69. Ibid., 3, 54, 65.

70. *EG*, 2 May 1769; *Diary of Mary Cooper*, 7, 8, 10, 20, 23.

71. Ibid., viii, 12, 26, 15, 17.

72. Sylvester Judd, *The History of Hadley, Massachusetts* (Springfield, Mass.: Huntting, 1905), 385. "Inventory of Capt. Moses Porter's Estate, July 20th, 1757," photocopy, Porter-Phelps-Huntington Papers, Amherst College Library.

73. Judd, *History of Hadley*, 423; Gen. 24, 91, 92.

74. "The Diary of Elizabeth (Porter) Phelps," *New England Historical and Genealogical Register* 118 (1964): 14, 12, 15.

75. Massachusetts Supreme Judiciary Court, Case Papers #15747, microfilm, Massachusetts State Archives; "Diary of Phelps," 17, 27, 29, 113, 222; Nylander, *Our Own Snug Fireside*, 90.

76. Joseph Barnard (1777–1785) Account Book, Pocumtuck Valley Memorial Association, microfilm 5302, 30 June and 8 Dec. 1762.

77. "Diary of Phelps," 22, 19, 27.

78. Ibid., 23.

79. Ibid., 13, 25, 111, 121; Judd, *History of Hadley;* Gen. 56. In February 1769, "one Mary Catling made a publick confession of her breach of the seventh commandment." On 26 July 1772, "Nicolas Bartlet and his wife made a publick confession of the sin of fornication—their child born the fore part of June."

80. "Diary of Phelps," 15, 19, 23, 26, 110, 123, 125, 218, 222, 225, 232, 305.

81. Ibid., 18, 23, 24, 27.

82. Ibid., 18, 113, 115, 117.

83. Jonathan Ashley, Sermon no. 1800, 23 Jan. 1749, MS, Union Theological Seminary Library, New York, quoted in David R. Proper, "Lucy Terry Prince: 'Singer of History,'" *Contributions in Black Studies* 9 (1990–1992): 194–95; "Diary of Phelps," 19, 113, 114, 115.

84. Ibid., 115, 119, 120, 223, 225.

85. Ibid., 120, 223, 225, 226, 228.

86. *EG,* 16–23 Aug. 1768.

## Chapter 6: A Bed Rug and a Silk Embroidery

1. Nathaniel Goodwin, *The Foote Family* (Hartford, Conn.: Case, Tiffany, 1849), 8, 80. The family genealogy spells the name "Elizabeth Foote," but Betty wrote her own name Elisabeth Foot. J. Herbert Callister and William L. Warren, *Bed Ruggs 1722–1833* (Hartford, Conn.: Wadworth Atheneum, 1972), 8, 9, 19.

2. William Warren Papers, Connecticut Historical Society, Hartford, Connecticut.

3. Gloria L. Main, "Gender, Work, and Wages in Colonial New England," *William and Mary Quarterly,* 3d ser., 51 (1994): 62–63, 65.

4. Cornelia Dayton, *Women Before the Bar* (Chapel Hill: Univ. of North Carolina Press, 1995), 157–230.

5. Elisabeth Foot Diary, Brainard Family Papers, box 16, Connecticut Historical Society, Hartford, Connecticut. This collection includes both the original and a typed transcription. Hereafter cited as EF.

6. EF, 20 and 21 Mar. 1775.

7. Barbara W. Brown, *Flintlocks and Barrels of Beef: Colchester, Connecticut, in the Revolution* (Colchester, Conn.: Bacon Academy, 1976), 1–3.

8. Richard Buel, Jr., *Dear Liberty: Connecticut's Mobilization for the Revolutionary War* (Middletown, Conn.: Wesleyan Univ. Press, 1980), 35; Richard D. Brown, *Knowledge Is Power: The Diffusion of Information in Early America, 1700–1865* (New York: Oxford Univ. Press, 1989), 247–49.

9. This may have been David *Wiles,* whose marker in Colchester Burying Ground says that he died on 20 Mar. 1815, in his sixty-second year. Beside him is his "relict" Elenor, who died 17 Jan. 1827, age seventy-four. Frank E. Randall, "Memoranda of All the Inscriptions in the Old Burying Ground at Colchester, Conn.," *New England Historical and Genealogical Register* 43 (1889): 363. Although Betty kept a watchful eye on Ellen's courtship, this behavior cannot have been unusual. In rural New England courting couples felt free to sleep together, a practice that contributed to the high premarital conception rates in the period. Betty herself may not have engaged in such behavior, but her friend Hannah Otis probably did. On February 17, Betty wrote that she had come home from the Otis house about midnight but that Elisha Wells had "Stay'd with" Hannah Otis. The phrase "stayed with" was probably a euphemism for "slept with."

10. EF, 17 and 20 Apr. 1775; Brown, *Flintlocks and Barrels,* 4–5.

11. The short involvement of Colchester's soldiers was typical; "two-thirds of Connecticut's marchers returned in ten days, driven back before they reached their objective by reports of scant provisions at Boston," Buel, *Dear Liberty*, 36–37.

12. Betty and Nabby noted only one other funeral in 1775, that of old Mrs. Caverly, whom Nabby had sat up with during her illness. Randall, "Memoranda," 358; EF, 11, 12, and 20 Apr., 14 and 21 June, 11 July, 1 Aug., and 27 Oct. 1775; Abigail Foot Diary, Brainard Family Papers, box 16, Connecticut Historical Society, Hartford, Connecticut (here-after cited as AF), 21 June, 8, 12, and 14 July, 1 and 22 Aug., and 4 Sept. 1775; EF, 15 Aug. 1775; AF, 17 Aug. 1775.

13. Ibid., 2 and 7 June, 10 and 11 Oct. 1775; EF, 7 and 8 June, 6 Sept. 1775.

14. Nabby's brief diary for 1776 does, however, note occasional visits to "David Wiles's house." AF, 26 Apr. and 22 May 1776.

15. EF, 23 Oct. 1775.

16. Elisabeth Foot to Mrs. Peggy Smith, Colchester, 5 Apr. 1774, in Brainard Family Papers, box 16.

17. Jerusha might have been Elisabeth's second cousin. Her great aunt, Sarah Foote, married a Thomas Olcott of Hartford, one of whose sons married a woman from East Hartford. Goodwin, *Foote Family*, 51, 56, 76–77, 80–82, 490.

18. EF, 22 and 24 Feb. and 1 Mar. 1775.

19. Elisabeth Foot poem and letter, 1772, Brainard Papers, box 16, Connecticut Historical Society.

20. Laurel Thatcher Ulrich, "Wheels, Looms, and the Gender Division of Labor in Eighteenth-Century New England," *William and Mary Quarterly*, 3d. ser., 55 (1998): 37–38.

21. AF, 5, 6, and 29 June, 9, 12, and 17 July 1775; EF, 23 July, 1 and 22 Oct. 1775.

22. AF, 25 and 17 July 1775.

23. EF, 3 July 1775.

24. EF and AF. In the early nineteenth century, some single women had begun to open their own store accounts, but most work was still listed under the name of the (usually male) head of household. See Thomas Dublin, *Transforming Women's Work: New England Lives in the Industrial Revolution* (Ithaca, N.Y., and London: Cornell Univ. Press, 1994), 41–43.

25. Main, "Gender, Work, and Wages."

26. EF, 26 Apr. 1775.

27. [Lydia Huntley Sigourney], *Sketch of Connecticut, Forty Years Since* (Hartford, Conn.: Cooke, 1824), 110; Marion Day Iverson, "The Bed Rug in Colonial America," *Antiques* 85 (1965): 107–9; Callister and Warren, *Bed Ruggs*, 10–19; Eric Kerridge, *Textile Manufactures in Early Modern England* (Manchester, U.K.: Manchester Univ. Press, 1985), 41.

28. Callister and Warren, *Bed Ruggs*, catalog numbers 4, 8, 9, 14, 19, 20, 22, 23, 26, 27, 33, 34. Number 25 might also be related.

29. H.F.K., *Antiques* 22 (Dec. 1932): 229.

30. Rita Buchanan, *A Weaver's Garden* (Loveland, Colo.: Interweave, 1987), 97, 99, 102, 104, 108, 119.

31. Lynne Z. Bassett and Jack Larkin, *Northern Comfort: New England's Early Quilts, 1780–1850* (Nashville: Rutledge Hill, 1998), 13–23, see especially plates 4 and 5; Ann P. Rowe, "American Quilted Petticoats," *Proceedings: Irene Emery Roundtable on Museum Textiles* (Washington, D.C.: The Textile Museum, 1975), 161–69, figure 3.

32. Donald Lines Jacobus, *The Bulkeley Genealogy* (New Haven, Conn.: n.p., 1933), 172;

Thomas Hopkins, *The Kelloggs in the Old World and the New* (San Francisco: Sunset Press, 1903), 1:172.

33. Among the eight rugs listed in twenty-six Colchester inventories taken in the 1770s there were two shag rugs, a green rug, a rag rug, and an old rug. The other three did not have descriptions. Colchester District Probate Court, book 4, Colchester, Connecticut.

34. *The Huntington Family in America* (Hartford, Conn.: Huntington Family Association, 1915), 844–46; George T. Chapman, *Sketches of the Alumni of Dartmouth College* (Cambridge, Mass.: Riverside, 1867), 15.

35. James P. Walsh, *Connecticut Industry and the Revolution* (Hartford, Conn.: American Revolution Bicentennial Commission, 1978), 20–25; Buel, *Dear Liberty*, 272–74; Frances Manwaring Caulkins, *History of New London, Connecticut* (New London, Conn., 1852), 545–72.

36. Ebenezer Punderson Account Books, Connecticut Historical Society, Hartford, Connecticut, book 1: 20 Aug. 1772; book 6: 26 Oct. 1774, 8 Nov. 1774.

37. Morey H. Bartow, Punderson Family History, MS, Punderson Papers, Connecticut Historical Society, Hartford, 69684, 11; Franklin Bowditch Dexter, *Biographical Sketches of the Graduates of Yale College*, vol. 1 (New York: Holt, 1885), 336–38.

38. Walter Geer, *The Geer Genealogy* (New York: Brentano's, 1923), 28–29, 48; *New London County Furniture, 1640–1840* (New London, Conn.: Lyman Allyn Museum, 1974), 9; John Wheeler Geer Account Book, MS, Connecticut Historical Society.

39. Chester M. Destler, *Connecticut: The Provisions State* (Chester, Conn.: Pequot, 1973), 11–13.

40. Inventory, Hannah Punderson v. Ebenezer Punderson, Copy, Punderson Papers, and Punderson Accounts, vols. 1–6, MS 69156.

41. Punderson Accounts, book 8: 7 May 1778.

42. Punderson Accounts, book 6: 7 Nov. 1774; book 1: 3 Aug., 9 Sept., 24 Aug. 1772; book 6: 13 Nov. 1774.

43. "Testimonials" and "Mr. Punderson's Narrative," in *The Narrative of Mr. Ebenezer Punderson, Merchant: Who Was Drove away by the Rebels in America from His Family and a Very Considerable Fortune in Norwich, in Connecticut* (London: Hawes, 1776), 5, 8.

44. Punderson Accounts, book 6: 25 Oct.–8 Nov. 1774.

45. Ibid., book 2: 24, 26, and 28 Oct. 1772.

46. I am indebted to Paul Costa-Grant for sharing his notes on African American and Indian customers at Punderson's store. Punderson Accounts, book 1: 24 and 28 Oct. 1771; book 2: 24 Dec. 1772, book 3: 30 May 1773; book 8: 27 July, 9 Aug. 1775; book 5: 12 Oct. 1774; book 3: 19 Mar. 1773; book 4: 3 July 1773; book 5: 23 and 29 Sept., 12 Oct. 1774; Laura J. Murray, ed., *To Do Good to My Indian Brethren: The Writings of Joseph Johnson, 1751–1776* (Amherst: Univ. of Massachusetts Press, 1998), 129, 133, 136, 137, 159.

47. Ibid., 109, 111–12, 115, 122, 126, 128–29, 131, 134, 135, 136, 138; Punderson's account book for early 1772 does not survive.

48. Ibid., 21–23, 168–74.

49. *Connecticut Gazette*, 21 Apr. 1775; *Narrative of Punderson*, 4–5.

50. Ibid., 5–8.

51. Letters of 30 July, 8 and 11 Aug., and 27 Sept. 1775, in *Narrative of Punderson*, 10, 11, 12, 14.

52. Attachment of Ebenezer Punderson Estate, 26 Aug. 1775; Record of the Punderson Family, MS, Punderson Papers; Punderson Accounts, book 8: May 1775–June 1778.

53. Jacobus, *Bulkeley Genealogy*, 173; Brown, *Flintlocks and Barrels*, 34, 62; "Captain Charles Bulkeley's Narrative of Personal Experiences in the War of the American Revolution from His Original Manuscript," *Collections, New London County Historical Society*, 2 (1933): 126–28.

54. "My dear Wife," 12 Feb. 1775[6], *Narrative of Punderson*, 24.

55. Inventory, Punderson Papers; John Wheeler Geer Account Book, Connecticut Historical Society.

56. David Conroy, who is working on a study of New London, points out that fully a third of the slaves in Connecticut in 1774 lived in New London County, and that in the town of New London, African Americans composed 10 percent of the population. Personal letter, 6 Mar. 1999.

57. William Warren, typescript, Connecticut Historical Society, suggests the Mary, Queen of Scots, connection but does not give his source. Since he corresponded with descendants, it may have been a family tradition.

58. Samuel Richardson, *Clarissa*, 3d ed. (London, 1751); *The Clarissa Project* (New York: AMS Press, 1990), 308–14.

59. Punderson Papers, folder 69877.

60. Prudence Punderson Journal, 20 Nov. 1778.

61. Ibid., 26 Jan. 1779.

62. Ibid., 9 May 1779.

63. Ibid., 15 Mar. 1779.

64. Ibid., Prudence Punderson to "Miss Mott," n.d.

65. Ebenezer Punderson to Prudence and Hannah, 13 Aug. 1779, Punderson Papers.

66. *Narrative of Punderson*, 9–10; Prudence Punderson Journal, 18 June 1780, July 1780. Clarina Punderson married Basil Bartow, son of John Bartow, the first regularly installed Anglican rector at Westchester. Robert Bolton, *The History of the Several Towns, Manors and Patents of the County of Westchester* (New York, 1881), 2:321, and genealogical inset between 350 and 351.

67. Prudence Punderson to Hannah Punderson, Journal, 30 Dec. 1780. Richard L. Bushman, *The Refinement of America: Persons, Houses, Cities* (New York: Knopf, 1992), 81–82.

68. Ibid., 14 Jan. 1782 and "Dear Granmma," East Hampton, [1782].

69. Morey Bartow, True Copy of Marriage Certificate, Punderson Papers, folder 2; *First Congregational Church of Preston, Connecticut, 1698–1898* (Published by the Society, 1900), 66–68.

70. Kenneth Walther Cameron, ed., *The Papers of Loyalist Samuel Peters* (Hartford, Conn.: Transcendental Books, 1978), 151.

71. "Letter written by Julia Avery Chamberlin, July 1922, aged 86 years," Punderson Papers, Connecticut Historical Society.

72. Ebenezer Punderson Will, photostat, Punderson Papers, folder 6968; Barbara W. Brown and James M. Rose, *Black Roots in Southeastern Connecticut* (Detroit, Mich.: Gale Research, 1980), 324, 216, 69; Jane Cato Estate, 1824, Probate Records, Connecticut State Library, Hartford.

73. *Huntington Family*, 844–46; Chapman, *Alumni of Dartmouth College*, 15; *Foote Family*, 56–57, 76–77, 80–82.

## *Chapter 7: Molly Ocket's Pocketbook*

1. Accessions Files, Maine Historical Society, Portland, Maine; William B. Lapham, *History of the Town of Bethel, Maine* (Bethel, Maine: Bethel Historical Society, 1981; repr. of 1891 ed.), 144–45.

2. Charles Willoughby, *Antiquities of the New England Indians* (Cambridge, Mass.: Peabody Museum, 1935), 255–56.

3. James W. North, *The History of Augusta* (Augusta, Maine: Clapp and North, 1870; repr., Somersworth, N.H.: New England History Press, 1981), 3–29; Alan Taylor, *Liberty*

*Men and Great Proprietors: The Revolutionary Settlement on the Maine Frontier, 1760–1820* (Chapel Hill and London: Univ. of North Carolina Press, 1990), 11–29; Bunny McBride, *Women of the Dawn* (Lincoln and London: Univ. of Nebraska Press, 1999), 7–10, 45–47; Bruce J. Bourque, "Ethnicity on the Maritime Peninsula, 1600–1759," *Ethnohistory* 36 (1989): 257–83.

4. "Journal of the Rev. John Pike," *Collections of the New Hampshire Historical Society* 3 (Concord, N.H., 1832, repr. 1870); 51, 58, 59, 60.

5. George Hill Evans, *Pigwacket* (Conway: New Hampshire Historical Society, 1939), 57–70; John Stuart Barrows, *Fryeburg, Maine: An Historical Sketch* (Fryeburg: Pequawket, 1938), 13–27; David Jaffee, *People of the Wachusett: Greater New England in History and Memory, 1630–1860* (Ithaca, N.Y., and London: Cornell Univ. Press, 1999), 95–100.

6. Evans, *Pigwacket*, 87, 90, 93; Bunny McBride and Harald E. L. Prins, "Walking the Medicine Line: Molly Ockett, a Pigwacket Doctor," in *Northeastern Indian Lives, 1632–1816*, ed. Robert S. Grumet (Amherst: Univ. of Massachusetts Press, 1996), 321–47.

7. N. T. True, "The Last of the Pequakets. Mollocket," *Bethel Courier*, copy at the Maine Historical Society with annotations by the author giving the source of various stories.

8. McBride and Prins, "Walking the Medicine Line," 326–27.

9. Cutter to Pepperrell, Saco Falls, 19 June 1744; Pepperrell to Cutter, Kittery, 22 June 1744, microfilm, Massachusetts Archives, Boston, 31:494–95.

10. *Journal of the House of Representatives*, vol. 21, 1744–1745 (Boston: Massachusetts Historical Society, 1946), 57–58, 63.

11. "Conference between his Excy & the Chief of the Indians brot up by Capt Cutter," 28 July 1744, microfilm, Massachusetts Archives, 32:501–3.

12. *Journal of the House of Representatives*, 21:152, 159, 179; Ruth Holmes Whitehead, "Every Thing They Make and Wear," in *Twelve Thousand Years in Maine*, ed. Bruce J. Bourque (Lincoln: Univ. of Nebraska Press, 2001), 315.

13. *Journal of the House of Representatives*, vol. 22 (Boston: Massachusetts Historical Society, 1947): 179, 182, 183.

14. *Journal of the House of Representatives*, vol. 23 (Boston: Massachusetts Historical Society, 1946–47), 29, 371; Noah Sprague, Account with Pigwackets for the Year 1748, microfilm, Massachusetts Archives, 32:632.

15. *Journal of the House of Representatives*, vol. 24, 1747–48 (Boston: Massachusetts Historical Society, 1949): 116–17; Mary Hall Leonard, *Mattapoisett and Old Rochester, Massachusetts* (New York: Grafton, 1907), 19.

16. "Treaty with the Eastern Indians at Falmouth 1749," in *Maine Historical Society Collections*, 1st ser. (Portland, Maine: Maine Historical Society, 1856), 4:145–67.

17. *Journal of the House of Representatives*, vol. 26, 1749–50 (1951): 160, 182.

18. McBride and Prins, "Walking the Medicine Line," 328.

19. When war began again in 1755, the Pigwackets had fled to St. Francis. When the mission was burned by English troops in 1759, they once again took to the woods, living in small bands in the mountainous country between Lake Champlain and the Kennebec, returning occasionally to the rebuilt church at St. Francis. McBride and Prins, "Walking the Medicine Line," 328–30.

20. Barrows, *Fryeburg*, 30, 31, 34–36.

21. Ibid., 49–50.

22. Ibid., 49–51.

23. Lapham, *Bethel*, 39–45, 458, 466, 563.

24. Henry Tufts, *The Autobiography of a Criminal* (Port Townsend, Wash.: Loompanics, 1993), 54–78. (This book was originally published as *A Narrative of the Life, Adventures, Travels and Sufferings of Henry Tufts* [Dover, N.H., 1807].); Gordon Day,

"Henry Tufts as a Source on Eighteenth-Century Abenakis," *Ethnohistory* 21 (1974): 189–98.

25. True, "Last of the Pequakets"; Lapham, *Bethel,* 620; Barrows, *Fryeburg,* 73.

26. Ibid., 38–40, 43, 44–45.

27. Colin G. Calloway, *The American Revolution in Indian Country* (Cambridge: Cambridge Univ. Press, 1995), 69.

28. The Sudbury-Canada raid was minor compared to British attacks on coastal Maine, but it terrified the new towns, who petitioned the General Court for money to build a fort. "The Captivity of Lt. Nathaniel Segar, during the Revolutionary War," in Lapham, *Bethel,* 50; ibid., 45–61; James S. Leamon, *Revolution Downeast: The War for American Independence in Maine* (Amherst: Univ. of Massachusetts Press, 1993), 181–82.

29. "Historical Record of Lucy M. Smith," 12 July 1889, manuscripts, Special Collections, University of Utah Library, Salt Lake City, 4.

30. Ruth B. Phillips, *Trading Identities: The Souvenir in Native North American Art from the Northeast, 1700–1900* (Seattle and London: Univ. of Washington Press; Montreal and Kingston: McGill-Queen's Univ. Press, 1998), 104–9, 293–97.

31. Margaret Swain, "Moose-Hair Embroidery on Birch Bark," *Antiques* 107 (1975): 726–29.

32. Phillips, *Trading Identities,* 107, 125

33. The work box is at the American Museum in Bath, U.K. Swain, "Moose-Hair Embroidery," 726–29; Phillips, *Trading Identities,* 125–26.

34. Ted Brasser, *A Basketful of Indian Culture Change* (Ottawa: National Museum of Man, 1975), 39–40.

35. Whitehead, "Every Thing They Make and Wear," 286, 320, 321–22. Willoughby, *Antiquities of the New England Indians,* 255–56.

36. Tufts, *Autobiography of a Criminal,* 53, 60–61, 72; *Luigi Castiglioni's Viaggio: Travels in the United States of North America, 1785–87,* trans. and ed. Antonio Pace (Syracuse, N.Y.: Syracuse Univ. Press, 1983), 39–40.

37. Charles E. Clark, James S. Leamon, and Karen Bowden, eds. *Maine in the Early Republic: from Revolution to Statehood* (Hanover, N.H., and London: Univ. Press of New England, 1988), plate 3, between 106 and 107; True, "Last of the Pequakets," 4.

38. Suffolk County Probate Records, Massachusetts State Archives, Boston, 44:185.

39. Massachusetts State Papers, microfilm, 29:279, Massachusetts State Archives.

40. Yolanda van de Krol, "Ladies' Pockets," *Antiques* 149 (Mar. 1996): 439–45. Martha Moore Ballard Diary, Maine State Library, Augusta, Maine, 19 Sept. 1797: "I Saw a Girl take a fan out of mr James Pages Seat and put it in her pocket. I informd mr Page who went to the Seat Shee was in and Shee Deliverd it up after denying Shee had Seen it. I Did not know her name but am informd it is Ellis." This was at Mr. Stone's meeting on a Sunday.

41. Judith Reiter Weissman and Wendy Lavitt, *Labors of Love: America's Textiles and Needlework, 1650–1930* (New York: Wings, 1987), 115.

42. *The Diary of Matthew Patten of Bedford, N.H.* (1903; repr., Camden, Maine: Picton Press, 1993), 219.

43. Maine State Museum, Conservation Laboratory Report, Curatorial Files, Maine Historical Society.

44. Lapham, *Bethel,* 16–25; Jean M. O'Brien, *Dispossession by Degrees: Indian Land and Identity in Natick, Massachusetts, 1650–1790* (Cambridge: Cambridge Univ. Press, 1997), 72–73, 77, 80, 85–86, 90, 186, 209.

45. Lapham, *Bethel,* 83, 149–50.

46. Curatorial Files, Maine Historical Society; Lapham, *Bethel,* 627, 577.

47. Tufts, *Autobiography of a Criminal,* 55, 65–66.

48. Sylvanus Poor, in True, "Last of the Pequakets," 6.

49. Ibid., 5.

50. Lapham, *Bethel*, 65, 115–18.

51. *Heads of Families at the First Census of the United States Taken in the Year 1790: Maine* (Washington, D.C.: Government Printing Office, 1908), 68.; Lapham, *Bethel*, 26, 38, 39, 43, 403, 458, 461, 466, 478, 512, 520, 535, 538, 541, 545, 558, 563, 571, 585, 599, 600, 606, 613, 614, 620, 626.

52. Ibid., 421–22.

53. Ibid., 298, 423.

54. True, "Last of the Pequakets," 4.

55. Barrows, *Fryeburg*, 153; Lapham, *Bethel*, 54.

56. Ibid., 151, 298.

57. True, "Last of the Pequakets," 3.

58. "Historical Record of Lucy M. Smith," 6; Lapham, *Bethel*, 478.

59. Ibid., 39, 43. On braided hair, see Henry Wansey, *The Journal of an Excursion to the United States of North America, in the Summer of 1794* (Salisbury, U.K., 1796), 52, and John M. Weeks, *History of Salisbury, Vermont* (Middlebury, Vt.: Copeland, 1860), 295.

60. "The Captivity of Lt. Nathaniel Segar," 50.

61. Lapham, *Bethel*, 419–20, 433.

62. True, "Last of the Pequakets," 1, 3, 5.

63. Lapham, *Bethel*, 421.

64. "Historical Record of Lucy M. Smith," 8–10.

65. Lapham, *Bethel*, 424–26.

66. Barrows, *Fryeburg*, 57–58, 267.

67. Lapham, *Bethel*, 421; Barrows, *Fryeburg*, 269–70.

68. Lapham, *Bethel*, 433–34.

69. "Historical Record of Lucy M. Smith," 7–8, 10.

70. True, "Last of the Pequakets," 4–5.

71. Ibid., 2–4; Catherine S. C. Newell, *Molly Ockett* (Bethel, Maine: Bethel Historical Society, 1981), 11–12.

72. True, "Last of the Pequakets," 2; "Mollockett," *Oxford Democrat*, 21 May 1901.

73. McBride and Prins, "Walking the Medicine Line," 326–28; McBride, *Women of the Dawn*, 56–67.

74. Charles E. Clark, "James Sullivan's History of Maine and the Romance of Statehood," in *Maine in the Early Republic*, ed. Clark, Leamon, and Bowden, 187–93.

76. Charles E. Clark and James S. Leamon, "Introduction," and Clark, "James Sullivan's History of Maine," in *Maine in the Early Republic*, ed. Clark, Leamon, and Bowden, 1–4, 186.

77. Taylor, *Liberty Men*, 79.

78. Charles E. Clark and James S. Leamon, "Introduction," and David C. Smith, "Maine's Changing Landscape to 1820," in *Maine in the Early Republic*, ed. Clark, Leamon, and Bowden, 2, 14–15; Taylor, *Liberty Men*, 61–87.

## Chapter 8: A Linen Tablecloth

1. See, for example, Stephan Thernstrom, *A History of the American People* (New York: Harcourt Brace Jovanovich, 1984), 208–11.

2. Henry Wansey, *The Journal of an Excursion to the United States of North America, in the Summer of 1794* (Salisbury, U.K.: Easton, 1796), 48, 49, 68, 83, 84; Gary Kulik, Roger

Parks, and Theodore Z. Penn, eds., *The New England Mill Village, 1790–1860* (Cambridge, Mass., and London: MIT Press, 1982), 18–19, 61–62.

3. Wansey, *Journal*, 47, 52, 53–55, 60, 64–65.

4. Drew R. McCoy, *The Elusive Republic: Political Economy in Jeffersonian America* (Chapel Hill: Univ. of North Carolina Press, 1980), 57–58, 148, 161, 166, 223–35.

5. James Hillhouse to Rebecca Hillhouse, 4 Nov. 1791, Hillhouse Family Papers, Sterling Library, Yale University, New Haven, Connecticut. Karen Kauffman kindly supplied this reference.

6. *The Diary of Matthew Patten of Bedford, N.H.* (1903; repr. Camden, Maine: Picton, 1993), 386, 440 (4 Feb. 1782). Jane C. Nylander, " 'Provision for the Daughters': The Accounts of Samuel Lane," in *House and Home*, ed. Peter Benes (Dublin Seminar for New England Folklife, Annual Proceedings, 1988), 11–27; Martha Moore Ballard Diary, Maine State Library, Augusta, Maine (hereafter cited as MMB), 31 July, 5 Aug. 1786; Laurel Thatcher Ulrich, *A Midwife's Tale: The Life of Martha Ballard Based on Her Diary, 1785–1812* (New York: Knopf, 1990), 75–80. The Ballard diary is now available in a transcription by Robert R. McCausland and Cynthia MacAlman McCausland, *The Diary of Martha Ballard, 1785–1812* (Camden, Maine: Picton, 1992), and online at dohistory.org.

7. MMB, 63; *Diary of Matthew Patten*, 535–36.

8. MMB, 28 May 1795.

9. A Virginia source said it took a bushel and a half to sow one acre of land. Martha Coons and Katherine Koob, *All Sorts of Good Sufficient Cloth: Linen-Making in New England* (North Andover, Mass.: Merrimack Valley Textile Museum, 1980), 36–38; S. W. Pomeroy, "Essays on Flax Husbandry," in *The New England Farmer; or, Georgical Dictionary*, ed. Samuel Deane, 3d ed. (Boston: Wells and Lilly, 1822), 138; MMB, 19 May 1786, 15 May 1787, 15 May 1788, 14 May 1791, 14 May 1793, 8 May 1794, 21 May 1799; *Diary of Matthew Patten*, 163, 194, 214, 301, 358, 369, 413, 430, 484, 505, 520, quote on 369.

10. Ibid., 6, 547–49.

11. MMB, 29, 30, and 31 July 1788. Other entries for pulling flax: 3, 4, and 5 Aug. 1786; 3, 4, and 15 Aug. 1787; 28 July 1788; 5 Aug. 1790; 7, 16, and 17 Aug. 1793; 13 Aug. 1796.

12. *Nailer Tom's Diary: Otherwise the Journal of Thomas B. Hazard of Kingstown Rhode Island*, ed. Caroline Hazard (Boston: Merrymount, 1930), e.g., 47 (9 May 1783), 305 (19 and 28 Apr. 1808), 100 (8 Aug. 1786), 50 (29 July and 1 Aug. 1783), 326 (27 and 29 July and 4 Aug. 1809); Coons and Koob, *All Sorts of Cloth*, 38.

13. *Tom's Diary*, 51 (29 and 30 Aug. 1783), 53 (10 Oct. 1783), 57 (22 and 31 Dec. 1783), 304 (16 Apr. 1808), 328 (24 Aug. 1809), 353 (4, 5, 13, and 14 Dec. 1810); *Diary of Matthew Patten*, 451 (6 Aug. 1782); Samuel Lane Accounts, New Hampshire Historical Society, Concord, New Hampshire. Also see Jerald E. Brown, *The Years of the Life of Samuel Lane, 1718–1806* (Hanover, N.H., and London: Univ. Press of New England, 2000), 115–20. Coons and Koob, *All Sorts of Cloth*, 23, 34.

14. *Diary of Matthew Patten*, 435; MMB, 22 Sept., 8 Oct. 1787; 20 Sept. 1788; 12 Sept., 1 Oct. 1796; 29 Sept. 1798; 23 Sept. 1800. *Tom's Diary*, 25 (5 Nov. 1781), 51 (23 Sept. 1783), 311 (10 Sept. 1808), 329 (4 Oct. 1809), 330 (24 Oct. 1809), 350 (5 Oct. 1810). Pomeroy, "Essays on Flax Husbandry."

15. *Diary of Matthew Patten*, 439, 210, 429; *Tom's Diary*, 336 (30 Jan. 1810); Samuel Lane Accounts, 5 Feb. 1752, 15 Mar. 1759, 16 Dec. 1758, 1 Mar. 1759, 7 Nov. 1759, 2, 3, and 26 Dec. 1760.

16. Coons and Koob, *All Sorts of Cloth*, 16–17, quoting from John Campbell diary, New Hampshire Historical Society, Concord, New Hampshire.

17. *Tom's Diary*, 326, 300.

18. Ebenezer Parkman Diary, quoted in Jane C. Nylander, *Our Own Snug Fireside: Images of the New England Home, 1760–1860* (New York: Knopf, 1993), 89.

19. *Tom's Diary*, 320, 113, 301, 350.

20. MMB, 16 and 19 June 1788, 19 Apr. 1799; Sarah Snell Bryant Diary, Houghton Library, Harvard University, Cambridge, Massachusetts, 10 Jan., 15 Feb., 12 Mar., 11 May, 4 Oct., and 20 Dec. 1810. Coons and Koob, *All Sorts of Cloth*, 38.

21. Diaries of Elizabeth Foot and Abigail Foot, Brainard Papers, Connecticut Historical Society, Hartford, Connecticut.

22. "Diary Kept by Elizabeth Fuller, Daughter of Rev. Timothy Fuller of Princeton," in Francis Everett Blake, *History of the Town of Princeton* (Princeton, Mass.: Pub. by the Town, 1915), 1:313, 315.

23. *The Diaries of Julia Cowles*, ed. Laura Hadley Moseley (New Haven, Conn.: Yale Univ. Press, 1931), 63; *Very Poor and of a Lo Make: The Diary of Abner Sanger*, ed. Lois K. Stabler (Portsmouth, N.H.: Peter Randall, 1986), 225, 304, 312.

24. J. E. A. Smith, *The History of Pittsfield, Massachusetts*, vol. 2 (Springfield, Mass., 1876), 53–54, 72, 73; *Cumberland Gazette*, 8 May 1788. *Cumberland Gazette*, 22 May 1805, recorded a similar event "a few days since . . . in Andover Society."

25. Diary of Ruth Henshaw Bascom, in Ruth Henshaw Bascom Papers, 1789–1848, American Antiquarian Society, Worcester, Massachusetts, microfilm edition, *American Women's Diaries*, reel one, 15 Sept. and 6 Oct. 1789, 27 Sept. 1807. Spinning frolics occurred before the war and continued long after. *The Diary of Mary Cooper: Life on a Long Island Farm, 1768–1773* (New York: Oyster Bay Historical Society, 1981), 8, 44, 48; Mary Beth Norton, *Liberty's Daughters: The Revolutionary Experience of American Women, 1750–1800* (Boston: Little, Brown, 1980), 169, 219; Laurel Thatcher Ulrich, "Daughters of Zion: Religious Women in Revolutionary New England," in *Women in the Age of the American Revolution*, ed. Ronald Hoffman and Peter Albert (Charlottesville: Univ. Press of Virginia, 1989); Christopher Clark, *The Roots of Rural Capitalism: Western Massachusetts, 1780–1860* (Ithaca, N.Y., and London: Cornell Univ. Press, 1990), 141.

26. Diary of Elizabeth Perkins Wildes, 1789–93, Maine Historical Society, Portland, Maine, 1 July 1789, 26 Oct. 1791, 12 Apr. 1793.

27. Ruth Henshaw Diary, 9 and 12 Apr. 1790, 24 Jan. 1792, 9 Feb. 1793, 1 Apr. 1793, 30 Dec. 1799.

28. Elizabeth Wildes Diary, 20 July, 21 Oct., and 16 Oct. 1789.

29. *Diary of Martha Ballard*, 21 Aug. 1786, 30 July 1791; Elizabeth Wildes Diary, 31 Oct. 1789; Sarah Bryant Diary, 16 Aug. 1810; Sarah Weeks Sheldon Papers, Weeks Family Papers, Sheldon Museum, Middlebury, Vermont, Feb. 1805. Stephen Innes, *Creating the Commonwealth: The Economic Culture of Puritan New England* (New York and London: Norton, 1995), 12.

30. Connecticut Valuations Lists, 1798, Connecticut Historical Society.

31. Gail Fowler Mohanty, "Unnoticed Craftsmen Noted: Commercial Handloom Weavers and Weaving in Essex County, Massachusetts, 1690–1790," unpublished typescript provided by author.

32. Sarah Anna Emery, *Reminiscences of a Nonagenarian* (Newburyport, Mass.: Huse, 1879), 6, 8, 28, 39.

33. There are two ways of reading diary entries that refer to "warping" at a neighbor's house. Because of the context, I have assumed that in this case Mrs. Wheeler was helping Henshaw set up her own weaving. In other cases, a woman might have borrowed a neigh-

bor's warping bars to prepare a web for her own loom. See Nylander, *Our Own Snug Fireside.*

34. MMB, vol. 1, 1 May and 11 Sept. 1788, 15 July 1791; Sarah Bryant Diary, 26 May 1810, 14 Oct. 1815; *Tom's Diary,* 302. Olwen Hufton notes the existence of similar networks among female spriggers and lace-makers in Great Britain in *The Prospect Before Her: A History of Women in Western Europe* (New York: Knopf, 1996), 169.

35. Elizabeth Foote Diary, 10 Apr., 9 Mar., and 23 Oct. 1775.

36. Stabler, ed., *Very Poor and of a Lo Make,* 500.

37. Plain "tabby" (over-under) required only two harnesses; patterned linens or twill required four. Sleys, which were equipped with fine slats made of wire or reed, varied according to the number of threads in a given piece of cloth. For sheeting, Sarah Weeks used a "2 and forty harness," noting that even with the help of her nine-year-old son, it took her all day Saturday and into Sunday to finish drawing the fine warp through the reed. Sarah Weeks Sheldon, Loose Journal, May 1832, Weeks Family Papers, Sheldon Museum, Middlebury, Vermont.

38. Martha Moore Ballard Diary, vol. 1, 20 Apr. 1790, 15 Oct. 1792. Ruth Henshaw noted that her mother bought a "two and thirty slay of a pedlar" in the fall of 1791. A sequence of entries in Tom Hazard's diary suggests he borrowed a sley from one man and carried it to another to get his blanketing woven. *Tom's Diary,* 335, 337.

39. Hannah Sanborn Philbrook, "A Few Memories and Traditions of Sanbornton," *Granite Monthly* 32 (1902): 181–82. Philbrook's paternal grandparents were Josiah and Tabitha Sanborn, who married in 1796 and had twelve children between 1798 and 1820. Her grandmother died in 1867.

40. Smith, *Pittsfield,* 2:162–70, 179–80.

41. *Tom's Diary,* ed. Hazard, 248, 250, 251; Ulrich, *A Midwife's Tale,* 264, 402 n. 2; Sarah Bryant Diary, inside cover of 1810 diary. Also see Clark, *Roots of Rural Capitalism,* 15, 95–117; Jonathan Prude, *The Coming of Industrial Order: Town and Factory Life in Rural Massachusetts, 1810–1860* (Cambridge, U.K.: Cambridge Univ. Press, 1983), 43.

42. 12 June 1801, Tolford-Patten Papers, New Hampshire State Library, Concord, New Hampshire, box 9.

43. *Tom's Diary,* ed. Hazard, 348 (17, 21, 26 Sept.), 350 (5, 6, 13, 18 Oct.); Ulrich, *A Midwife's Tale,* 264, 402 n. 2; Sarah Bryant Diary, 19 July, 10 Jan., 15 Feb., 12 and 29 Mar., 11 May, 25 Aug., 4 Oct. 1810. Also see Clark, *Roots of Rural Capitalism,* 15, 95–117; Prude, *Industrial Order,* 43.

44. Mary Edna Sullivan, "Women Weavers," in *After Ratification: Material Life in Delaware, 1789–1820,* ed. J. Ritchie Garrison, Bernard L. Herman, and Barbara McLean Ward (Newark, Del.: Museum Studies Program, University of Delaware, 1988), 100, 102, 106, 108, 110.

45. Tolford-Patten Papers.

46. William L. Warren and Lois North, "A Scrap of Paper," *Connecticut Historical Society* 25 (1960): 7–21.

47. MMB, 12 Sept. 1788; Elizabeth Wildes Diary, 25 Apr. 1791, 29 Nov. and 28 Dec. 1792, 9 Feb. 1793; Ruth Henshaw Diary, 1 May 1801, 16 and 18 Apr., 9 May 1791; Florence M. Montgomery, *Textiles in America, 1650–1870* (New York: Norton, 1984), 243; relevant entries in the *Oxford English Dictionary;* Mary Meigs Atwater, *The Shuttle-Craft Book of American Hand-Weaving* (New York: Macmillan, 1951), 119.

48. Montgomery, *Textiles in America,* 313; Robert Stone, *Connecticut Blankets, Coverlids, and Bed Rugs* (Lee's Summit, The Fat Little Pudding Boys Press, 1999), 29; Litchfield Probate, book 3, microfilm, Connecticut State Library; "The Diary of Elizabeth (Porter)

Phelps," *New England Historical and Genealogical Register* 118 (1964): 305; Reuben Trusselate, Perrystown, Hillsboro County, 1793, 5:248.

49. Annemarie Seiler-Baldinger, *Textiles: A Classification of Techniques* (Washington, D.C.: Smithsonian Institution Press, 1994), 98; Mary Meigs Atwater, *The Shuttle-Craft Book of American Hand-Weaving* (New York: Macmillan, 1951), 45, 123–128.

50. Deborah Sylvester weaving drafts, Gilder Lehrman Collection, Pierpont Morgan Library, New York.

51. Vivian Chapin, "An Analysis of Some Nineteenth-Century Weaving Drafts," unpublished typescript, Old Sturbridge Village, Massachusetts.

52. Glee Krueger owns Mary Palmer's draft; Vermont Historical Society, Montpelier, Vermont, miscellaneous file 1618, gift of Alice Swingle. Some names are quite literal ("Links and Wheels," "Block Work," "Double Block Work"), and others more poetic ("Sun, Moon, and Stars," "Church Windows," "Nine Snoballs"). The same collection includes "Jeffersons Fancy" and a draft for "N and O" written on the back of a manuscript receipt. Clearly more than one weaver was involved, since there are directions both for a "Compass Coverlet" and a "Compass Coverled."

53. Isadora Safner and Diane Piette, *The Weaving Book of Peace and Patience* (Brewster, Mass.: Two Cape Cod Weavers, 1980), based on pattern drafts by Patience Lawton Kirby and her daughter Peace Kirby Howland, Old Sturbridge Village, 26.60.1.2-31. On the range and complexity of early textiles and the difficulties in distinguishing local from imported fabrics, see Adrienne Hood, "Material World of Cloth," and Adrienne Hood and D. T. Ruddel, "Artifacts and Documents in the History of Quebec Textiles," in *Living in the Material World: Canadian and American Approaches to Material Culture,* ed. Gerald Pocius (St. Johns, Newfoundland: Institute of Social and Economic Research, Memorial Univ. of Newfoundland, 1991), 55–91.

54. New Hampshire Historical Society, 1983-5-7, Amherst, 22 Apr. 1793.

55. Susan Burrows Swan, *Plain and Fancy: American Women and Their Needlework, 1700–1850* (New York: Rutledge, 1977), 157–66, and figures 85 and 86; Susan Burrows Swan, *A Winterthur Guide to American Needlework* (New York: Crown, 1976), 126–33; Abbot Lowell Cummings, *Bed Hangings: A Treatise on Fabrics and Styles in the Curtaining of Beds 1650–1850* (Boston: Society for the Preservation of New England Antiquities, 1961), 33, figures 5, 43, 55.

56. Georgiana Brown Harbeson, *American Needlework* (New York: Bonanza, 1938), 155.

57. Ibid., 156.

58. Ruth Henshaw Diary, 2 Jan. 1794; 4 Feb., 3, 6, 11, and 12, Mar., 5 and 12 Sept., and 22 Dec. 1801; 21 Jan., 21, 22, and 24 May, 16 June, and 19 Aug. 1802.

59. Grace Rogers Cooper, *The Copp Family Textiles* (Washington, D.C.: Smithsonian Institution Press, 1971), figures 13, 25, 41, 42, 43, 44; pages 12, 23, 35–37. Cummings, *Bed Hangings*, figure 5, p. 43, illustrates a bed covering with a similar fringe made by a woman married in 1811 and a fragment of a curtain c. 1830.

60. New Hampshire Historical Society 1961.16.3, 5, 6; Domestic Linen, 989.294.9, Royal Ontario Museum, Toronto, Ontario.

61. Strawberry Banke Museum, Portsmouth, New Hampshire, set of curtains, 75.3795, 3795, 3796; Towel, 75.3799. Familysearch.org lists five Sarah Hodgdons born in New Hampshire between 1748 and 1807. Unfortunately, the files of the museum don't tell us which Sarah made the curtains, but the descendants said the textiles were probably made in Sanbornville.

62. Coons and Koob, *All Sorts of Cloth*, 82, showing a Maine tablecloth owned by the Society for the Preservation of New England Antiquities. Overshot tablecloths at the Maine

State Museum include 72.67.1 and 70, 83.39, 40. The diaper cloth with the cotton fringe is 71.110.1.

63. Ulrich, *A Midwife's Tale*, 90, 142–43.

64. Ruth Henshaw Diary, 6 June 1797.

65. Elizabeth Wildes Diary, 10 Aug., 12 Sept., 5 Oct., and 23 Dec. 1789; 4, 9, and 11 Jan., 8 Feb., 24 May, 4 Oct., and 3 Dec. 1790; 6, 8, and 24 Feb., 26 Nov., and 23 Dec. 1791; 11 Jan. and 14 Feb. 1792.

66. Ibid., 23 Aug. 1791, 22 Feb. 1792, 16 July 1790 (salt water cotton), 9 Mar. 1792; Joyce Chaplin, *An Anxious Pursuit: Agricultural Innovation and Modernity in the Lower South, 1730–1815* (Chapel Hill and London: Univ. of North Carolina Press, 1993), 220–26.

67. Elizabeth Wildes Diary, 29 Apr. 1790; 17 Oct. 1789; 6 Dec. 1790; 9 June 1792; 11 May 1790; 19 Mar., 13 Apr., 23 Aug., 19 Sept., 6 Oct., 13 Sept., 15 and 28 Mar. 1791; 7 Mar. 1792.

68. Ibid., 16 July, 15 and 25 Nov., and 14 Dec. 1789; 2 Jan., 25, 27, and 30 Mar., 12 May, and 6 Aug. 1790.

69. This appears to be the earliest reference in American sources to rubberized clothing. Nineteenth-century writers assumed that waterproof overcoats were first successfully manufactured by Charles Macintosh in 1821, but there must have been earlier attempts. Thomas Jefferson's invoices for 1803 mention a "superfine Waterproof Cassimere," and in a letter of 1 Jan. 1802 he mentioned "a surtout coat, which I have found entirely effectual against rain." Charles Goodyear, *Gum-Elastic and Its Varieties* (New Haven, Conn., 1855; repr., American Chemical Society, 1939), 52–53, and e-mail communications from Linda Welters, University of Rhode Island, and Linda R. Baumgarten, Colonial Williamsburg, 19 July 2000.

70. *Luigi Castiglioni's Viaggio: Travels in the United States of North America, 1785–87*, trans. and ed. Antonio Pace (Syracuse, N.Y.: Syracuse Univ. Press, 1983), 30, 32–33.

71. Seth Sprague, *Reminiscences of the Olden Times in the Old Colony Town of Duxbury* (1845), 7. Paula Marcoux of Plimoth Plantation, Massachusetts, kindly shared this reference with me.

72. John M. Weeks, *History of Salisbury, Vermont* (Middlebury, Vt.: Copeland, 1860), 291.

73. Ann Smith Diary, manuscript, Maine Historical Society.

74. Baron Louis de Closen, 1780, quoted in Helen Sprackling, *Customs on the Table Top* (Sturbridge, Mass.: Old Sturbridge Village, 1958), 19.

75. Mrs. John Farra, *The Young Lady's Friend*, quoted in Sprackling, *Customs on the Table Top*, 15.

76. Hillsborough County Probate Book 5:283 and passim, Hillsborough County Court House, Nashua, New Hampshire.

77. Albert Ten Eyck Gardner, ed., *101 Masterpieces of American Primitive Painting from the Collection of Edgar William and Bernice Chrysler Garbisch* (New York: American Federation of Arts, 1962), plate 38, 136.

78. MMB, 27 July 1790, 18 Nov. 1793, 4 Apr. 1802, 17 Mar. 1804; Ulrich, *A Midwife's Tale*, 162–63, 200–1, 264–65, 337.

79. Richard L. Bushman, *The Refinement of America: Persons, Houses, Cities* (New York: Knopf, 1992), 186–203, quote on 197.

80. *Diary of Sarah Connell Ayer* (Portland, Maine: Lafavour-Towers, 1910), 60.

81. Alan Taylor, *Liberty Men and Great Proprietors: The Revolutionary Settlement on the Maine Frontier, 1760–1820* (Chapel Hill and London: Univ. of North Carolina Press, 1990); Ulrich, *A Midwife's Tale*.

82. *A Girl's Life Eighty Years Ago: Selections from the Letters of Eliza Southgate Bowne* (New York: Charles Scribner's Sons, 1888), 100, 168.

## *Chapter 9: A Counterpane and a Rose Blanket*

1. Sandra Armentrout began her work on Eliza Bourne while documenting Federal period artifacts for the National Endowment for the Humanities–funded "Maine at Statehood" project. Sandra S. Armentrout, "Eliza Bourne of Kennebunk: Professional Fancy Weaver, 1800–1820," in *House and Home*, ed. Peter Benes (Dublin Seminar for New England Folklife, Annual Proceedings, 1988), 101–15; Sandra S. Armentrout, "Catalog Entry 139B," and Laurel Thatcher Ulrich, " 'From the Fair to the Brave': Spheres of Womanhood in Federal Maine," in *Agreeable Situations: Society, Commerce, and Art in Southern Maine, 1780–1830*, ed. Laura Fecych Sprague (Kennebunk, Maine: The Brick Store Museum, 1987). During the same period, Joyce Butler, also at the Brick Store Museum (Kennebunkport, Maine), completely transcribed the diary.

2. *Columbian Phoenix*, Providence, Rhode Island, 26 Mar., 7 May, 2, 16, and 23 July, 31 Dec. 1808; 1 and 15 July 1809; 30 June, 11 Aug. 1810.

3. Ibid., 1 Sept. 1810; *American Advocate*, Augusta, Maine, 11 and 24 Oct. 1810.

4. *New Hampshire Gazette*, 5 Jan. 1808, 10 July 1810; Drew R. McCoy, *The Elusive Republic: Political Economy in Jeffersonian America* (Chapel Hill: Univ. of North Carolina Press, 1980), 227, 230–31. The allusions to slavery were long-lived. The July essay quoted from James Warren's famous oration of 5 Mar. 1773: "If you from your souls despise the most gaudy dress that slavery can wear . . . you may have the fullest assurance that tyranny with her whole acursed train, will hide their hideous heads."

5. Tench Coxe, *A Statement of the Arts and Manufactures of the United States of America, for the Year 1810* (Philadelphia, 1814), xiii, xv, xxxix; Jacob E. Cooke, *Tench Coxe and the Early Republic* (Chapel Hill: Univ. of North Carolina Press, 1978), 492.

6. Edward Emerson Bourne, "The Bourne Family," typescript, Brick Store Museum, 2:1.

7. Ibid., 20–21.

8. Ibid., 403, 410, 441.

9. *Kennebunk Weekly Visitor*, 9 Feb. 1811.

10. Ibid., 236–37, 297, 300–1, and Armentrout, "Catalog Entry 139B," 218.

11. Armentrout, "Eliza Bourne of Kennebunk."

12. Bourne, "Bourne Family."

13. Edward Emerson Bourne, *The History of Wells and Kennebunk* (Portland, Maine: Thurston, 1875), 594–95.

14. Ibid., 686–89.

15. *Memoirs and Letters of Dolley Madison* (Boston and New York: Houghton, Mifflin, 1886), 39–40; Catherine Allgor, *Parlor Politics* (Charlottesville: Univ. Press of Virginia, 2000), 83; David Waldstreicher, *In the Midst of Perpetual Fetes: The Making of American Nationalism, 1776–1820* (Chapel Hill and London: Univ. of North Carolina Press, 1997), 166–72, 236–41.

16. There were similar ceremonials in other towns. In Hallowell, Maine, sixteen young women "clad in white, with black hats & cloaks, & white scarfs," represented the sixteen states of the Union in a parade that included the town's militia companies, judges, lawers, physicians, members of the fire society, and other dignitaries. In Bennington, Vermont, Jeffersonians used similar ceremonials to challenge the Federalist ascendancy. In one Fourth of July tableau, "Liberty" approached her seat in the meetinghouse to find that the "crown of royalty and the mitre of priestcraft had daringly usurped her place." With "peculiar dignity the beauteous Nymph removed the encumbrances, set them at her feet and seated herself to preside over the exercises of the day." Bourne, *Wells and Kennebunk*, 685; Laurel Thatcher Ulrich, *A Midwife's Tale: The Life of*

*Martha Ballard Based on Her Diary, 1785–1812* (New York: Knopf, 1990), 32; Robert E. Shalhope, *Bennington and the Green Mountain Boys: The Emergence of Liberal Democracy in Vermont, 1760–1850* (Baltimore and London: Johns Hopkins Univ. Press, 1996), 220.

17. Zilpah Wadsworth to Nancy Doane, letter-journal, Sept. 1799 (filed with 1797), Wadsworth-Longfellow Papers, Longfellow National Historic Site, Cambridge, Massachusetts. Also see Ulrich, " 'From the Fair to the Brave,' " 222–24.

18. Bourne, "Bourne Family," 1:441.

19. To Abigail Wildes, Dolley Madison Memorial Association, Inc., Guilford College, North Carolina. Thanks to Holly Shulman for providing me with a copy of this letter.

20. Abigail Wildes to Mrs. Madison, Madison Papers, University of Virginia, Charlottesville. Thanks to Holly Shulman for providing a transcription of this letter via e-mail, 2 June 2000.

21. Bourne, "Bourne Family," 2:247, 323–24.

22. Bourne, *Wells and Kennebunk,* 597–600.

23. *Memoirs and Letters of Dolley Madison,* 73, 78, 79.

24. Ibid., 91.

25. Allgor, *Parlor Politics,* 94–98.

26. I would like to thank Lois Thurston of Topsham, Maine, for alerting me to the existence of manufacturing data in the population census for her town and Edward McCarron for tracking down those and other records at the Government Document Center, Waltham, Massachusetts. For a list of extant manufacturing data, see Preliminary Inventory 161, *Records of the Bureau of the Census* (Washington, D.C., 1964), appendix 9, 132–34. In the following discussion, I have relied especially on manuscript census records, microfilm, National Archives, Washington, D.C., M252, reels 12, 18, 27, 49, 64, 65.

27. Topsham records suggest that probate records underestimate the extent of cloth-making in a living population. Probate records for the period 1800–1815 show 56 percent of households with wheels and 37 percent with looms. In the census, as we have seen, 88 percent of households claimed to have made cloth and 56 percent owned looms. Yet the ratio of loom-owning to wheel-owning households in the inventories (.66) is almost identical to that for loom-owning and cloth-making households in the census (.63), arguing for the accuracy of probate in revealing the structure of production.

28. 1810 Census, Manuscript Schedules: Essex County, Massachusetts, 2:113–18; Middlesex County, Massachusetts, 4:318–23; Orange County, Vermont, 1:361, 364, 366–402, 437–42, microfilm, National Archives Regional Center, Waltham, Massachusetts.

29. "A Series of Tables of the Several Branches of American Manufactures, Exhibiting Them in Every County of the Union," in Coxe, *Statement,* 4–31. Unless otherwise indicated, all state and county computations discussed below are derived from data published in these pages. Useful summaries also appear in Rolla Milton Tryon, *Household Manufactures in the United States, 1640–1860* (1917; repr. New York: Augustus M. Kelley, 1966), 161–82. Some of Tryon's numbers are in error, however. A typographical or computation error adds an extra million to Rhode Island's total. He also misinterpreted Maine's returns, lumping flax and mixed-fiber fabrics together in a catchall category he mislabeled "Cotton." On the general limitations of the manufacturing data, see Harold Hutcheson, *Tench Coxe: A Study in American Economic Development* (Baltimore: Johns Hopkins Press, 1938). Because returns were uneven, the results are imperfect, but they are nevertheless remarkably revealing.

30. [Albert Gallatin], *Report from the Secretary of the Treasury, on the Subject of American Manufactures* (Boston, 1810), 9–15, repr. in Gary Kulik, et al., *The New England Mill Village, 1790–1860* (Cambridge: MIT Press, 1982), 155–64.

31. Coxe, *A Statement*, 4–31, and 1810 Census, Manuscript Schedules, Hampshire County, Massachusetts, 3:207, 217, 219, 220–37, and Kennebec County, Maine, 1:943.

32. *Grandmother Tyler's Book: The Recollections of Mary Palmer Tyler, 1775–1866*, ed. Frederick Tupper and Helen Tyler Brown (New York, 1925), 141.

33. *Grandmother Tyler*, 282–83.

34. Jack Larkin, "Episodes from Daily Life: 'The Life and Writings of Minerva Mayo by Herself' as an Exercise in Microhistory," unpublished typescript, 5.

35. Hiram Munger, "Life and Religious Experience" and "William Davis Family Records," in *The New England Mill Village, 1790–1860*, ed. Gary Kulick, Roger Parks, and Theodore Z. Penn (Cambridge, Mass.: MIT Press, 1982), 403, 413–19.

36. Thomas Dublin, *Transforming Women's Work: New England Lives in the Industrial Revolution* (Ithaca, N.Y., and London: Cornell Univ. Press, 1994), 33–40, quote on p. 40, and Gail Fowler Mohanty, "Putting Up with Putting-Out: Power Loom Diffusion and Outwork for Rhode Island Mills, 1821–1829," *Journal of the Early Republic* 9 (1989): 191–216. For efforts to establish factories and employ artisan weavers see Mohanty, "Experimentation in Textile Technology, 1788–1790, and Its Impact on Handloom Weaving and Weavers in Rhode Island," *Technology and Culture* 19 (January 1988): 1–31, and Barbara M. Tucker, *Samuel Slater and the Origins of the American Textile Industry, 1790–1860* (Ithaca, N.Y., and London: Cornell Univ. Press, 1984), 47–66.

37. F. G. Comstock Account Book, MS71631, 27, Connecticut Historical Society, Hartford, Connecticut.

38. Manufacturers who failed to comply were fined. In 1713, officials penalized a member of their guild for "makeing one Stockfull of Cutts & one Stockfull of fine Midles without makeing any Shoots of Colloured yarn." Jane C. Nylander, "Textiles," in *The Great River: Art and Society of the Connecticut Valley, 1635–1820*, ed. Gerald W. R. Ward and William N. Hosley (Hartford, Conn.: Wadsworth Atheneum, 1985), 381–82; Charles E. Hanson, Jr., "The Point Blanket," *Museum of the Fur Trade Quarterly* (spring 1976): 5–10, and "Some Additional Notes on Trade Blankets," *Museum of the Fur Trade Quarterly* (winter 1988): 6–7; Court Book, B1/BC/A/6, Oxfordshire County Archives, Oxford, U.K.; Blankets at The Essex Institute, Salem, Massachusetts (133, 850; 103.641); Dewitt Wallace Gallery, Colonial Williamsburg (1970-159; 1970-160); New Hampshire Historical Society, Conway (1967.541 and 542; 1965.41.2; 1968.514); Society for the Preservation of New England Antiquities, Boston (1931.689; 1938.1430; 1938.1429; 1938.1429); Museum of American Textile History, Lowell, Massachusetts (62.69.B); Old Sturbridge Village, Massachusetts (26.113.7; 26.19.96; 16.19.167; 26.19.13; 26.19.83; 26.19.89; 26.19.149; 26.19.137); Daughters of the American Revolution Museum, Washington, D.C. (2501).

39. Solomon Stoddard Inventory, Hampshire County Probate Records, Hampshire County Courthouse, Northampton, Massachusetts, 5:4–5. *Vermont Centinel*, 20 Dec. 1805, 11 and 24 Dec. 1806; Florence M. Montgomery, *Textiles in America, 1650–1870* (New York: Norton, 1984), 169–70; Nylander, *"Textiles,"* 382; Pamela Clabburn, *The National Trust Book of Furnishing Textiles* (Viking, 1988), 121–22; Hanson, "Some Additional Notes," 6–7; *The James Alexander Papers*, New York Historical Society; *North Carolina Wills and Inventories* (Raleigh, 1910), 487; and conversations with Trish Herr, Shirley Brabner, and Robert Stone, a weaver who specializes in reproduction rose blankets.

40. Early Papers, B1/F/O/1, folder 4 and John Early, Sales and Purchase Ledger, B1/G/L1/1, pages 4, 22, 49, 50, 63, 65, 75, Oxfordshire County Archives.

41. Hanson, "Some Additional Notes," 7; Anna Wells Rutledge, ed. *The Pennsylvania Academy of the Fine Arts, 1807–1870* (Philadelphia: American Philosophical Society, 1955), 149.

42. *Columbian Phoenix,* 12 Feb. and 17 Aug. 1812.

43. The men and women who assembled New England's first textile collections assumed these blankets were made at home. Examples of English blankets attributed to New England weavers: Sturbridge 26.19.9, Sturbridge 26.19.1492; EI 129,437; New Hampshire Historical Society, 1965.41.2. Robert Stone, *Connecticut Blankets, Coverlids, and Bed Rugs* (Lee's Summit, Mo.: The Fat Little Pudding Boys Press, 1999), #111, 314, 321, 335, 352, 431, 501, 503, 900, 970, 987, 1052, 1054, 1078, 1080, 1171.

44. William J. Gilmore, *Reading Becomes a Necessity of Life: Material and Cultural Life in Rural New England, 1780–1835* (Knoxville: Univ. of Tennessee Press, 1989), 44–49, 357–58.

45. Betty Ring, *Girlhood Embroidery: American Samplers and Pictorial Needlework, 1650–1850* (New York: Knopf, 1993), 1:246; Glee Krueger, *New England Samplers to 1840* (Sturbridge, Mass.: Old Sturbridge Village, 1978), figures 25, 26, 46, 47, 67, 69, 81; Judith Reiter Weissman and Wendy Lavitt, *Labors of Love: America's Textiles and Needlework, 1650–1920* (New York: Wings, 1987), 125.

46. J. and R. Bronson, *Early American Weaving and Dyeing: The Domestic Manufacturer's Assistant and Family Directory in the Arts of Weaving and Dyeing* (Utica, N.Y., 1817; repr. New York: Dover, 1977), 169–71, 187, 189. I am greatly indebted to Adrienne Hood, who examined the blanket with me for the second time on 16 Apr. 1996.

47. J. E. A. Smith, *The History of Pittsfield, Massachusetts,* vol. 2 (Springfield, Mass., 1876), 322–23, 325.

48. Ibid., 171–72.

49. Elkanah Watson, *History of the Rise, Progress, and Existing State of the Berkshire Agricultural Society* (Albany, 1819), 2, 10, 12–16; Smith, *Pittsfield,* 2:336–37; Rodney H. True, "The Early Development of Agricultural Societies in the United States," *Annual Report of the American Historical Association for 1920* (Washington, D.C., 1925), 295–305; Wayne Caldwell Neely, *The Agricultural Fair* (New York: Columbia Univ. Press, 1935), 53–69.

50. Watson, *History,* 18–24; Smith, *Pittsfield,* 2:342.

51. Ibid., 199–201, 204–5, 209.

52. Ibid., 206–12.

53. Elkanah Watson, "Address Delivered before the Berkshire Agricultural Society" (Pittsfield, 1814), 6.

54. Thomas Gold, "Address Delivered before the Berkshire Association for the Promotion of Agriculture and Manfuactures" (Pittsfield, Mass., 1816), 10–12.

55. Smith, *Pittsfield,* 2:350–51.

56. Jane C. Nylander, *Our Own Snug Fireside: Images of the New England Home* (New York: Knopf, 1993), 179–81.

57. *New England Farmer* 1 (1823): 43, 66, 71, 74, 79, 81, 83, 86, 92, 93, 94, 97, 101, 109, 114, 115, 130, 154.

58. *Massachusetts Spy,* 30 Oct. 1822; 18 Oct. 1820; 28 Oct. 1818.

59. Ibid., 24 Oct. 1821; 9 Oct. 1822; 19 Oct. 1825; 18 Oct. 1826; 17 and 24 Oct. 1827; 14 Oct. 1829, and (for Hunter blankets) 20 and 27 Oct. 1830; 26 Oct. 1825.

60. Peabody-Essex Museum, Salem, Massachusetts, 104, 495; Society for the Preservation of New England Antiquities, Boston, 1949.3 and 1949.4; New Hampshire Historical Society, 1998. Sturbridge 26.19.164 also has flowers growing out of the circle.

61. *New England Farmer* 10, no. 14 (19 Oct. 1831): 109; 11, no. 17 (7 Nov. 1832); 15, no. 15 (19 Oct. 1836): 116; 16, no. 16 (25 Oct. 1837): 121. The rose blankets were among other gifts to the museum from her granddaughter, Rose Lawrence. Essex Institute, Accession Book, 1902–1915, p. 1465, 18 Dec. 1914.

62. *Vermont Gazette,* 13 Nov. 1832.

63. Joseph Philbrick Inventory, Hillsborough County Court House, Nashua, New Hampshire.

64. Eleanor Washburn Tracy to Royal Washburn, Royalton, Vermont, 1 Dec. 1819, MS letter, printed in "Clues and Footnotes," *Antiques* 107 (Apr. 1975): 686.

## Chapter 10: A Woodsplint Basket

1. Covered Basket, Peabody Museum, Cambridge, Massachusetts, 17-8-10/87266. The basket was purchased at a place called Pow-wow Station, near Plaistow, New Hampshire, in 1913 and given to the Peabody Museum five years later. See Madeline W. Fang and Marilyn R. Binder, *A Photographic Guide to the Ethnographic North American Indian Basket Collection* (Cambridge, Mass.: Peabody Museum, 1990), 1:456; Early Catalogs of the Peabody Museum, box 4, vol. 18, manuscript, Harvard University Archives; Sarah Peabody Turnbaugh and William A. Turnbaugh, *Indian Baskets* (West Chester, Pa.: Schiffer, 1986), 117. The donor, L. H. Jenkins, was the director of the Peabody Museum in Salem, Massachusetts.

2. Population Schedules of the Fourth Census of the United States, 1820, Vermont vol. 1, roll 126, microfilm, National Archives, Waltham, Massachusetts; Margaret R. Jenks, Poultney Cemetery Inscriptions, photocopy supplied by Daniell L. Roberts, Fair Haven, Vermont. The stone reads: "Infant son of Moses C. & Dorothy, d. Sept 8, 1821 age 3 w 5 d." The census schedule lists him as engaged in manufacturing, which suggests that he did not own land. Despite extensive searches in published genealogies, Vermont vital records, and earlier and later U.S. censuses for New England, New York, and Michigan, I have not been able to provide a firm identification. This Moses Goodrich could have been born in Connecticut, Massachusetts, or New Hampshire. Perhaps he died and his wife, Dorothy, remarried, but I can find no marriage records for either of them. Many records from this part of Vermont were, however, lost or burned in the nineteenth century.

3. Ted Brasser, *A Basketful of Cultural Change* (Ottawa: National Museum of Man, 1975); Sarah H. Hill, *Weaving New Worlds: Southeastern Cherokee Women and Their Basketry* (Chapel Hill and London: Univ. of North Carolina Press, 1997).

4. William J. Gilmore, *Reading Becomes a Necessity of Life: Material and Cultural Life in Rural New England, 1780–1835* (Knoxville: Univ. of Tennessee Press, 1989), 23, 85, 86, 150–51, 161, 177–78; H. P. Smith and W. S. Rann, *History of Rutland County, Vermont* (Syracuse, N.Y.: Mason, 1886), 215–16; Elsie C. Wells, *Bakersfield, Vermont* (Canaan, N.H.: Phoenix, 1976), 76; Tyler Resch, *The Rutland Herald History: A Bicentennial Chronicle* (Rutland, Vt.: Rutland Herald, 1995), 17–33.

5. *Rutland Herald,* 26 Dec., 5 and 19 Nov., 8 Oct., 24 Apr. 1821.

6. Colin G. Calloway, *The Western Abenakis of Vermont, 1600–1800* (Norman and London: Univ. of Oklahoma Press, 1990), 6–16.

7. Ibid., 183–85.

8. Randolph A. Roth, *The Democratic Dilemma: Religion, Reform, and the Social Order in the Connecticut River Valley of Vermont, 1791–1850* (Cambridge: Cambridge Univ. Press, 1987), 7; Calloway, *Western Abenakis,* 224–37.

9. Ibid., 226–27.

10. Ibid., 228–29.

11. Ibid.

12. Ibid., 234.

13. Robert E. Shalhope, *Bennington and the Green Mountain Boys: The Emergence of Liberal Democracy in Vermont, 1760–1850* (Baltimore and London: Johns Hopkins Univ. Press, 1996), 211–12; *Vermont Gazette,* 16 Aug., 6 Dec. 1802; *Farmer's Museum* (Walpole, N.H.), 23 Nov., 14 Dec. 1802. I would like to thank Randolph Roth for sharing his notes on the Gordon case.

14. Richard Newman, "Preface," and Helen MacLam, "Introduction," in *Black Preacher to White America: The Collected Writings of Lemuel Haynes, 1774–1833,* ed. Richard Newman (Brooklyn, N.Y.: Carlson, 1990), xi–xxxv, quote on p. xxiv.

15. Dawn D. Hance, *The History of Rutland, Vermont, 1761–1861* (Rutland: Academy, 1991), 511, 515–16, 636.

16. Mary Eva Baker, *Folklore of Springfield* (Springfield, Vt., 1922), 35–36.

17. William A. Haviland and Marjory W. Power, *The Original Vermonters: Native Inhabitants: Past and Present* (Hanover, N.H., and London: Univ. Press of New England, 1991), 247–50; Frederic Palmer Wells, *History of Barnet, Vermont* (Burlington: Free Press, 1923), 4.

18. Gaby Pelletier, *Abenaki Basketry* (Ottawa: National Museums of Canada, 1982); Jane C. Beck, ed., *Always in Season: Folk Art and Traditional Culture in Vermont* (Montpelier, Vt.: Vermont Council on the Arts, 1982); Chauncy K. Williams, *Centennial Celebration of the Settlement of Rutland, Vt.* (Rutland: Tuttle, 1870), 108, 109; Christopher McGrory Klyza and Stephen C. Trombulak, *The Story of Vermont: A Natural and Cultural History* (Hanover, N.H., and London: Univ. Press of New England, 1999), 201, 202.

19. Ann McMullen, "A Key into Technical Vocabulary," in Ann McMullen and Russell G. Handsman, *A Key into the Language of Woodsplint Baskets* (Washington, Conn.: American Indian Archaeological Institute, 1987), 170–71. Hill describes a similar process for preparing white oak splints among Cherokee, *Weaving New Worlds,* 122–26.

20. Ann McMullen, "Looking for People in Woodsplint Basketry Decoration," in McMullen and Handsman, *Key into the Language of Woodsplint Baskets,* 120–23.

21. McMullen, "Looking for People," 104–5; Richard Newman and Michele Derrick, Report on analysis of Algonkian basket, 3 Nov. 2000, Museum of Fine Arts, Boston Scientific Research, Peabody Museum files. This is an interesting example of the difficulties of working with understudied artifacts. The technology employed in this analysis was state-of-the-art, as the report indicates: "Small portions of each sample were analyzed by FTIR microspectrometry. The samples prepared for FTIR analysis were also examined by polarizing light microscopy. Gas chromatography/mass spectrometry (GC/MS) and high performance liquid chromatography (HPLC) were used to analyze some samples." But because the laboratory had "virtually no previous experience with an artifact of the type analyzed," it had few reference points for analysis. Projected future work at the Museum of Fine Arts on New England basketry may produce new information.

22. Frank G. Speck, *Eastern Algonkian Block-Stamp Decoration* (Trenton, N.J., 1947), 32; *Very Lo and of a Poor Make: The Journal of Abner Sanger,* ed. Lois K. Stabler (Portsmouth, N.H.: Peter Randall, 1986), 333–34, 352–53.

23. E.g., McMullen and Handsman, *Key into the Language of Woodsplint Baskets,* 30, 32, 88, 89, 94, 100, 110, 111, 116. On conditions of newspapers, conversation with Ed Hood and Nan Wolverton, Old Sturbridge Village, Massachusetts.

24. M. B. Cohn, "Description of Treatment," Center for Conservation and Technical Studies, Peabody Museum files.

25. Official records tell us that an indictment was filed with the Supreme Judicial Court in March. Purchase pleaded not guilty. His first trial, the following October, resulted in a

hung jury. In a second trial, a year later, he was found guilty of manslaughter. He appealed the verdict, and a year later, when that appeal was overruled, he was sent to the state prison in Charlestown, where he was to be kept in solitary confinement for three days, and afterward put to hard labor for three years. Middlesex County Supreme Judicial Court Record Book (1820–1824), 561; files, box 24, 1824–1826, Massachusetts State Archives, Boston.

26. *Rutland Herald,* 26 Dec. and 5 Nov. 1821.

27. James Fenimore Cooper, *The Last of the Mohicans: A Narrative of 1757* (repr., New York: Crowell, 1896), viii; Eva L. Butler, "Some Early Indian Basket Makers of Southern New England," in Speck, *Block-Stamp Decoration,* 39, 41, 44, 46, 47, 49, 50; Samuel Orcutt and Ambrose Beardsley, *The History of the Old Town of Derby, Connecticut* (Springfield, Mass.: Springfield Print., 1880), 23, 50; Jane Van Norman Turano, "Taken from Life: Early Photographic Portraits of New England Algonkians, ca. 1844–1865," in *Algonkians of New England: Past and Present,* ed. Peter Benes (Dublin Seminar for New England Folklife, Annual Proceedings, 1991), 121–43; Harriette Merrifield Forbes, *The Hundredth Town: Glimpses of Life in Westborough, 1717–1817* (Boston, 1889), 167–85; Octavia M. Sweetzer to Mrs. George B. Wells, 30 Aug. 1949, files, Old Sturbridge Village.

28. Ozias C. Pitkin and Fred E. Pitkin, *History of Marshfield, Vt.* (Marshfield: priv. pub, 1941), 9; Catherine S-C. Newell, *Molly Ockett* (Bethel, Maine: Bethel Historical Society, 1981); Bunny McBride and Harald E. L. Prins, "Walking the Medicine Line: Molly Ockett, a Pigwacket Doctor," in *Northeastern Indian Lives 1632–1816,* ed. Robert S. Grumet (Amherst: Univ. of Massachusetts Press, 1996), 321–47. For a semifictional but powerful account of Molly Ocket's life, see Bunny McBride, *Women of the Dawn* (Lincoln and London: Univ. of Nebraska Press, 1999).

29. Butler, "Early Indian Basket Makers," 47, 51; Alice Morse Earle, *Stage-Coach and Tavern Days* (1900; repr., New York: Dover, 1969), 95; Forbes, *Hundredth Town,* 176; N. T. True, "History of Bethel," and "The Last of the Pequakets," clippings from the *Oxford Democrat,* scrapbook, Maine Historical Society, Portland.

30. Forbes, *Hundredth Town,* 177, 179, 180.

31. Butler, "Early Indian Basket Makers," 40, 50; Forbes, *Hundredth Town,* 170, 173, 174.; Elizabeth C. Jenkins, "West Barnstable," in Donald B. Trayner, *Barnstable: Three Centuries of a Cape Cod Town* (Hyannis, Mass.: F. B. & F. P. Goss, 1939), 443; [Lydia Huntley Sigourney], *Sketch of Connecticut Forty Years Since* (Hartford, Conn.: Cooke, 1824), 59.

32. Forbes, *Hundredth Town,* 171, 180; Butler, "Early Indian Basket Makers," 48; True, "Last of the Pequakets," 1863; John Greenleaf Whittier, "Yankee Gypsies," in *Margaret Smith's Journal: Tales and Sketches* (Boston and New York: Houghton Mifflin, 1893), 338–39.

33. Forbes, *Hundredth Town,* 172–75.

34. Earle, *Stage-Coach and Tavern,* 93, 94; Butler, "Early Indian Basket Makers," 51.

35. Sigourney, *Sketch of Connecticut,* 34–38.

36. Ibid., 52–54.

37. Ibid., 55–59.

38. Ibid., 51, 52; Stephen Badger, "Historical and Characteristic Traits of the American Indians in General and Those of Natick in Particular," *Collections of the Massachusetts Historical Society,* 1st ser. (1798; repr. 1835) 5:41–42.

39. Walter J. Bigelow, *History of Stowe, Vermont* (not published, 1934), 239; Mary Hall Leonard, *Mattapoisett and Old Rochester, Massachusetts* (New York: Gafton, 1907),

118–19; True, "Last of the Pequakets"; Earle, *Stage-Coach and Tavern*, 95; Forbes, *Hundredth Town*, 173, 174; Pitkin and Pitkin, *History of Marshfield, Vt.*, 9.

40. Ann McMullen, "What's Wrong with This Picture? Context, Coversion, Survival, and the Development of Regional Native Cultures and Pan-Indianism in Southeastern New England," in *Enduring Traditions: The Native Peoples of New England*, ed. Laurie Weinstein (Westport, Conn.: Bergin & Garvey, 1994), 135, 123–50.

41. Thomas L. Doughton, "Unseen Neighbors: Native Americans of Central Massachusetts, a People Who Had 'Vanished,' " in *After King Philip's War: Presence and Persistence in Indian New England*, ed. Colin G. Calloway (Hanover, N.H., and London: Univ. Press of New England, 1997), 208–9. Also see Jean M. O'Brien, *Dispossession by Degrees: Indian Land and Identity in Natick, Massachusetts, 1650–1790* (Cambridge: Cambridge Univ. Press, 1997), 210–15; Patrick Frazier, *The Mohicans of Stockbridge* (Lincoln and London: Univ. of Nebraska Press, 1992), 194ff.; and Ruth Wallis Herndon and Ella Wilcox Sekatau, "The Right to a Name: The Narraganset People and Rhode Island Officials in the Revolutionary Era," in *After King Philip's War*, ed. Calloway, 114–43.

42. William S. Simmons, *Spirit of the New England Tribes: Indian History and Folklore, 1620–1984* (Hanover, N.H., and London: Univ. Press of New England, 1986), 272. Simmons's source is Frank G. Speck, "Native Tribes and Dialects of Connecticut: A Mohegan-Pequot Diary," in *Forty-third Annual Report of the Bureau of American Ethnology* (Washington, D.C.: Government Printing Office, 1925–26), 199–287. Other versions of carrying water in a basket appear in a 1761 account by Samson Occom, "An Account of the Montauk Indians, on Long-Island," *Collections of the Massachusetts Historical Society* 10 (1809): 105–11, and Arthur Peale, *Uncas and the Mohegan-Pequot* (Boston: Meador, 1939), 147–48.

43. Simmons, *Spirit of New England Tribes*, 142, 139.

44. Ibid., 95; Frank G. Speck, "A Modern Mohegan-Pequot Text," *American Anthropologist*, new series, 6, no. 4 (1904): 469–76.

45. Trudie Lamb Richmond, "Spirituality and Survival in Schaghticoke Basket-Making," in McMullen and Handsman, *Key into the Language*, 143.

46. "The Experiences of Five Christian Indians," in *On Our Own Ground: The Complete Writings of William Apess, a Pequot*, ed. Barry O'Connell (Amherst: Univ. of Massachusetts Press, 1992), 120–21.

47. Ibid., 123.

48. "A Description of Mashpee, in the County of Barnstable. September 16th, 1802," *Massachusetts Historical Society Collections*, ser. 2, no. 3 (Boston, 1846): 1.

49. "An Indian's Looking Glass," in O'Connell, ed., *On Our Own Ground*, 157.

50. Ibid., xxxiv–xxxviii.

51. "Experiences of Five Christian Indians," 152; Butler, "Early Indian Basket Makers," 40.

52. Klyza and Trombulak, *Story of Vermont*, 72–74; Harold A. Meeks, *Time and Change in Vermont: A Human Geography* (Chester, Conn.: Globe Pequot, 1986), 92–95.

53. Klyza and Trombulak, *Story of Vermont*, 72–74; Meeks, *Time and Change in Vermont*, 92–95.

54. The decline was substantial, from .168 per 1,000 persons to .137. Mary Beth Sievens, "Stray Wives: Marital Conflict and Gender Relations in Vermont, 1790–1830," Ph.D. diss., Boston University, 1996, 147–48. In the 1790s, 8 percent of women responded, but that had dropped to 3 percent by 1820. I have also profited from the as yet unpublished work of Kirsten Sword, whose comparative study of elopement notices in colonial newspapers is the first large-scale study of this phenomenon.

55. Sievens, "Stray Wives," quoting from *Rutland Herald,* Mar. 1795; Sievens, "Stray Wives," 96, quoting from *Rutland Herald,* 3 Dec. 1821.

56. Sievens, "Stray Wives," 94, from *Weekly Wanderer,* 23 July 1804.

57. Sievens, "Stray Wives," 95, 110, quoting from *American Register,* 15 Sept. 1826; 102, from *Vermont Journal,* 5 Aug. 1811.

58. *Vermont Journal,* 15 Dec. 1794, quoted in Sievens, "Stray Wives," 123.

59. Karen Halttunen, *Murder Most Foul: The Killer and the American Gothic Imagination* (Cambridge, Mass., and London: Harvard Univ. Press, 1998).

60. Lemuel Haynes, *Mystery Developed; Or, Russel Colvin, (Supposed to Be Murdered,) in Full Life: and Stephen and Jesse Boorn, (His Convicted Murderers,) Rescued from Ignominious Death by Wonderful Discoveries* (Rutland, Vt.: Fay and Burt, 1819).

61. Originally published Hartford, Connecticut, 1820. Reprinted in Newman, ed., *Black Preacher to White America,* 203–28.

62. Gerald W. McFarland, *The "Counterfeit" Man: The True Story of the Boorn-Colvin Murder Case* (New York: Pantheon, 1990); Halttunen, *Murder Most Foul,* 91–134.

63. Haynes, *Mystery Developed,* 25.

64. Ibid., 12, 32.

65. Ibid., 12, 13.

66. Halttunen, *Murder Most Foul,* 107, 115, 120.

67. Haynes, *Mystery Developed,* 21–23.

68. *Vermont Herald,* 21 Dec. 1821.

69. *Rutland Herald,* 5 Nov., 5 Dec. 1821.

## Chapter 11: An Unfinished Stocking

1. *Newport Mercury,* Newport, R.I., 13 Feb. 1769.

2. In contrast, Moulthrop portrayed her husband, the Reverend Ammi Ruhamah Robbins, surrounded by books with manuscripts and a quill pen in his hand. Jane C. Nylander, *Our Own Snug Fireside: Images of the New England Home, 1760–1860* (New York: Knopf, 1993), 150; *American Paintings in the Detroit Institute of Arts* (New York: Hudson Hills Press, 1991), 1:136–38, 526; *Diary of Thomas Robbins,* ed. Increase N. Tarbox (Boston: Beacon, 1886) 1:146, 526; Ralph W. Thomas, "Reuben Moulthrop, 1763–1814," *Connecticut Historical Society Bulletin* 21 (1956): 97–111; William Sawitzky, "Portraits by Reuben Moulthrop," *New York Historical Society Quarterly* 39 (1955): 401.

3. Silk Display, 50.2.1, 2, 3, 4, 5, 6, Accession Records, Vermont Historical Society, Montpelier, Vermont. "This exhibit is donated by a grandson, Edgar T. Flint, M.D. of Raritan, N.J., April 23, 1950."

4. Randolph A. Roth, *The Democratic Dilemma: Religion, Reform, and the Social Order in the Connecticut River Valley of Vermont, 1791–1850* (Cambridge: Cambridge Univ. Press, 1987), 117–30; Joyce Appleby, *Inheriting the Revolution: The First Generation of Americans* (Cambridge, Mass., and London: Harvard Univ. Press, 2000), 56–89. Biographical information on Laura Flint and her family provided by Jackie Calder, curator, Vermont Historical Society.

5. *Mr. Harper's Report to the Legislature of the State of New Hampshire on the Culture of Silk,* 13–15, in Stark Family Papers, Special Collections, University of New Hampshire; Accession Files, Vermont Historical Society.

6. *Mr. Harper's Report,* 16–18.

7. Ibid., 19–23.

8. Ibid., 24–25.

9. Ibid., 26–27.

10. Ibid., 5–15.

11. *Massachusetts Spy,* Worcester, Massachusetts, 21 Oct. 1829.

12. Someone used the little bit of silk the Bullocks preserved to embroider images of spinning wheels and reels on a linen napkin now at the Vermont Historical Society. Anna Gertrude Bullock, note on sericulture, Gifts and Loans File, Vermont Historical Society, 51.32.

13. Mary Tyler Silk, Vermont Historical Society, 32.5; Frederick Tupper and Helen Tyler Brown, *Grandmother Tyler's Book: The Recollections of Mary Palmer Tyler* (New York: Putnams, 1925), 353–54.

14. Ronald Savoie, "The Silk Industry in Northampton," *Historical Journal of Western Massachusetts* 5 (1977): 21–32.

15. Stark Family Papers, Special Collections, University of New Hampshire, MS 134.

16. *New England Farmer* 2 (1824): 114; *Massachusetts Spy,* 21 Oct. 1829, 26 Oct. 1831.

17. *Massachusetts Spy,* 28 Oct. 1818, 1 Nov. 1820, 5 Nov. 1823, 30 Oct. 1822; *New England Farmer* 1 (1823): 101, 110.

18. *Massachusetts Spy,* 9 Oct. 1822, 26 Oct. 1825, 31 Oct. 1832. The Rhode Island School of Design Museum has an unfinished pair of white cotton stockings "commenced by Aunt Mary Dexter in her 82nd year, 1805" (74.032.26 a and b). See Deborah Pulliam, "No Family Is Better Supplied with Handsome and Comfortable" (seminar paper, Univ. of Maine, Orono, May 2000), 6.

19. *Massachusetts Spy,* 26 Oct. 1831.

20. Sarah was born in Litchfield, Connecticut, in 1785, the fifth daughter and ninth child of Holland and Hannah Moseley Weeks, early settlers of Salisbury, Vermont. Her widowed mother's will and inventory, taken in 1813, shows that she was raised in a family both pious and industrious. The first item in the mother's will was a bequest to the Vermont Missionary Society, "an everlasting fund . . . for the benefit of the Heathen," a gift that represented 17 percent of the total value of the estate. Most of the mother's wealth was in homemade textiles—thirty bed sheets, eleven pillowcases; six diaper tablecloths, one with a fringe; and eleven blankets, including five "flowered" ones. Hannah Moseley Weeks Probate Inventory, Weeks Family Papers, Sheldon Research Center, Sheldon Museum, Middlebury, Vermont; John M. Weeks, *History of Salisbury* (Middlebury, Vt.: Copeland, 1860), 195, 196; C. S. Smith, *An Historical Sketch of Home Missionary Work in Vermont* (Montpelier, Vt.: Watchman, 1893), 2–7; and for larger context, William R. Hutchison, *Errand to the World: American Protestant Thought and Foreign Missions* (Chicago and London: Univ. of Chicago Press, 1987), 45–46, 62–69.

21. Sarah Weeks to John M. Weeks, n.d., Weeks Family Papers.

22. Sarah Weeks to "Dear Mother," Pittsford, 1810, Weeks Family Papers.

23. Sarah Sheldon, Loose Memoranda and Dye Book, 12, 14, 15, 16, 17, Weeks Family Papers.

24. Sarah Sheldon to Homer Sheldon, n.d., Weeks Family Papers; Sarah Sheldon, Dye Book, May 1832.

25. Sarah Sheldon to Homer Sheldon, 29 and 31 Mar., 7 Apr. 1833.

26. Sarah Sheldon to Homer Sheldon, 31 Mar., 16 June 1833.

27. Sarah Sheldon to Homer Sheldon, 16 June, 28 July, 12 Aug. 1833.

28. Persis Sibley Andrews Diary (typed transcription), Maine State Museum, Augusta, Maine; Persis Sibley Andrews Stockings, Maine State Museum, 81.100.2, 81.100.3; Pulliam, "No Family Is Better Supplied," 7–11.

29. Persis Sibley Andrews Diary, 11 Sept. 1841, quoted in Pulliam, "No Family Is Better Supplied," 19.

30. Nylander, *Our Own Snug Fireside,* 224.

31. Persis Sibley Andrews Diary, 2 Feb. 1845, 13 Mar. 1845, 7 Oct. 1849; Pulliam, "No Family Is Better Supplied," 12.

32. Persis Sibley Andrews Diary, 9 Aug. 1845.

33. Ibid., 12 Oct. 1845.

34. Ibid., 23 Oct., 16 Nov., 14 Dec. 1845.

35. Jeanne Boydston, *Home and Work: Housework, Wages, and the Ideology of Labor in the Early Republic* (New York: Oxford Univ. Press, 1990), 146 and passim.

36. *The Liberator,* Boston, 7, 23 Apr., 12 May 1837.

37. E. P. Thompson, "Time, Work-Discipline, and Industrial Capitalism," *Past and Present* 38 (1967): 56–97; Thomas Dublin, *Women at Work: The Transformation of Work and Community in Lowell, Massachusetts, 1826–1860* (New York: Columbia Univ. Press, 1979), 58–74; Jonathan Prude, *The Coming of Industrial Order: Town and Factory Life in Rural Massachusetts, 1810–1860* (Cambridge: Cambridge Univ. Press, 1983), 36–37, 126–57.

38. Jane Stevens to Jane Patten, Lowell, 22 Mar. 1835, Tolford-Patten Papers, box 6, New Hampshire State Library, Concord, New Hampshire.

39. Dublin, *Women at Work,* 20–21.

40. Gordon Francis Grimes, "A History of Dover, New Hampshire, 1790–1835" (honors thesis, Bowdoin College, 1971), vol. 2, Appendix 5: "Description of the Dover Factories"; Matthew Bridges to John Williams and Matthew Bridges to W. Shimmin, 29 June 1825, Dover Manufacturing Letter Book 1, New Hampshire Historical Society, Concord, New Hampshire.

41. John Williams to the directors, 31 Jan. 1827, and John Williams to W. Shimmin, 1 Aug. 1827, quoted in Grimes, "History of Dover," 1:140–42.

42. "If we succeed in preventing several of our workmen from promenading the streets this evening with flags bearing the motto 'FREE TRADE AND MECHANICS RIGHTS' in front of the principle stores with the music playing the 'rogues march' I believe the excitement will be brought to a close," one of the managers assured an investor. Grimes, "History of Dover," 1: 128–29 and Appendix 5.

43. "The First Strike," *New York Times,* 6 Feb. 1886, 3; John B. Andrews and W. D. P. Bliss, *Women and Child Wage Earners* (Senate Document, 61st Congress, Second Session), 10:23–49; Philip S. Foner, *History of the Labor Movement in the United States* (New York: International Publishers, 1947), 1:104–11; Philip S. Foner, *Women and the American Labor Movement* (New York: The Free Press, 1979), 30–37.

44. *Mechanics Free Press,* Philadelphia, 17 Jan. 1829.

45. Matthew Bridges to W. Shimmin, 6 Aug. 1828, Dover Manufacturing Letter Book 1.

46. Dublin, *Women at Work,* 86–98; Andrews and Bliss, *Women and Child Wage Earners,* 25–28; *The Man,* 20 Feb. 1834; *Boston Evening Transcript,* 17 Feb. 1834.

47. Almond Davis, "Memoir of Salome Lincoln (1843)," in *The New England Mill Village, 1790–1860,* ed. Gary Kulik, Roger Parks, and Theodore Z. Penn (Cambridge, Mass., and London: MIT Press, 1982), 511–16.

48. *The Man,* 20 Feb. 1834; *Boston Evening Transcript,* 17 Feb. and 6 Mar. 1834; Andrews and Bliss, *Women and Child Wage Earners,* 25–28.

49. Dublin, *Women at Work,* 98–104.

50. Grimes, "History of Dover," 1:167, 157–58.

51. *Boston Evening Transcript,* 25 Feb. 1834.

52. Undated broadside, Woodman Institute, Dover, New Hampshire.

53. Undated broadside, Woodman Institute.

54. "Farming Life in New England," *Atlantic Monthly* (Aug. 1858): 341, quoted in Thomas Dublin, *Transforming Women's Work: New England Lives in the Industrial Revolution*

(Ithaca, N.Y., and London: Cornell Univ. Press, 1994), 116; on the work habits of mill girls, 77–118, passim.

55. Persis Sibley Andrews Diary, 2 Nov. 1851.

56. Jane Stevens to Jane Patten, Lowell, 22 Mar. 1835, Tolford-Patten Papers, box 6; Hugh Tolford Estate Papers, 6 June 1823, Patten-Tolford Papers, box 9; [no author] *History of Bedford* (Concord, N.H.: Rumford, 1903), 1096–97; Benjamin Chase, *History of Old Chester* (Auburn, N.H.: priv. pub., 1869), 598–99.

57. Jane Stevens to "Dear Aunts," 24 Nov. [no year given], Tolford-Patten Papers, box 6.

58. Jane Stevens to E. Patten, 1 Sept. [no year given] Lowell, 2 June 1839, 5 Apr. 1840, 2 May 1847, Tolford-Patten Papers, box 6.

59. Dublin, *Transforming Women's Work*, 20.

60. Edgar Potter, "Who Made the First Straw Bonnet in Massachusetts?" *Old-Time New England* 11 (1920): 72–78; E. W. Carpenter, "Straw Bonnets," *Harper's New Monthly Magazine* 29 (1864): 576–84; Caroline Sloat, " 'A Great Help to Many Families': Straw Braiding in Massachusetts Before 1825," in *House and Home*, ed. Peter Benes (Dublin Seminar for New England Folklife, Annual Proceedings, 1988), 89–100; Jane Lancaster, " 'By the Pens of Females': Girls' Diaries from Rhode Island, 1788–1821," *Rhode Island History* 57 (1999): 81–86.

61. *New England Farmer* 2 (1824): 308–9.

62. Dublin, *Transforming Women's Work*, 48–75.

63. Donna Belle-Garvin, "The Warp and Weft of a Lifetime: The Discovery of a New Hampshire Weaver and Her Work," in *Textiles in Early New England: Design, Production, and Consumption*, ed. Peter Benes (Dublin Seminar for New England Folklife, Annual Proceedings, 1997), 29–47.

64. Gail Barbara Fowler [Mohanty], "Rhode Island Handloom Weavers and the Effects of Technological Change, 1780–1840," Ph.D. diss., Univ. of Pennsylvania, 1984, 293–96, 345–63.

65. Daniel Knapp to David Patten, 14 Mar. 1824, Tolford-Patten Papers, box 6.

66. "Almira Doty Stewart's Diary, Copied from her original diary which fell to pieces with Age," ms., Special Collections, Bailey/Howe Memorial Library, University of Vermont.

67. Donna Toland Smart, ed., *Mormon Midwife: The 1846–1888 Diaries of Patty Bartlett Sessions* (Logan: Utah State Univ. Press, 1997), 2–12; William B. Lapham, *History of the Town of Bethel, Maine* (1891; repr., Bethel, Maine: Bethel Historical Society, 1981), 467.

68. Smart, "Introduction," *Mormon Midwife*, 14–22.

69. Smart, *Mormon Midwife*, 99.

70. Ibid., 110, 113, 117.

71. Ibid., 29, 169–70.

72. Ibid., 10.

73. Historical Record of Lucy M. Smith, Special Collections, University of Utah Library, Salt Lake City, 41, 59, 61.

74. Ibid., 55.

75. Brigham Young and Heber C. Kimball, "The Fourteenth General Epistle to the Latter-day Saints," and Brigham Young, "Discourse," quoted in Anne L. Macdonald, *No Idle Hands: The Social History of American Knitting* (New York: Ballantine Books, 1988), 91–92.

76. Historical Record of Lucy M. Smith, 59–61.

77. Ibid., 51.

78. *New England Farmer* 11 (1832): 132–33.

79. *Farmer's Cabinet*, Amherst, New Hampshire, 15 Oct. 1831.

80. Ibid., 12 Oct. 1832, 3 Oct. 1834; Wayne Caldwell Neely, *The Agricultural Fair* (New York: Columbia Univ. Press, 1935), 71.

81. Information on current exhibit provided by Douglas Copeley, New Hampshire Historical Society, personal communication, 14 Mar. 2001. Patterson's will, dated 20 Sept. 1830, is in the Rockingham County Probate Records, New Hampshire State Archives, Concord. For more on the dispersal of the Patterson textiles, see Laurel Thatcher Ulrich, "In the Garrets and Ratholes of Old Houses," in *New England Textiles, Part Two*, ed. Peter Benes (Dublin Seminar for New England Folklife, Annual Proceedings, 1999).

## *Afterword*

1. The Smithsonian photo identifies the subject only as Mrs. Amos. According to Harvard's records, a Mashpee burden basket almost identical to that in Speck's picture came to the Peabody Museum in 1919 as the "gift of Mrs. Adaline Mills through Dr. L. C. Jones . . . Made by the Donors mother Marjory Mye (a full blood Mashpee Indian) about 1870." Frank Dorman, who is completing a book on Mashpee genealogy, helped me identify Mrs. Amos. Ella Gardner, who married Horatio Amos in 1881, was the daughter of Adeline Gardner Mills (b. 1842), who was the daughter of Margery Gardner Mye (b. 1818), the basket maker. Peabody Museum records do not identify the makers of the other Mashpee baskets in their collections, though the construction is similar. All appear to have been used extensively before they came to the museum. Madeleine W. Fang and Marilyn R. Binder, *A Photographic Guide to the Ethnographic North American Indian Basket Collection I* (Cambridge: Peabody Museum, 1990), 457; Peabody Museum, Catalogue of Collections, series 1, 14:62807, 18:87357, manuscript, Harvard University Archives; and Frank Dorman, e-mail communication, 19 Feb. 2001.

# Acknowledgments

This book began in 1990 as a conference paper on textile tools in eighteenth-century New Hampshire probate inventories. That project grew, like the proverbial sweater, an extra row on one side requiring an extension on the other, until it became wider and longer than I ever imagined. Early on I was blessed with a Veronica Gervers Fellowship that allowed me to spend several weeks in residence at the Royal Ontario Museum in Toronto, where Adrienne Hood taught me to look at cloth. I could not have found a wiser or more generous guide into the world of textiles. The Guggenheim Foundation provided additional support during that early period.

I might have finished sooner had it not been for the extraordinary generosity of the John D. and Catherine T. MacArthur Foundation, which awarded me a five-year fellowship in July 1992, and allowed me to offer summer employment to my University of New Hampshire graduate students and launch a more ambitious study than I had originally imagined. Edward McCarron, Jennifer LaMonte, Elizabeth Nichols, Edith Murphy, and Stacy Strader-Hogsett gathered much of the data that eventually went into "Wheels, Looms, and the Gender Division of Labor in Eighteenth-Century New England" (*William and Mary Quarterly*, 3d series, 55 [1998]: 3–38). When I moved to Harvard in 1995, a new group of students contributed their talents. Kirsten Sword, Sarah Pearsall, Mark Hanna, and Michelle Jarrett Morris taught me many things as they searched archives for elusive fabrics and persons. Along with other members of our early American dissertation group—Sharon Braslaw Sundue, Brian DeLay, Eliza Clark, and Paul Mapp—they have been perceptive readers and critics as well.

Museum research, unlike library research, is always collaborative. Some of my happiest moments have been spent examining objects alongside skilled and patient curators, registrars, and conservators. Some of them became informal advisors to my project, continuing to offer their advice by phone or through e-mails long after my visits. I am grateful to Lynne Bassett, formerly of Sturbridge Village; Susan Schoelwer and Richard Malley of the Connecticut Historical Society; Donna-Belle Garvin and Douglas Copeley of the New Hampshire Historical Society; Sandra Armentrout and Joyce Butler, formerly of the Brick Store Museum; Susan Haskell of Harvard's Peabody Museum; Paula Richter of

Peabody-Essex Museum; Celia Oliver of the Shelburne Museum; Diane Fagan-Affleck of the Museum of American Textile History; Linda Baumgarten of Colonial Williamsburg; Linda Welters and Margaret Ordonez of the University of Rhode Island; Jacqueline Calder at the Vermont Historical Society; Jennifer Jacobs and Judith Livingston Loto at the Litchfield Historical Society; Brock Jobe and Linda Eaton of Winterthur Museum; and many others.

Thanks, too, to Peter Benes, impresario of the Dublin Seminar on New England Folklife; Richard Candee, who claims to "know nothing about textiles" but has been a helpful and consistent supporter of this project; Florence Feldman-Wood, who taught me about spinning wheels; Craig Evans, who talked to me about looms; Tracy Smith, who tried to teach me how to spin and remained my friend; and Glee Krueger, who generously shared her knowledge of early American textiles. Within this wonderful world of "textilians" Jane Nylander is supreme. As a curator, museum director, scholar, and writer, she has done more to preserve and interpret New England textiles than anyone else I know. She is also a mean knitter. Her stockings are never unfinished.

At crucial points Janet Polasky, Eliga Gould, Joyce Chaplin, and Bruce Bourque offered helpful readings of particular sections or chapters. Michael McGiffert was a tough and helpful editor of "Wheels and Looms." Carla Pestana and Sharon Salinger improved and then published an early version of chapter four as "Pastoralism and Poverty in Colonial Boston," in *Inequality in Early America* (Hanover, N.H.: University Press of New England, 1999). Luke Beckerdite and Bill Hosley nurtured an early version of my work on Hannah Barnard's cupboard given as a lecture at the Wadsworth Atheneum and then published as "Furniture as Social History: Gender, Property, and Memory in the Decorative Arts" (*American Furniture* 3 [1995]: 35–64). Fredrika Teute and Ronald Hoffman helped move that study to the second stage with "Hannah Barnard's Cupboard: Female Property and Identity in Eighteenth-Century New England," in *Through a Glass Darkly: Reflections on Personal Identity in Early America* (published for the Omohundro Institute of Early American History & Culture by the University of North Carolina Press, 1997).

I tried out early versions of several chapters as the Anson Phelps Lectures at New York University; the Taft Lectures at the University of Cincinnati; the Kenin Memorial Lecture at Reed College; the Costa Lecture at Ohio University; the Carl Becker Lectures at Cornell University; the Teetzel Lectures at the University of Toronto; the Stice Lectures at the University of Washington; the Founder's Day Lecture at Harvard's Peabody Museum; and at the Massachusetts Historical Society and the Charles Warren Center for Studies in American History at Harvard. Many thanks to the organizers of these lectures and to the audiences who offered probing questions, useful comments, and family stories. The humanists and textilians in my family—Amy, Mindy, Julia, Nancy, and Naomi— offered practical help as well as encouragement. The engineers and scientists—Gael, Karl, Nathan, Thatcher, and Henry—kept their distance, though they, along with their spouses and siblings and our grandchildren—Griffin, Alena, Julia, Jamie, and Nathan—contributed squares to a commemorative quilt made for my sixtieth birthday, reminding me that there is more than one way to create textile history. In the desperate final stages of writing, my good friend Susan Gong read the entire manuscript, offering supportive and incisive criticism. The book is immeasurably better for her help.

Jane Garrett has now seen three of my books through production. I appreciate her wisdom and her patience. I am also grateful to Kathleen Fridella for managing the stygian labor of copyediting, to Anthea Lingeman for caring about the pictures, and to Alexis Gargagliano for keeping us all connected.

This book was spun and woven by many hands.

Laurel Thatcher Ulrich
Durham, New Hampshire
May 31, 2001

# Index

Note: Page numbers in *italics* refer to illustrations

Abenakis, 79–82, 83, 95, 98, 99–100, 107, 373, 439n65
  after Revolutionary War, 269–74
  in nineteenth century, colonial revival of, 30
  western, 343, 344–5
  *see also individual groups*
abolitionists, 389–90
Adams, Amos, 181, 183
Adams, Henry, 398
Adams, James O., 19
Adams, John, 19, 257
Adams, John Quincy, 420n13
Addams, Jane, 21–2
African-Americans, 232, 246–7, 344–6
  interracial marriages, 354, 360
  in New London County, Connecticut, 231, 457n56
  racism and, 345, 347
  slavery, *see* slavery
  voting rights, 24
age of homespun, 413–14
  Bushnell's speech naming the, *see* Bushnell, Horace, "Age of Homespun" speech
  nineteenth century idealization of, 17–40, 76–8, 139–40, 175, 377, 408–9, 413, 418
agriculture
  household production combined with, *see* household production of textiles, combined with farming
  progressive, 330, 377, 415
alcohol, 183, 184, 304
  Native Americans and, 124, 167, 255, 269, 354, 355, 356–7, 361, 363, 414
Alden, John, 27
Alexander, Betsy, 296
Algonkian basket, *see* Indian basket, Providence, Rhode Island, 1676
Algonkians, 414
  differences among, 44, 57
  gender division of labor, 44–5
  *see also individual groups, e.g.* Pigwackets
Allen, Ira and Ethan, 344
Allen, Mrs. Daniel, 194
Allen, Reverend Mr., 286
Allen, Samuel, 194

American Fur Trade Museum, 323
American Indian Archaeological Institute, 348–50
American Indians, *see* Native Americans; *individuals and individual Indian groups*
American Museum of Textile History, 89, 175, 188
American Revolution, *see* Revolutionary War
Amherst, New Hampshire, spinning demonstrations at, 26
Amos, Blind Joe, 365
Amos, Ella, 415–16, *416*
Andrews, Charles, 29
Andrews, Persis Sibley, 386–9, 395–6
Andros, Edmund, 84
Anglican Church, 229–30
Annawon, 60–1
*Antiques*, 132, 222
*Antiquities of the New England Indians* (Willoughby), 249, *262*
Apess, William, 363–6, *364*
apprenticing of sons, 196
Aquidneck Island, 69
archaeology, 29, 38, 44, 47, 50, 73, 249–50, 343
Arnold, Benedict, 228
Arnold, Mary Shippen, 260–1
Arnold, Richard, 71
Aron, Joseph, 356
Arrowhamet (Zachary) and wife Martha, 359
arson, 40, 201–2
Arthur, Mary, 161
"Articles of Pacification," 94
*Artist's Vade Mecum, The,* 231
arts and crafts movement, 17
Ashley, Jonathan, 205
Association of the House of Seven Gables, 32
Athanase, Agathe, 32, *33*
ax handles, 73
Axtell, Ann, 400

Backus, Ebenezer, 236
Baker, Captain Eliphalet, 212
Baker, Remember, 344
Ballard, Hannah, 287, 298

Ballard, Martha Moore, 4, 29, 72, 281, 282, 283, 285, 287, 288, 289, 290, 291, 298, 303–4, 319, *329*, 376
Bannocks, Tuggie, 355, 360
Baptists, 181, 199
Barbary pirates, 69, 70
Barker, Jonathan, 269
Barnard, Bridget, 129
Barnard, Francis, 124, 126
Barnard, Hannah, *see* Marsh, Hannah Barnard
Barnard, John, 125
Barnard, Joseph, 125, 127, 129
Barnard, Mary Colton, 125, 127
Barnard, Samuel, 125, 127, 129, 134, 137–8
Barnard, Sarah, 125
Barnard cupboard, Hadley, Massachusetts, 1715, 3, *108*–41, 415
    descriptions of, 109, 110, 117–23
    Hannah's name on, 122
Barrett, Samantha and Zeloda, 400
Bartlet, Sarah, 202
Bartow, Clarina, 244–5, 457n66
basket-making by whites, 217, 381
baskets, Native American, 29–30, 44–5, 47–50, 56–7, 60–1, 269
    conservation of, 42, 352–3
    decline of twined basketry, 72–3
    plaited, 60
    Providence, Rhode Island, *see* Indian basket, Providence Rhode Island, 1676
    sizes of, 45
    as textiles, 425n6
    wigwams as form of basketry, 45–6
    woodsplint, *5*, 73, 348, 414, *416*, 416–18, 478n1
        makers and sellers of, 341, 347, 354–7, *357*, 361, 362–3, 373, 399, 414–15
        Rutland, Vermont, after 1821, *see* woodsplint basket, Rutland, Vermont, after 1821
        uses of lidded, 342
*Basket Seller, The*, 357
Baym, Nina, 18
Beaman, Hannah Barnard Westcarr, 110, 124–5, 127, 128–9, *128*
Beaman, Simon, 128
Bean, Abigail, 269–70
Bean, Jonathan, 271
Beardsley, Cyrus, 372
bears, 271–2
beaver, 38, 257, 270
    trading of, 55, 56
    *see also* fur trade

Bedford, New Hampshire centennial speeches, 19–20
bed hangings, 222
bed rugs, 220–8
    flat darning stitch, 221
    Foot family, 3, 209, 221–8
    hand-embroidered embellishments, 222
    looping, 221
    shag, 226–7
bed ticking, 337, 404
Belknap, Jeremy, 101, 184–91, 206
Belknap, Ruth Eliot, 185
Bennet, Mrs. Joseph and Betsey, 398
Berkshire Country Agricultural society, 330–1, 332
Bethel, Maine (formerly Sudbury-Canada), 257, 258, 259, 265–6, 267–74, 404
Bible covers, 148
Billings, John, 129
birch bark
    boxes, 260, 269, 347
    embroidery, 260
Blackburn, Joseph, 153
blankets, *6*, 44, 53, 55, 228, 320, 331, 348, *349*, 383
    for Indian clothing, 55–6, *324*, 325, 414
    "point," 323, 325
    rose
        English, 307, 323–7, *324*, *326*
        homespun, 309, 322–3, *326*, *334–8*, 415
        New England, 1810, *see* rose blanket, New England, 1810
    as textiles, 425n
bonnet-making, 218, 299, 310, 381, 397–9, *399*
Boorn, Stephen and Jesse, 342–3, 369–72
Borden, Experience, 65
Borden, Joan, 63, 64
Borden, Mary Harris, 64, 65, 432n93
Borden, Mercy, 65
Borden, Meribah, 65–6
Borden, Richard, 63, 64
Borden, Thomas, 64, 65, 66, 69
Boston, Massachusetts, 154–5
    Atlantic commerce of, 144
    celebration Stamp Act repeal, 171–3, *172*
    the elite families of, 144, 146
    map, 1743, *158*
    social inequality in, 144
    spinning demonstrations, 26, 156, 157–8
    spinning factory to aid the poor, 145, 157–66
Boston, Sarah, 355–6, 361
Boston Common embroidery, 155–6, *156–7*
*Boston Evening Post*, 160
*Boston Evening Transcript*, 392, 394

*Boston Gazette*, 161, 178
*Boston News-Letter*, 295
Bourne, Edward, 310–11, 312, 314–16
Bourne, Elizabeth, *see* Wildes, Elizabeth
    Perkins (later Elizabeth Perkins
    Wildes Bourne)
Bourne, Eunice, *143*, 149, 173
    background of, 143–4, 173
    chimneypiece, *see* Bourne chimneypiece,
        Boston, Massachusetts, 1753
Bourne, John, 310, 311, 313–14, 350
Bourne, Joseph, 167
Bourne, Julia, 315–16, 333
Bourne, Melatiah, 145, 146, 159, 164
Bourne, Mercy Gorham, 144, 145–6, 149
Bourne, Richard, 143–4, 166–7
Bourne, Sylvanus, 144, 145, 146, 166–7, 168
Bourne, William, 146, 149
Bourne chimneypiece, Boston, Massachusetts,
        1753, 3, *142–73*, 231
    as cultural artifact, 153
    description of, 149
    details from, *151, 155*
    pastoral imagery of, 145
    pattern of, 143, 149–50
    questions raised by, 143
    technique used in, 149
Bourne counterpane, 1810, *306*, 307, 308–9,
        *313*, 337–9
Bowen, Ephraim, 176
boxes, 260–1, 269, 347
boycotts, 37, 176–9, 182, 309, 327
Bradford, Thomas, 71
Bradford, William, 57
Brattleboro, Vermont, 319
breakfast, mode of eating, 300–1
breeches, 190, 272, 280, 299
Brewster, John, Jr., *311*
Briant, Solomon, 167, 169, 171
Brick Store Museum, 307
broadcloth, 232
Brookfield, Massachusetts, 183, 186
brooms, 73, 354–5, 358, 361, 414
Brotherton, 233–4
Brown, Deb, 357–8
Brown, Elisha, 162
Browner, Deb, 358, 361
Bryant, Sarah, 281, 287, 288, 289, 290, 303,
        332–3
Bryant, William Cullen, 332
Buel, Elizabeth Barney, 32, 34–6, *35*
Bulkeley, Charles, 235
Bullock, Edmund, 380
bulrushes, mats from, 46

Bunker Hill, Battle of, 214, 266
Burns, Mary, 195
Burr, Esther, 147–8
Burton, Hannah Wolfe, 291
Busch, Julius, *12*
Bushman, Richard, 304
Bushnell, Dotha Bishop, 22, 23
Bushnell, Horace, 13, 79, 298
    "Age of Homespun" speech, 7, 14–17, 23,
        38, 372–3, 413, 414
    analysis of, 18, 20–2, 24–5
    background of, 22–3
    portrait of, *15*
    women's rights and, 23–4
Bushnell, Molly Ensign, 22

cabinetmakers' shop signs, 236, *237*
cabinets, 111
calico, 232, 281, 298, 390
Calloway, Colin, 343
Calvinism, 14, 16, 345
Camp, Lucy, 162
Campbell, John, 283–4
Camp Fire Girls, 30
Canada, French, 82, 144, 166, 343
    embroidery traditions of, 250
Canonchet, 58, 60
Canonicus, 63
Cape Cod, Massachusetts, 144, 145, 146
    Wampanoags of Mashpee, *see* Mashpee,
        Wampanoags at
carding, 51, 211, 214, 217, 218, 219, 222
    demonstrations, nineteenth century, 26
    mechanization of, 38, 289, 318
carpets, 236, 381, 407
Cary, Mary, 202–3
Cassasinamon, Robin, 58
Castle Island, 253, 254, 256
Cate, Patty, 194
Cato, Jane, 246–7
Cato, Sampson, 247
cattails, mats from, 46
cattle, 64, 67–8, 71, 196, 257, 431n76
cattle shows, textile exhibits at, 323, 329–33,
        335, 342, 380, 381–2, 399, 410
census of 1810, 308, 310, 317, 318, 320, 467n26
ceramic tableware, 279, 301
chair coverings, 148
chairs, repairing of, 354, 358, 414
Chandler, Samuel, 181
"changing works," *see* household production
        of textiles, exchange of work
Chapman, Eliphaz, 268

Chester, Prudence, 115, *116*
Chester Academy, Vermont, 328
chests, 111
 *see also* Hadley chests
Chicago World's Fair, 1892, 29, 32, *33*
child labor, 105, 321, 322
child mortality, 213
child-rearing, 389
chimneypieces, 412
 Boston Common embroidery, 155–6,
 *156–7*
 of Eunice Bourne, *see* Bourne chimney-
 piece, Boston, Massachusetts, 1753
chintz, 232, 299
Chipman, John, 181, 183
Chittenden, Elizabeth, 348, *349*
Christianity, *see individual sects*
*Christian Watchman*, 352
Church, Captain Benjamin, 42–3, 60–1, 251
Church, Judge Samuel, 13, 14
Churche's War, *see* King Philip's War
*Clarissa* (Richardson), 238–9
Clark, Aletta Clowes, 290–1
Clark, Jonathan, 270
Clark, Susanna, 193
Cleaveland, John, 181, 183, 212
click reel, 78, 186, *187*
clothing, 30, *31*, 32, 35, 54–6, 59, 95, 97, 101,
 130, 140, 144, 160, 181, 190, 197, 224,
 232, 233, 247, 254, 262–3, 270, 271,
 298, 316, 320, 321, 358, 372, 383, 384,
 385, 388, 396, 402, *411*
 *see also individual items of clothing, e.g.* shirts
"clouding," 396
Cochran, John, 283, 284
Cognehew, Reuben, 170–1
Colchester, Connecticut, 363
 during Revolutionary War period, 212–13,
 214, 217, 375
 rug weaving industry, 221
Coleman, D. C., 93
colonial revival, 17–40
Colton, George, 123–4
Columbian Tercentenary, 27
Columbia University, 34
Colvin, Lewis, 369–70
Colvin, Russel, 343, 369–72
Colvin, Sally, 369, 370, 372
combing, 52, 285
"Commemoration Ode," 252
commerce, 231, 414
 between colonists and Native Americans,
 55, 56–8, 257, 269
 embargo of 1807, 279

English-colonial, 44, 83, 84, 144
English-U.S., 281, 309
 rose blankets, 323–7
 tariffs to protect New England textiles, 393
 triangular trade, 196
 West Indies–New England, 38–9, 83–4, 85,
 104–5, 196, 231, 298, 414
compass
 motif for rose blankets, 324, *325*
 symbolism of the, 238, 324
Condy, Susanna, 149–50
Coney Female Academy, 386
Congregational churches, 181, 229
Connecticut, 3, 12, 57, 58, 60, 66, 67, 71, 86,
 102, 113, 125, 126, 189, 196, 280, 283,
 287, 293, 296, 301, 318, 322, 327, 333,
 341, 343, 345, 346, 348, 354, 356, 358,
 361, 376, 378–9, 380, 398, 400
 *see also individual towns*
Connecticut Historical Society, 24–25, *25*, 48,
 *49*, 140, 236
Connecticut River Valley, 106, 138, 342, 343
Connell, Sarah, 304–5
consumer revolution, 5, 21
Continental Congress, 234, 275
Cook, Elisha, 201
Cook, Esther, 117
Cook, Mary, 137
Cook, Philip, 347
Cooley, Timothy Mather, *345*
Cooper, Esther, 200–1
Cooper, James Fenimore, 354, 355
Cooper, John, 359
Cooper, Mary, 192, 199–200, 201, 206
Cooper, Reverend Mr. Samuel, 157, 165–6
Cooper, Simon, 200–1
Copley, John Singleton, 145, 153
cotton, 92, 289–90, 298–9, 312, 318, 319, 413
 English attitude toward, 83–4, 434n13
 factory-spun, 279, 318–19, 322, 396, 410
 Sea-Island, 298
 short-staple, 38
 West Indian, 38, 39, 83–4, 85, 196, 414
Cotton, Josiah, 104
cotton gin, 279
counted-thread embroidery, 226
counterpanes, 381, 399, *401*
 Bourne, 307, 311, 312, 315, 317, 332, 338
 1810, *see* Bourne counterpane, 1810
"Courtship of Miles Standish, The"
 (Longfellow), 27
coverlets, *6*, 194–5, 209, 292–3, *295*, 313, 314,
 332, 337, 400, *401*, 415, *417*
counterpanes, *see* counterpanes

finishing of, 295
Pennsylvania, 222
Cowles, Esther, 139
Cowles, John, 139
Cowles, Julia, 285–6
Coxe, Tench, 310
Crabbe, George, 152
craftsmen, 281–2
crewel, 149, 222, 265, 415
bed valance, 30, *227*
Crocket, Mary, 193
Crommet, John, 301
cross reels, *see* niddy-noddies
cupboard cloths, 112, 115
cupboards, 111
as containers for fine linens, 110–11, 112–17,
138–40
Hannah Barnard's, *see* Barnard cupboard,
Hadley, Massachusetts, 1715
joined, 111
Rowlandson, 111–12, *112*
curtains, 236, 296, 381
Cushing, John, 184, 185
cushion covers, tapestry, *121*, 123
Custis, George Washington, 330
Cutt, Ursula, 83
Cutter, Captain Ammi Ruhamah, 252
Cutts, Anna, 315
Cutts, Richard, 314, 316

damask, 113, 115, 145, 190, 316, 333
Damm, John, 79, 83
Damm, Martha, 82, 85, 86
Damm, Pomfret, 85
Damm, William, 78, 79, 105–6
garrison of, *see* Damm Garrison, William
inventory on his death, 78, 85, 86, 95, 103
Damm, William (nephew), 105
Damm Garrison, William, 175, 414
construction of, 76
history of, 82
restoration of, 76, *77*
spinning wheels at, *see* spinning wheels in
old log house, Dover, New
Hampshire
textile tools in garrett of, *75–6*, 175
Da Rosa, Antonio, 36
Daughters of Liberty, 177, 180, 183
Daughters of the American Revolution, 30,
32, 415
Litchfield, Connecticut, chapter of, 34, 35
*Manual for Immigrants,* 36
Sequoia Chapter of, 17

David, King, 65
Davis, William, 321–2
Dayton, Cornelia, 210, 211
Deane, Samuel, 286
"Death of Absalom, The," 147
de Brunes, Iohannis, *91*
Dedham, Massachusetts, 26–7
Deerfield, Massachusetts, 27–9, 109, 110
DeForest, John W., 24
de Pape, Abraham, *90, 187*
deVries, Jan, 105
Dexter, Hannah, 353–4, 360, 366, 368
diaper, 113, 291, 295, 296, 298, 302–3, 333, 337,
383, 402, 408
Dickinson, Rebecca, 205
Dickinson, Submit, 204
division of labor
of English textile industry, 50–3, 93, 428n27
gender based, 8, 37, 52, 196, 281
Algonkian, 44–5, 46–7
Dod, John, 94–5
Dominion of New England, 84
Dorchester Heights, siege of, 214
Doughton, Thomas, 360
Douglas, Ann, 18
Dover, New Hampshire, 79, 82–83, 105–6,
184–91, 393–4
settlement of, 79
spinning wheels at William Damm
Garrison, *see* spinning wheels in old
log house, Dover, New Hampshire
textile mills of, 390–1
strikes at, 391–2, 393–5, 476n42
Dover *Gazette,* 394–5
dresses, 30, 32, 299, 392, 402, 409
dressing, 52
dressmaking, 218–20, 299
ducks, 271
duffels or trucking cloth, 55, 325, 414, 429n34
Dunlap, John, 104
Dutch art, *see* Netherlands, art of the
Dwight, Timothy, 304
dyeing and dyes, 52, 217, 222, 262, 328–9, 332
"clouding," 396
indigo, 222–3, 227, 295, 332, 350
scientific analysis of, 350, 471n21

Eakins, Thomas, 17
Eames, Hitty, 398
Earle, Pliny, 380
Early Blanket Company, 324
Easton, John, 66
East Woodland period, 47

Eaton, Samuel, 181
*Eclogues* (Virgil), 150
education of women, 145, 148–9, 173, 210, 229,
    311, 323, 383, 386, 389, 404
  needlework, 146–8, 328, 381
  for teaching, 215
Edwards, Esther, 139, 140
Ellet, Elizabeth, 18
elopement notices, 367–8
Embargo Act of 1807, 309
*Emblemata of Zinne-Werck*, 91
embroidery, 348, *349*
  birch-bark, 260
  counter-thread, 226
  crewel, *see* crewel
  hanging, *119*
  moose-hair, 250, 259, 260–2, *261*
  pastoral themes for, *see* pastoral imagery
  Prudence Punderson silk, *see First, Second,*
    *and Last Scenes of Mortality, The*
  on rose blankets, 328–9
  samplers, 116–17, *118*
  teachers of, 146–7, 150, 381
  threads for, 147
  yarns for, 92
Emery, Sarah Ann, 287, 398
England
  civil war of 1640s, 83
  colonial rebellion and household
    production, 176–91
  commerce with the colonies, *see* commerce,
    English-colonial
  commerce with United States, *see*
    commerce, English-U.S.
  -French conflicts, 78, 98, 158–9, 257
  labor unrest in, 391
  restrictions on colonial manufacturing, 84,
    159
  Royal Council, Mashpee petition to,
    170–1
  taxation of colonies, 37, 171, 176, 179, 183
  War of 1812, *see* War of 1812
English textile industry, 414
  division of labor, 50–3, 93, 428n27
  as male-dominated, 4, 37, 52
  protection of, 84
  rose blankets, 307, 323–7
*Entertaining Passages Relating to Philip's War*
  (Church), 61
epidemics, 57
*Essex Antiquarian*, 32
Essex County, Massachusetts, 181
*Essex Gazette*, 176, 206
Essex Institute, 29, 32, 423n52
Ezekiel, prophet, 98

fancywork, 381, 410–12, *411*
farmer-weavers, *see* household production,
    combined with farming
Fay, William, 342
Fearing, Deborah, 199
Fearing, Hannah, 199
Federalists, 313–14, 316, 466n16
Fenner, Arthur, 70
Fenner, Dinah Borden, 42, 43, 61–3, 64, 65, 70,
    71, 414
Fenner, Thomas, 71
Fenner, Major Thomas, 42, 43, 61
Fenno, Oliver, 268
Field, Reverend Dr., 19
Field, Eleanor, 42, 43, 61, 72, 73–4
Field, Sarah, 42
Field, Wait, 42, 43
Field, William, 42
Firmin, Thomas, 91
*First, Second, and Last Scenes of Mortality,*
    *The*, 3, *208*, 209–10, 211, 231, 236–42,
    *237*, 247, 415
  as emblematical, 237–39
  family wealth reflected in, 236
  size of, 231
  subject matter of, 210
Flagg, Jared B., *15*
flannel, 228, 232, 332
flax, 51, 89, 92, 162, 272, 290, 319, 403
  production, steps in, 281–5, 304
  valuation of, 190
  value in rural economy, 202
Flint, Laura Riley, 377, 378
Foot, Abigail "Nabby," 209, 217, 228
  diary of, 209, 213–14, 218–19, 220, 228, 279
Foot, Elisabeth "Betty," 247, 375
  background of, 209
  bed rug, 3, 209, 221–8, *225*
  diary of, 209–20, 228, 247, 279, 288
  education of, 215
  letters of, 215–16
  marriage of, 209, 221
  as teacher, 220, 227, 247
Foot, Elizabeth Kimberley, 209, 218
Foot, Israel, 209, 222
Foot, Israel, Jr., 209, 216
  marriage of, 209, 212
Foot, Mary "Molly," 209, 211, 214, 216, 217–18
  bed rug of, 209, 221–8, *224*
  marriage of, 209, 212, 221
Foot, Sarah Otis, 212, 218–19, 221
  bed rug of, 209, 221–8
Foot bed rugs, Colchester, Connecticut, 1775,
    209, 211, 220–8, 415
  design for, 223–4, 226

dyeing of materials for, 222–3
pattern darning of details, 226
forks, 279, 301, 302, 303
Foster, Enoch, 271
Foundling Hospital
  Dublin, 160
  London, 160, *160*
Framingham, Massachusetts, 398
France
  -English conflicts, 78, 98, 158–9, 257
  French-Indian alliances, 80, 82
  *see also* Canada, French
Francis, Lydia, 355
Franklin, Benjamin, 183
Freeman, Pearson, 344–5
Freeman, Pearson Toussaint, 345–6
French knots, 150, 155
fringes, 223, 278, 296, 409
Frye, Colonel Joseph, 256, 258
Fryeberg, Maine, 257, 258
Fuller, Elizabeth, 285
Fulton, James, 318
furniture-making, 104–5, 111
  in Hadley, Massachusetts, 110
fur trade, 55, 56, 57, 58, 123, 124, 257
  *see also* beaver

Gage, John, 190, 206
Gallison, Captain John, 173
Gaylord, Samuel, 204
Geer, John Wheeler, 231, 236, 242
Geldorp, Gortzius, 113, *114*
Germany, spinning and weaving in, 95, 115–6
Gigger, Simon, 356, 357, 358
Gilead, Maine, 268
Gill, Massachusetts, 38
Gilman, Charlotte Perkins, 21
Gold, Thomas, 332
Goldsmith, Oliver, 242
Goodrich, Betty, 203–4
Goodrich, Josiah, 203
Goodrich, Moses, 341, 372
Goodrich, Sarah, 203
Goodwin family, 348, *349*
*Good Wives: Image and Reality in the Lives of
  Women in Northern New England,
  1650–1750* (Ulrich), 3
Gookin, Daniel, 54
Gordon, Stephen, 345
Gorham, John, 144
*Gospel Palladium*, 352
Gould, John, 103
Gove, Hannah, *417*
Governor's Council, Massachusetts, 144

gowns, 30–32, 281, 298, 299, 332
Graves, John, Sr., 435n
Green, Caty, 147
Green, Rufus, 147
"Greenfield Hill," 304
*Green Mountain Democrat*, 347
Gregg, Samuel, 104
Grimké, Angelina and Sarah, 23, 389
Gross, Elisha, 199
Groton, Connecticut, 229
gum elastic (rubber), 299

hackles, *see* hetchels
Hadley, Massachusetts, 110
  centennial, 26
Hadley chests, 110
  Hadley motif, 110
  with initials or names, 117, 128
  *MS* chest, 117, *118*, 121
  *RS* chest, 127, *128*
  *SH* chest, 117, *119*, 121
  *SW* chest, *120*, 133–5, 444n46
Hakluyt, Richard, 44
Hale, Enoch, 191
Haley, Moll, 193
Hall, Eliza Calvert, 18
Halttunen, Karen, 368
Hamilton, Alexander, 280
Hamlin, Hannibal, 273
Hancock, Thomas, 155, 156, 171
handkerchiefs, 299
hanks to measure yarn, 189
Harris, Howlong, 63, 70, 431n61
Harris, Susanna, 63
Harris, Toleration, 63, 66, 67
Harris, William, 60, 63–5, 67–8, 69, 70, 84,
  431n61, 432n93
Hartford, Connecticut, 12, 13, 109, 177, 279
*Hartford Courant*, 109
Hartford North Consociation, 14
Hastings, Abigail Marsh, 130, 131, *132*, 137,
  225–6
Hastings, Hannah Barnard, genealogy of, *132*,
  131–3, 226
Hastings, Waitstill, 131–2, *132*
hatcheling, 219, 403
Hatchet, Molly, 354, 355, 356
hats, 298, 397–9, *399*
  bonnet-making, 218, 299, 310, 381, 397–9,
  *399*
  woodsplint, 24–25, *25*
Haverhill Whittier Club, 32
Hawking, Steven, 71
Hawks, Sarah, *119*

Hawley, Gideon, 169, 170, 171
Hawthorne, Nathaniel, 252
Hayes, Joanna Critchet, 104
Hayes, Leah Damm, 104, 106
Hayes, Samuel, 102, 104, 106
Haynes, Lemuel, 345, *346*, 347, 369
Hazard, Thomas, 281, 282, 283, 289, 290, 319
Heath, Susannah, *154*
hemp, 92, 259
Hendricks, Bets, 358
Henshaw, Ruth, 281, 285, 287, 291, 292, 296,
    298
hetcheling, 284–5, 291
hetchels, 78, 281, 283, 284, 288
Hiller, Abigail, 147
Hillhouse, James, 280
Hillsborough (New Hampshire) Cattle Show
    and Fair, 410
Hincks, William, *187, 284*
Historic Deerfield, 135, 227, 327
histories of United States, themes of early,
    18–19
*History of the District of Maine, The*
    (Sullivan), 274–5
*History of the Indians of Connecticut from the
    Earliest Known Period to 1850*
    (DeForest), 24
*History of the United States during the
    Administration of Thomas Jefferson*
    (Adams), 398
Hobart, Dr. Mary, 29
Hodgdon, Sarah, 296
Hogarth, William, 160, *160*
Holley, George, 13
homespun, 92, 209, 222, 223
    English and American meanings of, 84
    as fabric name, 84, 85, 145, 146, 190, 193,
        201, 224, 279, 280, 299
    idealization of, *see* age of homespun as
        source of pride, 280, 281
    *see also* household production
Homestead, Stephen Robbins, *5*
Hope, Nathan, 360
Hopkins, Hannah, 302
household production of textiles, 153, 164, 232
    agricultural fairs, displayed at, 323, 329–33,
        335, 342, 399, 410
    colonial rebellion against English taxation
        and, 176–91, 375, 413
    combined with commerce, 196
    combined with farming, 86, 95, 104, 196,
        282–85, 291, 298, 312
    early republic (1790-1820), 278–304, 307–39
        before War of 1812, 308–17

exchange of work, 211, 212, 218, 219–20, 221,
        227, 279, 281, 285, 288, 289, 291, 383
    hardships of, 206–7
    hiring help for, 214, 284, 288, 320, 388
    industrialization's effect on, 400–1, 410
    in Ireland, 159
    from male perspective, 192–4
    by mid-eighteenth century, 103
    by mid-seventeenth century, 83–5
    for pay, 218, 219–20, 284, 288, 320, 322, 383,
        407
    pooling of resources, 84, 288
    social class and, 114–15
    as supplement to foreign imports, 5, 105,
        232, 279, 281, 298
    traded for store goods, 232, 383
    before War of 1812, 308–17, 413
housework, 212, 218, 219, 272
    labor-saving devices, 389
Howe, Daniel Walker, 18
Hudson, Thomas, 153
Hudson's Bay Company, 325
Hull House, 18
Hunter, Mrs. John, 333
Huntington, David, 228
Huston, Isaac, 281
"Huswifery" (Taylor), 94
Hutchinson, Anne, 27, 63
Hutchinson, Thomas, 166


illegitimate children, *see* out-of-wedlock
    children
Indian basket, Providence, Rhode Island,
    1676, 39, *41*–74, 414
    construction of, 47, 72
    dating of, 42, 47–8, 72
    label with history, 42, 61
    materials for, 47, 72, 73
    pattern of ornamental weaving, *48*
Indian Charity School, 184
"Indian's Looking-Glass for the White Man,
    The," 364
indigo dyeing, 222–3, 227, 295, 332, 350
industrialization, 21, 22, 105
    beginnings of New England (1790–1820),
        278–80, 289, 290, 410
    household production, effect on, 400–1, 410
    as savagery, 394
    textile mills of New England, *see* textile
        mills of New England
inkwell, *239*
Inman, Tabitha and Joanna, 103
Ireland, 231

linen production, 97, 101, 159, 160, 189, 283, *284*
Irish migration to New England, 79, 95–102, 409
ironing box, 115
Iroquois, 98, 124, 169, 234, 275

jackets, 299
Jacobs, Sarah S., *357*
James II, 98
James, Hannah, 104
Jefferson, Thomas, 279, 309
Jenness, the Widow, 193, 194
jewelry, Native American, 263
Jewett, Jedidiah, 181
Johnson, Joseph, 233–4
Johnson, Captain Samuel, 236
joined furniture, 111
Jones, Neptune, 247
Jordan, Captain, 253
Jordan, Samuel (Maine merchant), 146
Jordan, Samuel (of Massachusetts), 99, 437n44
Joseph, Pierre, 256
Josselyn, John, 45, 46

Kancamagus, 80–81, 393
*Keep Within the Compass,* 240
Kelley, Mary, 421n28
Kelley, Unis, 194
Kellogg, Hannah Barnard Hastings, *see* Hastings, Hannah Barnard
Kellogg, Nathaniel, 131
Kendrick, Sarah, 295
Kennebec Indians, 99, 100
Kennebec River, 99
Kennebunk and Kennebunkport, Maine, 281, 298, 307, 312
*Kennebunk Weekly Visitor,* 312
kersey, 60, 279, 325, 383
*Key into the Language of North America* (Williams), 54
Kimball, Fanny, 296, *303*
Kimball, Lucia, 249, 266, 273
Kimball, Peter, 106
King, Rufus, 305
King George's War, 168, 252–6
King Philip's War (Churche's War), 42–3, 60–1, 64–70, 78, 79, 110, 125, 251, 414, 416
Indian survivors of, 70–1, 72
start of, 58
Kingsley, James, 420n21

King William's War, 71, 110
Kirby, Peace, *294,* 295
Knight, Sarah Kemble, 113–14
knitting, 58, 211, 217, 281, 287, 376, 381–2, 383, *384,* 386, 407
patterns, 386
of stockings, 375–6, 408, 409–10, *411*
unfinished stocking, 1837, 3, *374–5,* 409
knitting frame, 375
knitting needles, 375
knives, 303
Kreighoff, Cornelius, *357*

lace, 59–60, 113, 146, 232, 279, 303, 335, 386
lacemaking, 36, 91, 92
Lake Champlain, 106, 124, 343
Lancaster, Massachusetts, 19, 58–9
Landon, Ebenezer, 12
Lane, Mary James, 192
Lane, Samuel, 206, 281–2, 283
account books of, 191, 192–94
*Last of the Mohicans, The* (Cooper), 354, 355
Leathers, persons changing their names from, 399–400
Leavit, Sarah, 194
Lebanon, Connecticut, 147, 177, 184, 233, 234
rug weaving industry, 221
Leslie, George, 181
Lexington, Massachusetts, 26
Lexington and Concord, Battle of, 198–9, 212, 234
*Liberator,* 389
Linebrook, Massachusetts, 186
Linen Bounty Act of 1943, Irish, 159
linen(s), 51, 84, 91, 92, 279, *292,* 293, 319, 428n27
fine, 91, 110–11, 112–17, 138–40, 300, 332, 415
Irish, 97, 100, 101, 159, 160, 189, 283, *284*
measurement of yarn for, 189
tablecloth, from early republic, *see* linen tablecloth from early republic
unfinished stocking of, 3, *374–5,* 409
linen tablecloth from early republic, 3, *277–8,* 291–8, *292*
fishnet trimming, 278
netting, 278, 295–7
weave structure of, 278
Lipson, E., *51*
Litchfield, Connecticut, 36, 383
bed rug, 226

Litchfield, Connecticut (*cont.*)
   Bushnell's "age of homespun" speech of
      1851, *see* Bushnell, Horace, "age of
      homespun" speech
   centennial, 1851, 12–17
   view of, in 1851, *11–12*
Litchfield Needle and Bobbin Club, 36
Little, Ephraim, 226
Londonderry, New Hampshire, 29, 98, 99, 100
Longfellow, Henry Wadsworth, 27, 252, 314
Long Island, 210, 235, 242–5
looking glass, *239*
looms, 196, 217, 310, 317–18
   construction of, 92
   fly shuttle, 312
   harnesses, 288, 289, 462n37
      four-harness, *94*
   "pair of," 85, 92, 435n18
   ratio to spinning wheels in household
      inventories, 103, 467n27
   sleys, 288, 463n37
   tape, 223
   warping (preliminary threading of loom),
      288, 462–3n33
   width of, 93
   at William Damm Garrison, 78, 85
   *see also* weaving
Louisbourg, French fortress at, 158–9, 191
Lovewell, Captain John, 251, 252, 273–4, 360
Lowell, Massachusetts textile mills, 390, 392,
      393, 396
Luther, Reverend Clair Franklin, 444n46

McBride, Bunny, 274
McCarron, Edward, 317
Mack, Robert, 29
McMullen, Ann, 360
Macpheadris, Archibald, 95–6
Macpheadris, Sarah Wentworth, 95–6
Macpheadris-Warner house, 95–7
   murals, *96–7*, 97–8, 102, 437n40
Madison, Dolley, 307, 313, 314, 315, 316
Madison, James, 280, 313, 316
Mahicans, 343, 355
   baskets, 341, 348, *349*, 352, 372
Main, Gloria, 210, 211, 219
Maine, 39, 99–100, 275–6, 281, 282, 286, 288,
      305, 318
   *see also individual towns*
Maine Historical Society, 249, 266
Maine State Museum, 249–50, 297
maize, 45
Maliseet Indians, 32
Manasseh, Henry, 24–25, *25*

Mann, Horace, 25–6
Mansfield, E. D., 17
*Manual for Immigrants* (Daughters of the
      American Revolution), 36
maps
   Boston, 1743, *158*
   major Indian groups at time of contact, *9*
   Narragansett Bay, circa 1676, *62*
   Northeastern settlement, *10*
   Pascataway (Piscataqua) River, c. 1660,
      *80–81*
Marie Agathe, *see* Ocket, Molly
Marion County, Pennsylvania, 27
market economy, male roles in, 105, 106
marriage, 161, 199, 200–1, 205, 206, 386–7
   elopement notices, 367–8
   polygamy, 405, 407
Marsh, Hannah Barnard, 109–10, 127, 129,
      130, 137–8
   cupboard of, *see* Barnard cupboard, Hadley,
      Massachusetts, 1715
   family background, 124–9
Marsh, Hannah Cook, 201–2
Marsh, John, 110, 129, 130, 444n46
Marsh, Moses, 202
Marshall, Lucy, 269–70
Martyn, Richard, 85
Marx, Karl, 91
Mary, Queen of Scots, 238, 457n57
Mashpee, Wampanoags at, 166, 364, 365,
      416–18, 478n1
   guardianship, attempts to free themselves
      from, 144, 166–71, 365
Mason, Moses, 268
Massachusetts, 79–80, 94, 100, 110, 114, 117,
      125, 128, 300, 321, 327, 333
   dissenters banished from, 63, 79
   Governor's Council, 143, 161, 166, 169, 253
   Indian lands, control over, 166–71
   seal, 54, *54*, 55
*Massachusetts Spy*, 333, *382*
Massachusetts Woman Suffrage Association, 27
Massasoit, 57, 66
Mather, Cotton, 127
Mather, Eleazar, 114–15
Mathews, Mercy Nonsuch, 354
Matthew, Hannah, 199
Mauwee, Eunice, 354
Mayo, Calvin and Sally, 321
Mayo, Minerva, 320–1
Meanwell, Deborah (pseudonym), 184
*Mechanics Free Press*, 392
Meequapew and son Peter, 69
Meloon, Rachel, 106–7, *107*
Melville, Thomas, Jr., 331–2

memorialization, 377, 387–8, 397, 409, 418

merino wool, 328, 329

Merrimac River, 251

Mesarvey, Thamsin, 83

Metacomet (King Philip), 44, 46, 58, 60, 66, 73
   *see also* King Philip's War

Metcalf, Betsy, 397–8, *399*

Methodism, 22

Miantonomo, 63

"middle landscape," 173, 304, 393

Middlesex County Agricultural Society, 410

Middletown, Connecticut, centennial
   speeches, 19

midwifery, 86, 203, 281, 405, 407

*Midwife's Tale, A: The Life of Martha Ballard
   Based on Her Diary, 1785–1812*
   (Ulrich), 4

migration from New England, nineteenth
   century, 401–9

milkweed, 48, 381, *382*

Minor, Lydia, 86

Minor, Manasseh, 86, 103

Miss Beach's Academy, Dorchester, 335

Missisiquoi Abenaki, 347, 372
   *see also* Abenakis

*Missouri Republican*, 323

Miss Stearne's School, New Worcester, 381

*Mr. Harper's Report to the Legislature of the
   State of New Hampshire on the Culture
   of Silk*, 378, 379

mittens, 299

moccasins, 263, 269

Mohanty, Gail, 287

Mohegan bag, 48, *49*

Mohegans, 57, 58, 67, 232, 358–9, 362
   educated, 233–4

Molloy, John, 304

Montgomery, Florence, 226

moose, 270

moose hair, 250, 259, 260–2, *261*

Mormons, 405, 407–8

Morrell, William, 46–7

mortise and tenon joints, 111

Morton, Thomas, 45, 55

Moulthrop, Reuben, 376, *376*, 474n2

"Mournful Elegy on Mr. Jonathan Frye, A,"
   252

movables, 111, 129, 161, 443n41
   provenance of, 131–5

Mulberry-Grove School, Leicester, 381

Mullins, Priscilla, 27

Munger, Hiram, 321

murders, 342–3, 345, 353–4, 366, 368–72

Murray, Elizabeth, 146–7

Museum of Fine Arts, Boston, 143, 149

muslin, 299

Mye, Marjorie, 416, *416*

Namumpum (later Weetamoo), 57–8, 59–60

napkins, 112, *115*, 115–16, 300, 301–3, 415
   initialing of, 116, *116*

Narragansets, 57, 58, 71, 361

Narragansett Bay, circa 1676, map of, *62*

Nash, Gary, 448n47

Nashua, New Hampshire, textile mills in,
   396–7

Natick, Massachusetts, 19, 350

Natick Indians, 265–6, 353, 360, 366, 368

Natick tribe, 342

Native Americans, 38, 104, 415–18
   alcohol and, 124, 167, 255, 269, 354, 355,
      356–7, 361, 363, 414
   basket-making, *see* baskets, Native
      American
   burial of material objects with their dead,
      78
   clothing of, 54–5, 263, *324*, 325, 414
   comparison to fabrics of Europeans and,
      50–1, 425n6
   "disappearing," 343, 353–6, 360–1, 364,
      414–15
   division of labor, 44–5, 46–7
   enslavement of, *see* slavery, Indians sold
      into
   ethnocentric descriptions of, 55–6
   folklore, 361–3
   hat, woodsplint, 24–25, *25*
   indentured, 69, 169, 266
   interracial marriages, 354, 360
   Israelites and, 431n70
   jewelry, 263
   major Indian groups at time of contact, *9*
   as naked savage, 54, *54*
   poverty of, 357, 361–2, 414
   racism and, 24, 347, 354–66, 399–400
   sellers of baskets and crafts, nineteenth
      century, 341, 347, 354–7
   violence, intrafamily, 357–8
   white stereotypes of, 233, 363–4, 366
   *see also specific types of objects made by
      Native Americans, e.g.* brooms;
      wigwams; *individual Indians and
      Indian groups*

needlepoint, 149

needlework education, 146–8, 150

Netherlands, art of the
   cupboards and textiles in, 113, *114*
   idealized visions of spinning in Dutch
      portraits, *90*, 95

netting, 146, 278, 295–7, 303, 409
Newburyport, Massachusetts, 178–80, *179*, 196, 287, 421n26
   niddy-noddy, *see* niddy-noddies; niddy-noddies, Polly Woodwell
   religious diversity in, 178–80
New England Company, 167, 169
*New England Courant*, 251
*New Englander*, 12, 14, 17
*New England Farmer*, 333, 410
"New England Kitchen of about 1750, A," scenes from, *28, 29*
New England Silk Convention, 380–1
New Hampshire, 278, 293, 295, 296, 301, 322, 333, 343, 378, 396
   furniture-making, 104–5
   relationship of Indians and colonists, 78, 79, 80–3, 95, 99–100
   settlement of, 79
   *see also individual towns*
*New Hampshire Gazette*, 309
New Hampshire Historical Society, 106, 375
New Haven, Connecticut, 57, 279
New London County, Connecticut, 231, 457n56
New Orleans Territory, 290
Newport, Rhode Island, 177, 235, 375
*Newport Mercury*, 177, 178, 181
newspapers
   to line lidded woodsplint baskets, 341, 342, 343, 352–3, 366
   *see also individual newspapers*
New Testament, 180
New York, 343, 344
New York City, nineteenth-century displays of household crafts in, 26
*New York Observer*, 12, 13
niche weavers, 400
niddy-noddies, 3, 78, 90, 92, *174*–207, 186–8, *187*, 188
   marked, 206
   Polly Woodwell, *174*–5, 175–7, 197
   purpose of, 175
Ninigret, 58, 71
Nipmuck, 58, 60, 354, 375
Nokes, Lydia, 194
Nonintercourse Act, 309, 327
Northeastern settlement, map of, *10*
Northhampton, Massachusetts, 19
Northhampton Historical Society, 115, *115–16*
Norwich, Connecticut, rug weaving industry, 221
Nusco, 124

Nute, James, 85
Nutter, Hatevil, 85


Occum, Samson, 233–4, 359
"Ocean-born Mary," *see* Wallace, Mary Wilson
Ocket, Molly, 269, 273–4, 355, 356
   as healer, 257–8, 266, 273, 360, 404
   during King George's War, 252–6, 274, 414
   money and, 266–7
Ocket's pocketbook, Bethel, Maine, 1785, 3, *248*–67, *264*, 414
   materials used in, 250, 259–61
   significance of, 250
   twining technique used in, 250, 260, 261–2, *262*
Olcott, Jerusha, letter to, 215–16, 455n17
"Old Draperies," 51
Old Testament, 64, 65, 97–8, 179
Oliver, Peter, 178, 184
Onerable, Darkis, 354
Onion River Land Company, 344
Orange, Vermont, 319, 321
Osgood, Mrs. Samuel, 272
Otis, Hannah (cousin of Eunice Bourne), 155, *156–7*
Otis, Hannah (friend of Betty Foot), 209, 211, 212, 220
Otis, James, 166, 168, 169
Otis, John, 144, 146
Otis, Mercy, 218
Otis, Nathaniel, 212, 216
Otis, Prudence, 218
Otis, Samuel, 146
out-of-wedlock children, 203–4, 210–11, 216, 454n9
overshot, 278, 292–3, 293, 294, 295


palm-leaf and straw hats and bonnets, 397–99, *399*
Pan, Jim, 363
parades, 13, 26, 156–7, 182, 314, 330, 392
Park, Linton, 27
Parker, Judge Amasa, 12–13
Parker, Jonathan, 301
Parkman, Ebenezer, 284
Parmalee, Syrena, embroidered blankets of, 334–5, *337*
Parsons, Jonathan, 178–9, 181
Partridge, Nehemiah, 97, 98
Pascatway (Piscataqua) River, c. 1660, *80–81*
Passamaquoddy, 263, *264*

*Pastorales, Les,* 150, *151*

pastoral imagery, 145, 150–5, 165–6, 405–6, 447n21

  rural hardships obscured by, 152, 173, 413

  sexual undertones of, 152–3

Patten, Matthew, 191, 195, 206, 265, 281, 283, 296, 396

Patten, Susanna, 195–6

pattern darning, 226

Patterson, New Jersey, 279, 392

Patterson, Thomas, 409–10

Paugussets, 354

Pawtucket, Rhode Island, waterpower spinning at, 279, 280

Payne, Anna, 314

Peabody-Essex Museum, 335

Peabody Museum, Harvard University, 32, *33,* 249, 341, 352

Pease, Widow, 170

Peat, Captain Robert, 101

Penacook, 80, 81–2, 98

Pennsylvania, male domination of weaving in, 105

Penobscots, 166, 263

Pepperrell, General William, 252

Pequawets, 249

Pequots, 57, 58, 232, 358–9, 361, 362

  last of the, 354

Pequot War, 60

petticoats, quilted, *223,* 224

Phelps, Charles, 204

Phelps, Elizabeth Porter, 192, 201, 202, 204–6, 206, 293

Philadelphia, Pennsylvania

  exposition of 1876, 27

  household crafts, nineteenth-century displays of, 26

Philadelphia Academy of Art, 325

Philbrick, Clara, *297*

Philbrick, Eliza, *6, 31,* 32, 415, *417,* 423–4n52

  "colonial gown" of, 30–2, *31,* 415

Philbrick, Joseph, 335, 337

Philbrick family embroidered blankets, 334, 335–7, *336,* 415

Philip, King, *see* Metacomet (King Philip)

Phillips, Ammi, 302, *302*

Phillips, Ruth, 260

Phinney, Cordelia, 149

Phips, Sir William, 437n40

pictures, framed, 236–7

Pierpont, John, 13–14, 15

Pigwackets, 250, 251–2, 260

  during King George's War, 252–6

  Revolutionary War and, 258–9, 269, 458n19

Pike, John, 82–3, 251

pincushions, 260, 299

Pioneer Museum, Salt Lake City, 409

pirates, 69, 70, 101–2

Piscataqua, 79

  *see also* Pascatway (Piscataqua) River, c. 1660

Pittsfield, Massachusetts, 286, 329–30, 331

*Pittsfield Sun,* 330

plain weave, 50

plantation agriculture in the South, 279, 413

plates, tin-glazed earthenware, *120,* 122

Plymouth Colony, 57, 58, 66, 79, 84

pocketbooks, 148, 264–5, *265*

  function of, 250, 263

  Molly Ocket's, *see* Ocket's pocketbook, Bethel, Maine, 1785

pockets, 263, 299

  English "pocket," 60

Pocumtucks, 124, 343

Pocumtuck Valley Memorial Association, 38

poetry, 20–1, 94, 154–5, 412

Pokanokets, 58, 67

politics

  pre-Revolutionary, 152, 154–5, 159, 176, 178, 182–4, 190

  early republic, 37, 280–1, 313–14, 394

  in fabric names, 293

Pollard, Captain John, 236

Pollard, Dorothy, *329*

Pollard, Merriam, 288

polygamy, 405, 407

Pomeroy, Eunice, 204

Pomham, Ruth, 356

Poor, Sylvanus, 267

Pope, Alexander, 152

Popmonit, Simon, 167

Poquiantup, Sampson, 232

porcupine quills, 32, 48, *49,* 262, 263

  linen strap ornamented with, 106, *107*

  woven into baskets, 45

Porter, Moses, 305

Portland, duke of, 437n40

*Portrait of a Family Saying Grace, 114*

Poughkeepsie, New York, nineteenth-century displays of household crafts in, 26

poverty, *see* social inequality

pregnancy, premarital, 203–4, 210–11, 216, 454n9

Presbyterians, 178–9

Prescott, Olive, 335, *336*

Prescott, Sarah, blankets of, 334, *334,* 335, *336*

Prince, Sarah, 147

Prins, Harold, 274

Printer, James, 350

probate records, 84, 101–2, 114–15, 127, 132, 139, 146, 189–90, 279, 287, 288, 293, 302, 467n27

   of William Damm, 78, 85, 86, 95, 102

   of Samuel Hayes, 102

*Proposal for the Imployment of the Poor, 91*

Proverbs 31, 14, 93, 180, 182, 215–16, 217, 238, 332

*Providence Evening Bulletin*, 74

Psalms 128:3, 113

pudding spoons, 414

Punderson, Ebenezer, 265, *265*

Punderson, Ebenezer, Jr., 242, 244, 246

Punderson, Ebenezer (father), 210, 228, 246

   as loyalist, 234–6, 242, 243

   slave Jenny, 246–7

   store of, 229, 231–3

Punderson, Ebenezer (grandfather), 229–30

Punderson, Ephraim, 235, 236

Punderson, Hannah, 243, 244, 245

Punderson, Prudence, 228–47

   background of, 229

   death of, 210, 245

   *The First, Second, and Last Scenes of Mortality, see First, Second, and Last Scenes of Mortality, The*

   letter-journal of, 210, 211, 228–9, 231, 240–5, *241*, 247

   other needlework of, 229–31, *230*

   the Revolution's effect on life of, 236–7, 242–5, 247

   thimble, engraved *PP*, 229, *229*

Punderson, Prudence Geer, 210, 235, 242, 244, 265

   crewel bed valance, *227*

Purchase, Joseph, 353, 471–2n25

Puritans, 57, 63, 79, 113, 124

Pynchon, John, 112, 123–4

Pynchon, William, 110, 124


Quakers, 63, 69, 181

Quebec, Canada, 257, 258

Queen Anne's War, 110

quilling, 214, 219

quill winder, 78, 92

quilting, 217, 219

quilts, bed, 223–4

   whole cloth, 224

quilts, patchwork, 382

Quinnapin, 60, 69, 430n49

Quinnipaiacs, 57

racism, *see* African-Americans, racism and; Native Americans, racism and

real property, inheritance of, 129, 130, 443n41

Rebecca Nourse Association, 32

Red Jacket, *324*, 325

refinement, rural, 278, 300–5, 415

   religious concerns about, 303

religious freedom, 63, 78, 79, 344

*Reporter*, 17

*Republican*, 17

Republicans (before War of 1812), 314, 466n16

Revere, Paul, 171–2, *172*

Revolutionary War, 4, 106, 198–9, 234, 235, 258–9, 412, 455n11, 458n19, 459n28

   bed rugs from period of, *see* Foot bed rugs, Colchester, Connecticut, 1775

   Bunker Hill, 214, 266

   early histories of, 18–19

   Lexington and Concord, 198–99, 212, 234

   Litchfield women's contribution to, 13

   Punderson family, effect on, 236–7, 242–5

   silk embroidery from period of, *see First, Second, and Last Scenes of Mortality, The*

   Tories, 210

Reyner, John, 84–5

Reynolds, Daniel, 301

Rhode Island, 333, 352, 360, 361, 375, 397, 400

   dissenters settling, 68

   Indian reservation, 71

   King Philip's War and, 66–9, 70

   triangular trade, 196

Rhode Island Historical Society, 42, 61, 73–4

Richardson, Samuel, 238–9

Richmond, Trudie Lamb, 362–3

rippling comb, 283, 284

Robbins, Elizabeth, 376, *376*

Roberts, Thomas, 101

Rochester, Massachusetts, 254–5, 256

Rockport, Massachusetts, 26

Rogers, John, 27

Rogers, Susanna, 252

rose blanket, New England, 1810, *308*, 308–9, 317, 322–3, *328*, 328–9, 337–9

   described, 307–8

Rosseter, Ann, 139

Rosseter, Sally, 243, 245

Rosseter, Sophia, 245

Rosseter, Thomas, 245

Rosseter, Timothy, 210

Rounds, Ellen, 76, 79

Rowlandson, Joseph, 112, 421n24

Rowlandson, Mary, 19, 58–60, 68, 111–12, 114,
    375, 416
  cupboard of, 111–12, *112*
Rowson, Susanna, 311
Royal Ontario Museum, 323, 328
rubberized clothing, 299
rugs
  bed, *see* bed rugs
  hearth, 381, 388
rum, 231, 232
Rutland, Vermont, 345, 347
*Rutland Herald*, 341, 342, 344–5, 353, 366, 370,
    372, 415

Sabbatus, 258, 269, 270
sable, 257, 270
sail cloth, 164
St. Francis, Quebec, 30, 256, 258, 269, 347,
    458n
St. Louis, Missouri, 26
St. Vitus Dance, 244
samplers, 116–17, *118*, 148, 225, 404–6, *406*,
    412
Sassamon, John, 58
Saul, King, 65
Schagticoke baskets, 341, 362–3
Scholfield, John, 289
Scituate, Massachusetts, 198–9
Sea Island cotton, 298
Sebastion, Tamer, 354
Segar, Nathaniel, 259, 270
Sekatau, Ella, 43
Seller, John, *80*
sericulture, 377–81, 395
Sessions, David, 404–7
Sessions, Patty Bartlett, 404–7
Seven Years' War, 191, 257
Sewall, Samuel, 114, 139–40
sewing, 217, 219, 299
sexual morality, 152–3, 210–11, 216–17, 238–9,
    247, 454n9
Shakers, 330
Shalloon, 193
Shaumpishuh, 57–8
shawls, 332
Shechem, 64, 65
sheep, 146, 287, 330, 332, 366, 377, 390,
    403
sheets, 278, 281, 293, 298, 383
Shelburne Museum, Vermont, 323
Sheldon, Homer, 383, 384–6
Sheldon, Samuel, 383, 385
Sheldon, Sarah Weeks, 382–6, 474n20

shifts, 160, 270, 383
Shirley, William, 156–7, 158, 159, 252–3
shirts, 299, 300, 332
short-staple cotton, 38
"Shred of Linen," 20–1
Sigourney, Lydia, 20–1, 61, 220–1, 358, 412,
    421n
silk, 51
  embroidery, Prudence Punderson, *see First,
      Second, and Last Scenes of Mortality,
      The*
  Massachusetts act barring wearing of, 125
  raw, 379, 380
  stockings, 377, 380
  "tow," 379
silk-making, 177, 377–81, 395
  history of, 379–80
Silliman, Abigail Williams Hinsdale Hall, 136
Silliman, Eunice, 136
Simcoe, Mrs. John Graves, 260
skeins, measurement of, 186, 188–9
skein winder, 78, 92
Slade, Alsa, *302*, 302
Slater, Samuel, 279, 322
slavery, 38, 145, 196, 204–5, 206, 236, 291,
      309–10, 394, 446n3, 466n4
  abolitionists, 389–90
  in early nineteenth-century New England,
      246–7
  expansion into western territories, 373
  Indians sold into, 57, 60, 67, 69–70, 80,
      169
smallpox, 57, 147, 446n3
Smith, Adam, 53
Smith, Ann, 301
Smith, Lucy, 271, 272
Smith, Lucy Meserve, 407–9
Smith, Peggy, letter to, 215
Smith, Deacon Philip, 126–7
snowshoes, *254*
social inequality, urban, eighteenth century,
      144, 153–65, 173
Society for Encouraging Industry and
      Employing the Poor, 145, 157–65
Society for the Preservation of New England
      Antiquities, *6*
Society of Blue and White, 27, 29
Sockabasin, Denny, *264*
socks, 331
*Son of the Forest* (Apess), *364*
Sons of Liberty, 171, 182–3
Southgate, Eliza, 305
Spears, Robret, 195
Speck, Frank, 350, 416

spindles, 281

spinning, 38, 86–7, 91–2, *93*, 211, 219, 222, 383, 403
- cotton-spinning factories, 279, 318–19, 322
- demonstrations, 156, 157–8, 178
  - nineteenth century, 18, 26, 27, 422n45
- during early republic (1790–1820), 285
- factory created to aid the poor, 145, 157–65, 173, 448n47
- as fallback job, 201–4
- frolics, 200–1, 286, 462n25
- household production, *see* household production of textiles
- idealized visions of, 93–5
- matches, 178, 309, 407
- meetings, 286
- persistence in rural areas, 38
- schools, 161, 162, 165, 177

spinning meetings, 37, 176–91, 206
- the churches and, 178–85
- colonial rebellion against English taxes and, 176, 178–84

spinning wheels, 29, 78, 89, 196, 387, 410
- accelerating heads, 38, 87
- bobbin-flyer wheels, 88, *89*, 90, 94
- distaff, 89, *89*
- double-flyer, 91
- double-handed, 38
- Dover, New Hampshire, *see* spinning wheels in old log house, Dover, New Hampshire
- drawing and twisting, 87
- drop spindle, 87, 88, 153–4
- flax wheels, 78, 88, *89*, 89–90, 115, 281–2, 408
  - displays of, 18
- foot treadles, 88–9, 101–2, 281
- heck, 281
- illustrations featuring, 90, *90–91*
- "lining wheels," 78, 90
- maidens, *89*
- mother-of-all, *89*
- nineteenth-century displays of, 17–18, 25, 26
- nomenclature in probate records, 101–2
- operation of, 86–7
- prevalence in New England by mid-seventeenth century, 83–4, 85, 138, 217
- ratio to looms in household inventories, 103, 467n27
- "Saxony wheels," 89
- spindle, or "walking wheel," 87, 89
- "wheel finger," 87, *88*
- with wooden axles, 92, 436n31
- wool wheels, 78, 87, *88*, 89, 281

spinning wheels in old log house, Dover, New Hampshire, 3, 75–107
- flax spinning wheel, 78
- William Damm Garrison, *see* Damm Garrison, William
- wool spinning wheel, 78, 87, *88*

spooling, 214, 218, 219

Sprague, Granny, 354

Sprague, Noah, 254–5, 260

Sprague, Seth, 300

Stamp Act, 171, 176, 179, 182, 183

stamping, 350–2, *351*

Stark, Henry, 381

Stella, Claudine Bouzonnet, 150, *151*, 153

Stella, Jacques, 150

Stevens, Jane, 390, 396–7

Stewart, Almira Doty, 402–4

Stewart, Sylvester, 402–4

Stiles, Elizabeth, 181, 183

Stiles, Ezra, 180–1, 187–8

Stirling, Isabel, 271–2

Stirling, Mary, 272

stockings, 59, 211, 219, 228, 263, 281, 299–300, 375–6, 383, *384*, 386, 388, 408, 409–10
- "clouded," 396, *397*
- fancywork, *411*
- imported, 375
- silk, 377, *378*, 380
- unfinished linen, 1837, 3, *374*–5, 409

Stoddard, Esther, 114–15, *115*, 139–40

Stoddard, Solomon, 114, 323

Stowe, Calvin, 19

straw and palm-leaf hats and bonnets, 397–99, *399*

strikes, 391–5

Sudbury-Canada, Maine, *see* Bethel, Maine

Sullivan, James, 274–5

Sullivan, John, 275

surtout, 299

Susup, Molly, 256, 269, 355

Sutherland, Massachusetts, 177

Swan, Caleb, 257

Swan, James, 258

Swan, Joseph, 272

Swan, Mary, 258

Swan, Nathaniel, 270

Sybil Carter Indian Lace Association, 36

Sylvester, Deborah, 192, 197–9, *198*, 206, 293


tablecloths, *6*, 112, 113, 278, 281, 298, 299, 300, 301–3, *303*, 332–3, 409
- from early republic, linen, *see* linen tablecloth from early republic
- finishing of, 295–7, 303, 409

table coverings, 148

*Tale of the Spinning-Wheel, The* (Buel), 32, 34–5

"Tammies," 51

tankards, silver, 135–6

Tantaguidgeon, Gladys, 361–2

tapestry cushion cover, *122*, 123

tassels, 278, 295

Taunton, Massachusetts, strike of textile workers at, 392–3

Taylor, Edward, 7, 93–4, 103, 112, 114, 123

tea, 176, 178, 179, 180, 234, 288, 386

teachers, 215, 220, 227, 247, 382–3

of embroidery, 146–7, 150, 381

tea dishes, 193, 281

tea kettle, 267, 301

teapots, 145, 231, 232, 303

tea table, *239*, 303, 402

temperance societies, 377, 389

tent stitch, 149, 150

textile mills of New England, 14, 38, 279–80, 318–19, 322, 390–7, 410

cotton-spinning, 279, 318–19, 322

outwork, 322

strikes at, 391–5, 476n42

wool carding, 38, 289, 318

textiles

primary types of, 425n6

warp and weft elements of, 425n6

*see also specific types of textiles, e.g.* baskets; blankets

thimbles, 229, *229*

Throgs Neck, *9*, 244

*Tobit and Anna*, *90*, *187*

Tolford, Isaac, 289–90

Tomhegan, 258, 259, 262, 269, 270

Topsham, Maine, 317–18

tow, 51, 283, 299, 337

carding of, *see* carding

tow cloth, 228

towels, *6*, 112, 278, 281, 293, 298, 299, 300

with netted fringe, 296, *297*

Townsend Duties, 176

Tracy, Eleanor Washburn, 338–9

Treaty of Aix-la-Chapelle, 159

Trinity Church, New Haven, 229–30

trucking cloth or duffels, 55, 414, 429n34

True, Dr. Nathaniel, 249

Trumbull, Faith, 147, 149, 231

Trumbull, John, 148–9

Trumbull, Jonathan, 234

Tufts, Henry, 257–8, 259, 262, 266

turkey feathers woven into mantles, 45

*Twelve Apostles*, 229, 231

twill, 50

twined textiles, 43, 47–59, 60, 361, 418

decline of twined baskets, 72–3

pocketbook, Molly Ocket's, *see* Ocket's pocketbook, Bethel, Maine, 1785

Twitchell, Eli, 250, 265, 266, 267, 268

Twitchell, Joseph, 265–6, 268

Twitchell, Peter, 268, 269

tyers, 281

Tyler, Mary Palmer, 319–20, 380

Tyler, Royall, 319, 320

Tyler, Winship, 380

U.S. Sanitary Commission, 26

upstreaming, 250

Vanderpoel, Emily, *34*, 34–5, 36

Veasey, Jonathan, 194

Vermont, 12, 18, 22, 39, 273, 291, 295, 300, 317, 318, 319–20, 323, 328, 333, 338–9

history of, 343–4

indigenous people of, 343, 344–5

literacy rates in early nineteenth century, 341–2

wool production, 366

Vermont Historical Society, 377

*Vicar of Wakefield, The* (Goldsmith), 242, 245

Vickers, Daniel, 169, 196

*Views of the Irish*, *187*

Virgil, 150, 154

voting rights for African-Americans, 24

Wadsworth, Zilpah, 314

wage economy, 377

Waldron, Richard, 79–82, 393, 434n4

Waldron, Thomas Westbrook, 185, 190

Wale, Dolly, 27

Wallace, Mary Wilson, 100–1, 409, *411*

Wallis, J., *93*

wall pocket, 32, *33*

Wampanoags, 57, 58, 60, 65, 66, 144, 416–18, 477n1

and Churche's War, 43–4

at Mashpee, *see* Mashpee, Wampanoags at

wampum, 124

as currency in fur trade, 56

sewing bag, *49*, 49–50

textiles from, 46, 60

Wampy, Anne, 366

Wangums, 354

Wansey, Henry, 279–80, 289, 318

Ward, Artemas, *254*

Ward, Edward, 321

War of 1812, 279, 316, 331–2, 412
  harassment of American shipping leading
    to, 308, 309
Warren, James, 154–5
Warren, Mercy Otis, 154–5
Washington, Martha, 296
Watson, Elkanah, 329–31
*Wealth of Nations, The* (Smith), 53
weaver's reeds, 78
weavers shuttles, *197*
weaving, 92–3, *93*, 217–18, 291–8, 317–18, 388,
    407
  as cooperative enterprise, 37, 104, 217
  demonstrations, 18
  feminization of, by late eighteenth century,
    4, 37, 103–6, 192–5, 196, 287, 318
  household production, *see* household
    production of textiles
  inexperienced results, 320
  as male occupation, 164, 287
    in seventeenth century, 4, 37, 52–3, 84–6,
      125–6
  mechanized, *see* textile mills of New
    England
  as metaphor for guiding hand of
    Providence, 7
  niche weavers, 400
  patterns and structures, 291–5, *292*, *294*
  *see also* looms
weaving reeds, 18
Webster, Mary, 126–7
Weeks, John, 300
Weeks, Sarah, 287, 463n37
Weetamoo, *see* Namumpum (later Weetamoo)
Weiner, Annette, 129, 137
Weir, Adam, 195
Welch, Alice, 214
Wells, Moses, 195
Wells, Sally, 213
Wells, Thomas, 214
Wequamunko, 124
Westcarr, Dr. John, 124
Westcarr, Hannah, *see* Beaman, Hannah
    Barnard Westcarr
Westcoat, Freelove Fenner, 42, 43
Westcoat, Samuel, 42
Western Nehantic, 354
Westford Public Library, 335
West Indian cotton, 38, 39, 83–4, 85, 196, 414
West Indies, 159
  –New England trade, 38–9, 83–4, 104–5,
    196, 231, 298, 398, 414
westward migration, nineteenth century,
    401–9
Wethersfield, Connecticut, 111, 124

Wetmore, Hannah Edwards, 140–1
whaling industry, 169
Wheelock, Eleazar, 184–5, 228, 233
Whigs, 25
White, Sally, 322
Whitfield, George, 178–9
Whitney, Eli, 279
Whittier, John Greenleaf, 356–7
Whittlesey, Hannah, 140
wife, derivation of word, 37
wigwams, 45–6, 56, 60, 170, 426n12
  moving of, 46
Wildes, Abigail, 311, 313, 314–15
Wildes, Elizabeth Perkins (later Elizabeth
    Perkins Wildes Bourne), 281, 286,
    287, 288, 291–2, 298–300, 301, 310–13,
    *311*, 316–17, 338, 375, 400
  counterpanes, 307, 311, 312, 315, 317, 332,
    338
    1810, *see* Bourne counterpane, 1810
Wildes, Israel, 298, 299–300, 310, 375
Wilds, David, 212, 213, 214
Wilds, Ellen, 211, 212, 213–14, 217
Willard, Joseph, 19
William Damm Garrison, *see* Damm
    Garrison, William
William III, prince of Orange, 98
Williams, Charles, 134
Williams, Esther, 121
Williams, John, 391
Williams, Penelope, 204
Williams, Roger, 45, 54, 56, 58, 63–4, 67, 72,
    143, 431n70, 432n93
Williams, Sarah, 134, 173
Williams, Solomon, 228
willie-nillie, *see* niddy-noddies
Willoughby, Charles, 249, 262, *262*
Wilson, Hannah (née Leathers), 399–400,
    *401*
Windham, Connecticut, 177
Windsor, Connecticut, 114, 124, 206
Winslow, Josiah, 84
Winters, Amanda K., 334, *334–5*
Winthrop, John, 56, 79, 113
witchcraft, 19, 126–8, 360, 420n21, 436n29
Witney, England, blanket-making in, 53, 55,
    323
wolves, 270, 272
*Woman Suffrage: A Reform against Nature*
    (Bushnell), 23
women
  Bushnell's "Age of Homespun" speech, *see*
    Bushnell, Horace, "Age of
    Homespun" speech
  education of, *see* education of women

exchange of work, 211, 212, 218, 219–20, 221, 227, 279, 281, 285, 288, 289, 291, 383
feminization of weaving, 4, 37, 103–6, 192–5, 196, 287, 318
freed African-American, 246–7
historians, 421n
household production, *see* household production of textiles
indentured as servants, 162
inheritance of, 111, 129, 130, 131, 133–8, 415, 443n41
marriage and, 161, 199, 200–1, 205, 206, 386–7
  elopement notices, 367–8
  polygamy, 405, 407
nineteenth-century holiday celebrations, role at, 26–7
rights of, *see* women's rights
sexual morality and, 210–11
store accounts, 399, 455n24
textile mills, working in, 390–7
work, different meanings for, 218–19
women's rights, 376
  Bushnell's thoughts about, 23–4
  Christian egalitarianism and, 23, 181
  legal disabilities, 23
  ownership of their own labor and product, 176, 191–8

Wood, William, 45, 54, 55, 56, 72
Woodman, Annie, 76
Woodman Institute, 76, *77*, 394
Woodside, Captain William, 263
woodsplint basket, Rutland, Vermont, after 1821, 3, *340–1*, 343, 347–8, 348–52, *351*, 372, 414–15
  described, 341, 348–52
  making splints, 348
  newspaper lining lid of, 341, 342, 343, 352–3, 366
Woodwell, Gideon, 191
Woodwell, Polly
  niddy-noddy, *174–5*, 175–7, 191, 197
wool, 51, 53, 89, 92, 298
  carding, *see* carding
  Foot bed rugs, *see* Foot bed rugs, Colchester, Connecticut, 1775
  merino, 328, 329
woolens, 51, 288, 319, 366, 428n27
Wooton, John, 153
worsteds, 51, 52, 92, 298
wrapped twining, 47
wraps as yarn measurement, 189

Yale University, Beinecke Library, 139
Yohicake bag, 48, *48*, 49, *49*, 50
Young, Brigham, 408

# A Note about the Author

*Laurel Thatcher Ulrich received her B.A. from the University of Utah, her M.A. from Simmons College, and her Ph.D. from the University of New Hampshire. She was previously professor of history at the University of New Hampshire and is currently Phillips Professor of Early American History and director of the Charles Warren Center for Studies in American History at Harvard University. She is the author of* Good Wives: Image and Reality in the Lives of Women in Northern New England, 1650–1750; A Midwife's Tale: The Life of Martha Ballard, Based on Her Diary, 1785–1812; *and* All God's Critters Got a Place in the Choir *(with Emma Lou Thayne).* A Midwife's Tale *won the Pulitzer Prize in history, the Bancroft Prize, and the American Historical Society's John H. Dunning and Joan Kelly Memorial Prizes, and Ulrich's discovery of Martha Ballard and work on the diary has been chronicled in a documentary film written and produced by Laurie Kahn-Leavitt with major funding from the National Endowment for the Humanities and the* American Experience *television series. Ulrich is also the author of numerous articles and reviews and the recipient of a MacArthur Foundation Fellowship and many other honors and awards.*

# A Note on the Type

*This book was set in Fournier, a typeface named for Pierre Simon Fournier fils (1712–1768), a celebrated French type designer. Coming from a family of typefounders, Fournier was an extraordinarily prolific designer of typefaces and of typographic ornaments. He was also the author of the important* Manuel typographique *(1764–1766), in which he attempted to work out a system standardizing type measurement in points, a system that is still in use internationally. Fournier's type is considered transitional in that it drew its inspiration from the old style, yet was ingeniously innovational, providing for an elegant, legible appearance. In 1925 his type was revived by the Monotype Corporation of London.*

*Composed by North Market Street Graphics, Lancaster, Pennsylvania*
*Printed and bound by Quebecor Printing, Fairfield, Pennsylvania*
*Designed by Anthea Lingeman*

JA 14 '02 **DATE DUE**